W9-AMY-312

Learning, Language, and Memory

PROVIDED BY THE BOL?

Learning, Language, and Memory

JOHN W. DONAHOE
UNIVERSITY OF MASSACHUSETTS, AMHERST

MICHAEL G. WESSELLS
VASSAR COLLEGE

HARPER & ROW, PUBLISHERS
New York, Hagerstown, Philadelphia, San Francisco, London

Sponsoring Editor: George A. Middendorf
Project Editor: Holly Detgen
Designer: Helen Iranyi
Senior Production Manager: Kewal K. Sharma
Compositor: American–Stratford Graphic Services, Inc.
Printer and Binder: Halliday Lithograph Corporation
Art Studio: Vantage Art Inc.

Learning, Language, and Memory

Copyright © 1980 by John W. Donahoe and Michael G. Wessells

All rights reserved. Printed in the United States of
America. No part of this book may be used or repro-
duced in any manner whatsoever without written permission except in the case of brief quotations embodied
in critical articles and reviews. For information address
Harper & Row, Publishers, Inc., 10 East 53rd Street,
New York, N.Y. 10022.

Library of Congress Cataloging in Publication Data

Donahoe, John W   date
  Learning, language, and memory.

  Includes bibliographical references and indexes.
  1. Learning, Psychology of. 2. Psycholinguistics. 3.
Memory. I. Wessells, Michael G., date   joint author. II.
Title.
BF318.D65   153.1   79-4586
ISBN 0-06-041685-8

To Millie and Sheila,
who know their many contributions.

Contents

Preface

Whether instructors or students, those who grapple with contempory problems in the field defined by this text are faced with special difficulties. The phenomena are extremely varied and the theoretical analyses are correspondingly diverse. Activities ranging from the relative simplicity of reflexes to the complexity of human cognition fall within the field and, not surprisingly, no single, unifying conception now exists.

The present text acknowledges and represents the genuine diversity while simultaneously elaborating a coherent perspective from which to view that diversity. Coherence is sought by interpreting each activity as the integrated expression of both phylogenetic and ontogenetic influences, of both the common ancestral environment of the species and the unique personal environment of the individual. This broad interactional, or epigenetic, perspective permits general themes to be perceived in what might otherwise be viewed as independent concerns. There are important conceptual continuities, for example, between such seemingly disparate phenomena as biological influences on the behavioral events in conditioning and structural limitations on the cognitive processes underlying language and memory.

While common conceptual and methodological issues are noted, no attempt has been made to translate or to reduce one theoretical orientation to another. Although our theoretical preferences are apparent, we have made a genuine effort to be problem-oriented rather than position-oriented. Believing that scientific evolution as well as organic evolution is based upon the selection of viable choices from among highly variable alternatives, we have sought to do justice to differing theoretical approaches. Most importantly, we have tried to provide readers with the information and analytical tools necessary to evaluate the various approaches for themselves.

TO THE STUDENT

Understanding what changes and maintains our behavior is central to understanding much of what is quintessentially human. Many societal institutions, for example education and psychotherapy, have the fostering of change as their explicit function and, most generally, an ever-changing environment demands an ever-changing organism.

In the pages that follow, we seek to identify the factors that influence thought and action (private and public events), to describe the major phenomena produced by these factors, and to integrate these findings theoretically. We begin the task with an examination of the phylogenetic legacy revealed in reflexive relationships between the environment and behavior and proceed to the study of learned relationships using classical and instrumental conditioning procedures. Having explored the processes involved in the change and maintenance of behavior in organisms whose relevant prior experience has been limited, we progress to the study of the behavior of experienced organisms such as ourselves. The understanding of language and memory in adult humans requires that the phylogenetic legacy be supplemented by knowledge of more than the prevailing environment. Linguistic and memorial phenomena are incomprehensible without recourse to the private events that are the legacy of earlier experiences. The logical and empirical analysis of private events—of cognitive processes—occupies a major portion of the latter half of the book and draws upon previous findings whenever appropriate.

Your efforts to understand those portions of the text selected by your instructor may benefit by a few suggestions for studying. No single method works best for all persons, but the following procedures work well for many. First, page through the entire assignment, noting major headings and gaining an overview of the major content and structure of the reading. Second, return to the beginning of the assignment and read each section carefully paying special attention to technical terms, which are *italicized* when first introduced. The central ideas are often contained in a topic sentence located at the beginning or the end of each paragraph. Third, through study questions supplied by your instructor or through brief outlines constructed by yourself, restate the major points of each section in your own words. Simply underlining or highlighting sentences in the text does little to improve either understanding or retention of the material. Fourth, upon completion of the entire assignment, review your answers to the study questions or your outlines and determine if they are still meaningful to you. If not, return to the relevant portions of the text and carefully restudy them. In your review, try not to lose sight of the major themes of the assignment as you learn the details that illustrate those themes.

If difficulties persist, consult a classmate, raise questions in class, or contact the instructor privately. Also, we would value a note from you indicating troublesome sections so that they may be improved in a future edition. Write either John W. Donahoe, Psychology Department, University of Massachusetts, Amherst, Massachusetts 01003, or Michael G. Wessells, Psychology Department, Vassar College, Poughkeepsie, New York 12601. We greatly appreciate your comments.

TO THE INSTRUCTOR

We believe that you will find this book to be quite comprehensive in its conceptual and empirical context, but not encyclopedic in the experimental examples which illustrate that content. Our preference has been to select examples that explicate several principles and phenomena. Stylistically, the first chapter employs a narrative prose that appears less frequently as the development progresses. Teaching makes one acutely aware that a text which is good in many respects may nevertheless fail in most respects if it is dull or irrelevant to the experience of its readers. The occasional interjection of applications of the material and of short biographical sketches of pioneers in the field—Pavlov and Ebbinghaus, for example—also improve readability.

Because of the length required to represent the breadth of the field, the entire text would probably not be assigned in a one-semester or a one-quarter course except with exceptionally well-prepared students—honors undergraduates or first-year graduate students. Accordingly, the *Instructor's Manual* suggests sections of the text that may be deleted for any of the following three types of courses: (1) a balanced coverage of learning and memory, (2) a more specialized coverage emphasizing animal learning, or (3) a more specialized coverage emphasizing cognitive psychology (information processing).

The *Instructor's Manual* also contains study questions keyed to the various sections of each chapter. Study questions are an effective means for facilitating student comprehension, as shown in classroom evaluations of earlier versions of the text, and you are encouraged to consider their use. Study questions greatly reduce the need to "cover" all assigned sections in lectures and permit the instructor to concentrate on topics of special difficulty or interest.

ACKNOWLEDGMENTS

Many persons contribute importantly to a book in addition to those whose names appear beneath the title. In this instance, appreciation is expressed to the students and colleagues with whom we have discussed these topics—especially Michael Crowley, William Millard, John Ayres, and John Moore—and to our most demanding reviewers—Charles Clifton and Philip Ziegler. They bear no responsibility, of course, for the imperfections that remain. We also thank Mildred Donahoe who obtained permissions and assembled the bibliography and thank Sally Ives, Judy Buck, Laura Blum, and Bonnie Thornton who typed portions of the manuscript. Gratitude is also due to Grant Donahoe for assistance with proofreading, to Lisa Donahoe for the concept of the cover design, and to Kirk Donahoe for relieving the first author of numerous responsibilities so that more time could be devoted to the preparation of the book.

JOHN W. DONAHOE
MICHAEL G. WESSELLS

Learning, Language, and Memory

1

The Origins of Behavior

INTRODUCTION

This book is concerned with learning—the processes that shape the behavior of living beings to the demands of an ever-changing environment. Before beginning our formal inquiry into these processes, it is well to examine some recent history for evidence of the urgent necessity of such knowledge.

In a city known as the Gateway to the West, the evening news reveals a group of public officials dedicating a new housing complex that is to serve as a model for the nation. A cluster of multistory buildings has replaced the rubble that once covered the area.

A few winters later, the evening news again shows us these same buildings—or are they the same? There are no officials in sight, nor many people of any description for that matter. Most of the windows of the buildings are broken and water, fed by broken pipes, cascades down the walls. As we watch, the buildings shudder. We hear the muffled roar of an explosion, and—in slow motion and instant replay—the buildings crumble and recrumble to the ground. The commentator tells us that to improve the livability of the housing complex, it has been necessary to reduce some of the buildings to rubble so that more space may exist among the remaining structures. When questioned for his reaction to the remodeling plan, a prospective tenant states that he believes that demolition is a step in the right direction.

In a city on the West Coast, a new mass transit system has opened. Streamlined cars move swiftly on rubber wheels along a smooth roadbed under the direction of computers. The system is to serve as a model for the nation.

One year later, city officials respond to a reporter's question, saying that while there have been the usual difficulties associated with the first year of such a complex operation, the major problem has been that the masses have not chosen to travel on the new system. People have preferred to use their own automobiles rather than the new facility. A massive transfusion of new money will be required if the system is to survive. The television segment closes with a scene of a nearby highway clogged with traffic. Those with color sets glimpse the sky overhead—it seems to grow perceptibly yellow as they watch.

In a metropolis in the Northeast, a charismatic mayor holds a news conference in September to announce that war has been declared on the educational problems of the city. New schools, new classroom configurations, new administrative procedures, new audiovisual aids—nothing has been withheld from the effort. It is to serve as a model for the nation. In June, the newspaper contains an article on page three which notes that the educational performance of the children in the city has fallen still further below the national average.

A nation's people and their elected representatives ponder the certainty of an approaching oil shortage. Should measures be immediately undertaken to conserve diminishing supplies or shall short-sighted self-interest cause the people to oppose modest restrictions now, even though the ultimate consequence is the severe deprivation of their children? Shall legislators vote for effective conservation now or shall the specter of defeat at the next election prevent such action? At this writing, the answers are unknown, but recent history is not a cause for optimism.

What is going wrong? Why have these proposals fallen short of the goals set by their designers? Was it because the goals were unworthy? Hardly! Few would quarrel with the idea of replacing substandard housing with new buildings, of substituting mass transit for the private automobile in order to reduce pollution, of helping children to learn, or of deferring the exhaustion of energy supplies. Were the failures, then, due to faulty engineering in implementing the proposals? Again, no. The new housing complex did accommodate many people in a minimum of ground space; the mass transit system did use the latest innovations in industrial technique; and the educational problems were combated with good facilities and teaching aids. Granted that the goals were worthy and the technology was adequate, why were the projects not successful?

As you have probably guessed, and as we believe, the projects failed because the designers neglected to appreciate fully that these are basically *human* problems, and solutions to such problems require an understanding of human behavior. People may not choose to live in housing that minimizes the use of land; the immediate convenience of driving one's own car may outweigh the reduction in the level of pollution in the future; there may be more to education than new buildings and the latest in audiovisual aids. Human problems require more than good intentions and good engineering if we are to find remedies for them. They require an understanding of human behavior. It is to that purpose—the understanding of behavior, and what changes and maintains it—that this book is directed. To fail to acknowledge that living creatures are at the heart of the matter, and not mere masonry and metal, is to risk the transformation of our dreams into nightmares.

Science and the Understanding of Human Behavior

Observation Of all the various ways of coming to terms with the world around us, modern man has often turned to science in his search for understanding. While some would have us believe that science is a strange and mysterious enterprise beyond the ken of common people and that scientists are high priests in some new and complex religion, the facts are quite otherwise.

Science proceeds first from a process in which we all engage—*observation*. Simply looking closely at the world—both the external world and that more private world within our skins—is the starting point of understanding for scientists and nonscientists alike. When we are content to view the world as it presents itself to us, we engage in *naturalistic observation*. Hiking through the woods to study the behavior of squirrels, watching a group of children at play in a schoolyard, and visiting a city to observe the behavior of people in crowds on a busy street are all examples of naturalistic observation.

Scientists, because they do not trust their ability to remember all that they have seen, will often engage in record-keeping of some type. Record-keeping, or *data collection,* may range all the way from making a few written notes of what has been seen to a highly detailed quantitative record automatically produced by an electronic instrument. Whatever the degree of sophistication of the record-keeping, the data are grist for the scientific mill to the extent that they are *reliable* and *valid*. A datum is reliable if it is repeatable, if at another time under similar conditions the behavior can again be observed by you or another. A datum is valid if it is relevant to the question being studied.

It should be noted that precision in data collection or measurement is not enough. An observation that is not importantly related to the question under investigation is not improved by a greater accuracy in measurement. Rubbish is rubbish whether we measure it to the nearest gram or kilogram. Note also that a reliable and valid datum may not have lasting worth if the experimental question has not been well-conceived. Scientists, like any of us, are not always able to tell what is a "good" question and what is a "bad" one until after the answer has been obtained. While prior knowledge is an indispensable guide to the formulation of scientific questions, the past provides no guarantee that the questions will be perceived as optimal from the perspective of hindsight. The important point is to keep asking the best questions you know how to ask, if for no other reason than that by chance alone some of the questions are bound to be "good" ones.[1] This book will contain many questions, both well- and ill-conceived, and some answers. You are encouraged to participate fully in this enterprise—science is not a spectator sport.

Naturalistic observation, although it provides the starting point for all scientific knowledge, is often superseded by *planned observations*, or *experiments*. In the experiment, the scientist intrudes into the natural flow of events in order to study more deeply the effect of one event upon another. By manipulating events, the scientist hopes to isolate and understand the variables that influence the phenomenon being investigated. The experiment is also a more efficient procedure than naturalistic observation since long waits must otherwise be endured if rare events are to be studied. Instead of trusting to luck that squirrels will be seen during a hike, the scientist may go to a zoo where squirrels are known to be or may capture some squirrels and observe them in the laboratory. Instead of waiting for a recess period to study the behavior of children at play, the scientist may invite two children to come to a playroom where their play is observed through a one-way vision window.

Experimental observations have potential hazards as well as advantages. Suppose that the scientist observing the behavior of squirrels was interested in answering questions about how squirrels behave in the wild—for example, in the events that cause squirrels to bury nuts which serve as a food source during the winter. Clearly, the behavior of squirrels in the zoo or in the laboratory might be quite different from that occurring in the wild. If the availability of food, the relative amount of light during the day, or the air temperature were important influences on the behavior of burying nuts, the zoo or the laboratory might be an unsuitable situation for making observations. Similarly, consider the scientist studying the play behavior of children; the answers which might be obtained to questions in the playroom situation could be very different from those based upon observations in the schoolyard. Perhaps children play differently just after being released from the classroom; perhaps two children play differently when they are alone in a playroom than when there are other children nearby. Again, the scientist interested primarily in answering questions about what determines how children play in a schoolyard must be on guard against these potential problems with a planned observation.

In short, there is always the risk that when planned observations are used, the situation may have been altered in critical respects so that the questions, and the answers which we obtain to our questions, have been fatally flawed in the process. When this happens, the scientist is in the position of the man who, when asked by a passerby what he was doing groveling on the ground underneath the streetlight, replied that he was looking for a coin that he had dropped. "Let me help you," said the passerby. "Where exactly did you drop the coin?" "Over there," said the man, pointing down the street to a particularly dark area. "Then why on earth are you looking here?" the passerby exclaimed. "Because the light is so much better here," said the man. Sometimes the scientist using planned observations may be looking where the light is good but the coin—the answer to the question—is not to be found.

Finally, there are some observations, such as the behavior of people in crowds, which cannot easily be planned because of practical reasons. When these circumstances arise, the scientist can arrange to be in a position to observe at times when the behavior of concern is most likely to occur; for example, at morning and evening rush hours, or, returning to the example of the squirrels, the scientist might locate a part of the forest where squirrels are plentiful and set up a blind from which observations could unobtrusively be made.

There is, however, another and more compelling reason than convenience for the scientist's frequent preference for experimental observations. In addition to placing less strain on the scientist's patience, planned observations allow the investigator some control over the events that influence the behavior being studied. That is, the scientist arranges observations so that the events which produce the behavior are limited to those few events of immediate interest.

Those conditions that the scientist chooses to vary are the *independent variables* of the investigation; those conditions that are held constant are *control variables*. For example, the scientist interested in the events that cause squirrels to bury nuts might plan observations in which the number of hours of light each day was varied and other factors, such as the availability of food or the temperature, were held constant or controlled. If squirrels bury nuts during days with little light and do not bury nuts during days with much light, then the scientist may conclude that the amount of daylight affects the behavior because other factors were held constant. In the wild, this insight might be difficult to attain since, as winter draws nigh in nature, the amount of daylight decreases, but there are simultaneous changes in the availability of food and in the temperature of the air. Which one of these changes is essential to the behavior of burying nuts would be a more complicated question to answer in the wild. The use of controlled observations, therefore, not only places fewer demands on the patience of the scientist but also often permits conclusions regarding the critical antecedents of behavior. Procedures involving controlled observations, particularly when these procedures are conducted in a laboratory situation, are called *experiments* and are the basis of much scientific knowledge.

Science and Everyday Methods of Knowing   Before going farther in this discussion of science as a way of knowing about the world, it should be pointed out that the experimental method of controlled observation is not unique to science. We all employ similar methods in seeking to understand our personal world, although the method is raised to its finest art in science.

Suppose you have an acquaintance who has always been pleasant in your previous chance meetings on the campus—who has smiled upon seeing you, raised a hand in greeting, or spoken a few words. One day, you pass each other but your acquaintance walks on with nary a sign of recognition, let alone greeting. What has happened? Was the person preoccupied and simply failed to notice you? Was the person in an ill temper and not talking to anyone? Or was the absence of recognition an indication that the person is now deliberately snubbing you?

How could you decide among these and the several other possible explanations of this behavior? Short of asking directly—and you could not rely completely on the truth of the answer in any event—you would probably carry out a controlled observation. For example, you might see the person on a subsequent day speaking to some other students. You could then go over to the group and place yourself in such a position that you could not avoid being seen. From overhearing the conversation, punctuated with laughter and friendly comments, you might infer that your perplexing acquaintance was in good humor. If the person fails to speak to you under these conditions, you conclude that you are being intentionally snubbed. Although you would probably not think of it in such terms, you have attempted to make a controlled observation so that the answer to a question about the behavior of another person might be achieved.

The Process of Science   Like you, the scientist has no guarantee that a single controlled observation—even a laboratory experiment—will produce a definitive answer to a question. Usually only a series of observations will suffice. The process of formulating questions, obtaining partial or complete answers to those questions, and then formulating new questions based upon the earlier answers is at the foundation of the scientific enterprise. This process reveals the *self-corrective* nature of science and accounts for continuity and progress in science. Science is truly a community activity in which each person is able to make use of all the answers obtained by his or her predecessors. This is in part what Newton meant when he said, regarding his theoretical work in physics, "I have stood on the shoulders of giants."

The self-corrective nature of science is also an important cause of the relatively high ethical standards in scientific work. Although there have been some notable exceptions, scientists are generally very accurate in the description of their methods and results. This happy state of affairs exists not because scientists are generally more ethical or honest than the rest of us, but because some other scientist will almost certainly pick up where the first scientist left off. In brief, if the first scientist had misrepresented any findings, the second would catch the error. Scientists are honest because only honesty pays off; it is the best policy in science in both the long and short run. In their other pursuits, scientists are probably no more or less honest or ethical than anyone else.

Some Assumptions   Lying behind the distinguishing features of the scientific process—the gathering of observations and the evaluation of these observations by self-corrective procedures—is an assumption that both scientist and nonscientist share: There is a *uniformity* in nature and that uniformity may be discerned. By uniformity we mean that the world in which we live is orderly, and that such order is essentially the same from one time to another and from one place to another if other conditions have been unchanged. Thus, the fabled apple which fell on Isaac Newton's head, and which purportedly stimulated his work on gravitational theory, would be assumed to fall in essentially the same manner now as in the seventeenth century, and in America as in Great Britain.

The belief in uniformity is so strong that when apparent exceptions are encountered, the scientist and nonscientist alike conclude that some other condition has changed and that this change is responsible for the difference in outcome. If an experiment is repeated but the result is different, the scientist casts about to discover some previously unsuspected conditions that may differ between the two studies. If a friend who has always previously greeted us when we pass on the campus now fails to greet us, we search for some condition that may have changed. Both the scientist in the laboratory and the person in the world at large have come to expect uniformity in nature, whether displayed in the fall of an apple or the behavior of a friend. When apples fall up or friends fall down, our belief in uniformity is unchallenged—we respond by seeking to understand the anomaly through further inquiry. We do not accept the conclusion that we live in a chaotic and capricious world, because in our experience there are so many instances to the contrary.

As stated before, however, it is not only the belief that there is uniformity in the world but also the belief that *we* can discern and comprehend that uniformity that provides the bedrock supporting scientific activity. A uniformity that is intelligible only to the gods would not suffice as a foundation for the development of science. The past successes of the application of controlled observation in conjunction with self-corrective procedures have produced this rather brash assessment of our capabilities as a species. Scientific procedures have worked as a way of understanding the world and, because they have worked, we have persisted in the use of these procedures.

When such procedures fail to work—as in the design of the housing complex with which we began this discussion, we start to question the utility of the scientific method itself as a road to knowledge. As with apparent failures to replicate experiments, however, we should first determine whether any of the conditions have changed between the old situations that gave rise to the principles and the new situations in which those principles are found insufficient. It is not that engineering principles are wrong but that they are incomplete as the basis for decisions regarding humans and other living things. It is not that scientific procedures are inadequate as a basis for understanding human behavior but that the results of the scientific study of behavior have not been fully incorporated into the solution of the problem.

Limitations of Science as a Means for Understanding Human Behavior

While we believe that the application of scientific method to human behavior has already led to important insights and holds great promise for continued understanding, the account of the preceding section should foster no illusions about the difficulties that must be faced. A controlled observation may not control some conditions that later work shows to be of great significance. The self-correcting method of science does not lead to straight-line progress in pushing forward the boundaries of knowledge. At the frontiers of the struggle, the battle lines surge first this way and then that. Although the overall direction of movement is toward greater understanding, there are always local skirmishes in which we flounder and—when truly unsuspected results are obtained—we may be obliged to fall back momentarily to regroup. However, unlike an army which grows weaker as the front expands and the lines of supply lengthen, science—through the discovery of ever more general laws—lives off the very land it occupies and therefrom grows stronger.

Character of Scientific Truths Even when the scientific process is going well, the understanding obtained is not the absolute truth spoken of in some philosophies but rather the transient truth of science. At any given moment, the current scientific understanding probably represents an advance over earlier knowledge but will, almost certainly, be superseded by a superior understanding in the future. Yesterday's brilliant insight may be today's outmoded idea and tomorrow's folly. In a relatively young science such as the study of behavior, we may expect the durability of our interpretations of observations to be less than that of the more mature sciences. The self-correcting nature of scientific inquiry is thus the source of our confidence in our ability ultimately to achieve a deeper understanding of ourselves and others, and the source of our humility in the assertion of the completeness of our present understanding.

If from what has been said about the scientific method of acquiring knowledge you have come to believe that the path to understanding is fraught with uncertainty, you are correct. If from what has been said about the fragility of our interpretations of observations, you have concluded that the quality of the answer received is no better than the quality of the question asked, you are also correct. Scientific method is not an alchemy which transmutes leaden questions into golden answers. There are golden answers to be found, but the search is best viewed as a slow advancement by successive approximations to more and more general formulations, rather than as a quest for the certainty promised by some philosophies.

Scientist as Behaver In addition to the uncertainty inherent in scientific knowledge, there is a second limitation, as true of a science of behavior as it is of all other sciences: The behavioral scientist stands squarely within the very system whose understanding is sought. The variables that affect the behavior of other persons affect the scientist with equal force. Therapists can behave in ways which, were they patients, would be labeled as symptomatic of repressed sexual urges; social psychologists may behave in ways which, were they laymen, would be labeled as prejudiced. In short, the fact that a scientist may have achieved insights into the origins of behavior does not confer any immunity from the effects described by those principles.

All behavior, including the behavior of scientists, is to be understood within the context of an adequate science of behavior. Accordingly, we may expect to see scientists stubbornly persist in ideas whose time has passed because these ideas are *theirs* or have served them well in the past, and we may expect them to become angered when such ideas are challenged. When we consider physical science, the ludicrous character of the notion that knowledge of a principle somehow confers immunity to the action of that principle is apparent. It is as if Newton would no longer have been troubled by apples falling on his head after having gained insights into the action of gravity. Of this at least you may be certain: Both we who write this book and you who read it are equally subject to the behavioral principles that are described herein.

The notion that science confers an immunity to the laws of nature upon its practitioners is absurd as a proposition, but it does reflect the fact that an understanding of scientific principles can permit us to avoid or delay what would otherwise be the consequences of such principles. Thus the airplane does not repeal the law of gravity but rather generates a force that opposes and exceeds the force of gravitation. As long as this opposing force originating in the flow of air over the wings is sufficient, the plane flies. But let the engines stop and the continued existence of gravitational force becomes apparent—sometimes tragically. So it is with an understanding of the principles which govern behavior; an understanding of these principles will permit us to design better lives for ourselves and others, but we must always work within the system. There is no hiding place. Accordingly, while knowledge of the antecedents of behavior confers no immunity from their action, it does hold the promise of their circumvention.

Science and Experience   Aside from the uncertain character of all scientific knowledge and the fact that the possessor of such knowledge does not thereby escape from its consequences, one other limitation of science as a basis for understanding behavior deserves to be mentioned. A scientific understanding of behavior, no matter how complete that understanding, is not equivalent to the experiencing of that behavior. The most thorough-going analysis of racial discrimination is not equivalent to the experience of that discrimination. The most detailed analysis of sexual behavior is not equivalent to the experience of that behavior. This same general point is often made by critics of science in their assertion that a scientific understanding is an impoverished understanding. What you have probably already realized is that this apparent conflict results from a confusion of the explanation of behavior with the direct experience of the behavior being explained. They are not the same, nor is direct experience a specific goal of science.

There are two senses in which scientific understanding may importantly contribute to experience, however. First, if you have learned to view a problem from the vantage point of science, then the achievement of an explanation can be an exhilarating experience indeed! To savor this experience requires a sophisticated palate, but so does an appreciation of Scotch whisky and it also can be heady stuff. Our hope is that your reading of this book will permit you to share, at least vicariously, in the pleasures of achieving a better scientific understanding of behavior.

The second and more broadly applicable sense in which science may contribute to experience is that while scientific explanations are not the equivalent of the experience, they can help in attaining and enriching the experience. By knowing the conditions under which the behavior or experience will occur, we may arrange for the realization of those conditions and hence of the experience. Thus while an exhaustive analysis of the physics of light will never capture the glory of a sunset, physics can tell us where to stand and when to look so that we may revel in that experience.

John Barth's comment about the relationship between technique and emotion in literature applies with equal force to the relationship between understanding and direct experience in science: "We tend to think of experiments as being cold exercises in technique. My feeling about technique in art is that it has about the same value as technique in love-making. That is to say, heartfelt ineptitude has its appeal and so does heartless skill; but what you want is passionate virtuosity."

Learning—The Change and Maintenance of Behavior

Before embarking on our journey, the goal of which is a scientific understanding of learning, it is well to take a few moments to consider what we mean by "understanding" and what we mean by "learning." To do otherwise is to risk not recognizing our goal when it is within sight.

Understanding Behavior   As used here, to understand a behavior is to be able to state the conditions under which that behavior will occur. If we know the conditions that are essential for the emergence of a given behavior, then we can predict when it will occur and can control its occurrence. That is, *the understanding, or explanation, of behavior consists of a statement of the functional relationship between the behavior and those prior events (antecedents) which influence the behavior*. This relationship may be stated in the symbols of everyday language, or in the more precise symbols of formal logic and mathematics. Both may be used to express the functional relationship between behavior (B) and its antecedents (A). The function may be stated verbally as in the sentence, "Burying nuts by squirrels is a decreasing function of the amount of daylight," or it may be stated more precisely as in the sentence, "Burying nuts is a negatively accelerated, exponential decay function of the amount of daylight." A graphic representation of the more precise sentence is given in Fig. 1.1.

Note that in either case some property of behavior, here the number of nuts buried per day, is expressed as a function of an antecedent condition, here

Fig. 1.1   A graphic representation of a functional relationship between behavior (the number of nuts buried per day) and an antecedent condition (the number of hours of daylight).

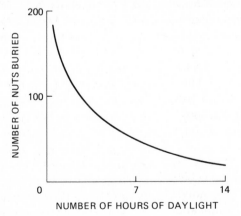

the number of hours of daylight. It is customary in graphic representations to plot the behavior, or dependent variable, on the vertical axis (ordinate) and the antecedent condition, or independent variable, on the horizontal axis (abscissa).

A more complete understanding develops as we are able to identify more of the antecedent conditions that affect the behavior of concern. Thus burying nuts might be affected by both the number of hours of daylight and the temperature. A more parsimonious understanding develops as we are able to give a more simplified and elegant account of the antecedent conditions. Thus the number of hours of daylight and the temperature might both affect the burying of nuts by their common effect on the production of a chemical substance. The more parsimonious understanding arises from the fact that we are able to identify a single antecedent, the chemical substance, as a function of the joint antecedents of the amounts of daylight and temperature.

It is important to point out that the parsimony referred to in the preceding example arises from the fact that two antecedents of the behavior have been replaced by a single antecedent, and not from the fact that the single antecedent is a physiological event—the production of a chemical substance. If the more parsimonious account results from the identification of an event that is observable outside the skin of the organism, that new, simpler antecedent also provides for a more parsimonious understanding of the behavior. If, for example, decreasing the amount of daylight and temperature were both found to decrease the general activity of squirrels and later work were to show that any procedure that decreased general activity would lead to an increase in the burying of nuts, then a more parsimonious account would also be achieved and a deeper understanding of the behavior would therefore have occurred. A deeper understanding provides a complete, yet parsimonious, account of the antecedents of behavior and is the product of an experimental analysis resulting from the making of controlled observations and the application of the self-corrective method of science.

Antecedents and Behaviors in Learning   Given that an understanding of behavior is achieved when we are able to state the antecedents of which the behavior is a function, we now turn to an examination of those antecedents and those behaviors that define the field of learning. What antecedents should the student of learning be concerned with? What behaviors are of interest to the student of learning? The answers to these questions are both complex and varied and, in a genuine sense, best come after and not before reading this book. After reading the book, the wide range of behaviors and antecedents discussed will form a basis for better answers than any short definition given at this point.

Nevertheless, it may be helpful to state at the outset that the study of learning focuses on those behavioral changes which occur as a function of the life experiences of the individual organism, particularly those events that are peculiar to the individual and are not routinely shared by all other members of the species. From the discovery of the functional relationships observed in the behavior of individuals and from the comparison of such relationships across time and across individuals, we seek to discern the continuities that describe human behavior and that constitute the laws of learning.

It should be obvious, though, that nature is not neatly divided into non-overlapping fields of study to suit the whim of the student of learning. Quite the contrary, it is more the rule than the exception to become fascinated with a problem having many ramifications and then to pursue its solution wherever it may lead. Thus the scientist who is interested in the learning of disadvantaged children may find it necessary to examine the effects of intrauterine nutrition on behavior, and the scientist who is investigating how stimuli affect learning may find it necessary to look at the effects of the early sensory environment on behavior. Problems, especially good problems, often enlarge rather than contract as their solutions are pursued.

Beyond paying particular attention to those antecedents that are not common to all members of a species living in their customary environments, the student of learning is especially concerned with antecedents whose effects on behavior are relatively enduring. Those antecedents with transitory effects, such as fatigue or drugs, are usually of less interest. If, however, there are longer-term effects that cause the person to avoid the fatiguing situation or to seek the circumstances in which the drug was administered, then the student of learning is apt to find his curiosity piqued.

Summarizing then, we may say that *the study of learning consists of the discovery and analysis of those antecedents that produce relatively enduring changes in subsequent behavior.*

What of the behaviors which are studied in the psychology of learning? If the antecedents that are of potential interest are many, the behaviors of potential interest are myriad. The species whose behavior has been studied range from amoeba to man and the types of behaviors range from the twitch of a single muscle fiber to the solution of a complex logical problem. It should be clear, then, that *behavior refers to the full scope of activities in which an organism may engage.* The briefest thought that flickers across awareness is behavior within the sense in which we use the term, and the fact of its evanescence is not grounds for ruling it outside the realm of behavior.

The fleeting character of thought and the fact that it is directly accessible to only one person means that such behaviors are more refractory to investigation than public behaviors. Private events fall within a science of behavior, but they present formidable technical problems for those who would study them. Because of the difficulties in investigating private events, we shall devote much of our effort toward the study of public behaviors, but our choice is made on pragmatic grounds and not because private events are, in principle, beyond the ken of a behavioral analysis.

Our search for an understanding of behavior will be illuminated by two fundamental principles—*the principle of natural selection* and *the principle of reinforcement.* The light which these principles provide is not that of the noonday sun which penetrates to the very bottom of the deepest crevasse but that of the rising sun which accentuates the prominences and depressions that mark the terrain over which, to reach our goal, we must travel. This more oblique light reveals those paths where progress may most likely be made and those places toward which the more intense and focused light of experimental observation may best be directed. At the conclusion of the journey lies a better understanding of our selves and of our society—even, perhaps, that "passionate virtuosity" of which we wrote earlier.

THE PRINCIPLE OF NATURAL SELECTION

It is September 15, 1835. A sailing ship of His Majesty's Navy has dropped anchor off the shore of a volcanic island, one of a chain of islands astride the equator some 600 miles from the western coast of the South American continent. A small landing party headed by a 25-year-old naturalist disembarks with provisions for a week to explore this sunblasted land of black lava sands—sands so hot that they burn the feet through the soles of boots. This strange island group, the ship's captain had called them "The Infernal Regions," is populated by equally strange creatures—huge tortoises weighing over 500 pounds, grotesque lizards which the naturalist refers to as "imps of darkness," and finches whose dark plumage stands in marked contrast to the brilliant hues of birds usually found at these tropical latitudes.

The naturalist who leads the little group has come to this place only through an improbable chain of circumstances. He had been an indifferent student as a boy, a failure as a medical student, and had received the invitation to join the ship on its circumnavigation of the globe upon the recommendation of a friend who had himself declined the offer. As unlikely as was this conjunction of ship, place, and man, it would forever alter the relationship of each of us with nature for the ship was the *Beagle,* the island chain was the Galápagos Archipelago, and the young naturalist was Charles Darwin.

Although Darwin's progress in formal education had not been noteworthy, he had been a keen observer and avid collector of animal and plant life throughout his boyhood and young adulthood, had been exposed to the best scientific minds at the Universities of Edinburgh and Cambridge, and had spent some weeks on a geological expedition in Wales in the company of a trained geologist. To these personal experiences that were to provide the foundation for Darwin's great insight must be added certain information that was generally available within the intellectual and social environment in which Darwin lived. Discoveries in geology had shown that the earth was much older than had previously been thought—the vast time required for the action of evolutionary processes was now available. Fossils lying at different geological strata had revealed transitional forms linking long-dead creatures with those which now inhabited the earth—the challenge to the doctrine of the special creation of each species was thus joined. Lastly, the air and pubs were full of wondrous tales by returning travelers of new animals and plants that had been discovered—the doctrine of special creation was again strained, now by the proliferation of species. It is within this context, supplemented greatly by his own explorations along the coasts of South America, that Darwin had written a letter three months earlier, as if he had a premonition of what was to come: "I look forward to the Galápagos with more interest than any other part of the voyage."

On the Galápagos, Darwin saw things which "haunted" him (his word) for over twenty years. "Here," Darwin wrote in his journal, "both in space and

(1)   (2)   (3)

Fig. 1.2   Sketches from Darwin's report of the voyage of the *Beagle*. (1) *Geospiza magnirostris*, (2) *Geospiza fortis*, and (3) *Geospiza parvula*.

time, we seem to be brought somewhat near to that great fact—that mystery of mysteries—the first appearance of new beings on this earth." While the tortoises and lizards held great fascination for him, the finches gave him perhaps the greatest pause: "The remaining land-birds form a most singular group of finches, related to each other in the structure of their beaks, short tails, form of body, and plumage. . . . The most curious fact is the perfect gradation in the size of the beaks. . . . The largest beak in the genus *Geospiza* (finches) is shown in [Fig. 1.2, left], and the smallest in [Fig. 1.2, right]; but instead of there being only one intermediate species, with a beak of the size shown in [Fig. 1.2, middle], there are no less than six species with insensibly graduated beaks. . . . Seeing this gradation and diversity of structure in one small, intimately related group of birds, one might really fancy that from an original paucity of birds in this archipelago, one species had been taken and modified for different ends."

Returning home to England after his voyage of almost five years, Darwin reflected upon what he had seen on the Galápagos. In private correspondence, he shared his momentous insight with friends—but he did not publish his conclusion. Instead, he began to amass evidence from the breeding programs of cattle and pigeons in domestication and from his own observations of animals, insects, and plants in the wild to evaluate the merit of his ideas. Finally, upon the urging of his friends, he consented to a brief, public report only when another scholar, Alfred Wallace, had independently arrived at a similar understanding. Following the initial brief report, *Origin of Species* was published in 1859.

Supported by a compelling set of observations and a closely reasoned argument, Darwin put forth the theory of evolution by means of natural selection. "As many more individuals of each species are born than can possibly survive, and as consequently there is a frequently recurring struggle for existence, it follows that any being, if it vary however slightly in any manner profitable to itself . . . will have a better chance of surviving, and thus be naturally selected. This preservation of favourable individual differences and variations, and the destruction of those which are injurious, I have called Natural Selection, or the Survival of the Fittest."[2]

With these words, the need had diminished for many special acts of creation to account for the diversity of nature and the possibility had appeared for a relationship between humans and animals of a kind hitherto undreamed of. No longer was it necessary for Darwin to be "astonished at the amount of creative force, if such an expression may be used, displayed on these small, barren, and rocky islands." In the place of astonishment, an exhilarating—if unproductive—emotion, the dark plumage of the finches could be interpreted as the result of natural selection against those lighter hues that would cause the small birds to stand out from the black lava and hence fall prey to the hawks that inhabited the islands. With regard to the gradations in the size of beaks, the availability of nuts with hard shells gave a selective advantage to those finches with heavier beaks, the availability of insects selected for a lighter beak, and the availability of fruits and flowers for still another form of beak. Finding different foods and no other species consuming those foods, the finches became progressively more in harmony with their environment through the action of natural selection. New species originated, not because of the attention given by a "creative force," but because of the isolation from competition with other species. Nature abhors a vacuum, whether that vacuum be organic or inorganic.

Natural Selection and Behavior

For those interested in understanding human behavior, what is to be gained by sharing Darwin's insight? What can the processes which shape beaks tell us about the processes which shape behavior? A few moments' reflection reveals that the relationship that exists between structure and behavior is an intimate one. The selective advantage that a large beak conveyed upon those finches living in environments in which hard-shelled nuts and seeds were available could be realized only to the extent that the finches behaved appropriately (i.e., pecked nuts and seeds). For a finch which did not peck at such sources of food, a large beak might provide no improved chance of survival.

In the case of some relatively simple behaviors, such as breathing, the relationship between structure and behavior is rather thoroughly understood. For most behaviors, however, the relationship between structure and behavior is not well understood. It is nevertheless assumed that every behavior—the merest thought that glimmers briefly in awareness as well as the gross movements of the limbs—is the product of physiological structure. To assume otherwise is to believe that we are made of other than the stuff of the physical world; a nonmaterial world is the province of mysticism, not of science.

In summary, since all behavior is mediated by physiological structures and since physiological structures are affected by evolutionary processes shaped in accordance with the principle of natural selection, natural selection may exert a profound influence upon behavior. Let us examine more closely how this influence might be realized.

Darwinian Fitness In order for the principle of natural selection to shape behavior, there must first be differences between individuals in their behavior, and these differences in behavior must produce differences in fitness. The meaning of "fitness" as the term is used in the study of evolution has a precise meaning. Differential fitness means a differential rate of production of surviving offspring. Men and women who accomplish great deeds that are applauded by society have high fitness in the Darwinian sense only if they produce viable offspring. A population composed of George and Martha Washington and Nicolai and Nadya Lenin would be of zero fitness since they left no offspring of record. They gave birth to nations, but not to sons or daughters. Charles and Emma Darwin, in an admirable example of the translation of theory into practice, had ten children, of whom seven survived childhood.

An additional requirement for the operation of natural selection is that the differences in structure that underlie the differences in behavior must be heritable. To say that a difference is heritable means that at least a portion of the determinants of the structure are transmitted from the parent to the offspring in the fertilized egg from which the offspring develops. It is important to note that Darwin was ignorant of the laws of heredity when he formulated the principle of natural selection. Darwin had slumbered in his grave at the feet of Newton for 18 years before Mendel's work was rediscovered in 1900. The principle of natural selection was thus basically a statement of a functional relationship and did not specify the precise nature of the mechanism which underlay that functional relationship; it expresses a relationship between the antecedent differential survival value and the consequent behavioral change. The modern sciences of genetics and molecular biology now provide a much deeper understanding of evolution, but they were unknown to Darwin.

The necessary conclusion from the fact of heritable individual differences in behavior—and the central insight of Darwin—is that those characteristics favored with greater fitness, even if that favor be ever so slight, will tend to increase in successive generations. Thus the selective action of the environment upon behavior will cause a progressive change in the relative frequency of the behavior through an increase in the relative frequency of the structures that underlie the behavior.

The principle of natural selection represents a deeper and more parsimonious account of the origin of behavioral differences and its implications are both pervasive and subtle. The characteristics that are favored or disfavored by the environment are only those characteristics with which the environment comes into direct contact. Only a realized characteristic, not a potential characteristic, results in differential fitness. If it were assumed, for example, that large size is favored over small size, large size must actually be attained before the environment may exert its selective effect. If nutritional deficiencies in the environment prevent persons with different potentials for size from realizing that potential, there can be no selection for size in such an environment. In short, *selection is on the basis of phenotype (realized characteristics) and not genotype (unexpressed hereditary, or genetic, potential).*

A second qualification is that the insight into behavior provided by *natural selection emerges with greatest force in the understanding of the behavior of groups of organisms and not of individual organisms.* Not all behaviors that are of benefit to the continuation of the group are also of benefit to the continuation of the individual. The individual soldier defending the nation against an

attacking army or the individual baboon defending the troop against a ma-
rauding leopard may perish, but their genetic endowment, shared with relatives in the individual's membership group, may thereby be preserved. In a
fundamental sense, it is the survival of the genes and not the individual possessing those genes that is the focus of natural selection (see Dawkins, 1976, for
a readable discussion of this theme). The individual is but the means to that
end.[3]

An Example Some points regarding the relationship between natural
selection and behavior are provided by observations of the behavior of two
species of gulls—the black-headed gull which nests in colonies in grassy, dune
areas and the kittiwake gull which nests on small ledges on coastal cliffs. The
young of the black-headed gull, whose shallow nests are easily accessible to
both flying predators such as the herring gull and the crow and to terrestrial
predators such as the fox, are vigorously defended by the adults of the colony.
Upon the intrusion of a predator into the colony area, a distinctive alarm call
summons a group of birds who, in the words of one predator, "fly toward it
calling noisily and defecating profusely while dive-bombing the enemy. I speak
with personal experience . . . when I say that this reception is an unpleasant
one. . . . The effect is unnerving to say the least, especially if the gull applies the
coup-de-grace, a not so gentle clip on the top of one's head with a trailing foot"
(Alcock, 1975, p. 272). While the response is quite effective when dealing with
herring gulls, crows, and tender-headed scientists, it is not so effective when
dealing with the fox. The half-eaten remains of black-headed gulls offer mute
testimony to the price which the individual must sometimes pay for the preservation of his genes in the group (Patterson, I. J., 1965).

The kittiwake, although it is also a member of the gull family, behaves
very differently. Because the cliffs are relatively free of predators—the narrow
ledges and gusting winds discourage avian enemies and the cliffs are inaccessible to the fox—the environment has not selected so strongly for responses to
predators. The rare predator is not typically met by an attack and is not lured
away from the nest by the adult birds. Remnants of the hatched eggs, whose
white inner surfaces draw attention to the young, are not removed from the
nest, and the young themselves neither hide nor are colored so as to be inob-
trusive (Cullen, 1957). These behaviors of the kittiwake are in marked contrast
to those found in its neighbor on the dunes, the black-headed gull (Tinbergen,
Broekhuysen, Feekes, Houghton, Kruuk, & Szulc, 1962). Natural selection has
shaped the behavior of the kittiwake and the black-headed gull populations to
different ends, but each end reflects the particular character of the environment to which the population is adapted. It is not meaningful to ask, "Which is
the better gull, the black-headed or the kittiwake?" Each is best for its particular environment, for its own ecological niche.

The differing behaviors of these two gulls in response to the common
problem of predation illustrates a further point—*fitness is not a general property of behavior that may be separated from the environment in which the be-*

havior occurs. Adaptiveness through the action of natural selection is not a property of behavior *per se,* but is a statement of the relationship between a behavioral characteristic of a population and a particular environment.

It would be an error to conclude, however, that all behaviors and all structures which are observed in living organisms are therefore adaptive for the prevailing environment. Because natural selection operates on the level of the population, other characteristics which occur in conjunction with the favored characteristic may fortuitously be maintained. Thus the kittiwake is thought to continue to lay eggs whose color matches that of the dune areas because of its origination from dune-nesting ancestors (Alcock, 1975). In the environment in which its ancestors evolved, camouflaged eggs had great adaptive significance; in the environment of the cliff, this characteristic is of less significance. As long as no opposed selective pressures arise, a characteristic may persist after the disappearance of the conditions which brought it into existence at the origin of the species. Living organisms are sometimes said to bear the "wounds of evolution." It is of some small consolation to reflect, however, that if the legacy of evolution is in truth a "wound," natural selection is currently acting to bind up that wound by reducing the frequency of adverse characteristics in the population. Evolutionary processes take time, even when the saltatory influence of mutations is admitted, and behavioral changes must perforce lag behind environmental changes.

The Adaptiveness of Behavior   Because the evolution of behavior is the result of the continuing process of natural selection and not a static condition, experimental analysis is required to determine whether any given behavior contributes to fitness, that is, whether it has adaptive significance in the present environment. Without the more focused light provided by experimentation, there is the danger that the concept of adaptation may give the appearance but not the substance of explanation. It is only too easy to fall into the logically circular argument that a behavior exists because it is adaptive and, in the next breath, to assert that the same behavior is adaptive because it exists.

As an example of how the adaptiveness of behavior may be evaluated, an examination of the black-headed gull is again instructive. As mentioned earlier, the black-headed gull—unlike the cliff-dwelling kittiwake—removes the broken pieces of eggshell from its nest. The color of the exterior of the eggshell is similar to that of the rest of the environment, that is, it is camouflaged, or cryptic. The interior of the eggshell is white, however, and visually conspicuous. The presumed contribution to fitness made by the behavior of eggshell removal is to camouflage the nest to predators, and hence to increase the likelihood of survival of the young. How can this assumption be tested?

First, the scientists wished to determine if the color of the eggs would in fact affect the extent to which the eggs were preyed upon by herring gulls and crows. Accordingly, they placed on the ground naturally colored eggs and eggs that had been painted a matte white. They found that within a maximum observation period of four hours, 81% of the naturally colored eggs but only 60% of the white eggs had survived intact. Thus light-colored eggs were clearly preyed upon more intensely than the cryptic natural eggs. It should be also noted that predators took a heavy toll of even the natural eggs—19% had been destroyed in four hours. Natural selection is very much at work among the black-headed gull.

Next, the scientists turned to the role of eggshell removal in survival. Does the presence in the nest of pieces of shell endanger the eggs and the chicks? To answer this question, naturally colored eggs with and without broken shell fragments were placed together in nest-shaped pits on the dunes. Thus the only difference between the nests was whether or not they contained pieces of shell with their telltale white inner surfaces. In observation periods lasting a maximum of five hours, 78% of the eggs in nests without shell fragments survived, while only 35% of the eggs with shell fragments remained. Clearly, the presence of pieces of shell greatly endangered the eggs and the behavior of removing the shell has adaptive significance.

Because they were careful observers, the scientists noticed a peculiar feature of eggshell removal from real nests: the shell fragments were not removed immediately after the chick had hatched! This was a surprising finding because of the risk of attack by the herring gulls and crows who prey upon both eggs and chicks. Natural selection would seem to favor prompt removal of the eggshell. Continued observation provided the solution to the puzzle. Some black-headed gulls themselves were seen to eat chicks who were newly hatched and still wet from the egg. These cannibals were driven away by nesting parents and seldom ate dry chicks because of difficulty in swallowing the fluffy young. But should the parent leave a wet chick in the nest in order to remove the shell, the chick would often be eaten (Tinbergen et al., 1962). Thus the selective pressure to remove the shell promptly was opposed by the counter pressure to remain in the nest until the chick was dry. Natural selection has favored the behavior of eggshell removal, but only if the removal is somewhat delayed.

This example of the fine tuning of behavior in accordance with the principle of natural selection illustrates a general finding that selection does not necessarily operate to produce extremes of behavior. If some of a behavior is adaptive, it does not follow that more of that same behavior is also adaptive. The opposition of selective pressures arising from different portions of the environment is the rule rather than the exception.

Natural Selection and Learning

Although we have seen that the environment may exert exceedingly subtle influences on behavior through the principle of natural selection, this principle does not provide a complete basis for the understanding of the origin of all behavior. The principle of natural selection describes the effect of common and relatively constant features of the environment on the behavior of a population of organisms which is exposed to that environment for long periods of time. If predators were attracted by shell fragments at one time but not at others or if predators developed an appetite for the eggs and young of the black-headed gull for a few years only, the behavior of the gull population would be markedly different. Thus while extensive and complex behavioral changes may be produced by the environment through natural selection, only a portion of the environmental influences may be illuminated by the light of this principle. Those environmental influences that are common to the *phylogeny* of a species—to its history as a group—are the province of the principles of natural selection. But each of us, whether human or gull, is not only a member of a species but also an individual. The behavior of each organism is shaped by its own individual genetic endowment as a legacy from its ancestral environment and its own individual experiences as a legacy from its contemporary environment. In short, what remains to be uncovered is an understanding of the principles that govern *ontogeny*—the development of the individual.

The study of ontogeny may be viewed as the analysis of the adaptation of the individual organism to its environment. Clearly, organisms whose behavior changes appropriately with changes in the environment have a reproductive advantage. Black-headed gulls which, after having sustained repeated attacks from foxes on one boundary of the colony, would congregate defenders at that boundary would better safeguard their genetic endowment. It is a certainty that the capacity of the behavior of the individual to be modified by the environment, that is, the ability to learn, would contribute favorably to fitness.

In the next major section of this chapter, we shall introduce the principle which bears the same relationship to ontogeny as natural selection bears to phylogeny. Of concern at present, however, is whether there is any evidence for the evolution of learning ability through natural selection. Unfortunately, behavior leaves no *direct* fossil record. It is structures themselves, and not how those structures were used, that are most clearly revealed when we journey back in time through the record which has been transcribed in the geological strata. Inferences can be drawn, and we shall have occasion to do so from time to time, but they remain inferences from observations, however plausible they may be.

Fortunately, the scientist may mimic the actions of natural selection on living organisms by instituting a program of artificial selection; that is, a program of selective breeding. With this strategy, the scientist imposes a criterion of fitness, and then determines whether the behavior of the animals changes over successive generations with respect to the selected characteristic. As applied to the evolution of learning, the question then becomes, "If we artificially select on the basis of performance in a learning situation, will the facility with which successive generations learn respond to this selective pressure?" If the selective breeding program is successful, we can conclude that evolution might select for those behavioral changes involved in learning.

Genetics and Learning Ability The importance of determining the influence of evolutionary processes was recognized by Tolman early in the study of learning and an extensive program of selective breeding was carried out by Tryon, one of Tolman's students. An enclosed maze, in which the rat had to learn the correct pathway to food, was chosen as the task to be learned. (See McClearn, 1963, for the history of this problem.) Tryon began with a large and heterogeneous group of rats and exposed each animal separately to the maze. The total number of errors (entrances into blind alleys) committed during 18 days of training served as the basis for artificial selection. In each generation, the males and females with the fewest number of errors were interbred in an attempt to form a so-called "maze-bright" strain of rats. Similarly, males and females with the greatest number of errors were interbred to form a "maze-dull" strain.

Was the experiment successful? Was it possible to produce through an artificial selection process two groups of rats which differed in their ability to learn the maze? A successful experiment would be consistent with the position that natural selection may occur for the adaptation of the individual to his environment.

The results of Tryon's experiment are shown in Fig. 1.3. The average number of errors made by the large group of rats with which the experiment had begun was slightly greater than 13. As the artificial selection procedure was applied to successive generations, two strains of rats emerged. The off-spring of the matings of animals which had learned the maze with few errors themselves made few errors when tested in the maze. Likewise, the offspring of pairs which had made many errors also made many errors. By the seventh generation, there was little overlap between the two strains. The poorest learners of the maze-bright group made fewer errors than the best learners of the maze-dull group. After seven generations, the bright strain made about eight errors in learning the maze, the dull strain about 18 errors. (See McClearn & DeFries, 1973, for a more detailed presentation of this experiment.) It is important to note that successive generations did *not* change the number of errors made on the *first* trial of their exposure to the maze. That is, the animals did not inherit the specific behavior of correctly running the maze. Rather, the

Fig. 1.3   The average number of errors to learn a maze as a function of successive generations of selective breeding by Tryon.   (From McClearn, 1963.)

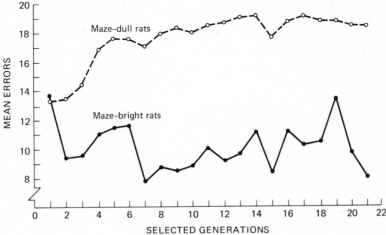

maze-bright and maze-dull rats began at the same point as their ancestors and then learned the maze with either fewer or more total errors respectively.

The data of the Tryon experiment are unambiguous—a selection process may exert a powerful effect on the number of errors made in learning a maze. The action of evolutionary processes may affect learning.

Identification of the *specific* behavioral characteristics responsible for changes in the number of errors is another matter, however. It strains credulity to believe that the environment in which the rat evolved as a species had resulted in specific genes that governed the ability to learn mazes. It is more reasonable to assume that in selecting animals based upon their maze performance, Tryon was selecting other component behaviors that influenced the number of errors made in the maze.

Subsequent research has supported this interpretation of Tryon's results. Specifically, maze-bright rats tend to be influenced by the spatial position of objects rather than the visual stimulation from those objects (Krechevsky, 1932). This finding probably reflects the fact that Tryon's maze was enclosed and hence provided minimal visual cues. Other work with the bright and dull strains showed that whereas the brights made fewer errors when given food for correct responses, dulls were superior in escaping from water (Searles, 1949). (See McClearn, 1963, for a summary and critique of other behavioral differences between Tryon's bright and dull strains.)

From these and other investigations, it is clear that Tryon's so-called bright rats are not generally more "intelligent" than the dull rats or "superior" to the dull rats. Artificial selection, like natural selection, has simply resulted in organisms which behave differently. To equate a difference in behavior with a difference in value is our doing, not nature's. Again, is the black-headed gull superior to the kittiwake? Each flourishes in its own environment and would likely perish if suddenly confined to the environment of the other. The notions of general superiority and inferiority seldom make either biological or behavioral sense.

The type of finding reported in Tryon's work—that artificial selection may produce differences in behavior and, particularly, differences in the ability to learn a specific task—has been repeated many times. In fact, *every selective breeding experiment that has been conducted in accordance with good experimental practice has been successful in influencing behavior.* The authors know of no exception to this statement. Examples of such behaviors include avoidance learning in rats and mice; trainability in dogs; aggressiveness in rats, mice and chickens; and emotionality in rats and mice. Thus the environment of the past, acting through the principle of natural selection, may modulate the effect of the present environment on the behavior of the individual. But through the action of what principle does the present environment affect the individual? What is the principle whose relation to ontogeny is that of the principle of natural selection to phylogeny? That is the subject of the next section of the chapter and to its answer we now direct our attention.

THE PRINCIPLE OF REINFORCEMENT

The principle of natural selection has caused new light to be shed on the relationship between man and the other species with whom the earth is shared. Instead of man and animal each expressing a portion of some common grand design, each species has been shaped by its particular environment through the processes of evolution. There is no single purpose or direction to evolution; indeed, there are as many purposes and directions as there are environments.

The turning of the focus of inquiry to the evolutionary history of a species was a crucially important redirection of effort since the past could be known, albeit imperfectly and with difficulty, by the methods of science. Thus the key which would unlock the future of a species could be discovered in the past and the present of that species. When a species flourishes and expands in the future, it is because the present and the past have fortuitously shaped the species to ends which happen to coincide with the demands of future environments. Preparations for the future depend utterly upon the existence of continuities between past and future environments.

While we might agree that the origins of groups, or species—even humans—may be found by looking at the environments of their ancestors, what of the origins of the behavior of individuals. Does not the behavior of individual men and women originate from some intelligence, or force, or mental faculty within each of us? Is not the key which would unlock the mystery of the individual to be found within and not without the person? The answer that dualistic Western philosophy has given since the time of Descartes (1596–1650) is as follows: The behavior of animals may be understood wholly in terms of physical principles but humans, although possessing a physical body, control that body through the free exercise of mind. Although Darwin had shown that the bodies of both animals and humans were shaped by the common action of evolution through natural selection, most people believed that the body was controlled by mental processes that were to some extent free of external influences. The Darwinian argument had won the bodies but not the minds of humanity; an understanding of human behavior was thought to require knowledge that transcended physical laws. The world was thought to be made of two stuffs—matter and mind.

The transformation from the dualistic view in which we stand halfway between the animals and the angels—a schizophrenic existence partaking of both worlds—is not as readily presented as is the change wrought by the theory of evolution. The chief difficulty arises from the fact that the transformation is not yet complete: We are now in the very midst of it. So close to the seminal events, proper perspective is not easily obtained for the eye of history is appropriately presbyopic (farsighted); like an older person it sees most clearly from a distance.

Whatever the ultimate judgment of history, the account sketched below will be included in the final story of the development of the fundamental principle of ontogeny. Although of equal moment, the story may lack some of the drama and color of the uncovering of the principle of natural selection. The

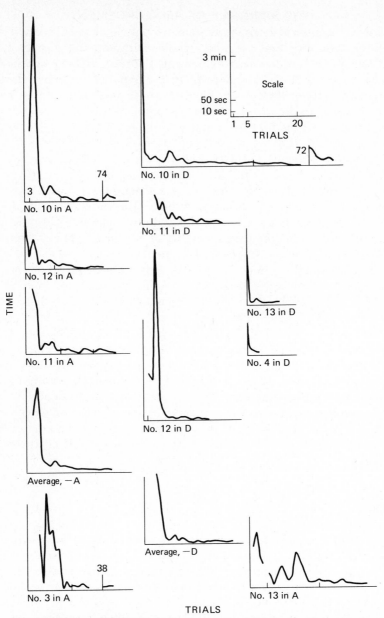

Fig. 1.4 Changes in the amount of time to operate the latch in puzzle boxes A and D as a function of the number of trials. A short vertical line above the abscissa and an associated number represent the number of days since the previous trial. A break in the curve represents a failure to operate the latch in 10 or 15 min. (From Thorndike, 1898.)

nature of science has changed since the time of Darwin's voyage on the *Beagle*. Science has become the vocation of the many and not the avocation of the wealthy few. It is now a part of the institutions of society and is carried out in universities and in the laboratories of government and industry. The golden answers are less often to be found in the form of nuggets lying on the surface, and are now more often the result of the mining operation of experimentation.

Edward Thorndike was born in 1874, only 15 years after the publication of *Origin of the Species*. After undergraduate work at Wesleyan College, he began graduate work at Harvard in 1895 with the intention of studying English. In addition to course work in English, Thorndike attended a lunch-period seminar held by the psychologist and philosopher William James. Thorndike had been introduced by chance to James's ideas while preparing for an examination at Wesleyan and had been so stimulated that he purchased *Principles of Psychology*, "the only book outside of the field of literature that I voluntarily bought during the four years of college." After two more courses with James during the spring semester, Thorndike decided to become a psychologist and embarked on a series of experiments that were to lead directly to his greatest achievement: He began his study of the origins of behavioral change.

Following the refusal of authorities to permit him to pursue his work with children, Thorndike turned to the chick as a subject. His landlady made him cease experimentation in his room because she feared the incubator would cause her house to burn down. After a futile attempt to find space in the Harvard laboratories, James ". . . with his habitual kindness and devotion to underdogs and eccentric aspects of science, harbored my chickens in the cellar of his home for the rest of the year. The nuisance to Mrs. James was, I hope, somewhat mitigated by the entertainment of the two youngest children."

The use of chicks rather than children as subjects had another advantage; it gave him a ready excuse to stop at the home of Bess Moulton in order to warm the chicks as they were brought from the farm to Harvard. Bess had just begun undergraduate work and, when she spurned his offer of marriage in Christmas of 1896, an unhappy Thorndike decided to leave Harvard to continue his work with a variety of animals at Columbia University. He wrote next year to Bess from his room in New York: "A mouse just ran across my foot. A lot of rats are gnawing the bureau; three chicks are sleeping within a yard of me; the floor of my room is all over tobacco and cigarette ends and newspapers and books and coal and a chicken pen and the cats' milk dish and old shoes, and a kerosene can and a broom which seems rather out of place. It's a desolate hole, this flat of mine. I will clean it Sunday and you come Sunday night. Don't just come and give me a piece of candy and sneak, but stay till the 11:03."

What Thorndike was seeking with his menagerie of animals—beyond the arousal of Bess's sympathy—was to uncover the course and origins of behavioral change. To this end, he constructed puzzle boxes in which he placed an animal that had been deprived of food. A mechanism operated by a latch would permit the animal to leave the box and eat. What Thorndike found is shown in Fig. 1.4. The behavior of individual animals changed; with continued exposure to the puzzle box the animals came more and more quickly to pull the latch.

Thorndike's insight was that the *consequences* of one's actions—what he had called "resultant pleasures"—were the basis for change. This insight was to become known as the *law of effect*. Responses followed by a "satisfying state of affairs" increased in strength while responses followed by an "annoying state of affairs" decreased in strength. In an attempt to dilute the mentalistic flavor of the law of effect, Thorndike defined the states of satisfaction and annoyance: "By a satisfying state of affairs is meant one which the animal does nothing to avoid, often doing things which maintain or renew it. By an annoying state of affairs is meant one which the animal does nothing to preserve, often doing things which put an end to it."

Although his initial work had been done with animals, Thorndike believed that "these simple ... phenomena ... which animal learning discloses, are the fundamentals of human learning also." This belief was rapidly translated into action when he joined the faculty of Teachers College, Columbia University in 1900. (He was simultaneously successful in persuading Bess Moulton to become his wife after all.) At Teachers College, he became the most prolific writer in the history of psychology as he applied his thinking and his research to the problems of education, concluding that "the law of effect is the fundamental law of teaching and learning."

In support of his denial of the mentalistic tradition and his assertion that "progress was not by seeing through things, but by accidental hitting upon them," Thorndike conducted human experiments on what he termed the "spread of effect." He believed this work to be his most important contribution to science. In a typical experiment, a list of words was read slowly with the subject asked to give a number from one to 10 following each word. Immediately after the subject had responded with a number, the experimenter labeled the response either Right or Wrong according to a prearranged schedule. At the conclusion of a number of repetitions of the list, a list intended to be long enough to prevent the subject from remembering his exact responses, the frequency with which a number was repeated in response to the various words was tallied. The results indicated to Thorndike that the law of effect applied with equal force to humans: numbers followed by *Right* were given more often as responses to the preceding word and this effect spread to adjacent responses as well. The phenomenon of the spread of effect was interpreted to mean that the consequence of a response may act automatically to strengthen a response with human subjects as had earlier been shown with animal subjects and, moreover, that other nearby responses were affected in a similar fashion.[4]

Thus for both animals and humans Thorndike identified the consequences of a response as crucially important. Whether a response was to continue or cease was determined by the environmental events which followed that response. Thorndike's words, spoken upon the 100th anniversary of Darwin's birth, best describe the implications of this finding as he saw them. "Our intellects and characters are no more subjects for magic, crude or refined, than (are) the ebb and flow of the tides or the sequence of day and night. Thus, at last, man may become ruler of himself as well as the rest of nature. For strange as it may sound, man is free only in a world whose every event he can understand and foresee. Only so can he guide it. We are captains of our own souls only so far as they act in perfect law so that we can understand and foresee every response which we will make to every situation. Only so can we control our own selves. It is only because our intellect and morals—the mind and spirit of man—are a part of nature, that we can be in any significant sense responsible for them, proud of their progress, or trustful of their future."[5]

Thorndike's great contribution to the understanding of the ontogeny of behavior was to direct attention to the environmental events that followed the behavior. Just as the future of a species was to be found in an examination of the environment of its ancestors, so the future of an individual member of a species was to be found in the history of its individual behavior. For both Darwin and Thorndike, the future did not pull the present toward itself, but rather the present was pushed into the future by the past. Purpose, both for the individual and for the species, was not a harbinger of the future but a residue of the past. Much remained to be done after Thorndike, and much remains to be accomplished still, as will be evident in Chapters 3 and 4, which deal with the modern statement of the law of effect—the principle of reinforcement. Nevertheless, Thorndike began the journey toward an understanding of the behavior of individuals with a giant step in a new and fruitful direction.

Reinforcement and Behavior

Most fundamentally, the law of effect holds that the fate of a response is determined by the environmental consequences that followed that response in the past of the individual. The events comprising such consequences might function to *increase* the frequency of the response relative to other behavior; that is, to function as *reinforcers* in modern parlance. Conversely the consequent events might function to *decrease* the frequency of the response relative to other behavior; that is, to function as *punishers*. When the emphasis is placed upon the *consequences* of responding, the very nature of the way in which we speak of behavior is fundamentally altered. Instead of saying that a person behaves in order to achieve a future good, we say instead that he or she behaves because such behavior was previously followed by a past good. It is not the anticipation of future delights, but the experience of past delights that causes us to behave as we do. People introduce themselves to others at a party, not only because they envision an enjoyable evening—though this may be—but because similar behavior has been followed by enjoyable evenings in the past. If the anticipation of the evening were sufficient for the occurrence of the behavior, then all would be bold and none would be reticent. Until the time of Thorndike, many psychologists believed that repetition or practice *per se* caused learning. After Thorndike, repetition was seen to be the *result* of learning, and not its cause. Those behaviors that endure are those which have been followed by reinforcing consequences; those behaviors that perish are those which have been followed by punishing consequences.

Functional Nature of the Law of Effect   While a comprehensive treatment of the principle of reinforcement must await later chapters, a few general remarks are in order concerning the nature of Thorndike's contribution. First, the law of effect is essentially a functional statement that relates the future frequency of a response to its past consequences. The value of the law of effect as an insight into the origins of behavioral change does not rest upon a knowledge of the processes that underlie and mediate the observed behavioral change—although such knowledge will ultimately deepen our understanding of a principle of reinforcement.

It is well to remember that the principle of natural selection, when first offered by Darwin, was also a functional statement similarly devoid of knowledge of the biological processes of which it was the expression. Both Darwin and Thorndike speculated about the mechanisms that gave rise to their functional statements. Darwin had his "gemmules," which purported to be the units of heredity, and Thorndike had his "confirming reaction," which was intended to represent the changes in the nervous system that were responsible for learning. Both Darwin and Thorndike were, of course, wrong about the processes underlying their insights, but the values of the principles of natural selection and reinforcement endure nevertheless.

Ultimately, the private events—whether described behaviorally or physiologically—that underlie the principle of reinforcement will be explicated and will enrich our understanding, just as knowledge of genetics and molecular biology has furthered our understanding of the principle of natural selection. Because of limitations of space, we shall not often pursue the study of the physiological processes responsible for behavioral changes. The study of these processes is an expanding and exciting enterprise, however, and will contribute substantially to a final statement of an adequate principle of reinforcement (for example, Glickman & Schiff, 1967; John, 1967; Kupferman, 1975; Pribram & Broadbent, 1970; Thompson, R. F., 1976).

By his early use of such diverse events as food for deprived animals and the word "right" for humans in his study of the law of effect, Thorndike freed the principle of reinforcement from a narrow and restrictive interpretation. These diverse events had in common only the functional property that they affected the relative frequency of the behavior that they followed. The insight that such disparate events as food, a kind word, and a lover's smile might all be subsumed under a single concept—reinforcement—was an abstraction of the highest order! While there are undeniable differences among these events—and an adequate analysis must reflect these differences—they share the property that they all may change the behavior which precedes them.

A case history (Bachrach, Erwin, & Mohr, 1965) illustrates nicely the functional significance of the principle of reinforcement. Mary, soon after her marriage and move to a distant city, began to lose weight for no known medical reason. Over a period of time, her weight fell from 120 to 47 pounds! Even upon returning to her parents' home, she did not gain weight and hospitalization was required. It appeared that Mary would soon die. What could be done for a person so disturbed that the basic biological need to eat had apparently become defective? Two psychologists in the hospital noticed that Mary spent a good deal of time talking to others or watching television if such activities were available. In Thorndike's terms, environments which permitted talking or watching television seemed to constitute "a satisfying state of affairs" for

Mary. Accordingly, the psychologists permitted Mary to talk to others or to watch television *only after* eating. At first, she would need to take but a spoonful of food when it was offered; later she had to feed herself. Over the course of one year, Mary almost doubled her weight and was able to leave the hospital. Note that this example indicates that even a response with a clear biological basis—eating—was made to increase by environmental events which were equally clearly social in nature.[6]

Importance of Temporal Relationships   A second general comment concerning the law of effect is that it asserts the importance of the temporal relationship among events in the generation of behavioral change. In order for one response to increase in frequency relative to other responses, what is required—other things being equal—is that the response be followed by a reinforcing environmental change. The response need not "cause" the reinforcer; it need simply be followed by the reinforcer in order for behavior to change. Thorndike's experiments on the spread of effect were specifically addressed to this point. By saying "right" after a response, not only that response but other, adjacent responses increased in frequency as well.

It remained for Skinner (1948) to make the point most effectively. Skinner placed a food-deprived pigeon in a small chamber and made food available "at regular intervals *with no reference whatsoever to the bird's behavior.*" Since some behavior must occur prior to the reinforcer, that behavior should increase because of the temporal relation only. Indeed, when the food hopper appeared every 15 sec, a readily identifiable behavior emerged in six of eight pigeons. Each bird behaved differently—one turned counter-clockwise, another thrust its head toward the ceiling, a third hopped from one foot to the other, etc.—but the behavior of each bird showed the effect of the reinforcer. Skinner labeled such learning superstitious by analogy with human superstitions. Once the response had been acquired, the interval between reinforcers could be lengthened to 1 or 2 min and the response was still maintained. The hopping behavior of a pigeon receiving food at one-min intervals is shown in Fig. 1.5. Clearly, the behavior was changed even though hopping was not necessary in order for the reinforcer to occur.[7]

Neither Thorndike's humans in the spread-of-effect experiment nor Skinner's pigeons in the *superstition experiment* could detect causes, only coincidences. Lest we leave this topic believing that the superstitious maintenance of a response is a phenomenon confined to our lesser bretheren, it should be noted that there is ample documentation with humans as well (Catania & Cutts, 1963). As the philosopher David Hume had indicated 200 years earlier, causation is a reaction of organisms to temporal succession and not a characteristic inherent in the physical world.

Implications for Applications   A third general comment that may be made is that by focusing upon behavior and its relationship to environmental events, Thorndike opened the way for us to control our own behavior. If supernatural forces arising from outside the physical world or private events arising

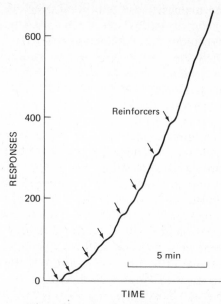

Fig. 1.5 The cumulative number of hopping responses as a function of time. Food was given independently of behavior at 1-min. intervals. Each occurrence of hopping caused the curve to move upward one unit. (From Skinner, 1948. Copyright 1948 by the American Psychological Association. Reprinted by permission.)

from within the individual are the wellsprings of the currents that shape our lives, the mastery of our destinies might forever elude us. If, however, the origins of behavioral change—of learning—reside in the environment, then we possess the resources to bring about systematic changes in our behavior.

While scientists are sometimes portrayed by themselves and others as engaged in a mysterious activity divorced from the concerns of the everyday world, history reveals that science often has profound effects on our daily lives. In fact, a science that has no such implications is suspect. An adequately formulated principle of reinforcement may be expected to have far-reaching consequences, and grave issues must be confronted if we are to avoid the potential dangers inherent in any technology (Skinner, 1971). Thorndike, with his applications of the law of effect to education, began the translation of principles into practice and we shall intermittently encounter other efforts as we proceed in our study of learning.

Some Potential Pitfalls Although the principle of reinforcement provides an essential leverage for many of the problems of individual behavior, there are potential hazards as well. As with the principle of natural selection, it is possible to "explain" too much by the principle of reinforcement. Just as the mere existence of a behavior is no guarantee that the behavior has current adaptive significance, so its existence is no guarantee that the behavior is presently followed by a reinforcer. To state that a behavior exists because it is reinforced, and then to maintain that it is reinforced because it exists is to argue in a logically circular fashion. What we shall be seeking is a formulation of a principle of reinforcement that defines a reinforcing relationship between the environment and behavior in a manner that is independent of the behavioral changes it tries to explain.

A second potential hazard arises from an overevaluation of the role of the temporal relationships between response and reinforcer. The superstition experiment demonstrates that a purely temporal relationship between observable responding and certain environmental events may lead to behavioral change. This finding does not exclude the possibility that other, perhaps unobserved, events may also play crucial roles in learning. Private events—for example, awareness in humans—may affect the outcome of a given temporal relationship in experienced learners. Similarly, acknowledging the importance of temporal relationships is not a claim that all responses and all reinforcers are interchangeable within a given temporal relationship. The ontogeny and phylogeny of the learner may differentially facilitate or hinder the development of new functional relationships. The precise contribution of the temporal relationship to learning is a matter for further analysis in our search for a principle of reinforcement. The precise expression in the individual of a given temporal relationship between behavior and its consequences is affected by both the prior history of the individual and the species of which that individual is a member.

In summary, although much remains unknown and there are potential dangers as well as advantages, an adequately formulated statement of a principle of reinforcement would provide a major insight into the development of individual behavior. This much is clear: *the behavior of every organism that has ever been studied is affected by its consequences.* The authors know of no exceptions to this general statement.

Reinforcement and Natural Selection

As you have no doubt recognized in reading the discussions of natural selection and reinforcement, there are many parallels between these two principles. The principle of natural selection states that the frequency of a behavior increases in subsequent generations of different organisms when that behavior is followed by certain consequences. The principle of reinforcement states that the frequency of a behavior increases in subsequent occasions for the same organism when that behavior is followed by certain consequences. The first is an assertion about the relationship of the behavior of groups and the environment, and deals with what have been called "the contingencies of survival." The second is an assertion about the relationship between the behavior of individuals and the environment and deals with what have been called "the contingencies of reinforcement" (Skinner, 1971).

What these principles have in common, in addition to their expression of a functional relationship between present behavior and its prior consequences is that both point outward from the person toward the environment as the origin of behavioral change. Natural selection points to environments in the past of the species; reinforcement points to environments in the past of the individual.

The relationship between the principles of natural selection and reinforcement is an intimate one. The capacity for behavior to be sensitive to its consequences, the basis of learning, is favored by natural selection. The capacity for behavior to have adaptive significance, the basis of natural selection, is favored by reinforcement. Since the behavior of all organisms is sensitive to both phylogenetic and ontogenetic consequences, we cannot neglect either principle in our effort to understand any behavior. The rich and varied tapestry which is the life of each of us is woven from the strands of both natural selection and reinforcement. These two principles are the very fibers—the warp and the woof—of the fabric. The shuttle that darts among the strands, and from whose action the tapestry emerges, is guided by the hands of the contemporary environment. But just as it is meaningless to inquire of the weaver, "Which is more important to the tapestry, the warp or the woof?" so it is meaningless to inquire of the behavior of any individual, "Which is more important, the environment of the distant past as reflected by the principle of natural selection, or the environment of the near past as reflected by the principle of reinforcement?" There is no tapestry without *both* warp and woof; there is no behavior without *both* natural selection and reinforcement.

Interaction of Reinforcement and Natural Selection   Although all behavior is affected by both the ancestral environment of the species and the more contemporary environment of the individual, population geneticists have found it convenient for some purposes to express the contribution of the ancestral environment by a measure called the *heritability* of the structure or behavior. The term heritability denotes that proportion of the differences between individuals in a characteristic that may be attributed to genetic variation. If in a given contemporary environment all of the differences among individuals in some behavior could be attributed to genetic variations, then the heritability of that behavior would be 1.0. If half of the differences could be attributed to genetic variation, then the heritability would be .50. In this section, we briefly examine the concept of heritability in order that we might better understand the interrelationship between the principles of natural selection and reinforcement.

First, the heritability of a characteristic does not reflect an immutable, invariant contribution of genetics to behavior. The heritability of a characteristic may change as the environment is changed. As a simple example, if heritability of skin color were assessed in Scandanavia, most of the differences would be due to environmental influences. Skin tones in this part of the world are due primarily to whether the person makes a living indoors or outdoors. In the United States, on the other hand, most of the variability in skin color is due to genetic factors. How then should we answer a question concerning whether variation in skin color is due primarily to environmental or genetic factors? As with all characteristics, the answer must be specific to a particular range of environmental conditions; the answer may vary as changes take place in the specific conditions under which the answer was obtained.

There is another more subtle sense in which the genetic contribution depends on the environment. From work with simple organisms, it is known that the expression of genes may change as a function of the environment, or conversely that the effect of the environment on behavior may change as a function of the genes. This phenomenon is referred to as *gene-environment interaction*. As an illustration, at one environmental temperature a fruit fly may develop wings which are capable of flight while, at another temperature, a genetically identical fruit fly may be incapable of flight. Both behaviors are equally influenced by the same genetic factors, but in one environment the animal soars and in the other it is confined to earth.

A second illustration of the interaction of genetic and environmental factors in the determination of behavior is provided by the differing reactions of organisms to stress. Through artificial selection based upon the effects of the ingestion of salt on blood pressure, two genetically different strains of rats have been developed which differ in their susceptibility to hypertension, or high blood pressure. When animals of these two strains are subjected to stress, by arranging that food-getting behaviors will also produce occasional electric shocks, only the strain susceptible to hypertension reacts with an increase in blood pressure (Friedman & Iwai, 1976). Thus the same environmental stress produces hypertension in some individuals and has no effect on others, depending on their genetic predisposition. Equivalently, the same genetic factors in the hypertension-susceptible strain are associated with a much elevated blood pressure in a stressful environment and with relatively normal blood pressure in a standard environment. Knowledge of neither the environment alone nor the genes alone is sufficient to predict the behavior of the individual—both sources of knowledge are essential. Behavior is the single, unified expression of the environments of both the near and distant pasts, and no one number can hope to capture the full richness of that expression.

Even with the qualifications that must be placed upon the interpretation of heritability, the usefulness of the measure for an understanding of the behavior of individuals is limited still further. The heritability measure is derived from the assessment of *groups* whereas the behavioral changes known as learning are characteristics of *individuals*. This is basically a reiteration of the point that natural selection is a principle which emerges from comparisons between different individuals whereas reinforcement is a principle that arises from comparisons over time within the same individual. Whatever its usefulness in behavioral genetics, a statement such as "50% of the differences in some behavior are due to heredity" has no clear meaning on the level of the individual. It does not mean that 50% of the behaviors are entirely due to natural selection and the remaining 50% are entirely due to reinforcement. Nor does it mean that half of each behavior is due to natural selection and the other half is due to reinforcement. The belief that we may neatly apportion behaviors into two independent entities—heredity and environment—reflects more the simplicity of our own thought processes than any simplicity to be found in nature. The behavior that we observe in each individual is the product of a unique combination of genetic and environmental antecedents.

Consider the following example: Two children are observed to perform differently on a numerical problem on an intelligence test. One child may have a known genetic defect, for example, Down's syndrome, and the difference in performance therefore might be attributed to genetic factors. However, that same child might then be put through a training program designed in accordance with behavioral principles (Reese, 1971) and subsequently perform on the numerical problem as well as the other child. The behavior on the numerical problem now has different origins in the two children, and while it may be possible by examining groups of individuals to conclude that 50% of the variation is due to heredity and 50% is due to environment, such a statement does not seem to be particularly helpful or meaningful in understanding the differences in the behavior of these two individual children. The environments of the distant past and near past, acting through the principles of natural selection and reinforcement, are inextricably intermingled in the individual. While for some purposes and because of the limitations of language they may be referred to separately, these two principles converge in the individual to find a complementary and unified expression.

If human problems are to be solved, we must find those contemporary environments in which each individual may best attain his or her personal objectives. The quest for human betterment through environmental change is known as *euphenics* and is to be contrasted with the approach through genetic change or *eugenics*. Because the environment influences the very manner in which the genes find expression in behavior and because the means for changing the environment are within our immediate capabilities, the best hope of avoiding the debacles with which the chapter began and of attaining the worthy goals on which most would agree is through euphenics. With this conclusion even the behavioral geneticist, who might understandably be thought to counsel otherwise, is in agreement (Thiessen, 1972).

A LOOK AHEAD

The principles of natural selection and reinforcement, acting together, are general statements that illuminate the origins of behavior in the ancestral and individual environments. Both principles contribute to the understanding of all the phenomena that we shall encounter, but each phenomenon also possesses characteristics that require additional insights. In this final section of our introduction to the study of learning, language, and memory, we shall look ahead to anticipate some of these phenomena and the special problems that they pose. In so doing, we shall also provide a brief overview of the structure of the presentation that is to come.

Fundamental Processes

The principles of natural selection and reinforcement both emphasize that behavior is influenced by its consequences. But the occurrence of every response is affected by events that precede it as well as those that follow it. Natural selection has produced in the black-headed gull a complex behavior pattern in which fragments of eggshells are picked up, carried some distance, and then deposited elsewhere. But natural selection has accomplished more than merely increasing the likelihood of a behavior. Natural selection has produced an animal which will engage in this behavior only in a special environment—one containing a nest, dry chicks, and shell fragments of a particular description. The black-headed gull does not indiscriminately pick up small pieces of material and carry them off under any and all circumstances. Only in the presence of specific environmental antecedents does the behavior occur.

Similarly, the reinforcer that increased hopping behavior in the pigeon in the superstition experiment does not then produce hopping under any and all circumstances. When removed from the experimental chamber and returned to its home loft, the pigeon behaves essentially as it had previously. Again, behavior has changed because of its consequences, but the change is restricted to only a portion of the total environment in which the creature must function.

Elicitation   When a stimulus controls a response, that environmental-behavioral relationship is called an *elicitation process* (Catania, 1971a). Elicitation processes may have their origins in the operation of natural selection—as with eggshell removal in the black-headed gull—or in the operation of reinforcement—as with hopping in pigeons in the superstition experiment. When the elicitation process is relatively independent of individual experience, the relationship between the environment and behavior is an instance of *unconditioned* stimulus control. When the elicitation process is heavily dependent upon individual experience, the relationship is an instance of *conditioned* stimulus control. Because the development of new functional relationships between the environment and behavior, that is, learning, arises from preexisting elicitation processes, we shall first examine elicitation processes *per se* before pursuing our search for an adequately formulated principle of reinforcement.

Reinforcement   Making use of preexisting elicitation processes, psychologists have sought an understanding of the principle of reinforcement in two simple learning procedures—classical conditioning and instrumental, or operant, conditioning. The best-known example of the classical procedure is Pavlov's work on salivary conditioning in the dog, in which an auditory stimulus acquires control of the salivary response after salivation has been elicited by food in the mouth. A well-known example of instrumental conditioning is Skinner's work, in which the pressing of a lever by a rat increases in frequency when lever-pressing is followed by the presentation of food, a potent eliciting stimulus.

Through the application of the classical and instrumental procedures, we shall identify the variables that promote learning, study the functional relationships between those variables and behavioral change, and—most importantly—seek to achieve a deeper understanding of the principle of reinforcement.

Stimulus Control   The presentation of elicitation processes in the classical and instrumental procedures does more than simply change the strength of responding; it also alters the stimulus control of the response. Food following an auditory stimulus in the classical procedure brings about the control of salivation by the auditory stimulus. Food following lever-pressing in the instrumental procedure brings about the control of lever-pressing by environmental stimuli such as the sight of the lever. Turning to an example closer to our own experience, another's thoughtful attention to our words makes it more likely that we shall speak to that person when encountered again at a later time. Salivating, lever-pressing, and speaking are not indiscriminately increased by reinforcing consequences; they are controlled by the environments in which those reinforcing consequences have been realized.

In the chapters dealing with stimulus control and motivation, we examine some of the specific and general effects of reinforcers on the environmental control of behavior. Following an experimental analysis of the variables affecting the development of stimulus control, we shall seek to understand the behavioral processes that determine the degree to which experience in one environment alters the control of behavior in other environments. While each experience is unique, these individual experiences change the performance of the learner in a variety of environments, and their effects appear to transcend the unique properties of the original experience.

The Experienced Learner

When we restrict our attention to the behavior of learners whose experience prior to the experimental situation may be tightly controlled, the fundamental processes of elicitation, reinforcement, and stimulus control may be viewed with considerable clarity. In order to understand the phenomena under investigation, we need look only at events that have occurred within the confines of the experiment as supplemented by species-typical behaviors from the ancestral environment.

When our concern is with the experienced learner who has a wealth of relevant prior experience, understanding is greatly complicated. If we confine our gaze to the present environment, an understanding of the phenomena of language and memory would forever elude us. By looking backward in time to the conditions of prior learning, the origins of these phenomena may become less obsure. But the task is an arduous one at best. Only rarely do we have access to the particulars of the relevant prior experience. We are in much the same position as the paleontologist who, having knowledge of only extant species and a few fragments of preexisting creatures, attempts to reconstruct the process of evolution through natural selection. Although the effects of selection may be amply demonstrated in the laboratory and the field with existing organisms, our knowledge of the precise sequence of events that led to any present species shall almost certainly remain imperfect and incomplete.

Because our knowledge of the antecedents of the behavior of the experienced learner is necessarily a partial one, we may question the generality of principles discovered from the study of processes in organisms whose experience may be more tightly controlled. Organisms with the rich and varied experiences of adult humans often appear to learn in new and, perhaps, fundamentally different ways from simpler organisms with more impoverished experiences. One thing at least is certain, stimulus control in the experienced learner is almost never completely determined within the experimental situation. Almost any event presented within an experiment already controls some response because of the learner's prior experience. Consequently, the response of the learner to that event must be taken into account in our efforts to understand the behavior. Even a seemingly simple stimulus such as a tone may evoke private events such as those which we call memories, thoughts, images, and the like. The tone may remind the learner of a bell signifying the end of class, may bring a popular song to mind or may conjure up an image of church bells ringing in a steeple. To the extent that these private events influence behavior in the experimental situation they must be incorporated in any adequate account of phenomena being studied in the experienced learner.

Language   Of the behaviors of which humans are capable, none distinguishes us more from our fellow creatures than our ability to produce and comprehend speech. Of all the stimuli that control human behavior and of all the responses that humans may emit, none are more important than those which comprise language. In our analysis of language, we shall be concerned with the contribution of both the ontogeny and phylogeny of the learner to language and speech, and whether the skills involved are language-specific or more general cognitive abilities. The study of language will also permit an analysis of creativity in behavior, since the experienced learner is capable both of producing and understanding sentences that have never previously been spoken or heard.

Memory   Our inquiry into human behavior is concluded with the study of memory. Memory is an appropriate final topic since its understanding requires a knowledge of almost all of what has gone before. The conditions in which the memories were acquired affect retention—this is the problem of storage. The conditions in which memories are recalled also affect retention—this is the problem of retrieval. Clearly, the principles governing reinforcement and stimulus control are relevant to the analysis of memory, and some continuity between the processes involved in learning and retention may be anticipated. Equally clearly, since much of our prior experience consists of linguistic stimuli and much of our retention is measured by linguistic responses, a knowledge of language is intimately related to the analysis of memory.

SUMMARY

We began the search for an understanding of human behavior with testimony that all is not well in the world. Some people are ill-housed and ill-fed; some portions of our cities have become nightmares that endure into the day; some children are not learning the skills that are necessary for the achievement of a decent adult life—the list of problems seems endless. It is our belief that the best hope for the remediation of human problems lies in the development of a scientific understanding of behavior, an approach to understanding that is a refinement and an elaboration of methods already used in daily life.

The application of scientific method to the study of behavior has resulted in the insight that behavior is influenced by its consequences—both the phylogenic consequences for the species as summarized by the principle of natural selection and the ontogenic consequences for the individual as summarized by the principle of reinforcement. Darwin's finches and Thorndike's chicks have pecked away at the old structure, in which humans were seen as the product of unknown and unknowable external and internal forces, until the structure has been fatally weakened. While we may mourn the loss of that structure, we take comfort in the realization that, by pointing to the environment as the origin of the forces that shape behavior, the principles of natural selection and reinforcement give promise that we may indeed acquire control of our destiny. In the pages which follow, we pursue our ultimate goal through an analysis of the basic phenomena and concepts of learning, language, and memory.

NOTES

1. There are, of course, no hard and fast rules for the formulation of "good" scientific questions. If such rules existed, the scientific enterprise would be a simple·one—and it is not. A provocative discussion of issues involved in the posing of scientific questions is contained in Platt (1964).
2. The preceding biographical material was obtained principally from Eiseley, 1958; Moorehead, 1969; and Bates & Humphrey, 1956—the last of which is a collection of selected readings and includes Darwin's brief and charming autobiography. For a full appreciation of Darwin's thinking there is no substitute for study of the original writings themselves.
3. Actions that favor the reproductive success of one's relatives but that diminish the reproductive success of the individual are labeled as instances of *altruism* by the population geneticist. Under certain general conditions, such actions increase the probability of survival of the genes that the individual organism shares with its relatives (Hamilton, W., 1964). The argument is most specifically documented with certain of the social insects (Trivers & Hare, 1976; Wilson, E. O., 1975). Under some circumstances, altruistic behavior may contribute to inclusive Darwinian fitness even among unrelated individuals (Trivers, 1971; Wilson, D. S., 1975).
4. While the findings reported by Thorndike on the "spread of effect" are largely replicable, their interpretation is more complex than Thorndike had imagined (see Buchwald, 1969; Hilgard & Bower, 1966, pp. 29-44; Hilgard & Bower, 1975, pp. 43-57, for discussions of these complications). The central point for present purposes is that by attempting to apply the law of effect to human verbal behavior as well as to the behavior of lower animals, Thorndike staked a claim to the full range of behavior for an adequately formulated principle of reinforcement.
5. The preceding sketch was drawn largely from a remarkably fine biography of Thorndike by Jonçich (1968). Some appreciation of Thorndike's substantive contribution can be obtained from the reading of *Animal Intelligence* (1911) and *Human Learning* (1931) and from a critical review of his work by Hilgard and Bower (1966).

6. The understanding of both abnormal and normal human behavior is more complex than indicated by the foregoing illustration. Seldom may behavior—such as undereating in our example—be adequately understood in isolation from other responses or from the full context of its environmental antecedents. In the instance of severe undereating (or *anorexia nervosa* as it is called), research indicates that treatment based upon learning principles is often successful (Halmi, Powers, & Cunningham, 1975) with little evidence of the development of other behavioral problems such as symptom substitution (Cahoon, 1968).

7. As with the spread-of-effect experiment, subsequent research has shown the interpretation of the superstition experiment to be more complex than originally thought. The reinforcing stimulus (here food) not only functions to increase the responses which precede it, but also acts as a powerful elicitor of other behaviors whose role must be considered in any comprehensive analysis (cf. Killeen, 1975; Staddon & Simmelhag, 1971).

2

Elicitation

Unconditioned
Stimulus Control

INTRODUCTION

Toward the end of the previous chapter, the concept of *stimulus control* was introduced. A stimulus is said to control behavior when some characteristic of responding varies systematically with changes in some property of stimulation. In the present chapter, we shall investigate one aspect of stimulus control, specifically *unconditioned* stimulus control, the control of behavior whose development shows clear evidence of the action of the principle of natural selection. Before beginning our inquiry, however, it is well to repeat that all behavior is affected by both phylogenetic and ontogenetic antecedents, and that elicited behaviors are simply those behaviors for which the ancestral environment plays a particularly important role. While the study of learning emphasizes the effect of the individual environment on behavior—and the great majority of the book will reflect that emphasis—a full understanding of behavior requires an appreciation of phylogenetic influences as well.

When the rich legacy of phylogeny is initially confronted, both scientist and layman alike must respond with wonder at its complexity. The lowly ant—and other social insects—walk in step to an ancient drum that first began to beat over 100 million years ago. Although we who began our journey only in the last three million years cannot hear that drum, we can see its effects in ritualistic insect societies in which each individual enacts a role whose subtleties rival those of diplomatic protocol. The legacy of phylogeny is also to be seen in the behavior of birds whose songs, courtship patterns, and nest building reveal their own special cadence. The vocal repertoire of a mockingbird would tax the skills of an accomplished musician and the nest of a Baltimore oriole those of a master weaver. In our fellow primates, we see the mark of phylogeny in the behavior of the mother monkey who clutches her stillborn infant to her breast protecting the infant from a harm that is dwarfed by the one which has already befallen it.

Faced with such complexities, and our inability to catch more than a glimmer of their origins among the meager and indirect fossil records left by the ancestral behavior, these sights have inspired some of humanity's most profound speculations. Consider the following words spoken by a woman in a Tennessee Williams' play. The woman is describing a journey with her son to the Galápagos Archipelago—the location of Charles Darwin's inspiration, it will be recalled.

> One long-ago summer my son, Sebastian, said, "Mother?—Listen to this!" He read me Herman Melville's description of the Encantadas, the Galápagos Islands. ". . . Take five and twenty heaps of cinders dumped here and there in an outside city lot. Imagine some of them magnified into mountains, and the vacant lot, the sea. And you'll have a fit idea of the general aspect of the Encantadas, the Enchanted Isles—extinct volcanoes, looking much as the world at large might look—after a last conflagration."[1] He read me that description and said that we had to go there. And so we did go there that summer on a chartered boat, a four-masted schooner, as close as possible to the sort of boat that Melville must have sailed on. . . . We saw the Encantadas, but on the Encantadas we saw something Melville *hadn't* written about. We saw the great sea turtles crawl up out of the sea for their annual egg-laying. . . . Once a year the female of the sea turtle crawls up out of the equatorial sea onto the blazing sand beach of a volcanic island to dig a pit in the sand and deposit her eggs there. It's a long and dreadful thing, the depositing of the eggs in the sandpits, and when it's finished the exhausted female turtle crawls back to the sea half-dead. She never sees her offspring, but we did. Sebastian knew exactly when the sea-turtle eggs would be hatched out and we returned in time for it. . . . Terrible Encantadas, those heaps of extinct volcanoes, in time to witness the hatching of the sea turtles and their desperate flight to the sea!
>
> —The narrow beach, the color of caviar, was all in motion! But the sky was in motion, too. . . . Full of flesh-eating birds and the noise of the birds, the horrible savage cries . . . over the narrow black beach of the Encantadas as the just hatched sea turtles scrambled out of the sandpits and started their race to the sea . . . to escape the flesh-eating birds that made the sky almost black as the beach! And the sand all alive, all alive, as the hatched sea turtles made their dash for the sea, while the birds hovered and swooped to attack and hovered and—swooped to attack! . . .
>
> My son . . . spent that whole blazing equatorial day in the crow's nest of the schooner watching this thing on the beach till it was too dark to see it, and when he came down the rigging he said, "Well, now I've seen Him!" and he meant God. —And for several weeks after that he had a fever, he was delirious with it. —He meant that God shows a savage face to people and shouts some fierce things at them, it's all we see or hear of Him. Isn't it all we really see and hear of Him now?*

* Tennessee Williams, *Suddenly Last Summer.* Copyright © 1958 by Tennessee Williams. Reprinted by permission of New Directions. Acknowledgment is also made to the British edition, *Five Plays* by Tennessee Williams, published by Secker & Warburg Ltd.

Sebastian had seen the events which followed upon the migration of the sea turtles to these volcanic islands and, in those events, he believed he had glimpsed the stern God of the Old Testament. The biologist looks upon these same events and ponders their meaning in the light of what is known of the action of evolution through natural selection. How can we understand the journey of the sea turtle to deposit her eggs upon this beach of cinders?

Stimulus Control and Evolution

In order for natural selection to produce stimulus control of behavior, at least three elements must be present: (a) greater fitness must accrue to those who display such stimulus control in their behavior; (b) the environmental conditions which are to control the behavior must be relatively constant; and (c) there must be sufficient time for the slow but irresistible forces of natural selection to operate. Could these elements have been present in the history of the sea turtle, and hence provide some insight into its migration from the grassy water pastures which border the continent to the distant islands upon which its eggs are deposited? How could natural selection have brought about such a complex environmental control of behavior?

Although we can seldom answer evolutionary questions regarding the natural history of the origin of stimulus control with the precision obtainable in laboratory experiments, a plausible account of the migratory behavior of the sea turtle may be given (Carr & Coleman, 1974). Assume that initially there was some reproductive advantage to the hatching of eggs on nearby offshore islands rather than on the beaches of the mainland. Perhaps land-based predators were more numerous on the mainland, thus causing greater fitness for the island-hatched turtles. The genetic endowment favoring swimming to the nearby islands to lay eggs would therefore become more frequent in the population of sea turtles.

Geologists believe, moreover, that the various continents were originally part of a single great land mass and that, with the passage of millennia, this central mass drifted apart to form the continents as we know them today. This analysis is referred to as the continental drift hypothesis (Wegener, 1966). Volcanic islands which formed at the boundaries of the continental plates would emerge and disappear, to be replaced by new volcanic islands at ever greater distances from the mainland. The offshore islands which were near the mainland at the birth of the species would very, very gradually become more distant from the feeding grounds near the mainland. The movement of the islands would amount to only a few inches each generation, however, and would be well within the capability of succeeding generations of sea turtles. Thus the relative constancy of the eliciting environment would have been present and 150 million years of time would have been available for the contingencies of survival to shape the extraordinary migration of the sea turtle (see Skinner, 1975, for an elaboration of this theme and for additional examples of phylogenetic shaping).

It must be recognized, however, that whether we see God on the Galápagos as did the character in Williams' play or the action of evolution through natural selection, our wonder and awe at the complexity of nature remains intact. We can never duplicate the origin of the sea turtle in the laboratory and, even granted that the contingencies of survival did produce the stimulus control of migratory behavior in the manner described, we remain relatively ignorant of the specific controlling stimuli and of the precise biological mechanisms of their action. With science, the solution of a mystery at one level of analysis often produces a new mystery at a deeper level. The principle of natural selection cautions us, however, not to mistake our ignorance of the controlling stimuli for the absence of such stimuli.

Unconditioned Stimulus Control and Learning

The early contributors to the psychology of learning acknowledged the existence of phylogenetic influences, but little more. Thorndike, for example, stated that, "The starting point for the formation of any association ... [between environment and behavior] ... is the set of instinctive activities which are aroused ... [by the environment]" (Thorndike, 1898). Once behavior had begun to change under the influence of the contemporary environment, however, little attention was given to the legacy of phylogeny. John B. Watson, a prime mover in the development of an objective approach to the study of behavior, argued forcefully for the overwhelming importance of ontogeny.

> Give me a dozen healthy infants, well formed, and my own specified world to bring them up in and I'll guarantee to take any one at random and train him to become any type of specialist I might select—doctor, lawyer, artist, merchant-chief and, yes, even beggarman and thief, regardless of his talents, penchants, tendencies, abilities, vocations, and race of his ancestors. (Watson, 1924)

Thus Thorndike and Watson, both of whom publicly stated their debt to Darwin at the outset of their careers, denied him in the end. Or better, the elaboration of their own contributions required so much of their energies that phylogeny was ignored rather than denied. Watson admitted as much when he added to the statement given above, "I am going beyond my facts, and I admit it, but so have the advocates of the contrary and they have been doing it for many thousands of years" (Watson, 1924).

Under the goading of more recent discoveries by those who take a biological approach to the study of behavior, modern work in the psychology of learning both acknowledges and incorporates knowledge arising from phylogenetic influences (for example, Bolles, 1970; Hinde & Stevenson-Hinde, 1973; Seligman & Hager, 1972; Shettleworth, 1972; Skinner, 1966). The almost exclusive emphasis upon the contemporary environment (environmentalism) or upon the ancestral environment (nativism) have been displaced in modern accounts by a recognition of the balance that is always struck between ontogeny and phylogeny in the determination of behavior. The view that behavior is the result of the complex interaction of both hereditary and environmental influences dominates the current analysis of learning and is termed the epigenetic approach (Kuo, 1967; Lehrman, 1970; Schneirla, 1949).

Our concern in this chapter is to introduce the concept of unconditioned stimulus control and to illustrate that concept with behaviors ranging from simple reflexes to complex social behaviors. We do this both because elicited behaviors are of considerable intrinsic importance and because even elicited behaviors may show the clear effects of the environments in which they occur. Thus a study of unconditioned stimulus control is well-suited to illustrate the interplay between the environments of the species and of the individual in the determination of behavior. A second general reason for studying elicited behaviors is that an investigation of their characteristics may shed some light upon, and suggest some parallels with, conditioned stimulus control. It is possible that there may be functional similarities between the manner in which the present environment controls behavior, whether that behavior arises chiefly from the distant past of the species or has been acquired in the recent past of the individual.

REFLEXIVE BEHAVIOR AND HABITUATION

The Reflex
The simplest illustration of unconditioned stimulus control is the functional relationship between the environment and behavior known as the reflex. In a *reflex,* some specifiable stimulus elicits a response; this relationship is found in essentially all members of a species. As with most examples of unconditioned stimulus control, the acquisition of the reflex occurred long before its appearance in the laboratory and is the expression of the genetic endowment of the species. Characteristically, both the stimulus and response are relatively simple, the functional relationship between them is precise, and the physiological mechanisms that mediate the reflex are better known than is true of other types of relationships. Examples of reflexes include such relationships as the knee jerk reflex in which a tap on the tendon below the kneecap elicits an extension of the calf of the leg, or the lacrimal reflex in which a particle on the schlera of the eye causes the eye to tear. In the first case, the response is muscular; in the second, the response is glandular.

The study of reflexes belongs principally within the field of physiology, that branch of science which deals with the biological functions of the organs of living beings. Our concern with reflexive behavior is chiefly to determine whether even this simplest of functional relationships between environment and behavior, having its roots in the phylogeny of the species, is affected by the experience of the individual.

Although the response to environmental change is a fundamental feature of behavior, few have held that behavior can be understood as merely a collection of reflexes. Descartes, the philosopher most responsible for the notion of mind–body dualism, suggested that an understanding of human behavior required other principles, but that the behavior of animals could be understood as a concatenation of reflexes. Sherrington, the great reflex physiologist, commented on Descartes' suggestion as follows: "But it lets us feel that Descartes can never have kept an animal pet" (1947, p. x). Sherrington thus rejected the idea that even the behaviors of animals could be viewed with profit simply as a collection of reflexes.

Classes of Reflexes   Although experience teaches us that clear-cut distinctions exist more often in our minds than in nature, many workers have found it convenient to categorize reflexes into one of two classes—*orienting reflexes* (ORs) and *defensive reflexes* (DRs) (Sokolov, 1963). The OR was first described in Pavlov's laboratory where he noted that a dog would prick up its ears at any novel sound and turn its head to face the source of the sound. Pavlov called the OR the "what-is-it?" reflex (Pavlov, 1927). The OR has been described as "the first reaction by means of which animal or man enters into a relationship with the surrounding environment" (Kirkukov as cited in Voronin, Leontiev, Luria, Sokolov, & Vinograda, 1965, p. 122). The OR has been characterized as a complex pattern of autonomic and central nervous system activities made in response to a novel, moderate-intensity change in stimulation and which has the effect of arousing the organism and increasing its responsiveness to other stimuli. An unidentified, barely audible sound occurring in a darkened house as we prepare to fall asleep might be a stimulus which would elicit an OR.

The DR is conceived of as a different pattern of activity in the nervous system which is produced by sudden, intense stimuli and which strongly elicits one response while decreasing responsiveness to other stimuli. A sudden noise that causes us to jump would exemplify a DR. In keeping with the descriptions given above, the OR is sometimes referred to as "preparatory" and the DR as "protective."

The utility of the distinction between the OR and DR requires continued scrutiny, however, for it is no great task to imagine a single stimulus—both novel and intense—that might elicit a strong startle response followed by an increased responsiveness to subsequent stimulation. Whether a stimulus elicits either an OR or a DR, or whether both processes are elicited in varying degrees by a single stimulus, awaits additional research.

The Startle Reflex

As a vehicle for the discussion of reflexive behavior, we have chosen the *acoustic startle reflex*—the response made when the individual is presented with a sudden, intense sound. If the OR may be described as the "what-is-it?" reflex, the acoustic startle reflex may be described as the "what-in-heaven-is-it!" reflex (or the "what-in-hell-is-it!" reflex, depending upon where one is accustomed to direct one's appeals at such moments). While any single reflex may have properties peculiar to that reflex, the acoustic startle reflex has been thoroughly studied and possesses a large number of features which are common to many other reflexes.

In the human, the acoustic startle reflex consists of the pattern of responses illustrated in Fig. 2.1. As determined by high-speed photography of the response to the unexpected sound of a pistol firing, the eyes blink, the head

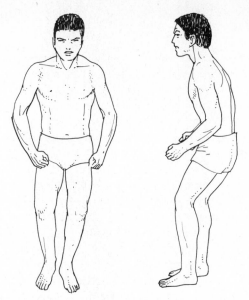

Fig. 2.1   Front and side views of the startle response of a human subject to a loud noise.   (From Landis & Hunt, 1939.)

moves forward, the mouth widens as though in a grin, the shoulders hunch forward, the abdomen contracts, and the elbows and knees bend (Landis & Hunt, 1939). The reflex occurs rapidly, being complete in less than .5 sec. In later work using a better controlled stimulus than a pistol shot, the reflex has been found to be elicited only by acoustic stimuli above 65 decibels (Hatton, Berg, & Graham, 1970). A decibel (db) is a unit of intensity in which the sound-pressure level is expressed as a ratio with a reference level of 20 microNewtons per square meter. The intensity of normal conversation is about 30 db and of a rock band about 120 db.

The response of the human to a sudden, intense sound is thus a "drawing in" of the body and has been found in infants and in a considerable variety of organisms including chimpanzees, orangutans, monkeys, ocelots, wolves, squirrels, and rats (Landis & Hunt, 1939; Horlington, 1968). A sequence of drawings depicting the course of the startle response in the rat is given in Fig. 2.2. Note particularly the closing of the eyes, the movement of the head and feet, and the general "drawing in" of the body. Many of the findings that are reported below arise from lower animals since the intense sounds that are required to elicit reliably the startle reflex may damage hearing, especially upon repeated stimulations.

Unconditioned Stimulus Control of the Startle Reflex   Let us examine the acoustic startle reflex to determine if it is under unconditioned control by properties of the eliciting stimulus. The specific properties of the stimulus that we shall study are the duration and the intensity of the eliciting tone.

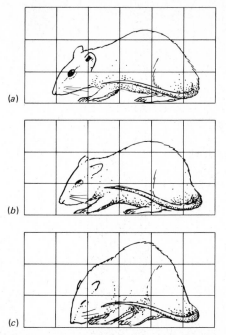

(a)

(b)

(c)

Fig. 2.2   The startle response of a rat to a loud noise. (*a*) The normal posture 5 msec after the onset of the noise but prior to the beginning of the startle response. (*b*) The startle response begins with closing of the eyes and laying back the ears 20 msec after the onset of the noise. (*c*) A complete startle response with the eyes closed, the ears laid back, and the back hunched 30 msec after the onset of the noise.   (After Horlington, 1968.)

A rat was placed in a small cage located in a sound-proofed room to prevent unintended noises from intruding into the experiment (Marsh, Hoffman, & Stitt, 1973). An electrical device, which was sensitive to movements of the cage floor, generated signals that were recorded by a pen on a moving strip of paper. The amplitude of the startle response could be determined by measuring the displacement of the pen on the paper after a tone was sounded. A tone of 6,900 Hz (cycles per second) and of seven different durations (.25, .5, 1, 2, 4, 8, and 64 msec) and six different intensities (80, 90, 100, 110, 120, and 125 db) was used. Thus there was a total of 42 different stimuli. During each of the daily test sessions, the animal was placed in the cage and each of the different tones was presented once, in random order. The time between successive tones (the interstimulus interval) was 30 sec. Did the startle reflex, which had not been elicited previously by these tones in this chamber, show evidence of unconditioned stimulus control, and if so what was the nature of that control?

The results of the experiment, averaged over animals and test sessions, are shown in Fig. 2.3*a*. The figure shows how the amplitude of the startle reflex (the dependent variable) was affected by duration and intensity (the independent variables). The first feature to note is that the startle response did change as the characteristics of the tone varied; that is, there was evidence of uncon-

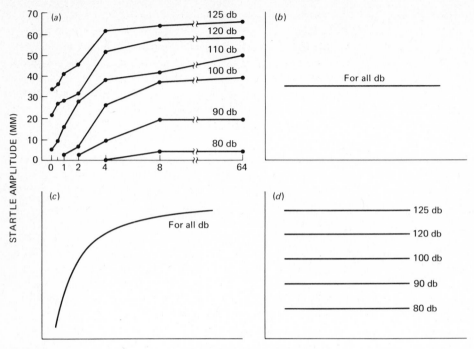

STIMULUS DURATION (MSEC)

Fig. 2.3   The effect of the duration and intensity of a 9,600-Hz tone on the amplitude of the startle reflex. (*a*) Actual results from Marsh, Hoffman, & Sitt, 1973. (*b*) Hypothetical results if the amplitude of the response was independent of both the duration and intensity of the stimulus. (*c*) Hypothetical results if the amplitude of the response was dependent upon only the duration of the stimulus. (*d*) Hypothetical results if the amplitude of the response was dependent upon only the intensity of the stimulus.   (*a:* Copyright 1973 by the American Psychological Association. Reprinted by permission.)

ditioned stimulus control. Proceeding to a more detailed examination of Fig. 2.3*a*, we note that both the duration and the intensity of the tone affected the startle response; that is, there was evidence that *both* the duration and intensity of the tone exerted uncondtioned stimulus control over the amplitude of the startle reflex. Finally, further study of Fig. 2.3*a* reveals the nature of the functional relationship. The amplitude of the startle reflex *increased* as the duration of the tone increased from .25 to 64 msec and as the intensity increased from 80 to 125 db. Thus the functional relationship that was discovered may be summarized by stating that the amplitude of the startle reflex is directly related to both the duration and the intensity of the eliciting stimulus.

While the empirical relationship between the dependent variable of amplitude of the startle response and the independent variables of duration and intensity of stimulation is as described in Fig. 2.3*a*, other relationships might have been obtained. The remaining panels of Fig. 2.3 illustrate some of these possible outcomes, and are intended to sharpen your skills in interpreting graphic representations of experimental results. In Fig. 2.3*b* neither duration nor intensity affect the startle response; responding is constant and stimulus control is absent. In Fig. 2.3c only duration affects the startle response; responding is controlled only by stimulus duration. Finally, in Fig. 2.3d only intensity affects the startle response; responding is controlled only by stimulus intensity.

We may have seemed to belabor the description of the methods used in this experiment and the interpretation of the figure displaying the results, but this was intentional. No experimental result can be adequately understood independently of the methods that were used to produce it. Often, later research indicates that some uncontrolled condition has influenced the findings of earlier work, and it is only through a complete description of the methods which were used that discrepancies between earlier and later work may be understood. In the case of the startle reflex, for example, even the time of day (Davis & Sollberger, 1971) is known to affect the amplitude of the response.

With respect to the interpretation of figures, the ability to understand graphic presentations of results is an essential skill for further progress. Some figures, such as Fig. 2.3a, are complicated by the fact that they illustrate the effect of more than one independent variable. In such figures, one independent variable is always indicated on the horizontal axis and the others are indicated within the field of the graph and are said to be *parameters* of the relationship between the dependent variable and the independent variable. In these terms, Fig. 2.3a shows the effect of stimulus duration on the amplitude of the startle response with stimulus intensity as the parameter.

Habituation

The control of the startle reflex by the duration and intensity of the eliciting stimulus illustrates the concept of unconditioned stimulus control. Given that the startle reflex illustrates unconditioned stimulus control, we may inquire whether even this relatively simple relationship between environment and behavior, which clearly owes much to phylogeny, may itself be modified by individual experience. That is, may even elicited behaviors be influenced by learning?

To answer this question, let us repeatedly elicit a startle reflex from an individual but let no external consequence follow each response. What happens? Does the organism continue to be startled afresh with each occurrence of the stimulus, or does the response change with repeated elicitations? The answer to this question is shown in Fig. 2.4 in which the startle reflex was elicited in different individual rats by acoustic stimuli of either 120 or 100 db. As can be seen, the frequency with which the startle reflex was elicited declined with repeated stimulations even though the intensity of the stimulus remained constant for a given animal (Davis & Wagner, 1969). The decrement in an unlearned response as a function of repeated presentations of the stimulus controlling the response is termed *habituation*. Habituation, since it depends upon the experience of the individual, is a form of learning and has been found in organisms ranging from protozoans to humans (Harris, 1943; Hinde, 1966; Thorpe, 1963).

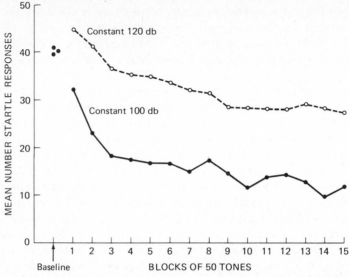

Fig. 2.4 The mean number of startle responses given to successive presentations of tones (in blocks of 50 presentations). The baseline point shows the mean number of startle responses to an initial 110-db tone. The groups then received either a 120-db tone or a 100-db tone during the habituation series. (From Davis & Wagner, 1969. Copyright 1969 by the American Psychological Association. Reprinted by permission.)

Figure 2.4 also demonstrates that the amount of habituation depends on the intensity of the eliciting stimulus. After 750 presentations of the 120-db tone, responding decreased by 38%, from 45 to 28 responses per block of 50 stimulations. After the same number of presentations of the 110-db tone, responding had fallen by 62%, from 32 to only 12 responses per block of 50 stimulations. Thus the amount of responding elicited by a constant stimulus underwent greater habituation as the intensity of stimulation decreased. In general, with intense stimulation responding shows less habituation and some components of the response may give little evidence of habituation at all (Gogan, 1970; Harris, 1943; Landis & Hunt, 1939).

Methodological Issues

Definition of Habituation Habituation is classified as an instance of learning because it is a change in behavior of a relatively enduring nature, resulting from the experience of the individual organism. Moreover, habituation cannot be attributed to purely sensory or motor factors.

An interpretation of habituation as the product of sensory factors may be eliminated as follows. It is known that receptors and other nerve cells are limited in the extent to which they may follow high rates of stimulation. For a short period of time after nerve cells have responded to a stimulus, they have a diminished capability to respond to a second stimulus (the so-called *refractory period*). Research in which the amplitude of the startle reflex has been studied as a function of the interstimulus interval indicates that there is indeed a di-minished response when successive stimuli are presented closer in time than approximately 4 sec (Davis, 1970b; Stitt, Hoffman, & Marsh, 1973). At these short interstimulus intervals, there is a reduction in the "effective stimulus in-tensity" (Wilson & Groves, 1973). However, by using interstimulus intervals longer than 4 sec, the diminished sensitivity can be avoided and a sensory con-tribution to habituation eliminated.

A purely motor interpretation may be ruled out via the phenomena of dishabituation. *Dishabituation* refers to a recovery of the strength of an habit-uated response when a novel stimulus is presented immediately prior to the habituating stimulus. This phenomenon is illustrated for the startle reflex in Fig. 2.5. In this experiment, two groups of subjects were given 14 presentations of a tone that elicited a startle response and habituation was observed. Imme-diately preceding the 15th presentation of the tone, half of the subjects (the experimental group) were shown a flashing light. As compared with the per-formance of the control group that did not receive the flashing light, the startle response recovered (dishabituated) in the experimental condition (Groves & Thompson, 1970). Clearly, recovery would have been impossible if a motor process such as muscular fatigue had been responsible for habituation.

In summary then, the term habituation is reserved for those decrements in behavior that cannot be attributed to either the purely sensory conse-quences of stimulation or the purely motor consequences of responding. This characterization of habituation illustrates a more general property of the ways in which behavioral phenomena are classified: a phenomenon is identified not only by a common behavioral outcome (in this case, an enduring decrement in

Fig. 2.5   Amplitude of the startle response to successive presentations of a 1,000-Hz tone at 110 db. The experimental group was given a flashing light immediately prior to the 15th tone. The control group continued to be presented only tones.   (From Groves & Thompson, 1970. Copyright 1970 by the American Psychological Association. Reprinted by permission.)

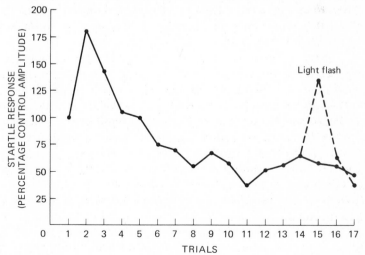

responding) but also by a common set of antecedents (in this case, changes that do not involve only peripheral sensory and motor mechanisms).

One last point needs to be made before we continue the identification of those behavioral changes which are labeled habituation. Habituation is confined to *decremental* changes in responding produced by repeated stimulation. Not all stimulus presentations cause decrements; some cause increments in responding. Reexamine Fig. 2.5 and note that the response to the second presentation of the tone was *greater* than to the first presentation. An increase in responding produced by preceding stimulation is called *sensitization*. Note also that by this definition of sensitization, dishabituation is a subclass of sensitization in which the increase in responding is produced by a preceding stimulus that *differs* from the test stimulus.

In completing this discussion of habituation, we may conclude that habituation refers to those enduring decrements in responding that occur to repeated stimulation when changes due to sensory and motor factors have been eliminated.

The Averaging of Behavioral Data   The behavioral changes that are of concern in habituation in particular, and in learning in general, are those that are the product of the individual environment of the individual organism. Groups do not learn, although individual members of a group may learn. Is there not a contradiction, therefore, between the assertion that learning is a behavioral process of the individual organism and the use of curves based on group averages to display that process? In Fig. 2.4, for example, average curves obtained by summing across the behavior of individual animals were presented as illustrations of habituation.

Averaging as a method of analyzing learning data is fully justifiable only when such averaging does not distort the basic nature of the behavioral processes being investigated, and when the only effect of averaging is to cancel out essentially random sources of behavioral variability. Thus as the precision of our experimental procedures improves and as we are better able to control undesired sources of variation, the need for averaging data should diminish. There is an element of *Catch-22*, however, in the decision of whether to average data: We should average data if only random variability is affected, but if the data are variable genuine differences in the behavioral processes are difficult to detect! The safest course is thus to control experimentally our observations so that we may reduce variability to minimal levels. To the extent that we are content to average behavioral data, then to that extent do we risk the distortion of behavioral processes and the acceptance of inadequately controlled experiments. At a minimum, individual observations should always be examined to ensure that averages faithfully represent the major features of the observations which give rise to them.

Let us turn to a more detailed consideration of the general issues of averaging in the specific context of the phenomenon of habituation. Consider first the possible distortions introduced when we average data across subjects in an effort to describe habituation. Figure 2.6 contains hypothetical average

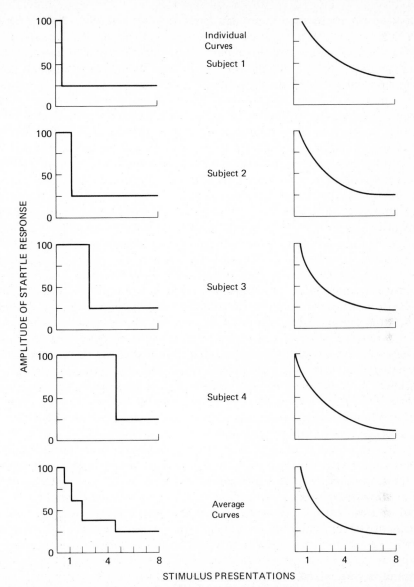

Fig. 2.6   Hypothetical habituation curves from individual subjects and group averages when habituation occurs abruptly (left column) or gradually (right column). Note that the group averages are similar although the individual curves are very different. The average curves would become even more similar with an increase in the number of individual curves upon which the average curves were based.

habituation functions that have been derived from two quite different sets of individual data. In the left column are individual habituation curves from four subjects, each of whom gave a constant high amplitude of startle response before shifting abruptly to a constant lower amplitude. In the right column are individual curves from four subjects, each of whom gave a gradually diminishing amplitude of startle response. Note, however, that in spite of these marked differences in the course of habituation in the individual subjects, the average habituation curves would be difficult to distinguish empirically.

It is of crucial significance to have carefully controlled procedures with which to study changes in individual subjects if behavioral processes are to be understood. Fortunately, although more work needs to be done to reduce variability, individual habituation curves generally show the gradual reduction of responding that is apparent in the average functions (Thompson, R. F., Groves, Teyler, & Roemer, 1973; but see Hinde, 1970, p. 3).[2]

The distortion of our understanding of behavioral processes is a potential hazard when any averaging is done—even when we do not average across subjects. A second, common type of averaging is to sum performance from a single subject across time. Averaging across events in time is also illustrated in Fig. 2.4 where each data point is the average frequency of responding summed over 50 presentations of the tone. When responding is measured as an average across 50 tones, it appears to show a progressive decline in frequency as the number of tone presentations is increased. In Fig. 2.5, where the amplitude of the startle response to each individual tone is presented separately, we see that responding actually *increased* on the second presentation of the tone—that is, sensitization occurred. Sensitization would have been entirely obscured if the average amplitude of the response across many presentations of the tone had been the sole measure of performance.

This discussion of methodological issues may be closed with the admonition that objective definition and measurement are no guarantee in themselves of a valid understanding of behavioral phenomena. Carved on the outside walls of Pavlov's laboratory were the words, *Beobachtung, Beobachtung, Beobachtung* (observation, observation, observation). Only close observation of the response of the individual organism to the individual event will provide an adequate foundation for useful definitions and meaningful measurement.

Phenomena Associated with Reflex Habituation

We have seen that even the reflex, that simplest of functional relationships between the environment and behavior which illustrates unconditioned stimulus control, may be modified by the experience of the individual organism. Thus the startle reflex, an ancient behavior pattern found throughout a wide range of the animal kingdom, may wane after its repeated elicitation.

Although our discussion of habituation has emphasized the laboratory study of a relatively simple reflex—because of the greater control of variables—the decrement following repeated elicitation occurs in more natural settings as well, and with more complex responses (Carew & Kupferman, 1974; Hinde, 1970; Peeke & Peeke, 1973; Petrinovitch, 1973). In nature, however, the sudden loud noise of a snapping twig or of a snarl may be followed by the attack of a predator. Should the intended prey be fortunate enough to survive the initial attack by "drawing in" its body and making a smaller target, the startle reflex would not show habituation upon subsequent exposure to similar loud noises. Quite the contrary—the startle response would be maintained and perhaps sensitized for a time. It is only when there are no extrinsic consequences of the response that repeated elicitation results in habituation.

The investigation of the consequences of responding is crucial to understanding behavior, but we shall defer its study until later chapters on reinforcement. For now, our attention is directed toward the unconditioned stimulus control of behavior and how experience may modify that control when the behavior has no external consequences. Of specific immediate concern is the examination of two characteristics of habituation—its retention and its stimulus specificity.

Retention   Among the defining characteristics of learned changes in behavior is that such changes are relatively enduring. While the exact duration of the change is dependent upon the conditions prevailing when the behavior was acquired and when it was tested for retention, learned changes are ordinarily quite long-lasting. It should be noted that the difference between acquisition and retention conditions is fundamentally quantitative and not qualitative (Osgood, 1953). In acquisition the time between successive stimulus presentations is typically short—on the order of seconds or minutes—while in retention the time between successive stimulus presentations is typically long—hours or days. In the instance of habituation, the similarity between acquisition and retention conditions is especially great because there are no extrinsic consequences of a response in either case. A retention test consists simply of another presentation of the eliciting stimulus but at a longer than usual interstimulus interval.

Let us examine the retention of habituation using the now familiar startle reflex as an example. With only a single presentation of a 112 db click, a reliable decrement in responding has been reported in the rat to a second click given 24 hours later (Horlington, 1968). Further evidence that habituation is retained is provided by the finding that habituation occurs more rapidly over successive habituation sessions when sufficient time has intervened between sessions to permit the response to recover (Lehner, 1941; Thompson, R. F., & Spencer, 1966, p. 24).

An extensive and well-controlled study (Davis, 1970b) provides information concerning some of the variables affecting the retention of habituation. In this experiment, rats were first tested to determine the initial level of the startle response to a 120-db, 4,000-Hz tone. Because responsiveness varies with the interval between stimulations, responding was measured at a number of interstimulus intervals—2, 4, 8, and 16 sec. The assessment of responding at the beginning of an experiment is a common procedure in behavioral studies, since it provides a baseline against which to compare the effects of the independent variable. The results of the baseline phase are shown in the left-hand panels of

Fig. 2.7. Startle responses to the tone occurred more frequently as the inter-stimulus interval increased from 2 to 16 sec.

Following the determination of the baseline level of the startle response, the habituation phase of the experiment began. To produce habituation, the tone was presented 1,000 times at 2-sec intervals for half the subjects, and at 16-sec intervals for the other half. The results of the habituation phase are shown in the middle panels of Fig. 2.7. As we have previously observed, re-peated presentations of the stimulus led to a decrease in responding, or habitu-ation. By the end of the habituation phase, the percentage of startle responses elicited by the tone had fallen below the baseline level for both the 2-sec and 16-sec interstimulus intervals.

With habituation now having been produced, a test of retention was given. During the retention phase, the tone was presented at different inter-stimulus intervals precisely as had been done during the baseline phase. For half of the subjects, the retention phase began 1 min after habituation; for the other half, retention began 24 hr after habituation. Thus both short-term and longer-term retention of habituation were measured. The difference between the level of the startle response during the retention phase and the baseline phase shows the effects of the intervening habituation phase. To the extent that retention levels are below baseline levels, to that extent has habituation been retained.

The outcome of the retention phase of the experiment is presented in the right-hand panels of Fig. 2.7. The results with the 1-min retention test are re-ported in the upper portion of the figure, those with the 24-hr test in the lower portion. First, under comparable interstimulus intervals, the percentage of tone presentations eliciting a startle response was lower after habituation. Thus there was retention of habituation. Second, by comparing the two retention tests, it is evident that there was less retention of habituation over a 24-hr in-terval than over a 1-min interval. Thus there was some recovery of the elicited response over the longer retention interval. The recovery of responding with the passage of time, but without specific additional experience within the ex-perimental situation, is called *spontaneous recovery*. Spontaneous recovery is, of course, merely the name, and not the explanation of a phenomenon. So-called spontaneous events are an anathema to science, the beginning and not the end of inquiry. We shall return to an analysis of spontaneous recovery later in this text.

Finally, retention of habituation was superior with the longer interstim-ulus interval between presentations of the tone during the habituation phase. That is, as shown in the right-hand panel of Fig. 2.7, the startle response recov-ered less completely when 16 sec had elapsed between presentations of the habituating tone than when only 2 sec had elapsed. This was found in both the retention test after 1 min and after 24 hr.

What are the processes that produce the facilitation of the retention of habituation by longer interstimulus intervals during habituation training? While the answers to this question are incompletely known, they may be pur-sued by employing a general strategy used to understand any behavioral phe-

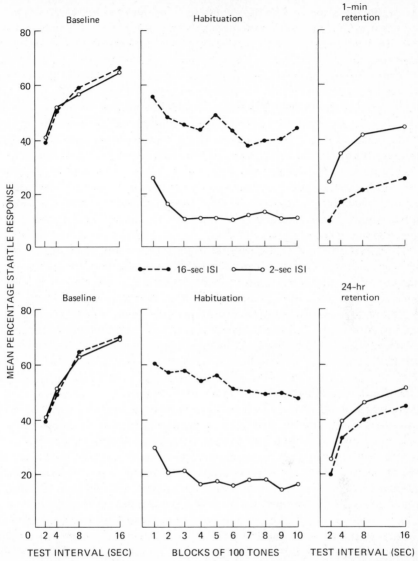

Fig. 2.7   The effect of the interstimulus interval (ISI) during habituation on the retention of ha-bituation with a 1-min retention interval (*top*) and a 24-hr retention interval (*bottom*).   (From Davis, 1970a. Copyright 1970 by the American Psychological Association. Reprinted by permission.)

nomenon: What is the role of the events that follow the behavior? What is the role of the events that precede the behavior? The origins of any present behavior are to be found in an examination of its consequences and of its antecedents.

First, are the consequences different when a reflex is elicited with long and short interstimulus intervals? With long interstimulus intervals, the reflex is elicited with higher probability and is followed by a more prolonged period without extrinsic consequences than occurs with short interstimulus intervals. Second, are the antecedents different when a reflex is elicited with long and short interstimulus intervals? Perhaps the stimulus conditions prevailing immediately prior to the elicitation of the reflex during habituation training are more similar to the conditions prevailing during the retention test with long rather than short interstimulus intervals. Thus because of the greater similarity between training and testing conditions with the long interstimulus interval, retention is superior.

The interpretation of differential retention as a result of the differential antecedents of the response presupposes that habituation is somewhat specific to the stimulus conditions under which habituation training has occurred. Fragmentary evidence does indicate that habituation is better retained if the stimulus conditions for the retention test are the same as those present during habituation training (Peeke & Veno, 1973), but only further research can determine the relative contributions of the antecedents and consequences of elicitation to the retention of habituation.

Stimulus Specificity   In asking whether habituation is specific to the particular properties of the eliciting stimulus, we are beginning an inquiry into a matter of importance for all learning: Are the behavioral changes that occur as a result of individual experience specific to the circumstances under which those changes are acquired, or do they occur subsequently in a broader range of circumstances? At stake is nothing less than the question of whether and to what extent past experience may influence present functioning. If behavioral change is confined to the precise environmental conditions of prior learning, then each of us is bound tightly to the peculiarities of our own experience and must face each new environment naively. If, however, learning affects behavior somewhat more generally, then present functioning in different environments may benefit by prior learning.

With respect to reflex habituation, the simplest of all learning, it is clear that the response decrement is greatest to the eliciting stimulus used in habituation training, but that some decrement occurs to other similar stimuli as well. While the observation of habituation to a range of stimuli after training with a single eliciting stimulus has been reported for a number of response systems (Graham, 1973; Groves & Thompson, 1970; Sokolov, 1963; Thompson, R. F., et al., 1973) and under natural as well as laboratory conditions (Hinde, 1970), we shall again focus upon the response to an intense acoustic stimulus. In this experiment (Rubel & Rosenthal, 1975), young chicks were first given habituation training consisting of five presentations of a 90-db, 1,000-Hz tone. The tones were presented only when the chick was resting with its eyes closed. Eye-opening within 2 sec of the tone was used as the response. After habituation training, each chick was given a series of 90-db tones varying in frequency from 800 to 1,200 Hz as a test of the specificity of habituation to the 1,000-Hz tone. Previous observations in this same study had shown that all frequencies of tone would elicit a response prior to habituation.

Figure 2.8 shows the response to the various tones following habituation training to the 1,000-Hz tone. The results are shown separately for 1-day-old and 3- to 4-day-old chicks. Notice that for both age groups the response decrement was greatest at the frequency of the habituating stimulus and that responding was also depressed to tones of similar frequency. As the frequency of the test tones departed from the habituation frequency, the percentage of responses increased. The curves shown in Fig. 2.8, which describe how responding changed as the stimulus varied, are called *stimulus generalization gradients*. In this case, they show the stimulus generalization of habituation.

You will remember that stimulus control was defined as a change in some characteristic of responding, as a function of variation in some property of stimulation. The generalization of habituation shows the stimulus control of habituation and, because habituation is a learned response, it is an example of *conditioned stimulus control*. The generalization of habituation exemplifies conditioned stimulus control because the stimulus control is dependent upon—conditional upon—the habituation experience of the individual chick. The fact that the stimulus control was less precise for the younger chicks than for the older chicks indicates, however, that habituation was not the only experience affecting the behavior. *Maturation,* which reflects the coaction of genetic and general environmental influences, also contributed to stimulus control. Thus in the stimulus control of this simple learned behavior, we see

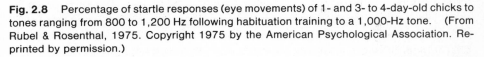

Fig. 2.8 Percentage of startle responses (eye movements) of 1- and 3- to 4-day-old chicks to tones ranging from 800 to 1,200 Hz following habituation training to a 1,000-Hz tone. (From Rubel & Rosenthal, 1975. Copyright 1975 by the American Psychological Association. Reprinted by permission.)

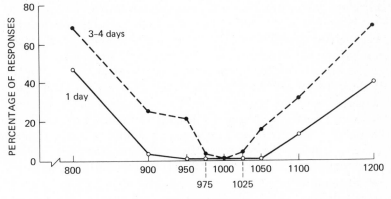

the joint effects of phylogeny and ontogeny. We see also the beginnings of evidence that past experience may influence present behavior beyond the narrow confines of the stimulus conditions that prevail when the behavior was acquired.

Theoretical Analysis of Reflex Habituation

The discussion of habituation has thus far consisted primarily of a statement of the variables that determine the occurrence and magnitude of habituation and some of the phenomena associated with it. We have found that repeated elicitation of a reflex produces a brief increment followed by a decrement in responding—and that this pattern of responding is influenced by such factors as the duration, intensity, and frequency of stimulation. Additionally, it has been determined that habituation may be retained for an appreciable length of time, and that it shows considerable stimulus specificity. In short, our concern has been with an analysis of the functional relationships between habituation and its antecedents. The identification of these functional relationships is the first step toward an understanding of the phenomenon of habituation.

Dual-Process Theory   We now move toward an attempt to achieve a deeper understanding by searching for a smaller number of antecedents that will permit the prediction of habituation and related phenomena. The approach that will be presented here is dual-process theory (Groves & Thompson, 1970; Thompson, R. F., & Spencer, 1966; Thompson, R. F., et al., 1973).[3] Dual-process theory is presented for its intrinsic merits and because it provides an opportunity for the discussion of issues in theory construction that will be relevant throughout the book.

The dual processes identified by the theory are the inferred physiological processes of excitation and inhibition.[4] It is first assumed that each stimulus presentation, in addition to eliciting a response, produces an excitatory process. The excitatory process causes a general increase in the tendency to respond that grows and then decays with continued stimulation or the passage of time. The greater the stimulus intensity, the greater the excitation. In addition to the excitatory process that causes an increment in responding, there is also assumed to be an opposed inhibitory process that is produced by the repetition of the eliciting stimulus. The inhibitory process is smaller with more intense stimuli and greater with more frequent stimuli, and is assumed to decay with the passage of time. The likelihood that a response will be elicited is determined by the difference in the strengths of the opposing excitatory and inhibitory processes. The notion that the net effect of stimulation on behavior can be profitably viewed as the synthesis of a response-enhancing process (excitation) and an opposed response-diminishing process (inhibition) is a venerable one having its roots in the physiology of reflexes (Sechenov, 1863; Sherrington, 1947) and extending its branches into modern learning theory (for example, Hull, 1943; Spence, 1937).

To evaluate the theory, a leg flexion response was studied in an animal with only its spinal cord intact. The use of a relatively simple nervous system and a relatively simple response was intended to enhance the chances of achieving a complete understanding of the physiological mechanisms of habituation.

The postulated relationship between the magnitude of responding in successive elicitations and the inferred processes of excitation and inhibition is shown in Fig. 2.9. At first, the magnitude of responding grows because the increase in the excitatory process is greater than the increase in the inhibitory process. Sensitization occurs. As the stimulus is repeated and the excitatory process decays, the inhibitory process continues to grow and the response habituates to approximately 50% of its original amplitude. By making certain assumptions about the relative rates of growth and decay of the excitatory and inhibitory processes, dual-process theory can give an account that is consistent with the known effects of variables such as the intensity, duration, and frequency of stimulation and with many of the phenomena associated with habituation. Through the use of two inferred processes—excitation and inhibition—the effects of many observable antecedents may be interpreted.

Model Experimental Preparations   The foregoing, all too brief, exposition of dual-process theory illustrates a number of general characteristics of much theoretical work in learning. First, in order to achieve a more precise understanding of the phenomena—here habituation—a *simplified experimental preparation* is employed. The use of a simple response (leg flexion) and a simplified nervous system (spinal cord) provides the experimenter with an enhanced possibility of exhaustively analyzing the mechanisms underlying the functional relationship.

Fig. 2.9   The amplitude of hindlimb flexion response (filled circles) with successive presentations of the eliciting stimulus. The difference between the inferred processes of excitation (E) and inhibition (I) is hypothesized to account for the observed amplitude of the response.   (From Thompson, Groves, Jeyler, & Roemer, 1973. Copyright 1973 by the American Psychological Association. Reprinted by permission.)

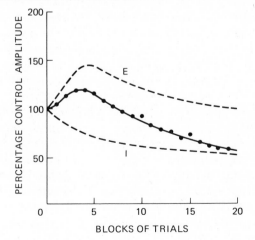

The strategy of reduction to a tractable model preparation is one that is commonly employed with profit (Kandel & Spencer, 1968), but it carries certain hazards as well. For one, the experimenter runs the risk of having a tractable preparation but one that is not well suited to display the full range of phenomena. In the case of dual-process theory, the theorists were aware of this potential problem and have demonstrated many comparable results between the spinal preparation and those obtained with intact organisms and more complex responses such as the startle reflex. An additional hazard with the simplified preparation is that the precise mechanisms of action in the more complex preparation must almost certainly be different. For example, the neural mechanisms involved in such diverse procedures as the elicitation of the startle reflex by an acoustic stimulus or of autonomic responses by a mild electric shock cannot be identical to the mechanisms involved in the elicitation of leg flexion in a spinal animal by stimulation of a sensory nerve. Again, the developers of dual-process theory were cognizant of this difficulty and have sought to determine the generality of their findings (Thompson, R. F., et al., 1973, pp. 265–266). In this regard, it may be anticipated that nature has solved similar behavioral problems in functionally similar ways, even though the precise biological means to the common end may differ widely. Thus a thorough analysis of one behavioral system may yield results that are functionally highly similar to those of another system having very different constituent physical mechanisms.

Inferred Processes A second characteristic of dual-process theory—one shared with many other theoretical efforts in the field of learning—is an attempt to account for the relationship between observable antecedents and behavior in terms of *inferred processes*. In the case of dual-process theory, the inferred processes are excitation and inhibition. Speaking generally, a danger in the postulation of inferred processes is that although there may be fewer inferred processes than observable antecedents, the theory may have the appearance but not the substance of parsimony. It should come as no surprise, for example, that the inferred processes permit the deduction of the observed relationships between antecedents and behavior: The processes were in fact inferred from those very same relationships. In the specific instance of dual-process theory, it should not be taken as strong evidence for the theory that its inferred processes correspond to the known observed relationships at the time of its formulation. Thus inferred excitation was assumed to grow and then decline because of what had been previously known about observed sensitization; inferred inhibition was assumed to grow with repeated stimulation because of what had been previously known about observed habituation; inferred inhibition was assumed to decay with the passage of time because of what had been previously known about observed spontaneous recovery. Consistency with the facts known at the time of the formulation of the inferred processes constitutes only minimal conditions for an acceptable theoretical analysis; the theory must also be able to predict as yet unobtained observations and to integrate as yet unrelated phenomena. Future research will determine the extent to which dual-process theory meets these criteria.

The use of inferred processes to account for behavioral observations is further complicated when the behavioral outcome is the result of an unspecified combination of multiple unobserved processes. Thus in the absence of additional independent evidence, a given amount of responding in dual-process theory could be the consequence of the net effect of many different combinations of the opposing processes of excitation and inhibition (Graham, 1973, pp. 203–212). Whether the opposing inferred processes are excitation and inhibition in the case of dual-process theory or Id impulses and reaction formation in the case of psychoanalytic theory, these processes must be assessed independently of the occurrence or nonoccurrence of the behaviors that they seek to explain. It would be logically circular to argue that a decrement in a reflex occurred because inhibition had increased and, simultaneously, to assert that inhibition increased because a decrement in the reflex had occurred.

The Analysis of Inferred Processes   Two general strategies exist for the independent assessment of inferred processes, and thereby the avoidance of logical circularity. In the first strategy, an experiment is sought in which the response is sensitive to variations in only one of the inferred processes. Having done this for each inferred process separately, the experimenter then attempts to predict performance in a situation in which the processes are acting in concert. As an illustration within the framework of dual-process theory, the experimenter might test responding to repeated stimulation when the subject had been given a drug thought to block excitation. The course of responding would then presumably reflect only the inhibitory process. Next, a comparable experiment might be done to reflect only the excitatory process. Having independent assessments of responding as a function of the inferred processes of inhibition and excitation, the experimenter then should be able to predict responding in a condition in which both processes act together. In terms of Fig. 2.9, the experimenter would have successively determined the excitatory and inhibitory functions and then measured responding in the standard habituation experiment.

A second strategy for the assessment of inferred processes is to devise a technique that will render the inferred process directly observable. Note that in the first strategy—*successive assessment*—the processes remain unobserved; it is only their effects that are observable. The second strategy—*simultaneous assessment*—is possible only when the inferred processes have genuine physical reality. The processes cannot be solely conceptual entities that serve as aids to the thinking of the theorist who seeks to understand the phenomenon. Again, we shall return to dual-process theory as a vehicle for illustration of this second strategy for dealing with inferred processes.

If there were physical inhibitory and excitatory processes, then nerve cells might be found in which these processes would be directly reflected. Thus there should be some cells which become less active when the stimulus is repeated (inhibitory cells) and others which become initially more active (excitatory cells). Exactly this type of experiment has been conducted (Groves & Thompson, 1970; Groves & Thompson, 1973). Moreover, the observed neural activity shown by the inhibitory and excitatory cells closely approximated the observed behavioral measure of the reflexive response. Thus a more detailed experimental analysis of habituation has opened the possibility for the direct observation of the previously unobserved processes of inhibition and excitation.

While the postulation of inferred processes having physical reality has the potential advantage of permitting the simultaneous assessment of those processes and of the behaviors that they seek to explain, the advantage remains unrealized until such direct observations have actually been made. The postulation of inferred behavioral or physiological processes when unaccompanied by independent observation represents merely the promise and not the fulfillment of an effort to relate the findings to the larger body of science and to secure a deeper understanding of the phenomenon. We must be on guard lest our attempts at explanation result in illusion and self-deception.

Summary Using dual-process theory as a vehicle, we have presented an analysis of the behavioral phenomenon of habituation and a discussion of some representative and related issues in theory construction. We have seen, in turn, how dual-process theory has attempted to come to grips with these issues. Ultimately, as with all theoretical efforts, only the test of future research will permit a final judgment of the value of dual-process theory in deepening our understanding of habituation. It may be well, at this point, to summarize the general issues that were raised. First, in order to increase the precision of observations, theoretical work often employs simplified experimental preparations. In so doing, some of the richness and complexity of behavior is intentionally diminished and we must guard against distorting our image of the very phenomena that we seek to understand. Our desire to be precise may impair our intention to be general and we may merely come to know more and more about less and less. Second, the explanation of behavioral relationships by means of a more parsimonious set of inferred processes may serve to disguise our real ignorance behind a mask of illusory understanding. A thorough experimental analysis of the behavior and its antecedents and consequences must be conducted if such self-deception is to be avoided. Theoretical analysis is necessary if an integrated understanding of diverse phenomena is to be accomplished, but a genuine theory must illuminate the facts and not obscure them behind murky rhetoric.

SOCIAL BEHAVIOR AND LEARNING

In the reflex, the simplest of functional relationships between the environment and behavior, phylogeny has determined that a stimulus of specified properties will control a response. The development of reflexive behavior demands relatively little from the environment, the demands being confined generally to those conditions that are essential to the viability of the species.

We turn our attention now to a more complex set of behaviors—social behaviors—but ones that also show the ubiquitous imprint of phylogeny. That social behaviors bear the mark of evolutionary pressures should come as no surprise. Relationships with other members of one's own species are a constant and enduring feature in the history of any species and the outcome of those relationships makes a clear contribution to fitness in the Darwinian sense. The study of comparative animal behavior under naturalistic conditions—*ethology* (Eibl-Eibesfeldt, 1975)—and of the application of population genetics to social behaviors—*sociobiology* (Wilson, E. O., 1975)—has forced the psychology of learning to reckon with the insights arising from a biological perspective on behavior.

Social behavior, as is true of all other behaviors, is a joint product of the action of both genetic and environmental factors. While the proportion of variation in human social behavior that is due to genetic variation is but a small part of the total variation, it is an essential part of a comprehensive analysis. As an illustration, the phenomenon of altruism whereby the life of the individual is forfeit to the survival of the group has been given a Darwinian justification: By increasing the survival of members of a genetically-related group, the altruist increases the contribution of his genes to the next generation. To the extent that altruistic behavior is influenced by genetic factors, the behavior will become more probable in successive generations (Hamilton, 1971; Wilson, E. O., 1975, pp. 106–129).

Our purpose in discussing the relationship between social behavior and learning is not to document the biological roots of social behavior. That has been done fully and often eloquently elsewhere (for example, Eibl-Eibesfeldt, 1975; Hinde, 1974; Wilson, E. O., 1975). Our purpose is the more modest one of demonstrating that the experience of the individual organism may alter the expression of the genetic legacy. Through the selection of a few instances of social behavior having acknowledged phylogenetic origins, we shall see that (a) unlike the simple reflex, the environmental stimuli that control social behavior often reflect the individual experience of the organism and (b) more so than the habituation of reflexes, the analysis of social behavior requires scrutiny of the consequences as well as the antecedents of responding.

Stimulus Control of Fixed-Action Patterns

Fixed-action patterns, as the term implies, are relatively invariant patterns of motor activity. These integrated motor patterns are typically more complex than the responses that are labeled reflexes but, like reflexes, are found in all members of a species, and often in related species as well. Examples of fixed-action patterns would be activities such as the turning around of a dog or a wolf prior to lying down or the species-typical song of many birds. Fixed-action patterns are thought by ethologists to reflect phylogenetic influences since these motor patterns may remain relatively unchanged under variations in the rearing conditions. Commonly employed variations in the rearing conditions include depriving the organism of the opportunity to engage in the behavior at the normal time of occurrence (*the deprivation experiment*) and rearing the organism with members of another species (the *cross-fostering experiment*).

Fixed-action patterns are often instances of social behavior since the stimuli that control their appearance are most frequently other members of the same species. For example, bird songs are important in protecting territories for courting and nesting, and occur upon sight of another bird of the same species. The stimulus that controls a fixed-action pattern is given a special name; it is called a *releaser,* or *sign stimulus.* For some fixed-action patterns, the releaser is confined to a high degree of precision to a specific characteristic of the other animal. Thus a particular patch of color on the breast of another male of the species may release a song that marks the territory as "occupied." For other fixed-action patterns, the characteristics of the releasing stimulus are defined only in a general way and a rather wide range of stimuli are potential releasers of the response.[5] We shall devote our discussion to such a fixed-action pattern—the following response of certain species of young birds.

Imprinting   Shortly after hatching, the young of birds that develop early the ability to locomote through the environment will follow any of a wide variety of moving stimuli. The moving stimulus (releaser) controls the following response (fixed-action pattern). Normally, the stimulus that becomes a releaser is the mother of the young birds, but birds such as chickens, ducks, and geese have been made to follow a wide variety of objects including wooden decoys, milk bottles carried about on electric trains, and humans. What is required for a stimulus to become a releaser for following is simply that the young bird be presented with a receding visual image of the stimulus (Moltz, 1963). One particularly perverse psychologist of our acquaintance went so far as to establish a live hawk as the releaser for the following response of a chick—a vivid demonstration of the role of individual experience.

The process whereby a stimulus is established as a releaser for the following response is called *imprinting* (Lorenz, 1935) and it is clear that the experience of the individual organism is crucial in determining which stimuli become releasers. In imprinting we have an integrated motor pattern that reflects phylogeny, but whose stimulus control shows with equal clarity the effects of ontogeny. Imprinting is therefore an instance of the acquisition of *conditioned* stimulus control. It is a special type of learning, however, in that acquisition in the natural environment is limited to a short period in the life of the young organism (the so-called *critical* or *sensitive period*) and affects the expression of other behaviors that emerge later in development (for example, sexual and aggressive behaviors). While imprinting is confined to certain species of birds, a case can be made that the basic behavioral processes that produce imprinting contribute to the development of social behaviors in a wide range of species, including humans and other primates (Bowlby, 1969; Hoffman & Ratner, 1973).

All functional relationships between the environment and behavior reflect both ontogeny and phylogeny. In the case of imprinting, the size, the shape, the rate of movement, and the auditory stimuli arising from the object have all been shown to affect the acquisition of control by the releaser (Bateson, 1971). The subtle interplay of the environments of the distant past and of the present in the control of behavior is nicely illustrated by the role of auditory stimuli in the control of the following response. Young ducklings show a preference for following objects that emit the normal call of the mother. The preference for the maternal call has been shown to be partially dependent, however, upon the ability of the young duckling to hear vocalizations while still in the egg (Gottlieb, 1971; Gottlieb, 1975). An illustration of the importance of both phylogeny and ontogeny on the effect of the releaser is the observation that birds which have been imprinted to humans are subsequently more apt to direct aggression rather than sexual behavior toward humans (Immelman, 1972). Can we blame them!

Effect of the Consequences of Social Behavior

Heretofore in our study of unconditioned stimulus control, we have analyzed a variety of behaviors with relatively little consideration given to the consequences of those behaviors—to the influences of the events that follow the response upon future occurrences of the response. Our attention has been directed chiefly at the antecedents of responding—at the eliciting stimulus for reflexive behaviors or the releasing stimulus for fixed-action patterns. We have seen how, even for behaviors that owe a clear debt to evolution, individual experience may modulate the elicitation of that behavior by its antecedents. In the discussion of the social behaviors which follows, however, we shall emphasize the necessity of also dealing with the consequences of responding. Darwin's insights must be supplemented by those of Thorndike and his intellectual descendents if behavior, especially complex behavior, is to be understood.

The present illustrations of how the consequences of social behaviors influence their expression will be restricted to two areas of undeniable biological significance—sexual behavior and maternal behavior. Which type of behavior should be discussed first is somewhat arbitrary. For our purposes, sex will take precedence over motherhood.

Sexual Behavior The expression of sexual behavior and related activities is the product of both phylogenetic and ontogenetic factors. Through the action of various behavioral processes, such as those operative in imprinting with birds, the sexual responses are normally directed toward a limited range of environmental stimuli, namely those stimuli associated with others of the same species.

The specific copulatory behaviors may be quite variable in a higher organism such as the rhesus monkey (see Fig. 2.10), but the development of these behaviors requires an environment that permits interaction with other monkeys during infancy (Harlow, 1962; Missakian, 1969). The consequences of sexual behavior are important. If other young monkeys are present during in-

Fig. 2.10 Some copulatory positions used by rhesus monkeys: (a) foot-clasp mount, (b) bite mount, (c) ventro-ventral mount, and (d) side mount. (After Hanby, 1972.)

fancy and adolescence—even if the mother is absent—the normal sequence of sexual behaviors occurs. In the normal sequence, there is inadequate and inappropriate sexual play and posturing during the first year of life, followed by the gradual development of more complete sexual behavior directed primarily toward members of the opposite sex during adolescence. Sometime following the production of sex hormones and the attainment of sexual maturity, adult sexual behavior occurs (Whalen, 1971).

   This sequence of events presupposes a social environment, however. If infant rhesus monkeys are reared in physical isolation from their own kind, they behave very differently. As chronological adults, they sit in the corner of the cage clutching their heads in their hands and slowly rocking back and forth. When presented with a similarly socially-deprived partner, only the inadequate and inappropriate sexual behavior of the infant appears, and when presented with a normally-reared, sexually experienced partner, either withdrawal or aggression occurs, dependent upon the relative size of the animals. At most, according to one investigator, "their hearts were in the right place but nothing else was" (Harlow, 1962). In keeping with other research (Beach, 1947), the sexual behavior of males was more affected by experience than that of females (Harlow & Harlow, 1969). By placing the socially immature monkeys with one-month-old infants, however, and permitting them to interact extensively, normal adult sexual behavior was recovered (Harlow & Suomi, 1971a; Harlow & Suomi, 1971b).

   These studies demonstrate the critical role of individual experience, and more particularly the role of the consequences of responding in the development of normal adult sexual behavior. Without experience in responding to social stimuli and in having such stimuli change in response to one's own behavior, adult sexual behavior failed to emerge. Furthermore, the evidence indicates that the importance of social interactions increases in the higher animals (Beach, 1967).

The following laboratory experiment further documents the fact that sexual behavior is sensitive to its consequences but, in addition, that the expression of sensitivity reflects the continuing imprint of phylogeny (Silberberg & Adler, 1974). Sexual behavior in male rodents is known to consist of a sequence of reflexive components (Beach & Jordan, 1956; Dewsbury, 1975). The sequence includes mounting the female, intromissions of the penis into the vagina accompanied by pelvic thrusting, and finally ejaculation. Under normal conditions, from 5 to 15 intromissions are required to produce ejaculation. In the experimental group of this study, male rats were permitted a maximum of only 7 intromissions in order to achieve ejaculation. Two control groups were given either the same number of sexual encounters each of which culminated in ejaculation, or the same number of ejaculations as the experimental group. Thus the first control group held the number of sexual encounters constant and the second control group held the number of ejaculations constant.

At the conclusion of 16 weekly encounters, 60% of the experimental group achieved ejaculation within seven intromissions, whereas only 20% of the control groups reached ejaculation. It is clear that the imposition of environmental consequences altered the expression of a sequence of reflexive behaviors. The manner in which the alteration was brought about is instructive, however. From other research it is known that increasing the time interval between intromissions will reduce the number of intromissions required for ejaculation. That is, like other reflexes, the elicitation of the ejaculatory reflex is facilitated by lengthening the interval between successive presentations of the eliciting stimulus. In keeping with this fact, ejaculation within 7 intromissions was found to occur by an increase in the time between successive intromissions. Thus while sexual behavior was sensitive to environmentally-imposed consequences, the manner in which that sensitivity was expressed reflected the phylogenetic legacy.

Maternal Behavior   The rich interplay of phylogenetic and ontogenetic factors is also readily apparent in maternal behavior. Female rhesus monkeys (Spencer-Booth, 1968) and humans (Brindley, Clarke, Hutt, Robinson, & Wethei, 1973) both interact with infants more than males, even when sexually immature (Chamove, Harlow, & Mitchell, 1967). However, only mothers move toward and vocalize upon hearing the tape-recorded cries of an infant monkey (Simons, Bobbit, & Jensen, 1967). While further work is needed to illuminate fully the interplay of heredity and experience influencing these results, it is clear that both factors are involved.

It is in the relationship between the infant and the mother that the interactions of phylogeny and ontogeny are particularly keen. Upon giving birth to her first infant, the rhesus mother will clasp the infant so that mother and infant are facing each other (ventro–ventral clasp). The infant may not be in a position to nurse, however, and may even be held upside down until the mother learns to position the infant properly (Bertrand, 1969; Hinde, Rowell, &

Spencer-Booth, 1964). Although infant monkeys have a grasp reflex that enables them to cling to the mother, the primary responsibility for maintaining ventro–ventral contact rests with the mother at first (Hinde & White, 1974). The consequences of holding the infant—including having milk removed from the distended mammary glands—is undoubtedly an important factor in the continuation of this behavior. With the passage of time, the proportion of the daylight hours spent on the mother declines until it is only 20% by the tenth month (Rosenblum, 1971). This change is brought about by changes in the infant's behavior, but more immediately by changes in the mother's behavior (Hinde, 1974; Hinde & White, 1974). The mother begins to reject the infant by stripping the infant from her body or by hitting or biting it. Maternal rejection is instrumental in inducing the young monkey to leave the mother as shown by the fact that infant monkeys will cling to an inanimate substitute mother or to peers for a longer period of time than occurs with a normal mother (Hanson, E. W., 1966; Harlow & Harlow, 1965).

Regardless of the specific relationship between genetic and environmental factors, there is common agreement on the overwhelming significance of individual experience in the determination of maternal and infant behavior (Gewirtz, 1961; Rosenblum, 1971). The importance of experience is nowhere more dramatically demonstrated than in the maternal behavior of those monkeys which have been raised in social isolation. After extraordinary efforts were undertaken to impregnate them, because of their deficient sexual behavior, these females finally conceived and gave birth. Their "maternal" behavior was described thus:

> Month after month female monkeys that never knew a real mother, themselves became mothers—helpless, hopeless, heartless mothers devoid, or almost devoid, of any maternal feeling. (Harlow, 1962)

EVOLUTION AND LEARNING

Our survey of the basic phenomena of reflexive and social behavior is largely complete. It is appropriate now to stand aside from the specifics of sea turtles, startle reflexes, and mother–infant relationships and consider what general principles have emerged from the study of these behaviors—all of which were chosen because they bear the imprint of evolution. More precisely, what have these behaviors to tell us of the interactions that exist between phylogeny and ontogeny in the determination of behavior?

In each of the behaviors that have been studied—whether it is the elicitation of a reflex or the complexities of maternal behavior—a common conclusion may be reached: It is not enough to know the evolutionary history of the organism, as reflected by its membership in a particular species, if its behavior is to be understood. The prediction and control of behavior—even those behaviors whose debt to evolution is generally acknowledged—require a knowledge of the particular experiences of the individual organism. With even so simple a functional relationship between the environment and behavior as exemplified by the reflex, the likelihood of a response is governed by both phylogeny and ontogeny.

An especially instructive, and ironic, illustration of the interplay between the effects of the near past through learning and of the distant past through genetics is provided by the feeding behavior of finches. It will be recalled that variations in beak size among finches inhabiting the Galápagos Islands provided a major impetus to Darwin's development of the principle of natural selection. Originally, it was assumed that each of the various species of finches innately selected that type of food which was best suited to its particular size of beak. Close observation has revealed this not to be true, however. The finches learn to peck at the seeds that are most easily opened by their beaks! While natural selection perpetuates the differing beak sizes, it is individual learning that provides the foundation for their natural selection (Hinde, 1959; Kear, 1962). Upon closer inspection, Darwin's seminal observation is an equally valid example of *both* learning and natural selection.

When we search for the mark of natural selection, we invariably also find evidence for the operation of individual experience. Consider a second example, this time of a classic study designed to establish the adaptiveness of a particular physical characteristic in a species of fish (Hoogland, Morris, & Tinbergen, 1957). Three species of prey fish were placed in a large aquarium. One of the species, the minnow, has no spines. Of the other two species, the ten-spined stickleback has small spines and the three-spined stickleback has large spines (see Fig. 2.11). A predatory fish, the pike, was then introduced into the aquarium. The purpose of the experiment was to determine if the presence of spines would deter predation by the pike, thereby demonstrating the adaptiveness of spines.

When first placed in the tank, the pike pursued and caught minnow and stickleback alike. The stickleback, however, was typically spit out immediately "and the pike would make violent coiling movements, and would 'cough' intensely several times." (Some drawings of a three-spined stickleback in the mouth of the pike are also given in Fig. 2.11.) After a few such episodes during which the pike was rarely successful in swallowing the sticklebacks, the pike preyed exclusively on the minnows. Thus the spines were adaptive only *after* the pike had suffered the consequences of trying to eat a stickleback. Learning was therefore necessary in order for the genetically-determined characteristic of spines to be adaptive. Findings such as these with beak sizes in finches and spines in fishes have caused zoologists to regard learning as a major factor in determining the pace of evolution (cf. Wilson, E. O., 1975, pp. 13–14).

Even the conventional wisdom that accepts as inherited those characteristics which appear in successive generations from a common ancestor may sometimes be in error. There are finches in a laboratory in England which have sung a distinctive, but unfinchlike, song for four generations. Is this the result, perhaps, of some genetic mutation that has been passed on from one generation to another? Because the experience of these birds is known from observations in the laboratory, the question may be answered—and the answer is "no." The great-grandfather of the present generation of finches was foster-reared by canaries, and because this species of finch learns its song from those which feed it, the great-grandfather finch had acquired a canary-like song.

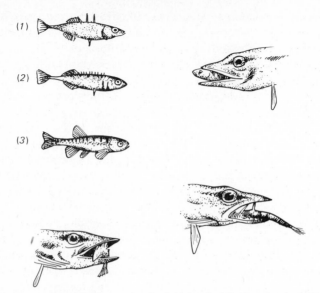

Fig. 2.11 Three prey fish: (1) three-spined stickleback, (2) 10-spined stickleback, and (3) minnow. Other drawings show the three-spined stickleback in various positions within the mouth of a predator fish, the pike. (From Hoogland, Morris, & Tinbergen, 1954.)

This song he then taught his progeny and they, in turn, have taught it to theirs (Hinde, 1974, p. 109). Thus individual learning provides the basis for tradition, a process which like genetic mechanisms may span the generations.

Because individual behavior is but the flow of one river fed by the two streams of phylogeny and ontogeny, the attempt to classify behavior as either innate or acquired is foredoomed to failure. The reasonable claim that the ability to learn is the greatest adaptation of all is testimony to the inseparability of genetical and environmental factors in the behavior of the individual. (See Schneirla, 1949; Schneirla, 1956; Wilson, 1975, pp. 26–27, for further comments on the utility of the distinction between innate and learned behaviors.) What is required for the understanding of behavior is a thorough experimental analysis of those variables which influence behavior—those events that precede the behavior and exert stimulus control over it, and those events that follow the behavior and reinforce or punish it. When these variables have been identified and their functional relationships to behavior determined, the motivation for an attempt to classify behavior as innate or acquired is largely swept away.

The foregoing is not intended as a rejection of the idea that the historical environment of the species influences present behavior through genetic mechanisms. Rather, it is an affirmation that what are truly inherited are genes and that these genes find expression in behavior only through the present environment. There is no behavioral talisman by whose presence the effect of phylogeny is invariably marked or by whose absence phylogeny is invariably denied. A behavior may exist in all members of a species because of either a common phylogeny or a common environment. Conversely, a behavior may exist in only one member of a species because of either a unique heredity or a unique environment.

To understand individual behavior, an experimental analysis must be conducted that makes use of controlled observations in the laboratory and, to the fullest extent possible, in the natural environment. The principle of natural selection provides a rich and powerful source of ideas for the direction of research, but there is no substitute for the experiment itself. The *observed* contingencies between behavior and the environment, and not vague appeals to "adaptiveness" by the naive evolutionist or to "experience" by the naive environmentalist, provide the genuine insights. The remainder of this book will consist largely of a presentation of the results of such experimental analyses of experience and efforts to integrate those results theoretically. The focused light of experimentation will most often be turned upon the contemporary environment as is appropriate in a book on learning, but we shall occasionally refer to the ancient environments of phylogeny as well. In the next chapter, which deals with reinforcement, we shall see that the effects of the consequences of responding have their roots in the phylogenetic earth of elicitation.

SUMMARY

The chapter on elicitation has focused upon behaviors—reflexes and fundamental social behaviors—that reflect phylogenetic influences. Using the startle reflex as a representative reflex, unconditioned stimulus control of behavior was illustrated. Repeated elicitation of a reflex was seen to produce habituation, a waning of the response and a simple instance of learning. Various behavioral phenomena including sensitization, dishabituation, retention, spontaneous recovery, and stimulus generalization were shown with habituated responses. In addition, issues of general significance to the study of learning were raised, using habituation as a vehicle. These issues concerned potential hazards in the averaging of behavioral data across individuals and across time, and in the use of simplified preparations and inferred processes in generating theoretical analyses of behavior.

In the treatment of social behaviors, the influence of the contemporary environment upon the expression of behavior became even more apparent. The particular stimuli (releasers) that control fixed-action patterns may be heavily dependent upon individual experience, and sexual and maternal behaviors are affected by their environmental consequences as well as by their antecedents.

A major conclusion from the study of reflexes and social behaviors was that a classification of behavior into innate and learned categories was neither meaningful nor useful and that what is required is a detailed experimental analysis of any given behavior in order to determine the conditions that are important to its occurrence.

NOTES

1. Herman Melville, the author of *Moby Dick,* had visited the Galápagos Archipelago as a sailor when a young man. In 1854, five years before the publication of Dar-

win's *Origin of Species,* Melville published a series of short sketches of this island group under the title: *A passage to the enchanted isles: Las Encantadas.*

2. More extensive general discussions of the relationship between individual and group functions are contained in Sidman, 1960, and Estes, 1956.

3. There are a number of other theoretical attempts to account for habituation including Horn, 1967; Ratner, 1970; Sokolov, 1963; Wagner, 1975; and Whitlow, 1975. The work of Sokolov and especially of Wagner and his associates represents instances of more general information-processing models of memory, and a detailed consideration of this type of theory is postponed until Chapter 10.

4. In dual-process theory, the processes that are called excitation and inhibition here are labeled sensitization and habituation respectively. The former labels are used to make clear the distinction between the inferred processes and the observed phenomena that those processes seek to explain.

5. See I. Eibl-Eibesfeldt, *Ethology, the biology of behavior* (New York: Holt, Rinehart, and Winston, 1975) for a thorough presentation of the ethological perspective on these and related matters.

3

Reinforcement

Classical Procedure

INTRODUCTION

We now begin in earnest our inquiry into how the behavior of the individual is shaped by the contemporaneous environment. An examination of elicited behaviors, our legacy from phylogeny, reveals that these behaviors—whether they are reflexes or social behaviors—cannot be understood merely as the product of the past environment of the species. Indeed, we have seen that an understanding of even reflexive behavior requires a knowledge of the unique environment of the individual as well as the common environment of the species of which that individual is a member.

There is a second and still more persuasive reason why elicited behaviors provide an incomplete account of the rich interplay between the environment and the organism: The life of each individual contains environmental challenges which are so idiosyncratic and fleeting that the demands of natural selection for time and constancy of conditions cannot be met. Faced with a changing environment, and therefore the unavailability of the relatively stereotyped solutions represented by elicitation, the capacity to develop new responses to the environment emerges within the lifetime of the individual. This capacity is the capacity to learn, and it too is a consequence of natural selection.

The emergence of learning through the action of natural selection presents a paradox, because through learning the course of evolution may itself be altered. Through changing the environment, we alter the very stuff upon which natural selection is based. Our ability to control the environment arises—another paradox—from our understanding of how the environment, in turn, controls behavior. Knowledge of how the environment produces behavioral change is the province of learning, and the uses to which we put that knowledge may determine whether humanity is to be judged ultimately as fallen angels or risen apes.

A Search for the Antecedents of Learning

This chapter seeks a deeper insight into the principle of reinforcement, primarily from the vantage point of the *classical conditioning procedure*. The subsequent chapter pursues the same goal, but from the perspective of the *instrumental conditioning procedure*. Whether these two procedures converge upon a common conception of the reinforcement principle is a matter of enduring concern to which we shall intermittently return.

Before directing our attention exclusively to the experimental and theoretical analysis of classical conditioning, the essential features of both the classical and instrumental procedures will be described. This description will clarify the defining feature of each procedure and will indicate something of its potential scope as a method for changing behavior. Let us see how the classical and instrumental conditioning procedures seek to dissect the flow of environmental and behavioral events so that the origins of learning can be uncovered.

Classical Conditioning   For much of their fundamental work, both Pavlov and Thorndike forsook the more turbulent flow of events that typifies our daily lives and searched for an understanding of the principle of reinforcement

Fig. 3.1   Dog restrained in a Pavlov frame in a classical conditioning experiment. The UCS is food contained in the bowl located in front of the dog. The salivary duct is externalized in order that saliva might flow into the tube connected to the cheek of the dog.

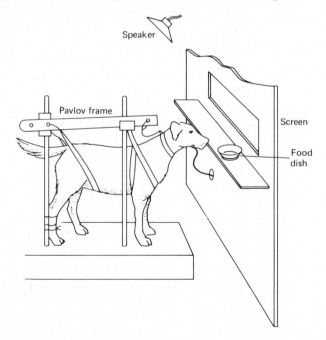

in the calmer waters of the animal learning laboratory. Through the use of animals, the relevant prior experience of the learner can be more completely specified; through the use of laboratory methods, the relevant environmental events might be better controlled.

In a typical experiment in Pavlov's laboratory, the following events occurred (Pavlov, 1927). A dog was lightly restrained in a harness (see Fig. 3.1) and a metronome began to tick. At the sound of the metronome, various orienting responses were observed—the ears of the dog pricked up, its head turned toward the sound. If appropriate instruments had been available, other responses mediated by the autonomic nervous system would have been observed—a change in heart rate or blood pressure. A few seconds after the sound of the metronome began, a bowl of food was given to the dog and the ticking stopped. Almost immediately after the food was presented, saliva was observed flowing copiously from a salivary duct that had been surgically diverted to the external surface of the cheek. This sequence of environmental and behavioral events—sound, food in mouth, salivation—was repeated perhaps some 10 or 20 times and then a *new* functional relationship between the environment and behavior appeared: The salivary gland began to secrete when the metronome alone was sounded and *prior* to the presentation of the meat powder. An environmental stimulus (the sounding of the metronome) had come to control a response (salivation) which that stimulus had not previously controlled.

Fig. 3.2 Dog restrained in a Pavlov frame in an instrumental (operant) conditioning experiment. The instrumental response is leg movement maintained by presentation of food in the bowl. The behavior which is monitored includes both leg movement and salivation.

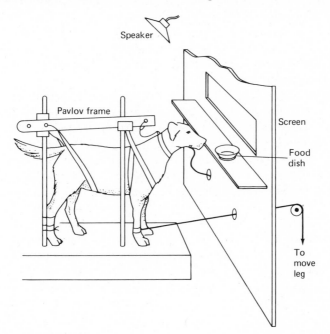

In more general terms, a procedure in which a "neutral" stimulus (the ticking sound) was followed by an elicitation process (food in the mouth elicited salivation) caused the neutral stimulus to control a response that resembled the elicited response. *It is the occurrence of an elicitation process contingent upon the presentation of a stimulus that is the defining feature of the classical, or Pavlovian, procedure.* The term contingent, as it is used here, signifies the succession of two events arranged by the experimenter. When an eliciting stimulus is contingent upon a neutral stimulus with the result that the neutral stimulus acquires control over some response, then the eliciting stimulus is said to function as a *reinforcer*.

Instrumental Conditioning   Our illustration of instrumental, or Thorndikian, conditioning comes from Konorski's laboratory in Poland (Konorski & Miller, 1937). This example is selected in preference to one of Thorndike's original studies because, in all respects except the critical one that distinguishes the instrumental from the classical procedure, it is identical to the previously described example from Pavlov's laboratory. Thus a close comparison of Konorski's and Pavlov's experiments is well-suited to highlight both the critical difference and the many similarities between the two procedures.

A dog is once again restrained in a harness and an auditory stimulus (a tone) is sounded (see Fig. 3.2). Again a number of orienting responses are given to the tone. While the tone is still sounding, the foreleg of the dog is raised by the experimenter (or the experimenter may wait until the foreleg is "spontaneously" raised by the dog) and only then is food introduced into the dog's mouth. Food then elicits the salivary response. After a number of repetitions of this sequence of events—tone, leg movement, food in mouth, salivation—a new functional relationship develops: The leg moves when the tone is sounded but *prior* to its movement by the experimenter and the introduction of food into the mouth. Once again, an environmental stimulus (the tone) has come to control a response (now leg movement as well as salivation) which that stimulus had not previously controlled.

Somewhat more generally, in an environment in which a response (leg movement) was followed by an elicitation process (food in the mouth elicited salivation) a change in the likelihood of the response was produced. *It is the contingency between a response and an elicitation process that is the defining feature of the instrumental, or Thorndikian, procedure.* If a contingent relationship between a response and an elicitation process results in an increase in the likelihood of the response, then the eliciting stimulus is said to function as a *reinforcer*.

Relationship Between the Classical and Instrumental Procedures
Learning occurred in both Pavlov's and Konorski's experiments because in both cases the environmental control of behavior was altered as a result of the experience of the individual organism. An auditory stimulus came to control the salivary response with the classical procedure and leg movement with the instrumental procedure. The procedures differed whereby these behavioral

changes were produced, however. In the classical procedure, the eliciting stimulus was contingent upon the occurrence of a stimulus; in the instrumental procedure, the eliciting stimulus was contingent upon the occurrence of a response. From the standpoint of the experimenter, the procedures are quite distinct, as shown in Fig. 3.3. In classical conditioning, the experimenter institutes a stimulus-reinforcer contingency while in instrumental conditioning a response-reinforcer contingency is arranged.

Although the procedural distinction between classical conditioning and instrumental conditioning is clear, it is a separate question whether that distinction is fundamental to the analysis of the principle of reinforcement. After all, it is the sequence of environmental and behavioral events as it is experienced by the learner, and not the description of that sequence by the experimenter, which produces changes in the behavior of the learner.

When the sequence of events in the classical and instrumental procedures are objectively examined, many similarities appear. In Pavlov's experiment, an orienting response may precede food and thus a response-reinforcer sequence may occur, as well as the stimulus-reinforcer sequence that defines the classical procedure. Similarly, in Konorski's experiment, the tone may precede the reinforcer and thus a stimulus-reinforcer sequence may occur in addition to the response-reinforcer sequence that defines the instrumental procedure. In short, the classical and instrumental procedures each contain within themselves the sequence of environmental and behavioral events that defines the other.

Learning is influenced by the complete sequence of events and is not restricted to those particular sequences directly instituted by the experimenter. Accordingly, because of the similarities in the actual sequence of environmen-

Fig. 3.3 Summary of the defining features of classical and instrumental conditioning. The wavy line indicates the contingency instituted by the experimenter in each procedure.

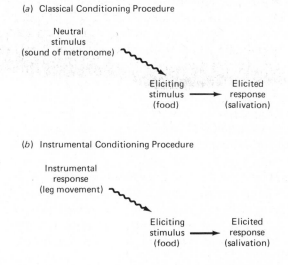

(a) Classical Conditioning Procedure

Neutral
stimulus
(sound of metronome)

Eliciting   Elicited
stimulus ⟶ response
(food)   (salivation)

(b) Instrumental Conditioning Procedure

Instrumental
response
(leg movement)

Eliciting   Elicited
stimulus ⟶ response
(food)   (salivation)

tal and behavioral events, we may expect to find similarities between the views of the reinforcement principle that emerge from the analysis of classical and instrumental conditioning. Each individual continuously behaves in an omnipresent environment, and we jeopardize the completeness of our understanding when we confine our attention only to those events directly manipulated by the experimenter. Experiments, even in the tightly controlled environment of the animal learning laboratory, are but intrusions into the continuous flow of events that characterize the life of any organism. William James, the psychologist who lured Thorndike from literature to science, spoke of "the stream of thought" (James, 1890, p. 239). Modern psychology realizes that the understanding of the course of that stream requires scrutiny of the full range of environmental and behavioral events (Schoenfeld & Farmer, 1970).

The Range of Effective Elicitors

In the experiments of Pavlov and Konorski, we saw how an elicitation process (food in the mouth elicits salivation) could be used in classical and instrumental procedures to bring about learning. A *reflexive* elicitation process could serve as a reinforcer in either procedure. Much subsequent work has confirmed that the elicitation of reflexes may function as reinforcers in a wide variety of circumstances. Thus a new functional relationship between the environment and behavior may develop through the phylogenetically old relationship embodied in the reflex. The seeds of the future are rooted in the earth of the past.

While reflexive elicitation processes are effective agents of behavioral change, and their utility is fully demonstrable with humans as well as other organisms, these processes do not often appear to be the direct source of learning in experienced organisms. Particularly in organisms having the richness of experience and complexity of structure of adult humans, it is a simple task to imagine a situation in which behavior changes in the apparent absence of a reflexive elicitation process. For example, when we continue to speak to those who pay attention to what we are saying and cease talking to those who ignore our words, our behavior changes, but a reflex is not evident. Paying attention and ignoring, respectively, increase and decrease the behavior of talking, but neither event is an eliciting stimulus for a reflexive response.

Our goal in this section is to determine whether events other than stimuli that elicit reflexes can serve as reinforcers. Upon the outcome of this inquiry rests the value of the classical and instrumental procedures as general methods for the production of behavioral change and for the attainment of insights into the principle of reinforcement.

Social Behaviors   In an effort to determine the range of eliciting stimuli that are effective in generating learning, we will first consider the release of fixed-action patterns. Can an elicitation process consisting of a releasing stimulus and a fixed-action pattern also be used to produce a new functional relationship between the environment and behavior? An answer to this question will be sought using the example of imprinting, whereby a releasing stimulus controls the fixed-action pattern of the following response.

Consider first some findings using the classical conditioning procedure (Hoffman, Barrett, Ratner, & Singer, 1972). A duckling, after being imprinted to the sight of a moving toy electric train, was placed in a chamber without the opportunity to see the imprinted stimulus. Deprived of the imprinted stimulus, the duckling began to emit a series of intense, "peep"-like vocalizations which are termed distress calls. Such vocalizations are known as distress calls since they occur when a predator is present or during painful stimulation (Sluckin, 1965). When the duckling was permitted to view the "mother" electric train through a transparent wall of the chamber, the distress calls ceased abruptly, only to begin with renewed vigor when the train again disappeared. For a duckling, out of sight is not out of mind.

Having established that the absence of the imprinted stimulus controlled distress calling, the experimenter then began to turn on a light prior to presenting the sight of the train. After a few repetitions of the light followed by the appearance of the train, the distress calls declined during the light alone. After some 50 repetitions of the light followed by the imprinted stimulus, distress calls were virtually eliminated during the light. A control group of other ducklings which also received the light, but not paired with the train, continued to emit distress calls when the light was presented.

The experiment was successful in showing that a new functional relationship between the environment and behavior can be produced if the occurrence of a releaser is made contingent upon a neutral stimulus. Thus the classical procedure is effective in producing learning when the elicitation process involves the release of fixed-action patterns as well as the elicitation of reflexive responses.

Now we turn to the question of whether the release of fixed-action patterns may also change behavior when presented in the instrumental procedure. Imprinting will again be used as the experimental illustration (Hoffman, Searle, Toffey, & Kozma, 1966; Peterson, N., 1960). After being imprinted to a moving electric train, a duckling was placed in a chamber containing a pole. Initially, the pole was seldom pecked by the duckling. But when the sight of the train was made contingent upon a peck, the pole was frequently pecked. A stimulus (the sight of the pole) gained control of a response (pecking) when the release of a fixed-action pattern was made contingent upon that response. Thus instrumental procedures may also change the environmental control of behavior through the elicitation of either fixed-action patterns or reflexive responses.

There is increasing evidence that the release of a wide variety of species-typical and social behaviors using either classical or instrumental procedures will produce learned changes in behavior. The elicitation of such social behaviors as the aggressive display in Siamese fighting fish (Hogan, 1967; Thompson, T., & Sturm, 1965), courting in quail (Farris, 1967), copulation in rats (Bermant & Westbrook, 1966)—even copulation without ejaculation (Sheffield, F. D.,

Wulff, & Backer, 1951), maternal behavior in mice (Frieman, J. P., 1965), and the sight of a conspecific in monkeys (Butler, 1954) have all been successfully used to bring about learned changes in the environmental control of behavior. Thus elicitation processes—whether they involve stimuli that elicit reflexive behaviors or complex fixed-action and social behaviors owing a clear debt to ontogeny as well as phylogeny—are all effective in promoting learning.

The fact that a new functional relationship between the environment and behavior may be produced through the elicitation of a reflex demonstrates that some learning is directly dependent upon the phylogenetic history of the species. The fact that behavioral changes may also be produced through the elicitation of social behaviors indicates that at least some learning is dependent upon the ontogenetic history of the individual as well.

Prior Learning   Since stimuli that elicit fundamental social behaviors also function as reinforcers, subsequent learning may show the effects of prior individual experience. A duckling for which the sight of an electric train is a reinforcer might be expected to learn very different subsequent behaviors than a duckling that was imprinted to its biological mother. We now examine the possibility that stimuli whose elicitation of behavior rests almost exclusively upon prior learning may serve as reinforcers.

The question of whether prior learned relationships between the en-

Fig. 3.4   The procedure for producing higher-order conditioning. In Phase I, a reflexive elicitation process is contingent on a neutral stimulus (S_1). As a result, S_1 comes to control a response that is similar to the reflexive response. In Phase II, a learned elicitation process is contingent on a second neutral stimulus (S_2). As a result, S_2—which has never been paired with the reflexive elicitation process—acquires control over a response that is similar to the learned response from Phase I. The wavy lines denote the contingencies imposed by the experimenter. The dashed lines denote the new, learned functional relationships between the environment and behavior.

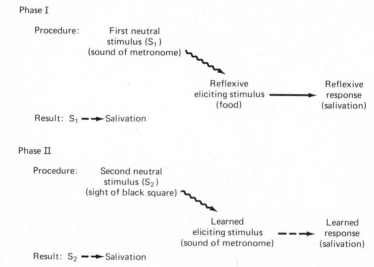

vironment and behavior could serve as the basis for new learning had occurred to Pavlov. He sought the answer in the following experiment (Pavlov, 1927, pp. 33–34). First a dog was trained to salivate to the sound of a metronome by pairing the sound with food. Next came the test of whether a learned relationship between a stimulus and behavior (the sound now controlled salivation) could be used to produce new learning. In this crucial phase of the experiment, a new stimulus—a black square—was paired with the sound of the metronome but food was no longer presented. Would the new stimulus also come to control salivation? After 10 pairings of the black square and the sound of the metronome, salivation occurred to the black square alone. The answer to the question was affirmative. In the classical procedure, learning may be produced by making a previously learned relationship between the environment and behavior contingent upon the presentation of a new neutral stimulus. The method for accomplishing this goal is summarized in Fig. 3.4 and was called *higher-order conditioning* by Pavlov. (See Rescorla, 1977, 1979, for recent work on higher-order conditioning.)

Can new learning also be based upon old learning when an instrumental procedure is used? In order to answer this question, it is first necessary to establish a learned functional relationship between a stimulus and a response, and then to determine whether a new behavior will change when that stimulus is made contingent upon the occurrence of the new behavior.

Such an experiment was conducted by Skinner (1938, pp. 82–83). In the first phase of the experiment, a learned functional relationship between a stimulus and a response was established by use of a classical procedure. A rat was placed in a test chamber and a distinct click was sounded immediately prior to the delivery of food into a small cup located on one wall of the chamber. After a number of pairings, the click was presumed to control responses, such as salivation, that were reflexively elicited by food. Once the learned relationship between the click and the food-elicited responses had been established, a response lever was introduced into the chamber. In the second phase of the experiment, an instrumental procedure was instituted in which the click was contingent on pressing the response lever, but food was no longer given. Would the frequency of lever pressing increase when the response was followed only by the click? The answer was again affirmative: The lever-pressing response was acquired when only the click was presented. The procedure and results of this experiment are summarized in Fig. 3.5.

The preceding experiment, and many others (see Hendry, 1969; Kelleher & Gollub, 1962; and Mackintosh, 1974, for summaries of related work), indicates that prior learning may provide the foundation for new learning using the instrumental procedure. In this fashion, it is believed that such diverse stimuli as the attention of a friend, a kind word, and money acquire the ability to function as reinforcers.

Skinner (1938) called the phenomenon whereby old learning may support new learning in the instrumental procedure *conditioned reinforcement*, "conditioned" because the new learning was conditional or dependent upon earlier learning. This phenomenon has also been called *secondary reinforcement*

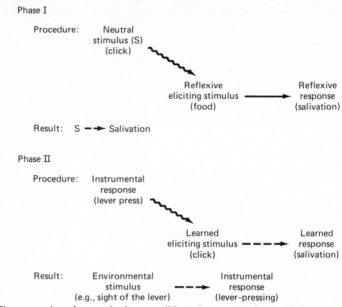

Fig. 3.5 The procedure for producing conditioned, or secondary, reinforcement. In Phase I, a classical procedure is instituted in which a reflexive elicitation process is contingent on a neutral stimulus (S). As a result, S acquires control of a response that is similar to the reflexive response. In Phase II, a learned elicitation process is contingent on an instrumental response. As a result, environmental stimuli acquire control over the instrumental response. The wavy lines indicate the two types of contingencies imposed by the experimenter. The dashed lines indicate new, learned functional relationships between the environment and behavior.

(Hull, 1943) to distinguish it from behavioral changes produced by stimuli such as food or water, which are effective elicitors relatively independent of specific prior experience. These latter stimuli are then termed primary reinforcers.

Concluding Comments   Our survey of the range of stimuli that are effective in producing learning is now complete. We may conclude that learning is initially dependent on reflexive elicitation processes, but that with continued experience, the number of potential reinforcers may increase enormously. Both stimuli that control fundamental social behaviors and stimuli whose control of behavior is almost entirely the product of individual experience become capable of functioning as reinforcers.

For a mature organism exposed to diverse sequences of environmental and behavioral events and having the complexity of structure required to appreciate those events, the number of elicitation processes capable of functioning as reinforcers must be legion. Thus the limits of learning for organisms such as humans arise less from the past of the species and more from the past of the individual as the organism develops. The word "good" may function as a reinforcer for the behavior of many people but not for the behaviors of those who fail to understand English or for those who understand English but are indifferent to the opinions of others. In either case, however, the environments of the past—both near and distant—guide and set the boundaries for future learning.

The classical and instrumental procedures have shown themselves capable of producing learning with a full range of eliciting stimuli, with conditioned as well as unconditioned elicitation processes. Accordingly, a more detailed analysis of the behavioral changes brought about by the classical and instrumental procedures has the potential for providing a deep and comprehensive understanding of the principle of reinforcement. In this chapter, we shall focus upon the experimental and theoretical analysis of classical conditioning. In the next, we explore instrumental conditioning. Through the study of these two procedures, we seek knowledge of the fundamental processes whereby the flow of environmental and behavioral events shapes our lives.

FUNDAMENTALS OF CLASSICAL CONDITIONING

The classical conditioning procedure, whereby a stimulus comes to control the behavioral component of the elicitation process with which it is paired, is believed to be the primary method through which the responses commonly labeled emotions are learned. A warm feeling upon seeing a person whose company we have previously enjoyed or fear upon confronting a situation known to be dangerous both owe much to the stimulus-reinforcer contingency of classical conditioning.

While most learned emotional reactions are veridical, some are without reasonable basis and are called *phobias*. If classical conditioning plays a role in the acquisition of phobias, perhaps the procedure may also play a role in their diminution. This insight has been exploited in a conditioning technique known as *systematic desensitization* (Wolpe, 1958). As an illustration, a claustrophobic person (someone who fears confinement in a restricted space) is first taught to achieve profound muscle relaxation. At the conclusion of the first phase of the technique, the word "relax" has acquired control over the behavior of relaxing. In the second phase, the person is presented with a graded series of stimuli which evoke the fear response. For example, pictures might be presented or the person might be asked to imagine being in an open-air stadium, an enclosed auditorium, a crowded bus, a train as it goes through a tunnel, and an elevator. Each stimulus is followed by the instruction to relax. The next stimulus in the graded series is given only when relaxation has followed the preceding stimulus. The state of relaxation could be objectively assessed by recording muscle tonus, that is, by electromyography. In this manner, the behavior of relaxation is conditioned to stimuli that were previously fear-arousing. This technique may be recognized as a variant of the higher-order conditioning procedure in which a stimulus acquires control of a response (the stimulus "relax" controls the response of relaxation), and then that stimulus is made contingent on other stimuli (the feared situations) until the new stimuli also control the response.

The notion of supplanting one response (for example, fear) with an antagonistic response (for example, relaxation) was first studied in Pavlov's laboratory. The method was called *counterconditioning*. In the original work, food was given to a dog immediately after a painful electric shock (Erofeeva, cited in Pavlov, 1928, pp. 29–30; see Pearce & Dickinson, 1975, for recent work on the problem). The result of counterconditioning was that the dog salivated and smacked its lips when shocked, with little evidence of the customary response to electric shock.

Pavlov's interest in the application of his work to human betterment occupied an increasing place in his later years (Pavlov, 1941). Before proceeding to examine in detail the findings obtained with the classical procedure, perspective on Pavlov's work may be enhanced by knowing something of the events that led to its development and of his hopes for his discovery. The behavior of both occupants of the laboratory—the scientist and the subject—can be understood through knowledge of their histories.

> Ivan Petrinovich Pavlov was a physiologist. Born in 1849, he spent all of his professional life until the age of 50 in an effort to understand the functioning of the body, particularly the reflexive secretion of gastric juices from the glands of digestion. This work would shortly (1904) bring him a Nobel prize. In the course of his work on digestion, however, Pavlov noted a curious thing: The juices that flowed from the externalized ducts of the digestive glands would often commence *before* food had actually been introduced into the mouth of the dogs which were his subjects. The mere sight of food or the experimenter or even the sound of his approaching footsteps were sufficient to cause the juices to flow! Instead of regarding such "psychical secretions" as merely an unwanted nuisance—which they were in his study of digestion—Pavlov realized that his techniques could be applied to the study of learned secretory responses as well as to unlearned, or reflexive, responses.
>
> While much of scientific progress begins with such unanticipated and casual observations, a properly prepared observer is also required if that progress is to be realized. In Pavlov's case, the preparation was there. Not only did he possess the laboratory techniques for the study of glandular secretions but also, and equally importantly, he was intellectually prepared to appreciate the significance of his observations through his reading of Darwin and Sechenov, his eminent predecessor among Russian physiologists.
>
> From Sechenov, he had been introduced to the idea that the behavior of the individual could be understood as a product of its environmental antecedents. In a remarkable book, *Reflexes of the Brain* (1863), published two years before *Origin of Species,* Sechenov had asserted: "the *initial cause of any human activity lies outside man . . . the initial cause of all behaviour always lies, not in thought, but in external sensory stimulation . . .*" (Sechenov, 1863). Armed with his technical skills as a surgeon and his philosophical commitments from Darwin and Sechenov, Pavlov turned at the age of 50 away from traditional physiology and toward the *terra incognita* of learning.
>
> He pursued the study of "psychical reflexes," or as he soon came to call them, "conditioned reflexes," with the same vigor that he had previously shown in his research on unlearned, or unconditioned, reflexes. From September first to June first of each year, he worked an invariant schedule: From 9 A.M. to 6 P.M. he was in the laboratory. Then returning home, he ate his evening meal, napped from 7 to 9, spoke with family and friends from 9 to 10 or 11, and—finally—studied and did calisthenics until 1 or 2 A.M. This procedure was followed seven days a week, including holidays, with the exception of Sunday, when he

stopped work at 3 P.M. and took a quiet walk. When summer arrived, however, Pavlov quit the laboratory entirely and spent his time in outdoor sports, gardening, and reading. He knew how to work and how to play.

Given such prodigious energy and discipline, Pavlov and his collaborators (who included some 200 workers over the years) produced such an avalanche of information that it is almost impossible for a modern investigator using the classical procedure to discover a phenomenon that was not previously found and commented upon by Pavlov. His first paper using the term "conditioned reflex" appeared in Russian in 1901 (cited by Gantt in Pavlov, 1928), only three years after Thorndike's initial report of the instrumental conditioning procedure. Following publication in England (Pavlov, 1906), Pavlov's work became known to an American audience (Yerkes & Morgulis, 1909) which rapidly proceeded to explore the implications of the procedure for the study of learning (Watson, 1913). While American psychologists were busying themselves with implications—and sometimes demonstrating an imperfect knowledge of the precise methods and findings (for example, Watson, 1914)—Pavlov continued with his research in spite of the turmoil brought upon by the Bolshevik revolution in 1917.

Many anecdotes during the post-revolutionary period reveal the character of the man. When offered extra rations, he refused to accept them unless all in his laboratory received food. When sons of priests were expelled from medical schools, he resigned his position at a medical school declaring that he too was the son of a priest. When ordered to remove from the lobby a portrait of the nobleman who had contributed to the founding of his school, he hung the portrait in his own office. When politicians first applied for admission to the Soviet Academy of Science, only Pavlov cast a dissenting vote. During the last three years of his life, Pavlov reconciled himself to the new government whose consistent financial support of science had finally won him over.

Pavlov's legacy to the scientific study of behavior is monumental. Whereas Darwin had sought to understand human behavior through the study of the ancestral environment, Pavlov looked to the environment of the individual. "The complex conditions of everyday existence require a much more detailed and specialized correlation between the animal and its environment than is afforded by the inborn reflexes alone" (Pavlov, 1927, p. 16). Because of his earlier work with "inborn reflexes" in which behavior was elicited by an easily identifiable stimulus, Pavlov focused upon the relationship between environmental stimulation and reflexes. It was left to Thorndike and his successors to study the relationship between behavior and elicitation. Pavlov saw Thorndike as a kindred spirit, however, stating, "Some years after the beginning of the work with our new method I learned that somewhat similar experiments on animals had been performed in America. . . . I must acknowledge that the honour of having made the first steps along this path belongs to E. L. Thorndike" (Pavlov, 1928, p. 39–40). The compliment has been returned by Skinner, an eminent successor of Thorndike: "Pavlov had shown the way. . . . I had the clue from Pavlov: control your conditions and you will see order" (Skinner, 1959, p. 362).

In concluding this brief digression concerning some of the forces which shaped Pavlov's work and some of the influences which flowed from that work, it is instructive to close with Pavlov's own hopeful and idealistic statement. ". . . I am deeply and irrevocably convinced that along this path will be found the final triumph of the human mind over its uttermost and supreme problem—the knowledge of the mechanism and laws of human nature. Only thus may come a full, true and permanent happiness. Let the mind rise from victory to victory over surrounding nature, let it conquer for human life and activity not only the surface of the earth but all that lies between the depth of the seas and the outer limits of the atmosphere, let it command for its service prodigious energy to flow from one part of the universe to the other, let it annihilate space for the transference of its thoughts—yet the same human creature, led by dark powers to wars and revolutions and their horrors, produces for itself incalculable material losses and inexpressible pain and reverts to bestial conditions. Only science . . . will deliver man from his present gloom, and will purge him from his contemporary shame in the sphere of interhuman relations" (Pavlov, 1928, p. 41). These are hardly the sentiments of the dispassionate scientist who held, at other times, that "There is nothing exceptional in my work; it is all based on facts from which logical conclusions were drawn. That's all." (cited in Babkin, 1949, p. 45).

Seraphima, Pavlov's talented wife who as a young woman was a participant in literary soirées with the likes of Dostoevski and Turgenev, reported that Pavlov would say to her: "I envy no one else, but I envy you your religious faith" (cited in Babkin, 1949, p. 28). The foregoing testament reveals that Pavlov had not lost the capacity for faith, but was simply expressing his faith in a different way. ". . . Like Darwin, Pavlov angered the nonscientists whose preconceived notions were threatened by his discoveries. But such anger is the way we pay our greatest men. It is a special tribute reserved for those whose work is especially significant" (Miller, G. A., 1962a, p. 192).

We have seen how Pavlov, with his prior history of work in reflex physiology, attempted to uncover the origins of behavioral change through introducing into the stream of ongoing behavior an elicitation process in conjunction with a stimulus. He was seeking the learned counterpart of the reflexes that he knew so well from his earlier work. In this section we shall examine the classical conditioning procedure more closely, paying special attention to basic terminology and types of procedures, and to the variables which must be controlled if the behavioral changes are to be understood. Equipped with this knowledge, we shall be in a position to return to the central question: What does the classical procedure have to tell us about the conditions that are essential for learning—about the principle of reinforcement?

Terminology of Classical Conditioning

The first aspects of a new field that must be mastered are the technical terms used to describe the important events in that field. Classical conditioning is no exception. Until this point in our discussion of classical and instrumental procedures, we have used the basic terminology of stimulus, response, and elicitation process. This frugality in terminology has been helpful in appreciating the continuities between the classical and instrumental procedures. When Pavlov began his work, however, special terms and symbols were proposed to denote the salient events of classical conditioning, and these special terms have persisted to the present time.

You will recall that in our earlier example of the classical procedure, a stimulus (the sound of a metronome) was correlated with an elicitation process (meat powder in the mouth elicited salivation). After a number of such paired presentations of the metronome with meat powder, the sound of the metronome alone came to control salivation. The stimulus of the metronome, which initially did not evoke salivation, is called the *conditioned stimulus* or *CS*. It is so called because its ability to control salivation is conditional upon, or dependent upon, the pairing of the stimulus with the elicitation process. The eliciting stimulus (food in the mouth) is called the *unconditioned stimulus* or *UCS*. The UCS is so named because the control of salivation by the UCS is not conditional upon the events occurring in the classical procedure. The response that is elicited by the UCS—salivation in our example—is called the *unconditioned response*, or *UCR* for similar reasons. The learned response—also salivation— that is controlled by the CS is called the *conditioned response* or *CR* since the control of behavior by the CS is conditional upon the sequence of events in the classical procedure. Finally, one last term should be reintroduced. The CS controls some behavior from the very outset of the experiment. No stimulus is truly neutral. These behaviors, it will be recalled, are labeled *orienting responses* or *ORs*. (All technical terms used in the classical procedure are summarized in Fig. 3.6.)

Varieties of Stimuli

Having introduced the basic technical vocabulary, we now examine the various types of stimuli that have been used in the analysis of learning through the classical procedure. Many different stimuli have been employed successfully as CSs and UCSs (see Gormezano, 1966; Gormezano & Moore, 1969; Grant, 1964; Kimble, 1961). Rather than simply list such stimuli, we shall consider the broad classes of events that have served as effective stimuli—first as CSs and then as UCSs.

The stimuli that have served as CSs in laboratory studies have most often been simple sensory events such as lights or tones. Usually only one stimulus is manipulated by the experimenter, but for some purposes a series or a combination of stimuli is presented. If two or more stimuli are administered succes-

Fig. 3.6 The symbols and technical terms used in describing the classical conditioning experiment. The wavy lines indicate the contingency arranged by the experimenter. The dashed line indicates the new, learned functional relationship between the environment and behavior.

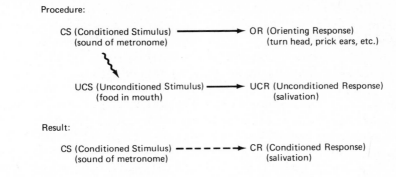

sively—for example, a light followed by a tone—then the procedure is described as *successive compound conditioning.* If two or more stimuli occur simultaneously—for example, a light and tone appearing together—then the procedure is called *simultaneous compound conditioning.* The latter procedure will prove very important in our analysis of the principle of reinforcement.

Complex stimuli such as pictures and words have also been used as CSs in classical procedures, although simple sensory events are favored when basic questions about the nature of reinforcement are being asked. Complex stimuli are chosen when there is some intrinsic interest in issues related to the CS itself, that is, when the classical procedure is used primarily as a tool for the study of other issues. Studies which use meaningful stimuli, such as words, as CSs are among this group and are designated *semantic conditioning* experiments (Razran, 1939). Semantic conditioning studies seek to investigate language and other related complex behaviors with the aid of conditioning methods (Grant, 1972; Razran, 1961). A second important group of studies is that in which the direct stimulation of internal organs—for example, the intestines or stomach—serves as a CS. These are called *interoceptive conditioning* experiments (Bykov & Gantt, 1957; Razran, 1961) and are directed at the capacity of internal stimuli to acquire control of behavior.

The diversity of stimuli that may serve as effective UCSs is also great. As we have seen, any stimulus that reliably controls a response is potentially usable as a UCS whether the control originates primarily from phylogenetic antecedents, as with reflexes, or from ontogenetic antecedents, as with learned behaviors. In higher-order conditioning (see p. 82), prior learning may establish a stimulus as an effective UCS (Ivanov-Smolensky, 1933). We have also noted another example in the use of the word "relax" as a UCS in systematic desensitization.

In addition to varying in the degree to which prior experience is important in determining the control of behavior by the UCS, UCSs also differ in the extent to which they produce observable UCRs. A major advantage of using behaviorally important stimuli such as those involved in elicitation processes is that the attention of the experimenter may be restricted to a specific subset of the many responses that comprise the stream of ongoing behavior. If the behaviors elicited by the UCS are readily observed and tightly controlled by the UCS (that is, present when the UCS is present and essentially absent otherwise) and if the CR resembles the UCR, then we are in a particularly favorable position to view the events that are involved in learning (Gormezano & Kehoe, 1975; Konorski, 1967, p. 303).

It must be realized, however, that our observation of the UCR is never perfect or complete. Even in the salivary conditioning preparation, we typically observe only a portion of the responses that occur when meat powder is placed in the mouth. Heart rate, respiration rate, and many neural changes also occur, but are not measured when we monitor salivation. The comprehensiveness of our measurements reflects in large part the state of technology. Observability is a fickle criterion upon which to decide whether a given procedure meets the definition of classical conditioning, although it may be a valid basis on which to judge the amenability of the procedure to rigorous experimental analysis.

A final distinction that has been made among stimuli which may serve as UCSs is whether they are appetitive or aversive (Spence, 1956). In *classical appetitive* (or *reward*) *conditioning*, the UCS is a stimulus that increases the frequency of responses that produce it when used in an instrumental procedure. In *classical aversive* (or *defense*) *conditioning*, the UCS is a stimulus that decreases responding when used in an instrumental procedure.

Classical Conditioning Paradigms

An organism may be said to be a theory of its environment (Weimer, 1973). From the events of prior environments, each of us must fashion a behavioral repertoire adequate for our survival in future environments. But from what features of the environment is that theory constructed? What is the nature of the sequence of events that comprise our personal theory of adaptation?

Classical conditioning seeks answers to these questions through varying the relationship between the CS and the UCS, the two events that are directly manipulable by the experimenter with this procedure. Three basic methods— or paradigms—may be defined by the relationship of CS onset to UCS onset. In the *forward conditioning* paradigm, the onset of the CS precedes the onset of the UCS. In the *simultaneous conditioning* paradigm, the onset of the CS and UCS are simultaneous. In the *backward conditioning* paradigm, the onset of the CS follows the onset of the UCS. Within the forward conditioning paradigm, two variations have been most frequently studied: *delay conditioning* in which the CS endures until at least the onset of the UCS, and *trace conditioning* in which the CS terminates prior to the onset of the UCS. (Figure 3.7 sum-

Fig. 3.7 Basic paradigms for the study of learning using the classical conditioning procedure. The horizontal line moves upward to indicate the onset of the stimulus and downward to indicate the termination of the stimulus.

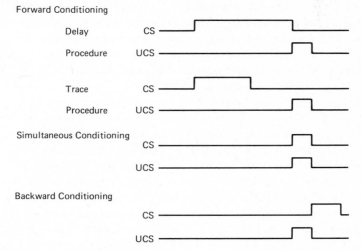

marizes the procedures just described.) Using the various CS-UCS relationships represented by these conditioning paradigms, investigators have searched for those circumstances that favor the enduring behavioral changes known as learning.

Control Procedures   The search for a principle of reinforcement is complicated by the fact that most responses, even the relatively simple ones often studied with conditioning procedures, are influenced by many factors. An experimental analysis of the effects of the CS-UCS relationship on learning must eliminate or hold constant all other factors that might affect performance. That is, the observations must be controlled to the fullest extent possible if the changes are to be attributed to the relationship between the CS and UCS.

In this section, we shall identify some of the common alternative sources of behavioral change that must be controlled in conditioning experiments. The precise nature of the extraneous factors varies somewhat with the characteristics of the particular experiment, but certain general sources may be identified. We shall illustrate many of these alternative sources of behavioral effects with the conditioning of the human eyelid response (blinking) as elicited by a puff of air to the cornea. An adequate methodology now exists for the study of human eyelid conditioning through the labors of a number of investigators (for example, Gormezano, 1966; Grant, 1964; Kimble, 1961; Spence, 1956), but only after some of the following factors had been identified, understood, and controlled.

One important consideration is the level of *baseline responding* in the response system of the CR. In the instance of the human eyelid response, for example, blinking occurs "spontaneously" at an appreciable frequency, even without a puff of air to the cornea serving as a UCS. How are we to distinguish a "spontaneous" blink that occurs during the CS from a blink that is the result of the CS-UCS relationship? Clearly, the experimental analysis of conditioning would be facilitated if responding in the absence of the CS or the UCS were a rare event.

It would be helpful also in analyzing the effect of the CS-UCS relationship on learning if no response to the CS occurred at the outset of the experiment. That is, unconditioned stimulus control by the CS should be minimal. In the case of the human eyelid response, an auditory stimulus may elicit a blink as a component of the startle reflex, and the onset of a light may elicit a blink if the retina is dark-adapted (Grant & Norris, 1947).

Habituation and sensitization may affect the monitored response as well. Regardless of the relationship between the CS and UCS, the classical procedure involves the presentation of two stimuli and, as we know from our earlier study of elicitation, the mere repeated presentation of a stimulus has effects on the responses elicited by that stimulus. The repeated presentation of the CS prior to a classical conditioning experiment might be thought to be a useful means of assessing the unconditioned stimulus control exerted by the CS. However, presenting the CS leads to habituation of the OR and the retardation of conditioning when the CS and UCS are subsequently paired. This retardation of conditioning has been termed *latent inhibition* (Lubow & Moore, 1959).

On the other hand, presenting the UCS may produce habituation of the UCR if the UCS is weak (Schneiderman, 1972) and sensitization of the response to the CS if the UCS is strong (Grant & Adams, 1944). Other more complex interactions resulting from the mere presentation of CS and UCS, and not from their relationship in the prior experience of learner, have also been reported (for example, Ison & Leonard, 1971; Marsh, Hoffman, & Stitt, 1976).

In addition to sensitization of the OR to the CS, new behaviors to the CS are sometimes seen as a result of UCS presentations. The evocation, as the result of unpaired CS-UCS presentations, of what would otherwise be labeled CRs to the CS is called *pseudoconditioning* (false conditioning). As an example, if a puff of air is applied to the cornea, the subsequent presentation of a tone will cause a blink to occur even though that intensity of tone was never previously observed to produce blinking (Grant, 1943). Pseudoconditioned responses have many origins, including the sensitization of previously subthreshold responses (Young, Cegavske, & Thompson, 1976) and the conditioning of CRs to other stimuli than the CS (Sheafor, 1975). In many respects, pseudoconditioning is a wastebasket term that encompasses a number of phenomena united by nothing so much as the incompleteness of our understanding of their antecedents. A complete understanding of pseudoconditioning will require a thorough knowledge of conditioning (cf. Dykman, 1976).

A short digression is appropriate in our discussion of efforts to achieve well-controlled observations. In the context of classical conditioning, a controlled observation is one that permits us to detect changes in behavior produced by the CS-UCS relationship when other causes of change have been eliminated or held constant. We have pursued this goal by making use of previous experimental work to identify potential alternative factors affecting the CR. The strategy of controlling for the effects of all previously identified antecedents of the behavior does not guarantee a completely controlled experiment, however. There may be other antecedents, as yet unidentified, that also contribute to the outcome. In a genuine sense, a completely controlled observation is possible—if at all—only after the phenomenon has been completely understood. But at that point, of course, there is no longer any need for the experiment—everything is known!

The decision to conduct an experiment is always a decision to step into the shadows. At best, prior knowledge may serve to lighten, but never eliminate, the darkness into which the experimenter moves. In the absence of certain knowledge of all relevant factors, the experimenter tries to anticipate likely candidates. The sources of alternative candidates arise from listing all possibilities that occur to the experimenter, from unsystematic hunches, and from the testing of well-defined theoretical hypotheses. The nature of the experimenter's theory, as well as prior experimental findings, enters into the design of a well-controlled experiment (Rescorla, cited in Teyler, Baum, & Patterson, 1975).[1]

We now return to the task of indicating some of the factors, other than the CS-UCS relationship, that may affect conditioning. So far, we have focused upon the contribution of events within the experiment. It is clear, however, that prior experience may also affect performance, especially with organisms whose extra-laboratory history may not be controlled. The effects of prior experience on the outcome of the CS-UCS relationship within the experiment is the major reason that it is extremely difficult to study fundamental conditioning processes in humans. Every event within the experiment is similar in some respect to events that have occurred prior to the experiment, and these similarities may affect the behavioral changes observed within the experiment.

Although much formal evidence exists regarding the intrusions of extra-experimental experience into conditioning with human subjects (for example, Grant, 1972), an anecdote will suffice. A colleague of one of the authors conducted an eyelid conditioning experiment, in which the CS was a spot of light that grew brighter just prior to the delivery of a puff of air to the eye. The responses obtained from the subject were unusual, however, and questioning at the end of the experiment elicited the statement, "Oh, wow! Like, it was like a giant moon rising over the horizon! Far out!" Such a CS is hardly a neutral stimulus. When further discussion revealed that the student had smoked an unlabeled cigarette just before the session, it became clear that uncontrolled prior experience had made a substantial contribution to the outcome of the experiment.

Careful selection of instructions and the use of procedures that disguise the true nature of the task have produced better-controlled observations with human learners in conditioning experiments (for example, Spence & Platt, 1967). Nevertheless, variations in the preexperimental environment complicate the endeavor enormously. Behavior within the experiment continues to be partially influenced by factors beyond the control of the experimenter. For this reason most investigations into the origins of behavioral change are conducted with infrahuman organisms whose extra-experimental experience may be directly controlled.

In searching for the origins of learning in the behavior of simpler organisms, we must contend with the risks as well as the advantages inherent in the use of simplified preparations. We believe that the advantages outweigh the risks in this instance. Each of the discoveries made under well-controlled conditions with the help of our furry and feathered friends can be compared with the results of the best-controlled experiments obtained with men and women. Where comparable experiments have been performed, the similarities in the functional relationships found between environment and behavior encourage us to believe that important continuities exist in the learning process. Discontinuities also exist, of course, and we shall point them out as well. The differences between lower animals and humans—or, for that matter, among lower animals of different species—are not confined to their individual preexperimental experiences. Their different ancestral environments have also bequeathed different legacies.

Basic Findings

Let us return to the central question with which our discussion of classical conditioning began: What relationship between environmental stimulation and an elicitation process must exist if learned changes in behavior are to occur? We now know that changes in behavior within the experiment may have origins other than the CS-UCS relationship, and that these other sources of variability must be controlled. Ideally, we seek a procedure in which the baseline level of activity in the response system of the CR is low, in which habituation and sensitization are not by themselves capable of accounting for the observed changes, in which pseudoconditioning is minimal, and in which the prior experience of the learner is controlled. To approximate these ideal conditions, we shift from the study of human conditioning to a simplified model preparation. Our primary interest in human behavior endures, but we seek the understanding of its fundamental processes in the behavior of another mammal.

The specific model preparation we shall consider is the conditioning of the nictitating membrane of the rabbit, a preparation developed by Gormezano and his students (Gormezano, 1972; Gormezano, Schneiderman, Deaux, & Fuentes, 1962; Schneiderman, Fuentes, & Gormezano, 1962; see also Patterson, Olah, & Clement, 1977 for related work with the cat). The nictitating membrane—or the third eyelid, as it is sometimes called— is a tough membrane that protects the eye from injury. The membrane may be extended laterally from the nasal side to cover the surface of the eye. The structure is vestigial in humans, represented only by the pinkish tissue in the corner of the eye, but it is present in many other species such as cats and rabbits.

As shown in Fig. 3.8, the rabbit is restrained and a wire connects the

Fig. 3.8   Rabbit in a restraint device for the conditioning of the nictitating membrane. The device above the head is connected to the membrane by a thin wire. The device controls an electrical signal that corresponds to the position of the membrane.   (After Gormezano, 1966.)

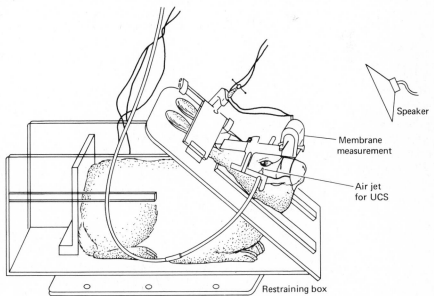

membrane to equipment that monitors movement of the membrane. In this research, the CS is typically a tone, and the UCS is either a puff of air to the cornea or an electric shock applied to the cheek, both of which reliably elicit movement of the membrane.

The results of experiments employing this procedure are clear: The CS comes to elicit the CR in the virtual absence of responses having origins other than the CS-UCS relationship. Specifically, independent control groups given neither CS nor UCS, CS alone, UCS alone, or unpaired presentations of the CS and UCS, make essentially no nictitating membrane responses when the CS is later presented. In order to obtain the 90–100% levels of responding to the CS obtained under optimal conditioning procedures, contiguity of CS and UCS is required. As used here, contiguity denotes that a specific temporal relationship between individual occurrences of the CS and UCS is necessary for learning.

CS-UCS Interval   Which of the various conditioning paradigms—forward, simultaneous, or backward—provides the CS-UCS relationship that best promotes learning? What is the most advantageous relationship of an environmental event to an elicitation process if that environment is to influence later behavior? The results from experiments that have varied the interstimulus interval between CS and US from -.50 msec (a backward paradigm in which CS follows UCS by .50 msec) to 1,000 msec (a forward paradigm in which CS precedes UCS by 1 sec) are shown in Fig. 3.9.

Fig. 3.9   Percentage of nictitating membrane (NM) responses to an auditory CS following classical procedures with various CS-UCS intervals for different groups of subjects. The response at C is for a control group given unpaired presentations of CS and UCS.   (Based upon the findings of Smith, M. C. 1968, and Smith, M. C., Coleman, & Gormezano, 1969. Copyright 1969 by the American Psychological Association. Reprinted by permission.)

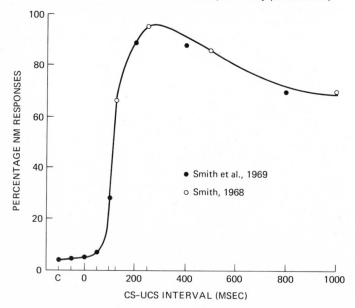

The optimal CS-UCS relationship is found in the forward conditioning paradigm. With a simultaneous or a backward paradigm, responses to the CS occur no more frequently than when CS and UCS are presented unpaired. With a forward procedure, the level of conditioning is optimal in the vicinity of 250 msec with the nictitating membrane, and then declines gradually as the CS precedes the onset of the UCS by longer intervals (Smith, M. C., 1968; Smith, Coleman, & Gormezano, 1969).

The precise value of the CS-UCS interval that is optimal for learning varies with the response system and the species—for example, 450 msec for the human eyelid response—but it is consistently a rather small positive value (cf. Gormezano & Moore, 1969, p. 136). Generally, the optimal interstimulus interval tends to be longer for response systems in which the latency and the duration of the UCR tend to be greater. For example, in the rabbit, conditioning of the cardiac response (heartrate)—a slower and longer-lasting response system than the nictitating membrane system—occurs at 6,750 msec, a CS-UCS interval at which conditioned changes are absent in the nictitating membrane (Van Dercar & Schneiderman, 1967).

A detailed examination of the form, or topography, of the nictitating membrane response is shown in Fig. 3.10 for forward CS-UCS intervals of 125, 250, 500, and 1,000 msec and for three intensities of UCS—1, 2, and 4 milliamperes (ma) of electric shock to the cheek. Consider first only one curve, the one which traces the amplitude of movement of the membrane with a UCS intensity of 1 ma at a CS-UCS interval of 125 msec (see upper panel of Fig. 3.10). Until about 100 msec after the CS, the membrane is motionless. Then the membrane extends over the eye a distance of about 4.5 mm before slowly returning to its resting position in the corner of the eye. The maximum extension of the membrane occurs at about the time at which the UCS was presented during conditioning trials (here, 125 msec after CS onset).

These characteristics of response topography were found for other combinations of UCS intensity and CS-UCS interval as well. For all conditions, the CR began to develop shortly after CS onset, rose to a maximum extension of the membrane in the vicinity of the usual time of UCS onset, and then declined thereafter (Smith, M. C., 1968). The data on response topography were obtained from occasional test periods of 2-sec duration in which the CS was presented without the UCS.

These results were obtained with a forward conditioning paradigm. Whether the classical procedure will produce a direct effect of the CS on the response system of the UCS in either the simultaneous or backward paradigms is in dispute. It is clear, however, that neither the simultaneous nor the backward procedures are as effective in fostering control of the CR by the CS as is the forward paradigm (Cautela, 1965; Mahoney & Ayres, 1976; Kimble, 1961).

It should be noted that events other than the nominal CS may become effective in controlling behavior in the backward procedure, since the UCS is preceded by whatever other stimuli are present in the experimental situation (so-called background stimuli). Thus learned relationships between the environment and behavior are possible but they may not directly involve that part of the environment which the experimenter has labeled the CS. It should

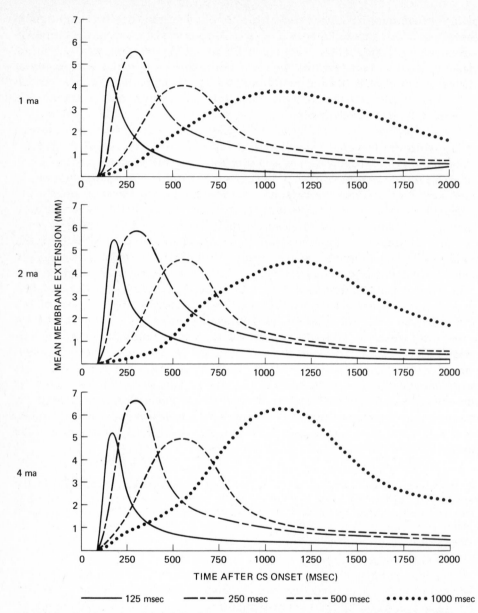

Fig. 3.10   Topography of the nictitating membrane response observed during 2-sec CS periods interspersed among CS-UCS pairings. Independent groups of subjects were trained using CS-UCS intervals of 125, 250, 500, or 1,000 msec and UCS intensities of 1, 2, or 4 ma.   (From Smith M.C., 1968. Copyright 1968 by the American Psychological Association. Reprinted by permission.)

always be borne in mind that even the relatively impoverished environment of the laboratory consists of a continuous succession of stimuli, only two of which—the CS and UCS— are under tight control by the experimenter in the classical procedure. In short, we must not confuse the absence of our control of an environment with the absence of that environment.

Having discovered that the forward conditioning paradigm constitutes the optimal CS-UCS relationship, we have not exhausted the information that can be extracted from our model preparation—the nictitating membrane response. We will consider now the effects on behavior of the delay and trace variations within the forward conditioning paradigm and of CS and UCS intensity. When the trace procedure is used instead of the delay procedure, upon which all of the previous conclusions have been based, the same general effects of the CS-UCS interval on conditioning are found but the absolute frequency of CRs is lower (Schneiderman, 1966).

The results of an experiment in which the CS-UCS interval was varied within trace and delay procedures are shown in Fig. 3.11. Note that performance under the delay procedure is superior to the trace procedure at all CS-UCS intervals. As in the backward paradigm, the trace procedure permits background stimuli present between CS offset and UCS onset to occur contiguously with the UCS, and to become effective in controlling the learned response. The control of the CR exerted by these other stimuli may affect the control of the CR by the nominal CS. Comparisons of the delay and trace variations of the forward conditioning paradigm indicate that for a variety of response systems and species, the delay procedure produces better control of the CR by the CS. The difference is most pronounced with rapid-acting response systems such as the nictitating membrane response, and less so for slower-acting systems such as the cardiac response (cf. Schneiderman, 1972, pp. 361–362).

Fig. 3.11   The effect of delay versus trace procedures on the classical conditioning of the nictitating membrane response at various CS-UCS intervals. Independent groups of subjects were used at each combination of delay or trace procedure with CS-UCS interval. The duration of thr trace CS was 200 msec.   (After Schneiderman, 1966. Copyright by the American Psychological Association. Reprinted by permission.)

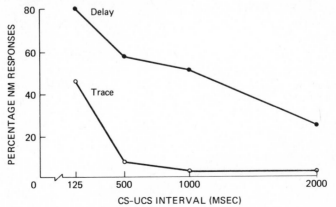

CS Intensity   The intensity of the CS also affects conditioning. In general, increased CS intensity produces an increase in the frequency of CRs. In an investigation with the nictitating membrane response using a 500-msec CS-UCS interval, CRs occurred during 67% of the presentations with a group receiving a 65-db CS and 84% of the presentations with a second group receiving an 86-db CS (Gormezano, 1972, pp. 158–160). In human eyelid conditioning, a similar effect is found when the same subjects are exposed to different CS intensities but the effect is much attenuated when independent groups receive different CS intensities (Grice & Hunter, 1964; Mattson & Moore, 1964).

UCS Intensity   Increases in UCS intensity also increase the frequency of CRs in the presence of the CS (Gormezano & Moore, 1969; Kimble, 1961). In the nictitating membrane preparation, increases in the intensity of electric shock (UCS) to the cheek produced increases in the percentage of conditioned membrane responses (Smith, M. C., 1968). As shown in Fig. 3.12, the level of responding after extended training (the *terminal* or *asymptotic level*) increased as the intensity of the eliciting stimulus increased from 1 to 2 to 4 ma for independent groups of subjects. Reexamination of Fig. 3.10, which depicts the topography of the CR, also reveals an effect of UCS intensity: As the UCS intensity increased, the amplitude of the conditioned membrane extension increased. In a similar fashion, human eyelid conditioning experiments have generally found higher levels of performance with higher UCS intensities (for example, Prokasy & Harsany, 1968; Spence, Haggard, & Ross, 1958).

Fig. 3.12   The effect of UCS intensity on conditioning at various CS-UCS intervals.   (After Smith, M.C., 1968. Copyright 1968 by the American Psychological Association. Reprinted by permission.)

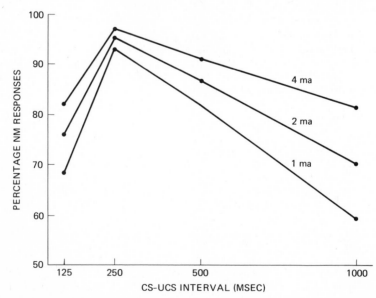

THEORETICAL ANALYSIS OF CLASSICAL CONDITIONING

In an experimental analysis, we seek to isolate the variables that control responding and to determine the form of the functional relationship between these variables and behavior. In a theoretical analysis, we seek to develop a set of principles that are consistent with the findings of an experimental analysis, and that serve to integrate the findings in an orderly manner. The most successful theoretical analyses not only integrate previous findings, but also have implications for the experimental analysis of other phenomena and suggest previously unappreciated relationships with other theoretical work. The experimental analysis of classical conditioning has been concluded; it is now time to consider how the findings obtained from that procedure may be integrated and understood. What are their implications for a principle of reinforcement?

Nature of the CS-UCS Relationship

In an effort to develop a principle of reinforcement based upon findings from the classical procedure, we shall attend successively to three aspects of those findings—CS-UCS contiguity, the discrepancy between the behavior controlled by the CS and UCS at the outset of the experiment, and the role of stimuli other than the nominal CS in the outcome of conditioning.

Contiguity A major conclusion which arises from our study of classical conditioning is that the temporal relationship between the CS and UCS is an important factor in the production of learned changes in behavior. For most response systems, the CS must precede the UCS by a short interval of time— usually a matter of seconds at most—if a new functional relationship between the environment and behavior is to develop. Thus with organisms for which relevant prior experience is minimal and for which the experimental situation is tightly controlled, the temporal contiguity of the environment with an elicitation process is necessary for learning to occur. The theory of the environment that enables the individual to function in the future is constructed from the moment-to-moment sequences of events which define the present.

Discrepancy Between Baseline and Elicited Responding New functional relationships between the environment and behavior depend upon the temporal proximity of a stimulus with an elicitation process. But while contiguity is often necessary for learning, is it sufficient? Is the mere presentation of a sequence of events consisting of a stimulus followed by an elicitor capable of producing learning?

Kamin sought the answer to this question through a type of classical conditioning experiment known as the *blocking design* (Kamin, 1968; Kamin, 1969). Two training conditions are involved. In the control condition, two stimuli (CS_1 and CS_2) are presented in a simultaneous compound paired with a UCS. Since both CS_1 and CS_2 are in a favorable temporal relationship to the elicitation process, both stimuli should acquire control over the response. In the experimental condition, a two-phase training procedure is used. During Phase I, one stimulus (CS$_1$) is paired with the UCS until the CR has reached a stable, terminal level of occurrence. Then during Phase II, both CS$_1$ and CS$_2$ are paired in a simultaneous compound with the UCS, as in the control condition.

If the temporal relationship of a stimulus to the elicitation process is sufficient for conditioning, then CS$_1$ and CS$_2$ should both control the CR in both conditions. Note, however, that unlike the control condition, the CS$_1$ portion of the stimulus compound already evokes the CR at the beginning of simultaneous compound conditioning in the experimental condition. Thus for the experimental condition—but not for the control condition—a smaller discrepancy exists at the beginning of Phase II between the behavior controlled by the compound CS and the behavior elicited by the UCS: At the beginning of Phase II, the compound stimulus (through prior conditioning of the CS$_1$ component) and the UCS both evoke activity in the response system of the UCS in the experimental condition.

In order to assess the control over behavior exerted by the CS$_2$ component of the simultaneous compound, CS$_2$ is presented alone during a final test phase. If the temporal relationship is sufficient for learning, both the experimental and control conditions should respond similarly to CS$_2$. If a discrepancy between the baseline, or entering, behavior to the CS and to the UCS is necessary for learning, then CS$_2$ should evoke behavior to a lesser extent in the experimental than in the control group. That is, control of behavior by CS$_2$ should be blocked by the preexisting control exerted by CS$_1$ in the experimental group.

In an experiment conducted in accordance with the blocking design, the nictitating membrane of the rabbit was conditioned using lights and tones in counterbalanced order as CS$_1$ and CS$_2$ (Marchant & Moore, 1973). During the test phase, CS$_2$ was presented alone without the UCS and responding in the experimental and control conditions was compared. The control subjects responded to 58% of the presentations of CS$_2$; thus simultaneous compound conditioning resulted in the acquisition of the CR by the CS$_2$ component. The experimental subjects, however, responded to only 5% of the CS$_2$ presentations; learning was blocked by prior conditioning of the CS$_1$ component. (A summary of the procedure and results of the blocking design is shown in Fig. 3.13.)

The significance of this complex, but extremely important, experimental design for a principle of reinforcement is clear: The development of new functional relationships between the environment and behavior requires both an appropriate temporal interval between the CS and UCS *and* an initial discrepancy between the behavior occurring to the CS and the UCS.

This insight has led to the development by Wagner and Rescorla of our clearest vision of an adequate theoretical analysis of the behavioral changes produced by the classical procedure (Rescorla, 1972; Rescorla & Wagner, 1972; Wagner, 1969; Wagner & Rescorla, 1972). To use Kamin's term, learning occurs in classical conditioning when the CS-UCS relationship "surprises" the subject through the elicitation by the UCS of a response which differs in strength from that which would otherwise occur during the CS.

Procedure:

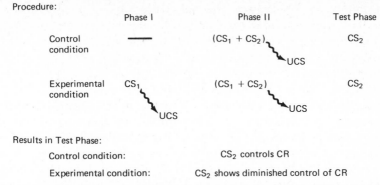

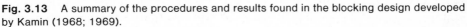

Results in Test Phase:

Control condition: CS_2 controls CR

Experimental condition: CS_2 shows diminished control of CR

Fig. 3.13 A summary of the procedures and results found in the blocking design developed by Kamin (1968; 1969).

These conclusions provide further support for the general proposition that the effect of present experience upon behavior depends on both phylogenetic antecedents (as reflected here by the elicitation process) and ontogenetic antecedents (as reflected here by prior conditioning during Phase I of the blocking design). Our understanding of the concept of reinforcement is deepened and extended by the results of the blocking experiment. Reinforcement in the classical procedure is not a property of a single stimulus (the UCS), but of a relationship between two successive stimuli, each of which controls different strengths of a given behavior. Thus, strictly speaking, it is never proper to speak of a reinforcing stimulus, but rather of a reinforcing function of elicitation processes. This view of reinforcement is hereafter referred to as the relational principle of reinforcement.

Role of Other Stimuli in Conditioning
At several points in our survey of the basic findings obtained with the classical procedure, we commented that the UCS may actually occur in a more favorable temporal relationship with other stimuli than with the nominal CS. For example, in the trace conditioning and backward conditioning paradigms, the UCS is immediately preceded not by the nominal CS, but by other stimuli comprising the background stimulation from the experimental environment. When stimuli other than the nominal CS stand in a more favorable temporal relationship to the elicitation process, a relational principle of reinforcement implies that the control of responding by the nominal CS should actually be reduced (Siegel, S., & Domjan, 1971). Let us see how that implication arises.

Since other stimuli (S_o) precede the UCS, a discrepancy exists between the baseline level of responding to S_o and the level of responding to the UCS. We shall label this discrepancy a *positive* discrepancy because the strength of the response elicited by the UCS is greater than the strength of that same response to S_o. As a result of the positive discrepancy, S_o should acquire control over the response.

Now consider the backward CS. Since the UCS never occurs in a favorable temporal relationship with the backward CS, no positive discrepancy exists. In fact, since the backward CS can be viewed as a compound CS consisting of the nominal CS and the ever-present S_0, a *negative* discrepancy arises when S_0 acquires control of responding. The discrepancy is negative because the strength of elicited responding during the nominal CS is less than that controlled by the S_0 component of the compound stimulus. The negative discrepancy produces a decrease in the control of responding by the CS component of the compound stimulus. As an experimental example, if the backward CS were a tone, the likelihood of responding to the tone should decline as a result of a backward conditioning procedure.

The foregoing analysis of the potential effects of S_0 on conditioning has two main purposes. First, the analysis indicates that stimuli other than those manipulated by the experimenter may contribute to the behavioral outcome of the classical procedure. Second, the analysis indicates that conditioning procedures may, under some circumstances, produce a reduction in the control of responding by a stimulus. If a stimulus is followed by a positive discrepancy, an increment in responding occurs. If a stimulus is followed by a negative discrepancy, a decrement in responding occurs. The former change is sometimes called *excitatory* conditioning, the latter *inhibitory* conditioning (Rescorla & Wagner, 1972). Both increases and decreases in responding will be considered in later discussions of the stimulus control produced by complex conditioning procedures.

In summary, an attempt to integrate the basic findings from the classical procedure has led to a relational principle of reinforcement. This principle accommodates the finding that an appropriate temporal relationship between the CS and UCS is necessary for learning, but must be supplemented by an initial discrepancy between the behavior elicited by the UCS and the CS. A relational principle of reinforcement also provides a rationale for understanding the effects of stimuli other than the nominal CS on behavior. We have thus come to the view that the organism acts as a detector of contiguous differences in elicitation processes, and from these discrepancies a theory of the environment is constructed. At the beginning of learning with the classical procedure, the response to successive environments (the CS and UCS) is discrepant; at the conclusion of learning that discrepancy has been resolved. The behavior of the organism has come into closer harmony with the demands of its environment.

Levels of Analysis

Observable changes in behavior, the data upon which our knowledge of conditioning is based, are incomplete reflections of the unobserved events that give rise to those observations. Even a behavior as simple as the movement of the nictitating membrane of the rabbit is the product of a multitude of physiological events (for example, Moore, J. W., 1978; Thompson, R. F., 1976). Because behavior may be affected by imperfectly known antecedents, some theorists (for example, Tolman, 1932; Hull, 1943) have preferred to reserve the term "learning" for the inferred processes thought to underlie behavior. Three sets of circumstances have been especially persuasive in the distinction made between learning (inferred processes) and performance (observed behavior).

First, the environmental determinants of behavior often antedate some appearances of the behavior by substantial periods of time. A friend whom one has known for years is for the first time observed playing the piano. Upon questioning, it develops that she took piano lessons as a child. The critical environmental antecedents (piano lessons) occurred many years earlier, and we attempt to bridge the temporal gap by saying that some representation of those environmental antecedents (habits, memories, and so on) endured across time to express themselves in behavior only at this late date.

Second, environmental determinants other than those extant when learning originally occurred may be important for the present emergence of the behavior. The friend who has revealed her heretofore hidden talent may say, upon further questioning, that she simply had not felt like playing the piano until that moment, or that no one had asked her to play until then, or that the particular piano reminded her of the piano upon which she practiced so many years ago. In short, other factors than those present when the behavior was originally acquired (motives, wishes, desires, and so on) are invoked in an effort to understand why the behavior has appeared at this point in time, and not at another.

Third, with organisms having the complex phylogenetic and ontogenetic histories of adult humans, the readily observed antecedents of behavior make up but a small portion of the total picture. The observation is that our friend sees a piano and plays a piece of music. The sheet music from which the piece was originally learned is gone; the long hours of practice are now unobservable; the initially halting movements of individual fingers have been replaced by the integrated execution of whole passages; the thoughts and emotions that accompany the playing are unseen. Only some of the products of experience are public and available to the senses of others; the remainder are private and available, if at all, only to the learner.

The observations that have fostered the learning-performance distinction—the temporal asynchrony between behavior and its antecedents, the multiple antecedents of any behavior, and inaccessibility of many of those antecedents—have led to the study of memory, motivation, and cognition respectively. We shall analyze these crucially important areas at some depth in later chapters. It is our position, however, that the learning-performance distinction is not the most fruitful approach to the very genuine difficulties confronted in dealing with the phenomena of memory, motivation, and cognition. Rather than regard performance as the observable consequence of the inferred, unobservable process of learning—a view in which the object of study, behavior, is but the symptom and not the substance of the psychology of learning—we prefer to distinguish between behavior and its underlying causes as simply different levels of analysis of the consequences of common environmental antecedents.

The problem of different levels of analysis is not peculiar to psychological science. It might be contended, for example, that the chemist is really not studying chemistry but physics, since the activity of atomic particles underlies all of the results. There is some truth in this contention, but it is a largely empty truth since a statement of similar import may be made of any scientific discipline. Behavior is undeniably a function of events on the physiological level, but physiology may be said with equal validity to be a function of events on the chemical level, and so on. In a sense we are all physicists, but the sense in which that is true does not force us to leave the subject matters studied in laboratories of psychology, physiology, or chemistry. Some questions are posed on the behavioral level and are best answered on that level: What are the events that caused Mary to sit down and play the piano at the party? Other questions demand answers at other levels of analysis—What are the neural events that control the pattern of finger movements responsible for the arpeggio which Mary played? Note that the answers to both questions refer to potentially observable events: The dimensions of both answers are those of the physical world.

None of this is to say that the various levels of analysis are independent of one another or that one level has nothing to offer the other in their different approaches to partially common problems. To the contrary, no laws discovered at the behavioral level may contradict any laws discovered at another level. Similarly, every law discovered at the behavioral level sets boundary conditions upon the laws to be discovered at other levels. Thus knowledge at the physiological level of analysis may extend and deepen our understanding of answers to questions posed at the behavioral level. Indeed, such mutually beneficial work is currently underway in the analysis of the physiological events underlying the behavioral changes produced by the classical procedure (for example, Thompson, R. F., 1976). In spite of the nexus of interrelationships that exist between adjacent levels of analysis, however, we have a continuing need for the sciences of behavior and physiology, just as we have a continuing need for the sciences of genetics and molecular biology.

SOME COMPLEXITIES IN THE CLASSICAL PROCEDURE

Through the use of a simplified conditioning preparation—the nictitating membrane of the rabbit—we have identified some of the major variables influencing learning within the classical procedure and have improved our understanding of the principle of reinforcement. While a simplified preparation has greatly facilitated the experimental and theoretical analysis of the behavioral changes produced by the classical procedure, our knowledge must ultimately be extended to the less tidy circumstances of more complex environments and organisms.

In moving to less well-controlled circumstances, we shall assume that the principle of reinforcement arising from our study of simplified preparations remains fundamentally valid. Our bias is that the principle of reinforcement will be supplemented, but not supplanted, by additional principles as new findings emerge. Of course, the belief that a simplified preparation provides a correct, but incomplete, basis for knowledge is just that—a belief. The validity of this belief must be evaluated, as are all such assumptions, by the self-corrective methods of science. Only after a thorough experimental and theoretical analysis will we know whether new findings require new principles or merely new additions to old principles.

We shall consider four types of complexities in the classical procedure: (a) those in which unobserved (private) events influence the monitored behavior; (b) those in which the relationship between behavior and the reinforcing elicitation process must be considered; (c) those in which interactions occur between the CS and the elicitation process; and (d) those in which reliable elicitation processes fail to function as reinforcers. While such complexities represent a challenge to existing principles, they also present an opportunity to extend the boundaries of knowledge.

Unobserved (Private) Events

Procedures in which the experimenter directly manipulates the presentation of CSs and UCSs and monitors the occurrence of CRs and UCRs offer obvious advantages for analysis. However, an appropriate relationship between the environment and the elicitation process will produce learning even when all of the important events are not observed by the experimenter. As noted at other points in our search for the origins of behavioral change, it is the learner's experience, and not the experimenter's description of that experience, which leads to learning.

In truth, the experimenter is never aware of all of the stimuli that affect the learner, or of all of the responses elicited by those stimuli—although in simplified preparations such knowledge may be closely approximated. In those circumstances in which the experimenter's knowledge is incomplete, it is assumed that the unobserved events have the same characteristics and are describable by the same laws as are observed events. These assumptions are instances of the scientist's more general belief in the continuity of nature. As a working hypothesis, unobserved events are believed to have the dimensions of public events—to be extended and localized in space and time—and to enter into the same functional relationships as public events—to act in accordance with the principles of conditioning.

Conditioned Suppression   As an example of a conditioning procedure whose analysis makes an appeal to unobserved events, we shall consider the phenomenon of conditioned suppression. Conditioned suppression is selected both because it is a relatively simple, well-studied example, and because the procedure is commonly employed to investigate questions of theoretical and applied significance. In fact, modern work on the blocking experiment, which played such an important role in the formulation of a relational principle of reinforcement, employed the conditioned suppression procedure (Kamin, 1968).

In conditioned suppression, the outcome of a classical procedure is not assessed by measuring directly activity in the response system of the UCS, but by measuring some other ongoing activity that is presumably suppressed by the CR (Estes & Skinner, 1941). As commonly implemented, the procedure involves three phases. In Phase I, an instrumental response—such as pressing a lever for food—is established during a baseline phase. In Phase II, the classical conditioning phase, a CS and UCS are presented in a relationship favorable for conditioning. For example, a tone might be followed by an electric shock. The classical procedure may be administered when the instrumental response is possible (on-the-baseline conditioning) or when the instrumental response is prevented, as by removing the lever from the experimental chamber (off-the-baseline conditioning). During the second phase, no direct measurement of the UCR or the CR is made although, returning to our example, the tone is assumed to acquire control over responses elicited by the shock. The UCR and the CR are thus unobserved events in the conditioned suppression procedure. In Phase III, conditioning is indirectly assessed by presenting the CS and measuring the extent to which the baseline instrumental response is suppressed by the unobserved CR. The assumption is that the learner cannot execute the CR without interfering to some extent with the baseline response, that is, that the CR and the instrumental response are incompatible.

Fig. 3.14 Cumulative records of bar-pressing responses made by a rat during successive stages of a conditioned supression experiment. In a cumulative record, each bar-pressing response causes the curve to move upward one unit. The passage of time causes the curve to move to the right. The CS period is indicated by the vertical lines cutting the cumulative records. The onset of the CS is indicated by the letter C, the offset by the letter S. (After Hunt & Brady, 1951. Copyright 1951 by the American Psychological Association. Reprinted by permission.)

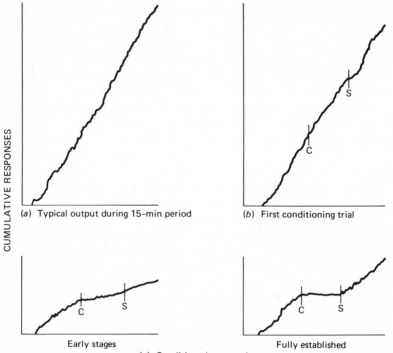

(a) Typical output during 15-min period

(b) First conditioning trial

Early stages

Fully established

(c) Conditioned suppression

CUMULATIVE RESPONSES

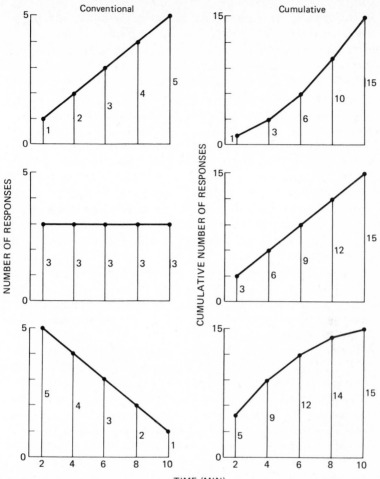

Fig. 3.15   Hypothetical conventional (left column) and cumulative (right column) records of the number of responses as a function of time in the experimental situation. Note the relationship between corresponding pairs of records displaying the same data. The number beneath each point represents the total responses which contribute to that point.

Figure 3.14 shows cumulative graphs of the baseline response of lever-pressing when the CS was presented for the first time, prior to being paired with shock (Fig. 3.14b). Note that responding is little affected by the CS prior to conditioning. The suppression of responding after a number of pairings of the CS with shock is shown in Fig. 3.14c. After conditioning, responding occurs normally when the CS is absent, but ceases almost completely when the CS is present.

Since cumulative records will be encountered again in this text, it is instructive to examine their relationship to the more familiar method of graphing. Figure 3.15 contains three pairs of graphs. The left member of each pair is a conventional graph; the right is a cumulative graph. The hypothetical data displayed in the graphs are frequencies of bar-pressing responses in five successive 2-min periods. Consider the top pair of graphs in Fig. 3.15. In the first 2-min period, one response occurs; in the second period, two responses; in the third, three responses; and so on. In the conventional graph on the left, these data describe a straight line with positive slope. In the cumulative graph on the right, the same behavior results in a function that rises at an increasing rate, that is a positively accelerated function. Each point in the cumulative graph is the sum of all of the responses occurring in that and all preceding time periods. Thus an increasing rate of responding may result in a positively accelerating cumulative record but a linear conventional graph. In the middle pair of graphs, a constant rate of responding results in a straight line with a slope of zero (a horizontal line) in a conventional graph and a straight line with a positive slope in a cumulative graph. Finally, the bottom pair of graphs, which depict a constant decrease in responding, are represented in the conventional graph by a straight line with negative slope and in the cumulative graph by a function that rises at a decreasing rate, that is a negatively-accelerated function. In summary, cumulative records never decrease and indicate changes in the rate of responding by departures from linearity (changes in slope). Satisfy yourself that you understand the relationship between cumulative records and conventional graphs and then reexamine Fig. 3.14 for its portrayal of the results from a conditioned suppression experiment.

Other conditioning phenomena that appeal to private events for their understanding might be cited. In *sensory preconditioning*, for example, two "neutral" stimuli, such as a light and tone, are successively presented a number of times. Then the second-appearing stimulus (say, the tone) is paired with a UCS. Upon testing, the first-appearing stimulus (say, the light) is observed to control the CR, although it has never been paired with the UCS (Brogden, 1939). What all such phenomena have in common is that unobserved stimuli and responses are inferred and are assumed to conform to the known effects of the classical procedure on observed responses. The general strategy of studying a phenomenon, whose direct effects are difficult or impossible to observe with existing technology, through examining its indirect effects on observed events is a common one in science. The unseen subatomic particles of the physicist, for example, are studied through the observable products of their collisions with other particles.

The validity of indirect means of assessing inferred processes rests upon the correspondence of the indirect effects with the conditioning of directly observable responses. There is much work of this type (for example, Annau & Kamin, 1961; Wickens & Cross, 1963). Ultimately, the unobserved neural and behavioral events that give rise to the indirect effects must be identified and studied directly. Again, there has been research directed to this end as well (for example, Black & de Toledo, 1972; Borgealt, Donahoe, & Weinstein, 1972; Cousins, Zamble, Tait, & Suboski, 1971; Reynierse, Scavio, & Ulness, 1970). The illumination of the underlying events and of the mechanisms whereby they produce their indirect effects is important because the interaction between various response systems may vary from one system to the next and with experience. Not all responses are incompatible with one another, and the degree and nature of the interaction may change with continued exposure. Moreover, the need to understand response interactions is not confined to the study of private events. As we shall see in the next section, response interactions may occur between observed responses in the classical procedure.

Response Interactions

The classical procedure is, by definition, a procedure designed to study the effects of the CS-UCS relationship on learning. Although the experimenter manipulates only the relationship between a stimulus and an elicitation process, relationships between other events are also simultaneously, but inadvertently, varied. As we noted in our preliminary discussion of the classical and instrumental procedures, since the learner is always behaving, there is always an opportunity for a relationship between responding and the elicitation process, even in the classical procedure.

Because we have previously restricted ourselves to experimental situations in which only activity in the response system of the UCS was considered, it has been possible to assume that the CS acquires control over a CR that is essentially identical to the UCR. This assumption—that the CS acts much like the UCS in the control of behavior—is known as the *stimulus substitution hypothesis*. The stimulus substitution hypothesis is the beginning, not the end, of wisdom in understanding the behavioral changes produced by the classical procedure.

A partial listing follows of the origins of responses that may affect the behavioral outcome of conditioning. Components of the OR may occur prior to the elicitation process and contribute to learning (for example, Konorski, 1967; Pavlov, 1927; Timberlake & Grant, 1975). Once the CR develops, it may occur prior to the elicitation process and influence the final form of the CR (for example, Brogden, Lippman, & Culler, 1938; Bruner, 1969; Wahlsten & Cole, 1972). Finally, the same elicitation process may lead to somewhat different behaviors controlled by the CS, depending on the manner of presentation of the UCS (for example, Soltysik, Kierylowicz, & Divac, cited in Konorski, 1967, p. 270).

Interactions Involving the CR Let us examine one of these potential sources of response interactions—the CR-UCS relationship. Even with the well-controlled nictitating membrane preparation, response-elicitation relationships—the defining feature of the instrumental procedure—inevitably develop. The maximum amplitude of the CR occurs in the vicinity of UCS onset (Smith, M. C., 1968), the overlap between the occurrence of the CR and UCS declines as performance deteriorates at nonoptimal CS-UCS intervals (Schneiderman, 1966), and shifts in the CS-UCS interval are followed by shifts in the time of the maximal CR to the new time of occurrence of the UCS (Coleman & Gormezano, 1971; cf, Boneau, 1958; Prokasy, Ebel, & Thompson, 1963; Pavlov, 1927). Thus there is an intimate relationship between the CR and the UCS: The opportunity for response-reinforcer as well as stimulus-reinforcer relationships is present in the classical procedure.

But which is primary and which is derivative? To what extent do the observed behavioral changes reflect the CS-UCS relationship manipulated by the experimenter or the CR-UCS relationship indirectly produced by that manipulation? Both interpretations of the origin of CR-UCS overlap are plausible. The point to be made here is that the issue may not be finally resolved using the classical procedure alone. If the effects of response-reinforcer relationships are to be thoroughly studied, then instrumental procedures must be used. It is, in principle, impossible to make an experimental analysis of the CR-UCS relationship within the classical procedure.

Keeping within the classical procedure, however, it is clear that the CR-UCS relationship is not necessary for the emergence and maintenance of the CR in at least some circumstances. The occurrence of the first CR cannot be so explained, and conditioning may take place at CS-UCS intervals too short to permit the occurrence of the CR prior to the UCS (Patterson, 1970). While it may be tempting to assert that the occurrence of the CR prior to the UCS benefits learning through "preparing" the subject to receive the UCS, such temptations should be resisted until required by an experimental analysis. Often terms such as "preparation," "expectation," and "anticipation" are used when all that is known is that a behavior occurs before a UCS. The beggar who salivates when looking through a restaurant window at a diner consuming his meal does not salivate in preparation, in expectation, or in anticipation of eating the meal. He salivates, if at all, because in the past the sight of food has been followed by the elicitation of salivation by food in his own mouth.

Whatever their origins, response interactions must be considered in the analysis of the final behavioral outcome of any given classical procedure. The fact that CRs may be dependent in part on the current status of other events would come as no surprise to a student of reflex physiology. The same stimulus may elicit different reflex responses depending on the position of the body. The expression of learned responses is no less complex. Consider the following example: A sheep, after learning to *flex* its leg to a CS that had preceded foot shock, *extended* its leg when placed on its back in the test apparatus (Liddell, James, & Anderson, 1935). As Hughlings Jackson observed, "The brain thinks in movements, not in muscles."

In summary, although the dominant theme in the classical procedure is stimulus substitution, the form of the CR may be modulated by interactions of the elicited response with other responses of diverse origins. Not only the elicited response, but these other responses as well must be considered if the final behavioral outcome of conditioning is to be understood.

Stimulus Interactions

With the exception of the earlier recognition that conditioning is affected by the intensity of the CS, our analysis has proceeded as if the choice of CS were a matter of indifference. This is not true; the choice of CS may have a profound effect on the course of learning with the classical procedure (for example, Holland, 1977).

In the nictitating membrane preparation, for example, the CR is acquired more rapidly with an auditory than a visual CS, and something is known of the physiology underlying this finding (Cegavske et al., 1976). In general, if the rate of acquisition differs among CSs, those CSs are said to vary in their *salience* (Rescorla & Wagner, 1972). For the rabbit, an auditory stimulus is more salient than a visual stimulus when a puff of air is employed as the UCS.

Differential Associability   The most interesting group of stimulus interactions are those in which the salience of the CS varies with the type of UCS. Such an interaction is known as *differential associability* and may be illustrated by the following experiment (Garcia & Koelling, 1966). A compound CS consisting of a taste component and an audiovisual component was paired with either of two UCSs for different animals. Specifically, rats drank salty (or sweet-tasting) water in the presence of a light and a clicking noise, and then either were made ill by the injection of poison or were shocked. Differential associability was demonstrated when it was later shown that the poisoned rats avoided the salty taste more than the light and click, but the shocked rats avoided the light and click more than the taste. Thus, which CS was more salient depended upon the UCS (poison or shock) with which it was paired.

Since these seminal observations by Garcia, the phenomenon has been demonstrated in many other species (see Revusky & Garcia, 1970; Rozin & Kalat, 1971; Seligman & Hager, 1972; and Shettleworth, 1972 for reviews). In man, for example, pictures of spiders and snakes—stimuli that are often the object of unreasonable fears (phobias)—are especially effective CSs for the aversive UCS of electric shock (Ohman, Fredrikson, Hagdahl, & Rimmo, 1976).

The origins of differential associability reflect both the phylogeny and ontogeny of the individual. A major finding illustrating the role of phylogeny is that a gustatory (taste) stimulus may become an effective CS for learned aversions even though poison-induced illness does not occur until *hours* later (for example, Smith, J. C., & Roll, 1967). Learning with such a long CS-UCS interval would be impossible with nongustatory CSs. This surprising result has been interpreted to mean that the intimate and constant relationship between taste and the consequences of ingestion in the history of the species has resulted in an adaptive specialization, in which the organism is biologically predisposed for conditioned aversions to be controlled by gustatory stimuli (Rozin & Kalat, 1971; Seligman, 1970). It is also true, of course, that gustatory stimuli and illness are related in the history of the individual as well as in the history of the species, and we may expect both sources to contribute to the behavioral outcome.

Aside from the long CS-UCS intervals over which such learning may occur, differential associability appears to be influenced by many of the same variables and to enter into many of the same functional relationships found with other instances of conditioning (for example, Best, M. R., 1975; Best, Best, & Mickley, 1973; Revusky, 1971). Blocking, for example, occurs with conditioned taste aversions (for example, Willner, 1978). A complete understanding of taste aversions will undoubtedly also depend on factors other than the CS-UCS relationship. Poisoning sensitizes the animal to novel stimuli generally (for example, Bitterman, 1975; Mitchell, Kirschbaum, & Perry, 1975), and habituation may occur with repeated presentations of an aversive UCS (Goudie, Thornton, & Wheeler, 1976). Whatever their origins, CS interactions once again illustrate that the understanding of any particular classical procedure requires that a principle of reinforcement be supplemented by information concerning the specific events by which the procedure is implemented.

Reinforcing Function of Elicitation Processes

As the final complexity in the classical procedure, we turn to the elicitation process itself. Through the process of evolution we have seen that elicitation processes may function as reinforcers to bring about alterations in the stimulus control of behavior. While abundant evidence indicates that an extremely wide range of conditioned and unconditioned elicitation processes serve as reinforcers, we may ask if *all* elicitation processes possess this function.

Quite clearly, there are some stimuli that reliably elicit behavior but do not function as reinforcers. Even well-controlled preparations may demonstrate the disjunction between elicitation and reinforcement. A shock to the face of the rabbit, but not delivered near the eye, will elicit a nictitating membrane response but will not function as a UCS (Kettlewell & Papsdorf, 1971). A dilute solution of acid will elicit salivation when introduced into the mouth of a dog, but will not serve as a UCS in a conditioning experiment (Konorski, 1967, p. 284). (See Bruner, 1965; Colavita, 1965; and Gerall & Obrist, 1962 for similar observations.)

How are we to understand these failures of elicitation processes to function as reinforcers? The first point to be made is that the observed stimulus and response that index the elicitation process are not the entirety of the process. As with the simpler learning exemplified by habituation, the observed response is the last in a sequence of events initiated by the stimulus—its overt occurrence is not necessary for conditioning to occur (for example, Beck & Doty, 1957; Solomon & Turner, 1962). Since natural selection operates only on expressed characteristics, the overt response was originally necessary for the learning capacity to develop, but the occurrence of the behavioral response is not now necessary for the occurrence of the neural events that underlie learning.

While the difference between elicitation processes that function as reinforcers and those that do not so function must reside in differences in these mediating neural events, this assertion is a truism, not an explanation. All differences in function must necessarily reflect differences in physiology, and to appeal to inferred, unknown "motivational" neural events is simply to give a name to our ignorance. Research on this problem at the physiological level must be done (Frey, Maisiak, & Dague, 1976), but we should guard against "solving" a problem at the behavioral level by substituting an equally puzzling problem at the physiological level of analysis.

A second approach to the problem of elicitation processes that do not function as reinforcers comes from the following observation: If organisms are given a choice between signaled and unsignaled presentations of an elicitor, signaled presentations are often preferred with both appetitive and aversive stimuli (for example, Cantor, 1971; Lockard, 1963). That is, an environment in which the elicitor is reliably preceded by a neutral stimulus is preferred to one in which the elicitor occurs without warning. Although the critical research remains to be done, it may be that elicitation processes that function as reinforcers are confined to those in which signaled presentations are preferred to unsignaled presentations. Only such elicitation processes may be capable of creating the critical discrepancy described by the relational principle of reinforcement.

SUMMARY

In his quest for an understanding of the currents that shape the flow of behavior, Pavlov chose to conjoin in time and space an elicitation process with a specified stimulus. The contingency between a stimulus (CS) and an elicitation process (UCS-UCR) is the defining characteristic of the Pavlovian or classical procedure. Using this procedure, Pavlov found that the CS came to elicit a new response (CR) that typically closely resembled the UCR. In order to determine which aspects of the CS-UCS relationship are critical to the production of learned changes in behavior, a well-controlled experimental situation was sought in which other factors influencing responding are eliminated or held constant. The selection of controlled conditions is a demanding task influenced by both empirical considerations and theoretical conceptions of the learning process. Based upon data obtained from a well-controlled situation—the nictitating membrane preparation—a forward conditioning paradigm is shown to be more effective in producing the control of the CR by the CS than either a simultaneous or a backward paradigm. Learning is also benefited by increased UCS and CS intensity and by the delay rather than the trace procedure.

A theoretical integration of the various findings indicates that the temporal relationship between the CS and UCS and a discrepancy in the strength of responding controlled by the CS and UCS at the outset of the procedure are both essential for conditioning. As shown by the phenomenon of blocking, the mere contiguity of a stimulus with an elicitation process is not sufficient. This theoretical analysis of conditioning is termed a relational principle of reinforcement. For an understanding of the effects of procedures in which some occurrences of the UCS are not contiguous with the nominal CS—for example, backward and delay procedures—the role of other stimuli (S_o) must be explicitly recognized, since S_o may acquire control over the CR and influence the control exerted by the nominal CS.

In the final section of this chapter, which deals with complexities in the classical procedure, an understanding of the full outcome of conditioning has been shown to require the consideration of unobserved (private) events, response interactions, stimulus interactions, and the further analysis of elicitation processes to identify those which may function as reinforcers. Variables of both phylogenetic and ontogenetic origins must supplement a principle of reinforcement in the analysis of any specific conditioning procedure. Each experiment tells us something of the general processes that govern learning, but also something of the general processes that govern evolution and of their particular expression in the individual.

NOTES

1. The most salient recent example of the contribution of theoretical differences to the analysis of conditioning comes from the contiguity and correlational views of the CS-UCS relationship (Ayres, Benedict, & Witcher, 1975; Benedict & Ayres, 1972; Quinsey, 1971; Rescorla, 1967). Space does not permit exploration of these theoretical differences, but further empirical and theoretical work has largely resolved the issue and led to the interpretation of conditioning presented later in this chapter (Rescorla & Wagner, 1972).

4

Reinforcement

Instrumental Procedure

INTRODUCTION

Our primary goal in this chapter remains the same as in the last—to achieve a deeper understanding of the principle of reinforcement. Findings obtained with the classical procedure indicate that learning occurs when a discrepancy exists between the behavior normally occurring in an environment and the behavior activated by the intrusion of an elicitation process into that environment. The environment acquires control over responses that, to a first approximation, resemble the elicited responses. As the result of individual experience, the learner comes to respond to an environment in a manner that is in harmony with the elicitation processes found in that environment.

The vision of the reinforcement principle that is provided by the classical procedure is a partial one, however. Learning does not consist solely of the control of already existing responses by new environments. Our behavioral capabilities are not confined to the mere rearrangement of the stimuli controlling elicited behaviors. The forces that shape individual behavior lead to new behavioral repertoires of great complexity and subtlety just as do the forces that shape species. Natural selection does not produce different species by the mere rearrangement of preexisting intact structures. Centaurs, satyrs, and unicorns—creatures composed of structures from different species—populate pre-Darwinian mythology, not the real world.

In evolution, the differential contribution of various genes to fitness together with the saltatory effects of mutation combine to bring about new structures and new functional relationships. What are the processes whereby novelty arises within the lifetime of the individual?

The best answer to questions concerning the origins of novelty in the behavior of the individual organism come from the application of instrumental, or operant, procedures. By making an elicitation process contingent upon some characteristic of behavior, the environment acquires control over responses that are not a part of the elicitation process. By gradually changing the response characteristics upon which the elicitation process is contingent, a complex and new behavior may be fashioned.

Both differential fitness in evolution and differential application of elicitation processes in learning are effective in shaping novelty. It strains the imagination to conceive of the ornate feathers of the peacock originating by natural selection from the hair cells of some primitive creature. Similarly, it taxes the mind to conceive of a great work of art originating by instrumental procedures from the scribbles of a child. But it is at least possible that our reluctance to believe reflects the limitations of our imaginations and our minds rather than any limitations inherent in either the principles of natural selection or reinforcement.

In the instrumental procedure, an elicitation process follows a response and thereby functions as a reinforcer to produce behavioral change. The notion that behavior is affected by its consequences is by no means a new one. Consider the following advice given by Benjamin Franklin to a military chaplain who was having difficulty attracting a congregation.

> We had for our chaplain a zealous Presbyterian minister, Mr. Beaty, who complained to me that the men did not generally attend his prayers and exhortations. When they enlisted, they were promised, besides pay and provisions, a gill [four ounces] of rum a day, which was punctually serv'd out to them, half in the morning, and the other half in the evening; and I observ'd they were as punctual in attending to receive it; upon which I said to Mr. Beaty: "It is, perhaps, below the dignity of your profession to act as steward of the rum, but if you were to deal it out and only just after prayers, you would have them all about you." He liked the tho't, undertook the office, and, with the help of a few hands to measure out the liquor, executed it to satisfaction, and never were prayers more generally and more punctually attended; so that I thought this method preferable to the punishment inflicted by some military laws for non-attendance on divine service.[1]

This advice by one of our founding fathers arises from everyday experience, but a scientific understanding—although it may originate with such experience—requires the more certain foundation of well-controlled observations in the laboratory. In this chapter, we shall examine the outcome of experiments using the instrumental procedure. Our goal will be to achieve an understanding of the principle of reinforcement which builds upon and supplements the understanding that resulted from the classical procedure.

While we shall focus upon the relationship between behavior and a subsequent elicitation process, it is well to remember that every behavior must occur in the presence of some environment. Although for ease of exposition the environmental context in which the elicitation process occurs may not be mentioned, to forget permanently that context cripples understanding. Just as a comprehensive account of the behavioral changes produced by the classical procedure requires us to acknowledge responses occurring prior to the elicitation process, so an adequate account of the results of the instrumental procedure requires us to acknowledge the role of *stimuli* prior to the elicitation process. As with the earlier treatment of classical conditioning, the presentation of the basic procedures and findings will be followed by a theoretical analysis of instrumental conditioning and a discussion of some of the complexities encountered with the procedure.

FUNDAMENTALS OF INSTRUMENTAL CONDITIONING

The lifetime of every organism is a rich and varied succession of responses and their consequences. Almost everything that we do brings us into contact with different environmental events, and these events in turn influence subsequent behavior. In order to disentangle the complex interplay of responses and their consequences that characterize the natural environment, those who seek an understanding of the principle of reinforcement using instrumental procedures have moved to the more placid and controllable environment of the laboratory. Like Pavlov, Thorndike and his intellectual descendants have searched for an understanding of the fundamental processes governing human behavior in the less turbulent arena of the animal learning laboratory.

The specific simple environments most often used in the study of instrumental procedures are the operant chamber, or Skinner box, and the runway. Both simplified environments trace their ancestry to the crude apparatus developed by Thorndike in William James' basement and in his cluttered room in New York. The operant chamber, in which a response such as bar-pressing is followed by the delivery of food, is the modern version of Thorndike's puzzle boxes, in which the operation of a latch by a cat would permit escape from confinement and access to a bit of fish. The runway traversed by the present-day rat is a more sophisticated version of the paths followed by Thorndike's chicks as they moved down passages whose walls were formed by stacks of books.

In this preliminary section, we shall examine some of the basic terminology and paradigms of instrumental conditioning and identify some of the important variables that must be controlled. Following this methodological information, we shall present the basic findings obtained with instrumental procedures.

Terminology of Instrumental Conditioning

Even though some of the events of interest in the instrumental procedure may be identical to those in the classical procedure, the two procedures developed independently of one another, with the result that different terms are often applied to the same specific events.

Reinforcing Stimulus (S^R)   Elicitation processes play a crucial role in both the instrumental and classical procedures but instead of the eliciting stimulus being designated as a UCS, it is named by its function—the elicitor functions as a *reinforcer* of an altered relationship between the environment and behavior. The eliciting, or *reinforcing stimulus,* is most commonly symbolized as S^R. Thus the same event, for example, food in the mouth of a deprived animal, is designated as a UCS in the classical procedure and as an S^R in the instrumental procedure.

Elicited Response   The elicited response, labeled the UCR in the classical procedure, did not occupy an important position historically in treatments of instrumental conditioning, and no commonly accepted symbol has been proposed. The elicited response may make a crucially important contribution to the complete behavioral outcome of the instrumental procedure, however, and we shall consider it somewhat later.

Instrumental Response (R)   The characteristic of behavior upon which the reinforcer, S^R, is contingent is called the instrumental response, or operant. If getting food in the mouth is contingent on the movement of the leg—as it was in Konorski's experiment with which we introduced the instrumental procedure—then leg movement is the instrumental response. If getting a grade of A on an examination is contingent on a correct answer to a question, then the correct answer is the instrumental response. Although various special symbols have been introduced by those who pioneered research in instrumental conditioning (for example, Guthrie, 1935; Hull, 1943; Konorski & Miller, 1937; Skinner, 1938; Tolman, 1932), we shall simply designate the instrumental response by the symbol R. The response is designated "instrumental" to signify that it is instrumental, that is, a means whereby S^R is produced. The response is called an "operant" to signify that it operates on the environment to produce S^R. As used here, R designates the characteristic of behavior that the experimenter has selected as a necessary condition for the occurrence of S^R: The experimenter has arranged for S^R to be contingent on R under some conditions.

Environmental Stimuli (S)   While it is true that instrumental conditioning is defined by the presence of a response-reinforcer contingency, it is also true that the contingency is usually in effect in only a limited range of environmental conditions. If Konorski's dog moved its leg while in its home pen, food would not be forthcoming. The contingency between leg movement and food was present only in the experimental situation. If the correct answer to an examination question occurs just as you leave the classroom, a grade of A is not obtained. Unfortunately, correct answers are reinforced by teachers when they occur in test situations, not when they occur in the hallway outside the classroom or while studying in your room.

Although the instrumental procedure is defined only by the presence of an R-S^R contingency, we must always bear in mind that the contingency is realized in some specific environmental context. Those features of the environment that come to control the instrumental response are called *discriminative stimuli*. In this chapter, the environmental stimuli are simply designated by S; in the next chapter, which deals exclusively with stimulus control, some additional symbols are mentioned.

Baseline Responding (Operant Level)   Having introduced the reinforcing stimulus (S^R), the instrumental—or operant— response (R), and the environmental stimuli (S) in which the response-reinforcer contingency is instituted, one last set of events must be considered. This set consists of those responses that occur in the presence of S at the beginning of learning—the *entering*, or *baseline*, *level* of responding.

The entering behavior of the learner is especially important in instrumental conditioning because one of its constituent responses is R, the instrumental response itself. Since the presentation of the reinforcer is dependent on the occurrence of R, the baseline frequency of R determines when and how often the learner initially experiences the response-reinforcer contingency. If the baseline level, or *operant level* as it is often called, is too low, behavioral change may never occur because the learner never comes into sufficient contact with the response-reinforcer contingency. Konorski's dog would never be presented with food unless its leg moved at least once. The student would never receive a grade of A unless the correct answer is given at least once. Two students who enter an algebra course with very different backgrounds in mathematics would experience very different degrees of success even though their responses are evaluated by the same criteria. Equal application of the contingencies of reinforcement to the unequal entering behaviors of different learners results in unequal opportunities for learning.

Instrumental Conditioning Paradigms

The response-reinforcer relationship, the R-S^R contingency, is the defining feature of all instrumental conditioning experiments. If the experimenter has arranged for an elicitation process to be dependent on the occurrence of a response, we are dealing with an instrumental procedure.

An understanding of the principle of reinforcement was sought, in the classical procedure, through the experimental manipulation of the relationship between an environmental event and an elicitation process (the CS-UCS relationship). The relationship between behavior and the elicitation process was allowed to vary as it would (for example, the OR-UCS and the CR-UCS relationship). In the instrumental procedure, we continue our search for a principle of reinforcement, but it is now the relationship between behavior and the elicitation process (the R-S^R relationship) that is varied experimentally. It is the stimulus-elicitation relationship (S-S^R) that is now left uncontrolled. Neither the classical nor the instrumental procedure is alone adequate to the development of an understanding of a principle of reinforcement. Together, these two procedures are powerful tools for the experimental analysis of behavior.

We shall use the instrumental procedure to study the effects of the R-S^R relationship on changes in behavior. As with the classical procedure, we shall focus primarily on two aspects of the defining contingency—the temporal relationship between the two events that define the procedure (the R-S^R interval) and the characteristics of the elicitation process.

Temporal Relations—Delay of Reinforcement   Given that some instrumental response has occurred, the elicitation process that is contingent on the response may occur either immediately or after some specified delay. The first method is called an *immediate reinforcement* paradigm; the second a *delayed reinforcement* paradigm. By observing the effects on behavior of varying the delay in reinforcement, we are able to determine whether the organism's theory of the environment is constructed from the relatively short time spans previously found with the classical procedure. Must a reinforcer in the instrumental procedure occur shortly after the instrumental response if that response is to change?

Characteristics of the Elicitation Process—Reinforcement and Punishment The characteristic of the elicitation process of greatest interest in the classical procedure was the intensity of the eliciting stimulus. We shall study the effects of this variable in the instrumental procedure as well. Of still greater interest, however, is the fact that some elicitation processes increase the frequency of responses upon which they are contingent, whereas others decrease the frequency of responses.

When the elicitation process increases the instrumental response, the eliciting stimulus functions as a *reinforcer*. When the elicitation process decreases the instrumental response, it functions as a *punisher*. In a laboratory situation, food for a deprived animal is often used as a reinforcer and electric shock as a punisher. Words of praise and reproof may function as reinforcers and punishers for persons. Stimuli that function as reinforcers are symbolized S^R as previously; stimuli that function as punishers are symbolized S^P. Instrumental procedures that employ such stimuli are known as *reinforcement* and *punishment paradigms,* respectively. These paradigms, together with the immediate and delayed variations of each, are depicted in Fig. 4.1.

We have encountered appetitive and aversive elicitation processes in our

Fig. 4.1 The (a) reinforcement and (b) punishment paradigms of the instrumental conditioning procedure showing immediate and delayed presentations of the eliciting stimuli. In the symbols, S is an environmental stimulus, R is an instrumental response, S^R is an elicitation process functioning as a reinforcer, and S^P is an elicitation process functioning as a punisher.

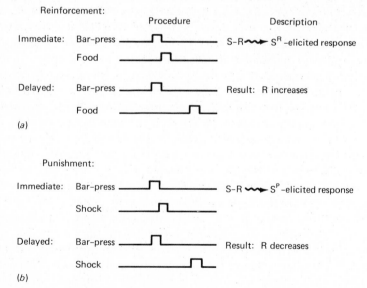

earlier discussion of classical conditioning, but the distinction did not assume the importance that it does in instrumental conditioning. In the classical procedure, the experimenter always monitors the response system activated by the eliciting stimulus. Salivation was monitored when food in the mouth was the UCS and leg flexion was monitored when shock to the foot was the UCS. In both cases, the environmental stimulus—the CS—came to control an increase in the monitored response.

In the instrumental procedure, however, the experimenter always monitors the instrumental response. The response system that is the object of the experimenter's attention does not change as the eliciting stimulus is varied. If a bar-press is followed by food, it is bar-pressing that is measured and not salivation. If a bar-press is followed by shock, bar-pressing continues to be measured, not jumping or vocalizing. Thus changes in an *invariant* response system are measured in instrumental conditioning, and not changes in *different* response systems as the eliciting stimulus varies. Both increases and decreases in responding are behavioral changes, and both are of interest to the student of learning.

Control Procedures

Our interest in instrumental learning stems from the desire to know what aspects of the R-S^R relationship produce learning. As indicated in the study of the CS-UCS relationship, however, behavior may be influenced by events other than those explicitly specified in the relationship. The same sources of complication arise in the instrumental learning situation. The need to rule out alternative interpretations of behavioral change calls for the development of controlled observations.

The achievement of controlled observations will be accomplished using the same general strategy previously employed with the classical procedure: We shall systematically assess the effects of those environmental and behavioral events and of their interrelationships that are not intrinsic to the R-S^R relationship. The environments of the past have exerted their effects upon behavior for many years and in subtle ways; it should come as no surprise that the disentanglement of those effects is an arduous task.

As with classical conditioning, and for the same reasons, most of the basic work on the R-S^R relationship has been conducted using infrahuman organisms. We seek the understanding of the behavior of men and women, but we are obliged to search for that knowledge among those whose relevant prior experience may be better controlled. We have seen that the range of effective elicitors is potentially very large—including reflexes, social behaviors, and conditioned reinforcers. For the human organism—even the child—the number of conditioned reinforcers is particularly large, a fact that makes it difficult to carry out well-controlled experiments on the fundamental features of the R-S^R relationship.

Test Environments—Operant Chamber and Runway The operant chamber consists of a rectangular space having a grid floor through which electric shock may be applied, a manipulandum by which responding may be monitored, and a tray into which food may be placed. The details of the apparatus vary somewhat with the species of animal; for example, the rat manipulandum is typically a lever that may be pressed and the pigeon manipulandum is a disk on the wall that may be pecked. (See Fig. 4.2a and b for drawings of the rat and pigeon chambers, respectively.)

The runway consists of a start-box into which the animal is placed, an alley which the animal enters when the startbox door is raised, and a goalbox into which food is placed. The start, alleyway, and goal floors sometimes consist of grids through which electric shock may be delivered. (See Fig. 4.2c for a sketch of a typical runway situation.)

Operation of the manipulandum in the Skinner box and locomotion in the runway define the instrumental response, and these behaviors are most often measured in terms of their frequency per unit time. In the operant chamber, the measurement is expressed as a rate (responses per minute) and in the runway as a speed (feet per minute).

Discrete-Trial and Free-Responding Methods Two general types of methods are used in the study of instrumental conditioning—*discrete-trial* and *free-responding*. With the discrete-trial method, the experiment is conducted in a series of more or less separate time periods, or trials, with the presentation

Fig. 4.2 Test environments frequently employed in instrumental procedures. (a) Operant chamber for the rat with bar-pressing as the monitored response. (b) Operant chamber for the pigeon with key-pecking as the monitored response. (c) Runway for the rat with locomotion from the startbox through the alley to the goalbox as the monitored response.

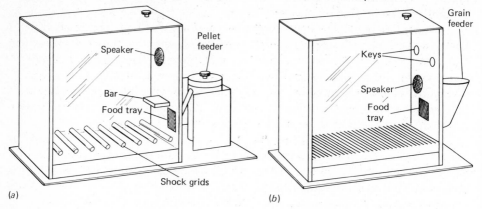

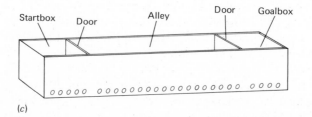

of S^R occurring at the end of the trial. Between trials, the manipulandum is not available to the organism. In the runway, the animal is typically placed in an intertrial interval box after being removed from the goalbox and before being placed in the startbox for the next trial. In the operant chamber, the bar may be retracted (for rats) or the entire box darkened (for pigeons) in order to prevent further responding until the onset of the next trial.

With the free-responding method, the learner is permitted unrestricted access to the manipulandum throughout the experimental session, and responding may recur immediately after the eliciting stimulus. The free-responding method cannot be instituted in the runway, but locomotor behavior may be studied with this method by using a circular running, or activity, wheel (for example, Morse & Skinner, 1958).

The discrete-trial and free-responding methods both have their particular strengths in providing controlled conditions for work with instrumental conditioning. By eliminating the possibility of responding after the eliciting stimulus, the discrete-trial method minimizes the possible effect of the elicitation process on the subsequent instrumental response. For example, if S^P were a shock that elicits the response of jumping, then the instrumental response of bar-pressing might increase momentarily if the bar is accidentally depressed as the animal jumps about the chamber. Thus a punishment paradigm in which bar-pressing produces shock might have the paradoxical effect of causing at least a temporary increase in the instrumental response.

Free-responding methods, on the other hand, do not require the animal to move through space, and hence reduce the effects of responding on changes in external stimulation. The experimental environment remains constant as the rat bar-presses but necessarily changes as the rat moves down a runway (for example, Donahoe, 1970). A free-responding method also entails many occurrences of R, thus providing sensitive estimates of the effects of variables. Often, these estimates are sufficiently reliable to permit observations of behavioral phenomena in single organisms without the need for averaging across individuals. In summary, it would be an oversimplification to assert that one method is superior to the other; the nature of the experimental question dictates the appropriate experimental method.

Baselines for Reinforcement and Punishment   The choice of an instrumental response that is a sensitive measure of behavioral change is complicated by the fact that elicitation processes may function as reinforcers and punishers. If a reinforcer is used, increases in responding are measured and it is in the experimenter's best interest to select an instrumental response having a fairly low operant level so that the increase may be detected. Bar-pressing in the operant chamber and locomotion in the runway are well-suited for the reinforcement pardigm since the baseline levels of these responses are quite low. There is little danger that the increase will be obscured by a "ceiling effect" such as might occur with responses that have very high operant levels and cannot increase further.

If a punisher is used, decreases in responding are measured and the experimenter should select an instrumental response that occurs at a relatively high baseline level so that the decrease may be detected. Because early workers employing instrumental procedures were more interested in the reinforcement than the punishment paradigm, the responses that they chose—bar-pressing and locomotion—are not ideally suited to the study of punishment because of their low operant levels. Since bar-pressing and locomotion already occur at low levels, it is difficult to obtain a sensitive measure of the decreases in responding produced by the punishment paradigm; that is, there is a "floor effect." In order to increase the sensitivity of these responses to punishment, a preliminary phase is often employed. Thus bar-pressing might first be maintained with food. Then in order to study punishment, electric shock as well as food would be presented following bar-pressing.

Effects of Elicited Responses The instrumental procedure, in addition to the response specified in the R-S^R relationship, contains other behaviors that may influence the outcome of the procedure. Clearly, the experimental environment influences the baseline level of the instrumental response and, as we have just seen, this has important effects on the sensitivity of the experiment to reinforcers and punishers. In addition, such factors as orienting responses and the habituation of responses to environmental and eliciting stimuli may influence the outcome of the instrumental as well as the classical procedure. In our treatment of instrumental conditioning, however, we shall examine in some detail only one source of uncontrolled variation—interactions between the instrumental response and responses elicited by the reinforcing (or punishing) stimulus.

The elicitation process may affect the instrumental response (R) independently of the response-reinforcer relationship. For example, if R is a component of the elicited behavior, then R may increase independently of the R-S^R relationship. We discussed an earlier hypothetical example in which shock elicited jumping that in turn caused an increase in bar-pressing. If R is incompatible with the elicited response, then R may decrease independently of the R-S^R relationship. If an animal tends to "freeze" after receiving many shocks, the frequency of bar-pressing might decline whether or not shock is contingent on bar-pressing.

Interactions involving elicited responses and the instrumental response have been the object of considerable recent research (for example, Bolles, 1970; Falk, 1971; Staddon & Simmelhag, 1971) and are discussed in a later section of the chapter dealing with complexities in instrumental conditioning. Our present concern is to describe briefly three control procedures used to assess such sources of behavioral variation—yoking, omission, and multiple-baseline procedures.

In the *yoking procedure* (Ferster & Skinner, 1957; Moore, J. W., & Gormezano, 1961), the control (yoked) subject in one test chamber receives the reinforcer whenever the experimental (lead) subject in a second chamber makes the instrumental response. Thus the temporal distribution and frequency of the reinforcer is identical for both lead and yoked subjects but the R-S^R relationship is present only for the lead subject (see Church, 1964, for a critical discussion of yoking as a control procedure).

A second control procedure for elicited effects is the *omission procedure*. In the yoking procedure there is no contingency between the behavior of the control subject and the occurrence of the reinforcer, but the reinforcer may nevertheless occasionally follow the monitored response and influence it through superstitious conditioning. A shock that occurs after a response by a yoked subject may decrease that response even though the relationship is temporal and not causal. The omission procedure may be used to ensure that the eliciting stimulus never occurs following the monitored response.

In an omission procedure, the control subject receives the eliciting stimulus only when the monitored response has not occurred during a specified period of time. In a discrete-trial procedure, food might be given only if the pigeon does *not* peck the disk during a stimulus period that is otherwise followed by food (for example, Williams, D. R., & Williams, 1969). In a free-responding procedure, food might be given only if pecking has not occurred for 30 sec (for example, Zeiler, 1971). By adjusting the size of the period during which responding leads to the omission of food, the control (omission) subject and the experimental subject may receive the eliciting stimulus equally often, but only the experimental subject receives food following the instrumental response. (See Jenkins, 1977, Mackintosh, 1974, pp. 114–124 and Sheffield, 1965, for discussions of the omission procedure.)

As we found in our earlier treatment of control procedures in classical conditioning, no single procedure provides a perfectly controlled observation. In the case of omission training, the procedure ensures that the instrumental response is never followed by the reinforcer, but it causes other responses (R_o) to be followed by the reinforcer. Thus some of the difference between the behavior of the experimental and control subjects may be due to the presence of an R_o-S^R contingency in the control condition as well as to the absence of the R-S^R contingency.

The last control procedure for elicited responses that we shall consider is the *multiple-baseline* procedure. In the multiple-baseline procedure, unlike those previously considered, a separate control group is not employed. Instead of observing a single response in experimental and control subjects, multiple responses are observed in a single subject. For example, the depression of either of two adjacent response levers might be followed by food but only one of the levers would also be followed by shock. Any elicited responses would presumably affect bar-pressing of the two levers equally, whereas the R-S^P contingency would affect one lever alone.

Again, no single control procedure is perfect. To the extent that the stimuli controlling the two responses of the multiple baseline are similar, then to that extent will the R-S^P contingency affect both responses equally. Thus two levers that look alike would both tend to be affected similarly by an R-S^R contingency present on only one lever. Two levers that are very different (for example, in size, shape, and position within the chamber) would tend to be affected less similarly.

Although the multiple-baseline procedure must be employed with care, it is a very useful technique when observations are costly. In applied work, when trying to evaluate procedures for changing behavior, a contingency may be placed on one activity (for example, studying science) but not for another (for example, studying English). If studying science increases but English remains constant, this is evidence for the effectiveness of the contingency. The contingency may then be subsequently instituted for studying English. In this way, successful procedures may be identified without the need to establish an independent control group which receives no treatment—an ethically troublesome control procedure (see Reese, 1977, and Sulzer & Mayer, 1977, for further discussion of control procedures in applied settings).

BASIC FINDINGS

Having surveyed the terminology, paradigms, and control procedures associated with instrumental conditioning, we shall now use the instrumental procedure to answer two primary questions. What effect does the temporal relationship between the instrumental response and the eliciting stimulus (the R-S^R relationship) have on the development of a new functional relationship between the environment and behavior? What effect does the intensity of the eliciting stimulus have on learning? Answers to these questions will be sought with both the reinforcement and punishment paradigms. Such answers are essential to a theoretical analysis of instrumental conditioning that will result in an improved understanding of the principle of reinforcement.

Delay of Reinforcement (R-S^R Interval)

We found in our study of the CS-UCS interval with the classical procedure that the stimuli present immediately prior to the occurrence of the elicitation process were in a temporally favored position to acquire control of behavior. Now, using the instrumental procedure, we inquire into the effect of the R-S^R interval on the control of R by the experimental environment, S. This inquiry would seem to be a straightforward matter: We simply arrange for the occurrence of R, follow R by S^R after some interval of time, and then measure the change in frequency of R. As shown by our experience with the classical procedure, however, things are not always as simple as they seem.

Consider first the following procedure. A food-deprived rat is placed in the startbox of a runway and then locomotes down the alleyway to the goalbox, where it is confined for a few seconds before being fed. This procedure is repeated for a number of daily sessions with different animals getting different delays of reinforcement until the speed of running stabilizes. The results from a study of this type are displayed in Fig. 4.3 (Logan, 1960). As can be seen, running speed was greatest with immediate reinforcement (0-sec delay) and decreased as the delay in reinforcement lengthened to 30 sec. The results of the foregoing experiment and many others agree in indicating that the temporal aspect of the R-S^R relationship is an important determinant of performance in instrumental conditioning.

Our familiarity with the outcome of the superstition experiment and with the phenomenon of conditioned reinforcement should alert us to some inter-

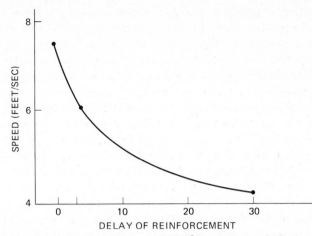

Fig. 4.3 Effects of the delay of reinforcement (R-S^R interval) on running in a runway. (After Logan, 1960.)

pretations of this finding, however. First, the superstition experiment indicates that behaviors which precede a reinforcer may be affected in the absence of any causal relationship between the two events. As applied to the delay of reinforcement paradigm, the implication of the superstition experiment is that the reinforcer delivered in the goalbox may increase the frequency of whatever other responses follow running in the alley. These other responses(R_o) may then interfere with the instrumental response (R) of running on subsequent trials (Spence, 1956). For example, if the animal were rearing up on its hind legs immediately prior to the delivery of food, rearing—which is incompatible with running—may increase with a consequent decrease in the speed of running.

The foregoing analysis implies that the deleterious effect of delay of reinforcement on the strength of R will vary considerably from situation to situation depending on the occurrence of R_o and on the interaction between R_o and R. An analogous conclusion was reached in the analysis of the delay paradigm with the classical procedure, in which it was necessary to consider the role of other stimuli (S_o) than the nominal CS if performance with appreciable stimulus-reinforcer (CS-UCS) intervals was to be understood.

In addition to the superstitious reinforcement of R_o, a second phenomenon that may contribute to the effect of delay of reinforcement is conditioned reinforcement. In a runway experiment, for example, the stimuli characteristic of the goal area are in an appropriate temporal and spatial relationship with food to become conditioned reinforcers. Thus the instrumental response of running may receive an *immediate* conditioned reinforcer upon entry into the goal area, thereby attenuating somewhat the deleterious effects of the delayed unconditioned reinforcer.

Origins of the Delay Effect In this section, we shall examine some of the evidence which suggests that both superstitious reinforcement of R_o and conditioned reinforcement of R contribute to the effects of delay of reinforcement on instrumental responding.

Although the contribution of other responses that intervene between the instrumental response and the reinforcer has been studied in runway situations (for example, Spence, 1956), a free-responding situation which permits the experimental control of responses analogous to R_o provides an apt demonstration of their effects (Catania, 1971b). A pigeon was placed in an operant chamber containing a left (L) and a right (R) response key. For our purposes, assume that a peck on the right key represents the instrumental response and a peck on the left key represents the other response. In order to obtain food, the pigeon had to execute a sequence of responses, consisting of an R response followed by a prescribed number of L responses. As examples, consider the sequences RL, RLL, RLLL, and RLLLL. The sequences differ in the number of L responses (R_os) intervening between R and the reinforcer. Since the execution of any response takes time, the sequences also necessarily differ in the time between the occurrence of R and the delivery of the reinforcer, and in this way are analogous to the relationship between the instrumental response, R_o, and S^R in the delay of reinforcement paradigm.

Under these conditions, we may again ask whether the effect of reinforcement on R varies with the time interval between R and reinforcement. The answer is shown in Fig. 4.4. The frequency of R responses declined as the position of R moved further from the reinforcing stimulus. It should be noted, however, that R responses that were removed from reinforcement by as many as 11 L responses still showed some effect of the reinforcer. In this longest sequence, the time between the occurrence of R and the presentation of food was approximately 7 sec (the average time required to make 11 L responses).

We now turn to the possible contribution of conditioned reinforcement to

Fig. 4.4 The rate of responses to key R as a function of the number of subsequent responses to key L required for food. The rates are corrected for the rate to key R when only key L responses were necessary for food. (After Catania, 1971b.)

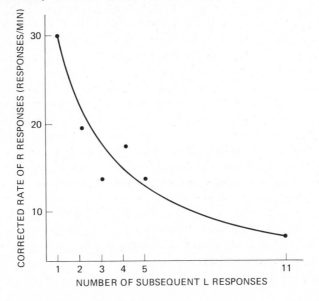

the observed effect of the R-S^R interval on behavior. A series of experiments has been directed at this issue, culminating in an experiment using a multiple-baseline technique (Grice, 1948). A modified runway apparatus was used in which the rat passed through either of two doors differing in brightness and entered a common delay chamber in which it remained until food was presented. Food was always given after a response to the door of one brightness and was never given after a response to the other door. The position of the correct door varied from trial to trial. By detaining the subject in a common delay chamber, whether the choice response was correct or incorrect, the conditioned reinforcement for both responses was equal. Any differences in choice would reflect only the R-S^R interval.

The results shown in Fig. 4.5 indicate that the correct door was chosen in a high proportion of trials with immediate reinforcement, but that preference declined sharply as the R-S^R interval lengthened. Thus when conditioned reinforcement is controlled, behavior is maintained by delayed reinforcement, but the time interval over which a reinforcer is effective is greatly reduced. In this case, the maximum tolerable delay was only a few seconds. (cf. Cohen, 1968).

Delay of Punishment   The preceding findings document the importance of the temporal relationship between the instrumental response and the eliciting stimulus, but they have been confined to the reinforcement paradigm. Do similar results occur with the punishment paradigm? The data are equally clear although somewhat less extensive: As the R-S^P interval lengthens, the ef-

Fig. 4.5   The effect of the R-S^R interval on the proportion of choice of the correct response using a common delay chamber to control for conditioned reinforcement.   (After Grice, 1948. Copyright 1948 by the American Psychological Association. Reprinted by permission.)

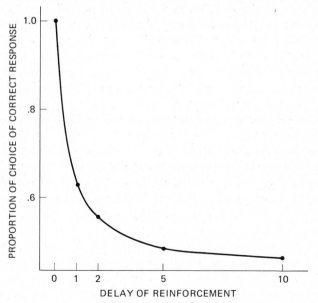

fect of punishment decreases (for example, Azrin, 1956; Camp, Raymond, & Church, 1967). Aversive stimuli, like appetitive stimuli, are most effective when presented immediately after the instrumental response.

As in the analysis of the origins of delay of reinforcement, both the relationship of other responses and environmental stimuli to the punisher and their joint relationship to the instrumental response must be considered (cf. Mackintosh, 1974, pp. 277–299). The possible contribution of stimulus-punisher relations to the decrement in the instrumental response is particularly interesting to consider. As an example, a rat whose bar-presses produce shock receives pairings of environmental stimuli with shock, as well as pairings of responding with shock. In our previous study of the behavioral changes produced by the classical procedure, we found that stimuli which are paired with an elicitor such as electric shock will acquire control over the elicited response. Thus, returning to our example, bar-pressing may decrease when it is followed by shock in a punishment paradigm, in part because environmental stimuli acquire control of shock-elicited responses that interfere with bar-pressing.

How can we determine the contribution of the R-S^p contingency to the decrease in the instrumental response (a specific punishment effect) apart from the contribution made by the S-S^p contingency (a general suppressing effect)? A yoked-control procedure has most often been used in the pursuit of an answer to this question: In an illustrative experiment (Church, 1969), two groups of rats were given the same number of shocks during a session in which bar-pressing was maintained by food. In the punishment (lead) group, in which shocks were response-contingent, bar-pressing was reduced to 7% of the pre-shock baseline. In the yoked-control group, in which the same number of shocks were given independently of responding, bar-pressing was only reduced to 54% of the preshock baseline.

Through specifying the contingency between bar-pressing and shock for the lead animals, the environment prior to the delivery of shock was precisely constrained. Most obviously, that environment was more apt to include the sight, touch, and smell of the bar for the lead than the yoked subjects. Hence these stimuli were in a particularly favorable temporal relationship to acquire control over shock-elicited responses. In keeping with the phenomenon of conditioned suppression (see pp. 107–108), bar-pressing is effectively suppressed by stimuli that reliably precede shock, even in the absence of a response-shock contingency.

There is little doubt that the punishment paradigm can be an effective procedure for producing behavioral change (Fantino, 1973; Premack, 1971a; Rachlin & Herrnstein, 1969). It is the direction of the behavioral change—increased instrumental responding in the case of reinforcement and decreased instrumental responding in the case of punishment—that distinguishes the two paradigms.

Magnitude of Reinforcement (Punishment)

We have seen that the temporal relationship between an instrumental response and an elicitation process importantly affects the development of new functional relationships between the environment and the instrumental response. We have seen further that the behavioral outcome of an instrumental procedure may require knowledge of elicited responses as well as the instrumental response. In this section we examine the effect of the intensity, or magnitude, of the eliciting stimulus on instrumental behavior.

Factors Affecting the Elicitation Process As with the classical procedure, we shall find that behavioral change is facilitated by more vigorous elicitation processes—whether the elicitation process functions as a reinforcer or a punisher. In order to study how the magnitude of the reinforcer or punisher affects learning, it is necessary to hold the vigor of the elicitation process constant throughout the experiment. With reinforcing stimuli, the elicitation process is usually established and maintained by depriving the organism of the stimulus. A rat might be deprived of food until it reaches 80% of its normal body weight, and then receive a limited number of small food pellets contingent upon the instrumental response. With punishing stimuli, a potent elicitor would be selected that would undergo relatively little habituation with repeated presentations. An electric shock provides an example of such a stimulus.

The importance of controlling deprivation and habituation in studying the effects of the magnitude of the reinforcer and punisher is well-documented (for example, Pavlov, 1927; Cotton, 1953; Clark, F. C., 1958) and has figured prominently in theoretical analyses of instrumental procedures (for example, Premack, 1965; Timberlake & Allison, 1974). We shall return to these and related matters in a subsequent chapter dealing with motivation.

Reinforcement Given that deprivation has been appropriately controlled, how does behavior change as a function of the magnitude of reinforcement? As found by many investigators (see Hall, 1976, pp. 300–301, and Pubols, 1960, for summaries), the asymptotic level of performance increases directly as a function of the magnitude of reinforcement. A discrete-trial runway procedure in which different groups of rats received either 2.5%, 5.0% or 10.0% solutions of a sugar (sucrose) at the conclusion of each daily trial illustrates the general finding (Kraeling, 1961). As shown in Fig. 4.6, the speed of running increased as the concentration of sucrose increased. Through separating the trials by a 24-hr interval, any contribution of the eliciting effects of the various concentrations to performance on the subsequent trial was controlled. Through employing a constant exposure time for all fluids, differential consummatory behavior, which would have occurred if different amounts of dry food had been used, was also controlled. Basically similar results have been found whether the magnitude of reinforcement is varied quantitatively, as in the preceding experiment, or qualitatively, as when produced by variations in the type of reinforcer (for example, Hutt, 1954).

Reinforcers and Evolution The finding that the vigor of the elicitation process affects learning in the instrumental procedure is further testimony to the initial debt that learning owes to phylogeny. As with the classical proce-

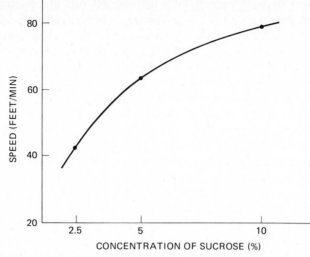

Fig. 4.6 The effect of the magnitude of reinforcement (sucrose concentration) on the terminal level of running. (From Kraeling, 1961. Copyright 1961 by the American Psychological Association. Reprinted by permission.)

dure, new functional relationships between the environment and behavior arise in the first instance from the prior functional relationships exemplified by unconditioned elicitation processes.

The fact that saccharin, a nonnutritive but sweet-tasting compound, may function as a reinforcer is especially interesting in this context. While appeals to environmental contingencies in the history of a species must always be speculative, it is the case that naturally occurring, sweet-tasting substances tend to be high in caloric value. The constancy and durability of this correlation between taste and nutritional consequences may have exerted pressure for the natural selection of organisms having a preference for sweet substances. During the first week of life, for example, human infants respond differentially to taste and show contented sucking behaviors to sweetness and distress reactions to sourness (Peterson & Rainey, 1910, cited in Hurlock, 1950, p. 121). When sweet-tasting but nonnutritive substances such as saccharin are encountered, they too are reinforcing as a legacy from the evolutionary history of the species. In an evolutionary history devoid of artificial sweetness, no differentiation between nutritive and nonnutritive sweet substances could have occurred.

An obvious instance of an elicitation process that serves as a reinforcer and that owes a debt to phylogeny are those environmental-behavioral relationships found in sexual behavior. There are few organisms for which sexual behavior is not reinforcing because the ancestors of such organisms have left few offspring. It must be reiterated, of course, that one's initial tastes may be greatly modified by experience. As we have seen, reflexes are but one source of those elicitation processes that are effective in producing learning.

Punishment   The magnitude of punishing as well as reinforcing stimuli affects the degree of behavioral change (Azrin & Holz, 1966). As an example, bar-pressing in rats was first maintained with occasional food presentations, using a free-responding procedure. Then separate groups were given different intensities of response-contingent shock that resulted in the suppression of bar-pressing (Boe & Church, 1967). To assess the enduring effects of the different shock intensities, test sessions were given in which neither shock nor food occurred. Since learned changes in behavior are relatively persistent, the differential effects of the intensity of S^p should be apparent even when the punishment paradigm is discontinued. The rate of responding in the test session, expressed as a percentage of the response rate during a previous baseline period when only food followed bar-pressing, is shown in Fig. 4.7. The decrease in responding was directly related to the intensity of the punishing stimulus used in training.

Summary   Our survey of the effects of the magnitude of reinforcement on behavioral change in the instrumental procedure is complete. We are drawn to the same conclusion reached after a comparable survey of the classical pro-

Fig. 4.7   The percentage of responding during a test period following punishment with differing intensities (voltages) of electric shock. Responding in the 1-hr test period is expressed as a percentage of the responding previously observed during a shock-free baseline period in which bar-pressing was followed by food alone.   (After Boe & Church, 1967.)

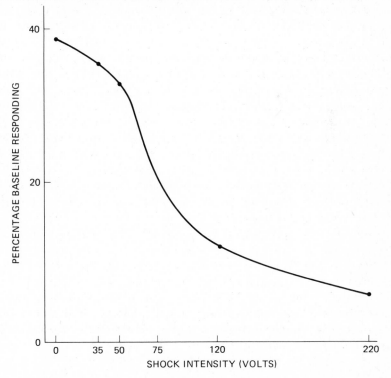

cedure: The final level of performance is a function of the intensity of the elicitation process. In the instrumental procedure, responding increased with an increasing magnitude of a reinforcing stimulus and decreased with an increasing magnitude of a punishing stimulus. The similar findings regarding the behavioral effects of the intensity of the elicitation process, together with the earlier results regarding the importance of temporal contiguity in both the CS-UCS and the R-S^R relationships, suggest a fundamental similarity in the behavioral processes involved in classical and instrumental procedures. The search for those common principles is described in the next section, which deals with the theoretical analysis of findings from the instrumental procedure.

THEORETICAL ANALYSIS OF INSTRUMENTAL CONDITIONING

Having experimentally identified some of the major aspects of the response-elicitation relationship that affect performance in the instrumental procedure, let us now attempt to integrate those findings theoretically. The theoretical analysis builds upon empirical findings, and in turn suggests further experimental work.

As in the theoretical analysis of classical conditioning, we begin by searching for those aspects of the response-elicitation relationship that are essential for learning. As before, our primary goal remains the formulation of an adequate principle of reinforcement—an understanding of how the environment of the individual fosters behavioral change. Following the effort to develop an adequate principle of reinforcement, we shall examine some of the implications of that principle for more complex instrumental procedures.

Nature of the Response-Elicitation Relationship

Instrumental conditioning is defined as a procedure in which the presentation of an elicitation process is made contingent upon the occurrence of a response. What features of the R-S^R (or R-S^P) relationship are necessary and sufficient for the production of behavioral change? Is it enough to have R occur in the presence of some environmental event, S, and then to present the eliciting stimulus? That is, is temporal contiguity of S, R, and S^R(S^P) sufficient for the emergence of an altered functional relationship between the environment and behavior? Or, as in the classical procedure, must a discrepancy also exist between the entering behavior of the learner and the behavior elicited as a part of the elicitation process? Let us see.

Contiguity The findings regarding the deleterious effects of delay of reinforcement and punishment on behavioral change testify to the importance of temporal relationships in the instrumental procedure. Under typical circumstances, other responses and stimuli intervene between the instrumental response and the elicitation process and render the R-S^R contingency ineffective over any but short temporal intervals (cf. Revusky & Garcia, 1970). The conclusions from both the instrumental and classical procedures concerning contiguity are, therefore, in harmony—the naive organism constructs its theory of the environment from environmental-behavioral contiguities that occur in proximity to elicitation processes.

In the experienced organism, of course, new learning may build upon old learning and the environmental-behavioral contiguities may be temporally distant from reflexive elicitation processes. The experienced organism may thereby appear to transcend the severe limitations of space and time that characterize the original conditions of learning. It should be remembered, however, that with conditioned reinforcers and punishers, the conditioned elicitation processes and not the original elicitors now must immediately follow the response. Contiguity remains important for learning in both the naive and experienced organism, but the origin of the elicitation processes may differ. A lover's smile may change behavior as effectively as more primitive reinforcing stimuli, but both events had best occur immediately after the behavior they would seek to change.

Discrepancy Between Baseline and Elicited Responding   In order for new functional relationships to develop between the environment and behavior, temporal contiguity with an elicitation process is usually necessary. But is contiguity alone sufficient for learning in the instrumental procedure? As in the classical procedure, we seek the answer to this question in the outcome of the blocking experiment.

In this experiment, it will be recalled, prior conditioning to one component of a compound CS attenuates conditioning to the other component when the compound CS is later paired with an elicitation process. As an illustration, if a tone is paired with shock and then a tone-light compound is paired with shock, the control of responding by the light component would be blocked. The blocking is attributed to a reduced discrepancy between the entering behavior of the learner to the compound CS and the behavior elicited by the shock.

Does blocking also occur with the instrumental procedure? Blocking would be expected if a discrepancy between the entering and elicited behavior is necessary for learning. If contiguity is sufficient with the instrumental procedure, however, control by the new component of the compound would be expected because the new component has been presented in temporal proximity to the elicitation process. For the resolution of these issues, let us turn to a blocking experiment conducted according to an instrumental procedure.

Using a discrete-trial procedure with pigeons, a control group was given compound stimulus training in which key-pecking was reinforced with food during a simultaneous compound consisting of a red key-light and a 1,000 Hz tone. In the experimental group, key-pecking was reinforced in the presence of a red key-light during the first phase, and in the simultaneous presence of a red key-light and tone during the second phase. During the test phase in which key-pecking was not followed by food, the light and tone components of the compound stimulus were presented separately (vom Saal & Jenkins, 1970). If contiguity is sufficient for instrumental conditioning, the control and experimental subjects should respond equally to the tone. If a discrepancy between the entering and elicited behavior is necessary, the control subjects should respond to the tone more than the experimental subjects.

The results were clear: While the control subjects responded to the tone an average of 67 times during the test phase, the experimental subjects responded an average of only 32 times. The two conditions were comparable in the number of responses to the red light, 87 for the control subjects and 90 for the experimental subjects. Blocking had occurred.

This experiment, which included a number of other control conditions, as well as a number of other studies employing instrumental procedures (for example, Chase, S., 1968; Johnson, D. F., 1970; Mackintosh & Honig, 1970; Miles, C. G., 1970) are consistent in indicating that contiguity of S, R, and elicitation process is not sufficient for learning; a discrepancy between entering and elicited behavior must also exist. Thus the roles of discrepancy and contiguity appear to be similar in both the classical and instrumental procedures.

Toward a Principle of Reinforcement

The outcome of an experimental analysis of the instrumental procedure has led us to the view that the temporal relationship between S, R, and an elicitation process, in which there is an initial discrepancy between the entering behavior and the elicited behavior, constitutes the conditions under which a new functional relationship develops between the environment and behavior. We shall expand on this view of the principle of reinforcement after considering some alternative accounts that have been proposed.

Some Alternative Approaches Historically, an understanding of the conditions that foster learning has been sought by attempting to identify some common feature shared by all reinforcing stimuli or by all responses to which those stimuli give rise. For example, many stimuli that serve as reinforcers—food, water, electric shock, and so on—clearly affect biological needs. Perhaps all reinforcers affect biological needs or, in the case of conditioned reinforcement, are based upon prior relationships to stimuli having this characteristic.

This conception of reinforcement, the *need-reduction hypothesis* (Hull, 1943), seeks the key to reinforcement in the properties of stimulation. It also represents an attempt to explain a behavioral observation (a change in response frequency) in terms of processes at another level (the physiology of the organism). While reductive explanations are expected and welcomed in a unified scientific conception of nature, it has already been noted that such efforts have the appearance but not the reality of explanation if the underlying process is itself not better understood than the behavioral process that it seeks to explain. Need-reduction theory, while it is consistent with much data, is found wanting in this respect.

Moreover, there are stimuli that are effective reinforcers when made contingent upon responding, but for which a need-reduction explanation is difficult to maintain. We have seen, for example, that sweet-tasting saccharin is a reinforcer and yet it has no caloric value. The fact that sweet-tasting substances often have high caloric value was almost certainly a potent factor in the natural selection of sweetness as an elicitor. Sweet substances often do reduce biological needs, but taste and not need-reduction is the property of stimulation upon which natural selection was apparently based in this case. In a sense, the natural selection of a preference for sweetness illustrates a superstitious selection resulting from the close, but by no means perfect, relationship between taste and caloric value (cf. Sheffield, Roby, & Campbell, 1954; Rozin & Kalat, 1971; Young, P. T., 1959).

Attempts to preserve the basic thrust of the need-reduction position led to the postulation of an inferred process of drive reduction. The *drive-reduction hypothesis,* in which drive has the status of a theoretical construct defined solely in terms of its relationship to observable antecedents such as hours of deprivation, is plagued by the difficulties commonly associated with inferred processes (Miller, N. E., 1963). Nevertheless, in the hands of Miller a definition of drive stimulus emerged whose connotations are similar to those of an eliciting stimulus: "A drive is a strong stimulus which impels action" (Miller, N. E., & Dollard, 1941). If the stimulus to which Miller referred is a physical event, not simply an inferred process, then drive stimulus and eliciting stimulus are kindred terms. Whether the *reduction* of stimulation is essential for learning is, of course, a separable issue from the position that eliciting stimuli are essential to learning.

A second set of observations that was difficult to reconcile with a drive- or need-reduction position, and that led some to emphasize the response rather than the stimulus as the locus of reinforcement, is illustrated by the following finding: Activities such as copulation without ejaculation serve as potent reinforcers (Sheffield, Wulff, & Backer, 1951). These activities by themselves can hardly be thought of as need- or drive-reducing. Again, as with saccharin, the experimenter has confronted the organism with a disjunction of environmental events that has not been encountered in the evolution of the species. Copulation has been conjoined with ejaculation in the history of the species as has sweet taste and caloric value. There had been little previous basis for a distinction between the two members of each pair of events upon which natural selection or individual experience could operate. Just as saccharin maintains responding in the absence of caloric value, so copulation functions as a reinforcer in the absence of ejaculation.

Because of the occurrence of vigorous consummatory responses with both the drinking of saccharin-flavored water and with copulation, it was suggested that perhaps it was the opportunity to make the elicited response that was essential to reinforcement (Sheffield & Roby, 1950; Sheffield, Roby, & Campbell, 1954). The notion that the occurrence of a dominant, or strong, response is itself the locus of reinforcement is termed the *prepotent-response hypothesis.* A variant of the prepotent-response hypothesis would restrict reinforcement to those responses that are consummatory in nature—for example, eating, drinking, and copulation (Glickman & Schiff, 1967).

The findings reviewed in the last chapter, which show that the overt expression of the UCR and CR is not essential in classical conditioning, should make us wary of assigning a critical role to the overt occurrence of the elicited response in the instrumental procedure. Indeed, reports soon appeared which demonstrated that liquids introduced directly into the stomach unaccompanied by consummatory behavior could increase the frequency of the behaviors that produced them (Kohn, 1951; Miller, N. E., 1963; Miller, N. E., & Kessen, 1952). Still later work revealed that direct electrical stimulation of certain brain areas would serve as a reinforcer without the elicitation of distinctive motor patterns in some instances (Olds & Milner, 1954).

To date, no single property of either the stimulus or the response that constitute the elicitation process has been shown to be necessary for reinforcement. Each effort to define the essential characteristic in this way has been found wanting in some respect; well-documented counterexamples exist in every case. Perhaps a different approach is called for. If neither the stimulational nor the behavioral aspects of the elicitation process alone provide the solution, perhaps it is the *relationship* of the elicitation process as a whole to preceding events that contains the answer.

Relational Principle of Reinforcement The finding from the blocking experiment, that a discrepancy between the entering and the elicited response is necessary for learning, is consistent with a relational interpretation of reinforcement. Consider the following illustrative example: A food-deprived rat is placed in a situation in which two responses of interest may occur. If the lever is sensed, the lever may be pressed; if food is sensed, the food may be eaten. The relative strengths, or preference, for bar-pressing and eating may be assessed by measuring the amount of time that the organism spends in each activity under baseline conditions in which free access to both activities is available (Premack, 1965). With a food-deprived rat, more time would be spent eating than bar-pressing in the baseline condition. If the elicitation process of which eating is a component is made contingent on the instrumental response of bar-pressing, a discrepancy is generated. When the discrepancy is positive, that is, the contingent elicitation process is more likely than the instrumental response, the instrumental response increases in frequency and a reinforcement paradigm is defined.

As an illustration of a punishment paradigm, consider the following situation: We confront our hypothetical rat with a new test chamber in which two activities are of interest—eating elicited by the sight of food and squealing elicited by electric shock. If during baseline conditions food is available in one part of the chamber and electric shock in another, eating will be preferred to squealing. Once again, we may assess preference by measuring the amount of time spent eating and the amount of time spent squealing (Premack, 1971a). If the elicitation process involving shock is made contingent on the instrumental response of eating, a discrepancy is generated. When the discrepancy is negative, that is, when the contingent elicitation process is less preferred than the instrumental response, the instrumental response decreases in frequency and a punishment paradigm is defined.

A statement of the principle of reinforcement that is consistent with findings from the instrumental procedure may now be given. The terminal, or asymptotic, strength of an instrumental response is a function of: (a) the baseline level of the instrumental response and (b) the discrepancy in strength between the elicited response and the initial level of that response determined in baseline conditions before the contingency has been instituted (Donahoe, 1977; Premack, 1959; Premack, 1965; Premack, 1971a). The greater the baseline level of the instrumental response, the greater the terminal level of the instrumental response. If the elicitation process is preferred to the instrumental response (a positive discrepancy), the instrumental response increases (reinforcement). If the instrumental response is preferred to the elicitation process (a negative discrepancy), the instrumental response decreases (punishment).

Our study of the behavioral changes produced by the classical and instrumental procedures has led us to a common conception of the principle of reinforcement. In both procedures, an elicitation process—a functional relationship between the environment and behavior that predates the learning situation—plays a critical role. Behavioral change occurs when environmental-behavioral contiguities occur in proximity to elicitation processes, and a discrepancy initially exists between the response to the eliciting stimulus and the response to the training environment (CS or S).

In the classical procedure, the elicitation process occurs following the CS, and the CS acquires control over a response (CR) that to a first approximation resembles the elicited response. The relationship of other behaviors to the elicitation process is not manipulated in the classical procedure, but these other behaviors may be affected if they are consistently followed by the elicitation process.

In the instrumental procedure, an elicitation process occurs following a response (R), and the environment (S) acquires control over a response that to a first approximation resembles the instrumental response. The relationship of other stimuli to the elicitation process is not manipulated in the basic instrumental procedure, but these other stimuli may also acquire control over behavior if they are consistently followed by the elicitation process. In both the classical and instrumental procedures, the final behavioral outcome is the result of an interaction between responses that are constituents of the elicitation process and responses that reliably precede the elicitation process.

The elicitation processes which have appeared in the examples of the classical and instrumental procedures given here have often been reflexive processes. Other elicitation processes having their origins more in the experience of the individual and less in the experience of the species could have been selected. Preexisting functional relationships between the environment and behavior, such as illustrated by the release of species-typical behaviors and conditioned reinforcement, can also be used to promote new learning. Because our purpose was to reduce the contribution of individual differences in experience to performance, reflexive elicitation processes were used as reinforcers and lower animals as subjects.

When dealing with learning in our own species, and in experienced organisms generally, conditioned elicitation processes more often serve as the basis for new learning. It is increasingly the prior experience of the individual and not the evolutionary history of the species that sets the boundary conditions for learning. This is not to deny the continued contribution of phylogeny to the behavior of all organisms, including humans. Anyone who has been tempted to kick a door upon which a toe has just been stubbed would be hard pressed to deny a role for phylogeny. Painful stimuli may elicit aggressive behavior in man as well as in many other species.

Experience alters the expression of the phylogenetic legacy, but it does not eliminate it. The experienced person who has stubbed a toe may utter a few choice words at the offending door, instead of actually kicking the door, but it is the expression of the phylogenetic legacy and not the legacy itself that has been altered. Acknowledging that legacy is the first step toward altering its expression.

Some Implications of a Relational Principle of Reinforcement Our study of the nature of the response-reinforcer relationship has resulted in the development of a relational interpretation of the principle of reinforcement. In this section, we examine some important implications of that principle. We begin with an illustrative experiment in human behavior and then document each implication with well-controlled animal experimentation.

Consider the following demonstration (Premack, 1959). During a baseline phase in which preferences were determined, children were given free access to either a machine that dispensed candy or a pinball machine. Some children spent more time with the candy machine and were labeled "eaters." Other children spent more time with the pinball machine and were labeled "manipulators." In the second phase, the opportunity to engage in one activity (for example, operating the candy dispenser) was made contingent on the occurrence of the other activity (for example, playing pinball). Consistent with a relational principle of reinforcement, the pinball-playing behavior of "eaters" was increased by the opportunity to operate the candy dispenser and the candy-dispensing behavior of "manipulators" was increased by the opportunity to play pinball.

There are four aspects of this rather simple demonstration that are particularly important to our understanding of a relational principle of reinforcement and to its application in our daily lives. First, *elicitation processes are not inherently reinforcing or punishing;* their effect on behavior depends on the preference of the organism for the elicitation process relative to the preference for the instrumental response. Neither the stimulus of the candy nor the response of eating candy is inherently reinforcing. Whether the elicitation process involving candy will increase behavior is dependent on the relative preference for manipulating and eating. The terms "reinforcer" and "punisher" are, therefore, functional terms that must, strictly speaking, always be used in connection with a specific instrumental response. The elicitation process whose constituents are the stimulus of candy and the response of eating will increase the frequency of pinball-playing behavior if the subject is an "eater," but not otherwise.

A laboratory example may be given of the implication that elicitation processes are neither inherently reinforcing nor punishing: The same amount of forced running in a motor-driven activity wheel will increase the frequency of the low probability response of bar-pressing, but will decrease the frequency of the high probability response of drinking (Terhune & Premack, 1975).

A second implication of a relational interpretation of instrumental conditioning is the *reversibility of reinforcement*. Eating candy was a reinforcer for the pinball-playing behavior of "eaters," but their roles were reversed for "manipulators." In the animal laboratory, the reversibility of reinforcement may be illustrated with the two activities of drinking and running in an activity wheel. If the access of rats to fluids is restricted, drinking will function as a reinforcer for running. If access to the running wheel is restricted, running will serve as a reinforcer of drinking (Premack, Schaeffer, & Hundt, 1964).

Third, if behavioral change is dependent on a difference in preference, *punishment and reinforcement may be treated in a strictly analogous fashion.* That is, if the discrepancy is produced by a more preferred elicitation process (a positive discrepancy), the instrumental response increases when the contingency is instituted. If the discrepancy results from a less preferred elicitation process (a negative discrepancy), then the imposition of the contingency produces a decrease in the instrumental response (Premack, 1971a).

Finally, a relational principle of reinforcement is *readily applicable to a wide range of reinforcers and organisms.* In order to change the strength of an instrumental response, two steps need to be taken. Initially the baseline, or operant level, of various activities must be assessed. Then a contingency must be instituted in which there is a discrepancy in preference between the instrumental response and the elicitation process that follows the instrumental response. Equal discrepancies in preference should produce equal changes in the instrumental response, regardless of the nature of the particular activities involved.

An application of the principle in the animal laboratory may be illustrated with the instrumental response of bar-pressing and the contingent elicitation processes of drinking a sucrose solution or running in an activity wheel (Premack, 1963). The preference for drinking was manipulated by varying the concentration of the sucrose solution; the preference for running was manipulated by varying the force required to turn the wheel. Whether drinking or running was used as the reinforcer, comparable discrepancies in preference produced comparable changes in the instrumental response of bar-pressing.

For an application to human behavior, consider the following example. A nursery school teacher wished to increase the amount of time that her students worked quietly at their desks—a nonpreferred activity for this age group. If given their choice, the children spent their time running about the room, playing, screaming, and so on. After noting these preferred activities during a baseline period, the children were told by the teacher that they could do such things as "run and scream" or "push the teacher around the room in her swivel chair" if they sat quietly and attended to the lesson. Occasionally, a bell would ring. If the desired study behavior was occurring when the bell rang, the children could then engage in the initially preferred activities. Within a few sessions, the children had increased their quiet study time to the desired levels (Homme, DeBaca, Devine, Steinhorst, & Rickert, 1963). An analogous application for a college student would be to make activities such as watching television, talking to one's roommate, or going to the student center contingent upon some specified amount of studying.

Much additional work remains to be done, of course, before a relational principle of reinforcement may be accepted as a useful formulation of a principle of reinforcement. Among the tasks is a determination of the suitability of the proportion of time in which an organism engages in an activity as a measure of the preference for an elicitation process (Donahoe, 1977; Dunham, 1977; Killeen, 1972). There are some elicitation processes, for example, those associated with sexual behavior, that are potent reinforcers but whose duration may be relatively short. It is important for such short-lived processes that the preference for the process be determined during the baseline condition under circumstances that are otherwise identical to those prevailing during the conditioning session (Premack, 1971a; but see Timberlake & Allison, 1974 for their discussion of momentary probability). Deprivation clearly plays an essential role in behavior change with a difference in preference producing learning only if the instrumental contingency maintains the deprivation for the contingent elicitation process (Premack, 1965). With appropriate eliciting stimuli, sexual behavior is highly preferred, but only if there is some minimal deprivation.

Extension to Multiple Responses

The relational principle of reinforcement has been developed in the instrumental procedure from the analysis of environments in which only one class of responses has been monitored—the instrumental response, or operant. Instrumental procedures with other arrangements between responses and elicitation processes are possible, and an analysis of these alternative arrangements is essential to understanding behavioral changes in many environments.

In this section, two alternatives will be considered—omission procedures and choice procedures. In *omission procedures,* the presentation of the reinforcer is contingent upon the nonoccurrence of the monitored response. Thus other responses (R_os) are temporally contiguous with the elicitation process. In *choice procedures,* two or more responses are monitored and reinforcers follow these responses according to independent contingencies. Thus there are two or more instrumental responses in choice procedures.

Omission Procedures: The Role of Other Responses (R_o)   The two basic instrumental procedures that have so far been considered are both procedures involving the presentation of elicitation processes contingent upon the occurrence of R. In the reinforcement paradigm, an elicitor follows R and R increases. In the punishment paradigm, an elicitor follows R and R decreases. It is possible, however, to devise procedures in which the *omission* of an elicitation process is contingent on the occurrence of R (Sheffield, 1965). As examples, rats might receive food if bar-pressing did not occur, or children might receive candy if they did not cry.

In trying to understand the effects of omission procedures on behavior, it is crucial to remember an observation made at the outset of our inquiry into the behavioral changes produced by classical and instrumental procedures: The organism is always behaving. Thus to assert that in an omission procedure the elicitation process never follows immediately after R is tantamount to asserting that the elicitation process does follow immediately after R_o. The child who does not get candy after crying does get candy after any number of other behaviors that the parent deems more desirable, for example, playing, talking, or running.

From the perspective that omission procedures ensure that the elicitation process follows R_o, these procedures are seen as special cases of the reinforcement and punishment paradigms in which it is the frequency of R_o that is directly affected by the contingency. An omission procedure may therefore be a reinforcement or a punishment paradigm with respect to R_o. In short, with respect to R_o, omission procedures are the already familiar procedures of stimulus presentation—reinforcement and punishment.

Since R_o must be incompatible with the occurrence of R in order for the elicitation process to be presented, the effect of the omission procedure on R_o may be indirectly measured by the frequency of R. The occurrence of R and R_o must necessarily be inversely related to one another, although it should be clear that the diversity of the various behaviors that comprise R_o must almost certainly be greater than those that comprise R. The child may gain candy in many ways but may lose it in only one—by crying.

When reinforcing elicitation processes are omitted upon the occurrence of R, the procedure is simply labelled an *omission procedure* if a discrete-trial method is used. In a free-responding situation, it is most often called a *differential-reinforcement-of-other-behavior*, or *DRO*, procedure (Zeiler, 1971; Zeiler, 1976).

As an illustration of a DRO procedure, bar-pressing in rats, which had been maintained by occasional presentations of sucrose in the first phase of the experiment, was placed on an omission procedure in which sucrose was presented following the nonoccurrence of bar-pressing of 20 sec (Uhl, 1973). Thus any behavior incompatible with bar-pressing constituted R_o. Under the DRO contingency, the frequency of bar-pressing declined even though the frequency of sucrose remained roughly constant. In addition to demonstrating the effects of a DRO procedure, these results indicate that the increase in bar-pressing when bar-pressing was followed by sucrose in the first phase of the experiment could not be attributed to any direct eliciting effect of sucrose on bar-pressing. It was not sucrose presentations per se, but the contingency between bar-pressing and sucrose that produced the original acquisition and maintenance of bar-pressing.

In summary, the omission procedure with appetitive elicitation processes leads to a decrease in the measured response, R. The decrease in R is most parsimoniously attributed to an increase in R_o due to the occurrence of a reinforcing elicitation process after R_o.

When punishing elicitation processes are omitted upon the occurrence of R, the procedure is commonly labeled an *escape procedure*.[2] Yelling at a child until his room is cleaned would illustrate an escape procedure. The aversive stimulus is applied until a specified response occurs and the stimulus is then omitted. The relationship between R_o and the elicitor now exemplifies the punishment paradigm. Since R_o and R are incompatible and since the organism is always behaving, the decrease in R_o produced by the escape procedure leads to an increase in R (Schoenfeld, 1969).

A typical laboratory method for the study of an omission procedure involving a punishing stimulus employs a runway in which the startbox and alley are electrified and the goalbox is made free of shock (Fowler & Trapold, 1962). Behaviors such as rearing up on the hind legs, squealing, biting the floor, and so on, are all followed by the continuous presentation of shock; only entry into the goalbox is followed by the omission of shock. Under these conditions, needless to say, the running behavior of the rat increases rapidly in speed.

Two behavioral outcomes of omission procedures involving aversive stimuli may be distinguished. If R occurs only during the presentation of the eliciting stimulus, then R is called an *escape response*. If, however, R occurs before the presentation of the eliciting stimulus—as is possible in some procedures that begin as escape procedures—then R is called an *avoidance response*. For example, suppose that the startbox door of a runway is raised 10 sec before the shock is turned on and, if the rat runs out of the startbox in less than 10 sec, the shock is not presented. Running from the startbox, since it occurs prior to the shock, would be called an avoidance rather than an escape response. The analysis of avoidance responses in omission procedures is postponed until the subsequent chapter on stimulus control.

The comprehensive description of R_o and its relation to R remains primarily a task for the future; only the beginnings of an adequate analysis have been made (for example, Dunham, 1971, 1978; Herrnstein, 1970; Laties, Weiss, & Weiss, 1969). However, one procedure has been specifically designed to study the interaction between different responses. In this procedure—the *choice procedure*—at least two behaviors are measured and the emission of both behaviors is studied as a function of the elicitation processes that follow each.

Choice Procedures: Multiple Instrumental Responses In moving from situations involving interactions between unmonitored other responses (R_o) and one monitored response to a choice procedure involving multiple monitored responses, it is crucial to recognize that the change is more striking for the experimenter than for the learner. Alternative responses, each with its own consequences, are available to the learner in every situation; the major difference is that the experimenter monitors more of the alternatives and manipulates more of the consequences in the choice procedure (concurrent schedule) (Herrnstein, 1970). Thus it is the experience of the experimenter more than that

of the learner that changes when we move to a choice procedure. For the behaving organism, as William James observed, ". . . the mind is at every stage a
theatre of simultaneous possibilities" (1890, p. 28). With the choice procedure,
we are afforded a glimpse of the drama in that theatre.

A typical choice procedure used in the laboratory involves an operant
chamber for pigeons containing two response disks. Key-pecking responses to
the left disk (R_L) are followed by food according to one rule; responses to the
right disk (R_R) according to a second rule. Technically, the rule that states the
conditions which must be met if a response is to produce a reinforcer is called
a *schedule of reinforcement* (Ferster & Skinner, 1957). In most choice procedures, the schedules of reinforcement associated with R_L and R_R are variable-
interval (VI) schedules. In a VI schedule, a variable interval of time must elapse
before an instrumental response is effective in producing the next reinforcer.
For example, with a VI 60-sec schedule, 60 sec elapses on the average before
the next reinforcer may occur. The intervals vary in size, although their average value is specified, with the result that a steady rate of responding is produced. Representative intervals that might appear in a VI 60-sec schedule are 5,
84, 33, 17, 168, and 53 sec (Fleshler & Hoffman, 1962). We have already encountered other reinforcement schedules, such as DRO, in our study of omission
procedures.

In the typical free-operant choice procedure, VI schedules having different average values are assigned to R_L and R_R. VI schedules are used since the
rates of responding may vary quite widely without appreciably affecting the
rate of reinforcement for the instrumental response. By examining the rates of
responding to the two alternatives, we may obtain a sensitive measure of the
effect of the reinforcers on choice behavior.

The findings from free-operant choice experiments may be summarized
by examining how the relative frequency (or time) of responding to one alternative varies as a function of the relative frequency of reinforcement for that
alternative. As shown in Fig. 4.8, the relationship is a simple one: The proportion of responses matches the proportion of reinforcers for that response. If
25% of the reinforcers follow R_L, 25% of the responses will occur to R_L; if 60% of
the reinforcers follow R_L, 60% of the responses will occur to R_L, and so on. This
simple relationship between relative responses and relative reinforcers is
called the *matching principle* (Herrnstein, 1970).

The matching principle has been found to describe the findings from a
wide variety of experiments, including those with human subjects (for example, Schroeder & Holland, 1969), and to be consistent with a relational principle
of reinforcement (Donahoe, 1977). Moreover, variations of characteristics of
the reinforcer other than its relative frequency may also be accommodated by
the matching principle—for example, relative magnitude (Keller & Gollub,
1977) and delay (Chung & Herrnstein, 1967) of reinforcement and comparable
characteristics of aversive stimuli (for example, de Villiers, P. A., 1974; de Villiers, P. A., 1977).

A central implication of the matching principle, and one which has considerable practical significance, is this: The relative frequency (or time) de-

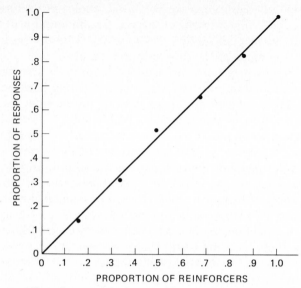

Fig. 4.8 The proportion of responses on one key as a function of the proportion of reinforcers for responses on that key. The key-pecking response of the pigeon in a two-key situation was used.   (From Herrnstein, 1961. Copyright 1961 by the Society for the Experimental Analysis of Behavior, Inc.)

voted to a given instrumental response may be changed either by varying the reinforcers for that response or by varying the reinforcers for other responses in the situation. In a choice experiment with pigeons, the frequency of responding on the left key may be increased by increasing the frequency of reinforcers for responding on the left key or by decreasing the frequency of reinforcers on the right key. In a classroom situation with young children, the teacher may increase the frequency of studying either by increasing the reinforcers for studying or by decreasing the reinforcers for other behaviors.

The implication of the matching principle, that we may change one behavior by varying the consequences of other behaviors, is especially significant for producing decreases in behavior. Although punishment procedures are often used to decrease the frequency of behavior, the matching principle tells us that the same purpose may be accomplished by increasing the reinforcers for other behaviors. Another way of expressing the content of the matching principle, and one which is in keeping with the relational interpretation of reinforcement, is that the effect of a reinforcer on behavior is not invariant—the effect depends on the total reinforcers available for all other alternative behaviors. A drowning man will clutch at a straw and beggars cannot be choosers because the alternatives that are available to them are so few and so lacking in value. Conversely, the behavior of "the man who has everything" can be changed only with great difficulty.

In the world outside the laboratory, of course, the alternatives available to the chooser differ in many respects simultaneously—in delay and magnitude of the reinforcer as well as in its frequency. For example, what would you do if you were invited to a party when you had planned to study for an important examination to be taken two days hence? Would the immediacy of the party outweigh the importance of the future examination? We may take little comfort in the finding that our fellow mammal, the rat, will select an immediate, small reinforcer in preference to a delayed, but larger reinforcer (Logan, 1965).

Acquisition

Terminal performance, following the institution of the contingency between responding and the reinforcer, has been the focus of the experimental and theoretical analysis of findings from the instrumental procedure. We have identified some of the variables that are important in producing change from the baseline to the terminal behavior, and have attempted to integrate the effects of these variables theoretically. A similar strategy—concentration on terminal performance—has been pursued in the analysis of the behavioral changes produced by the classical procedure. In both the instrumental and classical procedures, little attention has been given to the transitional behaviors that intervene between the baseline and terminal behaviors of the learner.

In this section, we remedy that omission as the focus shifts from the terminal behavior to the transitional behaviors themselves. The study of transitional behaviors is the study of the process of *acquisition*. In our study of acquisition, we shall introduce some of the procedures, such as shaping and chaining, that are employed to facilitate the transition from baseline to terminal behavior. We shall also examine more closely the full range of behaviors that are affected when a particular response is followed by a reinforcer—the issue of response classes, or operants. Finally, we shall consider various attempts to achieve a more precise description of acquisition—incremental and all-or-none models of the acquisition process.

Preliminary Considerations   The study of the process of behavioral change is a most demanding undertaking. When attention is restricted to baseline and terminal performance, a large number of observations may be made under relatively constant conditions. Thus a group of observations are obtained that are reliable at a minimum. When the objects of study are the transitional behaviors themselves, however, we are studying phenomena that are changing. For such a study, very reliable individual observations are necessary because one quick glance at the behavior may be all that is possible; the next time we look, the behavior may have changed. For this reason, some students of learning, chiefly those employing free-responding methods, have elected for the present to confine their study to periods of stable behavior, or steady-states. Other investigators, chiefly those using discrete-trial procedures, have also been concerned with an analysis of changing behavior, or transition-states. Clearly, there is an intimate relationship between the behaviors observed during the transition- and steady-states, and an adequate understanding of behavioral change will contain an integrated analysis of all stages of the learning process.

Acquisition functions obtained with some of the experimental procedures that we have examined are displayed in Fig. 4.9. Note that some depict the performance of individual subjects while others depict the average performance of a group, that some are from classical and others from instrumental procedures, and that some are conventional and one is a cumulative graph.

At the outset of our examination of acquisition, it is important to reemphasize that acquisition must begin from some baseline of entering behavior.

Fig. 4.9 Acquisition curves from a number of conditioning procedures. (*a*) Average curves from two groups of human learners in a classical procedure for conditioning the eyelid response at two different UCS intensities (air puff). (*b*) Individual cumulative records from a free-responding, instrumental procedures for food-reinforced bar-pressing in rats. (*c*) Average curves from groups of rats in a discrete-trial, instrumental procedure in an alleyway at three different magnitudes of reinforcement. (*a*: From Spence, Haggard, & Ross, 1958. Copyright 1958 by the American Psychological Association. Reprinted by permission. *b*: From Estes, 1959. *c*: After Kraeling, 1961. Copyright 1961 by the American Psychological Association. Reprinted by permission.)

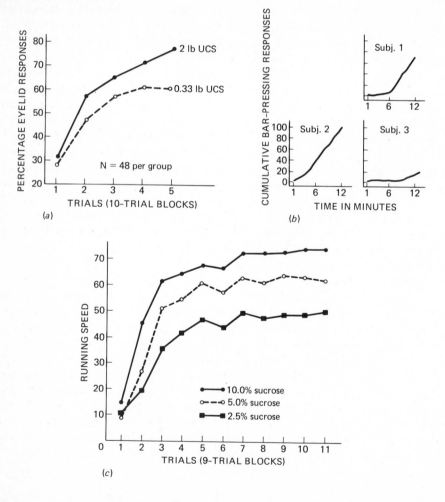

New experience never writes on a blank slate. With lower animals whose prior experience may be controlled, it is phylogeny which has contributed most of the preexisting writing. With experienced organisms, new experience must write upon a slate already crowded with the writings of both phylogeny and idiosyncratic individual experience. When prior experience has been held constant, the psychologist tends to speak of the experiment as a "learning" experiment. When prior experience has not been held constant or has been systematically varied, the psychologist explicitly acknowledges the contribution of factors other than those contained in the experiment, and speaks of a "transfer" experiment. In reality, all experiments dealing with behavioral change are to some extent transfer experiments—only the origins and our knowledge of the preexisting factors may vary, not the the existence of such factors.

The acquisition process has been most effectively studied using the classical procedure and—at the other extreme—using complex instrumental procedures with human subjects. This paradox arises because the study of acquisition requires the exhaustive monitoring of a well-specified response system if the entire process is to be observed. If behaviors other than those monitored are important constituents of the acquisition process, then vital links in the chain that extends from the baseline to the terminal behavior may be irretrievably lost. The classical procedure is well-suited to the study of acquisition because the response system of the eliciting stimulus is the locus of change in a well-controlled preparation. The instrumental procedure with human subjects is a tractable preparation when instructions are used to restrict performance to a small number of responses ("push button A or B," "say 'present' or 'absent,' " and so on).

Shaping   Instrumental procedures using lower animals as subjects have been less often employed in the study of acquisition. One of the primary reasons for this is that the standard methods used in instrumental procedures, such as runways and operant chambers, often require preliminary shaping of the criterion response. Specifically, in a runway the animal is often fed in the goal area and permitted to roam about the apparatus prior to the beginning of training. In the operant chamber, the animal is often first trained to eat from the food tray, and then behavior that successively approximates the terminal response is followed by food. For example, food might be given when the rat "looks at" the bar, then moves toward the bar, and then places a forepaw on the bar—all behaviors that do not include the terminal response but that make the terminal response more likely. The procedure of applying changing criteria that more closely approximate the terminal behavior is called *shaping*.

While shaping procedures may not be necessary in some instances, they do tend to produce greater uniformity in the topography of the response, and hence smaller differences in performance between subjects. An anecdote will illustrate the problems that may occur in the absence of shaping. A colleague of one of the authors regarded shaping as an unwarranted intrusion on the part of the experimenter into the "natural" learning process. Accordingly, after being trained to eat from the food tray, rats were simply placed in an operant chamber to learn "on their own." Shortly after one animal was put in the chamber, the research assistant noticed something unusual: The rat responded with an atypically long latency in the discrete-trial bar-pressing task and each response was preceded by an audible "thunk" that could be heard from outside the test chamber. Peering into the chamber, the assistant discovered the following: When the bar was inserted into the chamber, the animal leaped up, smashing its head on the ceiling—hence the "thunk"—and, as it fell down, its hind legs were extended, depressing the lever that caused the food to be delivered. Each occurrence of this demanding sequence—leap, smash, fall, extend leg—was followed by the reinforcer, and hence the sequence was maintained. The origin of this sequence of behaviors, most of whose constituents were superstitions, is unknown. Only bar-pressing was monitored. It is likely, however, that bar-pressing was an accidental accompaniment of the initial efforts of the rat to escape from the chamber. Since organisms detect coincidences, not causes, the entire sequence of activities was maintained by the subsequent reinforcer. In a genuine sense, the question is not whether to shape a response or to let it "freely" develop; the question is what shall do the shaping—the uncontrolled coincidences that may operate in any situation, or the more controlled contingencies instituted by the experimenter. Reinforcers exert their effects in either case.

Shaping is not a procedure whose importance resides simply in its utility as a training procedure for animals in operant chambers. Quite the contrary, much learning that occurs beyond the confines of the laboratory is, upon closer examination, the result of a shaping procedure. The goal of an English teacher who wishes others to read modern novels with understanding and pleasure is not attained by locking students in a barren room with a copy of Pynchon's *Gravity's Rainbow*. The parachute instructor does not push the novice from the plane with instructions to keep on jumping until he gets it right. In both these instances, the final goal is reached by a carefully planned sequence of behaviors that are successive approximations to the terminal behavior. The method of shaping by successive approximations, whereby the criterion for a reinforced response is gradually moved toward the desired terminal behavior, is one of the central techniques employed in programmed instruction (Skinner, 1954) and computer-assisted instruction (Atkinson & Wilson, 1969). The selection of optimal successive criteria remains an art guided by both the science of learning and those natural contingencies that shape all behavior—including the behavior of teaching.

Chaining   In addition to shaping, instrumental procedures—particularly those instituted outside of the laboratory—involve chaining. Rarely is a single response sufficient for reinforcement. Most often, a sequence of responses is required before the reinforcing stimulus is presented. A pigeon in an operant chamber must approach the disk on the wall, peck the disk, approach the food tray, and finally peck the grain before the food is actually ingested. A pigeon in the wild must engage in a still more complex sequence of responses involving such activities as flying, searching for food, and landing on a suitable surface while also keeping a sharp eye peeled for predators. A student in a classroom who is writing answers to questions based upon reading a textbook is engaged in a still longer sequence. The activities that must be executed before the instructor grades the paper are often demanding indeed!

In order for an instrumental sequence, or chain, of responses to develop, the components that are temporally closest to reinforcement are established first. More distant components are added later. Thus a pigeon is first trained to approach a feeder tray from which grain is available before being trained to peck the response key. The procedure of first reinforcing the final component of the chain and then progressively adding more remote components is called *backward chaining*. If circumstances permit the presentation of a reinforcer after each component during the acquisition of a behavioral chain, *forward chaining* may also be an effective method for producing sequences of behavior (Weiss, K. M. 1978).

Using backward chaining, successful demonstrations of rather long behavioral chains have been devised in the laboratory with lower animals. For example, a rat was trained to engage in a series of activities such as climbing a miniature staircase, scampering up a ladder, "playing" a toy piano, and crawling through a tunnel before finally pressing a bar that resulted in the presentation of food (Karen, 1974; Pierrel & Sherman, 1963). (See Fig. 4.10.) Even such heroic rodent performances, of course, pale in comparison with the elaborate and lengthy behavioral chains observed in highly experienced and structurally more complex organisms. The development of complex sequences of behavior

Fig. 4.10   A diagram of an apparatus used to demonstrate a 10-component response sequence in a rat. The components consisted of: (1) going through a doorway, (2) running up a spiral staircase, (3) going across a drawbridge, (4) climbing a ladder, (5) riding in a cart, (6) ascending a second stairway, (7) playing a toy piano, (8) crawling through a tunnel, (9) descending in an elevator to the floor, and (10) pressing a lever that resulted in the presentation of food. The sequence was established using the procedure of backward chaining.   (From Karen, 1974.)

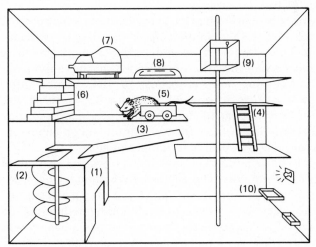

has received considerable experimental attention (see Adams, 1971; Bilodeau, 1966) and we shall study them further, particularly in connection with our inquiries into language and verbal behavior.

Response Classes The discussion of chaining should have made it clear that the notion that reinforcers affect only the probability of the immediately preceding response is a fiction. It is a convenient fiction because it has permitted us to describe the results of instrumental and classical procedures in a relatively simple and orderly manner. In reality, when an elicitation process is introduced into the stream of behavior, the ripples from that event may extend considerably beyond the place of its entrance.

What are some of the factors that determine the full range of behavior that is affected by the reinforcer? A number of matters are involved. First, the temporal proximity of the reinforcer to responses that precede the designated instrumental response is a factor. The discussion of chaining, and the earlier discussion of R_o in the delayed reinforcement paradigm, testify to the importance of the temporal variable.

Second, although reinforcers may be contingent upon only one property of a response, other simultaneously present properties of the response are affected as well. If the critical property is the depression of a response lever requiring a minimum static force of 20 gm, then all responses of greater force will produce food as well. Moreover, bar-pressing responses of a wide variety of topographies, or forms, will be followed by the reinforcer as long as all responses exert a force of more than 20 gm. Pressing with one paw, both paws, and the head will all be followed by food. Similarly, a verbal response to a question may be expressed in a wide variety of ways, any one of which may be followed by the approval of the questioner. The more restricted the definition of the properties of the criterion response, the smaller is the class of reinforced responses. By varying the range of activities that meet the criterion, the range of behaviors that are affected by the reinforcer may be determined (Logan, 1956; Skinner, 1938).[3]

Finally, factors operating prior to the learning situation make a very substantial contribution to the membership of the class of responses affected by reinforcement. These factors have their origins in both the ancestral environment of the species and the prior environment of the individual. The full contribution of phylogeny and ontogeny to the membership of response classes—to the "structure of behavior" (Catania, 1971a, 1973a, 1973b)—remains one of the crucially important, but insufficiently analyzed, problems for an adequate understanding of the effects of reinforcers on behavior. A few examples will indicate the dimensions of the problem.

One of the characteristics of most living organisms is their ability to move about in their environments. The means by which movement occurs may vary greatly, even for a single organism. Thus you may get from one place to another by a wide variety of ways—by walking, by swimming, or by driving a car, to name but a few. Suppose that you come upon a bakery with particularly delicious pastries while walking one day. It is likely that the behavior of walking to the bakery would be strengthened. But it is also likely that behaviors other than walking might also be affected by these events. Driving to the bakery in your car might also be strengthened, even though the behavior of driving had not occurred prior to eating pastries from that particular bakery. Thus the consequences of one behavior—walking—have also changed another behavior—driving. It is as if a response class of "movement behaviors" exists and when one member is affected, all members are similarly affected.

Experimental examples of such effects may be given. Rats that run a maze without error will then swim that same maze correctly on the first trial if the maze is later filled with water (MacFarlane, 1930). Running and swimming are different responses—although more similar than walking and driving a car, to be sure—and yet the consequences of one response have affected the probability of the other. Work of somewhat similar import has been conducted with visually-guided movements in monkeys. Unrestricted vision of forelimbs is necessary for the acquisition of visually-guided movement (Bauer & Held, 1975), but hand-eye coordination is sufficient for normal visual guidance of the movement of other parts of the body (Hein & Diamond, 1972). Thus visual observation of the consequences of arm movements also alters a class of functional relationships between the environment and bodily movement.

We shall examine transfer effects—including the effects of response similarity between earlier and later learning—in a subsequent chapter. Verbal responses will be examined primarily, since of all behaviors the structure of language has received the greatest study. Some research concerned with response classes has also been conducted with infrahuman organisms—particularly transfer effects between classical and instrumental procedures. As an illustration (Bower & Grusec, 1964), a classical procedure was first instituted in which food was presented to a pigeon following one stimulus (S_1) and was withheld following a second stimulus (S_2). Then in the instrumental procedure, the key-pecking response was reinforced with food during S_1 and was not reinforced during S_2. Positive transfer (a facilitative effect of the classical procedure on performance during the instrumental procedure) was found. The presence of common stimulus-reinforcer and response-reinforcer contingencies within the classical and instrumental procedures resulted in the control by S_1 of responses that were common to the two procedures. Thus, presumably, the response class of which key-pecking is a member includes some of the responses established by the classical procedure. (See Frieman & Goyette, 1973; Lawrence, 1950; Trapold & Overmeier, 1972, for related findings.)

While experimental evidence and casual observation are both consistent with the notion of response class, further analysis is required if its contribution is to be fully realized (Shick, 1971). It is one thing to assert that two responses are members of the same response class; it is quite another to establish the origins of their membership in that class. Unless class membership may be determined independently of the findings that the concept of response class seeks to explain, explanation is an illusion. Much additional work, especially conducted from a developmental perspective, remains to be done if the concept of response class, or operant, is to be rescued from such a fate. This task is a major item of unfinished business since reinforcers seem clearly to affect not only the specific responses that precede them but other related responses as well. "The unit of a predictive science is . . . not a response but a class of responses. The word 'operant' will be used to describe this class" (Skinner, 1953, p. 64; cf. Tolman, 1932, pp. 376–377).

Acquisition States   As we have seen, the acquisition of a response involves the transition from a baseline state to a terminal state of performance. For terminal states composed of complex sequences of responses, acquisition involves the reinforcement of responses that successively more closely approximate the desired terminal performance. The shaping procedure makes use of whatever knowledge is available concerning response classes and incorporates chaining procedures for longer sequences of responses.

For each task and organism, the transition states that intervene between the baseline and terminal states may be somewhat different, depending on the requirements of the task and the phylogenetic and ontogenetic history of the learner. Some tasks may require the accumulation of various component skills, others may involve the replacement of one set of elementary skills by more advanced skills, and most tasks probably involve transition states of both types (cf. Restle & Greeno, 1970).

Although the nature and number of transition states will vary from one learning situation to the next, it is useful to indicate something of the range of possibilities. At one extreme, performance may change in many small steps—or increments—as it progresses from the entering state to the terminal state (Hull, 1943; Thurstone, 1930). The conception of the acquisition process as involving an indefinitely large number of transition states is called the *incremental view* (Bush & Mosteller, 1955; Estes, 1950). As an example, we might imagine that the speed with which a rat traverses a runway begins at a low value and then gradually increases until some terminal value is reached. A hypothetical acquisition curve illustrating the incremental view is shown in Fig. 4.11a.

At the other extreme, performance might change from the entering to the terminal state in one abrupt step. The view that performance changes to its final level without occupying some intermediate, transition state is called the *all-or-none,* or *two-state view* (Estes, 1960). As an illustration, a simple conditioned response might go from the baseline to the terminal level in a single trial. For different learners, the "jump" in performance would occur after different numbers of trials, however. A hypothetical all-or-none acquisition curve for a single subject is shown in Fig. 4.11c.

Between the extremes represented by the incremental and all-or-none conceptions of the acquisition process lie other views in which the number of states is more than two, but less than an indefinitely large number (Restle, 1964). Such conceptions might be called *finite-state views.* Thus in a three-state process, performance would change successively from the baseline state, to the transition state, to the terminal state. A three-state model has, in fact, been

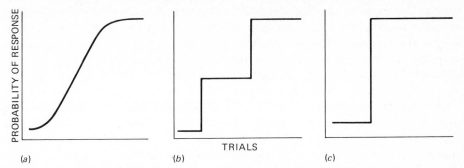

Fig. 4.11   Various representations of the transition states involved in the process of acquisition. (a) An incremental view, (b) a three-state view, and (c) a two-state (all-or-none) view.

found to provide a good description of the acquisition of the conditioned nictitating membrane response of the rabbit (Theios & Brelsford, 1966). Figure 4.11b illustrates an individual acquisition curve in a three-state model.

Regardless of the particular view of the acquisition process that best describes changes in performance in a given situation, several general points may be made. (See Atkinson, Bower, & Crothers, 1965 or Restle & Greeno, 1970 for more detailed surveys of various models of acquisition.) First, decisions among different conceptions of the acquisition process must be made on the basis of acquisition curves from individual learners. Consider, for instance, the distinction between the incremental and the all-or-none views. If the individual acquisition curves from various learners were averaged, the average curve would not distinguish between even these two very different conceptions of the acquisition process. The average of individuals, each of whom learned in an incremental fashion, would clearly be a gradually changing average curve. However, the average of individuals learning according to an all-or-none view would also be a gradually changing average curve since the abrupt change in individual performance would occur on different trials for different learners. We have encountered the insensitivity of average, or group, curves to underlying differences in behavioral processes in an earlier discussion of habituation (see pp. 52–54).

A second point regarding these various conceptions of the acquisition process is that it quickly becomes difficult to distinguish empirically a finite-state from an incremental model if the number of finite states increases beyond a few transition states—individual acquisition functions are not typically sufficiently reliable to permit the discrimination. Because the mathematics of finite-state views, that is, Markov chains, are more tractable than those of incremental views and because the description of characteristics of acquisition other than the average acquisition curve is generally superior, many modern analyses employ a finite-state approach.

Third, even after a particular conception of acquisition has been found to provide a good description of the process, an experimental analysis is necessary to determine the nature of the transition states. This point may be illustrated by comparing the acquisition of a conditioned nictitating membrane response in the rabbit with the acquisition of a simple verbal task in humans. Both learning tasks may be well-described by a three-state model of acquisition, but the behavioral processes represented by the various states are, of course, quite different. In the case of conditioning in the rabbit, the baseline state might be supplanted by a transition state in which the nictitating membrane response is sensitized by UCS presentations before the terminal state is reached, in which the CR is controlled by the CS. Thus the strength of responding might change from a low baseline value, to an intermediate value characteristic of sensitization, to a final high terminal value dependent on the CS-UCS relationship. As an example of a simple verbal task with humans, suppose that you are presented with a list of English words and are to learn to respond with the equivalent French words. The transition state might consist of learning the various French responses prior to the terminal state, in which the French words come under the control of the appropriate English words. The likelihood of responding correctly would therefore increase to an intermediate value, when you know the possible French responses, before rising to the terminal value when you know which French response goes with which English stimulus. Acquisition may be well-described by a three-state model in both situations, but the precise nature of the various states differs greatly and requires additional experimental analysis.

Other Transitions—Extinction In our discussion of transition states, we focused upon the process of acquisition—the changes that occur when a reinforcer is introduced and responding increases from the baseline to the terminal state. Other important transitions occur, however, as behavior changes in harmony with changing environmental conditions. For example, the schedule of reinforcement may be altered and responding changes accordingly (for example, Weiss, 1970). Such changes, as noted earlier, fall under the general heading of transfer effects.

Another important type of transition is that found in the process of *extinction*—the changes that occur when a formerly presented reinforcer is withheld and responding decreases from the terminal state to a new baseline state. Strictly speaking, extinction is a type of transfer effect in which the new schedule of reinforcement is one in which responding no longer has consequences that are determined by the experimenter. Thus key-pecking that formerly produced food may no longer do so, or conversing with another that formerly produced attentive listening may now be met with inattention. For both responses—key-pecking and conversing—the withdrawal of ·the reinforcer leads to a decline in responding.

Just as habituation occurs when a stimulus exhibiting unconditioned stimulus control is repeatedly presented without environmental consequences, so extinction occurs when a stimulus exhibiting conditioned stimulus control is repeatedly presented without consequences. The variables governing the process of extinction will be discussed in subsequent chapters dealing with stimulus control and motivation.

SOME COMPLEXITIES IN THE INSTRUMENTAL PROCEDURE

A theoretical analysis of the basic findings obtained with the instrumental procedure has led to the following conclusion: The stimuli occurring prior to the instrumental response acquire control over that response when it is followed by a discrepant elicitation process. Thus in a simplified preparation such as bar-pressing for food with the rat, the sight of the bar acquires control over the response of bar-pressing if the baseline level of responding is discrepant from the baseline level of eating. Only by means of the instrumental response of bar-pressing may the organism maintain the baseline level of eating.

While simplified preparations are essential to uncovering the principles governing learning in the instrumental procedure, the instrumental contingency may be realized in more complex preparations requiring a consideration of other principles. As we discovered with the classical procedure, understanding the complete behavioral changes produced by a procedure requires the recognition of factors other than those which define the procedure. In the classical procedure, events other than those involved in the contingency between the CS and the elicitation process influence the outcome of conditioning. Similarly, in the instrumental procedure, events other than those involved in the contingency between R and the elicitation process may also affect the final outcome of conditioning. Both classical and instrumental conditioning are procedures instituted by the experimenter, not exhaustive descriptions of the significant events affecting behavioral change.

In this section dealing with complexities encountered in the instrumental procedure, we shall consider two sources of additional factors. These sources are: (a) response interactions, particularly those between instrumental and elicited responses, and (b) stimulus interactions.

Response Interactions

The instrumental procedure is defined by the contingency between an instrumental response and an elicitation process. But as we have observed many times before, environmental stimuli are always present as well. To the extent that there is any constancy in the stimuli preceding the instrumental response, then to that extent does the instrumental procedure also contain an implicit contingency between environmental stimuli and the elicitation process. As an illustration, when bar-pressing is followed by food there exists not only a contingency between bar-pressing and the elicitation of eating but also a contingency between stimuli such as the sight and touch of the bar and the elicitation of eating. Thus, as with the classical procedure, the instrumental procedure contains both a response-reinforcer and a stimulus-reinforcer contingency.

What should be the effect of the implicit stimulus-reinforcer contingency on the outcome of the instrumental procedure? In seeking an answer to this question, it is well to remember the effect of stimulus-reinforcer contingencies in the classical procedure. In general, a stimulus preceding a discrepant elicitation process comes to control responses which, to a first approximation, resemble the responses elicited by the reinforcer. Applying this insight to the instrumental procedure, the stimuli preceding the instrumental response should acquire control over elicited responses. Thus the instrumental procedure leads to the environmental control of behavior having two origins—the response components of the elicitation process and the instrumental response that reliably precedes the elicitation process. Returning to the illustration of the rat bar-pressing for food, stimuli arising from the lever should acquire control over both salivation and bar-pressing.

When both origins of learned responses are acknowledged, the instrumental procedure is seen to differ from the classical procedure in that the former more precisely specifies the responses that precede the elicitor. The more precisely specified response is, of course, the instrumental response itself. The effect on the instrumental response of elicited responses, which are also controlled by the stimuli preceding the discrepant elicitation process, depends upon the compatibility of the two classes of responses. Both facilitating and interfering interactions may be anticipated between responses of these diverse origins.

Facilitating Interactions Facilitating interactions between instrumental and elicited responses are those in which the instrumental response benefits from the concomitant acquisition of responses elicited by the reinforcer. In the instance of bar-pressing for food, the instrumental response of bar-pressing and the elicited response of salivation interact little with one another (cf. Shapiro, 1960; Shapiro, 1962). However, biting, which is another response elicited by the sight of food, is sometimes observed to be the means by which the lever is operated.

By far the most extensive work on facilitative interactions has been conducted with the pigeon key-pecking for food. Since the instrumental response is pecking, and pecking is also a response elicited by the sight of food, considerable interactions may be anticipated. Indeed, research has shown that the classical procedure is sufficient to produce the stimulus control of pecking in the absence of any experimenter-imposed response-reinforcer contingency whatsoever. If a pigeon is simply given a number of trials in which the keylight is illuminated for a few seconds prior to the delivery of food, the pigeon will come to peck the key even if key-pecking is not necessary for the occurrence of food (Brown & Jenkins, 1968). This phenomenon—the acquisition of key-pecking in the absence of an explicit instrumental contingency between pecking and eating—is called *autoshaping*.

That the response elicited by the reinforcer is intimately involved in autoshaping is shown by the fact that the form of the key-pecking response varies with the nature of the reinforcer. When food is used as the reinforcer, the beak opens as the key is struck as if the pigeon were eating the key. When water is used, the throat of the pigeon pulsates as if drinking the key. If a female bird is presented after the illumination of the key, a male pigeon courts the key by bowing and cooing toward it (Jenkins & Moore, 1973; Moore, B. R., 1973). Thus the form of the instrumental response is clearly influenced by elicited responses and, in some instances, may be facilitated by them.

Many other examples of the facilitation of instrumental responses by elicited responses may be cited (see Shettleworth, 1975 for a particularly detailed study), including those employing aversive as well as appetitive elicitation processes (cf. Bolles, 1970). Moderate intensities of electric shock in the goalbox will actually facilitate running in the alleyway when the shock is applied only to the hindfeet, a point of application that elicits lurching forward. The same intensity of shock applied to the forefeet, a point of application that elicits lurching backward, interferes with running in the alleyway (Fowler & Miller, 1963).

Interfering Interactions   As the last observation indicates, elicited responses may also interfere with the instrumental response. Interfering interactions are especially pronounced in those instances in which the instrumental response and the responses elicited by the reinforcer or punisher are clearly antagonistic to one another. An everyday example that comes to mind is the parent who spanks the child in an effort to stop its crying. The instrumental behavior to be decreased—crying—is the very behavior elicited by the punisher! We should scarcely be surprised at the ineffectiveness of the procedure.

The key-pecking response of the pigeon with food as an elicitor may be used to illustrate interfering as well as facilitating response interactions if an omission procedure is employed. To be specific, suppose that the key-light is illuminated for a few seconds and that food is then delivered if key-pecking does not occur. If key-pecking does occur during the lighted key, food is omitted. An omission procedure of this type confronts the organism with a dilemma—responses other than key-pecking are required if food is to be presented, but pecking is the very response elicited by food. Clearly, the functional instrumental response (that class of responses other than key-pecking) and the elicited response (pecking) are incompatible.

What happens when the experimenter arranges conditions such as these which have never previously been encountered in the evolutionary history of the species? Under these perverse conditions, key-pecking is never completely eliminated; the pigeon continues to peck the key with an appreciable frequency even though such responses are never followed by food and, in fact, lead to the omission of food (Williams & Williams, 1969).

Other illustrations of interfering interactions between instrumental and elicited responses may be cited (for example, Breland & Breland, 1961), but only one more will be described here. This example is chosen because it also demonstrates that glandular as well as muscular responses may be acquired with an instrumental procedure.[4] The glandular response of concern is salivation in dogs, the response and species with which Pavlov carried out his original work with the classical procedure. An instrumental procedure was instituted in which water was introduced into the mouth of a water-deprived dog if a salivary response did not occur (Miller, N. E., & Carmona, 1967). Thus we again have an omission procedure in which responses other than salivation now serve as the instrumental response. Using water as the reinforcer, the dogs acquired "dry-mouth" responses.

The interference of the instrumental response of "dry-mouth" by responses elicited by the reinforcer is shown when the reinforcer is changed from water, which does not elicit salivation, to food, which does. Now with the instrumental contingency between the response of "dry-mouth" and the reinforcer of food, the dog is no longer able to keep its mouth dry (Sheffield, 1965). As was previously found with autoshaping of key-pecking in pigeons, an omission procedure using the salivary response of the dog with food as the reinforcer suppresses but does not eliminate salivation (Shapiro & Herendeen, 1975). Findings showing interfering interactions between the instrumental response and responses elicited by aversive stimuli have also been reported (for example, Azrin, 1970; Bolles, 1970). (For reviews of work on interactions between instrumental and elicited responses, see Hearst, 1975a, 1975b; Hearst & Jenkins, 1974; Jenkins, 1977; Wessells, 1974.)

Stimulus Interactions

Another source of complexity in the instrumental procedure is the potential interaction of the environmental stimuli that precede the instrumental response with the eliciting stimulus that functions as the reinforcer or punisher. We encountered a similar phenomenon in the classical procedure and labeled such interactions as instances of differential associability (see pp. 113–114).

The following experiment illustrates differential associability in an instrumental procedure and suggests one factor, the eliciting stimulus, that may contribute to the phenomenon. Different groups of pigeons were trained to press a pedal for either the presentation of grain or the omission of shock. Training occurred in the presence of a simultaneous light-tone compound stimulus. A test for the stimulus control of pedal-pressing was then conducted in which the light or the tone were presented separately and the elicitor was no longer presented. When grain presentation had been the elicitor, the light controlled pedal-pressing, whereas with shock as the elicitor, the tone controlled pedal-pressing (Foree & LoLordo, 1973; LoLordo & Furrow, 1976).

What was responsible for this demonstration of differential associability—the difference in procedure (presentation vs. omission) or the difference in reinforcer (grain vs. shock)? Subsequent work has shown that under a variety of procedures, the behavior of pigeons is more precisely controlled by the visual aspect of a compound stimulus as long as food occurs within the experiment (Foree & Lolordo, 1975). Thus, in this instance at least, differential associability is a function of the nature of the elicitation process.

A survey of recent findings, with both the classical and instrumental procedures, would uncover many instances in which response interactions and differential associability could be observed (for example, Bolles, 1970; Breland & Breland, 1966; Hinde & Stevenson-Hinde, 1973; Seligman, 1970; Seligman & Hager, 1972; Shettleworth, 1972). While the specific data contained in these reports represent important new contributions, the general proposition that behavior is affected by the environmental history of the species can hardly be regarded as a discovery in the post-Darwinian period. "Discoveries" such as this are possible only for those who have forgotten the past and, in so doing, have been forced to relive it. The psychology of learning was in dire need of a reminder concerning the contribution of phylogeny to the changes wrought by individual experience, but we have only been reminded of a truth that had been temporarily obscured by the excesses of early behaviorism.

What is needed is a thorough experimental analysis of the joint contributions of phylogeny and ontogeny to the ultimate behavioral expression of specific classical and instrumental procedures. From such an analysis will come, it is hoped, general principles describing stimulus, response, and reinforcer interactions. The available evidence is compatible with the notion that general laws of learning and genetics may be developed to aid us in the understanding of the behavior of all living organisms. While general principles of ontogeny and phylogeny may exist, neither set of principles is alone sufficient to cope with the complexity of the individual organism's behavior (cf. Gillan & Domjan, 1977; Lowe & Harzem, 1977; Revusky, 1971).

SUMMARY

In this chapter, we continued the search for a principle of reinforcement, but with the instrumental rather than the classical procedure. Once again, elicitation processes were used to bring about new functional relationships between the environment and behavior. Unlike the classical procedure, however, with the instrumental procedure the elicitation process is contingent on the occurrence of a response rather than a stimulus.

When elicitation processes are contingent on responses, they may increase the probability of those responses. Such elicitation processes are said to function as reinforcers (S^R). Under other circumstances, response-contingent elicitation processes may decrease the probability of responses that precede them. Such elicitation processes are called punishers (S^p). Whether acting as a reinforcer or a punisher in a given situation, elicitation processes are more effective when they are vigorous and when they follow soon after the instrumental response. When elicitation processes are delayed in their onset, other responses (R_o) occur in a more advantageous temporal relationship to the elicitation process and are more affected by the reinforcing or punishing function of the elicitor than is the instrumental response (R). As was found from our study of the classical procedure, we construct our theory of the environment—at least initially—from the moment-to-moment changes in the events that comprise our experience.

A relational principle of reinforcement emerges from the attempt to integrate the findings of an experimental analysis of the instrumental procedure. Although temporal contiguity between the instrumental response and the elicitation process is most often necessary for behavioral change, it is not sufficient. The blocking experiment has shown us that a discrepancy must exist between the behavior at the beginning of instrumental conditioning and the behavioral component of the elicitation process if learning is to occur. If the elicitation process is preferred to the instrumental response (a positive discrepancy), reinforcement occurs. If the elicitation process is less preferred than the instrumental response (a negative discrepancy), punishment occurs. Because the function of an elicitation process depends on its preference relation to the instrumental response, and is not an inherent property of the elicitation process, the functions of elicitors are both relative and reversible.

The acquisition process, whereby behavior changes from the baseline to the terminal state via various transition states, is difficult to study because, by its very nature, it involves a changing object of investigation. Various views of the process, ranging from an all-or-none to an incremental model of acquisition, were presented. Regardless of the conception of acquisition that describes the observed changes in behavior, an experimental analysis is required to specify the nature of the various behavioral states. By means of shaping procedures and the application of chaining techniques, complex and novel relationships between the environment and behavior may be developed.

Although by definition the instrumental procedure is directed toward the analysis of response-reinforcer relationships, these relationships must always be realized in some environment. With the classical procedure, the environment acquires control over behavior that—to a first approximation—consists of the response components of the elicitation process. However, responses that occur prior to the elicitation process may also be acquired and importantly influence the expression of the conditioned response. With the instrumental procedure, the environment acquires control over behavior that—to a first approximation—consists of the instrumental response that precedes the elicitation process. However, the response components of the elicitation process may also be acquired and importantly influence the expression of the instrumental response. Both response interactions between instrumental and elicited responses and stimulus interactions between discriminative and eliciting stimuli may affect the outcome of the conditioning procedure.

NOTES

1. Reprinted in the *Journal of Applied Behavior Analysis,* 1969, *2,* 247.
2. Another name sometimes given to the procedure whereby an aversive stimulus is omitted upon the occurrence of R is *negative reinforcement* (Skinner, 1953). The term, reinforcement, is employed because the monitored response is increased by the contingency. In this terminology, a stimulus whose presentation after R results in an increase in R is called a positive reinforcer; a stimulus whose omission after R results in an increase in R is called a negative reinforcer. This nomenclature has a number of ambiguities in usage (Michael, 1975) and will not be followed here.
3. For discussions that emphasize the contributions of intraexperimental factors to the membership of the response class, see especially the work of Skinner (1938; 1953; 1969), Shick (1971), and Hull (1934).
4. The question of whether glandular responses and other responses mediated by the autonomic nervous system, such as heart rate, may be acquired with instrumental procedures is an enduring problem in the psychology of learning (Konorski & Miller, 1937; Mowrer, 1947; Skinner, 1937; Skinner, 1938). Both statistical (Kimmel, 1975) and experimental (Miller, 1969) control procedures have been used in an effort to eliminate the effect of skeletal activity on the observed changes in autonomic activity. Although considerable positive evidence now exists, methodological difficulties continue to plague the research (cf. Miller & Dworkin, 1974; Miller, 1978) and some of the earlier more pronounced effects involving paralyzed rats (for example, Miller & DiCara, 1967) appear to occur only in selected cases.

5
Stimulus Control

INTRODUCTION

From our study of the classical and instrumental procedures, we have identified some of the conditions that foster changes in the environmental control of behavior, and have summarized that knowledge by a relational principle of reinforcement. In the present chapter, we proceed to an exploration of the origins and nature of the stimulus control that is produced by the reinforcement process.

Our primary goal remains the same—the understanding of how individual experience shapes human behavior. As was true of our search for a principle of reinforcement, we must seek many of the answers to fundamental questions about the origins and nature of stimulus control among those other species with whom we share the earth. Understanding the subtlety and richness of stimulus control in the adult human is our ultimate goal, but such complexity is the product of an equally subtle and rich legacy of ontogeny and phylogeny.

We assume that, were we able to trace the antecedents of adult human behavior, many of them would be resolvable into the conjunctions of environment, behavior, and reinforcer that constitute the origins of stimulus control in laboratory investigations. This assumption is admittedly an article of faith, not a statement of fact, but such beliefs underlie the continuity of explanation in science. Behavioral processes whose antecedents are not directly observed are assumed to operate in accord with principles found useful in the analysis of those behaviors whose antecedents are well understood.

The elicitation processes upon which behavioral changes are based always occur in the presence of some environment, whether that environment is explicitly specified as in classical procedures, or merely tacitly acknowledged as in the simplest instrumental procedures. Understanding the outcome of both procedures is impaired if we ignore the environment preceding the elicitation process. Similarly, the elicitation process always occurs after some behavior, whether that behavior is specified as in instrumental procedures, or merely acknowledged as in classical procedures. Understanding is hindered if we forget the behavior preceding the elicitation process. In short, behavioral change always involves a three-term contingency consisting of a stimulus, a response, and a reinforcer.

In many circumstances, the controlling stimulus is readily apparent, as in classical procedures and in those instrumental procedures in which the response-reinforcer contingency is operative only within a specified environment, for example, when leg movement is followed by food only if movement occurs during the sounding of a bell (Konorski & Miller, 1937). In other circumstances, the controlling stimulus is less clear, as in those experiments in which an adequate analysis compelled the consideration of other stimuli (S_o) in the treatment of findings with both classical and instrumental procedures.

Superstitious Stimulus Control

Because our interest in this chapter is stimulus control, many of the procedures that we shall consider contain an explicit environmental event whose properties are manipulated to determine if the behavior changes as the properties are varied. The development of stimulus control does not require, however, an explicit environmental event in whose presence the elicitation process reliably occurs. We have seen that an elicitation process may affect the strength of a response with which it is contiguous in the absence of a causal relationship between response and reinforcer. Similarly, a stimulus occurring prior to an elicitation process may gain control over behavior that occurs in its presence. Temporal contiguity, and not causation, leads to the environmental control of behavior. Not only may responses be "superstitiously" strengthened, but the environments that control responses may also acquire their controlling function from fortuitous coincidence.

Pavlov was aware of the possibility of fortuitous stimulus control arising within the classical procedure: ". . . it was observed in our earlier experiment (with the trace conditioning procedure) . . . that . . . other conditioned reflexes were very easily established to any chance stimuli which happened to coincide with the actual administration of the unconditioned stimulus. . . ." (Pavlov, 1927, p. 115). In the classical procedure, if the relationship of a stimulus to the elicitation process has only a chance basis, stimulus control eventually wanes as the elicitor will necessarily occur in the presence of other stimuli as well (Keller, Ayres, & Mahoney, 1977).

In the instrumental procedure, however, the situation is more complex. Once a response has occurred in the presence of a given stimulus and has been followed by a reinforcer, the response may become more probable in the presence of that stimulus. Then, to the extent that the response is controlled by the stimulus, the response will be less likely in the absence of that stimulus, and hence will be less likely to be reinforced in the presence of other stimuli. This state of affairs will perpetuate the superstitious control of responding by the stimulus in whose presence the response originally occurred. In short, it becomes a self-fulfilling prophecy that the response produces the reinforcer only in the presence of the stimulus. This effect is impossible within the classical procedure because of the independence of the response and the reinforcer.

Superstitious stimulus control of behavior within the instrumental procedure has been reported by Morse and Skinner (1957; see also Herrnstein, 1966). The key-pecking response of pigeons produced food on a variable-interval (VI) 30-sec schedule of reinforcement (that is, once every 30 sec, on the average, a response was followed by food). The response key was orange except for a brief 4-min period once each hour when the key was transilluminated with blue light *independently of the response or the reinforcer.* During the blue stimulus some pigeons came to peck slowly and others came to peck rapidly (see Fig. 5.1). Because there was, in reality, no causal relationship between the color of the key and the likelihood that a response would produce food, the rate during the blue stimulus varied both between animals and within the same animal over long time periods. By chance, for some subjects food had apparently occurred during the blue key-light, thereby leading to a high rate of responding during blue. Also by chance, for other subjects and at other times

Fig. 5.1   Stimulus control of key-pecking by the color on the key when the same variable-interval (VI) schedule was operating throughout the session. Although the rate of reinforcement was theoretically identical during the orange and blue key-lights, one pigeon decreased responding during blue (records A and B) whereas a second pigeon increased responding during blue (records C and D). The dashed lines mark the onset and the offset of the blue light.   (From Morse & Skinner, 1957. Copyright 1957. Reprinted by permission of the Board of Trustees, University of Illinois.)

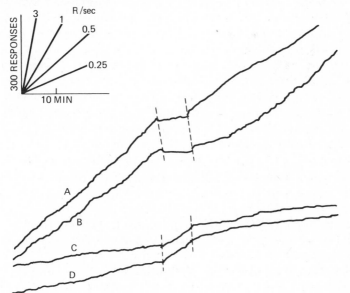

for the same subjects, food had not been encountered during the blue key-light and blue came to control a low rate of responding. Over the course of the experiment, all subjects displayed reliably different response rates during the blue and orange stimuli, even though the appearance of food was not causally related to the stimuli present when responding produced the reinforcer.

As with the effect of a reinforcer on responding, the environmental control of behavior develops out of the temporal relationship between environment, behavior, and reinforcer and not necessarily out of any causal relationship between these events. When we guide our decisions by horoscopes or judge others by the accent in their speech, might we not also be victims of superstitious stimulus control resulting from a fortuitous conjunction of environment, behavior, and reinforcer in our pasts?

Functional Definition of Stimuli

Almost every environmental event that we encounter as adult humans exerts some control over our behavior, has some meaning for us. An unidentifiable sight or sound is a rarity and we often express our consternation upon experiencing such an event by saying, "It was so strange I didn't know what to do!" Knowing "what to do" or "what to think" when an environmental event occurs is an indication that behavior is controlled by the event, that behavior is under stimulus control. If the control arises predominantly from individual experience, then the controlling stimulus is said to function as a *discriminative stimulus*. The term discriminative stimulus is most often used to denote stimulus control arising from the instrumental procedure, whereas the term conditioned stimulus (CS) denotes a stimulus of a similar function arising from the classical procedure.

It must be recognized from the outset that the influence which a stimulus has upon behavior is not an inherent property of that environmental event. To say that a stimulus controls a response is to indicate how that stimulus functions in a given situation and not some intrinsic property of the event. That same event may function in a number of different ways, only one of which may be to control behavior, and a different technical term is usually applied to indicate each of these functions. A similar practice is followed in everyday parlance. One object, a chair for example, may have many functions. It may serve as something to sit upon when we are tired, something to stand upon when we wish to replace a burned-out light bulb, something to prop against a door when we want to prevent others from entering a room, and so on. Thus the same physical object may function as a chair, a ladder, or a barricade depending on how it is used. Similarly, an environmental event that functions as a discriminative stimulus may serve other functions as well.

Consider the environmental event of electric shock. Electric shock presented for the first time to an organism evokes many responses—it is an eliciting stimulus and exemplifies unconditioned stimulus control. That same shock presented contingent upon another stimulus in a classical procedure is an unconditioned stimulus. When presented contingent upon a response in an instrumental procedure, the shock is a punishing stimulus. These are all functions that have previously been considered. Finally, as will be shown, the same shock may function as a discriminative stimulus and exemplify conditioned stimulus control.

The following experiment (Holz & Azrin, 1961) demonstrates the potential discriminative function of electric shock. Key-pecking in pigeons could occur in either of two successively presented environmental conditions. In one condition, key-pecking produced food according to a VI 2-min schedule of reinforcement and occurred at a moderate rate. In the second condition, key-pecking never produced food and occurred at a very low rate. The environmental event that distinguished these two conditions was electric shock: Shock was produced by responses that could also produce food and was absent when food was absent. As expected, shock functioned as a punisher in this experiment because key-pecking was reduced below the frequency maintained by a VI schedule of food presentation alone. However, shock also functioned as a discriminative stimulus since the rate of responding was higher when shock was presented than when it was absent. The discriminative function of shock is shown most clearly by a test phase in which food no longer occurred in either condition but the shock continued to be presented in one condition and not in the other. As shown in Fig. 5.2, key-pecking occurred frequently when shock was presented but slowly otherwise. By virtue of this special training procedure, responses occurred most when they were shocked and least when they were shock-free!

Were we to observe only the test phase of the preceding experiment, the

Fig. 5.2 Cumulative records of the key-pecking responses of two pigeons during a test phase in which responding had no experimental consequences (no shock) or in which responses produced electric shock (shock). Note that responding increased when it produced shock. See text for the training condition that produced this paradoxical result.   (From Holz & Azrin, 1961. Copyright 1961 by the Society for the Experimental Analysis of Behavior, Inc.)

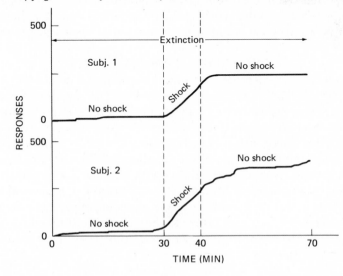

"masochistic" behavior of these pigeons would be a mystery. Knowing their conditioning histories, we recognize that shock has been the environmental context in which food has occurred, and that as a result behavior has come under the control of shock. How many of the seemingly inexplicable behaviors of ourselves and others could be understood if we but knew the stimulus conditions under which they were acquired?

Overview

Having noted the importance of temporal factors in the development of stimulus control and introduced the notion of discriminative stimulus, we may now proceed to the major content of the chapter. From previous work, it is known that stimuli which exert unconditioned stimulus control may function as reinforcers. Further, it is known from the phenomena of higher-order conditioning and conditioned reinforcement that stimuli which exert conditioned stimulus control may also serve as reinforcers. In the first major section, we inquire more deeply into the conditioned reinforcing function of stimuli, particularly regarding implications for the understanding of human behavior.

Following the treatment of conditioned reinforcement, we shall focus on two aspects of stimulus control—generalization and discrimination. Generalization is concerned with those factors that cause the effects of individual experience to transcend the boundaries of the specific events that comprise that experience. Individual experience is finite, but what are the limits of the *effects* of experience on the organism? Discrimination is concerned with those factors that circumscribe the effects of experience, that determine which of the many events within the environment are the ones that come to control responding. In a sense, generalization and discrimination are two sides of the same coin (cf. Brown, 1965) and we may anticipate that knowledge of both is essential to an analysis of stimulus control.

Finally, we shall move a step closer to our ultimate goal of understanding human behavior by considering the pioneering efforts of Ebbinghaus to study the events that control the learning and retention of verbal responses.

CONDITIONED REINFORCEMENT

With unconditioned reinforcers, an intimate relationship exists between the eliciting and reinforcing functions of stimuli. Effective elicitors of behavior are quite often effective reinforcers of behavior. If a principle of reinforcement derived from the study of unconditioned reinforcers is generally valid, then a similarly intimate relationship is to be expected between the discriminative and conditioned reinforcing functions of stimuli. Although conditioned reinforcement has been clearly demonstrated with humans (for example, Ferster & DeMyer, 1962; Staats, Finley, Minke, Wolfe, & Brooks, 1964), we shall pursue our expectation with lower animals whose relevant experience may be more completely controlled. We shall return to the role of conditioned reinforcement in human behavior at the end of this section, when generalized reinforcers and token economies are considered.

Elicitation and Conditioned Reinforcement

Stimuli that function as unconditioned reinforcers are most frequently potent elicitors of behavior. A hungry man will work for food, and food elicits a constellation of behaviors such as salivation. However, a hungry man will also work for money—a conditioned reinforcer. Although we sometimes make such remarks as, "I drooled when I saw all that money," we may ask whether conditioned reinforcers are also stimuli that control behavior.

We seek information regarding the relationship between the conditioned reinforcing and discriminative functions of stimuli from an experiment with the pigeon (Thomas, D. R., & Caronite, 1964). In this experiment, the wavelength on the key was first established as a discriminative stimulus. Then in a test period the wavelength on the key was varied, and changes in the discriminative and conditioned reinforcing functions of the various wavelengths were observed.

A 550-nm wavelength was established as a discriminative stimulus by presenting food on a variable-interval schedule for key-pecking. (The wavelength of the visible spectrum in humans ranges from 400 nm, for violet, through 550 nm, for greenish-yellow, to 700 nm, for red.) During testing when food was no longer presented, the discriminative function was evaluated by occasional response-independent presentations of a wavelength for 2 sec and recording the number of key-pecks during the wavelength. For other birds, the reinforcing function was evaluated by occasional response-dependent presentations of a wavelength for 2 sec and recording the number of key-pecks in the absence of the wavelength. The wavelength ranged from 510 to 590 nm and testing was conducted in blocks of presentations of the various wavelengths.

Fig. 5.3 Generalization gradients of the (a) conditioned reinforcing and (b) discriminative functions of various wavelengths following training in which key-pecking during a 550-nm stimulus produced food. Responding during each portion of the test session employed a different wavelength and is expressed as a percentage of the total responses during the entire test session.   (After Thomas & Caronite, 1964. Copyright 1964 by the American Psychological Association. Reprinted by permission.)

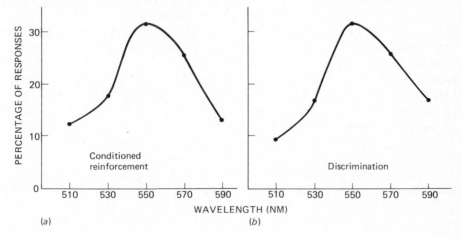

The covariation of the two functions of the test stimuli is shown in Fig. 5.3. The first aspect of the figure to note is that stimuli which were effective in maintaining responding to a darkened key were also responded to frequently. Thus effective conditioned reinforcers were also effective discriminative stimuli. Second, as the wavelength of the test stimulus was varied, both the conditioned reinforcing and discriminative functions of the stimuli varied together.

Curves, such as those contained in Fig. 5.3 that depict how responding changes as environmental stimuli are varied, are called *stimulus generalization gradients*. They are often used as measures of stimulus control. In these terms, the similarity of the stimulus generalization gradients of the conditioned reinforcing and discriminative functions of wavelength show the intimate relationship anticipated on the basis of earlier work with unconditioned reinforcers and elicitors. Other work also documents the covariation of the discriminative and conditioned reinforcing functions of stimuli (for example, Dinsmoor, 1950; Ellison & Konorski, 1964).[1]

Taken together, these findings are consistent with the view that the principle of reinforcement which emerged from the study of unconditioned reinforcers is equally valid for conditioned reinforcers. (For work of similar import with respect to the analysis of choice behavior, see Autor, 1969; Baum, 1974.) Conditioned reinforcers are also conditioned elicitors (discriminative stimuli) (for example, Denny, 1967; Hull, 1943; Keller & Schoenfeld, 1950; Skinner, 1938; Wyckoff, 1959).

Variables Affecting Conditioned Reinforcement

The phenomenon of conditioned reinforcement represents a bridge between our earlier concern with reinforcement and our present concern with conditioned stimulus control: Stimuli that have acquired control over behavior may function as reinforcers or punishers. Although the study of conditioned reinforcement must contend with a number of thorny methodological problems (see Bolles, 1967; Kelleher & Gollub, 1962; Mackintosh, 1974; Nevin, 1973), the validity of the phenomenon is now well-established.

Because the co-occurrence of a stimulus with a preexisting reinforcer is necessary for that stimulus to become a conditioned reinforcer, it should come as no surprise that the variables known to affect conditioning also affect the conditioned reinforcing function of stimuli, and in similar ways. Briefly, a stimulus becomes a more effective conditioned reinforcer as: (a) the number of pairings with the unconditioned reinforcer increases (for example, Bersch, 1951; Hall, 1951; Miles, R. C., 1956); (b) the interval prior to the presentation of the unconditioned reinforcer decreases (for example, Bersch, 1951; Jenkins, W. O., 1950; Stubbs, 1969); and (c) the magnitude of the unconditioned reinforcer with which it is paired increases (Butter & Thomas, 1958; D'Amato, 1955).

Although our illustrations have been confined to conditioned reinforcers, stimuli may also acquire the capacity to serve as conditioned punishers. Stimuli that precede unconditioned stimuli such as electric shock may later be used to decrease responses which produce them (for example, Mowrer & Aiken,

1954; Seligman, 1966). Once again, the variables that affect conditioning affect conditioned punishment similarly. (See Bolles, 1975; LoLordo, 1969; and Mowrer, 1960, for further discussions of conditioned reinforcing and punishing functions of stimuli.)

The development of conditioned reinforcing and punishing functions of stimuli through the nature of their prior temporal relationship with unconditioned reinforcers greatly extends the range of environmental events that are effective in producing changes in behavior. This is particularly true in organisms having the rich and varied legacy from ontogeny and phylogeny of humans. There can be little doubt that conditioned reinforcing and punishing stimuli must bear a heavy explanatory burden if the principle of reinforcement is to furnish important insights into the understanding of human behavior. The range of unconditioned reinforcers is often too narrow, the deprivation of unconditioned reinforcers is often too minimal, and the relation of unconditioned reinforcers to responding is often too delayed for human behavior in complex societies to be understood solely in terms of unconditioned reinforcement.

Conditioned Reinforcement and Human Behavior   Conditioned reinforcement, as it is demonstrated under the controlled conditions of the laboratory, is sometimes a fragile and evanescent phenomenon. For example, suppose that a rat has received food in a distinctively-colored goalbox at the end of a runway. Subsequently, the rat will select a goalbox of that color in preference to one of another color when food is no longer available in either goalbox, but only slightly more often than chance. In one such study, the color of a goalbox that had previously been paired with food was selected an average of only 8.3 out of 15 test trials—a statistically reliable but not powerful effect (Saltzman, 1949). Because of these and similar results with some laboratory methods, questions have been raised concerning whether the complex yet durable behavioral repertoires of humans may be sustained by conditioned reinforcers. However, there are a number of important differences between those laboratory methods that have yielded relatively feeble evidence of conditioned reinforcement and the circumstances that prevail in everyday human affairs.

The first difference, and one so obvious as to be easily overlooked, is that many laboratory demonstrations of conditioned reinforcement employ test procedures in which the unconditioned reinforcer no longer follows the conditioned reinforcer. In confirmation of this point, when the goalbox color in the preceding study continued to be paired with food outside of the preference test, the preference for that color increased by 40% (Saltzman, 1949). In daily life, conditioned reinforcers continue to be paired with unconditioned reinforcers. Money is not only banked; it is occasionally exchanged for such reinforcers as food. (For methods intended to minimize the weakening of conditioned reinforcers during testing, see discussions of chained reinforcement schedules, for example, Gollub, 1958, and second-order reinforcement schedules, for example, Kelleher, 1966; Nevin, 1973; Stubbs, 1971.)

A second difference between many laboratory demonstrations of conditioned reinforcement and the circumstances of daily living is that the conditioned reinforcer not only continues to be paired with unconditioned reinforcers, but the pairing is also intermittent. That is, outside of the laboratory, some presentations of the conditioned reinforcer are followed by an unconditioned reinforcer and some are not. For example, the attention of the parent to the child is sometimes followed by unconditioned reinforcers (food, caresses, and so on) and sometimes is not. For reasons that we shall uncover in the subsequent chapter on motivation, *intermittent reinforcement* (also called *partial reinforcement*) is an extremely effective procedure for increasing the persistence of learned behavior.

Using intermittent presentations of unconditioned reinforcers, conditioned reinforcers may be made more potent and longer-lasting (for example, Klein, R. M., 1959; Zimmerman, 1959). Thus parental attention, because it is intermittently followed by unconditioned reinforcers, should function as a durable conditioned reinforcer—or, in the case of some less fortunate children, as an equally durable conditioned punisher.

A final characteristic of the conditioned reinforcers encountered in daily living is that they are often paired with a wide variety of unconditioned reinforcers, not with only one type as in most laboratory demonstrations. The sight of the parent has preceded many reinforcing events of both unconditioned and conditioned origins—food, drink, warmth, caresses, playing, singing—a seemingly endless list of reinforcers.

Although more well-controlled research is needed, there is indirect evidence from the laboratory relevant to the contribution of multiple unconditioned reinforcers to the development of conditioned reinforcement. If the conditioned reinforcing function of a stimulus is related to its discriminative function, the more responses controlled by the stimulus the greater the potential reinforcing effect of that stimulus. Consistent with this expectation, studies have found that varied acquisition conditions (which presumably result in more varied behaviors controlled by the training stimuli) produce greater persistence of responding (Long, McNamara, & Gardner, 1965; McNamara & Wike, 1958). Research also indicates that a stimulus established as a conditioned reinforcer by pairing it with one unconditioned reinforcer (for example, water for an animal deprived of water) may function as a reinforcer under somewhat different deprivation conditions (for example, food deprivation) or under altered levels of deprivation (for example, less water deprivation) (Estes, 1949; Miles, R. C., 1956; Seward & Levy, 1953).

To the extent that varied acquisition conditions increase the durability of conditioned reinforcers and that conditioned reinforcers are effective beyond the specific acquisition conditions, to that extent will conditioned reinforcers play a substantial role in the analysis of everyday behavior beyond the confines of the laboratory (McClelland & McGowan, 1953). Stimuli such as parental attention that function as conditioned reinforcers in a wide range of environments are known as *generalized conditioned reinforcers* (Skinner, 1953).

Among the more effective generalized conditioned reinforcers in human society is money. Money in many different environments is temporally associated with many different unconditioned and conditioned reinforcers and symbolizes, or is a token of, a wide variety of other reinforcers.

The acquisition of a conditioned reinforcing function by tokens has been studied under laboratory conditions. In one type of experiment (Cowles, 1937; Wolfe, 1936), chimpanzees received food after inserting a poker chip token into a vending machine, thereby pairing the token with an unconditioned reinforcer. Other responses in a variety of learning situations were subsequently acquired and maintained by tokens alone as long as the tokens could occasionally be exchanged for food, even though the exchange might be delayed. In view of the postulated relationship between the eliciting and conditioned reinforcing functions of stimuli, it is interesting to note the behavior that was controlled by the tokens: "Often, they [the chimpanzees] held several poker chips in their mouths and rattled these against their teeth by vigorous head movements. All this activity was accompanied by high rates of responding as well as the screaming and barking which usually occurred during daily feedings in the home cages" (Kelleher, 1958, p. 288). Tokens that function as conditioned reinforcers also function as discriminative stimuli.

Token reinforcement procedures have been extensively used in applications of reinforcement principles to human behavior. Consider the following example of an effort to improve the social behavior of schizophrenic patients on a back ward in a mental hospital (Ayllon & Haughton, 1962). Most of the patients had been in the hospital for over 15 years and some had to be hand-fed by the attendants. A shaping procedure that ultimately employed token reinforcers was begun. At mealtime, the door to the dining room was opened but patients were no longer led to the room or helped to eat. Within a few days, all patients—including those who had required individual attention for years—entered the dining room during the 20-min period that the door was open. Once in the dining room, all patients ate without assistance. Apparently, the previous attention of the attendants inadvertently served as a reinforcer to maintain the "helpless" behavior of the patients.

Once the opening of the door was established as a discriminative stimulus for the response of entering the dining room, the second phase began. In this phase, entering the room was possible only when a token was placed in a collection box located at the door to the dining room. In order to encourage social interaction between patients, a token could be obtained only by a simple co-operative response. Specifically, tokens were obtained when two buttons were simultaneously pressed. Since the buttons were 7 ft apart, two patients had to work co-operatively. This rudimentary social response was acquired by all patients and related verbal responses were observed as well, even from patients who previously had spoken rarely. As an illustration, one patient directed another to the buttons saying, "Come on, lady, push the button; it takes two." In a second example, another patient commented, "I'll help her if she will help me sometime."

The foregoing application of token reinforcers illustrates only the first few steps of the chaining process culminating in the acquisition of a normal repertoire of social behavior. Much more complex procedures using tokens in institutional environments have been implemented in recent years. These procedures are known as token economies and they represent a major application of reinforcement principles to the remediation of behavioral dysfunctions (for example, Ayllon & Azrin, 1968; Kazdin, 1975). Such an application is an art grounded in the principle of reinforcement but supplemented by additional knowledge and a sensitivity to the ethical issues that always arise when we seek to change human behavior.[2]

Although more might be said about conditioned reinforcement (Gollub, 1977; Hendry, 1969; Kelleher & Gollub, 1962; Nevin, 1973; Wike, 1966), it is time to examine stimulus control for its own sake. We have seen that there is an intimate relationship between discriminative stimuli and conditioned reinforcers which parallels that between eliciting stimuli and reinforcers. However, the controlling, or discriminative, function of stimuli is important independent of its relationship to reinforcement, and we now proceed to study that function more closely.

STIMULUS GENERALIZATION

Viewed most broadly, conditioned—or discriminative—stimulus control includes the full range of functional relationships between the environment and behavior which have arisen from individual experience. As your car approaches an intersection the traffic light turns red and you step on the brake pedal. Someone asks you for the time and you glance at your watch and reply. You read a passage in a novel and are reminded of a similar event in your own life. You answer the phone and recognize the voice of a friend with whom you have not spoken in years. All of these are examples of conditioned stimulus control. In each case, the occurrence of some public or private behavior has been affected by an antecedent event from your individual experience. Indeed, much of what makes you a unique individual are the specific functional relationships between the environment and behavior that are the legacy of your personal history.

An understanding of the origins and nature of stimulus control is basic to an understanding of human behavior. In the analysis of conditioned stimulus control that follows, we shall focus on the general principles that illuminate a broad spectrum of such environmental-behavioral relationships. To aid us in our search for general principles of stimulus control, we shall study the behavior of both human and infrahuman organisms and shall employ both classical and instrumental procedures. Two aspects of stimulus control will be of greatest concern: (a) *stimulus generalization,* the study of how the stimulus control established in one environment is altered when the environment changes, and (b) *stimulus discrimination,* the study of the conditions that promote precise stimulus control.

Origins of Stimulus Generalization

We have found that stimulus control of behavior develops as a result of events occurring within the classical and instrumental procedures. In these procedures, stimulus control may be assessed by comparing the strength of the response in the presence and absence of the putative discriminative stimulus. For example, if bar-pressing by a rat produces food in the presence of a 1,000-

Hz tone, stimulus control by tone can be demonstrated by a greater frequency of bar-pressing when the tone is sounded than when it is silent. Note that in this method of measuring stimulus control, the stimulus used in testing for stimulus control is the same as that used in training.

In most of the studies that follow, however, stimulus control is evaluated by a more elaborate method. Following training, the learner is confronted with stimuli other than those present during training, and the strength of responding controlled by these stimuli is measured. A rat that had previously bar-pressed for food in the presence of a 1,000-Hz tone might be tested with tones varying between 800 and 1,200 Hz, for example. The strength of responding as a function of changes in the stimulus dimension of auditory frequency would ordinarily be represented by a generalization gradient (see Fig. 5.3). This more stringent measure of stimulus control, whereby responding varies systematically as a function of changes in a stimulus dimension, is called *dimensional stimulus control* (Hearst, Besley, & Farthing, 1970). In this latter method, we explicitly measure the extent to which experience in one environment affects behavior in other similar environments.

What are the origins of dimensional stimulus control? As with all environmental-behavioral relationships, we may be certain that both the past of the species and the past of the individual contribute to present performance. In the remainder of this section, we shall illustrate the joint contribution of phylogeny and ontogeny to stimulus control by reference to a common laboratory preparation—key-pecking in pigeons. We shall discover clear evidence of the phylogenetic legacy as well as the pervasive, and often subtle, effects of ontogenetic influences. Finally, an effort will be made to interpret these ontogenetic influences in the light of a relational principle of reinforcement.

Phylogenetic Origins   Although there were some early doubts about the reality of dimensional stimulus control (for example, Loucks, 1933; Razran, 1949), these doubts gave way to experimental evidence and were replaced by debates concerning the relative contribution of ontogeny and phylogeny to stimulus generalization (for example, Hull, 1943; Lashley & Wade, 1946). Let us examine one situation, the stimulus control of key-pecking in pigeons, as a means of presenting some of the issues involved.

As our training procedure, we shall employ an operant chamber for a pigeon. The stimulus is provided by a key that is transilluminated by light whose wavelength may be varied by the experimenter. The response is key-pecking that is maintained by a VI schedule (see p. 167) of food reinforcement (Guttman & Kalish, 1956). During training, the key is transilluminated by a single wavelength, for example, 550 nm. During testing for dimensional stimulus control, food is typically no longer presented and the wavelength transilluminating the key varies randomly from 490 to 610 nm in stimulus periods of 1-min duration. The frequency of responding during each of the test stimuli is plotted as a function of wavelength, yielding a stimulus generalization gradient along the wavelength dimension.

Is the acquisition and maintenance of key-pecking in the presence of only a single wavelength sufficient to produce dimensional stimulus control? The

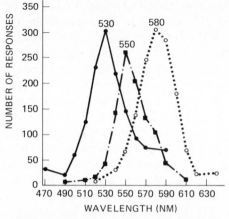

Fig. 5.4 Stimulus generalization gradients along the wavelength dimension obtained after a nondifferential training procedure. Each gradient was produced by an independent group of pigeons in which key-pecking had produced food on a VI schedule during a 530-, 550-, and 580-nm training stimulus respectively.   (After Guttman & Kalish, 1956. Copyright 1956 by the American Psychological Association. Reprinted by permission.)

answer is given in Fig. 5.4, in which average generalization gradients are presented for groups of birds each of which was trained with only one wavelength. Dimensional stimulus control is shown by the presence of generalization gradients that display maximal responding in the vicinity of the training wavelength and that decrease systematically as the test stimuli depart from the training environment. The absence of dimensional stimulus control would have been shown by flat generalization gradients, indicating that the frequency of key-pecking was the same for all test wavelengths.

Because no experience with different wavelengths was necessary, the results point to an important contribution of phylogeny to dimensional stimulus control by wavelength in the pigeon. Other work supports this conclusion. Even if the wavelength of light to which pigeons are exposed is restricted prior to the experiment, training with only a single wavelength is capable of producing dimensional stimulus control (for example, Oppenheim, 1968; Tracy, 1970). Thus preexperimental experience with other stimulus values is also not required. Moreover, still further research indicates that avian species have innate preferences for certain wavelengths, those that we label green and greenish-yellow (for example, Hess, 1956; Terrace, 1975). These colors correspond to the wavelengths reflected by the foods upon which these species customarily feed. Natural selection has been given the extended time and the constant conditions required for its contribution to dimensional stimulus control by wavelength in birds.

Ontogenetic Origins   While phylogeny undoubtedly makes an important contribution to stimulus control by wavelength in the pigeon, it would be a mistake to conclude that individual experience is irrelevant to the generaliza-

tion of responding. Even with visual stimuli in pigeons, both implicit and explicit characteristics of the training procedure may influence stimulus control.

An illustrative implicit characteristic of the usual training procedure is
that the stimulus is localized on the key. Because the training stimulus is not
present elsewhere in the operant chamber, pecks directed to locations other

Fig. 5.5   Stimulus generalization gradients along an auditory frequency dimension following
(a) nondifferential and (b) differential training with a 1,000-Hz stimulus. Each gradient was obtained from a different subject.   (From Jenkins & Harrison, 1960. Copyright 1960 by the
American Psychological Association. Reprinted by permission.)

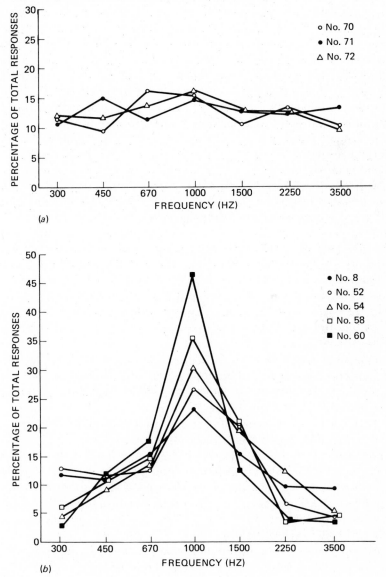

than the key do not contact the training stimulus and are not followed by food. Thus, implicitly, differential experience may occur with stimuli and with the consequences of responding to those stimuli. In confirmation of the possible role of this unintended source of differential experience, when the size of the training stimulus increases—thereby decreasing the possibility of pecking somewhere other than the training stimulus—the stimulus generalization gradient becomes flatter (Heinemann & Rudolph, 1963). Flat generalization gradients that are not sharply peaked in the vicinity of the training stimulus are indicative of poor dimensional stimulus control.

Still more compelling evidence for the contribution of ontogeny may be secured by substituting a pervasive auditory stimulus for a localized visual stimulus (Jenkins, H. M. & Harrison, 1960). Training consisted of pecking a white key for food in the presence of a 1,000-Hz tone, and testing consisted of the presentation of various tones between 300 and 3,500 Hz. As with the wavelength dimension, responding during testing did not produce food but pecking persisted for a considerable time because of the VI schedule used in training.

As shown in Fig. 5.5a, training with only a single value of the tone (that is, 1,000 Hz) did not produce dimensional control by the auditory stimulus—the gradients for individual animals were essentially flat. Thus, with a nonlocalized auditory training stimulus, very different results were obtained than with a localized visual stimulus.

Key-pecking in pigeons is, however, capable of dimensional control by auditory stimuli. In a second training condition with different subjects, periods with a 1,000-Hz tone alternated with periods in which the tone was absent. Responding during the tone produced food on a VI schedule as before, but no food was given for key-pecking in the absence of the tone (Jenkins & Harrison, 1960). During a generalization test conducted following this new training procedure, dimensional stimulus control was obtained (see Fig. 5.5b). After having been exposed to two stimuli during training and having received food differentially in these two stimuli, the generalization gradients peaked at 1,000 Hz and decreased sharply when other auditory stimuli were presented.

Theoretical Analysis   In this section, we shall try to understand how training with both the 1,000-Hz tone and its absence would facilitate the development of dimensional stimulus control. Our efforts will draw upon the earlier theoretical analysis of reinforcement.

Let us begin by describing more precisely the various stimuli present during training. The experimental environment during training consisted of two sources of stimulation, those stimuli unique to the 1,000-Hz tone—symbolized as S_1—and those other background stimuli in the situation—symbolized as S_0. For the learners exposed to only the 1,000-Hz tone during training, the stimulus present when responding produced a reinforcer was the compound stimulus $(S_1 + S_0)$. Since both S_1 and S_0 were present, both stimuli should acquire control over responding.

For the learners given differential training, the compound stimulus $(S_1 + S_0)$ was present when responding produced a reinforcer, but only S_0 was present when responding was ineffective. From the perspective of a relational principle of reinforcement, S_o should begin to acquire control over responding, but this control should decline with continued differential training. When the tone is absent, responding should occur at first because responding had previously produced a reinforcer when S_o was presented together with S_1. As training progresses and responding during S_o alone never produces a reinforcer, control by S_o should decline. Technically, a negative discrepancy (or inhibition) occurs, since the learned strength of responding during S_o exceeds the strength of the elicitation process during S_o. As control by S_1 increases and by S_o weakens, S_1 should progressively block control by other stimuli present during the $S_1 S_o$ compound stimulus. Thus at the end of differential training, responding is controlled by the stimuli comprising the 1,000-Hz tone—that is, by S_1—and not by S_o.

Now let us consider the implications of this difference in the source of controlling stimuli for the generalization test when other tones are presented. The auditory stimuli used in testing will be symbolized S_T and it will be assumed that the features or elements of S_1 become less numerous as S_T varies from S_1. In keeping with the earlier discussion of background stimuli, the test stimuli are compound stimuli consisting of $S_T + S_o$. In the training condition, in which only the 1,000-Hz tone is presented and in which S_1 and S_o both control responding, the compound test stimuli ($S_T + S_o$) should control appreciable responding since both components individually control responding: S_T controls responding to the extent that S_T and S_1 have stimulus elements in common, and S_o also controls responding. In the differential training condition, the compound ($S_T + S_o$) should control less responding: S_T exerts control to the extent that S_T and S_1 have common stimulus elements, but S_o does not control responding. In summary, the analysis indicates that generalization gradients obtained after training with only one stimulus should be flatter than gradients obtained after training with the presence and absence of a stimulus. (See Rescorla & Wagner, 1972; Wagner & Rescorla, 1972, for the original analysis of this problem.[3])

We may summarize our inquiry into the origins of stimulus control as follows: Both phylogenetic and ontogenetic factors contribute to all instances of stimulus control, with the ontogenetic contribution sometimes exerted in subtle ways through implicit characteristics of the training procedure. Although differential training with two stimulus values may not always be essential for the development of dimensional stimulus control, such training invariably facilitates the precision of stimulus control by reducing the control of responding that would otherwise be exerted by background stimuli (S_o).

The Nature of Stimulus Generalization

Through the joint action of phylogeny and ontogeny, stimuli present during conditioning acquire control over responding, and this control may extend to other stimuli on the same dimension as the training stimulus. The generalization of stimulus control, as measured by the generalization gradient, indicates that the effects of experience transcend the boundaries of the three-term contingency present during original learning and influence behavior in other environments. In a sense, the organism is capable of induction—a great economy in the construction of a theory of its environment.

Although stimulus generalization undeniably occurs, we have yet to discuss the behavioral processes that produce generalization gradients. We now examine the phenomenon of generalization more intensively and inquire into the behavioral processes that underlie it.

Convex Gradients   The generalization gradients that we have thus far examined have been *convex* in shape—that is, the frequency of responding was lower at either end of the gradient and rose to a maximum in the vicinity of the training stimulus in whose presence the reinforcer occurred. A gradient of this shape is often designated an *excitatory gradient,* although we prefer the theoretically more neutral label of convex gradient. To label a convexly shaped gradient as excitatory implies a direct relationship between the average frequency of responding and the strength of the behavioral processes giving rise to that average, an implication that we shall find to be false.

Concave Gradients   Stimulus control may also be demonstrated following situations in which the monitored response occurs at a low frequency during the training stimulus. Generalization tests following such training result in higher frequencies of responding at either end of the gradient and a minimum frequency in the vicinity of the training stimulus. A gradient of this shape is sometimes called an *inhibitory gradient,* but we prefer the more neutral term *concave gradient.* The use of the term inhibition implies that the behavioral process is weakest at the value of the training stimulus, and once again the term is misleading in this respect.

A training procedure in which extinction is correlated with one of the stimuli will be used to illustrate a concave gradient of stimulus generalization (Honig, Boneau, Burstein, & Pennypacker, 1963; see Pavlov, 1927; Bass & Hull, 1934, for earlier work). Once again, key-pecking in the pigeon serves as the experimental preparation. S_1 was a vertical black line on an otherwise white key. Key-pecking during S_1 did not produce food; that is, extinction was scheduled. S_0 was a blank white key during which key-pecking produced food on a VI 1-min schedule. The training procedure may therefore be expected to produce a low rate of responding during S_1 and a high rate of responding during S_0—the reverse of findings obtained with earlier training procedures. The stimulus generalization gradient was obtained during a testing procedure in which pecking no longer produced food and the orientation of the black line varied from horizontal through vertical.

As shown in Fig. 5.6, the stimulus generalization gradient was lowest at the line orientation present during S_1 and increased as the orientation departed from the value previously associated with extinction. Similar results have been obtained by others (for example, Jenkins, H. M. & Harrison, 1962). For a second group of pigeons, which received the line orientation associated with the VI schedule and the blank white key associated with the extinction schedule, a

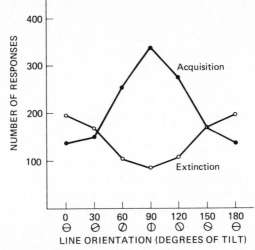

Fig. 5.6 Stimulus generalization gradients of acquisition and extinction effects obtained along a dimension of line orientation.   (After Honig, Boneau, Burstein, & Pennypacker, 1963. Copyright 1963 by the American Psychological Association. Reprinted by permission.)

convex stimulus generalization gradient was obtained as in previous work (see Fig. 5.6).

Because the organism is always behaving, whether or not the experimenter happens to be monitoring that behavior, the presence of concave generalization gradients after extinction training signifies that other responses (R_os) were, in fact, increasing as the test stimuli approximated S_1. The finding that the frequency of the monitored response decreased as the test stimuli became more similar to S_1 must reflect a corresponding increase in the frequency of R_o. The measurement of R_os during generalization testing is required before an adequate experimental analysis may be completed.

Other Responses During Generalization   The next experiment illustrates one means by which the R_os that intervene between occurrences of the monitored response may be measured. This method will prove useful in understanding the behavioral process that underlies the generalization gradient based upon the average frequency of the monitored response.

In this experiment, low frequencies of responding came under the control of the training stimulus, not through the use of an extinction schedule but through the use of a DRL schedule. With a DRL (differential reinforcement of low rate) schedule, the monitored response is reinforced only when at least *t* sec have elapsed since the preceding response. In this specific experiment (Gray, 1976), key-pecking in pigeons produced food on a DRL 8-sec schedule during a training stimulus having a wavelength of 570 nm. That is, at least 8 sec had to elapse between successive key-pecks in order for the second key-peck to produce food.

Following training, a generalization test was conducted in which 12 wavelengths ranging between 560 and 582 nm were presented in a number of random orders. The generalization gradient from one subject in this experiment is presented in Fig. 5.7a. Note that the gradient, obtained by averaging responses over the various test periods for a given wavelength, is relatively flat. Responding is lowest at the ends of the gradient, rises somewhat as the wavelengths approach the training stimulus, and then falls in the near vicinity of the training stimulus. The average gradient of the monitored response has some of the characteristics of a convex gradient and some of a concave gradient.

Let us attempt to understand the behavioral processes that yielded the average gradient. Although behaviors other than key-pecking were not directly measured, it is a necessary property of all responses that they require time for their execution. From this property, it is possible to devise a measure of performance that will permit us to describe the R_os. This measure is the interresponse time, or IRT, between successive occurrences of the monitored response (here, key-pecking) (Anger, 1956). Some R_os take relatively little time to execute (for example, looking away from the key between pecks); other R_os take a longer time to execute (for example, turning around in the chamber between pecks). The first R_o would produce a short IRT, the second a long IRT.

Fig. 5.7 Generalization gradient along a wavelength dimension obtained after training with a DRL reinforcement schedule. (a) Gradient based upon all responses. (b) Separate gradients for responses separated by the interresponse times (IRTs) indicated in the figure. (After Gray, 1976. Copyright 1976 by the Society for the Experimental Analysis of Behavior, Inc.)

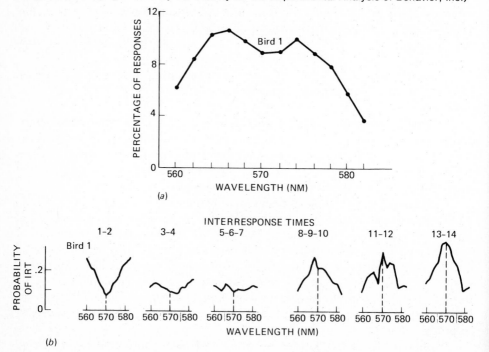

The generalization gradients, obtained when IRTs of different lengths were tabulated separately, are shown in Fig. 5.7b. When R_os taking from 1–2 sec were plotted, a concave gradient was obtained around the training stimulus. Short IRTs were very rare when 570 nm was presented, but were more likely at other wavelengths. When R_os of longer durations—which were differentially reinforced by the DRL schedule—were tabulated, the shape of the gradient changed dramatically. With IRTs in the ranges of 8–10 sec, 11–12 sec, or 13–14 sec, convex gradients were obtained. These longer IRTs were highly likely during the training stimulus and became rare as the test stimuli departed from 570 nm. Intermediate IRTs of 3–4 sec or 5–7 sec were about equally likely at all wavelengths.

The more detailed analysis of this experiment has proven instructive. Whereas the average gradient of the monitored response was relatively flat indicating poor stimulus control, the stimulus generalization gradients produced by tabulating the various IRTs separately indicated precise stimulus control. It was necessary to study the individual behaviors underlying the average gradient—other responses as well as the monitored response—in order to understand the generalization of stimulus control. In short, *the behavioral processes underlying stimulus generalization are incompletely specified by gradients based on the average frequency of the monitored response.*

Behavioral Processes Underlying Generalization   In this section, we shall use the technique of measuring the time between successive occurrences of the monitored response to provide insight into the behavioral process involved in generalization. Through the measurement of IRTs, we may examine more closely the behavior that occurs when we vary the similarity of the environment during generalization to the environment present during original learning.

For the first experiment, we return to a differential training procedure in which a VI schedule of reinforcement was present during S_1. Pigeons were used as subjects and auditory frequency as the stimulus dimension (Sewall & Kendall, 1965). With a VI schedule, food need not differentially follow IRTs of different lengths. Nevertheless, food *may* differentially follow different IRTs, dependent on the interaction of the entering behavior of the learner with the reinforcer (Morse, 1966).

Figure 5.8a shows the average rate of responding during various test tones following VI training with a 1,099-Hz tone. Below the gradient of average response rate, the frequency of IRTs that occurred during generalization is shown for each test tone. In order to indicate the IRT distributions found in generalization, all IRTs were plotted during each test stimulus. In the previous experiment employing the IRT measure, each IRT was plotted separately to produce its own generalization gradient. Each of the lower graphs in Fig. 5.8b is not a generalization gradient, but a frequency distribution of IRTs during the various test tones. Examination of the IRT distributions during generalization testing shows that a highly similar pattern of IRTs occurred to all test stimuli. When the subject responded in a new environment, the amount of responding

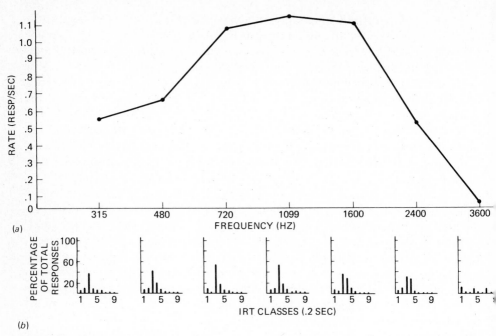

Fig. 5.8   Stimulus generalization gradient and associated interresponse-time (IRT) distributions obtained along the frequency dimension following training with a VI reinforcement schedule.   (From Sewall & Kendall, 1965.)

decreased as the new environment departed from the training environment, but the temporal pattern of the responses remained essentially the same.

The unchanging temporal pattern of responding in new environments— and hence the invariance of the responses (both the monitored response and other responses) controlled by the training and test stimuli—has been found with many species, stimulus dimensions, and training procedures (for example, Blough, 1963; Collins, J. P., 1974; Crites, Harris, Rosenquist, & Thomas, 1967; Crowley, 1979; Cumming & Eckerman, 1965; Migler, 1964). From these and other studies, the behavioral process underlying generalization may be summarized as follows: (a) *New environments control behavior previously conditioned in the training environment to the extent that the two environments have common features,* and (b) *New environments control the same responses conditioned in the training environment, only the likelihood of those responses changes as the new environment varies.*

In simple experiments of the type we have been considering, the common features between training and test environments may be specified rather precisely, and independently of behavior. For example, if training occurred in the presence of a wavelength of 550 nm and testing occurred in the presence of a wavelength of 555 nm, then a 5-nm difference exists between the two environments and that difference is smaller than would have existed with a test environment of, say, 560 nm. Indeed, with relatively simple sensory stimuli the number of nerve cells activated in common by the training and testing stimuli has been measured, and this measurement has been found to correspond to the amount of generalization (Thompson, R. F., 1965).

The notion that it is the number of features, or elements, in common between the training and testing environments that determines the extent of generalization is the *theory of identical elements*—one with a long history in psychology (for example, Atkinson & Estes, 1963; Bush & Mosteller, 1951; Guthrie, 1935; Thorndike, 1903). However, it is only in experiments involving well-defined sensory dimensions and organisms whose relevant experience may be well-controlled that the similarity between training and testing environments may be readily specified independent of the generalized behavior which the theory seeks to explain. To state that behavior generalizes because two environments are similar, and then to maintain that the environments are similar because of the existence of generalization is to engage in a patently circular argument. Common elements, including common private events, may provide the best conception of stimulus generalization in complex environments and with experienced organisms, but it is difficult to accomplish theoretical and experimental analyses of the precision attainable within simpler laboratory situations. The study of generalization, or transfer effects, will be pursued further in the subsequent treatment of learning in the experienced organism (see Chapter 7).

The conclusion that new environments control the same responses as were previously conditioned in earlier environments is obscured by stimulus generalization gradients based upon average response frequency (Migler, 1964). It is only apparent when the IRT distributions are examined. The gradual changes in response frequency indicated by the average gradient are the product of a varying probability of emission of the same behaviors conditioned during training. (For work of similar import at the physiological level of analysis, see John, 1967; Ramos, Schwartz, & John, 1976.) Once again, we are forcefully reminded of the hazards involved in averaging data, whether across time as in this instance or across individuals.

Ecclesiastes tells us that, "The thing that has been, it is that which shall be; and that which is done is that which shall be done; and there is no new thing under the sun." Do the findings obtained from the study of the generalization of stimulus control tell us that, in our response to new environments, we are limited to behavior previously learned in old environments? If we were able to trace the origins of our behavior in new situations, would we find them firmly rooted in the three-term contingencies of the past? We can never fully answer such questions with highly experienced organisms like ourselves, but what we know of generalization in organisms whose experience may be more completely analyzed suggests that it may be so. Our apparently creative response to new environments may be a complex mixture of previously established behaviors whose origins are lost in the imperfections of our memories.

Applied Implications To the extent that stimulus generalization is confined to environments sharing common features and is restricted to response classes established during conditioning, important limitations are placed upon the plasticity of the stimulus control. Consider the implications for applied programs which seek to train behavior in one situation for emission primarily in a second situation. Education, psychotherapy, correctional and drug rehabilitation all fall within such a description.

With drug addiction, for example, research indicates that the constellation of responses associated with the ingestion of drugs—those responses comprising addiction, withdrawal, and the development of tolerance—are all conditionable at least in part (Siegel, S., 1975, 1977, in press). A person who becomes addicted "on the street," is put in prison, and then returns to the street has learned the addiction in one environment, undergone withdrawal in a second environment, and has then been placed in the first environment again. If, under these circumstances, the person should again emit the constellation of responses comprising addicted behavior, should we be surprised? In view of the dissimilarity between the training and generalization environments, it would be surprising if the behavior did not recur.

While any application of psychological knowledge must involve additional factors, an important consideration is always the similarity between the training environment and the environment for which the training is intended to be relevant. How imperfectly many existing programs of education, psychotherapy, and rehabilitation approximate optimal conditions is all too apparent.

Some Complexities in Stimulus Generalization

Through the use of simple stimulus dimensions such as wavelength and learners such as pigeons whose prior experience may be controlled, we have advanced our knowledge of stimulus generalization. It must be realized, however, that neither the stimulus nor the learner is so easily characterized in the natural environment of the species. The natural environment contains complex stimuli whose dimensions are not easily identified and learners whose prior experiences influence their response to present conditions. In this section we acknowledge two complicating aspects of stimulus control in natural environments—multidimensional stimulus control and attentional phenomena.

Multidimensional Stimulus Control   Even in the simple circumstance in which a pigeon pecks a key transilluminated with monochromatic light (light of one wavelength), the controlling stimulus may include more than the wavelength on the key. The light is of a particular intensity as well as wavelength, the key is of a particular size and is located on the wall of the chamber and not the floor, and so on. In other words, although a generalization test may be conducted on only the wavelength dimension, the intensity, size, and location of the key may also be sources of controlling stimuli were we but to test for their influence.

Multidimensional stimulus generalization refers to the transfer of learned responses to new environments that differ from the training environment along more than one stimulus dimension. In an apt analogy, Osgood (1953) has drawn a parallel between the multiple generalization gradients that emanate from the training stimulus and a handkerchief that has been picked up at its center. The creases of the handkerchief move off in many directions, as do the gradients of stimulus generalization from any stimulus.

Multidimensional stimulus control has been studied in the laboratory; one example will suffice (Butter, 1963). Key-pecking in pigeons produced food on a VI schedule when directed at a key transilluminated by a 550-nm vertical line. Thus the training stimulus was defined both by wavelength and angular orientation. Following training, generalized responding was measured to test stimuli that varied simultaneously along the wavelength and line-orientation dimensions. The obtained generalization gradients clearly indicated stimulus control by both dimensions of the training stimulus.

Attention   Although training with multidimensional stimuli may produce simultaneous control by many aspects of the stimulus, such control does not always develop. Sometimes only one aspect of the training stimulus acquires control or one aspect exerts more control than others. When such findings arise, the concept of attention is often introduced. Generally, appeals to attention are made when environmental events within the situation do not appear sufficient to account for the stimulus control arising from that situation. At this point, an example may help.

For two pigeons, pecking a key produced food when the key was red and contained a white triangle. When the key was green and contained a white circle, food was not forthcoming. Subsequent testing revealed that key-pecking in one bird was controlled by color and not by shape but, for the second bird, by shape and not color (Reynolds, 1961a). Two learners exposed to the same key stimuli and reinforcers showed differences in the stimulus control of pecking.

The analysis of attentional effects requires knowledge of the phylogenetic and ontogenetic history of the learner. Knowledge of the present situation is not enough. In the prior experiment with pigeons, since pecking is controlled by stimuli at the point of contact of the beak (Jenkins, H. M., & Sainesbury, 1969), it is likely that by chance the two birds pecked different parts of the key during training. We shall analyze attentional effects as they present themselves at various points in our study of learning. Such phenomena have figured prominently in the history of learning (for example, Krechevsky, 1932; Lashley & Wade, 1946; Lawrence, 1950; Spence, 1937) and are of interest to modern theorists of many different persuasions (for example, Mackintosh, 1975; Moray, 1970; Posner, 1974; Thomas, Freeman, Svinicki, Burr, & Lyons, 1970; Trabasso & Bower, 1968).

STIMULUS DISCRIMINATION

From the behavioral processes responsible for stimulus generalization, the experienced organism brings to new environments a rich repertoire of responses previously acquired in similar environments. Stimulus generalization thus represents a great economy for the organism seeking to fashion a theory of its environment. But, as with all theories, there are boundary conditions beyond which the organism's theory is not sustained. If the organism finds itself in a world in which responding to one stimulus leads to a reinforcer, responding to similar stimuli is also likely to have similar consequences, but not necessarily. A bird that eats butterflies of one coloration is apt to find butterflies of similar coloration equally appetizing—but not necessarily. Some butterflies are poisonous and the bird must learn to eliminate these from its diet. A child is congratulated for saying "man" upon seeing other than its father, but is less apt to be similarly treated in the use of the word "Daddy." The breadth of generalization must often be constrained and the analysis of the procedures and processes whereby that constraint is realized is the focus of the present discussion of stimulus discrimination.

Three aspects are of central concern: (a) the methods for producing discrimination and associated phenomena; (b) the behavioral processes responsible for discrimination; and (c) the identification of the environmental features upon which the discrimination is based. In all of these efforts, a relational principle of reinforcement will provide valuable insights.

Basic Procedures and Phenomena

In our analysis of stimulus generalization, we found that the precision of stimulus control could be improved if responding has different consequences associated with the presence of the training stimulus (S_1) than with its absence (that is, with S_0 alone). A procedure involving the differential reinforcement of responding in the presence and absence of S_1 is called an *interdimensional* training procedure (Honig, 1970). A procedure involving only the reinforcement of responding in the presence of a single environment is called a *nondifferential* training procedure.

In the treatment of stimulus discrimination, we consider another differential training procedure, the *intra*dimensional procedure, that leads to even more precise stimulus control. With *intradimensional* training, in addition to S_1 and the background stimuli (S_0), a second training stimulus (S_2) is introduced that falls within the same stimulus dimension as S_1. Thus if S_1 were a 550-nm wavelength, S_2 might be a 570-nm wavelength. The reinforcement schedule during S_2 differs from that present during S_1.

The most common method for instituting intradimensional training with both classical and instrumental procedures is to confine the occurrence of the reinforcer to presentations of S_1 and to schedule extinction during S_2. Any procedure for differentially presenting the reinforcer during S_1 and S_2 meets the defining conditions of intradimensional training, however.

Classical Procedure Since the differential presentation of a reinforcer with S_1 (the CS) is inherent in the classical procedure, the classical procedure is always an instance of discrimination training. For this reason, prior comparisons between the stimulus control produced by nondifferential and differential training were confined to the instrumental procedure.

As an example of intradimensional training with the classical procedure, an experiment involving nictitating membrane conditioning with the rabbit will be described (Moore, J. W., 1972). The effects of two training methods were studied. In the first—interdimensional training—S_1 consisted of a 1,200-Hz tone paired with shock to the cheek and S_0 consisted of background stimuli from the experimental chamber. In the second—intradimensional training—a new stimulus, S_2, was introduced in addition to S_1 and S_0. During S_2 (a 2,400-Hz tone), shock never occurred. Thus in the latter procedure, one stimulus (S_1) was always present prior to shock and a second stimulus (S_2) was never present immediately prior to shock.

The results from a generalization test conducted after discrimination training with these two procedures are shown in Fig. 5.9. The *postdiscrimination gradient* of stimulus generalization following interdimensional conditioning gives clear evidence of stimulus control by the auditory dimension (see Fig. 5.9a). The postdiscrimination gradient following intradimensional conditioning (see Fig. 5.9b) shows even greater specificity of stimulus control: Responding dropped off more sharply as the test stimuli departed from S_1, particularly for auditory stimuli close to S_2 (2,400 Hz). Findings of similar import have been obtained with human subjects as well (for example, Gynther, 1957; Ross & Ross, 1972).

The finding that stimulus control was produced by both classical procedures and that it was more pronounced with the intradimensional procedure is consistent with the earlier analysis of the behavioral processes underlying generalization. With interdimensional training, the CS is assumed to consist of stimulus elements comprising the 1,200-Hz tone (S_1) and other stimuli (S_0). Since S_1 is reliably paired with reinforcement, it should block the acquisition of control by S_0, which is nondifferentially present throughout the experiment. During generalization testing, therefore, only the elements of S_1 should control responding and the postdiscrimination gradient should be peaked in the region of S_1 where those elements are most numerous. In intradimensional conditioning, only those stimulus elements that S_1 does not share with either S_0 or S_2 are reliably paired with reinforcement. Thus stimulus control by S_0 *and by those*

Fig. 5.9 Postdiscrimination gradients along the auditory frequency dimension obtained with the nictitating membrane preparation of the rabbit. The gradients were obtained following (a) interdimensional training with S_1 (1,200 Hz) and (b) intradimensional training with S_1 and S_2 (2,400 Hz).   (From John W. Moore, "Stimulus Control: Studies of Auditory Generalization in Rabbits" in Abraham H. Black, William F. Prokasy, *Classical Conditioning II: Current Research Theory*, © 1972, p. 214. Reprinted by permission of Prentice-Hall, Inc., Englewood Cliffs, N.J.)

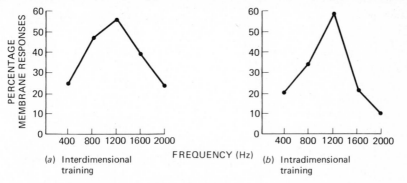

(a) Interdimensional training

(b) Intradimensional training

elements of S_2 which are not shared with S_1 should both be blocked in the in-tradimensional procedure. Since the elements shared by S_1 and S_2 should be found primarily on the side of the gradient nearest S_2, that side of the gradient should be most steepened by differential conditoning. A comparison of the shapes of the postdiscrimination gradients shown in Fig. 5.9 supports this analysis.

Instrumental Procedure   To illustrate intradimensional training with an instrumental procedure, the basic method may be modified to include a second stimulus (S_2) in which extinction is scheduled. Key-pecking in the pigeon again serves as the response and wavelength as the stimulus dimension. Generalization gradients were obtained after training with a nondifferential procedure and with either of two intradimensional procedures. For all three groups of pigeons, S_1 was a 550-nm stimulus during which food was presented on a VI l-min schedule. For the two discrimination groups, S_2 was either a 555- or 590-nm stimulus during which food was not available (Hanson, H. M., 1959).

Stimulus control is apparent in all three generalization gradients, and was especially precise in the postdiscrimination gradients found after intradimensional training with S_1 and S_2 (see Fig. 5.10). Thus the classical and instrumental procedures both reveal improved stimulus control following explicit differential reinforcement.

Fig. 5.10   Postdiscrimination gradients along a wavelength dimension obtained with the key-pecking response of the pigeon. The two discrimination groups received food on a VI schedule for responding during S_1 (550 nm) and responding was extinguished during S_2 (555 or 590 nm). The control gradient was obtained after nondifferential training with S_1.   (After Hanson, H. M., 1959. Copyright 1959 by the American Psychological Association. Reprinted by permission.)

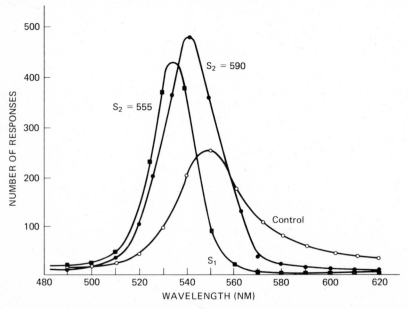

In addition, the instrumental procedure demonstrates two other possible consequences of discrimination training: peak shift and behavioral contrast. *Peak shift* occurs when the modal point of the postdiscrimination gradient is displaced away from S_2. *Behavioral contrast* occurs when responding increases during one stimulus (here, S_1) when the frequency of the reinforcer is reduced during a second stimulus (here, S_2). In the present context, the finding that the postdiscrimination gradients are not wholly contained within the generalization gradient of the nondifferential control group is evidence for behavioral contrast.

In a later section dealing with the identification of the controlling stimuli resulting from discrimination training, we shall inquire more deeply into the phenomenon of peak shift. For now, it is enough to note that the generalization of extinction effects from S_2 might lower responding to S_1, thereby causing a stimulus more remote from S_2 to control a higher frequency of responding. We shall not pursue the analysis of behavioral contrast. Behavioral contrast probably has a number of relatively independent origins, one of which is that the instrumental response (here, pecking) is also elicited by food in this preparation. Contrast, for example, is not found when pedal-pressing rather than key-pecking is the instrumental response for pigeons (Hemmes, 1973; McSweeney, 1978). (See the following for representative analyses of behavioral contrast: Bloomfield, 1969; Gamzu & Schwartz, 1973; Hearst & Jenkins, 1974; Marcucella & MacDonall, 1977; Premack, 1969; Rachlin, 1973; Reynolds, 1961b; Schwartz & Gamzu, 1977; and Terrace, 1968.)[4]

Fading   In the discrimination procedures that we have thus far considered, the values of S_1 and S_2 have remained constant throughout training. Pavlov observed, however, that a difficult discrimination could often be learned more rapidly when training began with stimuli that differed more widely than the final values of the discriminative stimuli (Pavlov, 1927). Further, Skinner noted that discriminations between widely differing stimuli could sometimes be acquired with the occurrence of little or no responding to S_2, that is, without "errors" (Skinner, 1938).

These two observations have led in recent years to the development of an efficient procedure for discrimination training known as fading. In a *fading procedure,* S_1 and S_2 are introduced at widely divergent values and then are changed to approach the desired terminal values through a series of gradual steps. Thus fading is a technique for successively approximating the terminal controlling stimulus, just as shaping is a technique for successively approximating the terminal instrumental response.

Early introduction of discrimination training prior to extensive reinforcement of responding during S_1 and progressive changes in S_2 both facilitate efficient performance with the terminal discriminative stimuli. Using the early and progressive introduction of S_2, a wavelength discrimination has been acquired without errors in pigeons (Terrace, 1963a) and errorless transfer from a wavelength to a line-orientation discrimination has also been accomplished (Terrace, 1963b). Techniques based upon similar fading procedures have been extensively used in applied work for teaching a variety of skills to children and adults. The following may be cited as examples: reading (Corey & Shamow, 1972), number concepts (Reese, 1977), and classroom learning (Sulzer & Mayer, 1977). As with shaping, the application of fading techniques to the solution of behavioral problems outside the laboratory requires both the knowledge of the scientist and the artistry of the practitioner.[5]

Behavioral Processes Underlying Discrimination

In our study of stimulus generalization, we had recourse to IRT distributions in order to understand the behavioral processes that contribute to the average generalization gradient. By examining the temporal pattern of responding, we found that new environments call forth old responses, but with a lower frequency than observed during the training environment. We now apply the same technique to an analysis of the behavior that gives rise to the average postdiscrimination gradient.

The analysis of the IRT distributions produced by intradimensional discrimination training is applied to the now familiar preparation of key-pecking in the pigeon with wavelength as the stimulus dimension. S_1 was a wavelength of 554 nm and S_2 was a wavelength of 569 nm. The reinforcement schedules associated with the discriminative stimuli were chosen so as to produce distinctive temporal patterns of responding during S_1 and S_2. By having different IRT distributions associated with S_1 and S_2—and hence R_os of different durations—it was possible to distinguish among the various R_os when they occurred during the test wavelengths (Collins, J. P., 1974).

The specific procedure was as follows. In training, key-pecking during S_1 produced food on a VI 1-min schedule for the criterion response. The criterion response was a key-peck that followed a previous key-peck within 1 sec. By having an IRT less than 1 sec as a criterion response, S_1 would control primarily R_os having short durations (that is, short IRTs). During S_2, food also occurred according to a VI 1-min schedule, but the criterion response was longer. The criterion response during S_2 was an IRT having a duration of greater than 3 sec. Thus S_2 controlled R_os of longer durations (that is, longer IRTs). The postdiscrimination gradient of stimulus generalization was based upon responding to test wavelengths randomly interspersed between presentations of the training stimuli. (A test procedure of this type is called a *probe procedure* to distinguish it from one in which all test stimuli are presented in a massed block of test stimuli.) During the probe tests, food was not presented as was also done in the massed test procedure used in earlier work.

The average postdiscrimination gradient for a single subject is shown in Fig. 5.11a. Although the average gradient is somewhat flatter than previously found when S_1 and S_2 were associated with VI and extinction schedules, respectively, there is clear evidence of stimulus control. The rate of key-pecking is highest in the vicinity of S_1, and declines as the test wavelengths depart from that value. It should be noted that this gradient demonstrates stimulus control under conditions in which the reinforcer occurred with equal frequency in both S_1 and S_2.

Although reinforcement frequency was equal, the rates of responding during S_1 and S_2 were not equal because of the different reinforcement sched-

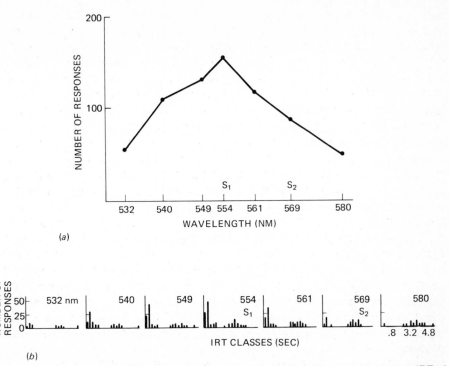

Fig. 5.11   (a) Postdiscrimination generalization gradient after training with a criterion IRT of less than 1 sec during S₁ (554 nm) and a criterion IRT of more than 3 sec during S₂ (569 nm). (b) IRT distributions observed during each stimulus presented in generalization testing. (After Collins, J. P., 1974.)

ules associated with the discriminative stimuli. The effect of the differential reinforcement of different IRTs is shown most clearly in the IRT distributions that arose from each test stimulus (see Fig. 5.11b). During S_1, responses having short IRTs predominated, but there were also some responses having the longer IRTs characteristic of S_2. During S_2, longer IRTs predominated, but short IRTs characteristic of S_1 were also observed (cf. Weisman & Davis, 1976). During a test stimulus intermediate between S_1 and S_2, for example, 561 nm, a mixture of S_1-controlled and S_2-controlled responses occurred as indicated by the presence of both short and long IRTs.

The findings obtained by examining the IRT distributions that occur after discrimination training agree with those after nondifferential training: New environments evoke responses previously established during the training environments. When different responses are controlled by the discriminative stimuli, as occurred here, test stimuli control a mixture of the previously conditioned responses. New environments continue to evoke old responses, but the proportions in which these old responses occur varies with the similarity of the test stimulus to the various training stimuli.

The view that discrimination training typically leads to a mixture of previously established responses in new environments, and not the emergence of qualitatively different responses, is supported by a number of studies with both infrahuman (for example, Crowley, 1979; Cumming & Eckerman, 1965) and human (for example, Donahoe & Miller, 1975) learners. The analysis has been extended to include responding maintained by electric shock and a variety of reinforcement schedules (Bushnell & Weiss, 1978; Weiss, S. J., 1976, 1977, 1978).

Identification of Controlling Stimuli

In our study of discrimination formation—its basic procedures and phenomena as well as its underlying behavioral processes—we have again employed simple stimuli and organisms whose relevant prior experience can be well-controlled. This approach has been a fruitful one in elucidating fundamental principles, but as was noted in the analysis of stimulus generalization it does not faithfully represent the complex conditions that prevail in the natural environment.

In the world of everyday experience, the discriminative stimuli are apt to differ multidimensionally—not in only one respect such as wavelength—and the learner is apt to have a long history of contact with similar stimuli in the past. Thus a child who learns to say "Daddy" in response to the sight of only one man may have differentiated his father from other men with respect to any number of stimuli (for example, facial features, size, and so on) and after having already learned to make many other discriminations (for example, man vs. dog, dog vs. ball, and so on).

Some sense of the complexities encountered in identifying the controlling stimuli in natural environments may be obtained by tracing the search for the controlling stimuli in the phenomenon of transposition. Moreover, in reviewing the course of laboratory work on transposition, general issues encountered in the identification of discriminative stimuli may be isolated.

Transposition Transposition refers to the transfer of an intradimensional discrimination such that responding in a transfer test preserves the *relationship* established between the discriminative stimuli. As an example, suppose that training first established a high rate of responding to S_1 (550 nm) and a low rate of responding to S_2 (560 nm). Transposition would be demonstrated if, in a subsequent test, responding was more frequent during a test stimulus (S_T) of 545 nm than during the original training stimulus of 550 nm. Note that the preference relationship for the shorter (that is, "bluer") wavelength shown in the transfer test is the same as that established in the original intradimensional discrimination. That is, 545 nm is "bluer" than 550 nm, just as 550 is "bluer" than 560 nm.

A number of experiments have demonstrated transposition with nonhuman animals with such stimulus dimensions as brightness (Kohler, 1918) and wavelength (Honig, 1962). The phenomenon is indisputable. At issue, however, are the implications of transposition for our understanding of the stimuli that control responding as a result of intradimensional training. Transposition suggests that responding is controlled by the relationship, or difference, between S_1 and S_2 and not by the specific values of S_1 and S_2 present in the experiment.

Appearances Can Be Deceiving   The notion that the difference between the discriminative stimuli is somehow controlling responding is consistent with the observations, but is it required by them? In an ingenious analysis, Spence (1937) showed that the phenomenon of transposition could, in principle, be accommodated by the view that responding was controlled by the specific values of S_1 and S_2 and not by the difference between them.

Suppose that S_1 and S_2 differ along some dimension such as wavelength. If responding produced a reinforcer during S_1, responding would increase and generalize to other similar wavelengths. The convex generalization gradient representing this outcome is designated the acquisition gradient in Fig. 5.12. Similarly, if responding failed to produce a reinforcer during S_2, responding would decrease and the decline would also generalize. The concave gradient representing this outcome is designated the extinction gradient in Fig. 5.12. The net tendency to respond following intradimensional discrimination training was then assumed to be the algebraic difference between the generalized tendencies to respond (acquisition) and not to respond (extinction). The difference is represented in Fig. 5.12 by the postdiscrimination gradient.

The critical feature of the postdiscrimination gradient for the analysis of transposition is that the net tendency to respond is not greatest for S_1 but for stimuli shifted away from S_2. To give a specific illustration of this shift, suppose that the learner was presented with a choice between a test stimulus (S_T) and S_1 following discrimination training (see Fig. 5.12). Since the net tendency

Fig. 5.12   An analysis of discrimination in which the postdiscrimination gradient is a function of the difference between the stimulus generalization gradients of acquisition and extinction.   (After Spence, 1937.)

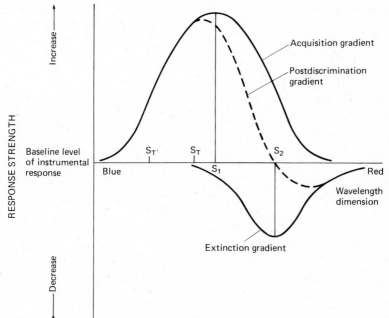

to respond to S_T is greater than the net tendency to respond to S_1, the new test stimulus would actually be preferred to the original training stimulus! Thus transposition, a phenomenon that appears at first glance to require another interpretation, may actually be accommodated by the view that responding is the result of the generalization of acquisition and extinction from the specific values of S_1 and S_2 used in discrimination training. Furthermore, this interpretation is consistent with the phenomenon of peak shift.

An implication of Spence's analysis, which differs from that of the alternative interpretation, may also be drawn. If a more distant test stimulus is presented, for example, $S_{T'}$, responding should be greater during S_1 than $S_{T'}$. The alternative view, without further assumptions, predicts that $S_{T'}$ would also control more responding than S_1 since the difference between the two stimuli is consistent with the relationship established during training. Transfer tests with more distant stimuli such as $S_{T'}$ confirm the interpretation based upon generalization gradients and not the alternative interpretation; S_1 is preferred to $S_{T'}$ (Ehrenfreund, 1952; Honig, 1962; see Hearst, 1969; Marsh, G., 1972, for related work).

Leaving aside for the moment questions concerning the range of application of Spence's interpretation of transposition, the analysis does indicate the need to explore thoroughly the alternatives in attempting to identify the controlling stimuli that result from discrimination training. A transfer result that appears to require control by the difference between stimuli may instead be accommodated by an analysis of interacting generalization gradients of acquisition and extinction controlled by the specific values of the stimuli present during discrimination training.

Implications about Capacity from Performance   In proposing his analysis of transposition, Spence (1937) stressed that it need not apply to transposition with organisms having the complex phylogenetic and ontogenetic histories of human learners. Subsequent work has confirmed these reservations about the completeness and generality of the analysis for humans possessing language skills (for example, Kuenne, 1946; see also Alberts & Ehrenfreund, 1951). Indeed, prior experience may affect the very generalization gradients that underlie the analysis of transposition (Thomas & DeCapito, 1966).

Even for nonhuman animals, it would be an error to conclude that the failure of intradimensional training to produce control by the difference between S_1 and S_2 implies an incapacity of the learner for such control. Strictly speaking, the results thus far presented indicate only that such control does not develop with this form of intradimensional training, not that pigeons or rats are incapable of transfer based on differences.

In order to determine whether an organism has the capability for a given type of stimulus control, it is minimally necessary that a procedure be devised in which only that property of stimulation covaries with the reinforcer. What the preceding experiments have shown is that when both the specific values of stimuli and the difference between stimuli covary with the reinforcer, the controlling characteristic of the stimuli is their specific value.

When procedures are instituted in which only the difference between stimuli is correlated with the reinforcer, the behavior of organisms such as rats and pigeons may be controlled by this property of stimulation (for example, Honig, 1965; Lawrence & de Rivera, 1954; Riley, 1958). One example will suffice.

Rats were trained to go to the right-hand of two doors when the top half of the stimulus card was darker than the medium gray that comprised the bottom half of the card. When the upper half was lighter than the medium gray on the bottom, they were trained to go to the left. The grays used to implement the darker and lighter values on the top of the card varied from trial to trial. If turning responses were controlled by the specific values on the top of the card, the dark grays should control right-going responses and the light grays should control left-going responses. If turning responses were controlled by the *difference* between the grays on the top and bottom of the card, the specific values used to implement the relationship should not affect performance. Transfer tests in which dark grays were used on both the top and bottom of the card, but in which the top was lighter than the bottom, controlled left-going responses. Thus it was the brightness difference and not the specific values of brightness that controlled responding. Results of similar import were found when light grays were used on both the top and bottom of the card. The rats turned right if the top was darker (Lawrence & de Rivera, 1954).[6]

The behavior of organisms other than humans is capable of being controlled by many complex environmental relationships if the reinforcer is differentially associated with those relationships. What is viewed as an incapacity of the organism may sometimes be better described as an incapacity of the environment to bring out the capacity of the organism. The potential variations in the learning environment and in the capacities of the learner are typically so great that it is rare when only one feature of the environment is capable of controlling behavior, or when the organism is capable of responding to the environment in only one way.

Discrimination and a Relational Principle of Reinforcement

A principle of reinforcement has already been invaluable in our analysis of stimulus control. The occurrence of a reinforcer during a stimulus leads to the control of behavior by that stimulus. Moreover, when the reinforcer occurs differentially in different environments, the specificity of stimulus control may be improved by eliminating control by background stimuli and by other nearby stimuli on the same dimension. Stimulus control may reflect the effects of reinforcers in more subtle ways, however. Two of these further influences will be considered here—edge effects and attentional phenomena.

Edge Effects   In the natural environment, stimulus control often develops after discrimination procedures involving many different stimulus values along a sensory dimension. The child's verbal response, "Daddy," is met with approval in the presence of only one man and is not similarly treated in the presence of any of a large number of other men. In this section, we examine phenomena—edge effects—that are found in such situations and that are interpretable via a relational principle of reinforcement.

Edge effects may be illustrated by the following experiment involving wavelength as the stimulus dimension and the pigeon as the learner (Blough, 1975). In one condition, 25 different wavelengths were presented a number of times in random order. Key-pecking produced food during 16% of the presentations of a central wavelength of 597 nm and during 10% of the presentations of all other wavelengths. In the second condition, a different group of pigeons was exposed to the same 25 wavelengths, but responding during the central wavelength never produced food, while food occurred during 10% of the other wavelengths as in the first condition. In short, responding was differentially reinforced through either an increase or a decrease in the frequency of food during the central wavelength relative to the other wavelengths.

The gradients of stimulus control are shown in Fig. 5.13. The gradients are based upon 25 wavelengths ranging from 470 to 617 nm, with a central wavelength of 597 nm in both conditions. The responses upon which the gradi-

Fig. 5.13 Postdiscrimination generalization gradients obtained when responding during a 597-nm stimulus signified (a) an increase or (b) a decrease in the frequency of reinforcement. (After Blough, 1975. Copyright 1975 by the American Psychological Association. Reprinted by permission.)

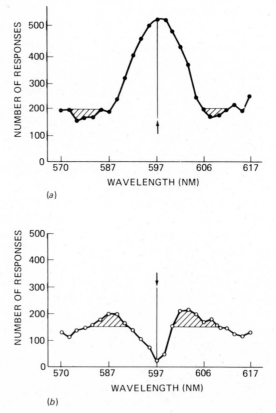

ents were computed were limited to those portions of each stimulus presentation in which responding was of moderate frequency. In this way, a measure that was sensitive to both increases and decreases in responding could be obtained. (See Blough, 1975, for a more complete description of the experimental and measurement techniques.)

In the condition in which the reinforcer occurred more frequently during the 597-nm stimulus, a convex (excitatory) gradient was found (see Fig. 5.13a). The shape of this gradient resembled that of an acquisition gradient. In the condition in which the reinforcer occurred less frequently during the 597-nm stimulus, a concave (inhibitory) gradient was observed (see Fig. 5.13b). Its shape was similar to that of an extinction gradient. While their shapes are generally similar to those previously observed with an extinction test procedure, the base of the gradients is narrowed by this training procedure. The bases of the gradients in Fig. 5.13 have widths of approximately 20 nm (from 587 to 606 nm), whereas generalization gradients obtained after discrimination training with only two stimuli were at least 40 nm wide at the base (see Fig. 5.10).

The gradients not only extended over a narrower range of the wavelength dimension, but they also showed other, new evidence of more precise stimulus control: The difference between responding during the 597-nm stimulus and stimuli at the base of the gradients was increased relative to that observed for stimuli at the ends of the wavelength dimension. Thus the difference in responding was exaggerated at the edges of the gradients. These areas of exaggerated differences are known as *edge effects* and are indicated in Fig. 5.13 by crosshatched areas. The functional significance of edge effects is that they increase the precision of stimulus control at the boundaries of differential reinforcement, the very places at which differential responding might otherwise be most difficult to develop.

Edge effects at the boundaries of gradients are consistent with a relational principle of reinforcement (Blough, 1975). They are presumed to arise in the following manner. Consider the concave gradient in Fig. 5.13b as an illustration. The 597-nm stimulus should control a low frequency of responding since key-pecking never produces a reinforcer in its presence. This reduced frequency of responding will generalize to adjacent stimuli, for example, 603 nm. Responding during these nearby stimuli would then also be infrequent. However, responses during adjacent stimuli sometimes produce a reinforcer with this test procedure. Thus there is an increased discrepancy, for nearby stimuli, between the generalized tendency *not* to respond and the direct effect of the reinforcer *to* respond. Since the increment in responding during a stimulus is a function of the size of discrepancy, the increased discrepancy produces an exaggerated effect of the reinforcer on responding to nearby stimuli. In the vernacular, the learner is "surprised" to find responding produce food during a stimulus so near to a stimulus in which responding never produces food that the effect of the reinforcer is magnified.

Aside from illustrating the sharpening effect of a relational principle of reinforcement on stimulus generalization, edge effects exemplify another general truth: The effect of a constant reinforcer does not produce a constant change in behavior. Depending on the similarity of the prevailing environment to other environments and to the prior occurrence of reinforcers in those environments, the effect of a given reinforcer may be exaggerated or diminished. Other work supporting this general point could be presented (for example, Kamin & Gaoini, 1974; Kremer, 1978; Rescorla, 1971), but we shall pursue the issue in a different context—that of attention.

Attentional Effects William James began his discussion of attention with the comment, "Everyone knows what attention is" (James, 1890, p. 403). While there is a sense in which this comment is undeniably correct, it is also true that psychologists differ widely as to what they mean by attention. As a modern worker observed, "Attention is not a single concept but the name of a complex field of study" (Posner, 1974, p. 1).

In the present exploration of attentional effects, we shall restrict ourselves to those phenomena that are illuminated, at least in part, by a relational principle of reinforcement. Two aspects of attention will be considered—selective attention and general attentiveness.

In the case of *selective attention,* prior experience causes a reinforcer occurring in the presence of a multidimensional stimulus to produce control by only one dimension of the stimulus. In the case of *general attentiveness,* prior experience causes a reinforcer to produce more precise stimulus control by a dimension than would have otherwise occurred. These opposing effects of prior experience on stimulus control may both be understood from the perspective of a relational principle of reinforcement.

As an illustration of selective attention, consider the following example (Johnson, D. F., 1970; see also Chase, S., 1968). Key-pecking in pigeons was first trained using an intradimensional discrimination procedure with the line-orientation dimension. In the presence of a vertical line, key-pecking produced food on a VI schedule; in the presence of a horizontal line, key-pecking did not produce food. Following this procedure, multidimensional discrimination training was given on the line-orientation and wavelength dimensions. In this second discrimination procedure, the vertical line on a 510-nm key was correlated with the VI schedule and the horizontal line on a 551-nm key was correlated with extinction.

From our earlier discussion of multidimensional stimulus generalization (see pp. 188–189), we know that key-pecking may simultaneously come under the control of both line orientation and wavelength. What effect did prior discrimination training on line orientation have on the development of stimulus control by wavelength? As shown by subsequent generalization testing, control by wavelength was attenuated by prior line-orientation training. As compared to pigeons given only multidimensional discrimination training, the wavelength generalization gradients were flatter in the pretrained pigeons. In the vernacular, the pigeons had continued to "pay attention" to line orientation and had not "shifted their attention" to wavelength. Attention was selective.

As you may have already realized, selective attention can be interpreted as an instance of blocking according to a relational principle of reinforcement. Pretraining with line orientation should block the acquisition of control by wavelength through eliminating the discrepancy between the strength of responding to wavelength and the vigor of the elicitation process activated by food. Without this discrepancy, the basis for learning is removed. Thus the blocking effect may be described in the language of attention as a selective attention effect (Rescorla, 1972; see also Lawrence, 1950; Mackintosh, 1975; Wagner, Logan, Haberlandt, & Price, 1968).

General attentiveness, which was identified by Reinhold and Perkins (1955) and studied most thoroughly by Thomas and his students (for example, Frieman & Goyette, 1973; Thomas, D. R., 1970; Thomas, D. R., Freeman, Svinicki, Burr, & Lyons, 1970), denotes a contrasting effect of prior experience on subsequent stimulus control. The phenomenon may be illustrated by the following study (Honig, 1969). During pretraining with the experimental group of pigeons, key-pecking a blue key produced food on a VI schedule, while pecking a green key was extinguished. Following discrimination training on the wavelength dimension, key-pecking a vertical line produced the reinforcer. A control group of pigeons also received key-peck training with the vertical line. To equate the two groups for exposure to wavelength and the amount of prior training, the control group first also pecked blue and green keys, but the VI schedule was not differentially correlated with the color on the key.

In order to assess the effects of prior wavelength discrimination training on stimulus control by line orientation, a generalization test was conducted along the line-orientation dimension. As compared to the control group, pigeons which had previously acquired a wavelength discrimination showed more precise stimulus control by line orientation. As shown in Fig. 5.14, the generalization gradient of the experimental group was more precise than that

Fig. 5.14 Stimulus generalization gradients along a line-orientation dimension following nondifferential training with vertical lines. The experimental group had received prior discrimination training on the wavelength dimension; the control group had not.   (From Honig, 1969. Copyright Academic Press.)

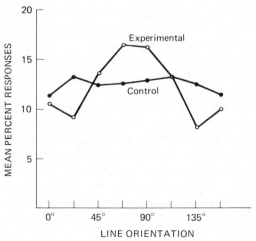

of the control group. Thus prior discrimination training on one stimulus dimension may enhance the control of behavior that is exerted by another dimension.

A relational principle of reinforcement is helpful in understanding the phenomenon of general attentiveness as well as selective attention. The analysis proceeds as follows. Unlike selective attention, the discriminative stimuli present during pretraining (that is, wavelength) were not present during training with the second stimulus (that is, line orientation). Thus pretraining with wavelength could not block control by the vertical line. More important, however, is the effect of other stimuli (S_o) on stimulus generalization along the line-orientation dimension. Prior discrimination training on wavelength would eliminate the control of key-pecking by S_o (see pp. 191–192), and subsequent control by the vertical line would continue to block control by S_o. When the generalization test was given on the line-orientation dimension, only those elements of the test stimuli that were common to the vertical line would control responding, and a sharp gradient should result.

In the control group, which did not receive prior discrimination training, S_o and the wavelength on the key should both control responding. Stimulus control by S_o would continue in the second phase of the experiment when the vertical line was on the key, since the second phase did not employ a discrimination procedure. Accordingly, during the generalization test on the line-orientation dimension, S_o would control responding at all values of line orientation and flatten the gradient. The foregoing analysis, which attributes some instances of general attentiveness to the elimination of stimulus control by S_o, is supported by other work in which S_o has been experimentally manipulated (for example, Tomie, 1976).

We have now concluded our exploration of some of the implications of a relational principle of reinforcement for the analysis of stimulus control. Our understanding of edge effects, selective attention, and general attentiveness has been deepened. Of perhaps greater significance than these specific analyses is the conclusion that the effects of a reinforcer in some present environment may be greatly influenced by previous experience. If we had not known of the different prior experiences of the learners in the attention experiments, the differences in the effect of reinforcers on behavior in the second phase of the experiments would have been mystifying.

Looking ahead to the analysis of behavior in highly experienced and complex organisms such as ourselves, we may anticipate formidable problems in the understanding of behavior if our knowledge is confined to only the events of the present. For persons with different prior experiences, the occurrence of the same reinforcer in the same environment in conjunction with the same response may well have very different effects on learning (cf. Rudy, 1974). Of course, attentional phenomena are diverse and may be analyzed from perspectives other than a relational principle of reinforcement (cf. Hickis, Robles, & Thomas, 1977; Mackintosh, 1977). We shall examine other attentional effects in later chapters.

Role of Stimulus Control in Selected Phenomena

There is scarcely a problem that is of interest to the student of learning that is not also touched by the processes involved in stimulus control. When we ask how the opinions of one person affect the attitudes of another, when we observe how the facial expressions of the parent affect the reactions of the child, when we see how the words of the therapist affect the behavior of the client— and how, in turn, the client's behavior affects the therapist—we are studying particular instances of stimulus control. In each case, understanding requires more than a knowledge of the general principles of stimulus control, but in each case understanding is incomplete without such knowledge.

Since our immediate concern is learning, we shall restrict ourselves to that field in pursuing some of the contributions that stimulus control can make to understanding. To illustrate that contribution, we shall examine in greater detail two phenomena that have been encountered earlier—extinction and avoidance.

Extinction   Much of our knowledge of stimulus control derives from generalization tests conducted during extinction. It is only fitting that we now reverse the process and determine some of the implications of stimulus control for the analysis of extinction.

In an extinction procedure the reinforcer that was presented during the acquisition of the response is withheld. The outcome of this procedure is that the learned response declines in strength. Although the events that we measure and manipulate in an extinction procedure—the learned response and the reinforcer—are most prominent in our description of the procedure, it is crucial to recognize that both of these events occur in a particular context. That is, because of the action of the reinforcer the response is not merely strengthened but is strengthened in a specific environment. An experimental example will document this point.

Rats received bar-press training in an operant chamber using a VI schedule of food presentation. Following the attainment of a stable level of baseline responding, extinction was begun under one of four stimulus conditions for different animals. In the constant condition, the prevailing stimuli were identical to those present during acquisition except, of course, for the omission of the reinforcer. In a second condition, the chamber was changed from brightly lit with metal walls to dimly lit with black plastic walls. In a third condition, the chamber remained the same, but the animal was transported to the operant chamber in a distinctive carrying cage rather than the normal home cage. Thus the stimuli immediately prior to testing were changed. In a fourth group, both the operant chamber and the method of transportation were changed (Welker & McAuley, 1978).

As shown in Fig. 5.15a, when extinction began the rate of responding fell below the baseline acquisition level and continued to decline throughout the 60-min test session. Of greater present concern, the greater the similarity of extinction to acquisition conditions, the greater the persistence of responding

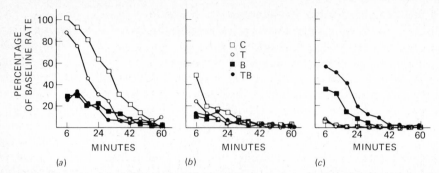

Fig. 5.15 Extinction curves obtained for the bar-pressing response after VI 1-min training. Responding in the control (C) subjects was extinguished under the same conditions as had prevailed during acquisition. The remaining subjects received changes in the way they were transported (T) to the test chamber, in the background (B) stimuli within the chamber, or both (TB). The figure shows performance during (a) the first extinction session, (b) the second extinction session, and (c) the sixth extinction session when all subjects were returned to the original acquisition conditions.   (From Welker & McAuley, 1978.)

during extinction. The stimulus conditions present during and immediately prior to acquisition had gained control over responding.

During a second extinction session (see Fig. 5.15b), responding declined throughout the session but not until after a partial recovery of responding had occurred at the beginning of the session. The increase in responding after the passage of time between extinction sessions is labeled *spontaneous recovery*. Spontaneous recovery occurs following training with both classical and instrumental procedures and has been known since the time of Pavlov (1927).

From the perspective of stimulus control, spontaneous recovery results from the limited opportunity for background stimuli characteristic of the first part of the session to be present during extinction. Since, by definition, such stimuli are present only or primarily at the beginning of the session, the extent of extinction training in their presence is necessarily limited (Guthrie, 1935; Estes, 1955; Skinner, 1950).

If the reinstatement of the controlling stimuli is responsible for spontaneous recovery, then the reinstatement of the presession and intrasession stimuli of the present experiment should also produce an increase in responding. Although a total of five extinction sessions were given and responding was essentially eliminated in all conditions, a sixth extinction session in which the original acquisition conditions were restored led to a sharp increase in responding (see Fig. 5.15c). The recovery of responding was especially pronounced for the learners in which both the method of transportation to the chamber and the chamber characteristics were returned to their former values.

While other factors also contribute to extinction and spontaneous recovery (cf. Hull, 1943), stimulus control provides a major insight into these phenomena (for example, Burstein & Moeser, 1971). Findings with human subjects point in a similar direction (for example, Adams, 1961).

Avoidance   An avoidance procedure, it will be recalled, is one in which the instrumental response is followed by the omission of an otherwise presented aversive stimulus. A child, having previously been burned upon touching a hot stove, now withdraws his or her hand upon seeing the stove. A rat, having been shocked in the startbox of a runway after a tone has been sounded, now runs from the startbox upon hearing the tone. In the vernacular, the child has learned to avoid the hot stove and the rat has learned to avoid the shocked startbox.

The understanding of avoidance has been challenging because of the apparent mystery surrounding the reinforcer of the avoidance response. What maintains the avoidance response, since the only consequence of the response that is directly manipulated by the experimenter is the omission of the aversive stimulus? How can the absence of an event function as a reinforcer?

The mystery of avoidance is largely one of our own making. It arises in great part from the tendency to equate the events which the experimenter manipulates with the totality of the significant events within the situation. In the case of avoidance, the two manipulated events are the stimulus preceding the avoidance response (for example, the tone in the startbox) and the stimulus following the nonoccurrence of the avoidance response (for example, electric shock). Ingenious appeals to each of these events have been made in an effort to account for avoidance behavior.

With respect to the stimulus preceding the avoidance response—the *warning stimulus*, attempts have been made to substantiate the termination of this event as the reinforcer. Thus the rat is said to avoid the startbox in order to terminate the tone that has in the past been paired with shock. Manipulations of the warning stimulus have expanded our knowledge of the variables affecting avoidance behavior, but termination of the warning stimulus is neither necessary (Kamin, 1957; Kamin, Brimer, & Black, 1963) nor sufficient (Kamin, 1956) to maintain responding. (See Anger, 1963; Mowrer, 1947; Miller, N. E., 1948; Rescorla & Solomon, 1967; Schoenfeld, 1950, for presentations of this theoretical work which is generally known as two-factor theory.)

The manipulation of the aversive stimulus has also added substantially to our understanding of avoidance behavior. In order to study the effects of the aversive stimulus in the absence of an explicit warning stimulus, a free-responding procedure was devised (Sidman, 1953, 1962). Briefly, the aversive stimulus occurs at a higher rate if the avoidance response fails to occur and at a lower rate (including a zero rate, that is, complete omission) if the avoidance response does occur. Note that no explicit stimulus distinguishes the preresponse from the postresponse environment.

The free-operant avoidance procedure was designed to investigate the effects of differences in the rate of preresponse and postresponse shock on avoidance behavior. As an experimental example, a rat in an operant chamber was given brief shocks at an average rate of six per min until a response bar was depressed, in which case shocks were temporarily given at a lower average rate of three per min (Herrnstein & Hineline, 1966). Avoidance responses were acquired and maintained with this procedure even though shocks continued to occur after bar-pressing—albeit at a lower rate. As with the manipulation of the warning stimulus, however, a reduction in shock rate is neither necessary (Benedict, 1975; Hineline, 1970) nor sufficient (Bolles & Popp, 1964) for the occurrence of avoidance behavior. In fact, "avoidance" responses are maintained by *increases* in overall shock rate as long as there is a delay imposed between the avoidance response and the occurrence of the next shock (Gardner, E. T., & Lewis, 1976). (See Herrnstein, 1969, for a presentation of this position, known as shock-frequency reduction theory, and Bolles, 1975, for a general review of this and related issues.)

Although the resourcefulness of living organisms makes it unlikely that any one factor is crucial to coping with aversive stimuli, we needlessly shackle inquiry when we restrict theoretical efforts to only two events—the preresponse environment (warning stimulus) and the aversive stimulus. Other events, notably the postresponse environment and responses other than the avoidance response, may contribute to measured performance even though they are customarily unmanipulated and unmonitored by the experimenter. Let us examine the avoidance situation with an expanded characterization of the environmental and behavioral events.

Behaviorally, we may partition the activity of the learner into two classes—those responses (R) to which the experimenter applies the omission (avoidance) contingency and those other responses (R_o) to which the contingency is not applied. The events that follow R are the omission (or delay) of the aversive stimulus and the availability of whatever other stimuli are present in the experimental environment. Although the experimenter manipulates only the aversive stimulus, every environment contains other elicitation processes that may function as reinforcers. After R, rats in an operant chamber may scratch or wash their faces, pigeons may preen their feathers or peck at the floor, humans may run their fingers through their hair or pursue daydreams. After R_o, however, the consequences are quite different. The aversive stimulus is presented immediately (or with a shorter delay) and the responses elicited by the aversive stimulus interfere with, and thereby deprive the learner of, the opportunity to engage in other elicitation processes. While receiving shock, rats cannot scratch, pigeons cannot preen, and people cannot dream.

The net effect of the different consequences of R (the avoidance response) and R_o would appear to be these: R feels the effects of the punishment contingency relatively less, and that of the implicit reinforcement contingency relatively more, than R_o. Both effects should favor the occurrence of R at the expense of R_o and thereby foster the development and maintenance of avoidance behavior.

If in fact implicit reinforcers contribute to the maintenance of the avoidance response, then manipulation of postresponse stimuli should affect the strength of the monitored response. The postresponse stimulus, or *safety stimulus,* should function as a conditioned reinforcer because it occurs prior to the opportunity to engage in preferred activities.

Evidence supports the foregoing expectation. Rats bar-pressing on a free-operant avoidance procedure were occasionally presented a 5-sec tone that was never followed by shock. To assess the reinforcing function of the tone, it was made contingent on the occurrence of the avoidance response. During one test period, the tone was presented according to a DRL schedule (that is, only after long IRTs). If the tone functioned as a reinforcer, it should increase the frequency of long IRTs and thereby lower the average rate of responding. During another test period, the tone was presented according to a DRH schedule (that is, differential reinforcement of high rates, or short IRTs). When presented according to a DRH schedule, the same tone should increase the rate of bar-pressing if the tone functioned as a reinforcer (Weisman & Litner, 1969).

As shown in Fig. 5.16, the effect of the tone on avoidance responding did change with the schedule according to which it was presented in keeping with its function as a conditioned reinforcer. A control stimulus not differentially correlated with shock-free periods did not appreciably change the frequency of avoidance responding from that found during the free-operant baseline sessions. (See D'Amato, Fazzaro, & Etkin, 1968; and Klein & Rilling, 1974, for related work; and Mackintosh, 1974, for a review of this literature.)

The potential role of implicit safety stimuli, other responses, and other elicitation processes in avoidance behavior remains to be experimentally evaluated (cf. Bolles & Riley, 1973; Dunham, 1971, 1972). Their explicit measurement and manipulation must be undertaken before the information is available to make a thorough analysis of avoidance as a special problem in stimulus control.

Fig. 5.16   The effect of presenting a stimulus, previously paired with a 5-sec shock-free period, contingent upon responding in a DRH and a DRL schedule. Avoidance responding was maintained by a free-operant procedure. A control stimulus, not differentially paired with shock-free periods, was also presented. Baseline sessions without differential pairings intervened between test sessions.   (From Weisman & Litner, 1969. Copyright 1969 by the American Psychological Association. Reprinted by permission.)

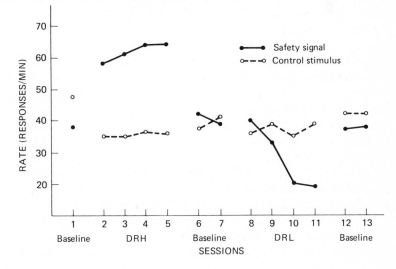

Aside from conditioned stimulus control, the contribution of phylogeny as represented by unconditioned stimulus control must also be considered. The history of the species affects avoidance responses as well as all other responses. Specifically, aversive stimuli are potent elicitors, and since the behavioral outcome of a conditioning procedure reflects both the instrumental response and the elicited response, the interaction of responses of these two origins is critical. For example, responses that are elicited by shock, such as running in the rat, are readily acquired avoidance responses whereas responses that are incompatible with shock-elicited behavior, such as key-pecking in the pigeon, are acquired with difficulty if at all (Fantino, Sharp, & Cole, 1966; Klein & Rilling, 1972). Responses that are elicited in environments in which aversive stimuli are presented have been called *species-specific defense reactions*. Their interaction with would-be avoidance responses may severely restrict the range of effective avoidance responses in some species and environments (Bolles, 1970, 1972), and must be accommodated in any analysis of avoidance as an instance of stimulus control.

VERBAL BEHAVIOR

In order to discern more clearly the behavioral processes that contribute to conditioned stimulus control, we have restricted ourselves largely to situations in which the environmental influences on behavior arose primarily from within the situation itself. We have, of course, intermittently acknowledged the contribution of phylogeny—as in species-specific defense reactions—or of prior experience—as in selective attention. Such acknowledgements, while they are essential to a complete understanding of stimulus control, have been more in the nature of diversions in our central pursuit—the discovery of the fundamental processes underlying stimulus control.

When we move from the key-pecking responses of pigeons in the presence of various wavelengths of light to the verbal responses of humans in the presence of complex verbal and social environments, what were formerly diversions now become the essence of the matter. If prior experience can alter the control of responding, as we determined in our study of transposition, how much more must we reckon with the prior experience of human learners in our efforts to understand verbal behavior?

While the beginnings of an intensive study of verbal behavior must await the completion of the subsequent chapter on motivation, it is appropriate that we recognize the dimensions of the problem before leaving the topic of stimulus control altogether. Verbal stimuli are among the most important events that influence our lives; verbal responses are among the most important events that comprise our behavior. An analysis of human behavior that stands mute on the subject of language has severely impaired its ability to contribute to an understanding of what is quintessentially human.

Our purpose in this introduction to verbal behavior is modest; we seek to illustrate by example the nature of some of the problems that must be faced by an adequate analysis of the factors which control verbal behavior. The examples are chosen from among those phenomena observed by Hermann Eb-

binghaus, the first psychologist with the audacity to probe complex verbal behavior using methods that satisfy contemporary standards of experimental
rigor. Before examining the specific fruits of his labors, however, we shall
spend a few moments considering the life of this remarkable man.[7] With Ebbinghaus, who now joins Darwin, Thorndike, and Pavlov, we have completed
the identification of the immediate progenitors of the scientific study of learning, language, and memory.

After playing his small role in Bismark's grand design for Europe during the
Franco-Prussian war, Hermann Ebbinghaus (1850–1909) returned to his studies
at the University of Bonn in 1871 to begin graduate work in psychology. His
dissertation, which was critical of von Hartmann's philosophical speculations
on the unconscious, reveals much of the felicitous writing style that led to his
reputation as the William James of Germany: "Wherever the structure [Hart-
mann's theory] is touched, it falls apart. . . . What is true is alas not new; the
new not true."

Among the specific propositions that he chose to defend in his doctoral examination were these: "psychology, in the widest sense, belongs under philosophy in no more intimate way than natural philosophy [that is, science] belongs
there" and "existing psychology consists more of logical abstractions and
verbal classifications than of knowledge of real elements of mind." The dissertation reveals much of the thrust and vigor that was to mark his thinking
throughout his life—both theses can provoke heated debate to the present day.
He was clearly among those who saw psychology as one of the natural sciences. A contemporary quotes Ebbinghaus as criticizing much of the then-cur-
rent philosophical and psychological theorizing as "impossible to anyone who
approached psychology from the side of biology" (Woodworth, 1909, p. 256).

Following receipt of his doctoral degree in 1873, Ebbinghaus studied natural
science in England and in France. While browsing through a secondhand
bookstore in Paris, he came upon a copy of Fechner's *Elements of psychophysics* (1860). In this work, the physicist Fechner sought to bring his quantitative
skills and mystical urges together to develop an "exact science of the functional
relations . . . between body and mind." Whereas Fechner had been content to
use simple sensory stimuli and to investigate problems that would now fall
under the rubric of perception, Ebbinghaus was inspired to attempt a similar
undertaking with respect to the more complex processes of learning and memory. Commenting on the arduous character of such an enterprise, Ebbinghaus
remarked, "At the very worst we should prefer to see resignation arise from the
failure of earnest investigation rather than from persistent, helpless astonishment in the face of their difficulties."

Equipped with missionary zeal and youth (not altogether independent qualities), and with the knowledge of science and British associationism garnered
from independent study, Ebbinghaus began his research. His sole subject was
himself. After completing the research and accepting a post at the University of
Berlin in 1880, he repeated much of the work before publishing the small book
that brings him to our attention—*Memory: A contribution to experimental psychology* (1885).

The book opens with a statement in Latin that may be rendered, "From the
most ancient subject we shall produce the newest science" (Boring, 1950). The
specific content of this newest science is deferred for a moment; for now it is

enough to note that the basic findings that Ebbinghaus uncovered in his work with himself as his only subject have endured into the present. Ebbinghaus's errors, if such be granted, were those of omission and not commission. In fact, much more so than other works of its time, *Memory* reads like a modern piece of research—a tribute to Ebbinghaus's genius and, perhaps, to our lack thereof.

Unlike Thorndike, Ebbinghaus published relatively little and, possibly for that reason and possibly for his experimental rather than philosophical biases, moved from Berlin to a lesser position at Breslau. On the subject of publication, Ebbinghaus wrote: "For certainly not every happy thought bolstered up perhaps by a few rough-and-ready experiments, should be brought before the public. But sometimes the individual reaches a point where he is permanently clear and satisfied with his interpretation. Then the matter belongs to the scientific public for their further judgment."

His later published scientific work was restricted to several papers on vision and to a type of sentence completion test that, a few years later, provided an impetus for the development by Binet of the intelligence test. He founded a laboratory wherever he went and continued to profess his commitment to the experimental method in his popular textbook in general psychology, viz: "When Weber in 1828 had the seemingly petty curiosity to want to know at what distances apart two touches on the skin could be just perceived as two, and, later, with what accuracy he could distinguish between two weights laid on the hand ... his curiosity resulted in more real progress than all the combined distinctions, definitions, and classifications of the time from Aristotle to Hobbes (inclusive)." This cavalier statement was made by no callow youth, but by an experienced man of 47 years!

Ebbinghaus, who had said that psychology had a long past but only a short history, began the history of the effort to understand the processes that govern verbal behavior. Before examining wherein he succeeded and wherein he failed, let us paraphrase some comments made by an historian of psychology (Watson, 1971) concerning Ebbinghaus's contribution: The sweeping claims to knowledge of the higher processes made by Ebbinghaus's more philosophical predecessors might be compared to those of monarchs during the age of discovery who staked a claim, not only to discovered lands, but also to any unseen territories that might lie beyond their immediate vision. Ebbinghaus saw the unknown lands, began their occupation, and even tilled their soil.

Ebbinghaus's Contributions

Ebbinghaus's philosophical predecessors were the British associationists, a group including such as Hobbes (1588–1679), Locke (1632–1704), Hume (1711–1776), James Mill (1773–1836), and John Stuart Mill (1806–1873). Mental events—for they were dualists—were seen as consisting of an association of ideas. But, in contradistinction to the dominant philosophical view, the source of these ideas was experience. The environment was the ultimate origin of thought for the British associationists. Even apparently new and complex thoughts were believed, upon analysis, to arise from new combinations of old ideas.

How was this philosophical position to be translated into experimental method? In Ebbinghaus's words, "how are we to keep even approximately constant the bewildering mass of causal conditions which, in so far as they are of mental nature, elude our control, and which, moreover, are subject to end-less and incessant change?" (Ebbinghaus, 1885, p. 7).

Ebbinghaus sought material, and a method that would satisfy his need for controlled observation. For his material, he devised a list of some 2,300 syllables containing three letters in the order consonant-vowel-consonant. Such syllables, or *CVC trigrams,* were referred to as "nonsense material" and were selected for "this very lack of meaning." Thus Ebbinghaus sought to control the effects of prior experience on the learning of verbal material by making that experience irrelevant.

For his method, he composed lists of nonsense syllables by random selection from his pool of items and then set about to learn those lists through a carefully prescribed procedure. The procedure consisted of reading each list through from the beginning to end at a constant rate governed by the ticking of his watch. As each syllable was read, he attempted to speak the next syllable before time obliged him to move on to its reading. The method that Ebbinghaus used has come to be called *serial learning* and the procedure for learning, *anticipation.* (The relationship of serial anticipation to the philosopher's notion of association of ideas is obvious.) During the 15-sec interval imposed between repetitions of the list, Ebbinghaus would record the time and number of the repetition.

He attempted to prevent his own opinions regarding the possible outcome of an experiment from influencing his learning. For those who were nevertheless uneasy regarding the separability of attitude and results, Ebbinghaus stated: "He who is inclined *a priori* to estimate very highly the unconscious influence of secret wishes on the total mental attitude will also have to take into consideration that the secret wish to find objective truth and not with disproportionate toil to place the creation of his own fancy upon feet of clay—that this wish, I say, may also claim a place in the complicated mechanism of these possible influences" (Ebbinghaus, 1885, pp. 29–30).

How well Ebbinghaus was able to exclude biasing factors is attested by the confirmation that his work has received from the efforts of thousands of college students who have subsequently served as subjects in verbal learning experiments. Among his major findings were that the number of repetitions required to anticipate a serial list correctly for two errorless repetitions increased disproportionately as list length increased. For example, Ebbinghaus took only one repetition to learn a list of up to seven syllables, but 13 repetitions for 10 syllables, and 38 repetitions for 19 syllables. A second finding was that retention improved with the number of repetitions—even beyond a perfect repetition—but that the increment in retention approached a point of diminishing returns.

As a method of measuring retention, Ebbinghaus used the *savings method.* The number of repetitions required to relearn the original list to a criterion of two errorless repetitions was determined and a savings score computed. The savings score was given by the difference between the repetitions needed in relearning and original learning, expressed as a percentage of the repetitions required in original learning. Thus if 10 repetitions were required originally and only eight repetitions in relearning, the savings score would be (10–8)/10 or 20%.

Perhaps Ebbinghaus's best known finding concerns the time-course of retention, the so-called *forgetting curve*. Forgetting was shown to occur rapidly at first and then more slowly as time progressed. Only half the repetitions were saved after as short a period as one hour; fully 25% were saved after as long a period as 6 days. These findings have been substantiated many times although later work has shown that Ebbinghaus, having learned so many lists of nonsense syllables, forgot them at a faster rate than subjects having only one list to learn.

Some Comments

Ebbinghaus's approach to the learning and retention of verbal material may be summarized as follows: Attempt to study verbal events through the use of nonsense materials in order that the experimenter may have direct access to all, or at least most, of the antecedents of the behavioral changes that occur within the experiment. Such a strategy runs a great risk and Ebbinghaus was aware of it. "Naturally the better one succeeds in this attempt the more does one withdraw from the complicated and changing conditions under which this activity takes place in ordinary life and under which it is important to us."

While recognizing the pitfalls, he concluded as follows: "But that is no objection to the method. The freely-falling body and the frictionless machine, etc., with which physics deals, are also only abstractions when compared with the actual happenings in nature which are of import to us. We can almost nowhere get a direct knowledge of the complicated and the real, but must get at them in roundabout ways by successive combinations of experiences, each of which is obtained in artificial experimental cases, rarely or never furnished in this form by nature" (1885, p. 26). Ebbinghaus's intellectual descendants, which included most workers in human learning for the next 75 years, shared this strategy and developed an impressive body of findings that sought to build an analysis of language and memory from the bricks of nonsense materials (see such surveys as Hall, 1971; McGeoch & Irion, 1952).

In spite of his immense and continuing legacy, modern analysis—with the benefit of hindsight—regards Ebbinghaus's strategy of research as fundamentally flawed as it was applied to the understanding of language and memory. Many phenomena of language and memory depend for their very existence upon the experience of the learner. Efforts to make prior experience irrelevant, to the extent that such efforts are successful, eliminate many of the very phenomena that we seek to investigate.

Ebbinghaus's strategy "solved" the problems of language and memory by controlling them out of existence. Somewhat similar logic was apparent in early methodological behaviorism when the problem of private events was "solved" by denying their existence (Watson, 1913). (For a different view see Skinner, 1953, 1974.)

It should be understood that it is not the experimental approach that was at fault. Quite the contrary, the application of the experimental method to the study of verbal behavior is Ebbinghaus's greatest contribution. It is, rather, the subject matter to which the method was applied that was the source of difficulty. The focused and intense light of experimentation is essential, but Ebbinghaus failed to direct the beam at the most promising places wherein reside the secrets of language and memory.

The argument has just been made that nonsense or meaningless material cannot serve as a fully adequate basis for the induction of knowledge concerning the fundamental behavioral processes undergirding language and memory. Such material is deficient, in principal, in the rich phylogenetic and experiential heritage that produces many of the phenomena of language and memory. A second argument is now made that a concern with such a heritage is unavoidable in any case since historical factors intrude themselves into the behavior of every person, even with the use of nonsense material. With other species, the relevant preexperimental experience may be more or less well-controlled. With the human organism—especially one capable of performing in a typical experiment dealing with verbal learning, language, or memory—the contribution of events prior to the experiment and outside of the view of the experimenter is unavoidable. When dealing with language and memory in humans, all learning experiments are truly transfer experiments.

The unavoidability of transfer effects from prior experience may be easily documented. As one illustration, subsequent research has shown that even nonsense syllables are not meaningless stimuli for human learners and that, moreover, the meaningfulness of these materials affects the acquisition and retention of serial lists (Underwood & Richardson, 1956b).

The meaningfulness of nonsense syllables, or of other verbal stimuli, is often measured by the number of verbal responses that are emitted when the stimulus is presented in a "free-association" test (for example, Noble, 1952). Imagine, if you will, the responses that come to mind when you see the "nonsense" syllables GOJ and FEM. Although neither syllable appears as a word in the English language, both almost certainly evoke some responses, albeit to different degrees. Note also the relationship between this method of measuring meaningfulness and our earlier discussion of stimulus control. A meaningful word and a discriminative stimulus are both events that control behavior.

The material to be learned is affected not only by the prior experience of the learner, but also by the serial learning method itself. The learner's task, as the experimenter defines it, is to give one syllable when presented with the immediately preceding syllable. However, the controlling stimulus is not simply the immediately preceding syllable (Young, R.K. 1968). For example, a subject might think when presented with the syllable RAJ in the third position in a serial list, "The third syllable is RAJ and RAJ is jar spelled backwards." The ontogeny of the learner has entered the situation through the notion of "thirdness" and through familiarity with the word jar. The controlling events are not confined to public stimuli within the serial list.

The idea that the behavior which is acquired in verbal learning studies is confined to the public response as defined by the experimenter is also an oversimplification. Such a fragmented conception of behavior has been questioned earlier. The concept of response class, or operant, was introduced to designate the class of behavioral changes that occur during learning.

In the serial learning task, there is abundant evidence that the functional unit of behavior is often not a single syllable within the list. When acquisition is closely examined for the individual subject, we note that subsets of adjacent words are often acquired together. If one member of the set is correctly anticipated, all members of the set are correctly anticipated (Martin & Noreen, 1974). As was true of the functional stimulus, the functional response with experienced organisms is not wholly determined by public events to which the experimenter has direct access within the experiment. The observed behavior is organized in ways that reflect not only the present environment, but past environments as well.

While this realization complicates the problem greatly, we need only echo Ebbinghaus: "We should prefer to see resignation arise from the failure of earnest investigation rather than from the persistent helpless astonishment in the face of their difficulties." Better to stumble in the effort to solve real problems than to triumph in the resolution of illusory ones.

SUMMARY

This chapter has been concerned with many topics—conditioned reinforcement, stimulus generalization, stimulus discrimination, applications of stimulus control to various phenomena, and the control of verbal behavior. As was noted at the outset, the analysis of stimulus control touches and provides a vantage point from which to view many of the diverse content areas of psychology.

In the treatment of conditioned reinforcement, we determined that conditioned reinforcers—like unconditioned reinforcers—function as elicitors of behavior and are accommodated by a relational principle of reinforcement. If the principle of reinforcement is to be of value in understanding human behavior, it must do so in the form of conditioned reinforcement.

The analysis of conditioned stimulus control yields evidence of the contribution of both phylogeny and ontogeny. Interdimensional discrimination training is not always essential for stimulus control, but it does invariably increase the precision of stimulus control and is necessary in many cases. When responding is acquired in one environment, dimensional stimulus control may develop, with the result that other environments containing stimulus elements in common with the training environment evoke the response but with a decreased frequency.

With intradimensional discrimination training, the range of stimuli that control the response is reduced still further. Environments that differ from those present during training evoke a mixture of the responses controlled by the discriminative stimuli. The determination of which aspects of the training environment control responding is a task for experimental analysis and not conjecture, as illustrated by the complexities encountered in the study of transposition. A relational principle of reinforcement also contributes greatly to our understanding of stimulus control as illustrated by such phenomena as edge effects and selective and general attention.

Many behavioral phenomena are illuminated by the findings uncovered in the analysis of stimulus control. Extinction, spontaneous recovery, and avoidance are representative examples within the field of learning.

Efforts to extend the analysis of stimulus control to the understanding of language and memory are greatly complicated by the extensive phylogenetic and ontogenetic background of the learner. Even the materials and methods devised by Ebbinghaus for the laboratory study of serial learning are not immune to the effects of important extraexperimental influences. It would be an error, however, to think of prior experience as merely a complication in the study of language and memory. The history of the species and of the individual are the very origins of the linguistic and memorial phenomena of greatest interest. The behavior of the experienced organism is not to be understood by an analysis of the contemporaneous environment alone.

NOTES

1. Some research has called into question the relationship between the conditioned reinforcing and discriminative functions of stimuli (for example, Kelleher & Gollub, 1962), but a plausible argument may be made for the failure to monitor the pertinent behavior rather than for the absence of such behavior.

   The relationship between elicitation and higher-order conditioning, a phenomenon allied to conditioned reinforcement (see pp. 82–83), has also received recent attention. In this research, the effects of alterations of the elicitation process in initial conditioning and in higher-order conditioning have been independently manipulated (for example, Rizley & Rescorla, 1972; Rescorla, 1973, 1977, 1979). The work has been primarily directed at the effect of subsequent changes in the elicitation process on performance established by earlier higher-order conditioning procedures. Through the use of higher-order conditioning, the stimulus and response components of the elicitation process may be independently manipulated and their contributions to learning studied.

2. The general term for the field in which knowledge of learning, especially reinforcement, is applied to the amelioration of dysfunctional human behavior is *behavior modification*. Much research dealing with the application of learning principles, and with ethical issues related to that application, may be found in periodical literature such as *Journal of Applied Behavior Analysis* and *Behavior Research and Therapy*.

3. The difference between generalization gradients obtained after nondifferential and differential auditory training is enhanced by the use of a lighted key during training (Rudolph & VanHouten, 1977). The great salience of visual stimuli with pigeons when food is present presumably blocks control by auditory stimuli.

4. There are a variety of other changes in responding that are brought about by interactions among stimuli differentially associated with reinforcement. These interactions also fall under the general heading of contrast effects and are reviewed in a number of other sources (for example, Bolles, 1975, pp. 412–423; Mackintosh, 1974, pp. 348–404).

5. Many studies have also been conducted regarding the effects of fading procedures on aspects of performance other than the efficiency with which the discrimination is acquired (see Terrace, 1966, and Rilling, 1977, for reviews).

6. The controlling stimulus in transposition experiments is also affected by many characteristics of the training procedure, notably whether a successive (multiple-stimulus) or a simultaneous (concurrent) discrimination procedure is employed. In general, simultaneous procedures, which provide for the appearance of both S_1 and S_2 on each training trial, favor control by the relationship between the stimuli. These and other matters are discussed in various reviews of the transposition literature (for example, Herbert & Krantz, 1965; Kalish, 1969; Mackintosh, 1974; Riley, 1968).

7. The biographical material was culled from the following sources: Boring, 1950; Shakow, 1930; Watson, R. I., 1971; Woodworth, 1909. To the best of our knowledge, no substantial biography of Hermann Ebbinghaus exists in the English language.

6
Motivation

INTRODUCTION

Through the action of differential reinforcement in our own lives and differential fitness in the lives of our ancestors, the stimulus control of behavior develops. The understanding of the changes wrought by these agents has moved us much nearer to knowledge of why we act as we do, but our journey remains unfinished. Among the issues that must still be confronted is motivation. Although it may be phrased in other terms, the study of motivation is largely an attempt to answer the following question: Why does the organism, in what appears to be the same environment, behave one way at one time and a different way at another time?

In the present section, we shall analyze the motivational question more closely in an effort to sharpen its focus and to discern possible routes to its answer. In subsequent sections, we shall discuss the basic findings in some detail and then examine two aspects of behavior often treated in motivational terms—the temporal patterning and the persistence of behavior.

The Problem of Motivation

There is no disputing the observation that the same organism sometimes behaves differently in what appears to be the same environment. At issue is how this observation shall be understood.

For some, the observation of variable behavior in an apparently constant environment is taken as a basic and unalterable limitation placed upon our understanding of behavior, particularly human behavior. From this perspective, variability is not a problem to be analyzed but a condition to be accepted. Science rarely adopts this attitude since, if behavior is truly capricious, continued investigation is to no purpose.

A second and equally unproductive approach is simply to attribute different motivations to the person when different behaviors are observed in ostensibly the same environment. Imagine the following hypothetical example.

You are seated in a quiet library and the person across the table from you reads a book without interruption for an hour. The next night, the same person with the same book fidgets in the chair, gazes into space, and leaves after a few minutes. Observations of this sort are commonly "explained" by an appeal to motivational terms. Thus the person might be described as "motivated" to read the first night and not the next. It should be clear, however, that appeals to "motives," "wishes," "desires," and the like are not explanations when used in this way. Such uses of motivational terms are simply an alternative means of describing our observations—we say the person was motivated in one case and not in the other only because we observed that person reading in the first instance and not in the second. Explanations of this sort are patently circular. Whereas we originally had the task of explaining why the behavior was variable, we now have the task of explaining why the motivation was variable. One mystery is simply exchanged for another when all we do is relabel observations in motivational terms.

A third approach to the problem of behavioral variability in an apparently constant environment is to examine the environment more closely in the hope of detecting some hitherto neglected feature that was present in one instance and not in the other. This approach represents a continued effort to account for the aberrant observation according to the principles of stimulus control. Returning to the example in the library, perhaps closer scrutiny would have revealed that the reader was wearing contact lenses on the first occasion and not on the second. Thus instead of a difference in "motivation" of the reader, there was a difference in ability to read the book.

Although the motivational question often yields to analysis as a subtle problem in stimulus control by the contemporaneous environment, a stubborn core of observations persists after such an approach has been exhausted. On many occasions, nothing in the present environment may be identified that is differentially available when the behavior occurs and when it fails to occur. In such cases, the explanation is sought in events that transpired prior to the observation, but whose effects have endured until the time of the observation. Organisms are historic creatures; they are the repositories of the effects of earlier environments and not passive reactors to present environments.

If stimuli from earlier environments bear a relatively specific relationship to stimuli from the present environment, the effects are most often classified as a crucially important subset of the field of stimulus control, namely *memory*. Referring to our example once again, the reader may have come upon something early in the book during the second night in the library that brought to mind an imminent appointment. Since the appointment was still some few minutes in the future, the person read a bit before leaving. A specific event in the past—making the appointment—might have been related to a specific event in the reading—perhaps a character in the book was of the same first name as the person with whom the appointment had been made. Memory may thus contribute to the variable behavior observed in a constant present environment. The study of memory and of the processes underlying memory will be pursued in later chapters.

More relevant to present purposes, however, are those instances in which prior environments affect present behavior, but in the absence of a specific relationship between observed (public) stimuli in the two environments. Under these conditions, the observations are most often classified as falling within the field of motivation. On coming into the library the second night, the person may have overheard a conversation indicating that a bomb threat had been phoned into the library. The person began to read, but slight noises normally ignored made the person jump, any movement caught the reader's attention, distracting thoughts interfered with reading, and so on. Faced with the inefficiency of the reading, the person left the library. Note that in this case, there was little specific similarity between the prior event—overhearing the bomb threat—and the present environment in which reading was disrupted. Also, many activities other than reading would presumably have been affected by the bomb threat. Finally, the satisfaction normally obtained from reading was decreased and the value of other activities, such as going outside the building, was enhanced. In short, the responsiveness of the reader to a wide range of stimuli was altered by news of the bomb threat.

Although no single example, much less one from everyday experience, illustrates purely any one effect, we are now in a position to be more precise concerning a technical definition of motivation. *Motivation* refers to a function of stimulation such that the presentation of a stimulus changes the strength of a wide range of elicitation processes. Just as a stimulus may serve reinforcing and discriminative functions, so it may also serve a motivating function to the extent that responding is altered to a considerable variety of other stimuli.

From this perspective, motivation is an additonal function of stimuli. As with the discriminative and reinforcing functions, the motivational function is not an inherent, invariant property of the stimulus. Furthermore, the various functions of stimuli are not independent of one another. If a stimulus having a motivational function changes the elicitation process involving a second stimulus, the ability of the second stimulus to function as a reinforcer is also affected.

Because of the intimate relationship between the eliciting and reinforcing functions of stimuli, we may anticipate that a major consequence of motivating events is that they alter the reinforcing function of other stimuli (Bolles, 1967; Catania, 1971a). Once again, a single event may have many functions and we should not regard events as belonging to mutually exclusive classifications of motivation, reinforcement, elicitation, and so on. A single event, such as an electric shock, may alter the organisms's response to many other stimuli (motivational function), decrease the frequency of responses that precede it (punishing function), and evoke a number of responses such as jumping and vocalizing (eliciting function). "Most cases are mixed cases, and we should not treat our classifications with too much respect" (James, 1902, p. 148).

One final point should be made regarding the view of motivation as a function of a stimulus that alters the responses evoked by a wide range of other stimuli. In this conception, the number of stimuli that may function motivationally is very large and may change with individual experience. Motivation is not a function of only those physiological deficits that are typically described as hunger, thirst, and the like—although procedures that produce such deficits are most often used in laboratory work. Other events—an overheard conversation about a bomb threat, for example—may also alter responding to a wide range of stimuli and thereby display a motivational function.

Overview

Motivation, as the term is used technically, refers to that function of stimuli whereby the strength of a wide range of elicitation processes is altered. The first major section of the chapter will be devoted to an analysis of motivation in this restricted sense.

Motivation is, however, a word from the everyday vocabulary, and as such possesses a richness of meaning that is only partially captured by the technical definition (Littman, 1958). For example, if we see one person working rapidly at a task and another working fitfully at that same task, we are apt to describe the first person as "motivated" and the second as "unmotivated." Thus differences in the temporal pattern of behavior are often interpreted in "motivational" terms. The second major section of the chapter will discuss some of the factors that affect the temporal pattern of responding. These factors include the motivational function of stimuli, but appeal chiefly to variables involved in schedules of reinforcement.

In the last major section, we shall discuss yet another aspect of "motivation" as that term is popularly used. If we see two persons engaging in the same task, neither with apparent success, and one persists and the other quickly desists, we are likely to call the first person "motivated" and the second "unmotivated." This difference in responding in the face of adversity will be designated as persistence. Again, the motivational function of stimuli, as used technically, will contribute to our understanding of persistence, but we shall also rely heavily on variables identified in the analysis of extinction following partial (intermittent) reinforcement.

MOTIVATIONAL FUNCTION OF STIMULI

Granted the restricted technical definition of motivation, we must come to grips with another issue before proceeding. Very often, the circumstances that lead to motivational effects may antedate the observation of those effects by an appreciable interval of time. A rat must be deprived of food for a few hours before the strengths of various elicitation processes begin to change. An overheard bomb threat may antedate by many minutes the heightened responsiveness that interferes with reading. How is the temporal disjunction between the initial motivating condition and the subsequent effect of that condition to be conceptualized?

Levels of Analysis

The question of temporal disjunction may be addressed on two levels—the behavioral level and the level of inferred processes. On the behavioral level, an attempt is made to discover orderly functional relationships between the observable motivating condition and the responses that are ultimately affected by that condition. Thus we might investigate how various responses change as a function of the number of hours of food deprivation. On the behavioral level, the inferred processes that intervene between the motivating condition and its behavioral effects are not of immediate concern. The behavioral approach will be used primarily in the present treatment of motivation.

The approach to the study of motivation via inferred processes postulated to underlie the observed relationships is a challenging, but hazardous, business—especially when the inferred processes are purely conceptual and not at the physiological level. As an example of the dangers inherent in some appeals to inferred processes, consider the following case history. A psychiatrist observed the behavior of a woman on a ward in a mental hospital. Wherever she walked, she carried a broom at her side, although she was never seen to sweep the floor. How could this behavior be understood?

The psychiatrist "explained" the woman's behavior in this way:

> Her constant and compulsive pacing, holding a broom in the manner she does, could be seen as a ritualistic procedure, a magical action. . . . Her broom would be then: (1) a child that gives her love and she gives him in return her devotion, (2) a phallic symbol, (3) the sceptre of an omnipotent queen . . . this is a magical procedure in which the patient carries out her wishes, expressed in a way that is far beyond our solid, rational and conventional way of thinking and acting. (Cited in Allyon, Haughton, & Hughes, 1965, p. 3)

Although there may be antecedents in the history of the psychiatrist that account for this explanation, the actual origin of the behavior was rather more mundane. For a number of days prior to the observation, her behavior of holding the broom had been reinforced on a VI 30-min schedule by the presentation of cigarettes. The study had been done as a part of a project on learning in chronic schizophrenic patients.

What may be learned from this example, apart from the fact that some psychologists enjoy fooling psychiatrists? Most generally, the antecedents of this seemingly bizarre behavior were to be found in the history of specific prior environmental-behavioral interactions. Knowledge of that history has largely eliminated the need to appeal to such motivations as love of a symbolic child, displaced sexual urges, or feelings of omnipotence. Rather than being "far beyond our solid, rational and conventional way of thinking," the behavior of carrying the broom exemplified a principle in the analysis of behavior, the principle of reinforcement.

None of this is to say that the private events inferred by the psychiatrist might not accompany similar behavior in some patients. The point is that it is hazardous to make inferences about such events from the very behavior that those inferred processes seek to explain. In the instance of broom carrying, a more complete knowledge of the antecedents of the behavior has dispelled much of the mystery. If we had comparable knowledge of the antecedents of other psychotic symptoms, would some of these also yield to more conventional analyses? We suspect so.

When inferred processes are pursued at the physiological level, and not solely conceptually, we are on firmer ground. (For a related discussion, see the treatment of inferred processes in the analysis of the dual-process theory of habituation, pp. 62–64.) The analysis of the physiological processes that intervene between the motivating condition and the observed changes in behavior is, in fact, one of the most active areas of research in physiological psychology. Although a survey of this research is beyond the scope of the present work, research is progressing rapidly on brain mechanisms (for example, Antelman & Caggiula, 1977; German & Bowden, 1974; Gold, 1973; Teitelbaum & Epstein, 1962), on peripheral mechanisms (for example, Friedman, M. J., & Stricker, 1976; Russek, 1971; Wade, 1972), and on sensory mechanisms (for example, Zeigler & Karten, 1974). The most complete understanding of the physiological processes underlying motivational effects comes from work with a simplified preparation—the blowfly (Detier, 1976).

Ultimately, of course, an understanding of motivational effects will draw upon information at both the behavioral and physiological levels, as well as the biochemical level. The fundamental unity of scientific inquiry demands no less. (See Hoffman & Solomon, 1974; Solomon & Corbit, 1974, for some initial efforts in this direction.)

The present approach to motivation focuses first on the consequences of deprivation and second on findings obtained with procedures involving more direct forms of motivational stimulation. Depriving an organism of food would illustrate the first procedure; administering electric shock or brain stimulation would illustrate the second. Most deprivation and stimulation work is concerned with the effects of motivation on a single monitored response—particularly the classically or instrumentally conditioned response. The third focus is *interim*, or *adjunctive, behavior*. These are the behaviors that occur in an environment during the interim between presentations of the motivating stimulus. Interim behaviors are dependent upon the occurrence of the motivator, but there is no experimenter-defined contingency between interim behavior and other events in the situation. Thus if an animal drinks water or attacks another animal when food is available only intermittently, drinking and attacking may be interim behaviors.

Deprivation-Produced Motivation

Left free to wander about their natural environments, individuals display a quite systematic pattern of contact with various stimuli. If we go without food or water for more than three or four hours, for example, we make an effort to reestablish contact. The nature of these patterns is determined by the joint action of the ancestral environment of the species (Collier, Hirsch, & Kanarek, 1977) and the past and present environments of the individual. The "hunger" that we feel when we see a picture of an ice-cream cone is complexly determined by the number of hours without food, our prior experience with ice cream, and having just seen the picture.

Elicitation When the normal pattern of contact with stimuli is disrupted, the eliciting function of those stimuli is enhanced and the eliciting function of other stimuli may also be altered. The simplest procedure for disrupting the normal pattern is to reduce the total amount of contact with the stimulus, a procedure called *deprivation*. Thus an organism that normally would have three meals over a 24-hr period might be totally prevented from eating. If you had not eaten for 24 hours, you would be more apt to salivate at the sight of an ice-cream cone, and at other stimuli that might not ordinarily evoke this reaction. Total abstinence is only the simplest deprivation procedure, of course, and other more complex procedures for altering the normal pattern are possible (Dunham, 1977; Premack, 1965).

Food deprivation in the rat provides an experimental example of how deprivation may alter the reaction to the environment. (For obvious reasons, deprivation studies are more readily conducted with organisms other than humans.) If a rat is deprived of food, food-elicited activities such as salivating and eating become more vigorous when food is ultimately presented. Food deprivation changes the response to other features of the environment as well. If deprivation takes place in an environment in which stimulation is held constant at a low level, activity—such as running in an activity wheel or moving about a cage—remains at a relatively low level. If, however, the environment is more variable and heterogeneous, large increases in activity occur (Teghtsoonian & Campbell, 1960). If stimulus change is introduced for only a short period of time each day, increases in activity are confined primarily to the period of stimulation (Campbell, B. A., & Sheffield, 1953). Finally, the relationship of stimulation to the presentation of food at the daily feeding may also affect the responding evoked by the stimulus. If the feedings occur immediately after a brief stimulus period, activity increases during that period. If there is no relationship between the stimulus and the occurrence of food, activity gradually declines (Sheffield, F. D., & Campbell, 1954). Thus deprivation affects not only the response to food but to other stimuli as well.

Reinforcement   Because elicitors of behavior are typically able to function as reinforcers, a major effect of deprivation is to alter the reinforcing value of stimuli. Food has been used as an example of a reinforcer at many points in this text, yet the ability of food to serve this function is dependent upon its having been established as a reinforcer through deprivation.

Indeed, recent work indicates that, in order for instrumental procedures to produce behavioral change, the contingency between the instrumental response and the reinforcer must restrict the organism's contact with the reinforcer below baseline levels (Premack, 1965; Timberlake & Allison, 1974). Unless the normal level of contact with the stimulus is reduced by the instrumental contingency, hence maintaining the eliciting properties of the stimulus, the stimulus does not function as a reinforcer. The precise restriction in the pattern of contact that is necessary to maintain the reinforcer is the subject of continuing study (Allison, 1976; Dunham, 1977; Terhune, 1978), but deprivation produced by reduced overall contact is clearly sufficient.

Not all elicitors are heavily dependent on deprivation for their effectiveness, as is food. Electric shock is an example of this second class of elicitors.

However, frequent contact with such stimuli does diminish their effectiveness to the extent that the elicited response habituates. Reduced deprivation and increased habituation have similar effects.

Stimulus Control   Deprivation affects the vigor of elicitation processes and the vigor of elicitation processes, in turn, affects the ability of stimuli to function as reinforcers. Since reinforcers bring about changes in the conditioned stimulus control of behavior, we may anticipate that deprivation will also affect learned responses.

The effect of food deprivation on responding in two instrumental conditioning procedures is shown in Fig. 6.1. Using a discrete-trial procedure involving a running response with rats in a straight alley, the terminal level of performance was an increasing function of the number of hours of food deprivation (Davenport, 1956; see Fig. 6.1a). Similar findings have been obtained using a free-responding procedure with rats in a bar-pressing task (Clark, F. C., 1958; see Fig. 6.1b).

Generalized responses are also affected by the level of deprivation. As an illustration, pigeons were trained to peck a response key transilluminated with a 550-nm wavelength under different deprivation levels. Deprivation was manipulated by varying the percent of normal body weight during training for different groups of birds. Following the attainment of stable rates of responding, a generalization test was conducted in extinction with wavelengths of 490 to 550 nm. The generalization gradients obtained from animals trained and then tested at 70%, 80%, and 90% of normal body weight are shown in Fig. 6.2. Generalized responding increased as the level of deprivation increased (see also Newman & Grice, 1965, and Thomas, D. R., 1962).

Behavioral Processes in Deprivation   On a behavioral level, two means by which deprivation may affect the frequency of a response have been identified. First, by increasing the vigor of the elicitation process the discrepancy, which is identified as critical to learning by a relational principle of reinforcement, is increased. In the instrumental procedure, this increased discrepancy may be described as an increased preference for the environment containing the reinforcer. If the reinforcer—for example, food—gains in preference relative to other elicitation processes, more time should be devoted to the instrumental response that is followed by the reinforcer than to other responses that are followed by other elicitors.

In confirmation of this analysis, the increase in the average rate of responding, produced when deprivation is increased, is accompanied by a decrease in other responses. In the runway, for example, activities such as rearing up on the hind legs or sniffing decline in frequency (Cotton, 1953). Thus average speed increases in part because as deprivation increases the stream of behavior consists more exclusively of the instrumental response.

A second means by which deprivation affects responding requires the assumption that deprivation gives rise to distinctive internal stimuli (private

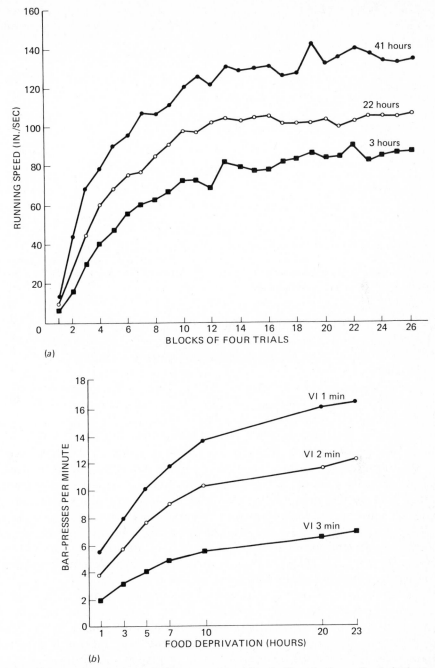

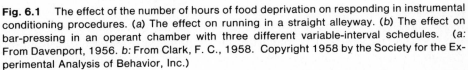

Fig. 6.1   The effect of the number of hours of food deprivation on responding in instrumental conditioning procedures. (a) The effect on running in a straight alleyway. (b) The effect on bar-pressing in an operant chamber with three different variable-interval schedules.   (a: From Davenport, 1956. b: From Clark, F. C., 1958. Copyright 1958 by the Society for the Experimental Analysis of Behavior, Inc.)

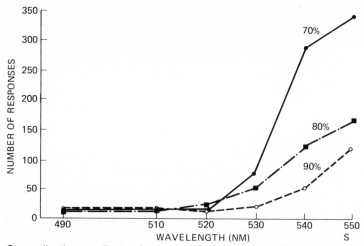

Fig. 6.2 Generalization gradients along the wavelength dimension obtained after training and testing at 70, 80, and 90% of normal body weight. Nondifferential training was given with 550-nm stimulus. (From Kalish & Haber, 1965. Copyright 1965 by the American Psychological Association. Reprinted by permission.)

events) (Guthrie, 1935). Stimuli arising from stomach contractions or from receptors that monitor the level of circulating nutrients might be examples of such events. The precise physiological events are not completely known but there is both indirect and direct evidence that these stimuli exist. The mere fact that we feel differently when we are "hungry" than when we are "thirsty" is one piece of evidence. Experimentally, rats in a modified T maze will acquire differential turning responses at the choice point depending upon whether they are food- or water-deprived (Hull, 1933; Leeper, 1935), or whether they have been deprived of food for 3 or 24 hrs (Bloomberg & Webb, 1949; Bolles, 1962).

If different deprivation conditions produce distinctive internal stimuli, these stimuli may acquire control over the response. That is, deprivation-produced stimuli should acquire stimulus control just as do observable (public) stimuli. In confirmation of this analysis, responses acquired at one deprivation level and then tested at a second level decrease in frequency as do responses acquired during one external stimulus and tested during a second external stimulus (Yamaguchi, 1952). Stimulus control generalizes whether the control is exerted by external or internal stimuli.

Furthermore, if deprivation-produced stimuli become more numerous as deprivation increases, a greater proportion of the stimuli present when the response is reinforced should be deprivation related. The consequence of the greater proportion of deprivation-produced stimuli is an increased likelihood that the stimuli controlling the response will be present (Estes, 1958).

Thus, through its joint effects on the vigor of the elicitation process and the occurrence of deprivation-produced stimuli, deprivation procedures alter the average frequency of responding. The behavioral processes that underlie the observed effect on average responding are those previously encountered in the relational principle of reinforcement and the generalization of stimulus control.

Stimulation-Produced Motivation

Thus far we have studied the motivational function of stimuli using deprivation as the procedure for the manipulation of such stimuli. In this section, we shall employ more direct procedures for the presentation of motivating stimuli. We shall examine the effects of motivating stimuli presented to the periphery of the organism—for example, electric shock—and presented centrally—for example, electrical stimulation of the brain.

Stimuli other than those arising from deprivation have clear motivational functions. The overheard bomb threat with which we began this discussion is one example; the parent's admonition to the child to "be careful" when leaving the house is another. In both cases, these words change the stimulus control of many responses. Because stimulation that has a potent motivating effect in laboratory procedures is often aversive or is often applied directly to the brain itself, we shall again turn to infrahuman organisms for basic information. (For a presentation of somewhat related work with human subjects on the effects of arousal on learning and memory, see Eysenck, 1976; and Walker, E. L., 1958, 1967.)

Aggressive Behavior   A particularly well-studied example of the motivating function of stimulation is provided by strong aversive stimuli. Electric shock applied to the periphery (Azrin & Holz, 1966) or direct electrical stimulation of certain hypothalamic brain structures (Flynn, Vanegas, Foote, & Edwards, 1970) will elicit attack on environmental objects. As expected, attackable objects will then function as reinforcers. Monkeys, for example, will acquire a new response that gains them access to an attackable object (Azrin, Hutchinson, & McLaughlin, 1965). Aggression to painful stimulation is not inevitable, however. If given the opportunity, organisms will escape or avoid such stimuli rather than attack (Azrin, Hutchinson, & Hake, 1967).

When electrical stimulation of the brain (ESB) is used to elicit aggressive behavior in cats, two types of attack may be distinguished. (See Hinde, 1974; Marler, 1976; and Theissen, 1976, for more extensive treatments of aggressive, or agonistic, behavior.) The first type is called *affective attack* and is characterized by an arched back, hissing and growling, and—most importantly—striking with unsheathed claws and savage biting. The second type, which is of greatest present interest, consists of approach to the object (usually an anaesthetized rat in laboratory studies), pushing the rat on its back, and biting directed at its head and neck. This second type is called *quiet-biting attack* (Flynn et al., 1970; Roberts, 1970).

In addition to simply eliciting attack, ESB also increases the number and intensity of elicitation processes. ESB expands the area of the muzzle of the cat from which orientation toward and biting of the object may be elicited (Flynn et al., 1970, pp. 163 ff.). In the absence of ESB, a stick touched to the side of the cat's muzzle elicits the turning away of the head. During ESB, the same touch causes the midline of the mouth to move toward the stick and the mouth to open. Moreover, the area from which touch is effective in eliciting quiet-biting attack increases with an increased intensity of ESB (MacDonnell & Flynn, 1966).

Although stimulation applied to an expanded surface area of the cat's body will elicit quiet-biting attack during ESB, it is important to note that the nature of the stimulation remains important. Cats attack rats, not elephants. If additional objects such as toy animals or horsemeat are available, it is only the rat that is attacked (Levison & Flynn, 1965). Quiet-biting attack does not occur in the absence of species-typical prey (for example, Hess, 1957). Experience also plays an important role in the determination of species-typical prey; cats reared in isolation do not direct their attack preferentially at rats rather than sponges placed in the cages (Roberts & Bergquist, 1968).

Thus in our examination of attack behavior produced by ESB, we see evidence of both the eliciting and motivating functions of stimulation, of the continued role of environmental stimulation, and of the importance of prior experience with that stimulation.

Reinforcing Brain Stimulation   Heretofore, we have relied upon deprivation procedures to establish elicitation processes that may then function as reinforcers. However, reinforcers as well as punishers may also be produced by electrical stimulation of the brain (Olds & Milner, 1954). ESB serves as a reinforcer in the absence of deprivation, although deprivation and hormonal conditions often modulate the magnitude of the effect (for example, Deutsch & DiCara, 1967; Hoebel, 1968; Olds, 1958), and may function as a reinforcer in many species, including man (Heath & Mickle, 1960, 1963). Moreover, reinforcing brain stimulation has many of the properties of other reinforcers (for example, Beninger, Bellisle, & Milner, 1977; Pliskoff & Hawkins, 1967; Trowill, Panksepp, & Gandleman, 1969), and enters into functional relationships in a manner consistent with a relational principle of reinforcement (for example, Hollard & Davison, 1971; Holstein & Hundt, 1965). In short, central stimulation of the brain seems to function as a reinforcer in much the same way as peripheral stimulation following deprivation.

With central stimulation, as with peripheral stimulation, the relationship between elicitation and the reinforcing and motivating functions of stimuli is an intimate one. Reinforcing brain stimulation often functions as an elicitor of behavior and may always so function if an appropriate environmental stimulus can be found (cf. Olds, Allan, & Briese, 1971; Valenstein, Cox & Kakolewski, 1968, 1970; von Holst & von Saint-Paul, 1963). As an example, if no clear-cut elicited response (a so-called *stimulus-bound behavior*) is observed during ESB, observers reported, "The behavior of the animals was most interesting and consistent ... the animal spent all of its time appearing to be 'searching' for the consummatory goal object" (Valenstein et al., 1969, p. 263, see also p. 256). Moreover, ESB may facilitate a wide range of elicitation processes depending upon the types of stimuli present in the environment. If food is present a rat may eat. If only water is present, ESB to the same brain site in the same animal may elicit drinking as a stimulus-bound behavior (Valenstein et al., 1968; see also Antelman & Caggiula, 1977, and Rowland & Antelman, 1976, for work of similar import using peripheral stimulation). Both unconditioned stimulus control, such as attack in the cat upon the sight of a mouse (Flynn et al., 1970), and conditioned stimulus control, such as bar-pressing in the rat upon the onset of a light (Beagley & Holley, 1977), may be facilitated by ESB. In summary, ESB facilitates a range of elicitation processes, that is, serves a motivational function.[1]

ESB, and perhaps every reinforcer (Beninger & Milner, 1977), facilitates a range of elicitation processes. As an experimental example using ESB, if a food-satiated rat finds both food and ESB in one goalbox of a T maze, eating will be elicited by food and the animal will learn to turn toward that goalbox at the choice point of the maze (Mendelson & Chorover, 1965). Thus ESB acts as a motivator to facilitate the elicitation of eating by the sight of food, and food then functions as a reinforcer for turning at the choice point even though the animal is satiated for food.

The preceding result may appear paradoxical if the term motivation is used in its everyday sense. The result seems to be saying that organisms learn in order to be motivated, rather than that they must be motivated in order to learn. As used here, however, the motivating function of a stimulus refers simply to its capacity to facilitate a range of elicitation processes. The following example may provide a better sense of the process. Imagine that you had exhausted your ability to perform sexually and that the movie star of your choice suddenly appeared and expressed an interest in sexual activity. If someone gave you a magic button that would restore the vigor of your sexual elicitation processes, would you push the button? If so, then you have responded to be motivated, as that term is used here. Or, more precisely, you have responded to put yourself in a condition such that your behavior may be reinforced by the occurrence of elicitation processes.

Interim Behavior

In our previous discussion of the motivational effects of deprivation and direct stimulation, the motivational function of a stimulus was assessed by examining its effects on an instrumental response or a relevant elicitation process. Thus the effects of food deprivation in the rat might be studied through measuring its effects on bar-pressing for food or on eating given the sight of food. But what happens when a motivating stimulus is presented and there is neither an effective instrumental response nor a relevant elicitor?

For an authoritative answer to this question, we turn to our resident expert—the laboratory animal. Suppose a food-deprived rat is placed in a test chamber containing a response lever, a foodcup, and a drinking tube. Suppose further that bar-pressing produces food, but only a small amount (45 mgm) once every minute. What happens in the interim between the occurrences of food when bar-pressing is ineffective and when there is no food to eat? The answer is, the rat drinks (Falk, 1961). In fact, the rat drinks approximately ten times as much water as it would otherwise consume under comparable conditions of deprivation if the same amount of food were available in a single large meal (Falk, 1969). Some other, less relevant, elicitation process is facilitated.

The behavior that is observed between occurrences of the elicitor, but which is dependent for its existence upon the presentation of the elicitor, is called *interim behavior* (Staddon & Simmelhag, 1971). Other related terms that have been proposed include *schedule-induced* (Falk, 1966), *adjunctive* (Falk, 1966), and *intercurrent* behavior (Smith, J. B., & Clark, 1974). When similar responses are found in the natural environment of the species, as opposed to a laboratory environment, they are termed *displacement activities* (Tinbergen, 1952, 1964; cf. Falk, 1977).

Characteristics of Interim Behavior Interim behavior is not confined to overdrinking (polydipsia) in food-deprived rats that receive food intermittently—although this is the most thoroughly studied case. The phenomenon is found with rats, pigeons, monkeys and humans, and with elicitors other than food (see Falk, 1971, 1972; Staddon, 1976, for reviews).

The following examples illustrate the generality of the conditions under which interim behavior has been observed. Rhesus monkeys drink water if given intermittent food (Schuster & Woods, 1966); pigeons peck visually localized environmental features if given intermittent food (Miller, J. S. & Gollub, 1974); pigeons attack members of their own species if given intermittent food (Flory, 1969); rats run in wheels if given intermittent water (King, 1974); squirrel monkeys drink water if given intermittent shock (Hutchinson & Emley, 1977); rats drink water if given intermittent access to running wheels (Wayner, Singer, Cimino, Stein, & Dwoskin, 1975); and humans smoke and eat if given intermittent access to problem-solving and money-winning tasks (Kachanoff, Leveille, McLelland, & Wayne, 1973; Wallace & Singer, 1976). Note that these examples also illustrate that the intermittent presentation of the same elicitor (for example, food) may result in different interim behaviors (for example, drinking or attacking), and that the elicited and interim behavior may be interchanged (for example, wheel-running and drinking). It should be noted also that the interim activity may have clear phylogenetic antecedents (for example, drinking in rats) or clear ontogenetic antecedents (for example, smoking in humans).

The import of all of this work is that the intermittent presentation of an elicitor facilitates other elicitation processes (Killeen, 1975, 1978). It is not simply that the unavailability of one activity (for example, eating) leaves more time for interim activities (for example, drinking), since the level of the interim activity increases above appropriate control levels (cf. Dunham, 1972). The findings that interim behavior occurs primarily in the time period immediately after the elicitor, that the amount of interim behavior is a function of the rate of presentation of the elicitor, and that deprivation of the elicitor enhances interim behavior all implicate the motivating function of the elicitor in the origin of interim behavior (Falk, 1966, 1967, 1969, 1971).

The specific interim response that is facilitated by the intermittent presentation of the elicitor is dependent upon the availability in the environment of the stimuli that control the response (Falk, 1977). Thus intermittent food leads to attack or drinking in pigeons depending on whether another pigeon (Flory, 1969) or water (Shanab & Peterson, 1969) is available. Similarly, intermittent food leads to drinking or chewing in rats depending on whether water or wood chips are available (Freed & Hymovitz, 1969). The motivating effect of intermittent food presentation is functionally identical to the motivating effect of intermittent brain stimulation, in that both are capable of facilitating a wide range of elicitation processes depending upon the environment in which they occur.

TEMPORAL PATTERNING OF BEHAVIOR

We have now completed the portion of the chapter that, in the strict technical sense, deals with motivation. However, as was mentioned at the beginning of our discussion, the term "motivation" connotes behavioral phenomena other than those associated with the facilitation of a range of elicitation processes. Among these other phenomena are the temporal patterning of behavior, to which we now address ourselves, and the persistence of behavior, to which we shall turn in the following major section.

Let us illustrate the motivational flavor of everyday descriptions of the temporal pattern of behavior by reference to the following laboratory example. Suppose that a rat occasionally receives food after bar-pressing, but only if less than 1 sec has elapsed since the previous bar-press. Suppose further that a second rat also occasionally receives food after bar-pressing, but only if more than 10 sec have elapsed since the previous response. Under these circumstances, although the level of food deprivation and the time between food presentations may be made essentially the same for both animals by reinforcing the criterion responses on different VI schedules, the first rat is typically described by observers as "hungrier," "more motivated," or "harder-working" than the second. Conversely, the second rat is described as "not very hungry," "unmotivated," or even "lazy." Not knowing the different rules whereby responses produced food for the two animals, the fact that the first rat responded rapidly with few pauses while the second rat responded slowly with many pauses is interpreted in motivational terms.

From an earlier discussion, you may remember that in the first case bar-pressing was being maintained by a DRH (differential reinforcement of high rate) schedule, but in the second case by a DRL (differential reinforcement of low rate) schedule. That is, the two animals did not differ in motivation but in the schedule of reinforcement. "By the manipulation of schedules, a wide range of changes in behavior can be produced, most of which would previously have been attributed to motivational or emotional variables" (Ferster & Skinner, 1957, p. 2).

Schedules of Reinforcement

A *reinforcement schedule* is a precise statement of the conditions under which a reinforcer occurs. This includes a complete description of the necessary and sufficient environmental, temporal, and behavioral requirements that must be met prior to the presentation of the reinforcer. The study of schedules of reinforcement had its origins both in laboratory convenience (Skinner, 1959) and in the desire to represent more faithfully the circumstances under which reinforcers occur in nature (Tolman & Brunswik, 1935). With reinforcement schedules, as with nature, not every occurrence of the instrumental response is followed by the reinforcer.

The free-responding procedure is most often used for the study of reinforcement schedules because of the greater ease in manipulating the various environmental, temporal, and behavioral requirements of the schedule (Ferster & Skinner, 1957; Skinner, 1933). The effects of schedules of reinforcement permeate every procedure and color every result, however, whether we choose to investigate them or to ignore them.

In every instrumental situation, some set of conditions must occur prior to every reinforcer, and the concept of schedules of reinforcement is simply an explicit acknowledgement of that truth. These conditions affect the stimulus control and temporal patterning of behavior whether they are obtained in a free-responding procedure in an operant chamber, a discrete-trial procedure in a runway, a verbal learning experiment in the laboratory, or in the less easily specified environments outside the laboratory.

The subject of schedules of reinforcement is too extensive to be fully explored here. Our goal will be to survey the behavioral effects of the elementary schedules of reinforcement, giving some sense of the means whereby they exert their effects on the temporal patterning of behavior. We shall conclude this section with discussions of interim activities in schedules of reinforcement and with some transfer effects between various schedules that are often given "motivational" interpretations.

Elementary Schedules of Reinforcement The elementary procedures devised for studying the effects of schedules of reinforcement on behavior may be divided into two classes—*interval schedules* and *ratio schedules*. Interval schedules are so named because reinforcers are delivered for the first response following a specified interval of time since the preceding reinforcer. Interval schedules may be of either the *fixed-interval (FI)* or *variable-interval (VI)* type.

In FI schedules, a fixed interval of time must elapse since the previous reinforcer before responding produces the next reinforcer. For example, the key-pecking response of a pigeon might be followed by access to grain if 60 sec had passed since the previous presentation of grain. Such a procedure would be described technically as a FI 60-sec schedule. An example that touches the human condition is as follows: A loved one is expected home from a trip at six o'clock in the evening. No matter how many times we go to the door and open it, door-opening will not lead to the sight of the loved one until the appointed time has arrived.

In the second type of interval schedule, VI schedules, a variable interval of time must elapse before a response is effective. Thus in a VI 60-sec schedule, a random selection from among intervals whose average was 60 sec would pass before responding produced a reinforcer. A VI schedule would be approximated by circumstances in which a loved one was expected to arrive on a given day of the week but the exact time of arrival was unknown. Note that in both FI and VI schedules, a response is still required in order for the reinforcer to occur. A temporal requirement has been *added* to the response requirement; time has not been substituted for the response.

So much for a description of FI and VI schedules. What effects do these procedures have on the temporal distribution of responding—on the "motivation" of the learner? Some representative findings in which key-pecking of deprived pigeons produced grain are shown in Fig. 6.3. Let us examine first the

Fig. 6.3 The temporal patterns of responding produced by (a) FI and (b) VI schedules of reinforcement. The cumulative records show the key-pecking of individual pigeons with food as the reinforcer. For ease of presentation the records have been closely spaced. The delivery of food is denoted by (a) downward and (b) horizontal movement of the recording pen.   (From Ferster & Skinner, 1957. Reprinted by permission of Prentice-Hall, Inc., Englewood Cliffs, New Jersey.)

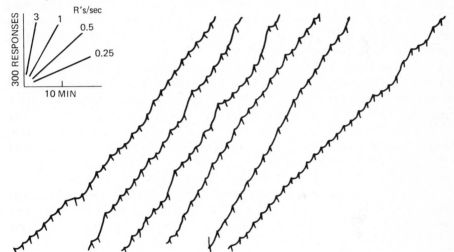

(a) Sustained reinforcement on FI 1 min

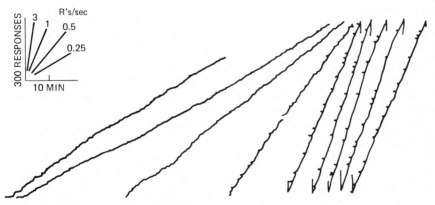

(b) Development of responding on VI 1 min

effects of FI schedules. After exposure to an FI schedule for some sessions, a distinct pattern of responding emerges: Responding seldom occurs in the early portion of the interval, but as the time draws nigh for delivery of the reinforcer the frequency of responding increases (see Fig. 6.3a). (The pattern of responding observed with FI schedules is, in the jargon of the laboratory, referred to as the "FI scallop.") The pigeon pecking the key for food and the person opening the door for the sight of a loved one both respond more often as the time for the reinforcer approaches.

When VI schedules are instituted, the frequency of responding occurs at a more nearly constant rate and the pause after the reinforcer is virtually eliminated (see Fig. 6.3b). The pigeon regularly pecks the key and the person checks the door, as responding may produce the reinforcer at any moment.

The second class of elementary schedules also includes two types—*fixed-ratio (FR)* and *variable-ratio (VR)* schedules. In FR schedules a constant number of responses must be emitted before the reinforcer occurs. Thus there is a fixed ratio between the number of responses and the number of reinforcers. As examples, a rat might be required to make 10 bar-presses to get food or a child might be required to complete 10 math problems before being permitted to go out to play. In either case, an FR-10 schedule would be in effect.

In VR schedules, a variable number of responses is the criterion for the delivery of reinforcers. On a VR-10 schedule, either 5, 10, or 15 responses might be required before food for the rat or play for the child would become available.

The behavioral effects of FR and VR schedules are displayed in Fig. 6.4. In FR schedules, particularly those with substantial response requirements, a period of not responding occurs after each reinforcer, and then responding abruptly increases to a high rate (see Fig. 6.4a). Speaking loosely, both the rat and the child are apt to procrastinate before getting down to work, but once work begins it will likely continue at a high rate until the ratio requirement has been satisfied. With VR schedules, high rates of responding are also produced, but the breaks in responding are largely eliminated (see Fig. 6.4b). The very next bar-press may be the one that produces food; the very next math problem may be the one that is followed by playtime.

As the foregoing brief survey indicates, schedules of reinforcement exert powerful effects on the temporal pattern of responding. Similar effects exist in other situations as well. Consider a discrete-trial situation employing a runway. To the extent that each trial consists of a number of running responses, to that extent does the runway situation resemble a ratio schedule (Keller, F. S. & Schoenfeld, 1950). Indeed, when environmental variables are equated, changes in the speed of running in a runway and in the rate of bar-pressing within a FR schedule display highly similar patterns (Donahoe, 1970; Donahoe, Schulte, & Moulton, 1968). In the natural environment, when the parent accedes to the child's request only after prolonged pleading, the child's verbal pleas have also produced a reinforcer on a ratio schedule. High rates of pleading on subsequent occasions may be anticipated in the latter case, just as high rates of bar-pressing and running are found in the earlier cases.

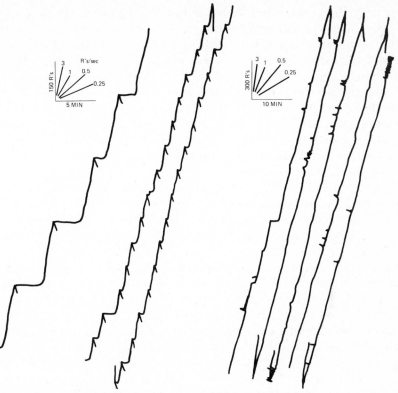

(a) Transition from FR 185 to FR 65   (b) Sustained VR 173

Fig. 6.4   The temporal patterns of responding produced by (a) FR and (b) VR schedules of reinforcement. Note the longer pauses following reinforcement with FR 185 than with FR 65. Note the virtual disappearance of pauses with VR 185. The response is key-pecking by pigeons and food is the reinforcer.   (From Ferster & Skinner, 1957. Reprinted by permission of Prentice-Hall, Inc., Englewood Cliffs, New Jersey.)

Experimental Analysis of Schedules   There is no doubt that the schedule of reinforcement exerts a profound effect on the temporal pattern of responding. What is yet in doubt is a very precise understanding of the behavioral processes that are responsible for the pattern. We now turn to that issue.

An extensive literature exists concerning the variables that affect the response patterns produced by various schedules of reinforcement (for example, Morse, 1966; Zeiler, 1977). Upon analysis, the so-called elementary schedules of reinforcement are complex procedures that provide many alternative sources for the stimulus control of responding (Ferster & Skinner, 1957). The identification of all of these sources exceeds the value of the knowledge for present purposes. However, to give some sense of the complexities, we shall consider briefly a few of the potential sources of stimulus control in one type of elementary schedule—the FI schedule.

With an FI schedule, it will be recalled, the rate of responding is low for some time after a reinforcer and then becomes higher as the time approaches for the delivery of the next reinforcer. In the vernacular, the learner is not "motivated" to respond after a reinforcer but "motivation" grows stronger as the next reinforcer draws near. What are some of the variables that may be important in generating the pattern of responding known as the FI scallop?

Let us first consider the responses that occur within the FI schedule. Since the instrumental response (R) does not produce a reinforcer until a fixed interval of time has elapsed, instances of R preceded by other responses (R_os) of longer durations are more apt to produce the reinforcer than when preceded by R_os of shorter durations. For example, if a pigeon receives food for key-pecking on an FI 60-sec schedule, an occurrence of R after R_o of 60-sec duration always produces food whereas an R following an R_o of a shorter duration is less likely to do so. Thus an R after an R_o of 20 sec produces food only if the R_o begins more than 40 sec after the previous reinforcer; all other occurrences of an R_o of 20 sec are ineffective. In short, an FI schedule implicitly arranges for the occurrence of reinforcers after longer as opposed to shorter IRTs, and we know that the differential reinforcement of longer IRTs reduces the rate of responding (cf. Platt, 1978; Reynolds & McLeod, 1970; Richardson, 1973).

Once the FI scallop has developed, there is a second potential role that responses occurring within the interval may play. If many Rs have already occurred within the interval, then it is likely that the next R will produce the reinforcer since that R is apt to be late in the interval. Conversely, if few Rs have occurred, it is not likely that the next R will produce the reinforcer since that R is apt to be early in the interval. Thus after considerable exposure to an FI schedule, the *number* of previous responses may be a source of stimulus control. It should be noted that there is no causal relationship between the number of responses and the likelihood of a reinforcer with an FI schedule, only a temporal one. As we know, a reliable temporal relationship is one constituent of the conditions necessary for the development of stimulus control.

Although response-produced stimulation may function as a discriminative stimulus (for example, Rilling & McDiarmid, 1965; Schulte, cited in Donahoe, 1970) and may play a role in FI schedules (Rilling, 1967), it can be shown that such stimuli are not essential to the maintenance of the FI scallop. Consider the following experiment that was designed to disrupt the usual relationship that exists between the number of responses in an interval and the likelihood of the reinforcer (Dews, 1962).

Key-pecking by pigeons produced food according to an FI 500-sec schedule. Occasionally, the diffuse light that normally illuminated the test chamber was turned off for 50 sec. During the dark periods, the interval continued to be timed, but few key-pecks occurred because pigeons normally roost in the dark. If key-pecking provided discriminative stimuli essential to the maintenance of the FI scallop, a dark period with little responding should "reset" the interval and cause subsequent key-pecking to return to the low rate characteristic of the beginning of the FI. If the FI scallop can be maintained by other sources of control, however, insertion of the dark periods would not disrupt the pattern of responding.

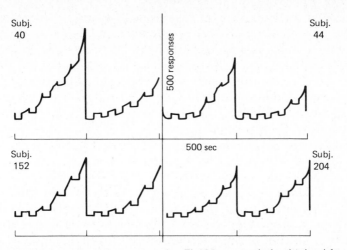

Fig. 6.5 Cumulative records of two successive FI 500-sec periods obtained from four individual pigeons. The five downward "notches" in each FI signify 50-sec test periods during which the chamber light was turned off. The downwards marks on the horizontal line under each cumulative record indicate the delivery of the reinforcers.   (From Dews, 1962. Copyright 1962 by the Society for the Experimental Analysis of Behavior, Inc.)

The results of the occasional insertion of five such dark periods within the FI 500-sec schedule are shown in Fig. 6.5 For all four subjects, key-pecking during the dark periods was largely eliminated, but yet the FI scallop remained basically unchanged. (See Dews, 1970, for a summary of this and related studies.)

These research findings show that response-produced stimuli are not necessary for the maintenance of the temporal pattern of responding found with FI schedules. What other sources of stimulus control exist? One further candidate that we shall consider is the discriminative function of the reinforcer itself. Because R is effective only after an appreciable length of time has elapsed since the presentation of the previous reinforcer, the stimulus consequences of the reinforcer may acquire control over subsequent occurrences of R. From this perspective, the insertion of periods without responding within the FI period would not disrupt the pattern because the time since the preceding reinforcer has not been disturbed.

In confirmation of the ability of the reinforcer to acquire a discriminative function, when food is occasionally omitted at the end of one fixed-interval, responding during the beginning of the next interval is greatly enhanced (Staddon, 1970, 1974; Staddon & Innis, 1969). Thus the reinforcing stimulus and its aftereffects are other sources for the stimulus control of responding within fixed-interval schedules.

The foregoing discussion of the possible effects of the implicit differential reinforcement of IRTs, and of the discriminative functions of the number of responses and of the reinforcer itself, gives some indication of the complexities encountered in the analysis of the sources of stimulus control in the "elementary" schedules of reinforcement. The capacities of living organisms for the stimulus control of their behavior are so extensive that it is naive to believe that only one variable is responsible for the temporal pattern of behavior in such complex circumstances. Experiments seeking potential sources of stimulus control with various schedules of reinforcement make an important contribution, but such findings establish boundary conditions on the capacities of organisms and should not be viewed as normative accounts of the sources of stimulus control (cf. Morse, 1966, p. 91).

Because of the complications encountered in the analysis of the "elementary" schedules of reinforcement, most recent work has employed synthetic schedules. In *synthetic schedules*, the necessary and sufficient conditions for the reinforcer are defined more exhaustively, with the result that potentially controlling stimuli are easier to study and independently manipulate. (The term synthetic is used to indicate that the contingency is a combination, or synthesis, of a number of different conditions rather than only one "elementary" condition, such as the passage of a fixed interval of time since the preceding reinforcer.) Although an understanding of the organism's potential sensitivity to sources of stimulation is essential to the analysis of the temporal patterning of behavior, it is not essential that the question be pursued with the "elementary" schedules of reinforcement (cf. Jenkins, H. M., 1970; Mackintosh, 1974, pp. 181–182).

Only one experiment employing a synthetic schedule will be described, an experiment to determine whether a pattern similar to the FI scallop could be *directly* shaped through following the pattern itself by the reinforcer (Hawkes & Shimp, 1975). The implementation of this synthetic schedule was accomplished with a digital computer, a common technique when complex contingencies are imposed on behavior. (See Schoenfeld, Cole, Blaustein, Lachter, Martin, & Vickery, 1972, for one system of synthetic schedules.)

After conditioning key-pecking in the pigeon, reinforcement was made contingent upon emitting a series of responses with successively decreasing IRTs. For example, the 10th key-peck in a series of consecutive key-pecks might be reinforced if the time between prior successive responses approximated 9, 8, 7, 6, 5, 4, 3, 2, and 1 sec, respectively. By requiring an ever closer approximation to the desired pattern, a scallop developed that was more regular in its temporal characteristics than the scallop produced by a conventional FI schedule. The terminal performance obtained with this synthetic schedule is depicted in Fig. 6.6.

If evidence is consistently forthcoming to substantiate the development of patterns of responding through the differential reinforcement of those patterns, the functional response, or operant, may be capable of a very complex definition indeed. For the experienced learner, an operant may consist of a behavioral pattern constructed from originally independent responses by the shaping effects of differential reinforcement. As with playing a guitar, in which the individual finger movements are replaced with practice by patterns of chording and plucking, so might a pattern of responses become a functional unit of behavior. These complex operants, or "chunks" of behavior, might then

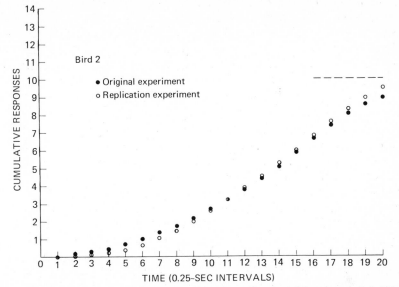

Fig. 6.6   The pattern of responding produced by direct shaping of the temporal distribution of responding by a computer-implemented synthetic schedule. The time over which the pattern was generated was 5 sec and performance was measured in .25-sec intervals. The horizontal dashed line represents the requirement that each interval contain 10 responses.   (After Hawkes & Shimp. 1975. Copyright 1975 by the Society for the Experimental Analysis of Behavior, Inc.)

be sensitive as a unit to the effects of further reinforcers. The possibility of complex operants complicates the understanding of the behavior of the experienced learner, but it increases greatly the flexibility with which organisms may respond to changing environmental conditions (cf. Shimp, 1975, 1976).

By-products of Schedules of Reinforcement
When pauses occur in the emission of instrumental responses, other responses occur. What is the nature of these other responses? When we recall that we are dealing with a deprived organism which is receiving intermittent presentations of small amounts of a potent elicitor, a likely candidate immediately comes to mind—interim behavior.

Interim Behavior   A variety of interim activities have been studied in the context of a number of schedules of reinforcement. We shall focus on aggressive behavior as it appears in some of the elementary schedules.

Interim behavior occurs most frequently during periods in which the instrumental response is not likely to be followed by the reinforcer. In order to study activity during such periods more directly, an explicit discrimination procedure may be instituted in which reinforcement is available during S_1, but is unavailable during S_2. S_2 is, therefore, a stimulus correlated with an extinction schedule. A number of theorists (for example, Amsel, 1958; Pavlov, 1927;

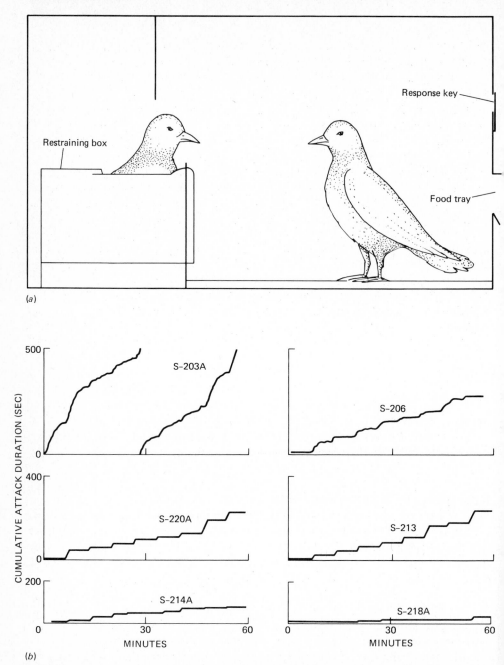

Fig. 6.7 (a) Test chamber showing the response key and the target pigeon. (b) Cumulative records of attack behavior shown for six different pigeons. Note that attack generally occurs at the onset of the extinction period just after the receipt of food. (From Azrin, Hutchinson, & Hake, 1966. Copyright 1966 by the Society for the Experimental Analysis of Behavior, Inc.)

Skinner, 1938; Spence, 1960) have suggested that "emotional" responses occur within extinction periods, particularly during the early stages of exposure to extinction.

As an illustration of extinction-induced attack, consider the following experiment using the pigeon (Azrin, Hutchinson, & Hake, 1966). Pigeons were placed on a discrimination procedure with alternating periods of reinforcement and extinction. In addition to a response key, the test chamber contained another pigeon that was restrained as shown in Fig. 6.7a. Attacks on the restrained pigeon, as well as key-pecking, were recorded.

The results are shown in Fig. 6.7b. Shortly after the discontinuation of the reinforcer, the restrained pigeon was attacked. (To avoid damage to live birds, stuffed birds and even mirrors were used as targets in subsequent research.) Using various control procedures, it was shown that attack was not dependent on the occurrence of key-pecking or on social interactions with other birds prior to the experiment. The insertion of time intervals between the delivery of reinforcement was sufficient to elicit attack during the interim periods (cf. Flory, 1969).

Since many schedules of reinforcement necessarily introduce intervals of appreciable duration between successive reinforcers, we might anticipate that aggressive behavior would also occur in such circumstances. Indeed, this is the case. When FR schedules are employed, attack occurs during the pause in responding that characterizes the beginning of each repetition of the schedule (for example, Gentry, 1968) and attack increases with increasing response requirements by the FR schedule (Cherek & Pickens, 1970). When FI schedules are employed, a similar phenomenon is observed during the early portion of the interval when the key-pecking response occurs with low frequency.

Because intermittent reinforcement facilitates the elicitation of attack, it would also be anticipated that the stimuli controlling attack behavior could function as a reinforcer. To evaluate this possibility, a pigeon was placed in a test chamber containing two response keys. Pecking one of the keys produced food according to an FI 2-min schedule; pecking the other key raised a door on one side of the chamber that provided access to a restrained target pigeon (Cherek, Thompson, & Heistad, 1973). As indicated in Fig. 6.8, responding on the food-producing key showed the usual pause after reinforcement followed by pecking until food was obtained. During the postreinforcement pause, however, the pigeon responded on the other key to produce the target bird, which it then promptly attacked. Thus the intermittent presentation of food to a deprived organism had a motivating effect on the elicitation of attack that permitted the stimulus controlling attack to function as a reinforcer.

Should we conclude from these results that aggression is the inevitable consequence of the intermittent presentation of reinforcers? Not at all. First, as we discovered in our earlier study of interim behaviors, the specific nature of the interim behavior varies with the stimuli present in the environment. If another organism is present, attack may occur; if water is present, drinking may occur. Second, even if a target for aggression is available, the level of attack behavior will vary with its consequences. If a target bird defends itself vig-

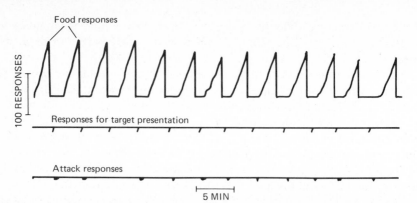

Food responses

100 RESPONSES

Responses for target presentation

Attack responses

├── 5 MIN ──┤

Fig. 6.8 The top record is a cumulative record of key-pecking maintained on a FI 2-min schedule for food reinforcement. The record is reset after each reinforcer. The middle record indicates pecks on a second key that caused a door to be raised which permitted access to a restrained pigeon. The bottom record indicates the occurrence of attacking pecks directed at the restrained target bird. (From Cherek, Thompson, & Heistad, 1973. Copyright 1973 by the Society for the Experimental Analysis of Behavior, Inc.)

orously, then attack toward that target is reduced (Azrin et al., 1967). Interim responses are affected by their consequences, as are other responses. Third, if an instrumental response is available that escapes the environmental stimuli present during intermittent reinforcement, the response will be acquired (Rilling, Askew, Ahlskog, & Kramer, 1969).[2]

Transfer Effects Between Schedules
In the laboratory studies considered thus far, only one type of reinforcement schedule has been operative. In natural environments, however, life is rarely so simple. The schedules according to which reinforcers are presented vary from situation to situation, and from time to time within the same situation. Since the entering behavior of the learner determines the specific manner in which responding comes into contact with the requirements of the schedule, differences in the entering behavior may lead to enduring differences in the behavior produced by the schedule. Although no general treatment of transfer effects between schedules is yet available, enough information is known to indicate the importance of such transfer effects. (See Ferster and Skinner, 1957; Weiss, B. 1970, for a discussion of some of the general issues.) We shall consider a few representative examples that have been studied in the laboratory and then comment upon some possible implications for the understanding of the behavior of experienced organisms beyond the confines of the laboratory.

Learned Helplessness. As a first example of transfer between schedules, let us examine the effect of prior response-independent presentations of an elicitor on the subsequent function of that elicitor in a response-dependent schedule. What happens, for example, when the learner is first given an aversive stimulus independently of what the learner does, and then is provided with a response that will escape or avoid the aversive stimulus?

To answer this question, dogs were first given a number of unavoidable, inescapable electric shocks. Then the dogs were separately placed in a test chamber divided into two parts by a barrier. A stimulus was given, and if the dog did not jump the barrier to the other side of the chamber within 10 sec, shock was administered. Under these conditions, dogs which had not received prior response-independent shocks quickly learned to escape and then to avoid the shock. Dogs which had first received unavoidable shock were severely retarded in learning to avoid or even to escape the shock (Overmeier & Seligman, 1967). The retarding effect of response-independent shock on the development of escape and avoidance responses is called *learned helplessness* (see Maier & Seligman, 1976; Seligman, Maier, & Solomon, 1971, for reviews).

A similar deleterious effect of response-independent presentations of an elicitor has been shown with appetitive stimuli. If deprived pigeons are given response-independent presentations of food and are then transferred to an autoshaping procedure in which the illumination of the key-light precedes food, the development of key-pecking is retarded (Engberg, Hansen, Welker, & Thomas, 1972). This phenomenon has been labeled—somewhat tongue-in-cheek—*learned laziness*.

What produces the phenomena of learned helplessness and learned laziness? No generally accepted theoretical analysis is yet available. Some investigators have proposed that during the response-independent phase of the experiment, the subjects acquire a "cognitive set" (an inferred process) in which they learn that there is no relationship between their behavior and the occurrence of important events (for example, Maier & Seligman, 1976). Other investigators have proposed that the subject acquires specific responses in the response-independent phase that then compete with the avoidance response in the response-dependent phase (for example, Glazer & Weiss, 1976a, 1976b; Bracewell & Black, 1974).

A third possibility should be mentioned. The co-occurrence of background stimuli with the elicitor during the response-independent phase may lead to the acquisition of components of the elicited response. Then the discrepancy between the behavior of the subject at the outset of the response-dependent phase and the behavior elicited by the putative reinforcer would be minimal and instrumental conditioning would be blocked. In short, under some circumstances the negative transfer effect of response-independent presentations of the elicitor may be understood from the perspective of a relational principle of reinforcement (see pp. 140–142; cf. Lawry, Lupo, Overmeier, Kochevar, Hollis, & Anderson, 1978; Rosellini & Seligman, 1978).

Shock as a Reinforcer   A final experimental example of transfer effects between schedules of reinforcement illustrates a particularly paradoxical finding: Following some prior experiences, an aversive event may maintain and even lead to the acquisition of responses that produce the aversive stimulus (Morse & Kelleher, 1977). After preliminary training with baseline schedules of reinforcement involving either food presentation (Kelleher & Morse, 1968) or shock omission (avoidance) (McKearney, 1969), an FI schedule of shock presentation was superimposed on the baseline schedule. Following a

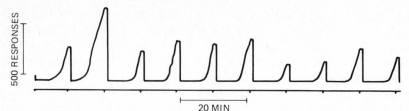

Fig. 6.9 Cumulative record of bar-pressing maintained by the presentation of electric shock. The response of the monkey produced shock according to an FI 10-min schedule followed by a 1-min period during which all responses produced shock.   (From Morse & Kelleher, 1977.)

period of training during which both the baseline and shock presentation schedules were operating simultaneously, the baseline schedule was eliminated. Now, with only the FI schedule of shock presentation operative, responding continued! The temporal pattern of responding was similar to that found with FI schedules of food presentation. (See Brown, 1969; Melvin & Martin, 1966, for related work.) That is, the pattern of responding was an FI scallop although the only consequence of responding was electric shock. If the monkeys had ceased responding, they would never have received any more shocks.

An example of a number of FI periods from such a procedure is shown in Fig. 6.9 (Morse & Kelleher, 1977). Not only is a previously acquired response maintained by shock, but another response may be acquired as well. When shock that had previously been administered for responding on the right response key was switched to the left key, the FI pattern was acquired on the left key.

Although experimental analysis of the origins of these various transfer effects remains incomplete, there is no disputing the fact and the potential significance of such effects. The entering behavior of the learner as well as the prevailing schedule of reinforcement must be incorporated into a comprehensive analysis of the patterning of behavior. The importance of what the learner brings to the learning situation—whether its source be the environment of the species or of the individual—should be a familiar theme. It was implied by a relational interpretation of reinforcement and was implicit in the very procedure of shaping a response. A pigeon placed in a test chamber with an FR 500 schedule of food presentation would starve to death. That same pigeon given food for every response and then gradually exposed to FR schedules of increasing requirements would prosper.

Extensions to Human Behavior   The similarity between transfer effects observed with schedules of reinforcement and certain phenomena observed in human behavior is provocative. The deleterious effects of earlier experience with response-independent events on later learning is seen by some as having implications for human depression and feelings of helplessness (Seligman, 1975). The concept of external vs. internal locus of control of behavior devised by personality theorists (Rotter, 1966) bears on a similar issue. People described as under external control are those who view the relationship between their behavior and its consequences as essentially capricious and determined by chance. People whose behavior is described as under internal control are those who view the events that follow behavior as being caused by their actions. Whether the relationship between behavior and subsequent events is perceived as capricious or causal might be affected by the experiences of the person with response-independent and response-dependent schedules and with the consistency and complexity of those schedules (Phares, 1976).

The nature of the response-dependent schedule of reinforcement is also relevant to some of the "needs" and "motivations" identified by personality theorists. One extensively studied social motive has been labeled "need-achievement" and has been described as the willingness of a person to continue at a demanding and effortful task until success has been attained (McClelland, Atkinson, Clark, & Lowell, 1953; McClelland, 1961). This description conjures up visions of ratio schedules to those familiar with schedules of reinforcement. Perhaps a conditioning history containing successively more extensive response requirements is one of the antecedents of need-achievement.

Proposals that link human depression, internal vs. external control, and need-achievement to schedules of reinforcement and to transfer effects between schedules are, of course, speculations. They are, at most, the sorts of notions that mark the beginnings of a rapprochement between diverse fields. Many serious efforts of this sort may be identified (for example, Bandura, 1969; Bandura & Walters, 1963; Krasner & Ullmann, 1965; Miller & Dollard, 1941; Mowrer, 1950; Wolpe, 1958, 1973), but the pursuit of these efforts is beyond the scope of this book.

PERSISTENCE OF BEHAVIOR

In order to capture more completely the meaning of "motivation" as that term is commonly used, we found it helpful to supplement findings regarding the general facilitation of elicitation processes with those relating to schedules of reinforcement. Knowledge of the motivating function of stimuli and of the schedule of reinforcement were both essential for understanding the temporal pattern of responding. In this section, we examine another aspect of behavior that is often described in "motivational" language—the persistence of responding. When someone persists at a task, especially when no obvious gain is accruing as a result of the activity, that person is often described as "highly motivated."

In our study of persistence, we shall find that the motivational function of stimuli—as that term is used technically—contributes importantly to the phenomenon. As in our analysis of the temporal patterning of behavior, however, other factors must be included. In particular, the motivational function of stimuli must be supplemented by the principles of stimulus control if persistence is to be understood. Before evaluating the contribution of motivation and stimulus control to persistence, we shall first describe the basic procedures and findings relevant to the study of persistence.

Basic Findings

In the laboratory, persistence is most often investigated by means of an extinction test following various acquisition conditions. Those conditions that produce the greatest resistance to extinction, as measured by a criterion such as the number of responses during the extinction test, are the conditions that favor persistence. Although resistance to extinction is affected by many variables, by far the most influential are those contained within acquisition conditions involving *partial reinforcement*. In partial reinforcement, only some of the conditioned stimuli or only some of the instrumental responses are followed by the reinforcer and resistance to extinction is greatly enhanced.

The finding that resistance to extinction is greater following partial reinforcement is paradoxical since it appears to be inconsistent with the known effect of reinforcers on responding. Because of this apparent paradox, the study of the increased resistance to extinction after partial reinforcement—the so-called *partial reinforcement extinction effect*—has attracted a great deal of experimental attention since its discovery in the 1930s (Brunswik, 1939; Humphreys, 1939; Skinner, 1938). We shall consider only a small portion of this vast literature here. (See Mackintosh, 1974, for a critical review of the effects of partial reinforcement on both acquisition and extinction.)

Most work on partial reinforcement has been conducted using discrete-trial procedures in the hope of reducing interactions between successive responses. (See Ferster & Skinner, 1957, p. 67, for a discussion of "percentage re-

Fig. 6.10 Acquisition with 100% reinforcement (Phase I); maintenance with 100, 50, 25, or 15% reinforcement (Phase II); and extinction (Phase III) of the nictitating membrane response of the rabbit. (After Gibbs, Latham, & Gormezano, 1978.)

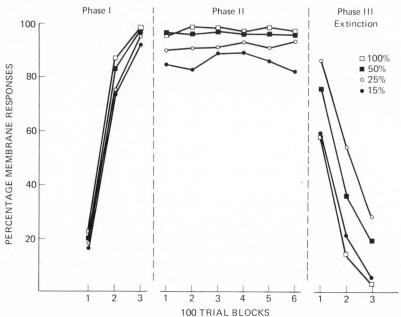

inforcement" in this regard and Staddon, 1970; Staddon & Innis, 1969, for examples of related work using free-responding procedures.) Typically, following initial acquisition of the response the reinforcer is presented on only a portion of the trials, and training is continued until performance has stabilized. Then an extinction test is given as a measure of persistence.

As an illustration of the partial reinforcement extinction effect, consider the following classical procedure employing the nictitating membrane response of the rabbit (Gibbs, Latham & Gormezano, 1978). Following initial training with 100% tone-shock pairings, different groups of animals were gradually shifted to 50%, 25%, or 15% reinforcement. As shown in Fig. 6.10, performance during partial reinforcement remained at or near the high levels maintained by 100% reinforcement. (For still lower percentages, for example, 5%, performance did decline.) Now to the major finding of present interest, the effect of partial reinforcement on persistence as measured by resistance to extinction: Responding continued at higher levels following partial reinforcement than following consistent (100%) reinforcement (see Fig. 6.10). Thus the partial reinforcement extinction effect occurred.

The greater persistence of responding following partial reinforcement is a hardy phenomenon, being reported for both classical and instrumental procedures and for many species (see Jenkins, W. O., & Stanley, 1950; Lewis, 1960; Robbins, 1971, for reviews). Many analyses have been offered of various aspects of the phenomenon (for example, Denny, 1946; Humphreys, 1939; Mowrer & Jones, 1945; Sheffield, V. F. 1949), but we shall focus upon only two sets of variables—those relating to the motivational effect (Amsel, 1958, 1967, 1972) and the discriminative effect of reinforcers (Capaldi, 1966, 1967, 1971).

Analysis of the Partial Reinforcement Extinction Effect

Partial reinforcement training consists of a series of trials, some of which terminate with a reinforcer and some of which do not. In an experiment conducted in a runway, food is present in the goalbox on some trials and not on others. We already know that the presentation of a reinforcer may generally facilitate other elicitation processes, depending upon the stimuli in the environment. Food may, therefore, function as a motivator and facilitate other elicitation processes, including those involving the instrumental response and interim behaviors. Responding on subsequent acquisition and extinction trials could then be influenced by the motivating function of food presentations, either directly via unconditioned effects or indirectly via conditioned effects.

In addition to serving a motivating function, the reinforcer may also function as a discriminative stimulus. Partial reinforcement consists of a sequence of reinforced and nonreinforced trials, and the outcomes of previous trials are in an appropriate temporal position to control responding on subsequent trials. From what we know of the generalization of stimulus control, we would expect responding to persist in extinction to the extent that the stimuli present during extinction are similar to the stimuli previously present when the response was followed by the reinforcer. We shall examine the partial reinforcement extinction effect to see if a discriminative function of the reinforcer contributes to the understanding of the pardoxically persistent responding after partial reinforcement.

Motivational Function of the Reinforcer   Elicitors that serve as reinforcers may also function as motivators for subsequent elicitation processes. What is the effect of omitting the reinforcer from an environment in which the reinforcer has previously occurred? This, of course, is the situation that obtains in partial reinforcement.

In runway procedures, the immediate effect of omitting the reinforcer from the goalbox is often not apparent, since successive trials are ordinarily separated by an appreciable intertrial interval. However, by the use of a double runway in which the goalbox of the first alley serves as the startbox of the second alley, the effect of omission of the reinforcer may be seen (see Fig. 6.11a). After 28 sessions in which food was presented in both goalboxes, food was occasionally omitted from goalbox 1. As shown in Fig. 6.11b, the speed of running in the second alley increased to a level above that found after the reinforcer (Amsel & Roussel, 1952; Wagner, 1959).

Reinforcer omission in an environment in which the reinforcer has previously occurred produces motivational effects (Skinner, 1938; Spence, 1937). In the case of the double runway, the motivational effect is shown by the facilitation of running in the second alley. By pairing stimuli from goalbox 1 with food, the goalbox stimuli should acquire control over the responses elicited by food. These conditioned responses will then occur on both food and nonfood trials since the environmental stimuli are the same in both cases. The occurrence of conditioned responses in the absence of the reinforcer produces the motivational effects observed in the second alley. This motivational effect of omission of the reinforcer is called *frustration* (Amsel, 1958).

Stimuli that have been paired with elicitors are known to acquire the capacity to function as motivators themselves. For example, a stimulus previously paired with shock will induce attack if an attackable environmental object is present (Hutchinson, Renfrew, & Young, 1971). Similarly, omission of food from a compartment in which food was previously available will induce attack or escape and lead to the acquisition of responses that permit either activity (Senowski & Denny, 1977).

Given that partial reinforcement will produce motivational (frustrative) effects, how may these effects aid the interpretation of the greater resistance to extinction after partial reinforcement? Amsel (1958) has proposed the following account. During partial reinforcement training, omission has frustrative effects. These frustrative effects result from responses conditioned to goalbox stimuli and may be evoked, via stimulus generalization, by other similar stimuli such as those found in the startbox and alleyway. Frustration, in turn, is assumed to have stimulus properties. On food trials, therefore, the stimuli in whose presence responding is reinforced have two origins: external stimuli from the apparatus and internal, inferred stimuli from frustration. Since both external and frustrative stimuli are present, both stimuli acquire control of the running response with continued training. When extinction is begun, frustra-

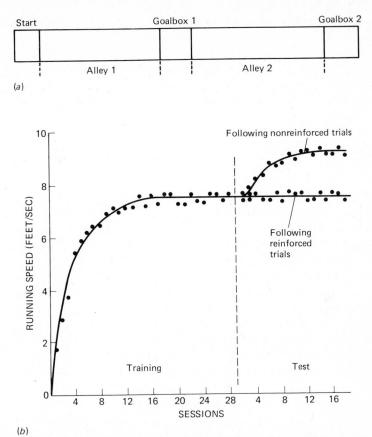

Fig. 6.11 (*a*) Diagram of the apparatus and (*b*) the effects of nonreinforcement on running speed in the second alley as a function of training sessions. The speed scores were obtained by taking the reciprocals of the median running times (in sec) in the original experiment and should, therefore, be regarded as approximate. (After Amsel & Roussel, 1952. Copyright 1952 by the American Psychological Association. Reprinted by permission.)

tive stimuli are produced because of nonreinforcement, but responding persists after partial reinforcement because frustrative stimuli have been established as discriminative stimuli for the instrumental response.

In learners exposed only to consistent reinforcement, however, the circumstances are different. Frustrative stimuli are also assumed to be produced when extinction begins, but responding has never previously been reinforced in the presence of such stimuli. Accordingly, extinction after consistent reinforcement is hastened because the stimuli during extinction are changed from those present during acquisition. In addition, the motivational effect produced by nonreinforcement may facilitate other elicitation processes—such as attack or escape—that compete with the running response.

While there is abundant evidence that omission of reinforcers will generate motivational effects, evidence also exists which shows that frustration is not essential for the occurrence of the partial reinforcement extinction effect.

In order for frustration to be produced by the omission of the reinforcer, the reinforcer must first have occurred in that environment. However, research indicates that partial reinforcement training consisting of only no-food followed by food trials will also produce the partial reinforcement extinction effect (Capaldi & Waters, 1970; Spear, Hill, & O'Sullivan, 1965). A sequence of nonreinforced (N) followed by reinforced (R) trials, for example, NNNRRR, also increases resistance to extinction. Thus frustration—even though it has a clear motivational effect and may contribute to the phenomenon through the inferred processes described earlier—cannot account for all instances of persistence following partial reinforcement.

Discriminative Function of the Reinforcer   Instead of appealing to the stimulus properties of frustration, a compelling analysis of the findings produced by partial reinforcement is possible if it is assumed that omission and presentation of the reinforcer have discriminative effects. Extinction consists of a series of nonreinforced trials. If it can be shown (a) that the stimuli on nonreinforced trials may exert discriminative stimulus control over responding on subsequent trials, and (b) that such control is established during partial reinforcement training, the partial reinforcement extinction effect is amenable to analysis as a problem in stimulus control.

What is the evidence regarding the discriminative effects of the outcome of previous trials on performance during subsequent trials? The answer to this question has been sought in a number of ways (Capaldi, 1966, 1967), but we shall consider findings from only one procedure—single-alternation patterns of partial reinforcement. If a rat is exposed to a strictly alternating sequence of food and no-food trials, for example, RNRNRN, responding becomes rapid on R trials and slow on N trials (Capaldi & Stanley, 1963). The effect is increased by larger magnitudes of food that make the outcomes on food and no-food trials more different (Campbell, Crumbaugh, Rhodus, & Knouse, 1971). Since responding always produces food after N trials and never after R trials, differential responding develops with a single-alternation pattern. The animals have not "learned the pattern" in some more general sense, because appropriate changes in running speed do not develop with double-alternation sequences, for example, RRNNRRNN (Bloom & Capaldi, 1961). The animal responds equally rapidly on all trials since the outcome of the previous trial is not differentially correlated with food on the following trial.

How may the finding that the outcome of the previous trial exerts stimulus control over responding on the subsequent trial be used to account for greater persistence after training with partial reinforcement? Capaldi (1966, 1967) has proposed that responding on a given trial comes under the control both of stimuli from the apparatus and of the aftereffects of stimuli from the previous trial. With partial reinforcement, these stimuli include the aftereffects of both R and N trials, whereas with continuous reinforcement only the aftereffects of R trials are present. Thus when extinction is begun and only N trials occur, responding persists in the partial reinforcement group because only in that group has responding produced food following the aftereffects of nonreinforcement from the previous trial. As can be seen, both the frustration and aftereffect accounts of persistence provide an interpretation based upon the discriminative effects of stimuli. In the frustration account, the critical stimuli arise from inferred frustrative responses controlled by stimuli within the same trial; in the aftereffects account, the critical stimuli arise from the outcome of the previous trial.

If the control of responding by the aftereffects of N trials is crucial to greater persistence, this implies that a nonreinforced trial followed by a reinforced trial (an NR transition) is the major origin of the partial reinforcement extinction effect. Only with an NR transition does the aftereffect of a no-food trial have an opportunity to be present on the next trial when responding produces food.

A number of lines of evidence support the view that the NR transition is crucial to the occurrence of persistence. First, if two partial reinforcement conditions are instituted, one condition having the sequence NNRR and the second the sequence RRNN, only the first condition shows the partial reinforcement extinction effect (Spivey & Hess, 1968). Both groups have an equal number of food and no-food trials and yet the first group, the one with the opportunity for the aftereffect of an N trial to function as a discriminative stimulus, persists in responding during the extinction test. Moreover, when sequences are used that vary the number of NR transitions for different groups, resistance to extinction increases as a function of the number of NR transitions (Spivey, 1967). The more NR transitions and the greater the number of N trials prior to an R trial, the greater the similarity of training to the stimulus conditions that prevail during extinction.

A second line of evidence comes from studies that use procedures to alter the aftereffects of the outcomes of the previous trial. Let us suppose, for example, that during the interval between trials a rat is fed in another box. If feeding occurs between trials of what would otherwise be an NR transition, the aftereffect of the interpolated feeding may interfere with the aftereffect of food omission from the previous trial. To the extent that this occurs, persistence should be diminished. Intertrial feeding placed within an RN transition, on the other hand, should have little effect since RN transitions do not contribute importantly to persistence. In accordance with this expectation, only the placement of food within an NR transition greatly diminished the partial reinforcement extinction effect (Capaldi, Hart, & Stanley, 1963).

While there is little question that the outcomes of previous trials function as discriminative stimuli for the control of responding, and that these stimuli provide a major basis for the understanding of persistence, some further comments should be made. When we appeal to the aftereffect of an event as a discriminative stimulus, we are squarely within the field of memory. Procedurally, research on memory is typically concerned with the effects of prior experience on later responding when the two are separated by appreciable time intervals. Recent work on aftereffects makes direct contact with the analysis of memory (Capaldi, 1971) and we shall pursue related matters in detail in subsequent chapters.

Findings that indicate the memorial character of the variables affecting persistence include the following: (a) The partial reinforcement extinction effect may be found with a 24-hr interval between trials (Weinstock, 1954). (b) The effect endures when a series of continuously reinforced trials are given prior to the extinction test (Jenkins, H. M., 1962; Theois, 1962). (c) Partial reinforcement in one situation enhances persistence in other situations in which only continuous reinforcement has occurred (Amsel, 1967; Brown, R. T., & Logan, 1965). Thus the study of partial reinforcement ultimately leads to the study of memory. It is encouraging to note that the analysis of the two phenomena converge (Capaldi, 1971; Tulving & Thompson, 1973) and that principles derived from the study of partial reinforcement in animals are helpful in understanding memory in humans (Halpern & Poon, 1970).

Conclusion   We began this section with the observation that differences in the persistence of responding are often described in motivational terms. Our inquiry into persistence, as it is manifested in resistance to extinction, has revealed that variables contained within partial reinforcement training exert the greatest effect on the continuance of responding. The motivational function of the reinforcer, as the term motivation is used technically, does affect responding as described by frustration. However, many of the effects of partial reinforcement on persistence appear to arise from the discriminative, rather than the motivating, function of trial outcomes. Whether using a frustrative or an aftereffects account, persistence occurs to the extent that responding has previously produced a reinforcer under the conditions that prevail during extinction—the frustrative and discriminative effects of reinforcer omission. In short, persistence grows from adversity. Those who persist are those who have in the past experienced failure and only then succeeded.

SUMMARY

Motivation is a word from the popular vocabulary and is used in a variety of ways in an effort to explain the elicitation, temporal pattern, and persistence of behavior. The appeal to motivation in this general sense is especially strong when the immediate antecedents of behavior are obscure to the observer.

As used here, motivation is a function of stimulation that denotes effects on the vigor of a broad range of elicitation processes. If a stimulus has a motivating function, it alters the responses that are controlled by many elicitors, both unconditioned and conditioned. Deprivation procedures are commonly used to enhance the motivating function of stimuli. Because motivating events affect the vigor of many elicitation processes and because the vigor of elicitation processes is intimately related to the reinforcing function of stimuli, motivational changes are often expressed through changes in the effect of reinforcers. Other responses than the instrumental response may also reflect the motivating function of stimuli. These responses—interim behavior—constitute a wide range of activities including aggressive behavior and excessive drinking.

Although motivation in the technical sense makes an important contribution to the temporal pattern of behavior through the augmenting of interim behavior, many of the differences in the rate of responding are attributable to the schedule of reinforcement. The schedule of reinforcement refers to the precise environmental, temporal, and behavioral conditions that must be met if the instrumental response is to produce the reinforcer. By varying the require- ments of the schedule of reinforcement, wide variations in the rate and tem- poral pattern of responding may be produced, even though motivation is held constant. Changes in behavior that are often attributed to differences in moti- vation may be understood as the effects of different schedules of reinforce- ment.

Finally, the persistence of behavior was analyzed. In the present context, persistence is measured by the extent to which behavior continues even though responding is no longer followed by a reinforcer. As with the temporal pattern of responding, the motivational function of stimuli provides only a be- ginning to the understanding of persistence. The use of a partial reinforcement procedure, in which only some occurrences of the response are followed by the reinforcer, favors the continuation of responding during a subsequent extinc- tion test. This finding is termed the partial reinforcement extinction effect. Frustration effects, which are motivational in nature, are helpful in under- standing observations such as an increase in the instrumental response or in interim behaviors immediately after nonreinforcement. In general, however, many of the phenomena associated with partial reinforcement are better un- derstood in terms of the discriminative function of the outcome of previous trials. This is especially true with respect to the effects of different sequences of reinforced and nonreinforced trials during training. A reinforced trial followed by a reinforced trial—an NR transition—is a major contributor to the partial reinforcement extinction effect. The understanding of persistence, especially with long intertrial intervals and with long intervals between partial reinforcement training and extinction testing, converges on the analysis of memory.

NOTES

1. The identification of the motivating function of stimulation with the facilitation of a range of elicitation processes bears some similarity to the notion of generalized drive (D) proposed by Hull (1943). In both conceptions, an interrelationship is im- plied between the reinforcing and motivating functions of stimuli, although the ra- tionale is different in the two cases. The notion of generalized drive differs in its contention that all habits (inferred processes underlying observed changes in be- havior) were assumed to be activated nonselectively.

2. There are a number of other matters that could be discussed under the heading, by-products of schedules of reinforcement. Chief among these are effects of vari- ous discrimination procedures on the presence of such by-products as schedule- induced aggression and behavioral contrast. Procedures in which discrimination training is begun early, before the instrumental response has been fully condi- tioned, and in which a fading procedure is used to introduce the discriminative stimuli are effective in achieving stable discriminations with few responses during the nonreinforced stimulus (Terrace, 1963a). These special procedures (Pavlov, 1927, pp. 121-123; Skinner, 1938, pp. 203-206) for the production of "errorless" dis- criminations were also thought to eliminate some of the usual by-products of dis- crimination (Terrace, 1966), but further work has in general not supported this position (see Rilling, 1977; Wessells, 1973, for discussions of these issues).

7

Learning in the Experienced Organism

INTRODUCTION

A recurring theme in our probing of the forces which govern human behavior is that the origins of many behaviors cannot be analyzed completely on the basis of the environmental context in which that behavior now occurs. How an organism responds in a contemporary environment depends upon the prior events in the lifetime of the organism. We have glimpsed the cumulative effects of the recent past upon the changes wrought by present environments in a number of earlier contexts. The effects of prior experience were explicitly acknowledged in our discussion of the relational principle of reinforcement. According to that principle, the effect of a new environment on present behavior depends upon the entering behavior of the learner. Similarly, in our study of stimulus control we saw that whether behavior comes to be governed by the relationships between stimuli or by the absolute values of stimuli is a function of the procedure used in prior discrimination training. In studies of human behavior, particularly verbal behavior (see pp. 210–216), the effects of prior learning have been our central concern.

In previous chapters, the emphasis was on the study of relatively simple behavior under controlled conditions. Most often, the prior experiences of the subjects, particularly nonhuman subjects, were relatively well known and controlled. The analysis of relatively simple responses having well-specified histories has yielded many fundamental insights into the origins of behavior. But we should be careful not to lose sight of our goal of understanding the relatively complex behavior that experienced adults exhibit in natural settings. An understanding of that behavior requires an analysis of the behavior of the experienced organism, and that is the task of this chapter.

Some Problems

To illustrate the phenomena we shall examine, and to identify some of the problems involved in analyzing them, consider the following example. Suppose we were to observe a tennis instructor give a lesson to two players, one a novice at racquet games and the other an expert at squash. Even if neither the novice nor the expert had ever played tennis, we would undoubtedly observe substantial differences between the two players at the outset. For example, the learners might watch the instructor demonstrate the proper way to swing. As a result, the swing of the learners might improve, and observational learning would be said to have occurred. But the novice might have observed only the arm movement and the general stance, whereas the squash expert might have observed the movement of the shoulder, the position of the knees, the action of the wrist, and so on. Since different aspects of the demonstration controlled the behavior of the two learners, the learners could be said to have attended to different features of the demonstration. When given the opportunity to play, the expert may reliably step into the ball on a variety of strokes and could be said to have mastered the concept of transferring the weight of the body from the back foot to the front foot. The wrist of the squash expert might snap at the moment of impact with the ball, an action that might have carried over or transferred from previous experience in squash. In playing a game of tennis, the novice might simply try to return the ball over the net, whereas the squash expert might formulate and execute strategies.

In this chapter, we shall examine the preceding behavioral phenomena in the context of two topics that are crucial for understanding the behavior of the experienced organism: transfer and concept formation. The study of transfer is critical for ascertaining how the experiences that occur at one moment influence the subsequent behavior of the organism. Through an analysis of concept formation, we shall identify some of what are often spoken of as the higher thought processes, and we shall see that those processes depend in part upon the earlier experience of the organism.

Now consider some of the complexities that are encountered in the attempt to analyze the behavior of the experienced organism. One of the primary problems is that the life history of the experienced organism is seldom known, particularly in the study of humans. That leaves the behavioral scientist in a disadvantageous position similar to that of the paleontologist who attempts to specify the origins of contemporary phenomena on the basis of fragmentary information about the past. Consider how difficult it would be to understand how the squash expert learned to play tennis. In the absence of information about prior experiences in squash, our analysis of this behavior would be highly inferential. The second problem, related to the first, is that learning in the experienced organism often involves little overt behavior. For example, our hypothetical squash expert apparently learned much by observing the behavior of the instructor. But the only overt behavior that occurred during that learning might have been a few eye movements and pensive facial expressions. In everyday terminology, the expert was thinking in ways that were not indicated by what action he did while observing the instructor. That brings us to the third problem: privacy. Many of the events that are important in the modification of overt behavior are private and typically inaccessible to direct observation. But science is by nature an enterprise that relies upon public observation. How then could we study the awareness and the strategies of the expert described above?

Some Strategies

There is no widespread agreement as to how best to resolve these problems. We shall outline briefly some of the strategies psychologists have adopted in their attempts to handle them. One strategy is to analyze the history of the experienced organism in an attempt to understand its present behavior. For example, one might perform longitudinal studies to ascertain what kinds of prior experiences lead to what kinds of subsequent behaviors. The behavior of the squash expert, for example, would undoubtedly be more intelligible if we had access to his or her prior experiences. But it is clearly an arduous task to observe behavior in settings outside of the laboratory over long periods of time. Moreover, many of the events one observes in the natural setting might be irrelevant to the behavior one wishes to understand. Accordingly, one might try to simplify the task of historical analysis by producing the behavior of interest in the laboratory where the experiences that lead to a particular behavior may be determined with precision. By combining observations made in the laboratory with those made in the field, the ontogenetic antecedents of the behavior of adults might be ascertained.

Behavior in present settings may be clarified substantially by an analysis of the history of that behavior, but it is very difficult to gain access to all of the pertinent information. In practice, the learning theorist, like the paleontologist, must reconstruct the past on the basis of partial information and with the aid of the inductive leap that is represented by any theoretical analysis. The inductive leap may fall short at first, but it is a risk all theorists must take in their efforts to provide the most consistent, simple, and general account of the phenomena they wish to explain.

The second strategy that has been adopted by many psychologists is to try to understand present behavior on the basis of inner events and processes—the processes traditionally called remembering, thinking, imagining, and so on. Since the processes that occur inside the organism are to some extent the product of prior experience, the analysis of inner processes in a sense represents an indirect analysis of the effects of prior experience. For example, from the overt behavior of our hypothetical squash expert, one might infer present knowledge of racquet games, and one might try to describe the expert's use of that knowledge. If he or she tended to make particular sequences of shots, one might infer a particular strategy. If aggressive play at the net were found to be ineffective and the expert subsequently played at the baseline, one might infer a change in strategy. If the expert first picked up a squash racquet and took a swing appropriate to squash, and then picked up a tennis racquet and took a swing appropriate to tennis, one might infer that he or she was covertly comparing the strokes of squash and tennis. In the preceding examples, the inferred strategies and comparisons were the product of previous experience. Thus the analysis of behavior on the basis of inner events makes indirect contact with the past of the organism.

The inner events and processes that are involved in complex psychological phenomena are most often inferred rather than directly observed. Although the physiological bases of complex psychological processes are not well understood, we should recognize a third strategy that is conceptually akin to the second. This strategy is to analyze the behavior of the experienced organism on the basis of inner events and processes that are directly observed in the neurophysiology of the organism. To the extent that present neurophysiological events depend upon the experience of the organism, the analysis of behavior on a physiological level makes indirect contact with the past of the organism.

We shall examine the merits and limitations of the various strategies as we proceed in our discussions of learning in the experienced organism. It should be noted at the outset that all three strategies have proved to be productive, and we believe that they will contribute to each other in significant ways. Whereas some theorists now prefer to account for behavior in terms of functional relationships between the environment and behavior, others now prefer an analysis based upon inferred inner events. Regardless of the strategy one adopts, however, a complete analysis of behavior requires the integration of the various strategies. Ultimately, we wish to fully understand both the private and the public events of the experienced organism. That understanding requires an historical analysis of both private and public events. We shall also want to determine the physiological bases of public and private events, for it is through physiological analysis that we may directly study private events. Furthermore, the observations from physiological analysis might eventually be integrated with observations from genetics and other biological sciences. In that way, a deeper understanding of the phylogeny and ontogeny of behavior may be attained.

Unfortunately, our goal of understanding behavior on a variety of levels is more inspirational than readily attainable. In the study of phenomena such as transfer and concept formation, we approach more closely the frontiers of scientific inquiry. We cannot help but be impressed equally by what remains unknown and by what is known.

TRANSFER

In everyday life, an experience that occurs at one time often affects behavior at some later time, and *transfer* is said to have occurred. Transfer effects may be divided into two broad classes—positive and negative. *Positive transfer* is said to have occurred if experience at one time facilitates learning at some later time. For example, having learned to drive one car, say a Ford with automatic transmission, we find it easier to learn to drive another large domestic car with automatic transmission than if we had not previously learned to drive the Ford. *Negative transfer,* on the other hand, is said to have occurred if experience at one time impairs learning at some later time. For example, the person who has had extensive driving experience in the United States may find it very difficult to learn to drive on the left side of the road in other countries. The distinction between positive and negative transfer is a functional one, for that distinction is made on the basis of the observed effects of prior experience upon subsequent learning.

The study of transfer is important for several reasons. First, it is necessary for an understanding of the ontogenetic origins of the seemingly mysterious behavior of the experienced organism. Second, the analysis of transfer has important practical implications. For example, education, broadly conceived, is an attempt to systematically provide the kinds of experiences that will facilitate learning all through life. In that sense, education is oriented toward the production of particular kinds of positive transfer. Conversely, prior experience often hinders the ability of the individual to learn and adapt to new situations, and the concern of psychotherapy is often to eliminate that negative transfer and provide experiences that may lead instead to positive transfer. Thus the analysis of transfer may lead to improvements in our educational and psychotherapeutic practices. We shall begin our analysis by examining the definition and the procedures used to study transfer.

The Definition of Transfer

In a paired-associate learning procedure, the subject is first shown pairs of items, typically words. Later, one member of the pair is presented and the task is to recall the other member. This procedure is often used to study transfer, as in the design outlined in Table 7.1a. Two equivalent groups of subjects are exposed to two successive paired-associate learning tasks. The letters "A," "B," "C" and "D" refer to entire lists of words, and the words in list A differ from those in lists B, C and D. In this procedure, both groups learn the same second list and differ only with respect to the list that was learned first. Assuming that other variables are controlled, any differences between groups in learning the second list must result from differences in previous learning, that is, from hav-

TABLE 7.1   Two Procedures Used to Study Transfer

Group	Phase I	Phase II
(a) Experimental	Learn A–D	Learn A–B
Control	Learn C–D	Learn A–B
(b) Experimental	Learn problem 1	Learn problem 2
Control	Rest	Learn problem 2

ing learned different first lists. In this particular case, negative transfer occurs. That is, the experimental group learns the second list (the A-B list) more slowly and with more errors than does the control group.

The design shown in Table 7.1a has several important features. In this design, the experimenter has direct control over the experiences of both groups, and the effects of prior learning upon subsequent learning may therefore be ascertained. Just as importantly, this design permits the experimenter to systematically manipulate the specific aspects of the lists that lead to positive and negative transfer. As might be expected from what is known about stimulus control, the similarity of the lists is a fundamental determinant of transfer, and this design permits one to assess the effects of the similarity of the stimulus terms, the similarity of the response terms, and so on. The preceding design is used to study transfer that results from specific commonalities between the two tasks. However, not all transfer effects are produced by specific intertask similarities, and alternative designs are used to analyze the latter effects.

Specific and nonspecific transfer　A transfer effect that results from specific commonalities between two tasks is called *specific transfer*. Conversely, a transfer effect that does not result from specific similarities between two tasks is called *nonspecific transfer* (for discussion of this distinction, see Osgood, 1953; Postman, 1969, 1971; Underwood, 1966).

The distinction between specific and nonspecific transfer may be clarified by considering the design outlined in Table 7.1b. This design might be used if one were interested in whether humans can improve their ability to solve mathematical problems. The experimental group first solves one problem and then a second one, whereas the control group first rests and then solves the second problem.

Assume that the experimental group solved the second problem significantly faster than the control group. Positive transfer might have resulted from specific similarities between the two problems and could possibly be classified as an instance of specific transfer. But other possibilities exist. Through solving the first problem, the experimental group might have become very alert and "prepared to think," whereas the control subjects might have been thinking about other things when they began the second problem. If that were the case, the effect would be classified as an instance of nonspecific transfer, and specifically of warm-up. A second possibility is that the experimental group learned something general that helped them to learn a diversity of problems. In that instance, the effect would qualify as an instance of nonspecific transfer, and specifically of learning-to-learn. Through learning-to-learn, humans come to solve successive problems faster and faster, as if their very ability to learn had been improved by experience.

To evaluate whether our hypothetical transfer effect is an instance of specific or nonspecific transfer, one would try to test whether that effect depends upon specific similarities between the two problems. If specific intertask similarities did not seem to contribute to the effect, then the effect could be classified as an instance of nonspecific transfer. This consideration raises an important point—nonspecific transfer is defined by exclusion. The traditional distinction between specific and nonspecific transfer is based on the ability of the experimenter to discriminate specific commonalities between two tasks. However, the commonalities between two tasks may be very subtle and may involve similarities in what is learned rather than, say, stimulus similarity. Nevertheless, the learned similarities may be just as specific as the obvious physical similarities, and both are amenable to an experimental analysis (Postman, 1969). The upshot of this discussion is that the distinction between specific and nonspecific transfer is best viewed with caution. That point shall become clearer as we discuss the phenomena of warm-up.

Warm-up Warm-up is a phenomenon of considerable generality. We are all familiar with warm-up in the performance of motor tasks such as playing tennis or playing a musical instrument. The influence of warm-up on learning in humans is illustrated clearly in an experiment by Thune (1950) concerning paired-associate learning. Before the experiment began, all subjects were exposed to six practice trials. Then the experiment proper began and was conducted on two successive days. All of the subjects were exposed to ten trials on a list (list 1) of fifteen pairs of two-syllable adjectives, but those ten trials were distributed across the two days in different ways for different groups of subjects. Whereas one group received all ten trials of list 1 on the first day, another group received eight trials of list 1 on the first day and two trials of list 1 on the second day. A third group received six trials on the first day and four trials on the second day, and so on up to the final group which received all 10 trials of list 1 on the second day.

On the second day of the experiment, following the completion of list 1, all groups were exposed to ten trials on a list (list 2) of fifteen pairs of one-syllable nouns that were unrelated to the words from list 1. All of the subjects had equivalent amounts of experience in paired-associate learning procedures, and the groups differed only with respect to the distribution over days of the trials of list 1. The results showed that the number of correct responses on list 2 increased as a function of the number of warm-up trials of list 1 on the second day. In a second experiment, Thune showed that similar effects are obtained when the task that precedes the learning of list 2 is a very dissimilar task, such as guessing which of five colors will appear in the window of a memory drum. In combination, the results of those experiments show that the rate of acquisition is an increasing function of the amount of warm-up, and the warm-up task need not be directly related or similar to the subsequent learning task (but see Schwenn & Postman, 1967).

Further experiments have helped to clarify the temporal characteristics of the warm-up effect. For example, Hamilton (1950) exposed subjects to a practice list of paired-associates and varied the amount of time that elapsed before the presentation of a second unrelated list of paired-associates. The principal result was that exposure to the practice list facilitated the learning of the second list, but the degree of facilitation decreased sharply as the delay between the practice and test lists increased. Thus the benefits of working on the practice list were short-lived, and the effects of warm-up may therefore be said to be temporary.

In closing this brief discussion of warm-up, several considerations are noteworthy. First, the term "warm-up" is a label for a nonspecific transfer phenomenon, but that term in no way explains the phenomenon. A second point is that warm-up effects are poorly understood, and they may involve such a diversity of processes that a common label may be inappropriate. For example, some warm-up effects, particularly in the area of motor skills, might result from peripheral factors such as an increased temperature and blood supply in the muscles used. Other warm-up effects might result almost entirely from central factors that are commonly grouped under the heading of attention. A third point is that some studies have suggested that the effects of warm-up depend upon the prior experience of the subjects. For example, warm-up substantially improves the performance of experienced subjects in paired-associate learning procedures, but warm-up has very small effects upon the performance of experimentally naive subjects (Schwenn & Postman, 1967). Although warm-up is classified as a type of nonspecific transfer, the effects of warm-up may be to increase the probability of specific activities or strategies that are relevant to the mastery of a task (Postman, 1969). In that sense, warm-up may not be best classified as an instance of nonspecific transfer. At any rate, specific factors seem to contribute to a wide variety of transfer phenomena, even those that have been classified traditionally as nonspecific in nature. We shall next consider some of those factors in detail.

Similarity and Transfer

One of the fundamental determinants of transfer is the similarity of the stimuli in the two tasks (for a review of the relevant literature, see Postman, 1971). A very straightforward procedure that has been used to investigate the role of stimulus similarity in transfer is to have the subjects (usually college students) learn two successive paired-associate lists in which the response words are identical and the stimuli vary in degree of similarity. For example, the experimental group could first learn the A'-B list shown in Table 7.2 and then learn the A-B list shown in that table. Thus the experimental group would first learn pairs such as *JAF-big* on list one and pairs such as *JOF-big* on list two. The control group could first learn the C-D list and then learn an A-B list in which the stimuli and responses are unrelated to those in the C-D list. By exposing both groups to two lists, the effects of warm-up and learning-to-learn are equated in the two conditions. Furthermore, both groups learn the same second list (A-B), and any differences in learning the second list must therefore result from having learned the first list.

As you might expect from what you know about stimulus generalization, substantial amounts of positive transfer are observed in the A'-B, A-B proce-

TABLE 7.2   Sample Transfer Paradigms in Paired-Associate Learning

First List						Second List
C-B	C-D	A'-B	A-B'	A-D	A-Br	A-B
PEM-big	PEM-bright	JAF-big	JOF-large	JOF-bright	JOF-hot	JOF-big
DAK-filthy	DAK-round	KUV-filthy	KEV-dirty	KEV-round	KEV-big	KEV-filthy
LIN-hot	LIN-green	FEX-hot	FAX-warm	FAX-green	FAX-fast	FAX-hot
GOX-fast	GOX-deep	TOB-fast	TEB-swift	TEB-deep	TEB-filthy	TEB-fast

dure (Dallet, 1962; Hamilton, R. J., 1943). The amount of positive transfer decreases as the similarity of the stimuli in the two lists decreases.

Just as stimulus similarity is an influential determinant of specific transfer, so too is response similarity. When the stimuli in the two tasks are identical and the responses are similar, as in an A-B', A-B procedure, positive transfer occurs (Gibson, 1940; Osgood, 1946). On the other hand, when the stimuli are identical and the responses are dissimilar, as in the A-D, A-B procedure, large amounts of negative transfer occur (Dallet, 1962; cf. Postman, 1971).

Numerous theoretical attempts have been made to provide a comprehensive account of transfer in terms of the combined effects of stimulus and response similarity (for example, Houston, 1964, 1966; Osgood, 1949). Although these attempts, particularly that of Osgood (1949), have helped to summarize some transfer effects and to stimulate research, they have met with limited success. The principal difficulty encountered is that transfer is affected by many variables other than similarity, and these variables often interact with the effects of similarity. For example, massive amounts of negative transfer are observed in the A-Br, A-B procedure (Kausler & Kanoti, 1963; Postman, 1962). However, in that procedure, the stimulus and response items are identical in the two lists, but the response items are paired with different stimuli. Since the negative transfer in the A-Br, A-B procedure does not arise from differences between the lists in stimuli or responses, that effect lies beyond the domain of theories that account for transfer solely in terms of stimulus and response similarity. As another example, consider the effects of response similarity upon transfer. Although considerable negative transfer is often observed in the A-D, A-B procedure, negative transfer does not occur in that procedure when the words that occur in the lists are low in meaningfulness (Jung, 1963; Richardson & Brown, 1966). Clearly, variables such as meaningfulness interact with similarity. Generally, the effects of stimulus and response similarity depend upon the history of the organism. A complete analysis of the effects of stimulus and response similarity upon the behavior of the experienced organism must take into account the effects of previous experience.

To analyze transfer in terms of stimulus and response similarity is to analyze transfer on a relatively molar level. However, that molar analysis is incomplete for the reasons described above. When molar theories fail to provide an adequate account of the basic observations, experimenters often begin to search for order on a more molecular level of analysis. Experimenters have begun to break down the overall transfer phenomena into a number of component processes, which we shall now consider.

The Componential Analysis of Transfer

Stimulus Discrimination The first component process involved in the overall transfer effects we have discussed is stimulus discrimination. In learning a list of paired-associates, the subject must discriminate between the various stimuli (Martin, 1967). Indeed, adult subjects can often recall the stimuli used in a paired-associate task in addition to simply discriminating between them.

An analysis of the role of stimulus discrimination in transfer procedures can help to clarify phenomena that cannot be accounted for in terms of stimulus and response similarity. For example, consider the observation that substantial negative transfer occurs in the A-D, A-B procedure when the stimulus words used are high in meaningfulness, but not when the stimulus words are low in meaningfulness (for example, Richardson & Brown, 1966). When the stimuli are high in meaningfulness, the subjects in both the experimental and the control groups can, on the basis of previous experience, discriminate reliably between those stimuli. Accordingly, the two groups should not differ with regard to stimulus discrimination, and on that account the experimental subjects should have no advantage relative to the control subjects. However, the story is quite different when the stimuli are low in meaningfulness. If the stimuli were nonsense syllables such as XJK and MLY, the subjects would have to learn within the experimental situation to discriminate between those stimuli. Furthermore, if the experimental subjects learned an A-D list followed by an A-B list, and if the control subjects learned a C-D list and then an A-B list, the experimental subjects would have a considerable advantage on the A-B list with respect to stimulus discrimination. Specifically, when the two groups are learning the A-B list, the experimental group has the advantage of the prior experience with the "A" words from the first list, whereas the control group does not. Thus when the stimuli are low in meaningfulness, the factors that typically lead to negative transfer in the A-D, A-B procedure are offset by the positive effects of stimulus discrimination, and the overall result is no negative transfer.

Although the foregoing account is plausible, it is possible to give alternative accounts of the effects of stimulus meaningfulness in the A-D, A-B procedure. For example, it is possible that when the "A" stimuli are low in meaningfulness, the stimuli that actually control responding in the A-D and A-B lists differ. In other words, the "A" items may be encoded differently in the two lists. That view is called the *encoding variability hypothesis* and may be clarified by the following example. Suppose, the stimuli were XJK, MLY, and so on. In list one, X and M might be the controlling or encoded stimuli, whereas in list two, J and L might be the controlling or encoded stimuli. In that case the procedure would actually resemble the C-D, A-B procedure! On the other hand, if the stimuli were high in meaningfulness (as in TIC and FUN), the subjects in the experimental group might, as the result of prior experience, have difficulty in responding selectively to different aspects of the stimuli in the two lists. In the study of the experienced organism, it may be a mistake for the experimenter to assume that the stimuli he presents are identical to the stimuli that actually control the subject's behavior (cf. Martin, 1968, 1972, for a discussion of the implications of this view). Whereas the experimenter may intend to arrange an A-D, A-B procedure, that procedure might be realized only when the stimuli are high in meaningfulness. (For some research that supports this interpretation, see Goggin & Martin, 1970; Martin, 1972; but see also Postman & Underwood, 1973).

Which of the preceding accounts of the effects of stimulus meaningfulness is most accurate remains to be determined, and both views may help us to understand behavior in somewhat different circumstances. At any rate, both accounts emphasize the contribution of stimulus discrimination to transfer phenomena.

Before examining other component processes, we should note here that stimulus discrimination is a fundamental determinant of transfer for a broad spectrum of procedures and species. For example, many experiments (for example, Bower & Grusec, 1964; Mellgren & Ost, 1969; Trapold & Overmier, 1972) have shown that discrimination learning in an instrumental conditioning procedure is facilitated by prior discrimination training with the same stimuli in a classical conditioning procedure. Moreover, within either the classical (Pavlov, 1927) or the instrumental conditioning procedures (Logan, 1966; Marsh, G., 1969; Mackintosh & Little, 1970), performance in a very difficult discrimination task involving similar stimuli may be improved considerably by prior discrimination training between less similar stimuli on the same dimension. Thus discrimination between two slightly different red lights may be facilitated by prior discrimination training between red and green lights. The transfer procedures in which an organism is given training on a simpler discrimination before being exposed to the more difficult discrimination are fading procedures (see pp. 193–194), and have been employed with a good deal of success to practical problems ranging from toilet training (Mahoney, Van Wagenen, & Meyerson, 1971) to learning to read and write (cf. Skinner, 1968).

Response Learning   As we continue our discussion of component processes that may contribute to transfer, we shall again focus upon paired-associate learning. The role of response learning may be clearly seen in the A-Br, A-B procedure in which the stimuli and responses of the first list are identical but are paired differently in the second list. When words high in meaningfulness are used in the A-Br, A-B procedure, a large amount of negative transfer occurs. However, that effect does not occur when the response words are low in meaningfulness (Mandler & Heinemann, 1956; Merikle, 1968). These different effects may result from differences in response learning in the two procedures (cf. Postman, 1971). With words that are high in meaningfulness, little response learning has to occur within the experimental situation, and there should be no differences between the experimental and the control groups in that respect. However, when the response words are low in meaningfulness, as in *VPN* and *HBS,* the subjects must learn the responses before they can learn the list of paired-associates. Furthermore, in that instance the experimental and control groups differ with respect to how much response learning must occur. For the experimental group, the responses are identical in the two lists, whereas for the control group which is typically exposed to a C-D, A-B procedure, the responses are different in the two lists. When the second list is presented, the control subjects have to learn new responses, whereas the experimental subjects do not. Thus the factors that can lead to negative transfer in the A-Br, A-B procedure are offset by the positive effects of response learning when the responses are low in meaningfulness.

Associative Relationships   The last two of the components we shall consider (for a discussion of other components, see Postman, 1971) involve not stimuli or responses alone but rather the associative relationships between the stimuli and responses. It should be recalled from our previous discussion of the British associationists and the research of Ebbinghaus (see pp. 211–216) that paired-associate learning was viewed as a process of forming associations between pairs of items. The associations were said to be of two kinds—forward (S-R associations) and backward (R-S associations). Both forward and backward associations are instances of stimulus control. For example, if the stimulus items presented by the experimenter reliably control the appropriate verbal responses, a forward association is said to have been formed. In previous chapters, we have spoken of stimulus control without reference to inferred associations. However, because associationistic theories have figured prominently in the analysis of transfer, we shall use the term "association," but only in a descriptive sense.

The effects of forward associations, backward associations, and the other component processes we have discussed are summarized in Table 7.3. As Table 7.3 shows, the component processes can have different effects in different transfer procedures. For example, in the A-B', A-B procedure, the forward associations lead to positive transfer (as designated by the plus sign; a zero indicates that there is neither a positive nor a negative contribution). But in the

TABLE 7.3   Component Analysis of Several Transfer Procedures

Component	Procedure				
	C–D A–B	A–B' A–B	A–D A–B	C–B A–B	A–Br A–B
Stimulus discrimination	0	+	+	0	+
Response learning	0	+	0	+	+
Forward association	0	+	−	0	−
Backward association	0	+	0	−	−

Source: After Postman, 1971.

A-D, A-B procedure, the forward associations lead to negative transfer (as indicated by the minus sign), since the control of the "D" response by the "A" stimuli that is established during the learning of list one is inappropriate for the A-B list. The most noteworthy aspect of Table 7.3 is that the various component processes interact to determine the direction and the magnitude of the overall transfer effects in the different procedures. In instances such as the A-B', A-B procedure, the component processes act in unison to produce positive transfer. However, in instances such as the A-Br, A-B procedure (and when the words used are high in meaningfulness), some component processes lead to positive transfer, whereas other components lead to negative transfer. In the latter instances, the direction and magnitude of the overall transfer effects depends upon the strength of the effects of the different component processes.

Reinforcement   Our discussion of the components involved in transfer would hardly be complete without acknowledging the importance of reinforcement. The role of reinforcement in transfer may be illustrated by an analysis of imitative behavior in humans. *Imitation* is said to occur when an observer's behavior is similar in form (topography) to that of a demonstrator or model and the observer's behavior is directly controlled by the behavior of the model.

In a number of studies, the role of reinforcement as an antecedent of imitative behavior has been investigated (Brigham & Sherman, 1968; Lovaas, Berberich, Perloff, & Schaeffer, 1966; Lovaas, 1976). In one experiment (Baer, Peterson, & Sherman, 1967), three severely retarded children of nine to twelve years of age served as subjects. These children had been observed extensively but had never been observed to imitate, and before the experiment began they were unresponsive to the experimenter's repeated requests that they imitate simple responses (for example, hand-clapping) of which they were otherwise capable. In the reinforcement phase of the experiment, the experimenter looked at a child, said "Do this," and emitted a response such as raising one arm. If the child then emitted a response similar in form to that of the experimenter, then the experimenter said "good" and gave the child food. But if the child did not emit a response within 10 sec that matched that of the experimenter, no reinforcers were delivered and the experimenter demonstrated the next response. In the course of the experiment, over one hundred different responses were modeled by the experimenter, and each response was modeled several times. Of course, the children never imitated at first, and it was therefore necessary to somehow increase the frequency of imitative responses to a level at which those responses could be followed by reinforcement. The procedure used for that purpose is called *guidance,* and it involved demonstrating a response and saying "Do this." Then the experimenter physically helped the child through the desired movements and presented food. After guiding the subject's responses on several occasions, the experimenter gradually began to reduce his assistance, and he used shaping procedures to bring about responses that matched those of the experimenter.

The results of the experiment are shown in Fig. 7.1. The main result was that as more and more responses were modeled by the experimenter, the subjects came to match their responses to those of the experimenter on the very

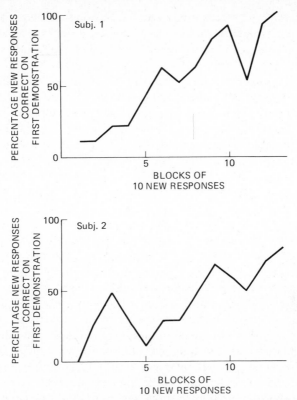

Fig. 7.1   The acquisition of imitative responses for two different subjects. As training proceeded, the children came to imitate novel responses readily, even before those responses had been reinforced.   (From Baer, Peterson, & Sherman, 1967. Copyright 1967 by the Society for the Experimental Analysis of Behavior, Inc.)

first demonstration of a particular response. Thus, after training, the subjects imitated the responses of the experimenter before those particular imitative responses had been reinforced. For example, if the imitative response, say pulling the window shade, had not previously been demonstrated by the experimenter, the subject at the end of training imitated that response on the first try even though that particular imitative response *had never before been reinforced.* Subsequent manipulations showed that when reinforcement was made contingent upon not imitating, the frequency of all imitative responses decreased sharply.

The preceding results show not only that reinforcement can be used to increase the frequency of imitative responses but also that the reinforcement of a variety of imitative responses leads to the establishment of a large class of imitative responses. After some members of the class had been followed by reinforcement, the frequency of many different and novel imitative responses increased. When a large class of imitative responses has been established and that class includes both novel and explicitly trained imitative responses, *generalized imitation* is said to have occurred. The exact boundaries of the class of imitative responses are not clear, and an important task for future research on imitation is to identify those boundaries and their antecedents. (For studies of the composition and the antecedents of classes of imitative responses see Garcia, Baer, & Firestone, 1971; Peterson, R. F., 1968; Peterson, R. F., & Whitehurst, 1971; Steinman, 1970a, 1970b; and Waxler & Yarrow, 1970.)

The fact that novel imitative responses can be rapidly acquired following the appropriate training has important practical implications. Specifically, by using reinforcement to establish a large class of imitative responses, the behavior therapist may swiftly bring about many different desired behaviors, for example, verbal behaviors, that would require much time and effort to shape individually. Of course, the goal of behavior therapy is not to simply teach individuals to imitate. After the desired responses have been conditioned through the imitation training described above, the therapist typically takes steps to bring those responses under the control of other variables so that they do not remain as simple imitative responses.

Next consider the theoretical implications of the preceding study. Following the reinforcement of imitative responses, the subjects would without explicit reinforcement imitate novel responses they observed. Think what would happen if we were to observe the subjects at that point without knowing their prior experiences. We might conclude that the subjects were learning new responses through observation independently of any effects of reinforcement. That is the same kind of conclusion one might reach by studying how adults behave in paired-associate learning procedures, for learning in that procedure often seems to proceed through observation rather than explicit reinforcement. Nevertheless, if we knew the history of the subjects who were imitating, we might conclude that the novel responses belong to the same functional class as the imitative responses that had previously received explicit reinforcement. Thus we might decide that the observational learning of the novel responses resulted from the prior reinforcement of other imitative responses.

We do not intend to imply that all instances of observational learning are the product of reinforcement. There is considerable debate as to whether observational learning involves processes that are fundamentally different from those involved in conditioning (Bandura, 1971a, 1971b; see also Gewirtz, 1971a, 1971b). Additionally, much evidence suggests that phylogenetic factors contribute extensively to observational learning phenomena such as the acquisition of bird song (for example, Marler, 1970b). For our present purposes, the central point is that many instances of learning in the experienced organism that do not seem to arise from reinforcement in the contemporaneous environment may involve reinforcement and transfer from the preexperimental experiences of the subject. The contribution of reinforcement may be obscured by the fact that after responses are acquired they may be maintained through very intermittent reinforcement, and the reinforcers may be conditioned reinforcers of a subtle nature (cf. Skinner, 1953, 1957, 1968). Indeed, some of the conditioned reinforcers may be self-administered, although the concept of self-reinforcement is quite controversial (cf. Bandura, 1976; see also Catania, 1975, 1976). In any case, there is little doubt that reinforcement may influence transfer, and that conclusion fits with our previous discussion of stimulus control (see pp. 176–189).

Mediation and Transfer

Having examined some of the fundamental processes involved in transfer, we may now inquire into some of the complex contributions of private events to transfer. Let us begin by asking what experienced organisms—typically, adult humans—do in learning a single list of paired-associates. Paired-associate learning may seem very simple and straightforward, but the veil of simplicity falls upon closer analysis (cf. Battig, 1968; Kausler, 1974). In learning pairs of words such as *girl-bicycle,* adults often state that they form covert visual images of a girl riding a bicycle. In fact, imagery seems to be one of the most influential determinants of paired-associate learning (Paivio, 1969, 1971b). Similarly, adults often learn pairs of words by making up sentences that include a pair of words (for example, *The girl rode her bicycle to school;* cf. Montague, 1972). The covert images and sentences described above are mediators in that they stand between the present environment and the overt behavior emitted in that environment. These mediational processes arise in large part from the prior experiences adults have had.

The privacy of mediational processes seriously complicates attempts to analyze learning experimentally. Mediational processes such as visual images have not yet been measured directly on a neurophysiological level. Moreover, it is questionable as to how much may be learned about mediational processes through introspection. What we introspect upon may be a product, and not a cause, of our behavior (cf. Pylyshyn, 1973; Skinner, 1974). Furthermore, introspective reports are often biased, for subjects often say what they think the experimenter wants to hear. For these reasons, mediational processes are most often inferred from behavior. Theories about the inferred private events yield predictions, and these theories are supported to the extent that the actual outcomes conform to the predictions.

This inferential strategy for studying private events has been employed extensively in contemporary analyses of concept formation, language and memory, but it is not free of problems. A complete analysis of behavior must specify not only the occurrence but also the origins of mediational processes. It is possible that the nature and the effects of mediational processes depend upon ontogenetic factors. Yet the exact ontogenetic origins of mediational processes are often unknown, for the experimenter typically lacks access to the history of the adult subjects. To handle those problems, some experimenters have adopted the strategy of building mediators into the repertoire of the subjects within the experimental setting (for example, Grover, Horton, & Cunningham, 1967; Jenkins, J. J., 1963; Potts, 1977). That strategy may be illustrated by an examination of the three-stage mediation paradigm.

Three-Stage Mediation Paradigms In one study of a three-stage mediation paradigm (Bugelski & Scharlock, 1952; for an analysis of various three-stage paradigms, see Horton & Kjeldergaard, 1961; Jenkins, J. J., 1963; Postman, 1971), adults learned three successive lists of word pairs. The lists were A-B, B-C and A-C, in that order. Notice that in this procedure, the subjects could learn the A-C list rapidly by applying what they had learned from the first two lists. Specifically, the learning of the A-C list would be facilitated if the presentation of the "A" words led to the occurrence of the "B" responses on a covert or private level. Those covert "B" responses could, as the result of training on the B-C list, in turn lead to the occurrence of the "C" responses. In other words, A-C learning could be facilitated by the establishment of a chain of stimuli and responses in which the "A" stimuli occasion the "B" response, which also function as stimuli that occasion the "C" responses. The results were that prior training on the A-B and the B-C lists facilitated the learning of the A-C list relative to a control condition in which the lists learned were A-B, D-C, and A-C. For the subjects in the experimental condition, the following chain of stimuli and responses was established: A → [B(r) → B(s)] → C, where "B" responses and stimuli are mediators that are inferred private events. For the subjects in the control condition, unlike the subjects in the experimental condition, no B-C relationship had been established that could mediate the learning of the A-C list.

Although the transfer procedures we discussed previously involved two stages and were not designed to study mediation, these two-stage paradigms may in certain cases be analyzed profitably as three-stage mediation paradigms. For example, the A-B', A-B paradigm may be viewed as a three-stage mediation paradigm in which the stages are B'-B, A-B', A-B and in which the first stage occurred before the experiment was begun. For example, if the A-B' pairs were *BOC-large* and *JAL-fast,* and if the A-B pairs were *BOC-huge* and *JAL-swift,* the learning of the A-B list might be facilitated on the basis of previously learned relationships between *large* and *huge* and between *fast* and *swift.* Specifically, *large* and *fast* might serve as mediators in the learning of the A-B list (cf. Barnes & Underwood, 1959; Russell & Storms, 1955).

Concluding Comments At present, there is considerable disagreement about the nature of private events and how to best study these events. Regardless of whether private events are conceived of as inferred theoretical constructs or as neurophysiological events, a full understanding of private events requires an analysis of their origins. In ascertaining the ontogenetic origins of private events, the strategy of explicitly manipulating the environment to bring about mediational processes seems promising.

The role of mediational processes in the behavior of experienced organisms is not well understood, and some important questions remain unresolved. For example, is there a unique involvement of mediational processes in learning in the experienced organism? The possibility exists that the experienced organism learns in fundamentally different ways than those discussed in preceding chapters. For example, adult humans seldom participate passively in experiments. Rather, they often form and test hypotheses about the purpose of the experiment, give instructions to themselves about how to respond, and so on. Even in a simple conditioning procedure, the behavior of adults may be influenced not only by, say, CS-UCS pairings but also by the subject's hypotheses about the relationship between the CS and the UCS. In fact, some theorists (for example, Brewer, 1974) have proposed that conditioning occurs in adult humans only if they are aware of the relationship between the CS and the UCS or between the response and the reinforcer. On that view, adult humans learn in conditioning procedures in ways that differ from those in which, for example, rats and pigeons learn. According to that position, prior experience may not only hasten or retard subsequent learning, but may also alter the processes through which that learning occurs. This possibility introduces a new dimension of complexity into the topic of transfer, and we shall examine that issue further in the following section.

Awareness and Learning

The potential importance of awareness in learning is apparent to investigators of classical conditioning. For example, in eyeblink conditioning procedures, many adults notice the onset of extinction and can state that the extinction procedure affects the conditioned response (Spence, 1966). In those subjects, extinction occurs very rapidly.

To analyze the role of awareness, investigators have sought relatively direct means of controlling awareness. One means of assessing the role of awareness is to vary the instructions that are given to adult subjects (Grings & Lockhart, 1963; Harvey & Wickens, 1971, 1973; Hill, 1967; Stern & Lewis, 1968). For example, Dawson & Reardon (1969) exposed four groups of subjects to a classical conditioning procedure in which the response system studied was the galvanic skin response. Three groups of subjects were given a detailed description of the classical conditioning procedure, and the CS (tone) and the UCS (shock) were identified. The three groups then received different instructions that were designed to facilitate, impair, or to not influence conditioning. The facilitory group was told that the most sensible and intelligent thing to do was to become conditioned. The inhibitory group was told the opposite, and the neutral group received no instructions about how sensible it is to become conditioned. The fourth group, called the pseudoconditioning group, was told only that a tone and a shock would be presented randomly. Following the delivery of the instructions, all four groups received 16 pairings of the tone and the shock.

The results, shown in Fig. 7.2, were that the instructions strongly influenced how much conditioning occurred. The magnitude of the conditioned response was increased by the facilitory instructions and decreased by the inhibitory instructions. The lowest response magnitude occurred in the pseudoconditioning group. Thus, depending upon the type of instructions given, the amount of conditioning that occurs may be increased or decreased. An important methodological implication of the results is that the instructions given to verbally competent humans is hardly a trivial procedural aspect of a study of conditioning. It is also worthwhile to point out that subjects may give themselves covert instructions that lead to modifications in their behavior. Thus even if the experimenter provides neutral or no instructions, the responding of the subject may nevertheless come under instructional control by covert verbal stimuli.

Numerous experiments have suggested that awareness does not simply

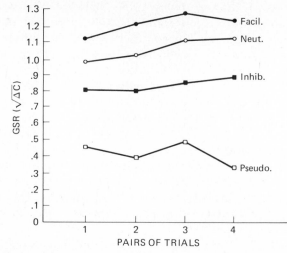

Fig. 7.2 The effects of instructions upon classical conditioning of the galvanic skin response. (After Dawson & Reardon, 1969. Copyright 1969 by the American Psychological Association. Reprinted by permission.)

contribute to conditioning in adults, but rather that awareness is necessary for conditioning (cf. Dawson, 1970; Dawson & Biferno, 1973; Dawson & Grings, 1968; DeNike & Spielberger, 1963; DeNike, 1964; Fuhrer & Baer, 1965; Spielberger & DeNike, 1966; for a review, see Brewer, 1974). Most of these experiments involved continuously monitoring both changes in the subjects' conditioned responses (for example, GSR or eyeblinks) and the subjects' statements about the events in the experiment. The chief evidence that supports this position is as follows. First, conditioning occurred only in subjects who were aware of either the stimulus-reinforcer or the response-reinforcer relationship. Moreover, variations in the instructions given to the subjects increased or decreased the probability that the subjects would become aware and show evidence of conditioning. Perhaps most significantly, conditioning and awareness developed at points very close in time. Specifically, the subjects verbally identified the CS-UCS relationship or the response-reinforcer relationship on one or several trials before there was evidence of conditioning. Since awareness preceded conditioning, it is unlikely that the awareness was the product of conditioning.

On the other hand, the results of numerous studies conflict with the view that awareness is necessary for conditioning. Specifically, there have been reports of conditioning without awareness (for example, Dixon & Oakes, 1965; Gavalas, 1967; Keehn, 1969; Kennedy, 1970, 1971; Johnson, H. J. & Schwartz, 1967; Oakes, 1967; Rosenfeld & Baer, 1969; Shapiro & Crider, 1967; Silver, Saltz, & Modigliani, 1970). Those studies and the problems involved in ascertaining whether conditioning occurs without awareness merit further study.

Conditioning Without Awareness   The most convincing demonstration of conditioning without awareness comes from a clever experiment by Rosenfeld and Baer (1970) on verbal operant conditioning. Deception played a key role in this experiment. The subjects were instructed to act as "experimenters" and to attempt to condition the verbal behavior of a subject who was presumably seated in an adjacent room. The presumed subject could not be seen but could supposedly communicate with the "experimenter" through an intercom. The "experimenter" was told to tell the subject to emit a word by saying "Next," "Go ahead," "O.K.," and so on. Following that prompt by the "experimenter," the subject said a word. If that word belonged to a particular category, for example, fluently spoken nouns, the "experimenter" awarded points to the subject by pressing a lever. The "experimenters" were asked to write down throughout the experiment their ideas about what might be responsible for changes in the verbal behavior of the subject. In reality, there was no subject in the other room, and the verbal responses of the "subject" were provided by tape recordings. And the recruited "experimenters" were in fact the subjects of the experiment. Although the "experimenters" had been led to believe they were reinforcing the fluent speech of a subject, the real purpose of the experiment was to condition the type of prompt (for example, "Next") said by the "experimenter." When the "experimenter" used a particular prompt, the speech of the "subject" was fluent; otherwise, the speech of the "subject" was disfluent.

The results of the experiment were that the verbal prompts of the "experimenters" were successfully conditioned. Furthermore, the written comments of the "experimenters" and a postexperiment interview revealed no signs of awareness. The "experimenters" showed no awareness that their verbal responses had been affected by the verbal behavior of the "subject." Indeed, the "experimenters" explicitly denied that their prompts had been influenced by the responses of the "subject." Besides establishing the gullibility of humans, the results suggest that conditioning may occur without awareness.

Some studies of conditioning without awareness have entailed the conditioning of private events (Hefferline & Bruno, 1971; Hefferline, Bruno, & Davidowitz, 1971). For example, Hefferline, Keenan, & Harford (1959) attempted to instrumentally condition a twitch of the thumb that was so small as to be classified as a private event. Indeed, that response was unnoticeable to the subjects and could be observed only by attaching electrodes to the hand and measuring the small electrical voltage changes (1 to 3 microvolts) produced by the response. There were several conditions in the experiment, but only one condition need be discussed here. The subjects were fitted with sets of electrodes on various parts of their bodies. They were told that the study concerned the effects on bodily tension of noise superimposed on music that was delivered through earphones. They were told to simply listen through the earphones and otherwise do nothing. The experimental procedure involved a combination of escape and avoidance contingencies. Specifically, an aversively loud noise was superimposed on the music, and a response turned off that noise for 15 sec.

Also, each response that occurred while the noise was absent postponed the onset of the noise for 15 sec.

The results of the experiment were that the escape and avoidance contingencies increased the rate of response above the baseline level for each subject. In the postexperimental interview, the subjects were astonished to learn that they had exerted any control over the noise, for they said they had believed throughout the experiment that they were passive victims with respect to the noise. Apparently, then, the responses of those subjects had been affected by reinforcement even though they had been unaware of both the response and the reinforcement contingency. From the viewpoint of the subjects, the thumb-twitch had remained a private event!

These results have implications not only for the relation between awareness and learning but also for our conception of private events. Historically, inner events have often been viewed as mental and indeterminate rather than physical and lawful. Additionally, these events have often enjoyed a privileged status in explanatory schemes. Results such as those reported by Hefferline et al. suggest a different conception of human behavior. Perhaps private events are physical and lawful and are affected by many of the variables that affect overt behavior. We saw previously that a private event may be affected by reinforcement contingencies in the same way that overt responses are. Furthermore, through differential reinforcement, private events may acquire discriminative control over overt responses, just as overt stimuli do (cf. Hefferline & Bruno, 1971). In short, private events may have the same functional status as public events. If so, private events as diverse as awareness and the humble thumb-twitch may be acquired through conditioning procedures. (For discussions of the role of reinforcement in the genesis of awareness and other private events, see Skinner, 1945, 1953, 1957, 1974; for discussions of the phylogenetic origins of awareness, see Gallup, 1970, 1977.) Much more research remains to be done before drawing firm conclusions regarding the functional status and origins of private events. Work in this area has already led to the use of operant conditioning procedures in the treatment of migraine headaches (for example, Sargent, Green, & Walters, 1973), epileptic seizures (Sterman, 1973), and many other disorders. Further probings into the nature of private events will undoubtedly extend our control of those events. Ironically, as our understanding of our outer behavior progresses, our understanding of our inner world may be simultaneously advanced.

Problems in the Analysis of Awareness   We have now seen that there is mixed evidence concerning the view that awareness is necessary for the occurrence of conditioning in adults. What are the reasons for the conflicting evidence on this issue? Although the answer to that question is not entirely clear, part of the answer has come from an examination of methodological variables. Many investigations have used postexperiment questionnaires or interviews to evaluate the awareness of their subjects. Unfortunately, different experimenters have used different questions to assess awareness, and therein lies one source of the discrepancies in results. For example, more awareness is generally found following extensive interviews than following brief interviews (Creelman, 1966). It is possible that conditioning without awareness appears to occur most often in studies that involve brief interviews rather than extensive ones. Additionally, the type of questions that are used determine whether awareness will be observed (Chatterjee & Eriksen, 1960; Eriksen, 1958). For example, awareness is often detected when the questionnaire includes recognition questions such as "shock (a) usually followed the highest tone; (b) usually followed the middle tone; (c) usually followed the lowest tone; (d) wasn't systematic; and (e) I couldn't tell." But awareness is less often detected when the questionnaire includes recall questions such as "Were you ever able to tell when you were going to be shocked?" In a study of GSR conditioning by Dawson & Reardon (1973), conditioning without awareness was observed when a recall questionnaire was used but not when a recognition questionnaire was used. In summary then, whether one finds evidence of conditioning without awareness depends in part upon how one measures awareness.

The problem of obtaining a reliable and valid measure of awareness is complicated by yet another problem. Questionnaires and interviews may not be neutral measuring devices, for awareness may actually be induced by asking particular types of questions. Adult subjects often seek to comply with what they believe to be the desires of the experimenter (for example, Orne, 1962). Relatively direct questions may lead the subject to look for relationships that were not observed during the conditioning phase of the experiment, and some subjects who are classified as aware after an experiment may not have been aware during the experiment. Conversely, indirect questions may encourage the subject to play dumb, and the awareness of that subject may go undetected. A related problem is that very subtle forms of bias may enter into experiments with humans despite the good intentions of the honest experimenter (Rosenthal, 1966). The experimenter may unknowingly influence the verbal responses of the subject in ways that are consistent with the experimenter's own expectations concerning the outcome of the experiment.

It may seem possible to circumvent these difficulties by studying conditioning and awareness in the context of a masking task such as classifying different tones. The use of masking tasks obscures the purposes of the experiment and can permit the mechanical assessment of awareness throughout an experiment. However, masking tasks are hardly trouble free. Masking tasks may interact with the conditioning tasks in ways that are not yet understood. The performance of some masking tasks may interfere with the occurrence of conditioning, whereas the performance of other masking tasks may facilitate the occurrence of conditioning. A distinct possibility is that awareness may be necessary for the occurrence of conditioning in some masking procedures but not in others. At any rate, the generality of results from experiments involving masking tasks remains to be determined.

In light of the preceding methodological complications, it is premature to draw firm conclusions regarding the relationship between awareness and conditioning. We believe that the weight of the evidence now available suggests that awareness is not necessary for conditioning in all situations. But it should be recognized that the boundary conditions of that conclusion have not yet been specified. There is no question that awareness may contribute to learning, and it may well be that awareness is necessary for conditioning in some circumstances but not in others. In short, there may not be a single answer to the question of whether awareness is necessary for conditioning in adults.

Concluding Comments Future research should explore further the definition of awareness. Most often, awareness has been defined in terms of the verbal behavior of the subject. That definition seems limited in that there are instances in which one seems to be aware of something but cannot quite put it into words. Whether one is playing tennis, driving a car in heavy traffic or having a peak experience, one has trouble describing all one is aware of. And even if one could state all one is aware of, the definition of awareness would still be in question. In order to be classified as aware in, for example, an instrumental conditioning procedure, must the subject simply be able to state that reinforcement is contingent upon responding? Or must the subject also be able to specify the exact response that produces reinforcement, the schedule of reinforcement, and so on?

Future research should also examine the causal status of awareness in conditioning experiments. The observations described above, that conditioning sometimes occurs only in aware subjects, have often led to the conclusion that awareness is a necessary condition for learning in adults. It is possible, however, that awareness is not a cause of conditioning but is the product of variables that lead simultaneously to both awareness and conditioning. In other words, awareness and learning may arise independently even when they are highly correlated in an experimental setting. Similarly, in some instances, the behavior changes produced through conditioning may bring about changes in awareness. At any rate, it is clear that private events play a major role in determining how the effects of one environment influence the effects of subsequently encountered environments. The pervasive influence of private events shall become even more apparent as we consider the topic of concept formation.

CONCEPT FORMATION

In our previous discussions of learning, and particularly in our discussions of stimulus control (see pp. 176–204), we have emphasized that responding often comes to be controlled by classes of stimuli. Technically, no two stimuli are ever exactly the same. Some stimulus classes are relatively broad and inclusive, whereas other stimulus classes are relatively narrow and restricted. For example, the class of stimuli that we call *animals* has many members and is very large relative to the class of stimuli we call *my blue coat*. Although responding is always controlled by a class of stimuli, not all behavior is said to be conceptual behavior. *Conceptual behavior* entails the control of responses by relatively large classes of stimuli, many of which are novel. For example, one could be said to have mastered the concept *dog* if one could identify many different dogs as members of the class *dog*. Furthermore, it is conventional to say that a person has mastered a concept such as *dog* only if the person can correctly identify dogs that he has never seen before as members of that class. If one could recognize only one's own dog and one's neighbor's dogs as members of the class *dog*, it would be inappropriate to say that that person has mastered the concept *dog*.

It should be noted that conceptual behavior involves both stimulus generalization and stimulus discrimination (Keller, F. S., & Schoenfeld, 1950). Continuing with the example of dogs, a person could be said to have mastered the concept *dog* if that person could correctly identify novel dogs (an instance of stimulus generalization) and if that person could discriminate between the member of the class *dogs* and the members of other classes such as *cats*, *wolves*, and so on.

By discussing conceptual behavior in the terminology of stimulus control, we have tried to show that conditioning theory may be applied to the analysis of conceptual behavior. However, many of the insights into conceptual behavior have come from analyses made by cognitive psychologists who have emphasized hypothetical, mediational processes in their theories and have not employed the terminology of conditioning theory. In an attempt to simplify our discussion and to recognize the contribution of mediational theories, we shall adopt some of the cognitive terminology here rather than attempt to translate between the cognitive and conditioning theories. It should be recognized that much of what may be said in one technical vocabulary may also be said in the other and that the substantive problems that confront conditioning theorists and cognitive theorists are very similar.

Before proceeding further, a word of caution is in order. Many philosophical and empirical problems arise in the use of cognitive terminology, and they are sufficiently deep and unresolved as to exceed the scope of this book. Some acquaintance with the problems may be gained by considering the term *concept*. When an organism responds in a similar fashion to a large class of stimuli some of which are novel, it is said to "have" the particular concept. To assert that an organism "has" a concept may imply that a concept is some sort of static mental entity that one carries around. However, we wish to avoid those implications in our discussions of concepts, for we do not believe that concepts are static, mental or entity-like in character. We shall use terms such as *concept* in a descriptive sense without implying that a concept is something more than a set of behavioral processes. In general, we view terms such as "concept" as theoretical constructs that have helped many scientists to systematically discuss and organize their observations. With these considerations in mind, we may begin our analysis of concept formation.

The Nature and Definition of Concepts

An appropriate way to begin our inquiry into concept formation is to examine some views concerning the nature of concepts, for those views have strongly influenced both theories of concept formation and metatheories of how to study the process of concept formation. We shall not attempt to explore the wide array of philosophical theories regarding the nature of concepts. Rather, we shall focus upon the two views of the nature of concepts that have guided most of the empirical research concerning concept formation.

The Attribute-Rule Hypothesis First consider a traditional view of the nature of concepts which may be called the *attribute-rule hypothesis*. According to that hypothesis, a concept is a category of events or objects that have common properties or features called attributes. For example, the members of the conceptual category that we call *circles* have in common the attribute or property of circularity. Of course, many everyday concepts are characterized by multiple attributes. For example, the members of the conceptual category that we call *dog* have in common numerous properties that may be described verbally as *has hair, has four legs, can bite,* and so on.

According to the attribute-rule hypothesis, concepts cannot be exhaustively described in terms of common attributes, for the relationships between those attributes are also important. In other words, concepts are defined both by their attributes and by *rules,* which are logical statements that specify how attributes may be combined. Several of the rules that may define how attributes may be combined to form a concept are shown in Fig. 7.3. The stimuli described in Fig. 7.3 can be classified in terms of three dimensions: brightness, size and shape. For each dimension, there are two attributes. Squareness and triangularity are the attributes for the dimension of shape, light and dark are the attributes for the dimension of brightness, and large and small are the attributes for the dimension of size.

In Fig. 7.3, the *affirmative* rule specifies that darkness is the defining attribute of the concept. Since the affirmative rule specifies that instances of the concept are defined on the basis of their brightness, the dimension of brightness is said to be relevant to the concept, and the dimensions of shape and size are said to be irrelevant. Basically the affirmative rule specifies simply that all of the stimuli that are instances of a concept must have a particular attribute such as darkness, triangularity, and so on.

Few concepts are as simple as those defined by affirmative rules. For example, the concept *water* is defined partially by the combination of several attributes such as *colorless, odorless, liquid,* and so on. When a concept is defined by the simultaneous presence of several attributes, that concept is said to involve a *conjunctive rule.* In Fig. 7.3, the concept *light square* involves a conjunctive rule since the concept is defined by the conjunction of the attributes of lightness and squareness. As shown in Fig. 7.3, an *inclusive disjunctive rule* involving the attributes of lightness and squareness would specify that all instances of the concept must be light and/or square. An everyday example of an inclusive disjunctive rule may be found in the concept *bad song* which may involve the attribute *bad lyrics* and/or the attribute *bad musicianship.* Another type of rule specifies that the relevant attribute of one dimension depends upon the presence of some other attribute, as in the conditional discrimination procedure. For example, as shown in Fig. 7.3, a *conditional rule* might specify that stimuli are instances of the concept if they are dark and they

RULE	□	⬜	▪	■	△	△	▲	▲
1. Affirmative (e.g., + if dark)	−	−	+	+	−	−	+	+
2. Conjunctive (e.g., + if light *and* square)	+	+	−	−	−	−	−	−
3. Inclusive disjunctive (e.g., + if light *and/or* square)	+	+	+	+	+	+	−	−
4. Conditional (e.g., if △, then dark; if □, then light)	+	+	−	−	−	−	+	+
5. Joint denial (e.g., + if not small and not △)	−	+	−	+	−	−	−	−

Fig. 7.3 Five rules that may define concepts. The stimuli that are positive instances of each concept are marked by a plus sign, and those that are negative instances are marked by a minus sign.

are triangles or if they are squares. As an everyday example of a conditional concept, a good citizen is one who votes regularly, pays taxes and works to improve society, but only if the person does not commit crimes such as murder. A variation of the conditional rule is the biconditional rule, which might state, for example, that triangles are instances if and only if they are light. The last rule we shall consider here is that of *joint denial*. As an example, the concept *peace* is defined in part by the joint absence of attributes such as fighting and fear.

Having described the attribute-rule hypothesis, we may use that view to introduce a distinction that has often been made in the analysis of concepts— the distinction between extension and intension (cf. Anglin, 1977; Fodor, 1975; Goodman, 1972; Miller, G. A. & Johnson-Laird, 1976). The *extension* of a concept is the set of all instances of the concept. The *intension* of a concept is the set of properties or attributes that define the concept. For example, consider the concept *light and square* from Fig. 7.3. The extension of that concept includes all of the stimuli that are positive instances of the concept. The intension of that concept includes the attributes *light* and *square*.

The distinction between extension and intension has important implications for both theories of the nature of concepts and theories of concept formation. The extension of many concepts, for example, the concept *animal,* is essentially infinite, for there is no limit to the number of instances of that category. Since the extension of that concept is infinite, that concept cannot be completely defined in terms of its extension. Rather, it must be defined in terms of its intension, or basic attributes. Similarly, in order to master a concept such as *animal,* one must learn something more than the instances of the concept, for in principle, one cannot be exposed to the infinite number of instances of a concept. One view of concept formation is that it entails learning about the attributes or the intension of the concept on the basis of the instances one is exposed to.

Most of the research that has been guided by the attribute-rule hypothesis has involved artificial concepts that are defined clearly by specifiable attributes and rules (for example, Heidbreder, 1946; Hull, 1920; for a review, see Bourne, 1966). By studying the acquisition of artificial concepts under controlled conditions, the experimenter is able to work with clearly defined concepts and to control and measure the effects of the subject's experience with instances of the concepts. The study of well-defined, artificial concepts is consistent with the widely used scientific strategy of studying a phenomenon under relatively simple and well-controlled conditions before addressing the complexities of the world beyond the walls of the laboratory. However, we have seen previously that one may err in the application of that strategy in an area. Many researchers have come to believe that the attribute-rule hypothesis and the research it has guided suffers from both oversimplification and limited generality, and we shall now examine the charges that have been made.

Problems with the Attribute-Rule Hypothesis The major criticism that has been posed against the attribute-rule hypothesis is that many natural concepts cannot be completely specified by a list of attributes that combine according to particular rules. For example, the philosopher Wittgenstein (1953) argued that a concept such as *game* cannot be described in terms of properties common to all members of the concept. Whereas some games involve boards (for example, checkers), others do not (for example, squash). Some games involve cards, others involve balls, racquets, bats and so on, while others (for example, tag) require no equipment. Many games have winners and losers, but other games (for example, catch or frisbee) do not. *Amusement* may seem to characterize all games, but amusement often seems to be lacking among professional chess players, soccer players, and so on. Indeed, the distinction between games and work projects seems to be difficult to make when considering professionals who earn their living by playing games before the public. As Wittgenstein emphasized, one may discern similarities and relationships among sets of games, but one cannot find properties common to all games.

Wittgenstein's argument may also be applied to concepts that include tangible objects as members (Herrnstein & Loveland, 1964; Herrnstein, Loveland & Cable, 1976). For example, consider the concept "dog." Many dogs have common properties such as *has four legs, is hairy, can bark, can reproduce by mating dogs of the opposite sex,* and so on. However, an animal could lack one or even all of the preceding properties and yet be classified as a dog. The reader is invited to risk frustration and try to formulate a list of attributes that are common to all dogs and that distinguish the members of that category from other categories such as *cat*.

The inability to define natural concepts such as *game*, *dog*, and *chair* in terms of common attributes has led both philosophers (for example, Wittgenstein, 1953) and psychologists (for example, Rosch, 1978; Rosch & Mervis, 1975) to believe that the members of many concepts bear a relationship of *family re-*

semblance. In a relationship of family resemblance, the members of a category share one or more attributes with one or more other members, but no attributes need be shared by all members of the category. In a family resemblance relationship, each category member bears some resemblance to at least one other member, but all of the members need not have common properties. When adult subjects are asked to list the attributes of items such as *chair, table, sofa,* and *rug,* all of which belong to the superordinate category *furniture,* they often do not list attributes that are common to all members of the category (Rosch & Mervis, 1975). That observation and others (see Rosch, 1978) indicate that the members of many natural categories bear a family resemblance to each other and do not necessarily have attributes common to all members. Thus although the attribute-rule hypothesis may adequately describe relatively simple concepts such as *square,* it does not seem to adequately describe many natural concepts such as *table.*

The second criticism of the attribute-rule hypothesis turns on the observation that many natural concepts lack well-defined boundaries and are said to be hazy or *fuzzy* (McCloskey & Glucksberg, 1978; Rosch, 1978). For example, what exactly is the distinction between a stream and a river, or between a bush and a tree? Much debate has arisen over the dividing line between life and death, between plant and animal, between acquaintance and friend, and so on. Resolving the fuzziness of current conceptual categories is one of the primary aims of scientific, philosophical and theological inquiry. Although fuzziness is a characteristic of many concepts, that characteristic is not captured by the attribute-rule hypothesis of concepts. The hypothesis, in its traditional form, states that stimuli either do or do not belong to a particular category that is defined clearly by a set of attributes and rules. Furthermore, the research that has been guided by the attribute-rule hypothesis has typically involved well-defined attributes and rules, and there has been no fuzziness in the boundaries of the artificial concepts used. The researchers who have adopted the view that concepts consist of attributes and rules may have devised and studied concepts that are unlike natural concepts that have fuzzy boundaries. Consequently, much of the research guided by the attribute-rule hypothesis may lack generality.

Now consider the third main criticism of the attribute-rule formulation of the nature of concepts. According to most traditional versions of the attribute-rule hypothesis, concepts are defined by attributes and rules, and concepts are not characterized in terms of their internal structure. In the research guided by that hypothesis, the stimuli used typically either have or lack the attributes that define the concept, and all members of the concept are seen as equally good instances of the concept. However, in natural concepts, not all instances are seen as equally good examples of the concept (Oden, 1977; Rips, Shoben, & Smith, 1973; Rosch, 1974, 1975; Rosch, Simpson, & Miller, 1976a; Smith, E. E., Shoben, & Rips, 1974). For example, both ostriches and robins are members of the category *bird,* but they are not seen as equally good examples of birds. Most adults in our culture see robins as "better" or "more typical" birds than ostriches are. Similarly, both chairs and footstools are instances of the category *furniture*, but chairs are seen as more typical of that category than foot-stools are. Moreover, of all the members of a category, some members may be seen as closely related to particular other members, while they are seen as less related to still other members. For example, robins and sparrows may be seen as more closely related than jays, robins, and chickens—even though robins, jays, sparrows, and chickens are all birds. Since some members are judged to be more typical of a category than other members, and since some pairs of members are seen as more closely related than are others, conceptual categories are said to have internal structure. In a metaphorical sense, some members are near the center of the concept whereas others are at the periphery, and some pairs are closer than others. These structural aspects of many natural concepts have often been overlooked in traditional statements of the attribute-rule hypothesis.

The preceding aspects of the internal structure of many natural concepts arise in part from the fact that the attributes of natural concepts are not independent; some attributes occur together, and attributes do not occur in all possible combinations (Anglin, 1977; Rosch, Mervis, Gray, Johnson, & Boyes-Braem, 1976b). For example, in the category *animal*, attributes such as *has beak, has feathers* and *can fly* are highly correlated, whereas *has hair, has beak* and *is cold-blooded* simply do not occur together. In the research that has been guided by the attribute-rule hypothesis, the attributes of the stimulus array typically have been independent, and all combinations of attributes have been presented with equal frequency. Thus it has been argued (for example, Anglin, 1977) that the attribute-rule hypothesis has generated research on concepts that are fundamentally unlike natural concepts.

We shall see in a later section that the preceding criticisms strike hard against traditional versions of the attribute-rule hypothesis, but that some of those criticisms may be handled adequately by formulating more sophisticated versions of that hypothesis. For our present purposes, however, the important point is that the criticisms outlined above have provided the impetus for the second major view of the nature of concepts that has guided research into the formation of concepts.

The Prototype-Transformation Hypothesis　In the preceding discussion, we observed that concepts have internal structure and that some instances of a concept are judged to be highly typical of a concept, whereas other instances are seen as relatively atypical. This type of observation has led some theorists to suggest that for each conceptual category, there is a basic pattern. That basic pattern or most typical pattern is called a *prototype* or *schema*. Recalling our spatial metaphor for conceptual categories, the prototype lies at the center of the category, and other instances of the category either may be close to the prototype or may lie far away from it on the boundary of the category. The membership in a category is defined not only by the prototype but also by a set of transformation rules that indicate the various ways in which the prototype may be modified to produce other positive instances of the category. Basically, the transformation rules specify the kinds of instances that can occur in a particular category, and therefore help to define the boundaries of the category (Laskey & Kallio, 1978). Transformation rules may specify numerous kinds of modifications of prototypes. For example, those rules may specify that the prototype may be inverted, rotated 90°, distorted randomly, combined with attributes not present in the prototype, and so on.

The prototype-transformation hypothesis may be clarified by considering briefly a set of experiments (Posner & Keele, 1968; Posner, 1969, 1970) designed to study prototypes in conceptual categories involving visual stimuli. The stimuli were random arrangements of nine dots such as those shown in Fig. 7.4. The stimuli included three prototype dot patterns and four distortions of each prototype that were generated by subjecting the dots in the prototype to small, random displacements. For each set of four distortions, the prototype represented the central tendency of the set. In Phase I of the experiment, adult subjects were exposed to a paired-associate learning procedure in which they learned to give a particular name in the presence of each of the distortions that had been generated from a particular prototype. The prototypes were never presented during Phase I, and that phase continued until the subjects reliably classified the distortions into the appropriate categories. In Phase II of the experiment, the subjects were asked to classify a variety of stimuli into the categories they had learned in Phase I. The stimuli included some of the distortions that had been presented in Phase I, some novel distortions of the prototypes, and the actual prototypes, which had never before been seen by the subjects. The novel distortions and the prototypes were equally similar to the distortions that had been presented in Phase I.

The principal results of the experiment were that the subjects classified the prototypes quite well. In addition to categorizing the prototypes more accurately than the novel distortions, the subjects in some instances categorized the prototypes as accurately as the distortions they had learned to classify in Phase I. Furthermore, following a delay of one week, accuracy in classifying the prototypes did not decline, whereas accuracy in classifying the distortions of the prototypes did decline. In an experiment similar to the preceding ones, the subjects were asked to indicate whether each stimulus had or had not been presented during Phase I. In keeping with the results described above, the subjects reliably identified prototypes that had not actually been presented before

Fig. 7.4 Examples of random dot patterns. The top row includes three prototypes and the bottom row shows four distortions of the right prototype.   (From Posner, 1973.)

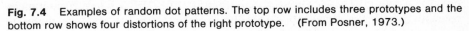

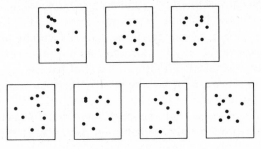

as stimuli they had previously seen. Taken together, the results of these studies support the view that concepts may be described in terms of prototypes and transformations thereof (see also Attneave, 1957; Franks & Bransford, 1971; Laskey et al., 1978; Reed, 1972; Rosch, 1978).

A Critique of the Prototype-Transformation Hypothesis The prototype-transformation hypothesis escapes some of the chief criticisms that have been aimed at the attribute-rule hypothesis. For example, the prototype-transformation hypothesis is consistent with the observation that the members of many conceptual categories do not all have common properties, but rather bear a relationship of family resemblance. The degree of family resemblance of a category member to other members has been defined in terms of the extent to which a particular member possesses attributes in common with other members (Rosch & Mervis, 1975). Although the prototypes of natural concepts such as *furniture* often lack attributes that are common to all members of the category, the prototypes bear a very high degree of family resemblance to other members of the category. In other words, the degree of family resemblance of an item is highly correlated with the rated prototypicality of the item, where prototypicality is defined as the degree to which an item is judged to be representative or typical of the category (Rosch & Mervis, 1975). Since the prototype does not necessarily share attributes in common with all category members, the prototype hypothesis escapes the problems involved in defining concepts in terms of attributes possessed by all category members.

Another advantage of the prototype-transformation hypothesis is that it accords with the observation that conceptual categories have internal structure. For example, the prototype is by definition the most typical or representative instance of the category. Generally, the closer an instance is to the prototype, the more typical it is judged to be of the entire category. Furthermore, the prototype-transformation hypothesis has begun to guide much research concerning natural concepts that do not readily conform to the attribute-rule hypothesis.

The prototype-transformation hypothesis, however, does have some notable disadvantages in addition to its merits. One of the primary problems concerns the nature of prototypes. It is possible that a prototype may be defined in terms of a set of attributes, some of which may be more important or heavily weighted than others (cf. Neumann, 1974, 1977). That possibility is consistent with the observation that the prototype has the greatest degree of family resemblance (as defined by common attributes) to other members of the category. But that view is ironic when one considers the fact that the prototype-transformation hypothesis has been seen as fundamentally unlike the attribute-rule hypothesis. It may be that the two hypotheses are less discrepant than was originally envisioned (Palmer, 1978; but see Laskey et al., 1978), and it may be possible to integrate the two by modifying the traditional version of the attribute-rule hypothesis.

A related problem is that the prototype-transformation hypothesis in some domains may not provide substantial advantages relative to the attribute-rule hypothesis. For example, the natural geometrical concept *square* may be defined satisfactorily in terms of attributes and rules, and prototypes may not help to define such logical concepts. The same may be said with regard to the observation that many concepts have fuzzy boundaries. The prototype hypothesis is consistent with the observation that the category boundaries are often poorly defined, for many atypical instances of a category may lie near the border of the category. However, upon closer inspection it seems that the prototype, together with a list of acceptable transformations, could identify any stimulus as either a member or a nonmember of a particular category, just as a list of attributes and rules would do. Thus in order to account for the fact that it is often difficult to decide whether or not a stimulus belongs to a particular category, both the prototype-transformation and the attribute-rule hypotheses need to be supplemented by some sort of decision mechanism (for example, signal detection theory; cf. Green & Swets, 1966; Posner, 1969) that operates probabilistically.

Concluding Comments   One objection that may be raised against the research that has been guided by the attribute-rule hypothesis is that it concerns artificial concepts and is therefore of limited generality. However, the study of concepts that do not occur outside of the laboratory is not a problem in itself. Indeed, the study of natural concepts does not necessarily confer immunity from the problem of limited generality, for the conditions of any laboratory study, questionnaire, and so on may not resemble the typical conditions outside the laboratory. Furthermore, a particular natural concept may not be representative of all natural concepts. The key question to be asked of any experiment in evaluating generality is whether and to what extent the materials and procedures have properties in common with those that occur in so-called natural settings. It should also be recognized that artificial concepts have been used in the research guided by both hypotheses discussed above (for example, Bruner, Goodnow, & Austin, 1956; Rosch, Simpson, & Miller, 1976a).

In the study of natural concepts such as *bird,* the experimenter has little control over and no knowledge of the subject's prior experiences with the members of the category. Consequently, one may specify the structure and composition of natural concepts in adults, but the ontogenetic origins of that structure and composition cannot be discovered by studying adults. We believe that one fruitful way to address that problem is to study artificial concepts with reference to which the subjects' experience may be specified and controlled. (For an alternative strategy of a developmental orientation, see Anglin, 1977; Flavell, 1977; Piaget, 1953). Moreover, the concepts and acquisition conditions studied in the research guided by the attribute-rule hypothesis may yet prove to be similar to some of the concepts and acquisition conditions that are encountered outside the laboratory.

Numerous unresolved problems confront both the attribute-rule and the prototype-transformation hypotheses. One unresolved problem may be called the problem of *contextual variation.* We have so far discussed conceptual categories as if they were unitary and static in nature. In fact, just the opposite may be true. For example, physicists have devised different concepts of light that they use for different purposes. Under some conditions, they conceive of light in terms of waves, whereas under other conditions they think of light in terms of particles. Similarly, some of the life forms we may categorize as *insects* when talking to children or friends may not be classified by us as *insects* when we are in a biology class. Furthermore, as we experience new aspects of our environments, our conceptual categories may be modified sharply. It is simply too soon to tell whether these and other problems such as the definition of conceptual boundaries are best handled by the attribute-rule hypothesis, the prototype-transformation hypothesis, or by some combination of the two. For that reason, we shall include the research and principles that are the progeny of both hypotheses in our discussion of the antecedents of concept formation.

The Determinants of Concept Formation

Our analysis of the antecedents of concept formation must begin with a description of the experimental procedures that are typically used to study concept formation. Most experiments involve one of two methods: the method of reception or the method of selection (Bourne, Ekstrand, & Dominowski, 1971). In the *method of reception,* the subject is shown a series of stimuli such as those given in Fig. 7.5. The stimuli are presented successively in an irregular order. In the presence of each stimulus, the subject says "yes" or "no" to indicate whether the stimulus shown belongs to the concept that has been designed by the experimenter, and the subject is then told whether the response is correct or incorrect. For example, if the concept were *circle and three borders,* a conjunctive concept, the subject would be shown a series of cards one at a time and would respond "yes" or "no" to each. The subject is told the response is correct if it was "yes" to a card that contained a circle and three borders or "no" to a card that did not contain both a circle and three borders. Of course, the subject must guess on the initial trials which stimuli do and do not belong to the concept.

In the *method of selection,* the subject is shown the entire array of stimuli and is allowed to choose one that he or she thinks is an instance of the concept. If the choice is correct, the subject is told so by the experimenter. As in the method of reception, the subject is forced to guess at the beginning of the experiment, and the experiment continues until a large percentage of the subject's responses are correct. The main difference between the methods of reception and selection lies in who controls the sequence of stimuli to which responses are given. In the reception method, the experimenter controls the sequence, whereas in the selection method, the subject controls the sequence. An additional difference between the method of reception and the method of reflection concerns the demands placed on the memory of the subjects. In the method of selection, the subject has available the stimuli responded to on previous trials. But in the method of reception, the subject has access to those stimuli memorially rather than by way of direct exposure.

As you can well imagine, the two methods have different advantages and limitations. For example, the method of selection permits the experimenter to

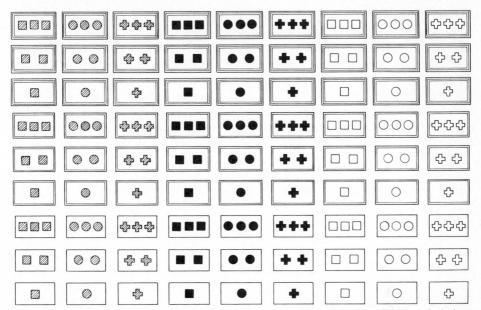

Fig. 7.5 Stimuli from a laboratory experiment in concept learning. The stimuli varied along three dimensions: shape, color, and number of borders. For each dimension, there were three attributes (e.g., red, black, or green). (From Bruner, J. S., Goodnow, & Austin, 1956.)

see how the subjects arrive at the concept when the experimenter does not intrude. If the subjects were systematically forming and testing hypotheses, it would be relatively easy for the experimenter to describe those hypotheses on the basis of the sequence of choices by the subject. Although the method of selection in a sense leaves the subject free to respond, that method also takes the control over the stimuli out of the hands of the experimenter. The method of reception gives the experimenter direct control over the sequence of stimuli, and that method can be arranged so that it is still possible to assess how the subjects are going about their task (Levine, 1966).

With the necessary experimental tools in hand, we may now examine some of the determinants of concept formation. In concert with the central theme of this chapter, we shall see that the effects of different variables upon conceptual behavior depend upon the prior experience of the organism.

Type of Rule We saw previously that concepts can involve different kinds of rules, and the possibility exists that some rules are intrinsically more difficult than others. In a variety of experiments (for example, Neisser & Weene, 1962; Wells, 1963), the effects of the type of conceptual rule upon concept acquisition have been assessed. In one experiment (Bourne, 1967), adult subjects were divided into groups that learned concepts involving different rules: the conjunctive, the disjunctive, the conditional, and the biconditional rules. After the subjects in a group learned one concept characterized by a particular rule, for example, the conditional rule, they were required to learn a second concept with a conjunctive rule. The experiment continued until the subjects in the different groups had learned nine successive concepts, each of which involved a particular rule. Each successive concept involved different attributes, and the subjects were told at the outset of each problem what the relevant attributes were. By identifying the relevant attributes for the subjects, the experimenters were able to study the learning of rules, rather than the learning of rules in combination with the learning of the relevant attributes.

The results of the experiment are shown in Fig. 7.6. One important aspect of the results is that on the first problem there were significant differences in the number of trials required to learn the various rules. Whereas the concepts that involved the conjunctive and the disjunctive rules were learned fairly rapidly, the concepts that involved the conditional and the biconditional rules were learned quite slowly. However, the initial differences in the difficulty of learning the various rules did not arise from some permanent structural feature of humans that makes some rules easier to learn than others. With added experience, the subjects came to learn the various concepts very rapidly, and the difference in the rate of learning the different rules disappeared. In further experiments (for example, Bourne and Guy, 1968; Dodd, Kinsman, Klipp, & Bourne, 1971), it has been shown that subjects who have had training with different kinds of rules can learn to solve problems involving different rules in equal numbers of trials.

We may conclude that it is not necessarily the nature of humans to learn

Fig. 7.6   The mean number of trials required to learn various types of conceptual rules.   (From Bourne, Ekstrand, & Dominowski, 1971.)

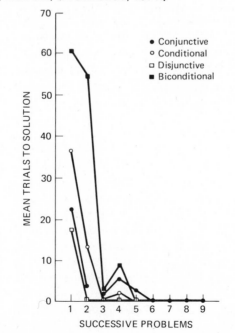

some conceptual rules more easily than others. Rather, it seems that the subjects' preexperimental experiences transfer positively to the learning of some rules and negatively to the learning of others. The differences that arise from prior experience may be eliminated through subsequent experience, and the same conclusion applies with equal force to the learning of attributes (cf. Bourne, 1967).

Typicality   We pointed out earlier that many conceptual categories have internal structure in that some category members are judged to be more typical of the category than are others. Recent experiments indicate that the internal structure of conceptual categories has implications for how categories are formed (Rosch, 1978). For example, not all members of a category are learned at an equal rate, as the following study (Rosch et al., 1976a) shows.

The experimental task involved learning to classify nonsense patterns of dots, similar to those shown in Fig. 7.4, into four categories. Each category consisted of a prototypical pattern, which represented the central tendency of the category, and numerous dot patterns that were distortions of the prototypes. Some of the distortions were minor whereas others were extreme, and there was a total of five degrees or levels of distortion. The subjects were shown the prototype and one pattern from each level of distortion for each of the four categories. The stimuli from the various categories were presented in an irregular order, and the items from, for example, category one were sometimes followed by an item from category three or from category four, and so on. The stimuli were presented one after another in a paired-associate procedure, and the experimenter provided immediate feedback concerning the correctness or incorrectness of the response. That procedure was continued until the subjects had made two errorless runs through the list. After completing the learning task, the subjects rated on a five-point scale how typical each item was of the category it belonged to.

The main results of the experiment were twofold. First, there were large and reliable differences in the number of errors that occurred in learning the various items within each category, despite the fact that the various items were presented with equal frequency. Second, there was a relation between the number of errors made in learning to classify an item and the rated degree of typicality of that item. The more typical of a category a stimulus was judged to be, the fewer the errors that were made in learning to categorize that stimulus correctly. Furthermore, when the subjects were asked to remember and reproduce in drawing as many of the presented patterns as possible, they more often produced relatively typical items rather than atypical ones, and they tended to produce the most typical items first. Subsequent experiments (Rosch et al., 1976a) showed that the effects of typicality upon rate of acquisition cannot be explained on the basis of the frequency of exposure to various items or the overlearning of the prototypes. For now, the point of central importance is that there is a high positive correlation between the judged typicality of an item and the rate at which that item comes to be classified as an instance of a particular concept.

The research described above is relatively recent, and some broad questions confront that research enterprise (for example, Neuman, 1974; 1977). One class of questions concerns the interpretation of correlational effects. Does the rapid learning of particular items lead those items to be rated as highly typical? Or does the high degree of typicality of particular items lead to the rapid learning of those items? Finally, could there be a third, unidentified variable that determines both the degree of typicality and the rate of learning? Until unequivocal answers to these questions are provided, the exact origins of typicality effects shall remain uncertain. One approach that has been taken in addressing these questions will be examined in the following section.

Information and Concept Formation We stated previously that the prototype of a category bears the highest degree of family resemblance to other members of the category. Relative to other members of the category, the prototype has the most attributes in common with other members of the category. Additionally, of all the members of a category, the prototype has the fewest attributes in common with the members of other categories (Rosch & Mervis, 1975).

For these reasons, the prototype is said to convey more *information* than any other members of a particular category (Rosch et al., 1976b). Information has been defined as the reduction of uncertainty (cf. Garner, 1962; Hunt, E. B., 1962), and we shall see later that the concept of information plays a prominent role in contemporary analyses of memory. Figuratively speaking, if there are many members of many different categories, there may be considerable uncertainty as to whether a stimulus does or does not belong to a particular category. The presence of a particular attribute reduces that uncertainty to the extent that the attribute is unique to a particular category. And since the prototype of a category has the most attributes in common with other members of that category, and the fewest attributes in common with members of other categories, the prototype is the most informative member of the category.

What determines the degree of informativeness of the various items within a category? One suggestion that has been given (Rosch et al., 1975; Rosch et al., 1976a, 1976b) is that the structure of the environment an individual is exposed to determines the informativeness of an item. According to that view, a prototype is the most informative member of the category by virtue of the fact that the prototype consists of a unique cluster of attributes that are highly correlated and distinctive in the environment. For example, the stimuli that we call *birds* are generally characterized by numerous attributes such as *can fly, has beak, has feathers,* and so on. The latter attributes are highly correlated in that they tend to occur together in the environment when they occur at all. Moreover, those attributes are highly distinctive and informative in that they do not occur in other categories such as *dog* or *squirrel.* In this view, the distinctive correlations of attributes in the environment are mirrored in the prototypes of the categories we form. Thus the structure of the environment determines how informative a particular item is. If one were trying to determine whether a particular stimulus is, for example, a bird, a lizard, or a flying squirrel, that stimulus would be highly informative if it had attributes such as *has beak* and *has feathers* and lacked attributes common to all three categories.

The view outlined above has important implications concerning concept formation. Since prototypes are believed to be the most informative members of categories, which items are prototypes may be determined by the structure of the environment. If that hypothesis is valid, the structure of the environment may be the central factor that underlies both the degree of typicality and the rate of learning of the items within a category. On a deeper level, the structure of the environment may be one of the chief determinants of which stimuli will be grouped together or treated as functionally equivalent by the organism (see Rosch, 1978; Rosch et al., 1976b, for further discussion).

The claim that the structure of conceptual categories reflects the structure of the environment may not now be evaluated adequately on an empirical level. However, it is appropriate to note here that similarities in the structure of the environments of different societies may contribute to the formation of similar conceptual categories in very different cultures. This point shall be of considerable importance in our subsequent discussion of language development. Conversely, differences in the structure of the environments of different societies may lead to the formation of very different conceptual categories in different cultures.

It is also important to recognize that the structure of the environment is not the only, or even the primary, determinant of the formation and internal structure of categories (cf. Rosch et al., 1976b). Stated simply, not all aspects of the environment come to participate equally in the control of behavior. Which stimuli or attributes thereof come to be grouped into a particular category depends in part upon the prior experiences of an individual and the contemporaneous contingencies to which that individual is exposed. For example, two individuals who have been exposed throughout life to the same birds may nevertheless categorize those birds in very different ways. One who enjoys simply watching birds may not notice many of the subtle differences and similarities that might be apparent to one who has studied ornithology and has often been reinforced by friends for making subtle distinctions. Similarly, the attributes that are important for some purposes may be relatively unimportant for others. Attributes such as *has feathers* and *has beak* may be important in discriminating between birds and other animals, but those attributes are far less important in discriminating between different species of birds. In short, both structural and functional factors may contribute to the formation of concepts. This point should be kept in mind as we now examine the importance of information in the context of the question of whether a concept is best learned on the basis of positive instances of the concept.

In several early experiments (for example, Smoke, 1933), adults learned concepts readily on the basis of exposure to positive instances of the concept, but they benefitted little from being told which stimuli were not instances (that is, were negative instances) of the concept. One account of that observation is that the negative instances carried less information than did positive instances (Hovland, 1952). This account gained credibility from the consideration that in many of the early laboratory studies of concept formation, there were many more negative than positive instances. To test this, a procedure was designed in which the positive and negative instances carried equal amounts of information (Hovland & Weiss, 1953). Nevertheless, in that procedure it took adults longer to learn concepts solely on the basis of negative instances than solely on the basis of positive instances.

The preceding studies show that adults may have difficulty using the information supplied by negative instances. Is that difficulty intrinsic to all humans, or could it arise from the prior experience of the adults who were studied? If the difficulty arises from previous experience, it should be possible to overcome that problem by providing extensive experiences in learning concepts on the basis of negative instances. To evaluate the latter possibility, Friebergs & Tulving (1961) had adults learn 20 successive concepts. Each concept involved a conjunctive rule, and for each problem there were exactly four positive instances and four negative instances. Half of the subjects were shown only the positive instances and half of the subjects were shown only the negative instances. The task of the subjects was to name each concept. The results of the experiment were that the subjects who had been shown the positive instances learned the first few concepts much faster than the subjects who had been shown the negative instances. Following the learning of numerous concepts, however, the subjects in the two conditions required approximately equal amounts of time to learn the concepts.

The preceding observations show that, given the appropriate experiences, adults can learn concepts equally well on the basis of positive or negative instances. But an important question remains: why must adults be given special training before they can readily learn concepts on the basis of negative instances? The best answer that may now be given to that question appeals to the principle of negative transfer. In learning many natural concepts such as *dog*, the negative instances greatly outnumber the positive ones, and the negative instances carry less information. Additionally, we are seldom if ever required to learn natural concepts solely on the basis of information from negative instances.

In concluding this section, it should be reiterated that informational analyses alone do not, and are not intended to, provide complete accounts of concept learning. Although informational analyses point out the importance of the structure of the environments to which organisms are exposed, they do not specify the conditions under which various aspects of the environment will actually be involved in the formation of categories. For example, the information provided by negative instances may contribute to the formation of concepts under some conditions but not under others. What is needed now is a thorough analysis of the conditions under which the information that is potentially present in the environment is actually used by the organism. It is hoped that the description of the task in cognitive terminology has not obscured the fact that this task also confronts students of conditioning. Stated in the vocabulary of conditioning theory, the task involves specifying the conditions under which the various attributes and dimensions of complex stimuli will acquire control over responding.

Stimulus Variables and Concept Formation As we mentioned previously, the formation of a concept involves the development of stimulus control by a relatively large class of stimuli. Many of the variables that influence the development of stimulus control affect the formation of concepts. One of those variables is stimulus salience. For example, Hull (1920; see also Brown, F. G., & Archer, 1956) used a large number of Chinese letters to study the formation of concepts. The Chinese letters were grouped into several categories, and all of the members of a particular category had a particular visual feature in common (for example, one feature was ⟍⟍). In one condition, the features that defined the various categories were painted red so as to make them highly noticeable or salient. In the second condition, the letters were completely black so that the critical features did not stand out. The result of the experiment was that the subjects in the first condition learned to correctly classify the letters faster than the subjects in the second condition did. Clearly, salience contributed to concept formation.

In a similar vein, the degree of difference between the attributes of a dimension affects the formation of concepts. One relevant experiment (Archer, 1962) involved stimuli that included several dimensions such as size and shape. For some dimensions, for example, form, the particular attributes that were presented were very discriminable (for example, circular forms versus elliptical forms), whereas the attributes of other dimensions were very similar. The result of chief interest was that the rate of learning depended upon the extent of the difference between the attributes of the relevant dimension. If the relevant dimension had very different attributes, learning occurred rapidly. Conversely, if the dimension had very similar attributes, concept formation occurred slowly.

Another stimulus variable that influences concept formation is the variability or the degree of diversity of the instances of a concept to which a subject is exposed. For example, Posner & Keele (1968) arranged many dot patterns that included four prototypes and several different levels of distortion of the prototypes. The subjects were shown only the minor distortions of the prototypes of some categories. Thus the stimuli presented from those categories were low in variability and were said to comprise a tight category. For other categories, both minor and more extreme distortions of the prototypes were presented, and those categories were said to be loose. The subjects were shown the same number of instances from each category in a paired-associate procedure, and the learning task continued until all of the patterns were classified correctly and reliably. After the subjects had learned to classify the patterns, they were shown novel, extremely distorted patterns and were asked to classify each into one of the four learned categories. For the tight and the loose concepts, the novel distortions were equal in overall distance from the originally presented members of the category.

The results were that the novel stimuli from the high variety (loose) categories were classified correctly more often than were the novel stimuli from the tight categories. Thus the degree of variability of the presented instances of a category affects how novel instances of the category will be classified. In other words, stimulus variability is one determinant of the boundaries of concepts (for further discussion, see Posner, 1969; see also Homa, 1978; Homa & Vosburgh, 1976). An important task for future research is to determine more precisely the nature and antecedents of concept boundaries.

In many instances, the influence of stimulus variables on concept learning depends upon previous experience. For example, if responding in the past had been differentially reinforced in the presence of stimuli along the dimension of hue or color, but not in the presence of stimuli lying along the dimension of size, then it would be easier to learn a concept in which the relevant dimension was color rather than size. Of course, that difference could be overcome by the appropriate training, but the point remains that attention plays a role in concept learning (Kendler & Kendler, 1975), and prior experience is one of the chief determinants of which aspects of stimuli one attends to.

The contribution of prior experience to the effects of stimulus variables in concept learning procedures may be seen clearly in the case of verbal concepts. In a concept learning procedure involving verbal stimuli, the subject is required to respond in a particular way to a class of verbal stimuli. For example, Underwood & Richardson (1956a; see also Mednick & Halpern, 1962) presented subjects with lists of 24 nouns. In each list, there were four instances of each of six different concepts. The subjects were told that the lists contained six sets of four common nouns, and that the nouns within a set could be described by the same word. When each word in the list was presented, the subject tried to say the correct response for each word, and the experimenter indicated whether the response was correct. In all, the list was presented 20 times, and the order of the words varied from trial to trial.

The result of primary importance was that the rate at which the subjects arrived at a concept depended upon the extent to which the different instances of the concept were associated with the name of the concept. For example, if the concept were *white*, the subjects arrived at that concept rapidly when the instances of that concept were *snow*, *tooth*, *chalk*, and *milk*, for those instances are strong verbal associates of *white*. The concept *white* was arrived at less rapidly if the instances of the concept were, for example, *onion*, *paste*, *sheep*, and *collar*, all of which are only weakly associated with *white*. Thus the speed with which one can induce a verbal concept from a set of exemplars depends upon the strength of association between the exemplars and the verbal concept. The strength of association is in turn the product of the prior experiences of the subjects. Clearly, experience contributes to the speed with which one can induce a verbal concept on the basis of verbal stimuli, and that conclusion undoubtedly applies with equal force to nonverbal concepts and stimuli.

Procedural Determinants of Concept Formation The last variable we shall consider is the type of instructions and training procedures used in experiments on concept formation. Subjects may be deceived about the actual purpose of an experiment, or they may be asked explicitly to assign stimuli to categories designated by the investigator, and so on. As the following study

(Brooks, L., 1978) shows, the different types of instructions may lead to very different outcomes.

The stimuli used in the experiment were sequences of letters such as X, V, M, R, and T. There were two classes of letter sequences that were produced by two different grammars. In simple terms, a *grammar* is a set of rules that specify how particular elements (letters in this case) may be combined to form sequences of elements. We shall have much more to say about grammars in our subsequent discussion (see pp. 324–332) of the grammars of natural language that specify how words may be combined to form sentences. For now, the important point is that two artificial grammars were used to produce two different categories of letter sequences. Although the two sets of sequences conformed to different rules, the sequences of both categories appeared very similar, for most letters appeared in both types of sequence. For example, two of the sequences that belonged to one category (Category A) were VVTRXR and XMVRXR, and two sequences from the other category (Category B) were VVTRVV and MRMRTV.

In one condition, called the memorization condition, the subjects learned lists of paired-associates in which the stimuli were letter sequences from the two categories, and the response items were either names of cities or types of animals (for example, baboon and giraffe). The subjects received no instructions pertaining to the two classes of letter sequences. Rather, they were simply told to say the appropriate word in the presence of each stimulus. The paired-associate procedure continued until the subjects had gone through the thirty different pairs successively without making any errors.

In the second condition, called the concept learning condition, a different set of subjects were asked to learn to correctly classify into two categories the same thirty letter sequences that were shown in the memorization condition. A reception procedure was used in which the sequences were presented successively. The subjects stated whether a particular stimulus belonged to Category A or to Category B, and they were given feedback concerning the correctness of their responses. That training procedure continued until all of the sequences had been presented successively without errors on the part of the subject.

Following completion of the two learning tasks, the subjects from both conditions were shown novel letter sequences and were asked to classify them into the three categories: Category A, Category B, or neither. The subjects in the memorization condition had not been told previously that the sequences shown in the training procedure belonged to two categories. Moreover, the subjects in the memorization condition stated that they had not noticed that there were two different categories of stimuli. To aid those subjects in the classification of the novel sequences, the experimenter told them that some of the stimuli had come from Category A and others had come from Category B, but the rules that defined the categories were not described. Although the subjects from the memorization condition giggled or complained that they did not know how to classify the novel stimuli, they agreed to try.

Interestingly, the subjects in the memorization condition classified the novel stimuli at a level of accuracy (60% correct) that far exceeded that expected on the basis of guessing (about 33% correct). In contrast, the subjects from the concept learning condition classified only about 46% of the novel stimuli correctly. Indeed, their performance was very little better than that of a control group that had participated in neither the paired-associate nor the concept learning procedures.

These observations are important in several respects. First, they show that the instructions and procedures used strongly influence concept formation. Since different instructions and procedures may lead to very different outcomes, it is unwise to try to ascertain the nature and antecedents of concept formation by using any one procedure. Although the reception procedure may lead to concept formation for some kinds of stimuli, it clearly does not do so for all types of stimuli. Second, the learning of individual stimuli (as in the paired-associate procedure) may lead to concept formation. Many theories emphasize that concept formation involves the detection and abstraction of regularities among the members of a category. However, the results from the memorization condition suggest that concept formation need not involve the extraction of attributes or the formation of prototypes (Brooks, L., 1978; Medin & Schaffer, 1978; Nahinsky & Oeschger, 1975; Robbins, Barresi, Compton, Furst, Russo & Smith, 1978); we shall return to this point in the next section. The third important implication of the results is that at least some conceptual knowledge may be tacit (for a discussion of tacit knowledge, see Polanyi, 1966). Stated in different terms, concept formation does not necessarily involve the awareness of the subject. In concept learning procedures, adult humans often state that they are searching for regularities, consciously evaluating their responses, and so on. But the preceding results suggest that the awareness of the subject is not necessary for the formation of a concept.

Concluding Comments   In closing, we must note that there are many other determinants of concept formation, including IQ (Harter, 1965), age (Strong, 1966), developmental level (Flavell, 1977), anxiety (Dunn, 1968), and concreteness of the stimuli (Heidbreder, 1946). For more complete reviews of the literature see Bourne (1966), Bourne, Ekstrand & Dominowski (1971) and Kintsch (1977).

Theoretical Aspects of Concept Formation

Since the behavior of the experienced organism is determined only in part by the contemporaneous environment, that organism is often said to make an active contribution to the learning that occurs in a particular situation. In particular, concept formation has been described as a process in which subjects adopt higher-order strategies, form and test hypotheses, and so on. In this section, we shall first examine some of the strategies that have been inferred and then explore the view that concept formation involves the formation and use of hypotheses or prototypes.

Strategies in Concept Formation   One of the first systematic analyses of the strategies involved in concept formation was made by Bruner, Goodnow, & Austin (1956). They used the method of selection so that they could observe consistencies in the pattern of responses of their subjects and then infer the strategies of those subjects (for a discussion of the problems involved in inferring strategies, see Johnson, E. S., 1978).

We shall consider two of the strategies identified by Bruner et al. The first strategy is called *conservative focusing*. As the name implies, that strategy involves concentrating upon and systematically testing the relevancy of one attribute at a time. Assume that the first correct choice the subject makes is a card containing one red cross and three borders (see Fig. 7.5). In this instance, there are many attributes that may have made the card a "correct" choice. For example, it may have been the presence of three borders that was critical, or it may have been the presence of a cross, and so on. In the strategy of conservative focusing, one presumably considers all of the potentially relevant attributes simultaneously and then systematically tests one attribute at a time. Thus after choosing the correct card, the subject might test the relevancy of the attribute *redness*. Accordingly, the next choice might be a card containing one green cross and three borders. If that choice also turned out to be correct, the attribute of redness could be rejected from the class of possibly relevant attributes. The subject might then go on to pick a card containing one red cross and two borders (the original correct card had three borders). If that choice were incorrect, the attribute of three borders would be retained as an attribute relevant to the concept. If the subject proceeded in that manner to test out each attribute one at a time, the conjunctive concept of "one form and three borders" would eventually be arrived at.

Another strategy that was discerned by Bruner et al. is called *focus gambling*. This strategy, unlike conservative focusing, involves changing two or more attributes at a time. If the first correct response were, as before, a card containing one red cross and three borders, a subject who was following the strategy of focus gambling might next choose a card with one red square and two borders. In that instance, the subject would have simultaneously changed two attributes: *cross* and *three borders*. As you can see, the focus gambling strategy carries both greater potential risks and greater potential payoffs than the conservative focusing strategy. Focus gambling is riskier in that errors are not very informative. If one varies two attributes at once and is wrong, one does not know which attribute is relevant and which is irrelevant. On the other hand, focus gambling offers considerable benefits in that if one simultaneously changes two attributes and is correct, then two irrelevant attributes would have been identified very quickly. Thus following the focus gambling strategy might lead to either very rapid or very slow concept learning, but whether learning is rapid or slow is largely a matter of chance.

In many of the procedures traditionally used to study concept formation, adult humans seem to learn more rapidly by following the conservative focusing strategy than by following any others that have been identified. However, conservative focusing is not necessarily the most effective strategy for forming concepts that are more complex than simple attributive ones (Johnson, E. S., 1978). Moreover, the conservative focusing strategy is not the logically most efficient strategy. To perform with maximal efficiency in the concept learning procedure described above (in which the concept was *one form and three borders*), one would have to remember each card that had been selected, which attributes had and had not been tested, which attributes had been found to be relevant, and so on. Thus the most logical and efficient strategy imposes heavy burdens upon memory. Most people have not had the training required to handle such a large memory load, and concept learning may be facilitated through the use of procedures for improving retention (Dyer & Meyer, 1976). Extreme memory demands do not arise when the conservative focusing strategy is followed, for the subject who adopts that strategy need not remember all of the presented stimuli and tested attributes. In conservative focusing, the subject begins by forming the global hypothesis that all of the attributes of the first correct stimulus are relevant. Then the subject tests each attribute, rejecting those that do not always occur in a correct choice and keeping those that do. Rather than remember all of the particular cards that have been chosen, the subject need only remember a small number of attributes that are either relevant or not yet tested.

Both the conservative-focusing and the focus-gambling strategies discussed above entail the analysis of attributes of the presented stimuli and the evaluation of their relevance to the concept. It is important to note, however, that there are strategies for forming concepts that do not involve analyzing and evaluating attributes. The latter strategies are called *nonanalytic,* whereas strategies such as those described previously are called *analytic* (see Brooks, L. 1978, for a full discussion of analytic and nonanalytic processes).

The distinction between analytic and nonanalytic strategies is best illustrated through examples. If one were learning the concept *dog* by following an analytic strategy, one might first analyze various instances of that category into attributes such as *has fur, has four legs, can bark* and so on. Then one might systematically test out the relevance of the various attributes or combinations thereof according to, for example, the conservative focusing strategy. By using the feedback provided by other people, one would reject the irrelevant attributes and keep the relevant attributes and attribute combinations, thereby acquiring the concept *dog.* In contrast, the formation of the concept *dog* according to a nonanalytic strategy would not involve the discrimination and evaluation of attributes. Rather, one would learn one or several instances of the category *dog* and then evaluate whether other stimuli belong to that category on the basis of similarity to the learned instances. If a novel animal were encountered, one might classify it as a dog if it were similar to a stimulus known to be a dog, for example, the family fleabag. The chief difference between analytic and nonanalytic strategies is that the latter involves the learning of particular instances of a category whereas the former involve the learning of particular attributes.

Nonanalytic strategies have not yet been studied extensively, but it seems that they should be. First of all, nonanalytic strategies do seem to characterize responding in procedures other than the traditional selection and reception procedures. For example, recall from our discussion of procedural determinants of concept formation (see pp. 296–298) that a paired-associate procedure facilitates concept learning relative to a standard reception procedure. The advantage of the paired-associate procedure may be that it promotes the learning of individual items. The learning of individual items, in turn, may facilitate the formation of a concept via a nonanalytic strategy (see Brooks, L. 1978 for further evidence on this point). A related point is that nonanalytic strategies may be more effective than analytic strategies under some conditions (Johnson, 1978). For example, some natural categories such as *animal* may include a very large number of instances and dimensions, and many of the important dimensions (for example, *mode of reproduction*) may not be clear to the learner. Under those conditions, the task of learning the concept may be simplified by learning particular instances of the category rather than trying to first isolate and remember all of the relevant attributes. Of course, after numerous instances have been learned, analytic strategies may also be adopted. Thus the two types of strategy may be complementary rather than mutually exclusive. Future research should describe and evaluate the relations between analytic and nonanalytic strategies and the role that nonanalytic strategies play in the formation of natural concepts.

It is important to recognize that strategies originate not only from present procedures but also from the previous experiences of the subject. This point may be clarified by considering the phenomenon of learning-to-learn or learning set (Harlow, 1949).

Learning-to-Learn   Consider an experiment by Harlow (1950) concerning the learning of a large number of discriminations by rhesus monkeys. The procedure for each discrimination involved six trials. On each trial, the monkey was shown two objects, for example, a red barrel and a yellow cube, that differed along a number of dimensions. Beneath each object was a small well that could hold a piece of food. If the yellow cube was correlated with reinforcement in a particular discrimination problem, the monkey would obtain food on each of the six trials by moving that cube. If the incorrect object was chosen, the monkey did not obtain food and had to wait a brief period before the next trial began. In order to prevent the responses from coming under the control of spatial stimuli (for example, left or right), the position of the object correlated with food was varied from trial to trial in an irregular manner. Only six trials were given on each problem regardless of whether the discrimination had been mastered. Then another discrimination problem with novel objects was begun, and so on for a total of 312 different, six-trial problems of equivalent difficulty.

The results of the experiment are shown in Fig. 7.7. The result of primary interest is that as the monkeys were exposed to more and more different discrimination problems, they came to learn the discriminations more and more rapidly (see performance on trial 2) and to a higher level of mastery. For example, on the first eight problems, the percentage of correct responses gradually increased over trials to a level that was above that expected on the basis of random guessing (that is, the 50% level). However, the monkeys did not master the first eight problems, for on the sixth trial of those problems, only about 75%

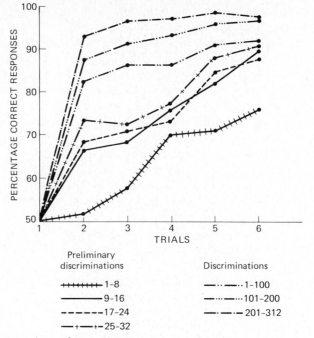

Fig. 7.7 The percentage of correct responses as a function of the number of trials within blocks of successive problems. Performance on a problem improved gradually during the early problems, but after extended experience with similar problems, performance improved very rapidly within each problem. (After Harlow, 1959.)

of their responses were correct. In contrast, on the later problems, for example, problems 201 to 312, the percentage of correct responses increased sharply after the first trial to a very high level of accuracy. Indeed, many of the later discriminations were learned in essentially one trial and with few or no errors. The errors that occurred on trial one were necessary, for there was no way of knowing which object was correct on the very first trial of a problem. Since the monkeys learned the successive discriminations faster and to a higher level of accuracy, there was a large amount of positive transfer from the early to the later discriminations. In a sense, the monkeys learned how to learn through experience with various problems.

Similar results have been obtained in studies of humans (Postman, 1969; Postman & Schwartz, 1964). For example, humans learn successive lists of words in fewer and fewer trials even though the lists are roughly equal in difficulty (Ward, 1937).

Learning-to-learn seems to come about through numerous processes. One process is the reduction of errors such as continuing to respond to particular stimuli that are no longer correlated with reinforcement (that is, stimulus perseveration; see Harlow, 1950, 1959; but see also Bessemer & Stollnitz, 1971; Darby & Riopelle, 1959; Mackintosh, 1974; and Schusterman, 1962, 1964). The primary process that is believed to be involved is the development of a general strategy that can be applied to diverse problems (Hull, 1952; Restle, 1958; Levine, 1965). Levine (1959, 1965) has characterized that general strategy as a *win-stay, lose-shift strategy*. Following that strategy, one would continue to select an object after receiving food for choosing that object, and following the choice of an incorrect object, one would shift over to the other object on the next trial. That strategy would clearly lead to a high frequency of correct responses in the learning set procedure.

The win-stay, lose-shift strategy clearly originates through experience and is a transfer phenomenon in the fullest sense. Indeed, in the experiment described above, hundreds of trials were required for the development of that strategy. Once that strategy was developed, each problem was solved with few errors and the rapid solution may have appeared to be insightful. Thus the ability to solve problems and make subtle discriminations through insight or other cognitive processes depends in part upon ontogenetic factors. These and similar observations (cf. Birch, 1945; Schiller, 1952) suggest that it is an oversimplification to characterize learning as either a gradual process of trial and error or a rapid all-or-none process involving insight. There may be no simple, unitary "nature" of learning, and the characteristics and contemporaneous antecedents of learning may change as the behaving organism is changed by experience.

The observation that conceptual strategies arise through experience has significant implications. First, a variety of different experiences may give rise to the development of a variety of different strategies. Consequently, we may expect that adults will be flexible in their use of strategies. That expectation will be confirmed in our subsequent inquiry into memorial processes. The second noteworthy point is that the use of a particular strategy may lead to either positive or negative transfer. For example, training in an object-alternation procedure, in which the correct object on trial n is the incorrect object on trial n + 1, requires a win-shift, lose-stay strategy. As one would expect, prior training on the alternation procedure produces large amounts of negative transfer in subsequent exposure to the learning set procedure. A full understanding of conceptual behavior requires an analysis of not only the origins of strategies but also of the conditions under which various strategies will transfer or be applied to new situations.

In closing, it should be recognized that conceptual strategies may also have important phylogenetic antecedents. Although learning-to-learn is general across a wide range of species—for example chimps (Schusterman, 1962), dolphins (Herman & Arbeit, 1973), cats (Warren, J. M., 1965) and bluejays (Hunter & Kamil, 1971)—there have been reports (for example, Warren, 1965; see Harlow, 1959 for a review) of substantial differences between species with respect to performance in the learning set procedure. At one time, there was some hope that performance in the learning-to-learn procedure could be used to rank different species according to their level of "intelligence" or general ability to learn. More recently, that hope has all but disappeared and for several reasons. First, the attempt to rank animals with respect to learning ability is poorly conceived, aside from the problems in defining and measuring general abilities and intelligence (Hodos & Campbell, 1969), for there is no linear evolutionary progression from, for example, unicellular organisms to humans. Moreover, comparisons of different species are meaningful only when the different species are exposed to comparable tasks. Unfortunately, it is exceedingly difficult to equate the testing conditions for two different species, and differences that appear to be due to differences in ability to learn are often due to differences in the sensory and motor capacities of different species and to differences in the procedures that are used to study different species (cf. Clark, F. C., 1972). For example, if the objects used in a learning set procedure differ in color, rhesus monkeys reliably perform better than cebus monkeys (Devine, 1970). However, the superiority of the rhesus monkeys in that procedure probably arises from differences between species with respect to color vision (De Valois & Jacobs, 1968), and the differences between species disappear when the objects used in training do not differ in color (Devine, 1970). Evolution has undoubtedly given rise to different learning abilities in different species (Bitterman, 1965), but the specification of those differences must await an enormous amount of further careful research.

Hypothesis-Testing and Concept Formation   We have seen that subjects often adopt strategies that involve forming and testing hypotheses about the relevant attributes of a category (for a review of hypothesis-testing, see Brown, 1974). However, it is frequently difficult to determine the exact nature of the hypothesis that a subject may be testing. For example, if a subject chooses a card containing a small blue circle with three borders, the hypothesis might be "small is relevant," or that some combination of attributes is relevant. An important step forward in the analysis of concept formation occurred when researchers devised procedures that made the inferred hypotheses more directly accessible to the experimenter, and those procedures will now be examined.

Special procedures (Levine, 1966, 1969) have been used in the analysis of hypotheses in concept learning procedures. The first important feature of these procedures is that they involve the method of reception in which the experimenter rather than the subject has control over the sequence of stimuli. Another important feature of these procedures is that following each trial in which feedback is given, there are four "no-feedback" trials. If the subject were testing a hypothesis regarding a particular attribute on a feedback trial and that hypothesis is correct, the subject should continue to respond in accord with that hypothesis on the following four no-feedback trials. The stimuli that are presented in the four no-feedback trials are cleverly arranged in a way that allows the experimenter to determine the hypothesis, if any, that is being tested.

The stimuli that were used and the patterns of responding that indicated which hypothesis was being tested are shown in Fig. 7.8. The stimuli used were characterized by the dimensions of color, form, size and position, and there were two attributes (for example, large or small) for each dimension. The concept that was devised by the experimenter always consisted of a single attribute, for example, white. On the first trial of the experiment, a stimulus was presented, and the subject was told which of the letters was correct. Then

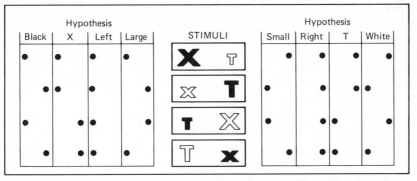

Fig. 7.8   The stimuli that were used in the experiment by Levine. The various hypotheses that might be followed are listed on the left and right of the stimuli. In the column below each hypothesis is shown the pattern of responding over the four trials that would indicate that a particular hypothesis was being followed. For example, if the hypothesis were "black," then the pattern of responding would be left, right, left, right.   (From Levine, 1966. Copyright 1966 by the American Psychological Association. Reprinted by permission.)

there were four trials in which a stimulus was presented, the subject chose one of the two letters ("X" or "T") and no feedback was given. Then there was another trial in which a stimulus was presented, the subject chose a letter, and feedback was provided concerning the correctness of the response. That feedback trial was followed by four no-feedback trials, and so on for a total of three cycles. Since there were eight attributes, the subject could in any particular cycle respond according to one of eight measurable hypotheses such as "left is correct." Which hypothesis was being tested was revealed in the pattern of responses within a block of four no-feedback trials. For example, if the hypothesis were "left is correct," then the subject would always choose the letter on the left. Likewise, if the hypothesis were "large," then the subject would always pick the large letter, as shown in Fig. 7.8.

The results of the experiment provided striking confirmation of the view that subjects in concept learning procedures form and test hypotheses. In about 92% of the patterns of responding within a block of no-feedback trials, there was a pattern that was consistent with one of the eight admissible hypotheses. Furthermore, if a hypothesis was confirmed on a feedback trial, that hypothesis was retained throughout the following block of no-feedback trials 95% of the time. In contrast, if an hypothesis was not confirmed on a feedback trial, then 98% of the time, that hypothesis was not followed during the subsequent no-feedback trials. Thus the subjects could be said to have been following a win-stay, lose-shift strategy.

Having devised a procedure that permitted relatively direct assessment of hypotheses, Levine was able to determine whether the subjects were simply testing one hypothesis at a time or whether they were following a more sophisticated strategy. If the subject was testing only one hypothesis at a time, the subject would not learn all that was possible from a single response. For example, if one of the stimuli was presented and the hypothesis was "white," the subject would choose the white letter, for example, the small "T" in the top row of Figure 7.8. If told this choice was incorrect, the subject would then reject only the hypothesis that white was correct. However, the subject could have learned much more during that feedback trial. If the subject chose the small white "T" on the right and was told this was wrong, the hypothesis "white," could be rejected, as well as the hypothesis that "T" was correct, that small was correct or that the right position was correct. In other words, each feedback trial could potentially be used to eliminate half of the hypotheses that had been viable before that trial.

On the basis of the observations that had been obtained in several experiments, Levine (1966) estimated how many hypotheses the subjects were testing on each feedback trial; the results are shown in Fig. 7.9. The top line in Fig. 7.9 (labelled "no memory") shows the results that would be expected if the subjects were testing only one hypothesis at a time and did not remember which hypotheses had or had not been tested. The bottom line (labelled "perfect processing") shows the results that would be expected if the subjects were eliminating as many hypotheses as possible on each feedback trial and were flawless in remembering the hypotheses and outcomes. As Fig. 7.9 shows, the subjects actually eliminated more than one hypothesis on the basis of what

Fig. 7.9 The number of hypotheses that were tested over successive feedback trials. (From Levine, 1969.)

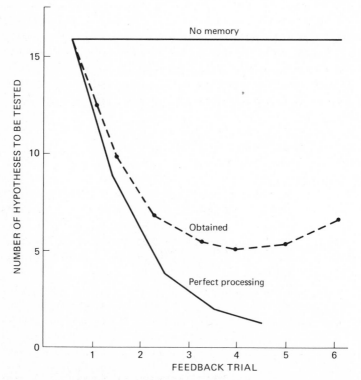

happened on a feedback trial, yet they did not eliminate hypotheses with maximal efficiency.

The preceding results have significant theoretical implications. In various mathematical theories of concept learning (for example, Bower & Trabasso, 1964; Restle, 1962), it has been assumed that adult subjects have very poor or no memory for the hypotheses that have been tested previously. That view was consistent with observations (Trabasso & Bower, 1964) that subjects in some procedures are very poor at recalling the particular instances that they had seen in the learning procedure. However, subsequent observations (Chumbley, 1969; but see also Kellogg, R. T., Robbins, & Bourne, 1978) have suggested that although subjects readily forget particular stimuli, they do remember the pertinent hypotheses. Furthermore, the observations from the experiments by Levine show clearly that the subjects remember the potentially relevant hypotheses from trial to trial and reject hypotheses on the basis of the outcome of responses in the feedback trials. Clearly, memory can contribute to concept learning, and how well one remembers depends upon a variety of conditions within the experimental setting. Consequently, we can expect that memory will contribute strongly to concept learning under some conditions, and less so under others (for supporting evidence, see Bourne, Ekstrand, & Dominowski, 1971; Erickson & Zajkowski, 1967). That conclusion is clearly consistent with our previous statements concerning nonanalytic strategies.

Another theoretical implication of Levine's observations is that adults learn a good deal on all feedback trials, regardless of whether the responses on those trials had been correct or in error. Some early theories (Bower & Trabasso, 1964; Restle, 1962) involved the assumption that the subjects learn only on those trials in which an error occurs. But Levine (1966) observed just the opposite: the subjects were able to eliminate more hypotheses on trials in which correct responses occurred than on trials in which incorrect responses occurred. Thus the view that learning occurs only on error trials is inaccurate (Brown 1974).

Concluding Comments Theories of hypothesis-testing have provided valuable insights into concept formation, but their generality remains to be determined. Many investigators now believe that concept formation is best conceived along the lines of the prototype-transformation theory. In that view, learning a concept involves forming a prototype of the category of stimuli that are presented. As more and more members are encountered, the prototype is modified so that it continues to bear the greatest degree of family resemblance to other instances of the category. When novel stimuli are presented, the subject determines whether they belong to the category by comparing them to the prototype. If a novel stimulus is sufficiently similar to the prototype, it will be classified as a member of the category (Reed, 1972). How similar an item must be to the prototype in order to be classified as a member of the category depends upon numerous factors such as the variability of the previously presented members of the category, the accuracy requirements of the task, and so on.

Prototype models of concept formation were proposed very recently, and it would be premature to evaluate those models in detail here. It is more productive here to point out some of the problems that confront both prototype-transformation and hypothesis-testing models.

One significant problem concerns the theoretical representation of conceptual knowledge. As stated previously, prototypes may in many instances be described in terms of the attributes or features that are used to describe conceptual knowledge in hypothesis-testing theories (Neumann, 1977; Palmer, 1978; Rosch, 1978). Accordingly, it is possible that the formation of prototypes may be analyzed as a process of testing hypotheses about which features of stimuli are relevant and central in a category.

Another problem is that contemporary models of concept formation are based upon observations from a somewhat restricted set of procedures. We have seen that different procedures give rise to different outcomes. If general models are to be formulated, we must look beyond the boundaries of the paradigms now used to study concept formation. Similarly, we must investigate many different types of concepts ranging from the concrete and well defined to the abstract and vague.

Finally, it should be acknowledged that much that can be said in terms of hypothesis-testing, forming prototypes, and so on may also be said using the vocabulary of stimulus control. When one learns an affirmative concept such as *small,* one's behavior comes to be controlled by a class of stimuli that share the attribute of smallness. The question that arises is whether an account of the conceptual behavior must necessarily appeal to inferred processes such as hypothesis-testing. We believe that the most productive theories may combine features of both conditioning theories and mediational or cognitive theories such as those concerning hypothesis-testing. Conditioning theories emphasize the contribution of prior experience and can help specify the environmental antecedents of conceptual behavior. Cognitive theories emphasize inferred inner processes and can help identify the private events that are important in concept formation. Because we ultimately seek an understanding of both the public and the private antecedents of behavior, we may draw upon the insights of both conditioning theories and cognitive theories. In our subsequent discussion of language and memory, we shall turn increasingly to cognitive analyses, but we shall continue in our effort to reap the benefits of both types of theory.

SUMMARY

Prior experience makes a large contribution to the behavior of the adult organism, but we often lack access to those prior experiences and to the private events that are the product thereof. In the absence of information about prior experiences, the behavior of the experienced organism often appears to be mysterious and functionally unrelated to the relatively simple behaviors that were the focus of earlier chapters. Seemingly mysterious and unique phenomena such as the imitation of novel responses in the absence of explicit reinforcement or the sudden solution of a problem often become more intelligible when we know something about their historical origins.

The experimental analysis of transfer represents an attempt to determine under controlled conditions exactly how the effects of exposure to numerous environments combine in the determination of behavior. We have seen that the direction and the amount of transfer depend upon the similarity of the stimuli and the responses that occur in the various environments an organism is exposed to. We also saw that the effects of similarity were not best analyzed on a molar level but rather in terms of components such as stimulus discrimination and response learning. The analysis of private events such as visual imagery, verbal mediators, and awareness is central in the analysis of adult behavior. Due to present technological limitations, inner processes are most often inferred rather than directly observed.

In our analysis of concept formation, we saw that some conceptual categories may be defined in terms of attributes combining according to rules. Yet other concepts defy attempts at description in those terms. Many natural concepts have no common attributes and are best characterized in terms of family resemblance relationships, fuzzy boundaries, and internal structure. To accommodate the latter features, it has been proposed that concepts are best described in terms of prototypes and transformation rules. Although the attribute-rule hypothesis and the prototype-transformation hypothesis have yet to be fully tested, both hypotheses have generated research that has begun to clarify the determinants of concept formation. Among the latter determinants are the type of rule, the typicality and information value of the stimuli, the variability and salience of the stimuli, and, of course, the type of procedure employed. Throughout our discussion, we emphasized that the prior experience of the subjects influenced the effects of each of the preceding variables. Given the appropriate training, subjects learned from negative instances as well as from positive instances, they learned conditional rules as rapidly as conjunctive rules, and so on.

As in the analysis of transfer, inferred inner processes were of central importance in the study of conceptual behavior. The development of strategies and prototypes and the formation and testing of hypotheses occupied the center of the theoretical stage. Eventually, a deeper understanding of behavior may come from the integration of the attempts to infer inner processes from the behavior of the organism, to specify the historical origins of private and public events, and to use physiological procedures to directly observe and manipulate processes within the organism.

With this chapter, we have crossed the boundary that divides the relatively simple and the undeniably complex phenomena of learning. In the subsequent chapters, we shall address two of the most intricate phenomena in all of psychology: language and memory. There we shall encounter many of the problems that were discussed in this chapter, and we shall again encounter the various strategies that psychologists have used to resolve those problems. In our inquiry into language and memory, it will be helpful to keep in mind the insights that have come from the study of learning in the experienced organism.

8
Language

One of the most significant of all the products of our evolutionary history is our capacity for language. The significance of language is apparent in our day-to-day experiences, for it is the basis of much of our communication, thought, and art. Language extends the effects of our environment, for language permits us to learn about events and places that are remote in space and time. Through talking, we learn about dangers that we might not survive through direct exposure, and we acquire more effective ways of producing reinforcing events.

Language is also important for theoretical reasons. First, the capacity for language probably played a central role in the evolution of *Homo sapiens* as a cultural animal (Hewes, 1977). Through language, we may acquire the insights, skills, and customs of preceding generations and pass them on to the next. Thus the use of language helps a culture to bring about important changes in behavior through rapid cultural training rather than slow genetic alteration over generations.

The theoretical significance of language also stems from the view that we alone have the biological capacity for language (Chomsky, N., 1972; Lenneberg, 1967; McNeill, 1970) and that language lies at the heart of human nature. The possibility exists that we are unique not only in having language but also in learning it. Specifically, we may learn language in part through processes that differ qualitatively from those involved in the acquisition of communicative and conceptual behavior in nonhumans (but see Marler, 1977). And once acquired, language may permit us to learn in unique ways, for the use of language entails symbolic processes that may be beyond the capacities of other animals. Furthermore, humans may learn language in part through specialized processes not involved in, for example, learning to play a musical instrument or to solve a mathematical problem. The preceding issues are presently the subject of considerable debate, and we shall pursue them further in this and the following chapter.

Regardless of the uncertainty surrounding the preceding issues, no doubt exists that an analysis of language is required for an understanding of learning and memory. For example, we saw in the preceding chapter that verbal mediation contributes to learning and retention in the experienced human. What is less certain is how language is best analyzed. Recently, many theorists have become dissatisfied with traditional psychological analyses of language, and they have turned to the field of linguistics, where far-reaching and productive breakthroughs have occurred in the study of language. Accordingly, we shall draw upon concepts from both linguistics and psychology in our examination of language and language development.

At the outset, it is important to acknowledge the differences between linguistic theories and the psychological theories we have considered thus far. In general, linguists have studied adults with complex and unspecified histories and have tried to devise theories of the knowledge that users of language may be said to have. Theories of linguistic knowledge are concerned with *linguistic structure*, for those theories specify the linguistic concepts we have and the relationships between them. Linguistic theories do not, and are not intended to, specify how linguistic knowledge is used or acquired. For example, linguistic theories do not account for the ways in which we speak or read or remember sentences. The latter phenomena are aspects of *linguistic function*. Linguistic theories are well suited for analyzing questions concerning linguistic structure, but other theories of a more psychological orientation must be turned to for analyses of how language is actually used. As we shall see, structural and functional analyses of language may be complementary (Catania, 1972, 1973b; Chomsky, N., 1972; Clark, H. H., & Clark, 1977; Segal, 1977), as are analyses of anatomy and physiology. The view that theories of linguistic structure and linguistic function complement each other provides the basis for the recently evolved field of psycholinguistics. As we shall see, psycholinguistic theories are designed to account for linguistic functions such as speaking and reading, and they are often built upon linguistic theories of the knowledge that language users are said to have.

In our inquiry into language, we shall begin with a linguistic analysis of an aspect of language and then consider the implications of that analysis for an understanding of linguistic functions such as speech perception, sentence comprehension, and so on. Having examined the fundamental aspects of language, we shall consider the question of whether language is unique to humans, and in the following chapter we shall examine the development of language.

LANGUAGE, COMPETENCE, AND PERFORMANCE

When thinking of language, one tends to think of the distinctive ways of speaking that characterize the many different ethnic groups of humans. Anyone who has learned a second language knows that languages differ with regard to speech sounds, expressiveness, the importance of word order, and so on. Yet these differences may not be as crucial to the definition of language as they may seem. For one thing, the differences in the ways humans speak in different communities may obscure the underlying similarities in the knowledge that all language users may have. Furthermore, language consists of far more than speech or customary patterns of speaking, for language users may know more than they can say. Consequently, contemporary students of language have tried to define language in terms of the kind of knowledge that language users have. This knowledge is called *linguistic competence* and is distinct from the ways in which humans actually speak, which are aspects of *linguistic performance* (Chomsky, N., 1957, 1965, 1975). Theories of linguistic competence are concerned with linguistic structure, whereas theories of linguistic performance are concerned with linguistic function. Because the distinction between competence and performance is central in many analyses of language, we shall examine the distinction further.

The Distinction Between Competence and Performance

Chomsky (1957, 1965, 1975) defines linguistic knowledge as an abstract system of knowledge that is reflected in our ability to speak and comprehend grammatical sentences, to identify anomalous sentences such as *The bachelor is married,* to discriminate that sentences such as *Flying planes can be dangerous* have two interpretations, and so on. In contrast, linguistic performance refers to the use of linguistic knowledge, for example, in carrying on a conversation or writing an essay. Thus the processes involved in, for example, talking and reading are aspects of linguistic performance, and these aspects of performance reflect to some extent our linguistic competence or knowledge.

One of the main reasons for making that distinction is that linguistic performance is affected by many factors, only one of which is linguistic competence. For example, we seldom speak sentences as long as those contained in Lincoln's Gettysburg Address, even though we have the knowledge required to produce very long sentences. Speaking very long sentences places heavy demands on one's memory and our failure to produce very long sentences in everyday situations results from memorial factors rather than competence factors. Similarly, we have the linguistic knowledge required to produce grammatical sentences such as *The plumber the doctor the nurse met called ate the cheese,* but that sentence would be very difficult to comprehend if it were spoken at normal speed during a typical conversation. Fatigue, emotional factors, and memorial factors all contribute to performance, and linguistic performance is therefore an imperfect reflection of linguistic competence. By distinguishing between competence and performance, linguists may bypass the effects of emotion, fatigue and so on, and focus on only those aspects of performance that seem most pertinent to the topic of language.

The second reason for drawing a distinction between competence and performance is that some aspects of competence in principle cannot be reflected in performance. Imagine what it would be like to try to list all of the different well-formed sentences that can occur in the English language. One would cease to exist in the effort, for the time required to enumerate so many sentences exceeds the life span of humans. In fact, it is theoretically impossible to enumerate all possible well-formed sentences of a language such as English since an infinite number of well-formed sentences can occur in natural languages.

Since an infinite number of sentences can occur in a language, language is said to be a productive system, and speakers of a natural language are said to exhibit *linguistic productivity* or *linguistic creativity*. The linguistic creativity of language users will rapidly become apparent to the observant person. It is a relatively rare occurrence for the same exact sentence to be repeated, except of course for the many idioms and cliches of our culture. Most of the time, we are productive in our daily speech.

Now consider what would happen if there were no, or very limited, linguistic productivity. Not only would our experiences become even more repetitive than they already are, but it also would be difficult to speak of novel events in a meaningful fashion. There are obvious disadvantages to a system of communication in which one grunt means roughly *Come over here* while another grunt means *We must travel 10 miles north*. If humans are to adapt readily to diverse and rapidly changing environments, humans as social animals need to be able to communicate about a great variety of events and experiences. This line of reasoning leads one to suspect that linguistic productivity is not merely a result of chance factors. Rather, linguistic productivity may be a critical aspect of human language that arose because it conferred reproductive advantage on individuals who were most productive. In other words, linguistic productivity may have originated and been maintained and refined because of its functional significance in the evolution of human beings.

The phenomenon of linguistic productivity has important implications for the study of language. The major implication is that language cannot be fully understood by merely describing and accounting for the speech or performance of different groups of people. In order to understand language, one must understand the linguistic competence that is only partially manifest in performance. The daily occurrence and importance of linguistic productivity pose a critical problem that must be resolved by any comprehensive theory of language. The problem is how finite humans with limited capabilities can produce and understand an infinite number of utterances. The latter problem provides a focal point for much of the later discussion of competence.

The third reason for distinguishing between competence and performance is that humans all over the world may, as the result of their evolutionary history, share common aspects of linguistic knowledge. But the common knowledge may not be apparent in observed speech, which varies widely across cultures. To formulate a general theory of language, linguists have tried to look beyond differences in observed speech to ascertain the general properties of language that are part of our biological heritage.

The distinction between competence and performance is now well established, although some theorists question the value of the distinction (for example, Salzinger, 1978; Skinner, 1974). Regardless of one's view on the merits of the distinction, there is no doubt about the importance of the phenomena that the distinction is intended to reckon with. We should keep in mind that both structural and functional theories of language must eventually accommodate the differences between linguistic and memorial factors, the phenomenon of linguistic creativity, and the possibility of general features of language that transcend cultural boundaries.

Components of Linguistic Competence

Having distinguished between competence and performance, we now may distinguish between various aspects of competence. Human speech consists of certain classes of elementary sounds, called *phonemes,* and combinations of those basic sound classes. The study of the classes of elementary sounds of human language and the rules governing their combination is called *phonology.* Phonemes may be combined in certain regular ways to form the minimal units of meaning called *morphemes,* which are roughly similar to words. The study of *morphology* is concerned with the ways in which phonemes may be combined to form morphemes and the ways in which morphemes may be combined to form words. Words may be combined in many ways to form sentences, and the study of how words may be ordered is called *syntax.* Language, however, is much more than a system that describes elementary sounds, meaningful units and the rules that describe the ways in which those sounds and units may be combined. The combinations of phonemes and morphemes that we call sentences have meaning, and the study of meaning is known as *semantics.* In summary then, there are four principal aspects of linguistic competence: phonology, morphology, syntax, and semantics.

We shall now consider briefly the major aspects of competence and focus primarily upon the theory of syntax, which has had a profound impact on psychological research. Linguistic theory will be discussed in the context of the English language, but remember that many of the concepts we examine may be applicable to many languages and may lend insight into the nature of human language.

PHONOLOGY

Humans are capable of producing many different speech sounds; these sounds are called *phones.* Two phones are seldom if ever exactly alike, just as no two nonverbal responses are ever exactly alike. For example, each time one says *pin,* one emits the initial sound in a unique way. Conventionally, phones are denoted by enclosing symbols within square brackets. Thus the initial phone in the word *pin* is [p]. The linguistic analysis of a language typically begins with a description of the phones that are used in that language. Phonetic description is usually accomplished by using the International Phonetic Alphabet, which has symbols for the speech sounds of many different languages and allows linguists to obtain comparable observations for a wide variety of languages.

Although all phones are different, only some of the differences between phones are important. The difference between two phones is unimportant if those phones may be substituted for one another without changing the meaning of a word in a particular language. In English, many different [p] phones may occur in the word *pin* and speakers of English nevertheless hear the same word, *pin*. Since the various [p] phones may be interchanged without producing a different word, these phones are said to be in free variation.

Now consider the phones [p] and [b]. The difference between those phones is important in English since that difference alone can lead to two words with different meanings. For example, the difference between the [p] and [b] phones distinguishes between pairs of otherwise identical words such as *pin* and *bin*, *pet* and *bet*, *pun* and *bun*, and so on. Since the [p] and [b] phones cannot be interchanged in particular words without changing the meanings of the words, these phones belong to different functional classes of phones.

The classes of phones that are functionally important in a language are called *phonemes*. A phoneme may be defined as a class of similar phones which are functionally equivalent in a particular language. By convention, a phoneme is denoted by a symbol enclosed by oblique lines. Thus the phones [p] and [b] belong to different phonemes that are denoted as /p/ and /b/.

Different languages are characterized by different phonemes, and this is a source of difficulty in learning another language. For example, speakers of English usually do not distinguish between the initial sounds of *keep* and *cool*, and these sounds do not belong to different phonemes in English. However, in languages such as Arabic, the initial sounds of *keep* and *cool* sometimes distinguish between words and therefore belong to different phonemes. Similarly, the phones [l] and [r] belong to different phonemes in English (for example, these phones distinguish between the words *look* and *rook*), but not in Japanese. In Japanese, the phones [l] and [r] may be substituted for one another without changing the meanings of the words in which they occur.

The Theory of Distinctive Features   Although functional differences between phones may be analyzed at the level of phonemes, these differences may also be analyzed on a more molecular level. By analyzing functional differences on a molecular level, it is possible to account for a broad range of linguistic observations with a very small number of theoretical terms. The molecular analysis of the functional differences between speech sounds has come from the theory of distinctive features. According to this theory (Jakobson, Fant, & Halle, 1963; Chomsky, N., & Halle, 1968), all phonemes can be described as configurations of a small number (about twelve) of *distinctive features*. These features are binary, and one or more of the binary features provide the basis for distinguishing between a pair of phonemes. For instance, the phonemes /d/ and /t/ are very similar except that /d/ is said to be voiced (since the vocal cords or folds vibrate), while /t/ is said to be voiceless (the vocal folds do not vibrate).[1] The voiced-voiceless feature is distinctive for this pair of phonemes. The voiced-voiceless feature also distinguishes /p/ and /b/ as well as /s/ and /z/. Other pairs of phonemes may be differentiated on the basis of several distinctive features.

The theory of distinctive features is important here because it shows that general linguistic principles can be formulated. Languages differ with respect to phonemic structure, but the phonemes of all human languages can be described in terms of the theory of distinctive features (Jakobson et al., 1963; Stevens & House, 1972). For this reason, the distinctive features are called *linguistic universals* and are held to be one basic aspect of human language.

Sequences of Phonemes

The sounds that are important in a language cannot be analyzed solely in terms of either phonemes or distinctive features, for the individual sounds that are important are often combined to form larger linguistic units. The phonemes of a language may be combined to form morphemes, but only certain types of phonemic combinations are permissible in a given language. To illustrate, no morpheme in the English language begins with more than three consonants (Hockett, 1958). Combinations such as *splb* and *mpsg* simply do not occur in the English language. Phonemes are combined only in certain orderly and predictable ways to form morphemes (for further discussion of morphemes and morphology, see Lyons, 1968).

Just as there are many acceptable sentences in a language that do not actually occur in speech, so there are many permissible combinations of phonemes that are seldom if ever produced by speakers. Language is a productive system on various levels of analysis. To describe competence, one must describe not only the combinations of phonemes that actually occur in a language but also all of the possible combinations that are permissible in a language. Linguists have attempted to describe the phonemic aspect of competence by formulating rules that can be used to enumerate or generate all of the phonemic combinations that are possible in a language (see Chomsky, N., & Halle, 1968).

A linguist might go about formulating rules for combining phonemes in the following manner. First, a large representative sample of performance for a certain language would be obtained. Then the combinations of phonemes would be studied to determine which combinations occur regularly and which do not. The linguist might then present native speakers with sequences of phonemes that did not occur in the sample of behavior and ask which sequences are acceptable or sound right, and which are unacceptable. Finally, on the basis of the linguist's own observations and those of other linguists, the simplest and most economical set of rules would be formulated that could be used to enumerate all acceptable phonemic combinations and none of the unacceptable ones.

In order to provide a foundation for the later discussion of the grammatical system of a language, several general features of *linguistic rules* will be considered here. First, the rules are descriptive of the competence of natives rather than prescriptive of the ways in which natives should speak. Linguistic rules are not like the rules of grammar that became such potent conditioned aversive stimuli to many of us in elementary school. Rather, linguistic rules are formal and abstract descriptions of some aspect of competence. Furthermore, even though linguistic rules may describe the acceptable combinations of phonemes in a language, linguists do not contend that a speaker consciously uses those rules when emitting some sequence of phonemes. The rules are aspects of competence rather than performance, and speakers are said to know linguistic rules only in an abstract sense. The concept of linguistic rules will be very important for the discussion of language acquisition in the next chapter, for many psychologists and linguists now believe that the acquisition of language involves the acquisition of rules.

Phonology and Linguistic Performance
The theory of phonology is concerned with linguistic competence. Yet the principles of competence may have important psychological implications,

Fig. 8.1 (a) The sound spectrogram for the utterance "to catch pink salmon." (b) The spectrogram that was used to produce the same phrase by means of the pattern playback. (After Liberman, Mattingly, & Turvey, 1972.)

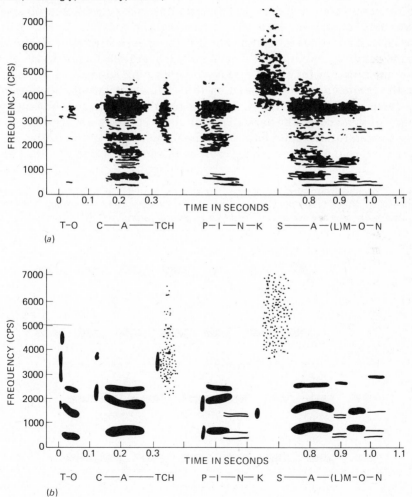

which psycholinguists try to specify. In this section, we shall examine some psycholinguistic analyses of speech perception that are rooted in the principles of phonology.

The first important point is that phonemic analysis provides information concerning the stimuli that exert control over the behavior of listeners in a particular verbal community. In other words, phonemic analysis identifies functional classes of verbal stimuli. To illustrate that point, we will consider the phenomenon of categorical perception of speech. Before describing that phenomenon, however, we must first examine briefly some of the research tools that are used in the study of speech perception (see Wilder, 1975, for a detailed discussion).

When we speak, we produce sound waves that have two main properties: frequency and amplitude. The frequency of sound waves determines their pitch, whereas the amplitude of sound waves determines their loudness. In order to study acoustic patterns of speech, a device called a speech spectrograph is used. Stated simply, a speech spectrograph converts acoustic patterns of speech into a visible record. Specifically, the speech spectrograph shows the frequency and the amplitude of speech stimuli over time. Figure 8.1a shows the speech spectrogram for the utterance *to catch pink salmon.* In this spectrogram, the frequency is represented on the vertical dimension, the duration is represented on the horizontal dimension, and the amplitude is shown by the darkness of the record. The darker regions of the spectrogram are areas of high energy concentration called *formants.* The formants are produced by the passage of air through the resonating cavities of the throat and mouth. The for-

Fig. 8.2 The spectrographic patterns of the speech stimuli that sounded like either /b/, /d/, or /g/. (After Liberman, Harris, Hoffman, & Griffith, 1957. Copyright 1957 by the American Psychological Association. Reprinted by permission.)

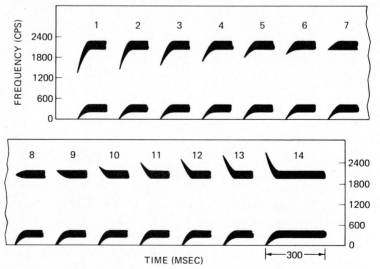

mants are important in that they carry much of the information that is required for speech perception (cf. Massaro, 1975, for a review).

In order to study speech perception, it is necessary to have a high degree of control over the acoustic stimuli that are presented to a listener. Acoustic stimuli may be precisely controlled by means of a device called the pattern playback, which converts visual spectrograms back into sound. By devising one's own visual spectrograms (for example, by painting), one may vary properties of the spectrograms to determine which properties control the listener's behavior and which do not. Figure 8.1b shows the spectrographic pattern that was used to produce *to catch pink salmon* by means of the pattern playback.

Categorical Perception   Now let us turn to the phenomonon of categorical perception. In an early experiment (Liberman, Harris, Hoffman, & Griffiths, 1957), a set of 14 speech stimuli, shown in Fig. 8.2, were made using the pattern playback. The stimuli were constructed in such a way as to sound like the consonants /b/, /d/, or /g/ in the context of the same /a/ vowel, which led the stimuli to sound like *ba, da* or *ga*. It should be noted that the stimuli differed only with respect to the direction and the extent of the transitions of the upper or second formants. Furthermore, the physical differences between pairs of adjacent stimuli were equal. For example, the physical differences between patterns 3 and 4 were equal to the physical differences between patterns 4 and 5 or between patterns 10 and 11.

In a test for stimulus control, the stimuli shown in Fig. 8.2 were presented

Fig. 8.3   The identification functions for the /b/, /d/, and /g/ sounds. The numbers on the abscissa correspond to the stimuli illustrated in Fig. 8.2.   (From Liberman, Harris, Hoffman, & Griffith, 1957. Copyright 1957 by the American Psychological Association. Reprinted by permission.)

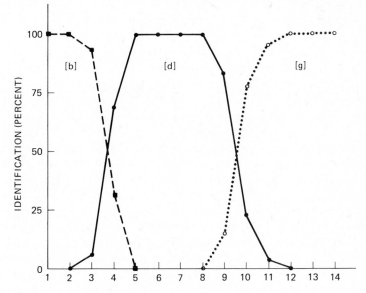

to adult subjects in an irregular order, and the subjects identified each stimulus as /b/, /d/ or /g/. The results are shown in Fig. 8.3. Stimuli one through three were identified as /b/, stimuli four through nine were identifed as /d/, and stimuli 10 through 14 were identified as /g/. Stimulus generalization occurred since, for example, various physically distinct stimuli occasioned the response /g/. Stimulus discrimination occurred since some stimuli occasioned the response /g/, whereas other stimuli occasioned the response /d/, and so on. In summary, the identification functions shown in Fig. 8.3 show which stimuli belong to the three phonemes /b/, /d/, and /g/.

One question left unanswered by the results of the preceding procedure is whether adults can discriminate between the different sounds that were classified together as /b/, between those that were classified as /g/, and so on. The subjects had been instructed to classify each stimulus as either /b/, /d/ or /g/, and it may be that the subjects classified different stimuli as, say, /d/ even though they detected the differences between those stimuli. In a second experiment, this possibility was evaluated through the use of a discrimination procedure. The procedure involved a series of trials in which three stimuli were presented successively and briefly. The first two stimuli in a trial always differed physically, and the third stimulus was identical to one of the first two stimuli. The task of the subject was to indicate whether the third stimulus matched the first or the second stimulus. If the subjects can discriminate between the first two stimuli, then they should correctly indicate on a large percentage of trials which of the first two stimuli matched the third stimulus. But if the subjects could not discriminate between the first two stimuli, then they should guess and emit the correct response on only about 50% of the trials. By presenting all of the possible pairs of the stimuli shown in Fig. 8.2, the experimenters determined the stimuli the subjects could or could not discriminate between.

The results of the discrimination procedure were in striking agreement with the results of the preceding identification procedure. For example, the subjects classified stimuli two and three as belonging to the phoneme /b/, and in the subsequent discrimination procedure, they failed to discriminate reliably between these two stimuli. Similarly, the subjects in the identification procedure assigned stimuli three and four to different phonemes (/b/ and /d/), and they reliably discriminated between those two stimuli in the discrimination procedure. In general, the subjects discriminated better between pairs of stimuli that belonged to different phonemes than between those that belonged to the same phoneme. Discrimination across phonemic boundaries was better than discrimination within a phoneme. That was true even when the physical difference between stimuli from different phonemes was smaller than the difference between stimuli from within the same phoneme. Thus the subjects discriminated more reliably between stimuli three and four (across the /b/-/d/ boundary) than between stimuli five and eight, even though the physical difference between stimuli five and eight was much greater. Since adults discriminate between stimuli belonging to different phonemes but not between stimuli belonging to the same phoneme, phonemes are said to be perceived *categorically*. Speakers of English hear the differences between categories but do not hear the differences within categories.[2]

Although categorical perception has been demonstrated for a variety of phonemes (cf. Liberman, Cooper, Shankweiler, & Studdert-Kennedy, 1967), this phenomenon occurs neither for all speech sounds nor under all experimental conditions that have been studied. For example, the stimuli belonging to the phonemes /b/ and /p/ appear to be perceived categorically in some discrimination procedures but not in others (Pisoni & Lazarus, 1974; see also Barclay, 1972; Pisoni & Tash, 1974). Moreover, the phenomenon of categorical perception appears stronger in consonants than in vowels (Pisoni, 1973). Furthermore, the ability to discriminate between different phonemes clearly depends upon experience (for example, Kuhl & Miller, 1975; Streeter & Landauer, 1975), and that is as it should be, given that languages differ with respect to phonemic structure. Considerable work remains to be done to clarify the exact antecedents and implications of the categorical perception of speech stimuli. On one hand, some research (which will be discussed in Chapter 9) suggests that the categorical perception of consonants appears very early in infancy and implies that the categorical perception of speech is part of our biological capacity for language. On the other hand, some research has shown that categorical perception occurs for nonverbal stimuli (for example, Jusczyk, Rosner, Cutting, Foard, & Smith, 1977; Kopp & Lane, 1968; Pisoni, 1977) and in nonspeaking organisms such as the chinchilla (Kuhl & Miller, 1975). It is simply too early to determine whether categorical perception of speech in humans reflects a language-specific biological capacity. At any rate, the important point for our purposes here is that the phonemic analyses that are carried out by linguists do in some instances convey important information about linguistic performance, and specifically about the perception of speech.

Further evidence of the importance of phonemes in linguistic performance comes from studies of the errors that occur in speech. For example, in spoonerisms, the initial phoneme in one word is mistakenly interchanged with that of another word (for example, MacKay, 1970). The often embarrassing result is that a phrase such as *wasted the whole term* becomes *tasted the whole worm,* or *our dear old queen* becomes *our queer old dean.* Similarly, Fromkin (1973) has observed that the initial sound in *church* functions as a unit in speech errors. Thus one might say *chee cane* rather than *key chain.* Both consonants move together when errors are made and therefore seem to function as a unit. Clearly, slips of the tongue are revealing in both psycholinguistics and psychoanalysis.

Just as the analysis of phonemes has implications for linguistic performance, so too does the analysis of distinctive features. For example, two sounds that differ with respect to only one feature are judged by adults to be more similar than two sounds that differ with respect to two features (Greenberg & Jenkins, 1964). Similarly, adults are more likely to confuse two sounds that differ with respect to one feature than sounds that differ with respect to two features (Cole & Scott, 1972; Miller, G. A., & Nicely, 1955; Studdert-Kennedy & Shankweiler, 1970).

Phonemes and the Units of Speech Perception   The preceding discussion has shown that the concepts of phonological theory are helpful in the analysis of how we perceive speech. Some theorists (for example, Liberman, Cooper, Shankweiler, & Studdert-Kennedy, 1967; Liberman, Mattingly, & Turvey, 1972; Studdert-Kennedy, 1974) have taken phonological theory one step farther and contended that the phoneme is the basic unit of speech perception. According to that view, perceiving a word, for example, *bag*, involves the perception of three individual phonemes: /b/, /a/ and /g/.

The question of whether phonemes are basic units of speech perception is complicated by the occurrence of the acoustic phenomena called parallel transmission and context-conditioned variation (cf. Liberman, Mattingly & Turvey 1972). *Parallel transmission* is said to occur when acoustic information concerning the different phones that occur in, for example, a word is transmitted simultaneously rather than successively. For example, in the word *bag* parallel transmission is said to occur if acoustic information concerning the [b] phone is transmitted at the same time during which information concerning the [ae] phone is transmitted. Figure 8.4 shows in schematic form a spectrogram that can be converted by the pattern playback to the syllable [b ae g]. Note that acoustic information about the vowel extends throughout the entire syllable. Thus the acoustic information concerning the vowel is transmitted in parallel with the information concerning the consonants. The acoustic stimulus that we describe as *bag* could not be divided into three separate sections to

Fig. 8.4   Schematic spectrogram for the syllable "bag." The acoustic representation of that syllable does not consist of a sequence of acoustic stimuli that correspond to each of the three phones. Rather, the information concerning each phone is transmitted in parallel with information about other phones.   (From Liberman, 1970. Copyright 1970 by Academic Press, *Cognitive Psychology*.)

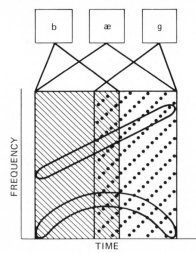

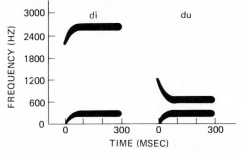

Fig. 8.5   Spectrographic patterns that can be used to produce the syllables [di] and [du]. The acoustic stimulus for the [d] sound is dependent upon the following vowel and is said to be context-conditioned.   (From Liberman et al., 1967. Copyright 1967 by the American Psychological Association. Reprinted by permission.)

produce the three phones [b], [ae] and [g]. The information concerning these three phones is transmitted simultaneously as a unit, and the word *bag* does not consist of three separate phones chained together in a series.

Now consider *context-conditioned variation*. Context-conditioned variation is said to occur when the acoustic representation of a phone varies according to the context in which it occurs. For example, consider the spectrographic patterns shown in Fig. 8.5. The patterns can be used to produce the syllables [di] and [du], respectively, and these patterns differ markedly with respect to the second formant. Thus very different acoustic stimuli give rise to the [d] sound. The acoustic stimulus for the [d] sound is clearly not invariant and is conditional upon the following vowel. Interestingly, if only the initial portion (0 to 50 msec) of either pattern is fed to the pattern playback, the [d] sound is not produced. Rather, a short chirping sound is produced. Apparently, the acoustic stimulus for the [d] sound is transmitted in parallel with that for the following vowel.

Taken together, these phenomena show that the speech code is not like an alphabet in which phonetic elements are always represented in about the same way and are strung together to form larger units such as words. Apparently, the perception of speech is not a process of discriminating acoustic stimuli that invariably correspond to particular phonemes. Furthermore, the perception of a word does not involve the successive discrimination of a series of phonemes. Beyond that statement, however, it is unclear as to exactly what is involved in the perception of speech. As we have pointed out, phonemes do not have invariant acoustic representations, but the acoustic representation of a syllable is relatively invariant. This type of observation has led some theorists (for example, Massaro, 1975, 1976) to suggest that syllables rather than phonemes are the basic units of speech perception. However, responding to phonetic stimuli may come to be controlled by the context in which they occur, and it does not seem to be necessary to postulate that the syllable is the basic unit of speech perception (cf. Liberman et al., 1967). Although it is too soon to tell definitely, it may turn out that both phonemes and syllables (and perhaps other linguistic units) can function as units of speech perception under different conditions (cf. Healy & Cutting, 1976).

Concluding Comments   Two central points may be drawn from the preceding discussion of phonology and performance. First, principles of linguistic competence may have important implications for the analysis of linguistic performance. Just as importantly, the units of linguistic analysis such as the phoneme may or may not be suitable units for the analysis of linguistic performance. Thus while the theory of competence may have implications for the understanding of performance, the theory of competence is not, and was not intended to be, a theory of performance. Keeping that in mind, we may now resume our exploration of the nature of linguistic competence, and we shall next consider the syntactic aspect of competence.

SYNTAX

The study of syntax involves a formal description of the ways in which the morphemes of a language can be combined to form grammatical sentences. The first requirement of a theory of syntax is that it must account for the observation that native speakers with presumably finite capabilities can produce and understand an infinite number of well-formed sentences. In order to account for the latter feature of competence, linguists (for example, Chomsky, N., 1957, 1965) have proposed that a theory of syntax should consist of a finite set of rules that can generate the infinite number of grammatical sentences in a language and no ungrammatical sentences. The set of syntactic rules is part of the grammar of a language.

What types of rules should be included in a theory of syntax? Although the answer to that question must be developed throughout our discussion of syntax, it will be helpful here to identify some of the criteria that are often used to evaluate different types of rules. Speakers of a language can not only discriminate sentences from nonsentences, but can also discriminate the internal structure of sentences, as the following example shows.

To native speakers, sentences consist of distinct word clusters or *constituents* rather than simple left-to-right sequences of elements (Levelt, 1970). For example, one can easily discriminate the major constituents of the sentence *The ambiguous question confused the bright students*. The two major constituents may be diagrammed as follows:

The ambiguous question confused the bright students.

The ambiguous question   confused the bright students

This diagram indicates what most native speakers of English observe: *the, ambiguous* and *question* seem to naturally belong together and *confused, the, bright* and *students* seem to belong together. Furthermore, the phrase *confused the bright students* can be divided into two constituents:

confused the bright students

confused   the bright students

The constituent structure of the entire sentence can be specified as follows:

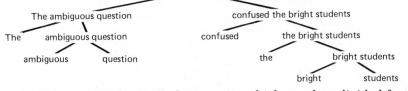

Because a sentence may be divided into units which are then divided further, sentences are said to have a hierarchical structure.

Speakers of a language may be said to know more than which word sequences form grammatical sentences, for they also have knowledge of the internal structure of sentences. This knowledge is critical for understanding sentences, particularly ambiguous ones such as *Flying planes can be dangerous.* For now, the main point is that a speaker's knowledge of language includes the ability to discriminate sentences from nonsentences, to discriminate the internal structure of sentences, to discriminate the ambiguity of particular sentences, and so on. These discriminations that native speakers can make with respect to their language are called *linguistic intuitions.* Because a theory of competence is intended to account for the linguistic knowledge of native speakers, a theory of competence should account for the linguistic intuitions that speakers are said to have. Accordingly, models of syntax have been formulated to account for those intuitions, and we shall next examine two of these models.

Phrase-Structure Grammar

In order to devise a grammar that specifies the constituent structure or phrase structure of sentences, linguists have formulated rules called *phrase-structure rules* (Chomsky, N., 1957). A single phrase-structure rule might, for example, analyze a sentence into its immediate constituents of noun phrase and verb phrase. Another phrase-structure rule might divide a noun phrase into an article and noun. A system of phrase-structure rules is called a *phrase-structure grammar.*

Figure 8.6 shows a very simple phrase-structure grammar that consists of seven phrase-structure rules. The arrow in each rule means *can be rewritten as.* The application of a phrase-structure rule results in the rewriting of one larger constituent as one or more smaller constituents. For example, rule 1 specifies that the element *Sentence* may be rewritten as NP + VP. Rule 2 specifies that the element *NP* may be rewritten as *Art + Adj + N*, and so on. The brackets around the *Adj* element indicate that it is optional; a noun phrase must include the elements *Art* and *N*, but the phrase need not include the *Adj* element. The braces around the elements in rule 4 indicate that the items listed belong to the same class and any of the items may be selected.

The lower portion of Fig. 8.6 shows diagrammatically the derivation of the sentence *The angry man hit the dangerous person.* Beginning with rule 1, *S*

Phrase–structure rules:

  (1) sentence (S) → Noun phrase (NP) + Verb Phrase (VP)
  (2) NP → Article (Art) + [Adjective (Adj)] + Noun (N)
  (3) VP → Verb (V) + NP
  (4) N → { person, man, woman . . . }
  (5) V → { greeted, saw, hit . . . }
  (6) Adj → { cheerful, bright, dangerous, angry . . . }
  (7) Art → { the, a, that . . . }

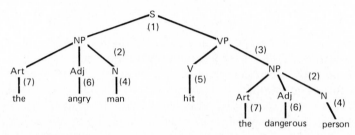

Fig. 8.6 A simple phrase-structure grammar and the constituent structure of one of the sentences that can be generated by this grammar. The numbers in parentheses indicate the operation of particular rules.

is rewritten as the constituents *NP* + *VP*. Applying rule 2, the *NP* is rewritten as *Art* + *Adj* + *N*. Next, rule 7 rewrites *Art* as *the*, rule 6 rewrites *Adj* as *angry*, and rule 4 rewrites *N* as *man*. The elements *the*, *angry* and *man* are called terminal elements since they cannot be rewritten with any of the rules listed. Rule 3 then rewrites *VP* as *V* + *NP*. *V* is then rewritten as *hit*. Finally, the *NP* is analyzed by the application of rules 2, 7, 6, and 4 to yield the terminal elements *the*, *dangerous* and *person*. The diagram of the constituent structure shown in Fig. 8.6 is called a phrase marker. Many more simple sentences could be generated by the grammar shown in Fig. 8.6.

    The preceding example shows that the generation of sentences by a phrase-structure grammar entails a description of the constituent structure of the sentence. Since phrase-structure grammars can specify the constituent structure of sentences, these grammars can account for some interesting linguistic intuitions that native speakers have concerning their language. For example, we know that the sentence *They are visiting parents* can have either of two meanings. Thus the sentence is ambiguous. Presumably, the ambiguity arises from the fact that the same sequence of morphemes can have two different grammatical structures. A phrase-structure grammar can account for the ambiguity of the sentence by specifying the different grammatical structures of that sequence of morphemes. The two different constituent structures are shown by the phrase markers of Fig. 8.7. The first sentence of Fig. 8.7 might occur as a reply to the question *Who are those people?* while the second sentence might occur as a reply to *What are they doing today?* Generally, phrase-structure grammars can clarify ambiguities that arise from a sentence having two different constituent structures.

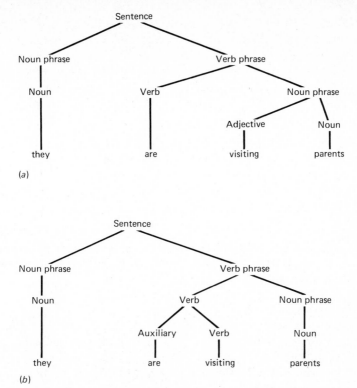

Fig. 8.7 Two alternative constituent structures of *They are visiting parents*, an ambiguous sentence.

An Evaluation of Phrase-Structure Grammar As models of syntax, phrase-structure grammars have several merits. Phrase-structure grammars can be formulated to generate an infinite number of grammatical sentences and no ungrammatical ones. Furthermore, these grammars can provide systematic descriptions of the hierarchical structure of sentences, and they can account for some of the ambiguities in sentences.

Phrase-structure grammars also have some serious limitations, and linguists have put forth strong arguments that a phrase-structure grammar cannot provide a comprehensive account of syntax (Chomsky, N., 1957). Although phrase-structure grammars sometimes clarify the ambiguity that arises in the interpretation of sentences, these grammars often fail to provide all of the structural information that is necessary for the interpretation of sentences. A sentence such as *Shooting police can be dangerous* is ambiguous. This sentence could be either a warning not to shoot at police or to avoid situations in which police are shooting. Some of the other examples that have arisen in the literature are *Visiting relatives can be a nuisance, The shooting of the hunters was awful, They were made by the machine* and *The police were ordered to stop drinking.* The foregoing type of ambiguity is not apparent in the constituent structure of a sentence, and the ambiguity is not resolved by varying the stress on different words in the sentence. Clearly, the phrase structure of a sentence does not provide all of the information that is necessary for interpreting all sentences.

There are many other linguistic intuitions that cannot be accounted for by phrase-structure grammars. To native speakers of English, certain families of sentences are clearly related. Native speakers agree for example that the following sentences are related.

(1) The chimp questioned the humans.
(2) The humans were questioned by the chimp.
(3) The chimp did not question the humans.
(4) The humans were not questioned by the chimp.
(5) Who questioned the humans?

Phrase-structure grammars cannot account for the preceding observations (cf. Chomsky, N., 1957) and therefore cannot serve as a complete model of syntax. Accordingly, linguists have proposed a more powerful model of syntax called transformational grammar.

Transformational Grammar

As discussed above, sentences such as *Fighting chimps can be dangerous* are ambiguous, and this type of ambiguity cannot be clarified through a description of the constituent structure of the sentence. The constituent structure or the surface structure of a sentence shows only some of the important structural features of sentences. In order to describe all of the relations between morphemes that are essential for interpreting a sentence, linguists have proposed that a distinction must be made between the *surface structure* and the *deep structure* of a sentence. A sentence such as *Fighting chimps can be dangerous* has only one surface structure but two deep structures. Thus the ambiguity of the sentence is clarified at the level of deep structure rather than surface structure.

To further explicate the need for distinguishing between deep and surface structure, consider sentences (6) and (7):

(6) The professor is easy to understand.
(7) The professor is anxious to understand.

These sentences have similar surface structures but in (7), *professor* is the subject while in (6), *professor* is the object. In this example, one can again see that the surface structure does not indicate all of the important grammatical relationships in a sentence. Sentences (6) and (7) are similar only in a superficial sense: they have similar phrase structures but very different deep structures, as Fig. 8.8 shows. Chomsky (1965) contends that only the deep structure of a sentence contains all of the information necessary for the semantic interpretation of a sentence. In short, the surface structure of a sentence determines the phonological aspects of a sentence but is not critical for the interpretation of a sentence.

There is another important reason for distinguishing between deep and

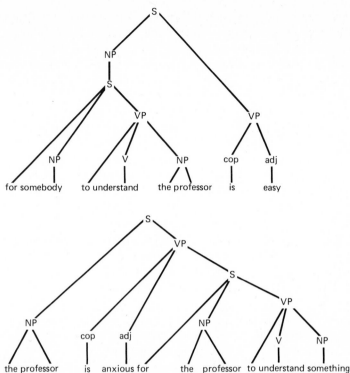

Fig. 8.8 The deep structures (simplified) of the sentence *The professor is easy to understand* and *The professor is anxious to understand.* (From Cairns & Cairns, *Psycholinguistics*, copyright Holt, Rinehart, and Winston, Inc., 1976. Reprinted by permission of Holt, Rinehart, and Winston.)

surface structure. An analysis of the phrase structure of sentences does not reveal the relationship between such sentences as (1) through (5) above. However, the relationships between sentences (1) through (5) can be specified at the level of deep structure. The relationships between the members of a family of sentences can be elucidated by showing how the various surface structures are derived from a similar underlying or deep structure. Hence, if a theory of syntax were built upon the distinction between deep and surface structure, then that theory could potentially account for both the ambiguities of many sentences and the relationships between the members of a family of sentences. For these and other reasons (see Chomsky, N., 1965) the distinction between deep and surface structure has been incorporated into recent models of grammar.

In Chomsky's influential theory of transformational grammar, the distinction between deep and surface structure is of central importance. In this theory, there are two types of syntactic rules. The first type of rule is the now familiar phrase structure rule. The phrase structure rules generate the deep structures of sentences. The second type of rule is called a *transformation rule.* Transformation rules rearrange elements in the deep structure in such a way as to form the surface structure of a sentence. In a sense, transformation rules translate the deep structure into the surface structure.

A detailed description of transformational grammar is beyond the scope of this chapter (the interested reader should refer to Akmajian & Heny, 1975; Chomsky, N., 1957, 1965). However, a very simple and abstract example should help to clarify the nature of transformation rules and the process through which sentences are derived by transformational grammar.

Figure 8.9 shows part of a very simple transformational grammar. This grammar consists of phrase structure rules that generate deep structures and transformation rules that transform the deep structures into surface structures. For example, assume that the set of phrase-structure rules shown in Fig. 8.9a have generated the following string of terminal elements:

$$p + v + k + a + x + h + t + e$$

The hypothetical phrase structure of that string of elements is shown by the phrase marker of Fig. 8.9b. The phrase marker shown in Fig. 8.9b corresponds to the deep structure of the sentence. The deep structure can be converted into

Fig. 8.9 A very simple and abstract transformational grammar. The phrase-structure rules listed in (a) generate the deep structure that is shown by the phrase marker in (b). The application of the two transformation rules to the deep structure in (b) produces the phrase marker in (c).

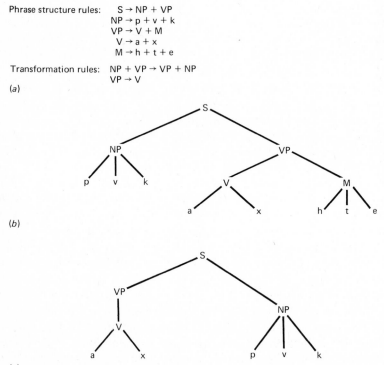

Phrase structure rules:
$S \rightarrow NP + VP$
$NP \rightarrow p + v + k$
$VP \rightarrow V + M$
$V \rightarrow a + x$
$M \rightarrow h + t + e$

Transformation rules:
$NP + VP \rightarrow VP + NP$
$VP \rightarrow V$

(a)

(b)

(c)

the surface structure shown in Fig. 8.9*c* by the operation of the transformational rules NP + VP → VP + NP and VP → V. The application of these transformation rules results in the deletion of the M constituent and the permutation of the NP and VP constituents. Operations such as deletion and permutation are the same sorts of operations that are performed by the transformational rules used to describe language.

The rule NP + VP → VP + NP, like all transformation rules, differs from phrase structure rules in various ways. First, as Fig. 8.9 shows, transformation rules convert one phrase structure into another while phrase structure rules do not. Whereas phrase structure rules rewrite a single element as one or more different elements, transformation rules may apply to a string of numerous elements (such as NP + VP). Finally, transformation rules involve relatively complicated operations such as deletion and permutation, while phrase structure rules involve the simple rewriting of elements.

As another example of the fundamental properties of transformational rules, consider the following very simplified version of a passive transformation:

$$NP_1 + V + NP_2 \rightarrow NP_2 + be + en + by + NP_1$$

This rule might be involved in the generation of a sentence such as *The mouse was chased by the cat,* and involves several elementary operations. First, the two noun phrases are inverted so that NP_2 precedes NP_1. Second, the element *by* is added before NP_1. Third, an auxiliary form of *be* and a participial affix are added to the verb. Thus the transformation rule operates on an entire string of elements and performs numerous operations.

The transformational grammar that has been formulated by linguists can formally and precisely describe many of the relations between sentences that seem to "go together" to native speakers. Consider the following family of sentences:

(8) The chimp defied the humans.
(9) The humans were defied by the chimp.
(10) The chimp did not defy the humans.
(11) The humans were not defied by the chimp.

In a standard transformational grammar (Chomsky, N., 1965), the relationship between sentences (8) through (11) is expressed at the level of deep structure. For example, the deep structure that underlies these sentences shows that *chimp* is the subject and *humans* is the object. Notice that sentences such as (8) and (9) have very different surface or constituent structures. The surface structure cannot show that *chimp* is the logical subject (that is, it is the chimp that does the defying), and *humans* is the logical object of both sentences (8) and (9). More generally, many of the important grammatical relationships between sentences are apparent only at the level of deep structure.

The exact nature of the deep structure that underlies sentences such as (8) through (11) is quite abstract and will not be described here. For the purposes of this discussion, it is sufficient simply to understand that sentences (8) through (11) have similar deep structures and that various transformation rules convert those deep structures into the various surface structures of these sentences. A passive transformation must be applied to the deep structure in order to generate the surface structure of sentence (9). A negative transformation rule must operate on the deep structure to produce the surface structure of sentence (10). Both the passive and the negative transformations must operate in order to generate the surface structure of sentence (11), and so on.

To summarize briefly, a transformational grammar consists of two types of generative rules: phrase structure rules and transformational rules. The phrase structure rules generate the deep structures that underlie sentences. The deep structure of a sentence provides all of the structural information that is required for the interpretation of a sentence. The transformation rules convert the deep structures into the surface structures of sentences. The interrelatedness of different sentences can be accounted for by a transformational grammar since superficially different sentences may have a common underlying structure.

For a variety of reasons many linguists now believe that transformational grammar provides the best available model of syntax (Chomsky, N., 1965, 1971, 1975). Transformational grammar can presumably generate the infinite number of grammatical sentences of a language such as English, and no ungrammatical sentences. Additionally, many different types of ambiguous sentences can be accounted for by a transformational grammar. This grammar can provide a formal account of the intuitive relations between various sentences. Furthermore, transformational grammar requires fewer rules than other grammars, such as phrase structure grammars. Finally and most importantly, some features of transformational grammar appear to be general across languages. For instance, although the syntax of different languages may include different transformational rules, certain operations (for example, displacement and permutation) performed by the transformation rules may be general across languages (Slobin, 1971a). Also, the general form of a transformational grammar may be universal (Chomsky, N., 1965). For example, the distinction between deep and surface structure may be necessary in all languages.

The transformational grammar that we have considered here is by no means a complete model of syntax, and that model is, like all scientific theories, best seen as tentative. For our purposes, the theory of transformational grammar is as important for the profound influence it has exerted upon psychological research and theory concerning linguistic performance as it is for what it says about language.

Syntax and Performance

In this section, we shall examine some of the attempts to employ concepts such as transformation rules, deep structure, and surface structure in the analysis of how we comprehend and remember sentences. Throughout our discussion, we shall explore some of the complexities involved in the attempt to interrelate theories of competence and performance.

Surface Structure and Performance   In an early experiment concerning the relation between surface structure and performance (Johnson, N. F., 1965a, b), adults were exposed to a paired-associate learning procedure in which the stimuli were digits and the responses were complete sentences such as *The tall boy saved the dying woman* and *The house across the street burned down*. The result of primary interest was that the pattern of errors that occurred in this learning task depended upon the surface structure of the sentences. Figure 8.10 shows the surface structure of the two sentences, and the lower panel shows the pattern of errors that occurred in learning those sentences. Specifically, Fig. 8.10*b* shows the probability of an error in recalling each word given that the preceding word had been recalled correctly. In other words, Fig. 8.10*b* shows the probability with which errors occurred at the transitions from one word to the next.

The main result was that most errors occurred at the transitions between phrases. For example, the most errors for sentence one occurred at transition three, which was the boundary between the noun phrase and the verb phrase. The probability of recalling *boy* given the correct recall of *tall* was much higher than the probability of recalling *saved* given the correct recall of *boy*. Similarly, for sentence two, most errors occurred at the transitions between

Fig. 8.10   (*a*) The surface structures of the two sentences used in the experiment by Johnson (1965). (*b*) The probability of an error in recalling each word given that the preceding word had been recalled correctly.   (From Johnson, N. F., 1965a. Reprinted by permission of Macmillan Publishing Co., Inc. Copyright © 1965 by The Free Press, a Division of The Macmillan Company.)

The tall boy saved the dying woman.

(*a*)

The house across the street is burning.

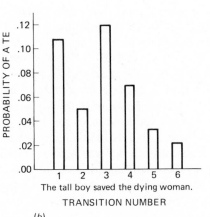

The tall boy saved the dying woman.

TRANSITION NUMBER

(*b*)

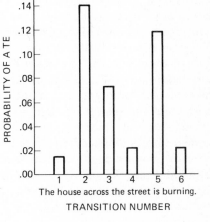

The house across the street is burning.

TRANSITION NUMBER

words that belonged to different phrases. The probability of recalling *house* given the correct recall of *The* was much higher than the probability of recalling *across* given the recall of *house*. In further experiments, it was shown that isolated word pairs such as *house-across* are as readily learned in a simple paired-associate procedure as are word pairs such as *across-the*. Thus the difference in the transitional errors that had been observed in the sentence learning task were not attributable to differences in the difficulty of learning particular pairs or to prior experience with the word-to-word constraints that are inherent in the English language.

The results of the preceding study show that the learning of sentences is not simply a matter of learning a simple sequence or chain of words in which each word occasions only the immediately following word. Rather, through experience, verbal behavior comes to consist of large functional units such as phrases that are specified at least in part by the phrase structure analysis of sentences. In some sense then, phrase structure has some degree of psychological reality, and that conclusion has been supported by a wide variety of investigations (cf. Clark, H. H. & Clark, 1977; and Johnson, N. F., 1968, for reviews).

Subsequent studies have shown that the phrase structure of sentences has considerable influence upon reading. In one experiment (Aaronson & Scarborough, 1976), subjects were instructed to read and remember a series of sentences such as *The newly designed outboard motor, whose large rotary blades power the boat, was of high quality*. On each trial, the subjects read a sentence one word at a time. The word *ready* appeared on a screen at the start of a trial, and the first word of the sentence for that trial was presented when the subject pressed a button. Similarly, the subject gained access to the second word of the sentence by pressing the button a second time, and so on throughout the sentence. The amount of time spent reading each word was of primary interest. The results were that the reading time per word varied according to the phrase structure of the sentence. The longest reading times occurred at the major constituent breaks of the sentence, for example, at the words *motor* and *boat* in the sentence described above. One plausible account of this effect is that the subjects grouped the words belonging to a single constituent into a functional unit. Grouping the words presumably takes time, and that could account for the longer reading times at the constituent boundaries.

The preceding observations show that phrase structure may influence performance, but it is important to recognize that the effects of phrase structure depend upon the nature of the task and the type of strategy employed by the subjects. For example, if adults in the reading task described above are required to comprehend the sentences rather than remember them verbatim, the phrase structure does not affect reading times (Aaronson et al., 1976). Fine-grained analysis of reading times showed that subjects in the comprehension task spend more time viewing semantically important words than syntactically important words, whereas subjects in the recall task do the opposite. Apparently, subjects use different strategies in executing different tasks (cf. Aaronson et al., 1976; Clark, H. H., & Clark, 1977). The flexibility and diversity

of the strategies subjects use in performing linguistic tasks is of central importance for any theory of performance. Although the exact nature and origins of
these strategies are unknown, it seems clear that the effects of linguistic variables such as phrase structure depend upon many other variables. We shall see
that this complicates attempts to relate theories of competence and
performance.

Performance and Deep Structure Next consider the distinction between
surface structure and deep structure. We noted earlier that sentences such as
(12) and (13) have similar surface structure but different deep structures.

(12) John is eager to please.
(13) John is easy to please.

In (12), *John* is the subject whereas in (13), *John* is the object. Blumenthal &
Boakes (1967; see also Blumenthal, 1967) had subjects learn a set of sentences
such as (12) and (13). Next, the subjects were asked to recall each sentence, and
various words from the sentences were presented as prompts during the retention test to facilitate memory. The result of primary interest was that *John*
was a more effective prompt for the recall of sentence (12) than for sentence
(13). Presumably, that result was due to the fact that *John* is the underlying
subject of sentence (12) but not of sentence (13).

This result gave rise to the possibility that the underlying subject of a
sentence is in general a more effective prompt than is the underlying object of a
sentence. Unfortunately, the deep structural relations of sentences do not always predict which words will serve as effective prompts (Perfetti, 1973). This
is not too surprising when one considers the effects of semantic and nonlinguistic factors in the use of language. For example, in a sentence in the passive
voice such as *The magnificent ship was constructed by one hundred hardy
sailors, ship* is the object of the sentence. Yet *ship* might be highly effective as a
prompt if the ship referred to were the topic of a long conversation. Similarly,
ship might be an effective prompt if the person trying to remember the sentence had formed a visual image of sailors building a ship. The syntactic role of
a word is only one determinant of how effective a word is as a cue to remember, and the effects of syntactic role may be outweighed by the effects of other
variables. To test the effect of syntactic variables upon linguistic performance,
one must know about and control for the effects of nonsyntactic factors, and
this consideration will assume increasing importance as we continue our
discussion.

The Derivational Theory of Complexity Many of the early attempts to
build a theory of performance upon the theory of linguistic competence involved the prediction of performance on the basis of transformational rules
(for a review, see Greene, 1972). More specifically, the attempts involved predicting performance in sentence memory and sentence comprehension tasks
on the basis of the *derivational complexity* of sentences. In early versions of

transformational grammar (Chomsky, N., 1957), families of sentences such as (14) through (21) were said to be based upon one *kernel sentence,* which was simple, active, affirmative and declarative in nature.

(14) The boy hit the ball. K
(15) The ball was hit by the boy. P
(16) The boy did not hit the ball. N
(17) Did the boy hit the ball? Q
(18) The ball was not hit by the boy. PN
(19) Was the ball hit by the boy? PQ
(20) Did the ball not hit the boy? QN
(21) Was the ball not hit by the boy? PQN

Whereas sentence (14) is a kernel sentence, sentence (15) is derived from that kernel by the application of the passive transformation. Similarly, sentences (16) and (17) are derived from the kernel sentence by the application of the negative and the question transformations, respectively, and so on. Since sentences (20) and (21) are derived linguistically through the application of a greater number of transformation rules than sentences (14) and (15), sentences (20) and (21) are said to be of greater derivational complexity.

In early psycholinguistic experiments (for example, Mehler, 1963; Miller, G.A., 1962b; Miller, G.A., & McKean, 1964), the assumption was made that adults comprehend and remember sentences by covertly transforming them into kernel form and then remembering the kernel form along with "transformational tags" that indicated which transformations had been applied to it. Furthermore, it was assumed that time was required to perform each transformation that was applied to produce the kernel form. It followed that sentences that involved, for example, three transformations would take longer to comprehend than sentences that involved only one transformation. In these early studies, the time required to comprehend sentences was in general observed to increase with increases in derivational complexity (although there were notable discrepancies in the results of different experiments; cf. Fodor & Garrett, 1966; Garrett & Fodor, 1968; Greene, 1972). Similarly, the results of early studies of sentence memory (Savin & Perchonock, 1965) conformed to predictions made on the basis of the theory of derivational complexity. Later research (cf. Glucksberg & Danks, 1975; Matthews, 1968) showed that many of the observations that the derivational theory of complexity accounted for were also explainable on the basis of performance factors such as sentence length. We shall now examine some of the difficulties encountered by the derivational theory of complexity.

To illustrate the problems involved in the view that sentence comprehension time is predictable on the basis of derivational complexity, consider some of the observations concerning the relative comprehension times for active and passive sentences. Passive sentences involve a passive transformation and are therefore derivationally more complex than simple, active, affirmative sentences. Accordingly, passive sentences should take more time to comprehend than active sentences. In several studies (for example, Gough, 1965), that prediction was confirmed, and the attempt to predict performance on the basis of what was known about syntactic competence seemed feasible. However, in subsequent experiments it was shown that under some conditions the derivationally complex passive sentences take no longer to comprehend than simple active sentences. For example, Slobin (1966) observed that passive sentences such as (22) take no longer to comprehend than active sentences such as (23):

(22) The flowers are being watered by the girl.
(23) The girl is watering the flowers.

The passive sentence (22) is said to be nonreversible since the object (*flowers*) cannot be reversed with the subject (*girl*) to produce an acceptable sentence (that is, *The flowers are watering the girl* is unacceptable). On the other hand, passive sentences such as (24) may be reversed to produce grammatical sentences such as (25), and it takes longer to comprehend reversible passive sentences such as (24) than active sentences such as (26).

(24) The cat was bitten by the dog.
(25) The dog was bitten by the cat.
(26) The dog bit the cat.

Thus the hypothesis of derivational complexity predicts that passive sentences will take longer to comprehend than active sentences, but in fact, that prediction is confirmed only for reversible passive sentences.

Subsequent studies have shown that in some instances the comprehension time for even reversible passive sentences is not predictable on the basis of derivational complexity (Herriott, 1969). For example, equivalent amounts of time were required for the comprehension of sentences (27) and (28).

(27) The doctor treated the patient.
(28) The patient was treated by the doctor.
(29) The doctor was treated by the patient.

Sentence (28) is reversible syntactically, for sentence (29) is grammatical. However, sentence (28) is nonreversible on a semantic level since it is the doctor who typically treats the patient, not vice versa. Herriott (1969) observed that semantically reversible passive sentences such as *The dog was bitten by the cat* took more time to comprehend than the corresponding active sentences, but semantically nonreversible sentences such as (28) did not take more time than the corresponding active sentences. Clearly, semantic factors contribute to sentence comprehension time, and linguistic performance cannot be predicted on the basis of syntactic considerations alone.

Problems Involved in Assessing the Relationship Between Syntactic Competence and Performance   The fact that linguistic performance cannot be predicted solely on the basis of syntactic factors may be interpreted in a number of different ways. This observation may indicate that there is no direct relation between competence and performance and that the attempt to build a theory of performance upon the theory of competence is fundamentally flawed. On the other hand, that observation may indicate that accounts of performance must be based upon various aspects of competence rather than upon syntax alone. Although linguistic theory in the 1960s was more concerned with syntax rather than with semantics, it became clear in the early stages of psycholinguistic research that semantic factors contribute substantially to linguistic performance, even in procedures that are designed to assess syntactic factors. The fundamental importance of semantic factors in linguistic performance may be seen by simply pondering what happens in the production of a sentence. Loosely speaking, in composing a sentence one first thinks of what to say, which involves semantics, and then translates that thought into an acceptable sentence, which involves syntax (see Clark, H. H., & Clark, 1977). Because semantic factors strongly affect performance and are not easily separated from syntactic factors, it may not be possible to evaluate the contribution of syntax to performance solely by manipulating syntactic variables. Thus the failure to predict performance on the basis of syntactic competence may indicate simply that syntax is only one factor among many that affects performance.

Building a theory of performance on the basis of the theory of competence, then, requires a rather complete understanding of the relationships between various aspects of competence such as syntax and semantics. Unfortunately, we presently lack that understanding, and this impedes attempts to specify the relation between competence and performance. The problem is magnified by the fact that theories of linguistic competence are the subject of intense research and, like other scientific theories, are dynamic and subject to revision. Revisions in the theory of competence may produce serious problems for theories of performance. For example, in the early versions of the theory of transformational grammar (Chomsky, N., 1957), passive sentences were of greater derivational complexity than active sentences. In the later revisions (for example, Chomsky, N., 1965, 1971) of that theory, however, active and passive sentences were considered to be of equal derivational complexity. Thus when the theory of competence was modified, some of the fundamental assumptions of the early psycholinguistic enterprise were undercut. That problem exists currently, for linguists are undecided about the optimal form for a theory of transformational grammar.

A similar problem involved in determining the relationship between competence and performance is that one must know a good deal about performance variables such as memorial factors before the theory of competence can be adequately tested. As we have seen, humans bring a wide variety of strategies and hypotheses to bear upon tasks such as sentence comprehension (Clark, H. H., & Clark, 1977). Psychologists knew very little about these performance factors when they first began to evaluate the relationship between competence and performance. In hindsight, we may state confidently that psychologists asked for too much when they sought a very direct and simple relationship between competence and performance. As the preceding discussion has shown, there are many complexities inherent not only in the relationship between competence and performance but also in the attempts to ascertain that relationship. The relationship between competence and performance will receive additional attention as we proceed with our inquiry into the nature of competence.

SEMANTICS

A complete analysis of language must include a systematic treatment of semantics, for meaning provides the basis for communication, the primary function of language. Unfortunately, semantics is probably the least understood of all aspects of linguistic competence, and the length of our discussion of this complex topic must necessarily be disproportionate to its importance.

The conditions that must be satisfied by a theory of semantics are analogous to the conditions that must be met by a theory of syntax. Just as a theory of syntax should generate all permissible sentences of a language, so should a theory of semantics assign semantic interpretations to the grammatical sentences of a language. Furthermore, a theory of semantics should formally describe the linguistic intuitions of native speakers. For example, a semantic theory should account for the observation that sentences that are not ambiguous syntactically may be ambiguous semantically. Sentence (30) is semantically ambiguous, although it is not ambiguous with respect to syntax. Also, a semantic theory should account for the observation that sentence (31) is contradictory.

(30) The bill is large.
(31) The bachelor's wife spoke softly.

Theories of Semantics

Katz and Fodor (1963) proposed that a semantic theory should consist of two components. First, it must have a dictionary that specifies the meaning of different words. Second, the theory should contain a set of rules (called projection rules) that systematically describe the meanings of sentences on the basis of the meaning of individual items and the deep structural relations between those items.

The semantic dictionary describes the meaning of single words in terms of syntactic markers, semantic features and selection restrictions. The syntactic markers indicate the syntactic roles that can be assumed by a given word. A word such as *shot* can be either a noun (as in *The shot was fired*) or a verb (as in *He shot the can*). In the interpretation of a sentence containing the word *shot*, an analysis of the deep structure of a sentence indicates the syntactic function of the word. If the sentence were *The shot was fired*, the syntactic analysis would indicate that only the features of *shot* as a noun need be considered in further semantic analysis.

Associated with each syntactic marker for an item is a set of *semantic features* which are similar to the attributes that were discussed in our examination of concept learning (see pp. 280–284). Each feature conveys part of the meaning of the word, and the meaning of a word consists of a combination of semantic features, just as a phoneme consists of a combination of phonological features (but cf. Bolinger, 1965). The word *bachelor* consists of such semantic features as (human), (male) and (unmarried), and the word *wife* includes such features as (human), (female) and (married). Since the word *bachelor* can only be a noun, it has only one syntactic marker and one set of semantic features. In contrast, a word like *shot* has two syntactic markers and two sets of semantic features.

In many instances, a single dictionary item with a given syntactic marker has more than one list of semantic features. In the sentence *The bill is large,* the word *bill* clearly functions as a noun. Nevertheless, the sentence is ambiguous since the noun *bill* has at least two separate meanings. Ambiguities that arise from multiple word meanings are accounted for in terms of multiple lists of semantic features. In the case of the noun *bill,* one list of features might define the meaning of that word as it is used in *My telephone bill could induce cardiac arrest in a wealthy person.* A separate list of features would define the meaning of the noun *bill* as it is used in *The bird with the large bill glided across the lake.* In this manner, a semantic theory can explain many different instances of semantic ambiguity.

Finally, there are certain *selection restrictions* for each dictionary item. The selection restrictions define the permissible ways in which words may be combined. A word combination such as *bachelor's wife* is impermissible since that combination violates the selection restrictions listed in the dictionary for the words *bachelor* and *wife. Bachelor* includes the feature (unmarried) while *wife* includes the feature (married); therefore, *bachelor's wife* is contradictory.

The syntactic markers, the semantic features and the selection restrictions define the meanings of individual items in the semantic dictionary. However, the meaning of a sentence is obviously not determined entirely by the meanings of the different words in a sentence. Sentences have internal structure, and the meaning of a sentence depends upon the relationship between the words that together comprise the sentence. The meaning of a sentence depends upon the operation of *projection rules.* Projection rules derive the meaning of sentences by combining word meanings in a manner that is consistent with the grammatical structure of a sentence and the selection restrictions listed in the dictionary.

Interpretive and Generative Semantics   The preceding theory of semantics is said to be an *interpretive theory* since it depicts the semantic component of competence as interpreting the deep structures that were generated by the syntactic component of competence. One assumption that is fundamental in that theory is the hypothesis that the deep structures of sentences contain all of the information necessary for a semantic interpretation of those sentences. That assumption is troublesome in that it is contradicted by numerous observations. For example, in sentences (32) and (33), *John* and *Bill* bear the same semantic relationship and these sentences appear to have very similar meaning.

(32) John sold the car to Bill.
(33) Bill bought the car from John.

The semantic relatedness of sentences (32) and (33) cannot be accounted for by an interpretive theory of the type described above, for John is the subject in (32) but is the object in (33). The deep structures of sentences such as (32) and (33) do not carry information about the relatedness of those sentences, and there are many other sentences of a similar nature. Therefore, the semantic theory described above is incomplete.

The preceding sorts of observations have in general led linguists down either of two paths. One path has involved revising the interpretive theory of semantics in ways that permit the theory to account for the relatedness of sentences such as (32) and (33). In the revised version of that theory, semantic interpretation involves not only the deep structures but also the surface structures and structures intermediate between deep and surface structures. The other path that linguists have followed has led to the theory called *generative semantics* (Lakoff, 1971; McCawley, 1968). In that theory (and others, see Fillmore, 1968), there is no deep structure like that in the theory proposed by Chomsky. Rather, the underlying representations of sentences are primarily semantic in nature, and transformations operate on those semantic structures to derive the surface structures of the sentences. Thus the theory of generative semantics postulates a very different relationship between syntax and semantics than does the interpretive theory. The relative merits of the interpretive and the generative semantics theories is currently very controversial in linguistics, and no adequate analysis of semantics will be available until that controversy is resolved (for discussion of that issue, see Steinberg & Jakobovits, 1971).

One interesting aspect of the controversy over the nature of semantics concerns the relationship between competence and performance. Since semantics are primary in the generative semantic theory of competence, that theory may provide a more useful base for a theory of performance than the linguistic theory in which syntactic deep structures are fundamental. For example, semantically based theories of language have figured prominently in the analysis of language development. Although many linguists would argue that a theory of competence should not be evaluated in terms of its suitability as a basis for a theory of performance, others have argued that a theory of competence must have rather direct implications for a theory of performance and should be evaluated accordingly. Regardless of the outcome of that controversy, there is little doubt, as we have seen, that competence and performance are related indirectly, and we shall now consider the relation between semantics and linguistic performance.

Semantics and Performance

In the preceding section, we noted that some semantic theories have postulated that the meaning of a word consists of a set of semantic features. That view is consistent with a variety of observations concerning linguistic performance. For example, consider a study by Brown and McNeill (1966) concerning the *"tip-of-the-tongue"* phenomenon. Most of us have experienced that phenomenon, for we often have the feeling that we know a particular word or name but cannot remember it. Indeed, that is often what makes taking tests so frustrating. Brown and McNeill induced that state by giving adults dictionary definitions for infrequent words and asking them to recall the word that had been defined. An example of the definitions they presented is "a navigational instrument used in measuring angular distances, especially the altitude of sun, moon and stars at sea." If subjects said that they were certain they knew the word but could not remember it, then those subjects were said to be in the tip-of-the-tongue state. When subjects were in that state, they were asked to guess the number of syllables in the word, to indicate the initial letter, to identify words of similar meaning, and so on.

The results of greatest importance for our purposes were that the subjects were able to indicate which words were similar in meaning to the word they were trying to remember. For example, the subjects that were given the definition stated above indicated that the word they were trying to remember was conceptually related to *astrolabe, compass, protractor,* and so on. Also, the subjects were able to indicate that the word sounded like *secant* and *sextet* (in case you are in the tip-of-the-tongue state, the target word is *sextant*). These observations suggest that a word is represented psychologically as a group of features that may be visual, phonological or semantic in nature. Although each word may be represented by a particular set of features, different words may have semantic features in common, just as different simple stimuli may have common elements. Words that share semantic features (for example, *woman, girl* and *lady* share the semantic feature *female*) are seen as semantically related (cf. Clark, H. H., & Clark, 1977). The conception of word meanings in terms of semantic features has strongly influenced theories of how we remember over long periods of time.

We noted previously that there are semantic restrictions on the ways in which words may be combined, and we noted that sequences such as *honest thief* are impermissible since they violate the semantic selection restrictions. Just as the semantic features identified by linguists may contribute to performance, so it is with the semantic selection restrictions identified by linguists. For example, semantic selection restrictions contribute to sentence perception. Entwisle and Frasure (1974) played tapes of sentences such as (34), (35) and (36) for children of various ages and asked the children to repeat each sentence verbatim after it had been played.

(34) Bears steal honey from the hive.
(35) Trains steal elephants around the house.
(36) From shoot highways the passengers mothers.

Sentence (34) is both grammatical and meaningful. Sentence (35) has appropriate syntactic structure but is semantically anomalous, for semantic selection restrictions are clearly violated in that sentence. In (36), words are presented in an irregular or scrambled order, and that string of words is both syntactically unacceptable and semantically anomalous. The three types of sentences were played against a background of acoustic noise that, like noisy traffic, increased the difficulty of perceiving the sentences.

The results of the experiment were that for children of age six, the three types of sentences were equally difficult to repeat. For the older children, however, performance was better when the sentences were semantically appropriate than when they were semantically anomalous, even though both types of sentences had appropriate syntactic structure. Clearly, performance was affected by the semantic relationship between the words in the sentences. Another result was that performance was better for the anomalous sentences than for the scrambled ones, thus indicating that syntactic constraints also contributed to performance. These results show that as children grow older and have more experience with the English language, they learn the semantic selection restrictions that are characteristics of English, and that learning can facilitate aspects of performance such as sentence perception. A spoken sentence is a complex stimulus sequence in which the stimuli that occur initially place constraints upon the kinds of stimuli that can occur later. Learning which stimuli can go with which others is an important part of language acquisition, and the analysis of syntactic and semantic structure goes hand in hand with the study of linguistic function.

The Representation of Complex Semantic Relationships   In our previous discussion of syntax, we saw that there is no complete and widely accepted theory of syntax or semantics currently available. It is therefore a very tenuous undertaking to try to build a theory of performance upon theories of semantic and syntactic competence. Accordingly, psychologists (for example, Kintsch & van Dijk, 1978) have adopted the research strategy of formulating independent theories of performance that do not stand or fall on the basis of a particular linguistic theory.

To illustrate the kinds of performance models that have been suggested, consider Fig. 8.11. Figure 8.11 shows how the semantic information underlying the sentence *John murders Mary at Luigi's* has been represented in one model (Rummelhart, Lindsay, & Norman, 1972) of performance. In this model, knowledge is represented in a network in which the circles or "nodes" stand for concepts and the lines connecting the nodes stand for semantic relationships. This knowledge is said to be represented in a *propositional* format, for the knowledge is represented in terms of abstract interpreted concepts such as *actor* and *instrument*. In general, a proposition specifies a relationship between two or more concepts. The relationship is specified by a relational term, and the concepts that are related are called the arguments of the proposition. For example, the proposition

climb (cat, tree)

specifies the relationship (climb) between the concepts *cat* and *tree* which are the arguments of the proposition. Propositions shall be of considerable importance in our subsequent discussions of memory, but they are mentioned here only to introduce the model shown in Fig. 8.11.

The model makes certain assumptions about how the information is used, and from these assumptions certain aspects of performance may be ac-

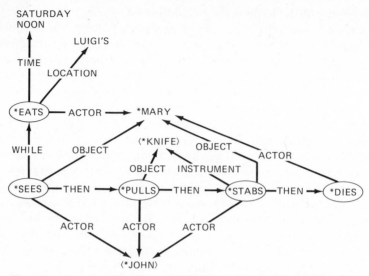

Fig. 8.11   The semantic network said to underlie the sentence *John murders Mary at Luigi's*. The circles or nodes stand for concepts and the lines connecting the nodes stand for semantic relationships.   (From Rummelhart, Lindsay, & Norman, 1972.)

counted for. The details of the theory are not our primary concern here, however, for we will consider semantically based performance theories further in Chapter 11. At this juncture, we would like to use the model shown in Fig. 8.11 as a vehicle for discussing the relationship between competence and performance and for discussing the nature of cognitive theories of performance.

Competence, Performance, and Cognitive Psychology   The first important point to be made here is that knowledge is represented in very different ways in theories of competence and in contemporary theories of performance. Thus the representation shown in Fig. 8.11 is very different from the deep-structural representations that were described earlier in the chapter. Furthermore, the psychological processes for analyzing sentences such as *John murders Mary at Luigi's* into its underlying conceptual representation need not correspond to the steps involved in deriving a sentence linguistically. In short, theories of linguistic performance need not be, and are not, based upon either the structures or the rules specified by linguistic theory. Whereas psycholinguists were at one time hopeful that they could use the theory of competence to build a theory of performance, that approach has now been abandoned. There is currently sparse evidence of a direct relationship between competence and performance (Bever, 1970; Cairns & Cairns, 1976; Clark, H. H., & Clark, 1977; Fodor & Garrett, 1966). Just as theories of competence are not designed to account for performance, so current theories of performance are not designed to include or account for linguistic competence. Theories of competence and performance are intended to provide systematic accounts for different sorts of observations, and these theories must be evaluated according to different criteria.

However, this is not to say that linguistics and psychology are unrelated. To the extent that the nature of knowledge is important in both competence and performance models, we can expect to see extensive interchange between these two fields. Indeed, psychological theories of language acquisition have been powerfully influenced by linguistic theory.

Another important point about the type of performance model shown in Fig. 8.11 is that it is a cognitive model. Broadly speaking, cognitive psychology is the study of knowledge and how that knowledge is acquired and used. Unlike conditioning theory, cognitive theories attempt to account for behavior not in terms of functional relationships between the environment and behavior but in terms of private events occurring within the behaving organism. Cognitive theories have figured prominently in the analysis of language acquisition and memory. For now, it is sufficient to note that the cognitive approach has arisen in the attempt to deal with three fundamental and interrelated problems.

The first problem is that there is in the experienced organism a large discrepancy between what the organism does and what it can do. Just as that discrepancy has led to the formulation of motivational theories (see pp. 219–222), so too has the discrepancy led to cognitive theories. Generally, cognitive theories, like linguistic theories, have dealt with that problem by distinguishing between knowledge (what an organism can do) and performance.[3]

The second problem is that in studying the experienced organism, there is often very little observable behavior that occurs, and the prior experiences of the organism are unknown. For example, when an adult reads a paragraph and then answers written questions about what has been read, the observable behavior consists of perhaps a set of eye movements and fixations and a few strokes of a pen. Those responses are clearly not the only important behavioral events that occurred, and it is no wonder that the easily observable behavior of the adult is often seen as the shadow and not the substance of the processes that have occurred. Furthermore, the antecedents of responding in contemporary settings are typically unknown, and psychologists have therefore often adopted the strategy of formulating theories that are based upon the processes that occur within the organism (see pp. 258–259). By emphasizing the importance of knowledge, cognitive theorists are led to study the private events that contribute so strongly to the behavior of the experienced organism. Moreover, they are led to systematically describe the knowledge of the organism. Since that knowledge results in large part from prior experience, they are able to relate prior experience to current behavior in an indirect manner.

The third problem is that the organism always contributes to learning, and many past learning theories have not, as far as cognitive psychologists are concerned, captured the contribution that the organism makes. For example, some early versions of behaviorism (for example, Watson) did not adequately recognize the importance of the biological heritage of the organism. Contemporary cognitive theories attempt to recognize the importance of phylogenetic determinants of behavior by attempting to specify knowledge that has phylogenetic origins and by specifying on a conceptual level the structures through which experience operates (for example, short-term memory and long-term memory; cf. Chapters 10 and 11). Moreover, some associationistic theories that have been built upon the work of Ebbinghaus depicted learning as a process of passively forming internal, mental associations between stimuli and responses. If a stimulus and a response occurred contiguously, an association was presumably formed as a result. Contemporary students of human behavior believe that the adult organism makes a very active contribution to learning. For example, the hypothesis-testing model of conceptual behavior (see pp. 304–307) depicted humans as actively constructing and testing hypotheses about complex relationships between stimuli. The richness and the complexity of the internal events that humans bring to bear on many tasks is now believed to be better accounted for in terms of knowledge and subtle performance strategies than in terms of the formation and utilization of associations.

Of course, cognitive theories represent only one type of attempt to handle the preceding problems. Those same problems may be dealt with by studying directly the contribution of the phylogenetic and the ontogenetic environments to observable behavior and by studying private events by means of physiological analysis. The approach which will ultimately turn out to be most fruitful remains to be seen, and we believe that both approaches can contribute to each other. At any rate, there is no question that cognitive theorists have set out to tackle the intricacies of the experienced organism far more systematically than most other theorists have. Accordingly, we shall increasingly turn to cognitive theory as we explore the behavioral subtleties of the experienced organism.

We have now completed our description of language and the psychological implications of theories of competence. What remains to be considered are the problems involved in defining language. We shall now consider some of those problems within the context of a question that is both fascinating and profound in its own right: Do nonhumans have the capacity for language?

LANGUAGE, HUMANS, AND APES

The question of whether nonhumans have the capacity for language rubs harshly against the grain of one of our most cherished views: that we are unique and fundamentally superior in the kingdom of living things. That assumption lies at the roots of many of our governmental and religious institutions. It is no light matter to question the assumption that humans are unique and special among animals, and even in contemporary schools, teachers have been scorned for presenting the theory of evolution through natural selection. At the outset of this inquiry, we should be on guard against our culturally instilled belief that humans are unique, and that the capacity for language must lie above the level of "the animals."

The view that language is unique to humans is supported by casual types of observations. Cats do not speak, dogs are notably inarticulate and our closest relatives, gorillas and chimps, do not seem to chatter among themselves as humans do. Rather casual observations have been used at various times to characterize the human as the tool-making animal, the tool-using animal, the reasoning animal, and so on. However, conclusions that are based on casual observations often melt away under the intense light of scientific investigation, and so it has been with many conclusions about the uniqueness of humans. For example, the extensive naturalistic observations of chimps (vanLawick–Goodall, 1968; Teleki, 1973) have helped to discredit the view that humans are unique as makers and users of tools. Chimps have been observed to feed on termites by finding tree branches of a particular size, stripping off the leaves and dipping the sticks into the termite mound. Thus the chimps obtained a few crunchy morsels of their favorite food. Casual observations cannot be taken as compelling evidence for the uniqueness of tool-making in humans, and we must be wary of casual observations that suggest language is unique to humans.

Although systematic naturalistic observation has distinct advantages over casual observation, it too is of limited value in inquiring whether nonhumans have the capacity for language. The method of naturalistic observation can be used to determine what animals do in their species-typical environments, but that method does not indicate what animals are capable of doing. Throughout our inquiry into learning, we have seen that the behavior of individual animals depends in large part upon the effects of the ontogenetic environment. Exposure to radically different ontogenetic environments may result in the occurrence of radically different behaviors.

Questions concerning behavioral capacities are best analyzed experimentally. By adopting an experimental approach, one may expose nonhumans to environments that might never occur naturally. Using this strategy, the behavioral capabilities of a species may be assessed more thoroughly. In the last few decades, psychologists have taken an experimental approach to the problem of whether nonhuman primates have the capacity for language. Specifically, psychologists have sought to communicate with chimps by means of languages that have many characteristics in common with those typically used by humans, and these attempts will now be examined.

Project Washoe

Before 1965, there were at least five reported attempts to teach chimps to talk (Kellogg, 1968). In some cases (for example, Hayes, 1951), the chimps were reared in a home as a child might be. The attempts to teach chimps to speak were both ingenious and elaborate, but each attempt was an unequivocal failure. For example, Viki, the chimp reared by Hayes (1951), learned to follow numerous spoken instructions but could only say the words *mama, papa,* and *cup* even after extended training. The pride of humans remained intact.

Recently, Gardner and Gardner (1971, 1974, 1975) have taken a very different approach to the question of whether chimps have the capacity for language. They noted that chimps were very "handy" and that the captive chimps in the early studies spontaneously communicated with humans by gesturing although those same chimps rarely did so by vocalizing. Chimp vocalizations may be controlled more by antecedent stimulus conditions than by their consequences. For example, Viki, the Hayes's chimp, was a crafty burglar of sweets but she frequently got caught later since the sweets elicited loud plea-sure grunts. The foregoing observations led the Gardners to suspect that the failure of chimps to learn spoken language showed only that chimps cannot use speech as a medium of communication. Accordingly, the Gardners decided to attempt to teach language to a chimp by using a gestural system of communication.

Gardner and Gardner chose American Sign Language (Ameslan) as the gestural medium to be used because it is widely used by humans in the United States. By using an established system of human communication, it was possi-ble to circumvent the problem of deciding whether the gestural system met the formal criteria that define language. Those criteria are still a matter of debate among linguists, but it is clear that sign language bears important similarities to spoken languages (Bellugi & Fischer, 1972; Bellugi & Klima, 1975; Schlesinger & Meadow, 1972). Also, Ameslan was chosen so that the verbal behavior of the chimp could eventually be compared with that of human children.

The subject for the project of the Gardners was Washoe, a female chimp who was approximately one year old at the start of the project. Washoe lived in a house trailer that was situated on a fenced lot with trees, shrubs and play-things. Her environment was arranged so as to provide a maximally interesting environment that would be optimal for the acquisition of verbal behavior. Each day, Washoe interacted with a variety of human companions, all of whom were adequately proficient in Ameslan. Washoe's companions used Ameslan to provide a continuous commentary on daily events. Thus they signed appropriately during all of the routine activities such as feeding and dressing, and they signed continuously while playing games, looking at maga-zines and visiting new places.

The Acquisition of Signs   Washoe learned new signs through a variety of procedures. A shaping procedure was used to teach Washoe the signs for *more* and *open*. For example, when Washoe was tickled (tickling was a power-ful reinforcer), she often made playful protective movements that resembled the sign for *more*. Washoe was tickled after she emitted responses that pro-gressively approximated the *more* sign, and she soon came to make the appro-priate sign for *more*. Other signs, such as that for *sweet*, were acquired by observing others make that sign while dessert was being served.

The most rapid procedure for teaching new signs to Washoe was a train-ing method called *guidance* (cf. Fouts, 1972). As the name suggests, the method of guidance involved holding Washoe's hands in a certain way, moving her hands to complete the appropriate gesture, and then tickling her. That method proved to be especially useful in that it permitted the experimenters to teach new signs without having to wait for Washoe to spontaneously emit a particu-lar gesture or an approximation of the gesture. For example, the sign *tickle* is made by moving the index finger of one hand across the back of the second hand. The second hand is held open with the fingers together and with the palm facing downward. As one might imagine, such behaviors could be quite difficult to shape, and having to wait for those behaviors to occur without training would most likely provide the conditions for the extinction of the experimenter's behavior. The effectiveness of the guidance technique also resulted from the fact that each new gesture could be reinforced immediately and under well-controlled conditions.

Perhaps the most remarkable aspect of Washoe's acquisition of gestural responses was the fact that she occasionally invented her own signs. For example, Washoe came to make an impatient gesture that was interpreted as *hurry.* She would raise her arm and shake her hand vigorously at the wrist even though she had neither been taught that gesture nor observed it in others. As another example, Washoe once observed a swan but had no sign for *swan.* Ingeniously, she made up a new sign by combining two signs that had already been acquired: she called the swan a *water bird* (Linden, 1975).

A startling example of invention occurred in the case of the sign for *bib.* Washoe had just learned to use the Ameslan sign for *napkin* in referring to bibs as well. The *napkin* sign is made by touching the mouth with an open hand and making a wiping movement. During month 18 of the project, a person held up a bib at dinner and asked Washoe to name it. Washoe signed *please* and *come-gimme* but she did not make the *bib* sign. Washoe then proceeded to move her index fingers from behind her neck, along the edge of her chest to the region of her naval; she had just traced the outline of a bib on herself!

Naming   Naming various objects and events is an important feature of linguistic performance in humans. We are able to emit appropriate verbal responses in the presence of particular aspects of the environment, and we are able to generalize those responses to novel environments. In other words we can name various objects such as chairs, chimps, chandeliers, and so on, and we can correctly name many objects that we have never seen before. So it was with Washoe.

The Gardners assessed Washoe's ability to name objects by showing her a series of objects inside of a box with one transparent side and asking her to name what she saw. In her worst performance, Washoe was shown three different exemplars of each of 33 items, and she named 53 of the 99 exemplars correctly. If Washoe had been gesturing randomly, she should have named only about three of the exemplars correctly. Additionally, the errors made by Washoe were illuminating. As an example, Washoe made 12 errors on trials in which grooming articles such as brushes and combs were to be named. Of the 12 errors that were made by Washoe, 7 errors consisted of Washoe having made a sign for other grooming articles. Thus Washoe's errors were systematically related to the category to which a particular exemplar belonged; that phenomenon is remarkably similar to the effects of semantic relatedness on human memory. Washoe's emission of nounlike signs was clearly controlled by the appropriate environmental features (see also Patterson, F. G., 1978; Gill & Rumbaugh, 1974).

When Washoe had learned a sign, she often emitted that sign in a wide variety of novel situations. For example, after she acquired the sign for *food,* she could identify novel magazine pictures that contained food objects (like many humans, Washoe loved to look through magazines). Similarly, after Washoe had learned the sign for *open,* she emitted that sign in the presence of drawers, boxes, jars, and even water faucets! Clearly, Washoe's signing responses were not confined to the original training environment, and those responses met the criteria that define conceptual behavior (cf. pp. 278–279).

Sign Combinations As Project Washoe continued, it became clear that Washoe would readily combine signs to form longer utterances, just as humans combine words to form sentences. Interestingly, Washoe did not have to be trained explicitly to combine signs. Within a little more than two years after she first combined signs, Washoe had emitted 294 different two-sign combinations.

An important feature of Washoe's sign combinations was that within a combination, there were certain privileges of occurrence, just as there are in the English language. Although Washoe would sign *Greg tickle* or *Naomi hug*, she seldom emitted such combinations as *tickle hug*. Furthermore, there were a small number of signs that tended to occur in many different combinations, just as a small number of words tend to occur frequently in the earliest word combinations of some children (Braine, 1963). As is the case with children, the combinations of signs emitted by Washoe were under stimulus control of the appropriate features of her environment. For example, on 12 separate occasions on which Washoe was confronted with a locked door and a human who held the key to that door, Washoe signed *gimme key, more key, gimme key more, open key, key open, open more, more open, key in, open key please, open gimme key, in open help, help key in,* and *open key help hurry.*

Concluding Comments The results of Project Washoe left little doubt that Washoe communicated via sign language with humans, and there are many striking similarities between Washoe's signing behavior and human verbal behavior. Just as humans speak more slowly when addressing someone who is not proficient in their language, so it was with Washoe. To facilitate communication with humans who had not mastered Ameslan, Washoe signed slowly and carefully. Several humans commented upon the humiliation they felt when an ape signed more slowly so that they could keep up! Furthermore, just as humans (particularly children) talk to themselves, so Washoe talked to herself. When sneaking off to forbidden places, she sometimes signed to herself *quiet* (Gardner & Gardner, 1974). When she was late or had to get to the potty, she sometimes signed *hurry* to herself! Finally, she used signs to swear at other animals, and she was once observed to call a rhesus macaque a *dirty monkey* (Linden, 1975). On another occasion, she commented slightingly upon some unfamiliar chimps—she called them *black bugs* (Linden, 1975).

Although there is little doubt about Washoe's ability to communicate via Ameslan, the question remains as to whether chimps have the capacity for language.

Language in Chimps?

Many difficulties arise in attempting to answer the question of whether Washoe has the capacity for language. Competence has been defined by linguists on the basis of what adult humans can do. But should one say that an animal has the capacity for language only if it has the competence of an adult human? If so, then one is led to the conclusion that children who are just acquiring language lack the capacity for language, for those children cannot do all that adult humans can do. This conclusion seems unsatisfactory since children who are just beginning to speak surely have some sort of rudimentary capacity for language. The question of whether Washoe has language seems unfair if an affirmative answer is to be given only if Washoe can do all that adult humans can do. Linguists have defined language solely from an adult human perspective, and the definition of competence may be so narrow as to necessarily exclude nonhumans and young children at the early stages of language development.

Another problem that is encountered in resolving the question of whether Washoe has the capacity for language is that competence, as it is defined for adults, is difficult to assess in animals other than adult humans. The assessment of competence typically entails an examination of linguistic intuitions, and it is very difficult to assess the linguistic intuitions of animals such as chimps and young children (for example, de Villiers & de Villiers, 1978). In short, hypotheses concerning the competence of animals other than adult humans are difficult to test. These difficulties are far from resolved, and much theoretical and empirical work in this important area is needed.

For the reasons described above, it seems best to approach the question of whether chimps have the capacity for language by comparing the linguistic behaviors of chimps to the linguistic behaviors of humans. The difficulties and prejudices that bear on the question of whether other creatures have the capacity for language may not be brought to bear so readily upon questions of observable behavior. By studying the linguistic behaviors of different species under many different conditions, valuable information might be obtained about the nature and evolution of language. Such information should also help to clarify the issue of whether unique learning processes are involved in the acquisition of language by humans. Encouragingly, it was in this spirit that the Gardners undertook Project Washoe.

Washoe and Children   Two very important features of human language are semanticity, or meaningfulness, and productivity; the verbal behavior of Washoe and humans may be compared with respect to those two features (Brown, R., 1970, 1973; Gardner & Gardner, 1971, 1974). Consider first the question of whether Washoe's utterances were meaningful or semantically appropriate. As described earlier, the Gardners presented very convincing evidence that Washoe used single signs appropriately in a variety of situations. When Washoe was shown numerous items in a box, she could frequently name those items appropriately. Furthermore, the use of signs by Washoe was not restricted to the situations in which those signs first occurred. After Washoe had used *more* to request more tickling, she used that sign appropriately in a wide variety of situations, as in *more milk, more swing* and *more grapefruit juice* (Brown, R., 1970) even without further training. Washoe's use of such signs as *more* bears a marked resemblance to a child's earliest use of words (Brown, R., 1970).

A deeper question is whether Washoe combined signs as children combine words to form meaningful rudimentary sentences. Washoe's sign combinations did not seem to be sequences of unrelated signs in that her combinations were segmented just as English sentences are. In English, sentences are segmented as the result of certain patterns of intonation, as when one ends an interrogative sentence with a rising pitch. Segmentation in Ameslan is accomplished by starting and ending sign combinations in a nonlinguistic position of repose. When emitting sign combinations, Washoe moved her hands in the upper regions of her body while at the end of a combination, she moved her arms to the lower part of her body and relaxed her hands in fistlike positions. Without explicit training, Washoe came to segment her combinations by using gestures that are quite similar to those made by deaf humans who are fluent in Ameslan (Gardner & Gardner, 1971, 1974).

Further evidence that Washoe was indeed combining signs in the ways humans combine words to form sentences comes from analyses of her replies to "Wh-questions" (Gardner & Gardner, 1975). "Wh-questions" include questions such as *Who are you?*, *What is that?*, *Whose is that?*, and so on. Each of those questions calls for an instance of a particular grammatical category. For example, *What is that?* calls for a noun, *Who is that?* calls for a proper noun, and so on. Since Wh-questions call for major sentence constituents, answers to those questions provide information about one's knowledge of grammatical relations within a sentence (Brown, R., 1968; Ervin-Tripp, 1970). Washoe's replies to Wh-questions contained the appropriate sentence constituents at least 84% of the time. When Washoe's replies to a wide range of Wh-questions were compared to children's replies to similar questions, it was found that Washoe consistently outperformed children who have begun to combine words to produce two-word sentences. Thus Washoe appeared to have mastered some of the same kinds of grammatical relations that young children have mastered.

Gardner and Gardner (1971, 1974) have also investigated whether Washoe's combinations of signs are semantically similar to the early combinations of children as they have been described by Brown (1970; 1973). The early two-word combinations of children seem to express semantic relationships that are independent of the particular words that occur in a pair. Brown reported that 75% of the early combinations of children could be described by a small number of semantic-structural relationships such as agent-action (as in *Adam put* or in *Eve read*) and possession (as in *Adam checker* or in *Mommy lunch*). Gardner and Gardner were able to classify Washoe's two-sign combinations into structural categories similar to those used by Brown for children. They found that Brown's classificatory scheme described 78% of Washoe's combinations. Thus the early combinations of Washoe bear substantial resemblance to the early combinations of children (cf. Gardner & Gardner, 1971, 1974, for further evidence concerning this point).

The observation that Washoe combined signs that fit together into larger meaningful units gives rise to the question of whether there was evidence of syntax in her sequences of signs. So far, there is incomplete evidence on this point. All that can be said now is that word order, which is the major indicator of structural relationships in English, was not especially important to Washoe.

In English, the order of *Washoe* and *Roger* is critical in sentences such as *Washoe tickle Roger* and *Roger tickle Washoe*. Washoe apparently tended to use such combinations interchangeably (Brown, R., 1970). The order of the signs was consistent in only some of Washoe's combinations (for example, *you me out* and *you me in*). For several reasons, however, these observations need not lead to the conclusion that Washoe's utterances show no evidence of syntax. First, sign order may not have been consistent in the utterances of Washoe's human companions, and Washoe may have been imitating the human primates. Also, Gardner and Gardner (1971) point out that Washoe's companions may have responded to Washoe's utterances in the same way regardless of the order of her signs. Finally and most importantly, the order of signs is not the only or even the major syntactic device in all languages (Bloom, L. M., 1973; Braine, 1971; Slobin, 1973) and order is not as important in Ameslan as it is in, say, English (Bellugi & Fischer, 1972; Bellugi & Klima, 1975). Although consistent word orderings are regularly observed in many children who are learning to speak English (Brown, R., 1970), the occurrence of regularities of word order is not characteristic of all children for all languages (Slobin, 1973). Until the syntactic features of Ameslan have been described fully and until the signing responses of deaf children have been analyzed systematically, the question of whether Washoe has the capacity for syntax must remain open. As matters now stand, Washoe appears to have the syntactic competence that children may be said to have at the earliest stages of language development (Brown, R., 1973).

   With respect to linguistic productivity, Washoe once again seems a little less hairy and a little more *Homo*. Washoe actually invented several signs that she had never seen before. The most striking case was her invention of the *bib* sign that was described above. Washoe's creation of that sign was especially important since the Gardners later learned from fluent speakers of Ameslan (at the California School of the Deaf at Berkeley) that Washoe's sign for *bib* is in fact the correct Ameslan sign for a bib. Thus it is unlikely that Washoe's invented signs were arbitrary in form. Rather, Washoe seems to have understood some of the more systematic principles of Ameslan. It should be noted here that Washoe is not a special case. Numerous chimps have now been taught sign language (cf. Fouts & Couch, 1976; Linden, 1975; Patterson, F. G., 1978), and linguistic productivity is hardly rare among the apes. For example, a chimp named Lucy once lacked a sign for *watermelon* and so she invented a new one: *drinkfruit* (cf. Fouts & Couch, 1976, for further examples).

   Whether Washoe was creative in her combination of signs is more difficult to determine. Washoe did combine signs without special training, and soon after she came to emit sequences of two signs, she began to emit sequences of three signs by adding appeal signs to her two-sign sequences. Instead of signing *tickle more,* she came to sign *please tickle more.* However, the possibility remains that Washoe was imitating rather than "creating" in combining signs. To assess that possibility, one would have to examine all of the utterances that had been emitted in the presence of Washoe. This same problem arises in the assessment of linguistic productivity in children. Even if Washoe was productive in her combinations, she was probably not nearly as productive as children. The Gardners reported that Washoe made 294 two-sign combinations in a period of 26 months. That number of combinations contrasts sharply with Braine's (1963) report of a child who in successive months produced 14, 10, 30, 261, and 1,050 different combinations of two words. In order to further evaluate the extent of Washoe's productivity, her linguistic behaviors should be compared to the verbal behaviors of deaf children who are learning Ameslan as a first language and who have a vocabulary of comparable size.

In conclusion, Washoe's verbal behavior seems to be similar semantically and structurally to that of children who are in the earliest stage of language development (referred to as Stage I by Brown, R., 1970; 1973). Thus Washoe may be said to have a rudimentary capacity for language.

Further Experimental Analysis
of Linguistic Behavior in Chimps

There are many factors that might contribute to the failure of chimps to acquire a particular language. Foremost among these factors are the nature of the language (for example, the degree of complexity) and the type of training procedure used to teach chimps to use the language. The effects of these factors are difficult to assess in an uncontrolled situation in which a chimp freely communicates with others by means of a complex human language. The effects of the nature of the language and the nature of the training procedure might be clarified by using a variety of rigorous training procedures to teach chimps simpler languages that were devised experimentally. This approach to the study of the linguistic behaviors of chimps has been undertaken by Premack (1970, 1971b, 1971c, 1973, 1976; Premack, Woodruff, & Kennel, 1978) and by Rumbaugh (1977). Thus far, this research has suggested that chimps have at least a rudimentary capacity for reading. Also, given the appropriate training, chimps can acquire concepts such as *name of,* and they can use logical connectives (for example, *if . . . then*), compose compound sentences, comprehend a variety of yes-no questions and wh-questions, and so on.

The preceding observations give us good reason to believe that future studies of linguistic abilities in nonhumans will be both worthwhile and exciting. The Gardners are now studying sign acquisition in two infant chimps who will be reared for an extended period by people fully proficient in Ameslan (Gardner & Gardner, 1975). Washoe is now at a primate reserve with other chimps who have been taught Ameslan, and there is evidence that those chimps communicate with each other via Ameslan (Linden, 1975). A multitude of intriguing questions may be elucidated by these projects. Will a chimp who is competent in Ameslan teach the language to her hairy associates? Will chimps teach Ameslan to their offspring and use sign language to pass on the knowledge acquired by successive generations? Chimps now acquire sign language only through explicit training, but will chimps be able to teach each other signs without explicit training as adult humans do with their children? At the limits of their capacity, how will the verbal behavior of chimps compare with that of adult humans, particularly with respect to productivity and syntactic competence? Just what will they have to say to us?

Although studies regarding the linguistic capabilities of nonhumans are fascinating in their own right, these studies will help to clarify the definition of language (Fouts, 1974). To interpret studies of nonhumans, we shall have to formulate criteria for deciding when an organism other than an adult human may be said to "have" language. These criteria will undoubtedly help us to analyze language acquisition and the linguistic abilities of children. While existing definitions of language are based primarily upon analyses of what speakers can do and are structural in nature, we can expect to see more concern with linguistic function in the definition of language (for example, Brown, R., 1973; Brown, R., & Herrnstein, 1975; Premack, 1976). Ultimately, language may be defined not only in terms of what an organism can do, but also in terms of what that organism actually does, how it comes to do it, and so on.

Furthermore, studies of language in nonhumans should provide fresh insights into the relationship between language and other behavioral events. Stated loosely, by examining the conceptual abilities of, for example, chimps before and after language training, it may be possible to ascertain how language affects thinking and conceptual behavior. Conversely, it may be possible to specify how the conceptual abilities of the chimp affect its verbal behavior. Just as studies of language in nonhumans may help to clarify the relation between language and thought, so too may they help to clarify the relation between language and memory. We have only begun to discern the relationships between language, concepts, and memory, and the chimp may serve as a useful vehicle to facilitate our journey down that most complex path (cf. Premack, 1976; for an analysis of this approach, see Terrace, 1979).

SUMMARY

Language has been characterized by linguists as an abstract system of knowledge that underlies our ability to produce and understand an infinite number of sentences, to discriminate sentences that are grammatical, ambiguous, related to other sentences, and so on. Our linguistic competence has been accounted for theoretically in terms of the theory of transformational grammar, which postulates several different aspects of linguistic knowledge: phonology, syntax, and semantics. Of central importance in that theory are linguistic rules. Rules describe how phonemes may be combined to form morphemes and words, how words may be combined to form sentences, and so on. The description of languages in terms of rules recognizes that language is a productive and combinatorial system, and the rules systematically describe in an abstract way the knowledge that could be used to create novel words and sentences. Two types of syntactic rule are particularly important in the theory of transformational grammar: phrase structure and transformational rules. Phrase-structure rules generate the deep structures that provide the information required for the semantic interpretation of a sentence. Transformational rules operate on the deep structures by rearranging, adding, and deleting elements to produce the surface structures of sentences, which carry the information required for the phonological representation of the sentences. Although each language has its own unique rules, words, and so on, some aspects of language appear to be general or universal. For example, the distinction between deep and surface structure is believed to be common to all human languages. The universal features of language help to define on a conceptual level our biological capacity for language.

The formal elegance and power of the theory of transformational grammar, together with Chomsky's arguments that linguistic knowledge must in some sense underlie verbal behavior, gave rise to attempts to build theories of performance upon the theory of competence, and the field of psycholinguistics blossomed forth. Although it has been established that phonemes may play an important role in speech perception, that syntactic factors contribute to verbal learning, and so on, the relation between competence and performance has turned out to be exceedingly complex. Attempts to ascertain the relation between syntactic competence and linguistic performance have been hindered by changes and gaps in the theory of competence, difficulties in separating the effects of syntax and semantics, and by the lack of understanding of the effects of performance variables such as memorial factors. The latter considerations, together with the increasing evidence for the contribution of semantic factors to linguistic performance, have led psychologists to formulate independent models of performance that are based upon semantics rather than syntax. Although attempts to forge theories of performance out of the substance of linguistic theory have largely been abandoned, linguistic theory has left its mark upon psychological analyses of language, particularly upon cognitive approaches to language. The principal aim of cognitive theories is to specify the knowledge that actually underlies performance and to determine how that knowledge is used.

Many unresolved problems remain in the analysis of language, and some of the problems are highlighted by studies of communication between chimps and humans. The definition of language itself is unclear, for we have no set criteria for deciding when chimps or even young children can be said to have mastered language, and many questions remain as to whether animals other than primates have some capacity for language (for example, Hewes, 1977; Marler, 1970, 1975). On the basis of the evidence now available, we may say that chimps have a rudimentary capacity for language, but it remains to be seen whether that capacity is rooted in psychological processes that are fundamentally similar to those involved in the linguistic performance of humans. It also remains to be seen whether language may be analyzed fruitfully as a phenomenon separate from conceptual and memorial processes (Premack, 1976), and functional analyses of language are needed in the future to supplement linguistic structural analyses. The interrelatedness of linguistic and nonlinguistic factors will become apparent in the following chapter in which we shall explore the question of how language is acquired.

NOTES

1. Lisker and Abramson (1964) have suggested that this feature be discussed in terms of voice-onset time. Voice-onset time is the latency to the vibration of the vocal folds following the release of the stop closure involved in producing the consonant.

2. An alternative account of the phenomenon of categorical perception is that subjects can discriminate between the stimuli within a category but respond on the basis of the verbal label assigned to those stimuli because of problems in remembering the sounds themselves (cf. Massaro, 1976).

3. Many cognitive theories distinguish between knowledge, motivation and performance. Although these distinctions may be convenient for some purposes, they are associated with a variety of problems (see pp. 220–224) and may not be necessary. For example, the distinction between knowledge and performance creates a gap between thought and action (Miller, G., Galanter, & Pribram, 1960) that has been difficult to bridge.

9

The Development of Language

The question of how language originates within the lifetime of an individual is for several reasons the focus of extensive research. First, humans have a unique biological basis for language (Lenneberg, 1967), and an understanding of how we acquire language may clarify the role that biological factors play in making each of us what we are. Second, the acquisition of language may involve unique processes and may lie beyond the domain of the principles of learning discussed in previous chapters. Finally, in virtually every known area inhabited by our species, children come to master language at an early age without the aid of special training. The sheer enthusiasm and virtuosity with which each child undertakes the complex task of mastering his or her native language is sufficient to capture our interest in the origin of language. Contemporary research has established that biological and experiential factors are interwoven throughout the development of language. Therefore, we shall consider in this chapter the contributions made by both phylogenetic and ontogenetic factors to the development of language. In our discussion of language development, we shall divide the path that development typically follows into several parts or stages. However, it is important to note that the divisions that we have made exist for the sake of expository convenience and do not necessarily reflect differences in functional processes.

FROM CRYING TO THE FIRST WORDS

Children typically utter their first words at about one year of age, to the delight of parents everywhere. Although a full year may pass before the first words are spoken, many events that appear to contribute to language acquisition occur well before the first year has passed. During the first year, extensive parent-infant interactions occur, and the child's vocalizations and nonverbal responses come to control the behavior of the parents. The acquisition of language may be rooted partly in the nonlinguistic, communicative interactions between parent and child. Furthermore, the things, people, and events that adults speak of may not be discriminable for the newborn. In their first year, children come to distinguish between different objects and people and between many other aspects of the environment. As children develop, verbal behavior will be "mapped" onto these discriminations and they will begin to tell us what they know (and ask us for what they want!). The purpose of this section is to consider in more detail the major events during the first year that seem to play a role in the development of language.

Preliminaries to the First Words

The important precursors of spoken words may be divided into four interrelated categories: communicative, linguistic, cognitive, and anatomical/physiological. Understanding of the subsequent discussion may be facilitated by noting here the principal differences between those categories. The difference between the communicative and the linguistic precursors of language is that much early communication is nonlinguistic—for example, gestural. Some of the processes involved in nonverbal communication may differ fundamentally from those involved in linguistic communication (for example, the processes involved in speech perception). Cognitive precursors are said to differ from those that are communicative or linguistic in that we can learn or come to know things without verbal or nonverbal communication. Indeed, one of the banes of our existence is the frustration that arises from not being able to effectively communicate what we know. Anatomical and physiological precursors refer to the physical changes that occur during the development of language and that are specifically related to language rather than to, for example, overall motor coordination.

At the outset of this discussion, it should be stated that the preceding distinctions are more heuristic than substantial. For instance, we agree with many other theorists (for example, Chomsky, N., 1976; Skinner, 1974) that at some level all changes in cognition and communication entail anatomical/physiological changes. Another caveat is that it is not known whether or to what extent fundamentally different learning processes are involved in the development of nonlinguistic and linguistic communication. The distinction between language and communication is closely akin to the distinction between competence and performance. Both distinctions have arisen from the work of Chomsky (1957, 1965, 1975; see Lenneberg, 1967), who argued that language involves specific biological abilities that differ from those involved in communication or performance. At this stage of research, however, it is simply unclear as to what the differences are (if there are any) between communication and language and the processes involved therein. The final point to be made here is that what is stated in terms of cognition or communication can often be stated in terms of behavior, stimulus control, and so on (cf. Catania, 1973b; Segal, 1975, 1977; Skinner, 1953, 1957, 1974; Salzinger, 1978). To provide continuity with the preceding chapters and to promote some integration between the behavioral and cognitive approaches to the study of language development, we shall in this chapter use both behavioral and cognitive terminology and shall try to identify some of the relationships therein. Let us now examine the precursors of the first words.

Crying The first vocalizations of children can hardly be said to foreshadow the elegance, complexity and beauty of human language as we often think of it. Indeed, the earliest vocalizations of children please few and disturb many, for they consist mainly of crying. Only the most general voicing mechanisms are involved in crying, and little articulation is required. As the child ages, vocalizations come to include cooing sounds, intense cries, less intense discomfort sounds, and a variety of vegetative sounds such as coughs, burps and so on (Stark, Rose, & McLagen, 1975; Wolff, P. H., 1966).

Cries and other nonlinguistic sounds may contribute at least indirectly to the development of language. Crying is among the first responses of the infant that systematically modify the behavior of the parents and other adults. In turn, crying responses may be modified by the responses of the parents, for crying appears to be affected by reinforcement (Gewirtz, 1978). Since crying responses modify the behavior of others and are in turn modified by the behavior of others, crying may be said to serve a communicative function. Indeed, by 7 or 8 months of age, children emit a variety of different cries, and parents can accurately discriminate the various cries as requests, signs of hunger, greetings, and so on (Ricks, 1975). Crying may play an important part in the development of a repertoire of communicative responses, and that development may subsequently facilitate communication via language.

Early Nonverbal Communication During their first year, children communicate with parents and siblings not only by vocalizations but also by means of gestures. For example, parents often show and give objects to infants. Children who are 6 or 7 months old often reciprocate by spontaneously showing and giving things to adults (Escalona, 1973). Similarly, young children often point at novel or desired objects, and they sometimes emit open-handed reaching and grasping responses (Carter, 1975; Ingram, 1971).

Although all nonvocal gestures may seem to be very similar, different gestures may in fact serve different functions and belong to different functional response classes. Pointing and reaching often have different consequences. Whereas a pointing response may be followed by a parent looking at and naming an object, a reaching response (which is often accompanied by whining) may be followed by reception of the object (Clark, H. H., & Clark, 1977). Thus pointing and reaching are typically correlated with different consequences. Accordingly, these responses have been described as serving different communicative functions. Specifically, pointing is said to *assert* the presence of something, and reaching is said to *request* something (Bates, E., 1976; Bruner, J. S., 1975). Assertions and requests occur often in linguistic communication, and although the details are now obscure the roots of linguistic assertions and requests may lie in the nonlinguistic communicative episodes that occur very early in life (Bruner, J. S., 1975). An important task for future research is to specify the nature and extent of transfer from early gestural communication to later linguistic communication.

Early Linguistic Ability   The early absence of speech, together with the crude nature of many early vocalizations, might be mistaken as a general lack of linguistic ability on the part of infants. However, that conclusion is not fully warranted, for infants have some of the same phonological skills that adults show (see Morse, 1974, 1978). As an example consider the following experiment (Eimas, Siqueland, Jusczyk, & Vigorito, 1971) that tested the ability of 1-month-old and 4-month-old infants to discriminate between the adult phonemes /b/ and /p/. First, Eimas et al. prepared separate recordings of several phones belonging to the /p/ phoneme and several other phones belonging to the /b/ phoneme. Next, the recording of a particular phone was played continuously for infants whenever the infants sucked a pacifier at a high rate. Whenever the rate of sucking declined below a preestablished criterion (habituation) the volume of the recording decreased. If the rate of sucking remained low for two consecutive minutes, a recording of another phone was presented, and again the volume depended upon the rate of sucking. In some conditions, the second phone belonged to the same phoneme as the first phone (for example, both might have been variants of /p/), whereas on other occasions, the first and second phones belonged to different phonemes.

The result of major interest was that when the second phone belonged to a different phoneme than the first phone, the rate of sucking increased significantly when the second phone was presented, and dishabituation could be said to have occurred. In contrast, the rate of sucking did not increase when the second phone belonged to the same phoneme as the first. Thus the infants responded categorically to the /p/ and /b/ phonemes, just as adults do (see pp. 319–322). Moreover, the infants discriminated between the phones of different phonemes even though they could not produce those phones. In other words, their production lagged behind their comprehension. Apparently, some listening that is important for the development of language may be occurring even when the child produces no speechlike sounds.

The observation of categorical perception of speech in infants as young as 1-month has led to the suggestion that human infants have innate feature detectors that are sensitive to particular acoustic properties of speech (Eimas, 1975a, 1975b). However, that suggestion should be viewed with caution. For one thing, the same sort of categorical perception that has been observed in young infants has been observed in such decidedly nonlinguistic animals as the chinchilla (Kuhl & Miller, 1975) and the rhesus monkey (Waters & Wilson, 1976). Clearly, the occurrence of categorical phonemic perception does not require the postulation of linguistically specialized feature detectors. Rather, the contrasts between speech sounds that fall into different phonemic categories may be highly distinctive to the auditory systems of humans and certain other mammals. Indeed, the phonemic structure of human languages may reflect the functional characteristics of the auditory system. Of course, the categorical perception of speech sounds in humans may involve linguistically specialized processes that do not occur in nonhumans, but that remains to be determined by future research. Another problem with the postulation of innate linguistically specialized feature detectors is that the contribution of experience to the occurrence of categorical perception in infants is unclear (cf. Butterfield & Cairns, 1974). Until the effects of early experiences have been ascertained, it seems premature to call "innate" the aspects of the auditory system that are involved in categorical phonemic perception.

Early Anatomical Development   In the preceding section, we mentioned that the vocalizations of human infants consist of cries. The predominance of crying over speechlike vocalizations in the early months seems to reflect neither a hostile disposition nor original sin, for newborn humans simply lack the peripheral anatomy required for the production of speechlike sounds. Before infants can produce the sounds of speech, a variety of complex changes must occur in the shape of the mouth, teeth, and throat, in the connections between the brain and speech muscles, and so on (Lenneberg, 1967; Lieberman, 1975).

The importance of changes in the peripheral anatomy for the development of language are illustrated by the following example. The larynx of newborn humans (and of nonhuman primates) opens almost directly into the oral cavity, whereas the larynx of adult humans exits into a portion of the pharynx. Thus in adult humans part of the pharynx lies in the airway above the larynx as shown in Fig. 9.1. By changing the size and shape of that portion of the pharynx, adult humans can produce such speech sounds as [i], [a], [u], [k], and [g]. Indeed, these sounds are found in a wide variety of languages. Newborn humans simply cannot produce the adult form of such sounds, for the growth processes that lead to the development of the adult form of pharynx are incomplete before the age of two (Lieberman, 1973).

These findings concerning the role that changes in the pharynx play in the development of language are important for several reasons. First, they relate certain apects of language development to specifiable maturational changes. Just as importantly, these findings clarify the biological basis of what appears to be a universal aspect of language: the use of one of the vowels /i/, /a/ or /u/ (Lieberman, 1973). Clearly, our biological heritage for language may be reflected in at least some of the universal aspects of language. Finally, these findings are important because they identify an aspect of our biological capacity for language that appears to be quite unique. Like newborn humans, chimps and other nonhumans lack the peripheral anatomy required to produce all the sounds of human speech (Lieberman, 1973, 1975). Chimps can acquire a gestural language, but try as they may, Washoe and friends cannot learn to speak as adult humans do.

Although changes in peripheral anatomy may be necessary for the production of particular speech sounds, these changes alone may not be sufficient. Speaking is an activity of awesome intricacy and subtlety. Speech requires the simultaneous control and coordination of breathing, the tension of the vocal

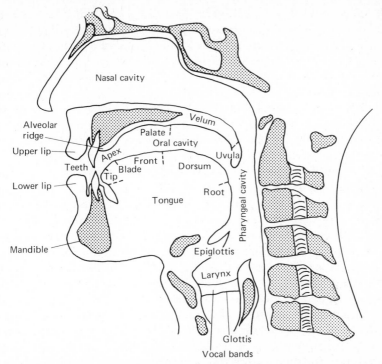

Fig. 9.1   The anatomy of the speech organs of the adult human. Note the elongated portion of the pharynx that lies above the larynx is called the supralaryngeal portion of the pharynx and plays an important role in the production of some universal sounds of speech.   (From Francis, 1958. Copyright 1958 by W. Nelson Francis. Reprinted by permission of John Wiley & Sons, Inc.)

folds, the configuration of the oropharyngeal cavity, the position of the tongue, the shape of the lips, and so on (cf. Lenneberg, 1967, for details). Fortunately, evolution seems to have provided a vehicle for some of the changes in muscular strength, control and coordination that are required for speech. That vehicle is the babbling that infants engage in.

Babbling   By the time they are 6 months old, children produce a wide variety of speechlike sounds in an unsystematic manner, and the children are then said to be babbling. In babbling, children emit sounds that are not part of the language of adults around them, and adults who are struggling to learn the gutteral sounds of the German language may be astonished to find that infants spontaneously "babble" these sounds. Interestingly, babies all over the world, and even deaf children, emit the sounds of diverse languages while babbling. Babbling typically continues to the age of 1 year, and babbling often occurs after the child has begun to produce acceptable words in his or her native language.

Babbling appears to contribute to the development of language in helping to strengthen the muscles involved in speech and in providing a means for children controlling and coordinating their speech. Moreover, babbling seems to serve a communicative function, at least for some children. For example, children seem to vary their intonation patterns during babbling to make requests, to reject items, and so on (Dore, 1975; Halliday, 1975). Thus during the babbling period vocalizations come to serve some of the same communicative functions that are served by nonverbal gestures (see Bruner, J. S., 1974/5; for further discussion).

Another way in which babbling is related to language development is that babbling can produce the "raw material" that can be operated on by the environment. Specifically, once speech sounds are babbled, they may be differentially reinforced by, for instance, the parents, thus facilitating the production of actual words. A study by Routh (1969; also see Bloom, K., 1977) shows clearly that the verbal responses of infants can be affected by their consequences. Routh studied the vocalizations of several groups of infants aged 2 to 7 months. For both groups that are relevant to this discussion, there were two baseline and three conditioning sessions. During the two baseline sessions, the experimenter stood expressionless and unresponsive before the infant and recorded the number of vowel and consonant sounds that the infant emitted. During the three conditioning sessions, all vowel sounds were reinforced for the vowel group and all consonant sounds were reinforced for the consonant group. The reinforcer consisted of the experimenter smiling and saying "tsk, tsk, tsk" while touching the infant's abdomen. As before, the vowel and consonant sounds emitted by each infant were recorded.

The results for the vowel group were that reinforcement produced large increases in the number of vowel sounds and a small increase in the number of consonant sounds. Similarly, reinforcement in the consonant group increased the number of consonant sounds but not the number of vowel sounds. Thus through selective reinforcement vowel sounds and consonant sounds were differentiated into distinct response classes.

Children at the age of 9 to 12 months may not have reliably produced acceptable words in their native language, but they may nevertheless be emitting wordlike responses during the babbling period. For example, one child was observed to say [gaga], [gaegi] and [gagi] in pleasurable situations such as those in which she could handle toys, chew crayons, and so on (Dore, Franklin, Miller, & Ramer, 1976). These syllabic sequences seem to be relatively stable units in that they are set off by pauses, they are emitted regularly, and they occur under similar conditions. We may speculate that these early wordlike responses have been acquired and maintained by adventitious reinforcement. If parents or siblings attend to children or give them things they are reaching for while they utter a particular sequence of syllables, the probability of occurrence of that response may be increased under similar conditions. The early utterances that seem to be the child's spontaneous inventions may have specifiable environmental antecedents. An important goal for future research is to specify rigorously the behavior-environment interactions that influence the verbal behavior of the developing child.

A great deal remains to be learned about the relationship between babbling and the development of language. One point should be clear: babbling is not strictly necessary for the development of language. For example, cases have been documented of people who could not speak but who nevertheless came to understand language to the same extent as people who do speak (Fourcin, 1975; Lenneberg, 1962). Furthermore, there is sometimes a period of silence between the period during which children babble and that in which they utter their first words (Dale, 1976). Also, many of the sounds that are produced frequently during the babbling period (for example, [l] and [r] sounds) occur infrequently during the period in which the first words are produced. These observations have led some theorists (for example, Jakobson, 1968) to propose that the processes that occur in the period in which the first words are produced are discontinuous with and fundamentally different from the processes underlying vocalizations in the babbling period. However, other research (Oller, Wieman, Doyle, & Ross, 1976) indicates that some of the sounds that occur most often during babbling also occur frequently in the production of the first words. Given that babbling may serve a variety of functions, there may be both continuities and discontinuities between babbling and speaking words. Careful analyses of the environments in which different children are reared may help clarify these issues.

One-Word Utterances

At about 1 year of age, children typically utter the first genuine words of their native language. Not surprisingly, the first words of children are relatively simple and reflect some of their primary interests: food, toys and animals (Nelson, K., 1973). Among the most frequently occurring words in those categories are *milk, cookie, dog, cat, ball,* and *block.* Of course, *mama, dada,* and *baby* also occur frequently. Unsurprisingly, many of the first words that are emitted are names of objects that the child can act upon. However, the generality of the preceding observations is uncertain, for many of the data concerning early utterances have been obtained from the study of a rather small number of children from a rather restricted range of socioeconomic settings.

The relative simplicity of children's first words displays little of the communicative, cognitive and linguistic complexity that is inherent in these utterances, and we shall now consider these complexities further.

Communicative Functions   Generally, the one-word utterances of children may be said to serve two communicative functions: assertion and request (Clark, H. H., & Clark, 1977; Greenfield & Smith, 1976). Note that these communicative functions are the same ones that were characteristic of gestures at an earlier stage of development. Assertions often consist of an utterance combined with a gesture. For example, a child might point to a ball and say "Ball." In emitting such gesture-word combinations, children may show no sign of wanting to receive or hold the thing named. Indeed, that is about all that distinguishes assertions from requests. Requests consist of a word accompanied by a reaching gesture or a whining sound.

There is no sharp and widely accepted dividing line between assertions and requests, but these types of utterances may have different antecedents. In general, early verbal assertive responses involve naming, and naming responses are often shaped and maintained by social reinforcers (Skinner, 1957;

Winokur, 1976). Parents often seek to engage their children in naming games in which the parents point to something, ask "What's that?" and then show their approval when the child emits the appropriate response. If the appropriate response is not emitted, parents may name the object and ask the child to imitate them.

Exactly how naming comes about in children is not yet known, but early communicative interactions may be of central importance. For example, well before the naming game occurs, children and parents carry on nonvocal dialogues in which they take turns pointing at objects or pictures (Ninio & Bruner, 1978). Learning to take turns in nonlinguistic interactions may transfer positively to subsequent linguistic interactions such as the naming game. Naming in children may also come about through the same sorts of reinforcement procedures that were used to bring about naming in Washoe (see pp. 348–350). By explicitly building a repertoire of naming responses, the members of a social or verbal community increase their chances of coming into contact with important objects, processes and changes in the environment. And in fact it has been observed that children, like adults, often talk about what is new—at least for them (see Greenfield & Smith, 1976).

In contrast to assertive responses, requests may be maintained by material reinforcers, such as the receipt of milk, a toy, the opportunity to hold a cat, and so on. Thus assertive responses and requests, whether verbal or nonverbal, may be divided into broad but different functional response classes.

As the parent and child become skilled in very simple communicative interactions, more complex and bidirectional interactions begin to occur (Bruner, J. S., 1975), and they pave the way for the occurrence of task-oriented social activities that may involve a division of labor. These activities may involve little more than a parent holding up a box of toys while the child reaches in. Throughout these activities, there is often much eye contact and vocalization. Eventually, even simple tasks may be structured according to roles in which each participant does a particular thing and in which the roles may be reversed (Garvey, 1975).

At first glance, the interactions described above may seem little more than child's play. However, a little reflection raises the possibility that the development of some of the more subtle and complex aspects of language may depend in part upon the pressure applied by others to induce the child to communicate and interact in more subtle and complex ways. Of course, the communicative functions that are served by language must to some extent be based not only upon communicative factors but also upon cognitive abilities and processes. We shall now examine the relation between cognition and one-word utterances.

Cognition and One-Word Utterances The development of language is of necessity tied closely to the development of cognition (Moore, T. E., 1973; Sinclair-de Zwart 1973; Slobin, 1973), and what children say reflects to a considerable extent what they know. Piaget (1951, 1953, 1955a) has studied cognitive development extensively and it is worthwhile to consider here some of his observations and suggestions that pertain to the development of language.

From birth to about 15 months of age, infants are said to be in the *sensory-motor stage* of development. That stage involves the development of action schemas such as sucking, feeding, reaching, and so on. During the early parts of the sensory-motor period (about 0–4 months), infants treat objects as if they were extensions of themselves. For example, young infants will visually follow a moving object, but if the object disappears from view, the infant seems to lose interest and shows no sign of searching for the object. That seems to be more than a case of "out of sight, out of mind," and it appears to many students of development that infants do not know that objects have a permanent and independent existence. Later in the sensory-motor period, the infant will search visually but not manually for an object that has disappeared, and the interaction within the child's nervous system between the visual and the tactile modalities may be limited at that point. Gradually, the child comes readily to search for and find objects that have disappeared, and shows surprise if the object does not turn up in the place where it had been hidden, and so on. By the end of the sensory-motor period, children are said to have mastered the concept of *object permanence*. Mastery of that concept may be a prerequisite for talking about objects that are not present, that are receding from view, and so on (but see Corrigan, 1978). As an aside, nonhumans such as rhesus monkeys may be said to master the concept of object permanence, and they even pass through the same stages as humans in doing so (Wise, Wise & Zimmerman, 1974).

Once children have begun to discriminate between permanent objects and themselves, they can discriminate between different objects such as a ball, a cookie, and so on. Just as importantly, they may come to discriminate between different higher-order classes of stimuli. For example, they may come to discriminate between objects that are movers or agents (for example, siblings, adults, pets) and those that are only movable (for example, inanimate objects such as rocks). Similarly, they may come to discriminate between objects that are used as instruments (for example, spoons and knives) and those that are not. As we shall see, abstract categories of knowledge such as "agent" and "instrument" may constitute some of the fundamental conceptual-semantic distinctions upon which the early development of language is founded. It should also be noted, however, that although knowledge of these categories has often been attributed to children, few steps have been taken to define rigorously the child's conceptual categories and the boundaries thereof. In defining those categories empirically, the procedures that have been used to study stimulus control (see Chapter 5) and concept learning (see pp. 278–308) in relatively simple conditions should prove helpful (cf. Braine & Wells, 1978).

The attainment of object permanence is also important in that it seems to mark a significant developmental milestone: the ability to represent events and objects internally. At the end of the sensory-motor period, children make and use tools, they emit imitative responses over long delays, and they engage in symbolic play. These activities are typically said to involve the formation and utilization of internal representations. Although speaking in terms of internal and symbolic representations poses sundry conceptual problems (cf. Pylyshyn, 1973; Skinner, 1957, 1964, 1974), there is little doubt that activities such as tool-making involve private events. In the following discussion, we shall for the sake of expository convenience speak of internal representations rather than of private events, but we believe that the phenomena that are spoken of in terms of internal representations are amenable to an analysis in terms of private events. In short, "internal representations" is a metaphorical phrase and does not imply the existence of literal internal copies.

The ability to form and use internal representations is fundamental for the development of language (Piaget, 1955b; Premack, 1976). Communicating through language entails the use of arbitrary symbols (that is, words) that are abstract representations of objects and events, attributes, relationships, and so forth. Speaking the sentences that can occur in human language entails, as we shall see, the production and covert editing of representations of the things we talk about. Without internal representations, there would be no thought or language as we know it. Since these representations are absent at birth, it is no surprise to find that language is also missing at birth. Although the exact nature of the relevant cognitive and symbolic abilities and the development thereof are not yet understood well, it seems clear that cognitive development provides some of the necessary groundwork for language (Bloom, L. M., & Lahey, 1978; Clark, H. H., & Clark, 1977; Edwards, 1973; Macnamara, 1972).

One-Word Utterances and Language   During the period in which one-word utterances are the predominant form of speech, the linguistic skills of the child have clearly only begun to develop. Yet to produce words that others can understand, children must have learned some of the differences in speech sounds that are phonemic in their language.[1,2] Additionally, children must have discriminated to some extent which parts of the relatively continuous speech stream they are exposed to can stand by themselves. In other words, children must have learned to segment the speech stream into the appropriate syllables and words. The difficulty of that task can be readily attested to by anyone who has tried to learn a foreign language. When one is first exposed to a novel language, it seems to "all sound alike," and it almost seems impossible that anyone could isolate discrete words out of the speech stream. Of course, at the one-word stage, the speech heard by the child is much simpler than that to which adults are typically exposed (cf. deVilliers & deVilliers, 1978; Snow, 1977), but the segmentation problem nevertheless remains.

Syntactic Properties   Recall that one-word utterances, together with situational information, can often be interpreted in various ways. Whether *ball* is interpreted as an assertion or a request depends largely upon the gestural accompaniments of the utterance, the location of the ball relative to the child, and so on. These observations have led some theorists (for example, DeLaguna, 1927) to call one-word utterances *holophrases* to indicate that single words may express as much as whole sentences. That position is consistent with the observation that children who produce only one-word utterances can comprehend multiword utterances (Sachs & Truswell, 1978).

On the other hand, adults may tend to read too much into one-word utterances (cf. Olney & Scholnick, 1978). If one-word utterances are really reduced sentences, why is only one word produced? The problem does not seem to be a limitation in the span of memory or attention (Olson, 1973). Moreover, the production of single words stems neither from vocabulary limitations nor an inability to represent multiword utterances, for 1-year-olds can understand some multiword utterances. In fact, soon before two-word utterances are produced, children produce sequences of one-word utterances such as *Baby, Chair* that will later appear as two-word utterances such as *Baby chair* (Bloom, L. M., 1973). Perhaps the child's communicative needs can be met early on by the production of single words. At any rate, it is too soon to conclude that one-word utterances reflect the same linguistic competence as is reflected in full sentences. At the present time, we have no clear rules for deciding which phenomena of children's language reflect linguistic competence and which stem from performative factors such as communicative and cognitive ones (Brown, R., 1973; deVilliers et al., 1978; Limber, 1976). Separating competence and performance in child language constitutes a significant challenge for future research.

Semantic Properties Consider next the semantic properties of the first words. One of the most striking aspects of words at the one-word stage is their semantic composition. Although the child's early words overlap adult words in meaning, these words are often either overextended or underextended (Bowerman, 1976; Bloom, L. M., 1973; Clark, H. H., & Clark, 1977). *Overextensions* are said to occur when the child applies a word more broadly than adults do. For example, the child might say *doggie* in the presence of all four-legged, furry mammals rather than only in the presence of dogs. *Underextensions* are said to occur when the child applies a word in a more restricted manner than adults do. For instance, the child might say *doggie* in the presence of the family dog but not in the presence of other dogs.

To help clarify the origins of the semantic composition of the first words, consider the situations that the child is exposed to when learning to talk. When a child hears the word *dog* said by others, dogs alone may sometimes be present, but at other times cats or other animals (or no animals whatsoever) may be present. Simply put, the child has no way of discerning what it is exactly that others are talking about.

The task that confronts the child who is determining what a word means bears many similarities to concept identification tasks (see pp. 288–308). Just as concept learning may be viewed as a process involving the formation and testing of hypotheses about various attributes, so too may the process of learning word meanings be viewed as one that entails hypothesis-testing (Clark, E. V., 1973, 1975). According to the hypothesis-testing model, the child forms hypotheses about the meanings of the words heard and then tests them out. In principle, hypotheses about early word meanings could be based on a broad range of stimulus dimensions such as color and texture. However, most early words are controlled by stimulus dimensions such as shape, movement, function, size and sound (Bowerman, 1976; Clark, E. V., 1973, 1975; Clark, H. H., & Clark, 1977; Nelson, K., 1974). It is not known whether the predominance of hypotheses based on the latter attributes reflects biological factors, experiential factors or some mixture of the two. At any rate, once the initial hypothesis is formed about the meaning of a word, that hypothesis can be modified on the basis of the feedback the child receives. Thus if the initial hypothesis concerning the meaning of *ball* is based upon say, shape, the child would erroneously call everything from balls to apples and eggs *ball*. Most objects that children talk about are defined by the conjunction of numerous attributes, and the child must encounter numerous instances of the category *ball* before the relevant attributes and the conceptual rule whereby those attributes are combined can be determined.

Whether a child overextends or underextends the meaning of a word depends upon which dimensions of the object being spoken of control his or her verbal behavior. We believe that the child's history of reinforcement determines in part which stimulus dimensions control the child's verbal behavior. If a child has previously received differential training on the dimension of size but not on the dimension of shape, the child may be more likely to respond verbally to new objects on the basis of size rather than on the dimension of shape. The result could be overextensions based upon similarities in the size of the objects that are talked about. For example, the child might call all adults *mama* or *papa*. Of course, underextensions could also result. For instance, if the child had learned the word *dog* in the presence of a large dog, and if the child responded on the basis of size, that child might call only large dogs *dogs*. Through differential reinforcment, the child's verbal responses eventually come to be controlled by the same classes of stimuli that control the verbal responses of adults.

Language, Communication, Mapping, and Cognition   It is important to note that the child's verbal behavior, like that of adults, may not indicate what the child knows about the world. For example, a child who overextends *doggie* by saying that word in the presence of both dogs and cats may be able to discriminate between dogs and cats. Language serves communicative functions, and the child who does not yet produce the word *cat*, may say *doggie* in the presence of cats to request holding them, to draw the parents' attention to them, and so forth. Indeed, it has been observed that some words that are overextended in production are not overextended in comprehension (Clark, H. H., & Clark, 1977). For instance, one child overextended *apple* to many spherical objects in production, but that same child could consistently identify apples when shown groups of spherical objects and asked to pick out the apple. Similarly, a child who says *doggie* only in the presence of the family dog (an underextension) may categorize this dog with other dogs, but may also discriminate that the family dog is treated differently by the parents. Accordingly, that child may communicate only about the family pet with the word *doggie*.

The main point of the preceding discussion is that children, for communicative reasons, may not always map their verbal behavior onto the conceptual categories they may be said to have. In other instances, overextensions or underextensions may occur because children have simply not learned to map their verbal behavior onto the appropriate conceptual categories. For example, if a child has observed others say *dog* in a room containing both a dog and a cat, the child may learn to say *dog* in the presence of both types of animal. That overextension would result not from communicative factors but from inappropriate semantic hypotheses.

A final consideration is that many overextensions or underextensions may occur for neither communicative nor semantic reasons but rather for cognitive or conceptual reasons. That is, children may use words inappropriately when they simply do not make the distinctions between events and objects that adults do. Children who call all four-legged hairy animals *doggie* may in fact group all such animals into one and only one category. In that case, the verbal behavior of the children would accurately correspond to their conceptual knowledge, but the response *doggie* would be inappropriate on both conceptual and semantic grounds.

An important point of the preceding discussion is that the road between language and cognition runs in both directions. Our conceptual knowledge affects our language at least to the extent that we cannot talk about things we do not discriminate. And coming the other way, our conceptual behavior may be shaped by the linguistic distinctions that the members of our society encourage us to make (Whorf, 1956). The infants of a social group may not discriminate between different types of snow, but if these differences are important to the members of the group, for example, a tribe of Eskimos, then the society will teach both the appropriate nonverbal and verbal behavior and the appropriate conceptual distinctions. Given the intimate relationship between language and cognition, future studies of language development, and particularly of semantic development will need to include assays of the cognitive development of the child (cf. Bloom, L. M., & Lahey, 1978; deVilliers & deVilliers, 1978).

EARLY WORD COMBINATIONS

The production of two-word utterances constitutes another significant milestone in the development of language: speaking in sentences. To be sure, these sentences are quite simple. Indeed, two-word utterances are sometimes referred to as *telegraphic speech* since function words such as *on, to, the,* and *and* are often omitted, just as they are in a telegram. Only the critical content words such as nouns, verbs and adjectives are included. The simplicity of two-word utterances belies their importance in the development of language and in the study thereof. As pointed out previously, language is a combinatorial system and some of the combinatorial power of language becomes available to children when they begin to combine words systematically. Moreover, the production of sentencelike combinations of words marks the development of the rudiments of syntax. And on a methodological level, semantic, grammatical and cognitive relations are easier to assess in two-word utterances than in one-word utterances, and considerable research has accordingly been devoted to two-word utterances. In this section, we shall describe the regularities in two-word utterances, examine some of the grammars that have been suggested to account for them, and inquire into their antecedents.

Structural Regularities of Early Word Combinations

Two-word utterances, like the multiword sentences of adults, are character-ized by numerous regularities in structure. For example, there are regularities in the ways words are distributed in these early utterances (Braine, 1963). A few words (sometimes called pivot words), such as *there, move* and *my* are used often, they appear in many different combinations, and they tend to occur in particular positions. Thus a child might say *there doggie, there chair, there truck,* and so on. Other words such as *chair, shoe* and *mommie* are called open words and they occur in fewer combinations and vary freely in position. These regularities in the distribution of words appear to be general across a wide va-riety of languages (Brown, R., 1973), and it should be recalled that they were also characteristic of the sign combinations emitted by Washoe. However, not all of the words spoken by children may be classified as either pivot or open words (for example, Bowerman, 1973; Braine, 1976), and part of the problem in maintaining a strict pivot-open classification is that the ordering of words in early word combinations is often variable (Braine, 1976). The classification of words as either pivot or open words is at best a very rough one.

The regularities in two-word utterances that are described by the pivot-open classification scheme are surface regularities. However, two-word utter-ances are also characterized by a variety of deeper, semantic regularities. The basic semantic relationships that appear most frequently in early word combi-nations are shown in Table 9.1. There are several important points to be made in regard to those semantic relationships. First, two-word utterances that have similar surface structures may have very different semantic interpretations. For example, utterances such as *Eve lunch* and *Adam checker* appear similar in that both consist of a person's name followed by an object. However, *Eve lunch* is said to express the agent-object relation, whereas *Adam checker* is said to express the possessor-possession relation (Brown, R., 1970, 1973).

Just how does one ascertain the semantic relationship that is expressed by an utterance? The best available answer to that question is that the seman-tic relations are inferred from two types of observation: the context in which an utterance occurs and the stress that is placed on different words. For exam-

TABLE 9.1 Prevalent Semantic Relations of Two-Word Sentences of Children in a Variety of Languages

Semantic Relations	Examples
Agent and action	*Adam put; Bambi go*
Action and object	*See sock; Hit ball*
Agent and object	*Eve lunch; Mommy sock*
Action and locative	*Walk street; Go store*
Entity and locative	*Baby room; Sweater chair*
Possessor and possession	*Adam checker; Mommy lunch*
Entity and attributive	*Big train; Red book*
Demonstrative and entity	*That book; This cat*

Source: Adapted from R. Brown, 1973.

ple, *Adam checker* could be said in reply to the question "Whose checker is that?" and with the accent on *Adam* (Wieman, 1976). Under these conditions, *Adam checker* would be said to express the possessor-possessed relationship. Similarly, a statement such as *Christy room* could be said to express the possessor-possession relationship, but *Christy room* could also be said to express the entity-locative relationship. Of course, the semantic interpretation of two-word utterances is not always clear,[3] and we shall return to that matter shortly.

Another important point about the semantic relations expressed in two-word utterances is that they appear to be general across a variety of languages such as English, German, Russian, Finnish and Samoan (Slobin, 1973). Interestingly, the same semantic relations that are present in early word combinations are also present in the early sign combinations of deaf children (Bellugi & Klima, 1972, 1975; Bellugi & Fischer, 1972). The generality of the semantic relations shown in Table 9.1 is so impressive that those relations have come to be seen as characteristic features of linguistic competence at the two-word stage of language development (referred to as *Stage I* by Brown, R., 1973).

The third important point concerning the early semantic relations is that they include categories and relations that are abstract and inferred, and the functional significance of those relationships remains to be determined. A persistent problem that arises in the study of child language is that of "reading too much into what the child says." Our skill in interpreting what others say is a tribute to our linguistic and communicative knowledge and helps us in everyday situations. However, that skill is of limited scientific value until rigorous, empirical criteria are devised to permit researchers to interpret early utterances validly and reliably. The semantic relations on which we now focus in the study of language development may exist more for the convenience they afford the observer than for their functional importance. For example, it may be helpful to classify some utterances in the agent-action category, but it is another matter to assert that all agent-action constructions are similar for the child (cf. Braine & Wells, 1978; Schlesinger, I. M., 1974). Indeed, the things that are classified as "agents" by the child may differ considerably from those of adults (Bowerman, 1976; Braine, 1976; Clark, H. H., & Clark, 1977). The wisest policy at this point is to treat the semantic relations discussed in this section as tentative, working hypotheses about the meanings of early word combinations.

Grammar and Stage I

Linguists and psycholinguists have argued that the task of analyzing language acquisition can proceed only after we have specified what it is that develops or is learned. They argue further that what is developed is not simply performance or verbal behavior but rather linguistic competence, and knowledge of syntax is one central aspect of linguistic competence. In this section, we shall examine two models of Stage I grammar that have been proposed, and we shall use those models as vehicles both for discussing the nature of grammatical knowledge at Stage I and for discussing the problems involved in specifying the linguistic competence of children.

Transformational Grammar and Stage I   Recall that the theory of transformational grammar postulates two levels of linguistic structure: surface structure and deep structure. Bloom (1970) has applied the transformational model to child language and has argued that the distinction between deep and surface structure is part of the linguistic competence of children at Stage I of language development. For example, the statement *mommy sock* can mean either *mommy's sock* or *mommy put on my sock*. The fact that *mommy sock* can be interpreted in two ways can be accounted for by postulating two different deep structures underlying that utterance. Figure 9.2 shows (*a*) the deep structure for the agent-object interpretation of *mommy sock,* and (*b*) the deep structure for the possessor-possessed interpretation of that utterance.

For the sake of brevity, we shall forego a complete discussion of transformational models of language at Stage I (see Bloom, L. M., 1970; Brown, R., 1973, for more detailed discussions). For our purposes, it is sufficient to note that current transformational grammars for Stage I attribute to children knowledge of the subject-verb-object relationships that adults are said to have. Indeed, that attribution is made even though utterances at Stage I typically consist of two words and do not include subject, verb and object. Basically, the theory holds that the child knows the subject-verb-object relationship but lacks the competence to produce all three in a single utterance. For example, the absence of a verb in the utterance *mommy sock* is accounted for by the application of an obligatory reduction transformation which deletes the verb from the underlying verb phrase.

Transformational grammars for language at Stage I have the advantage of relating the competence of the child to that of adults. However, these models encounter the difficulty that they fail to provide a principled way of distinguishing between competence and performance. For example, children at Stage I sometimes produce three-word utterances (Bloom, L. M., 1970; Brown, R., 1973). Therefore, the failure to produce utterances including subject, verb and object does not result from an inability to produce utterances longer than two words. Since children at Stage I can produce three-word utterances, why should they lack the competence required to produce three-word utterances that contain subject, verb and object? Could the failure to produce

Fig. 9.2   Two different deep structures underlying the utterance *mommy sock*. The symbol "φ" is a dummy element.   (From Dale, *Language development*, copyright Holt, Rinehart, and Winston, Inc., 1976. Reprinted by permission of Holt, Rinehart, and Winston.)

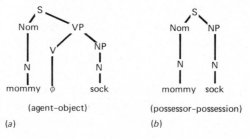

the latter kinds of utterance result from performative factors? We are often unable to obtain the linguistic intuitions of children. Consequently, competence is often inferred directly and solely from the utterances that are said to reflect that competence, and there is considerable uncertainty regarding which phenomena reflect competence and which lie in the realm of performance.

The upshot of the preceding discussion is that the transformational grammar that has been proposed to account for Stage I language is at best controversial (for further criticisms, cf. Braine, 1974, 1976; Brown, R., 1973), particularly with regard to the postulated reduction transformation. Accordingly, psycholinguists have proposed alternative models of linguistic knowledge at Stage I, and we shall now consider the case grammar model.

Case Grammar and Stage I   Case grammar has recently begun to command considerable attention in the field of developmental psycholinguistics. However, this grammar was initially devised to apply to adult language, and it is worthwhile to consider briefly the conceptual origins of case grammar.

Fillmore (1968), like generative semanticists, has pointed out that the semantic relatedness of many sentences is not accounted for by standard versions of transformational grammar. For example, consider sentences (1) and (2). Those sentences have different deep structures, and key is the subject in (1) whereas it is the object of a preposition in (2). However, in both sentences, the

(1) The key opened the door.
(2) John opened the door with a key.

key plays a similar role: it is the instrument used to open the door. Transformational grammars do not adequately capture the fact that key plays similar semantic roles in sentences such as (1) and (2). One basic problem with standard transformational grammars is that they rely heavily upon categories such as "subject" and "object" and these categories are too broad. The subject of a sentence may be an agent, as in (2), or it may be an instrument as in (1) (cf. Fillmore, 1968, 1971, for further discussion), but the distinction between, for instance, agents and instruments is not included in transformational models of grammar. Case grammar is a semantically based model that breaks syntactic categories such as "subject" and "object" down into semantic categories such as "agent" and "instrument." Broadly speaking, the goal of case grammar is to specify more precisely than transformational grammar the various relations that nouns may bear to verbs.

The various relations which can hold between a noun and a verb are called case roles or case relations. The main case relations that are common to numerous languages are shown in Table 9.2. As Table 9.2 shows, the Agentive case identifies the instigator of an action named by the verb. The Instrumental case is filled by nouns that name inanimate forces or objects that are causally involved in the action specified by the verb. The Experiencer case includes nouns that name animals that are in a psychological state or are having an experience that is specified by the verb. The Factitive case includes animate or inanimate objects that result from the action or state named by the verb.

TABLE 9.2   Basic Case Relations Specified by Case Grammar

Case Name	Definition	Example (italicized noun is in designated case)
Agentive (A)	The typically animate, perceived instigator of action	*John* opened the door. The door was opened by *John*.
Instrumental (I)	The inanimate force or object causally involved in the state or action named by the verb	The *key* opened the door. John opened the door with the *key*.
Dative (D)	The animate being affected by the action named by the verb (includes possession)	John gave the book to *Bill*. *Daddy* has a study.
Experiencer (E)	The animate being having a given experience or mental disposition	*Tom* wanted a drink. *Adam* saw Eve.
Factitive (F)	The object or being resulting from the state or action named by the verb	God created *woman*. John built a *table*.
Locative (L)	The location or spatial orientation of the state or action named by the verb	The sweater is on the *chair*. *Chicago* is windy. John walked to *school*.
Objective (O)	The semantically most neutral case; anything representable by a noun whose role in the state or action named by the verb depends on the meaning of the verb itself	Adam sees *Eve*. The *sweater* is on the chair. John opened the *door*.

Source: From Bloom, *Language Development,* by permission of The MIT Press, Cambridge, Massachusetts. Copyright 1970 by Lois Bloom.

Nouns in the *Locative* case specify the location for the action or state named by the verb. Nouns in the *Objective* case have a role in the state or action named by the verb that depends directly upon the meaning of the verb. Although case grammar is quite new and is not yet fully developed, the preceding cases are widely agreed upon (but see McCawley, 1968).

The relevance of case grammar to Stage I language is apparent from what we have said about language development to this point. The semantic relations that characterize two-word utterances (see Table 9.1) are precisely the kinds of case relations specified by case grammar. Moreover, the cognitive-semantic relations that have been inferred from one-word utterances are similar to the case relations specified by case grammar. According to the case grammar model, language acquisition involves the development of various categories such as agent and action, rules for combining these categories for various verbs, rules that map deep structures onto surface structures, and so on.

An Evaluation of Case Grammar   In comparison to the transformational model of language at Stage I, the case grammar model has several advantages. One is that the categories of knowledge proposed by case grammar provide a more accurate description of children's linguistic knowledge than does transformational grammar. Recall that transformational grammar includes very broad and abstract syntactic categories such as subject and object. As indicated earlier, there is some evidence that suggests that children in the first two years develop categories such as "agent" whereas there is little hard evidence that they have developed categories such as "subject" by that age.

Although the case grammar model provides a good first step toward describing linguistic competence at Stage I, that model currently confronts numerous difficulties. One problem is that verbs are often absent in two-word utterances, yet the verb is of central importance in case grammar. Why is such a central part of the sentence not included? One might argue that the answer to that question is to be provided by a theory of performance and not by a theory of competence. However, it is well to remember that competence is inferred from performance, and it is all too easy to attribute to children knowledge that they do not possess. That consideration brings us to the second problem with the case grammar model: it equates the categories of child knowledge with those of adult knowledge. Case grammar models can indicate that particular verbs may have different case frames or roles for children and adults. Similarly, these models can indicate that particular roles that may be obligatory in adult language may be optional in child language, and so on. Nevertheless, case grammar models ascribe knowledge of the basic semantic categories to both children and adults. In fact, there is very little empirical information available concerning comparisons of the child's and the adult's knowledge of categories such as "experience," "locative," and so on (but see Braine & Wells, 1978), and further research in this area is needed badly.

Grammatical analyses of Stage I language have made a valuable contribution to the analysis of language development. The case grammar model in particular has helped to guide research and to draw attention to questions concerning the nature of the child's conceptual knowledge, the relationships between language and cognition, and the importance of semantic knowledge in language development. Models of grammar, however, do not specify how language develops as it does. In the next section, we shall inquire into the antecedents of the early word combinations of children.

The Origins of Early Word Combinations

The question of how language is acquired is so immense and intricate that many contemporary theorists, particularly those of the psycholinguistic orientation, have adopted a strategy that is intended to clarify and simplify the task of analyzing language development. Specifically, they have viewed the first step in studying language development as that of defining the biological bases for language. By defining the aspects of language that are rooted in phylogeny, they have hoped to define more precisely which aspects of language are acquired. Moreover, they have tried to define what it is that ontogeny operates upon.

The preceding strategy has brought many benefits, primary among which is the continued recognition of the contribution of phylogeny to language development. However, that strategy has given rise to several problems. The first problem is that some theorists have been led to draw strict dichotomies between phylogeny and ontogeny and have essentially placed the problem of language acquisition within the unacceptable framework of the nature-nurture dichotomy. A second problem is that for ethical and technological reasons, it is very difficult to obtain physiological or genetic data concerning the contribution of phylogeny to language development. Accordingly, much of the evidence that has been offered concerning the role of phylogeny is behavioral and, in many instances, conceptual in nature. This is not necessarily a problem, but in the absence of hard physiological and genetic evidence, it is perhaps too easy to prematurely or unnecessarily ascribe some aspects of language development to our biological heritage. The third problem is related to the second: The curiosity of behavioral scientists (particularly nonbiologists) is often put to rest once a particular phenomenon is said to be part of our biological heritage. The problem is that we may fail to notice instances in which a phenomenon of language development is attributed incorrectly to our phylogenetic legacy.

None of the preceding problems are inherent in the strategy of beginning the analysis of language with an analysis of the biological foundations of language. Nevertheless, these problems have arisen all too often in the study of language, and it is wise to keep them in mind during the following discussions of the origins of language.

Phylogenetic Antecedents Much of the evidence concerning the contribution of phylogeny to early word combinations is behavioral rather than physiological or anatomical. Perhaps the main evidence for a strong biological contribution to early word combinations comes from the observations concerning structural regularity and universality (see pp. 372–373). Recall that early word combinations seem to involve a rather small number of combinations of conceptual-semantic categories such as agent and object, and that these combinations are general across a wide variety of languages.

Why is it that the early word combinations of children who speak such different languages and who live in such different locations share such striking underlying similarities? One answer that has been offered is that the universal aspects of language development reflect our biological heritage for language (for example, Lenneberg, 1967; McNeill, 1970). Indeed, those universal aspects of language development, like the universal aspects of adult language (see pp. 315, 332), have been said to reflect our innate knowledge of language (for example, Chomsky, 1972).

The claim that the universal aspects of language development reflect our biological heritage is problematic. The main problem with this view is that it is circular, given the evidence upon which it is currently based. Presently, the strongest evidence that the universal aspects of language development result from biological factors is that these aspects are universal. But that is exactly what needs to be explained. The assertion that these universal aspects arise from biological factors is best viewed as suggestive until more specific genetic and physiological data are available.

In the past, some theorists (for example, Lenneberg, 1967) have argued that it is not the universals of language development alone that suggest a strong contribution of phylogeny to language acquisition. Rather, it is the observation that those aspects of language development are species-specific that gives strength to that argument. However, the evidence reviewed in Chapter 8 (see pp. 346–355) concerning the linguistic abilities of chimps has called into question the view that the universals of language and language development are specific to humans. Indeed, the early sign combinations of Washoe are characterized by many of the same semantic relations that occur universally in the early word combinations of humans. Would we attribute innate linguistic knowledge to nonhumans that acquire language under conditions similar to those under which humans do? Much more research remains to be done, but it is too early to claim with confidence that all of the universal aspects of language development are specific to humans.

A very important question that we have only begun to explore concerns how phylogeny affects language development. Some theorists (for example, Chomsky, N., 1965, 1972; Lenneberg, 1967) have proposed that many of the deeper aspects of language develop through the growth and maturation of language-specific structures and processes, with the ontogenetic environment simply activating what is latent within the organism. However, other possibilities exist. For example, to a considerable extent, language development may be mapped onto or synchronous with cognitive development (for example, Bloom, L. M. & Lahey, 1978; Clark, H. H. & Clark, 1977; Schlesinger, 1977). Some aspects of language development may reflect cognitive development, and the universals of language development may reflect the universal aspects of cognitive development (cf. Slobin, 1973). In turn, the universal aspects of cognitive development may reflect some of the universal features of the environments that humans inhabit. For example, linguistic relationships such as agent-action may be based upon nonlinguistic knowledge of those relationships. Furthermore, cognitive knowledge of these relationships may be based upon the occurrence of universal events, such as animate beings acting upon the inanimate aspects of the environment in the ways we call "chasing," "holding," "throwing," "building," and so on. It is hoped that future research will clarify the contribution of phylogeny and the nature of the interplay between phylogeny and ontogeny in the universal aspects of language development.

Ontogenetic Antecedents of Early Word Combinations   During their first two years, children come to distinguish between various objects, and they also come to discriminate the relations that the objects can enter, such as the object-locative relation. Knowledge of the object-locative relation could provide the cognitive basis for utterances such as *sweater chair,* just as knowledge of the agent-locative relation could provide the basis for utterances such as *Mommy sock.*

The contribution of knowledge about nonlinguistic events to the occurrence of early word combinations may also be seen in the linguistic creativity of the child. Once the child begins to combine words, the child soon produces a considerable number of two-word combinations, many of which are novel. The novelty of these word combinations arises in part from the novelty of the nonverbal events that the child speaks of. A child who knows the words *doggie* and *run* may say *doggie run* upon first seeing a dog running. That view is supported by the results of an experiment by Whitehurst (1972). Social and food reinforcers were used to teach two-year-olds to say certain nonsense syllables in the presence of various colors and unusual figures. Then he combined some of the colors and figures and taught the children to respond to each color-figure combination by naming first the color and then the figure. Finally, he presented novel combinations consisting of colors used in previous combinations and figures that had not appeared in previous combinations. The results were that the children correctly named the novel combinations although they had never before seen them or been reinforced for responding to them. Thus novel utterances can be based upon novel stimulus combinations, and at least some linguistic creativity seems to follow from the novelty of the stimuli that occur in the environment of the child.

We have much to learn about the antecedents of cognitive knowledge. Exactly why is it that children seem to divide the world up into categories such as agent and action? One possibility is that these categories are part of the biological heritage of our species and arise relatively independently of the ontogenetic environment. Another possibility is that the ontogenetic environments that humans are exposed to contain events that may be most efficiently categorized as agents, actions, and so on. At any rate, questions concerning the nature and origin of cognitive categories are similar to questions concerning the nature and origin of stimulus classes. Just as phylogeny and ontogeny jointly determine the stimulus control relations that develop in an individual's lifetime, so they may determine the cognitive categories that develop in an individual's lifetime. This view is already supported, albeit for categories other than those we have been discussing, by an impressive amount of developmental research (cf. Flavell, 1977).

In concluding, we should note that very little is known about how cognitive knowledge is utilized in language. What is the nature of the transfer processes whereby children come to map language onto cognitive knowledge? The process whereby children do so has been said by many authors to involve the formation and testing of hypotheses, but it remains to be specified what these hypotheses are, where they originate, how they are modified, and so on.

Communicative Linguistic Antecedents   Earlier in the chapter, we mentioned that parents engage their children in communicative exchanges at an early age. As children develop, most parents continue to apply pressure to the child to communicate. Moreover, adults change their conversational demands according to the linguistic and nonlinguistic communicative skills of the child (de Villiers & deVilliers, 1978; Lewis & Rosenblum, 1977; Snow, 1977). Almost anything a newborn infant does will be accepted by the mother as an appropriate "turn" in a "conversational" interchange, as the following interaction illustrates:

MOTHER: Hello. Give me a smile (*then gently pokes infant in the ribs*).
INFANT: (*Yawns*)
MOTHER: Sleepy, are you? You woke up too early today.
INFANT: (*Opens fist*)
MOTHER: (*Touching infant's hand*) What are you looking at? Can you see
  something?
INFANT: (*Grasps mother's finger*)
MOTHER: Oh, that's what you wanted. In a friendly mood, then. Come on,
  give us a smile.   (Clark, H. H., & Clark, 1977, p. 329)

As the child's linguistic skills develop, the parents may no longer accept a
smile or a grasping gesture as an appropriate conversational turn. Rather, they
seem to demand verbal interaction, often by repeatedly asking a question.

The exact role played by increasing conversational demands has yet to be
determined, but it does seem likely that these demands contribute to the occurrence of early word combinations. For example, parents often ask children
questions that cannot be answered in a single word, and encouraging children
to answer these questions may facilitate the development of multiword utterances. An important path for future research in language development is to
specify carefully the nature and the effects (for example, discriminative, reinforcing, and so on) of the social stimuli that are described by the phrase "communication pressure." Of course, the blade of communication cuts both ways.
As the child comes to produce multiword utterances, the child may more effectively alter the behavior of others and the inanimate aspects of his environment. Thus another important topic for research is the question of what the
consequences of the child's utterances are and how they contribute to language development.

To this point, we have seen that adults pressure children to communicate,
but exactly what do parents and others say to young children? In the past, it
has sometimes been assumed that children are typically exposed to a complex
corpus of utterances that is characterized by grammatical errors, hesitations,
and so on. That description may accurately describe adult speech, but recent
research has shown conclusively that children are, as most parents know, typically exposed to a very different type of speech than adults are exposed to (cf.
Lewis & Rosenblum, 1977; Snow & Ferguson, 1977). Compared to speech addressed to adults, speech addressed to younger children (for example, 2-year-
olds) by both adults and older children is slow, simple, grammatical, and repe-
titious (de Villiers & de Villiers, 1978; Sachs, Brown, & Salerno, 1976). For
example, the utterances that adults address to 2-year-olds typically contain
fewer than four words, whereas utterances that adults address to other adults
typically include over eight words (Phillips, 1973). The simplicity of the utterances that are addressed to young children does not arise from brevity alone,
for those utterances usually do not contain function words (for example, articles and prepositions), negative clauses, negatives, and so on.

Overall, the available evidence suggests that older children and adults
modify their speech to match the linguistic skills of the young child. It is as if

others in the child's environment give the child a series of "language lessons" that are graded in difficulty and that are just one step above the level of the child's linguistic skill at a particular moment (for further discussion of this topic, see Clark, H. H. & Clark, 1977; de Villiers & de Villiers, 1978). Further research should elucidate whether these lessons are necessary or merely sufficient for the segmentation of individual words, the production of two-word combinations, and so on (cf. Sachs & Johnson, 1976).

Up to this point, we have considered only the development of the rudiments of language during the first two years of life. Let us now examine the development of some of the more complex aspects of language that occurs beyond the age of two.

ELABORATIONS OF LANGUAGE

Shortly after children first combine words, they begin to produce three-word utterances. And soon after that they begin to produce four-word utterances. The remarkable rapidity with which children's utterances increase in length is illustrated in Fig. 9.3 which shows the mean utterance length for three children

Fig. 9.3 The increase in the mean length of utterance for three children between the ages of 1½ and 4 years. (From Brown, R., 1973. Copyright © 1973 by the President and Fellows of Harvard College.)

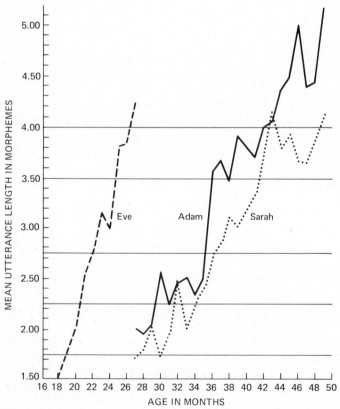

during the period from one and a half to just over four years. As the mean utterance length increases, so too does the structural complexity of these utterances. Whereas the 2-year-old typically produces very simple utterances that have a telegraphic quality and often require the aid of contextual factors for proper interpretation, the 5-year-old can produce a rich array of grammatical sentences, including passives, questions, those with subordinate clauses, and so on.

A complete description of later language development is beyond the scope of this discussion (see Clark, H. H., & Clark, 1977; de Villiers & de Villiers, 1978). For our purposes, it will be sufficient to consider those aspects of phonological, syntactic and semantic development that are currently seen as having important implications for theories of how language acquisition occurs.

Phonological Development

One of the most striking features of phonological development is the gap between comprehension and production. For example, Smith (1973) put drawings of a mouse and a mouth in another room and asked his son on several occasions to bring him a particular drawing. He observed that his son could reliably retrieve the requested drawing, thus indicating that his son could distinguish between the two words. Yet his son was unable to produce that difference himself, for he said (maus) for both drawings. Many similar observations have been reported in the literature (for example, Dodd, 1975).[4]

The observations that children often fail to produce distinctions they comprehend suggests that many of the phonological errors children make reflect problems in production. Children often simplify adult words (cf. Smith, N. V., 1973) by omitting final consonants (for example, *ball* becomes [ba]), reducing clusters of consonants (for example, *cry* becomes [ai]), omitting unstressed syllables (for example, *away* becomes [we]), and by duplicating one syllable (for example, *kitchen* becomes [KIKI]). The frequency of the simplifications decreases markedly between the ages of two and four years, and that decrease seems to reflect not so much the child's knowledge of phonology as the child's articulatory skills (Clark, H. H., & Clark, 1977).

The observation that many phonological errors stem from problems in production has important implications. One is that it may be difficult to determine the occurrence of imitative utterances. For example, consider the following dialogue:

FATHER: Say "jump."
CHILD: Dup.
FATHER: No, "jump."
CHILD: Dup.
FATHER: No, "jummmp."
CHILD: Only Daddy can say "dup!"   (Smith, N. V., 1973, p. 10)

In this type of interchange, the child appears to be trying to imitate the father's pronunciation of "jump," yet the child is unable to match the father's pronunciation (and clearly knows it). Since the form of the child's response depended upon the form of the father's response, the child's response *Dup* could be said to be imitative. The problem is that the response *Dup* is typically not emitted by adult speakers of English, and adult observers may tend to view that response as a linguistic creation of the child rather than an imitative response. Consequently, imitation may seem to be less pervasive than it actually is (see Whitehurst, 1978), and that consideration will become important when we later examine the role of imitation in the development of language.

There is another important implication of the observation that many phonological errors stem from production or articulation problems: The child's knowledge of phonology may not be accurately reflected in the child's own speech (cf. Dodd, 1975). Since the child's knowledge of phonology is not accurately indicated by what he or she says, a complete assessment of a child's phonological knowledge must include tests of both comprehension and production. In general, theories of knowledge must be based upon tests of both comprehension and production. Ultimately, theories of language development must not only incorporate but also account for the differences between production and comprehension.

The Development of Rules We pointed out above that children may make many of the phonological distinctions that adults do, although they do not produce all the sounds they can distinguish. A child who can discriminate the [s] sound in *stick* and *stop* may be unable to produce that sound and may instead say *tick* and *top*. According to that view, once a child can articulate the [s] sound when it is followed by a consonant, the child should be able to emit that sound in a wide variety of the appropriate linguistic contexts. Thus the child should be able to say not only *stick,* but also *stop* and other similar words (Clark, H. H. & Clark, 1977). In fact, this seems to be what happens, for once a new speech sound is produced, that sound tends to be produced in a variety of words (Smith, N. V. 1973, 1975). Thus it appears that children do not learn to produce each sound in each word separately. Rather, they seem to learn and produce particular sounds systematically. This observation, which is supported by experimental results, has led to the view that children learn not only which speech sounds are phonemic in their language but also rules governing the occurrence of those sounds in their language.

At this point, a few words of caution are in order. The knowledge and speech of children may not always be as systematic as a description of knowledge in terms of rules may imply. For example, it has been reported that children sometimes come to make an appropriate phonemic contrast in some instances but not in others (Ferguson & Farwell, 1975). The acquisition of knowledge about phonemes and how they may be combined may not be an all-or-none affair. The range of linguistic rules may be like the boundaries of many natural concepts (cf. pp. 279–288): They may be loosely defined at a particular instant and may be subject to considerable changes during development. Thus the statement that a child has learned a particular phonological rule may have some heuristic value, but it only begins to define the child's knowledge.

Syntactic Development

Now we shall consider some of the elaborations of syntax that occur in child language beyond Stage I. Some of the changes that occur seem to be continuous with the linguistic skills that were present at Stage I. For example, many of the child's three-word utterances are agent-action-object constructions, which are extensions of the agent-action and action-object constructions that occurred during Stage I. Other changes in child language seem to bear no such clear relation to the linguistic skills that developed during Stage I. One of those changes concerns the acquisition of grammatical morphemes.

The Acquisition of Grammatical Morphemes   In most of the two-word combinations of children, grammatical morphemes are conspicuously absent. Articles, prepositions, and the markers for possession, plurality, past tense, and so on are all missing. These grammatical morphemes develop gradually over a period of several years. Of primary interest is the observation that these morphemes develop in a very regular order (Brown, R., 1973; de Villiers, J. G., & deVilliers, 1978). These morphemes and the order in which they are acquired are shown in Table 9.3. Interestingly, the order of acquisition of these morphemes can be predicted fairly well on the basis of grammatical and semantic complexity. For example, the present progressive morpheme -ing is derived by the application of the progressive affix transformation. In contrast, the contractible auxiliary is derived by the application of the progressive affix transformation and three others (cf. Brown, R., 1973). Accordingly, the contractible auxiliary is said to be grammatically more complex than the present progressive. And as Table 9.3 shows, the present progressive morpheme is acquired before the contractible auxiliary. In general, morpheme X will be acquired before morpheme Y if morpheme X is derivationally simpler than morpheme Y. Similar analyses have shown that the acquisition order of the grammatical morphemes is predictable on the basis of the relative semantic complexity of these morphemes (Brown, R., 1973). Relative semantic complexity is determined by comparing the number of semantic dimensions correlated with the various morphemes. For example, the third person singular (-s) is said to be semantically more complex than the plural (-s) since the former morpheme is correlated with the dimensions labelled "number" and "earlier in time," whereas the latter morpheme is correlated only with "number." The correlation between either grammatical complexity or semantic complexity and order of acquisition is about .80 (Brown, R., 1973).[5] The important point for our purposes is that there is a relatively high correlation between the order in which the morphemes are acquired and the linguistic complexity of those morphemes (Deutsch & Pechman, 1978).

The Development of Syntactic Rules   Another feature of the acquisition of grammatical morphemes is that they are acquired and applied in a highly systematic fashion, and that often results in both linguistic advances and errors. As an example, consider the acquisition of the past tense form of verbs in English. Children come to produce the correct past tense forms of verbs in

TABLE 9.3   Fourteen Grammatical Morphemes (Suffixes and Function Words) Listed According to the Order in which They Are Acquired

Morpheme	Meaning
1. Present progressive: *-ing*	Ongoing process
2. Preposition: *in*	Containment
3. Preposition: *on*	Support
4. Plural: *-s*	Number
5. Past irregular: e.g., *went*	Earlier in time relative to time of speaking
6. Possessive: *-'s*	Possession
7. Uncontractible copula *be:* e.g., *are, was*	Number; earlier in time
8. Articles: *the, a*	Definite/indefinite
9. Past regular: *-ed*	Earlier in time
10. Third person regular: *-s*	Number; earlier in time
11. Third person irregular: e.g., *has, does*	Number; earlier in time
12. Uncontractible auxiliary *be:* e.g., *is, were*	Number; earlier in time; ongoing process
13. Contractible copula *be:* e.g., *-'s, -'re*	Number; earlier in time
14. Contractible auxiliary *be:* e.g., *-'s, -'re*	Number; earlier in time; ongoing process

Source: After R. Brown, 1973. Copyright © 1973 by the President and Fellows of Harvard College.

four stages. At first (in Stage I as described above), few or no past tense forms are produced. When children first begin producing verbs in the past tense, they usually use the correct past tense forms of irregular verbs such as *come* and *break.* Thus children initially say *came, broke,* and so on. In the next stage, children use the past tense morpheme for regular verbs (*-ed*) and produce words such as *walked, baked,* and so on. At that stage, a curious thing occurs: The child stops using the correct past tense forms of the irregular verbs which were previously mastered and applies *-ed* to all verbs, thereby producing ungrammatical forms such as *camed* and *breaked* (Ervin, 1964). The errors are called *overgeneralizations* or *overregularizations,* and they often persist for several years until the final stage is attained. In the final stage, children distinguish between regular and irregular verbs, and they are usually correct in converting verbs to the past tense form. Similar stages characterize the acquisition of other suffixes and function words, and these stages occur in a variety of languages (cf. Ferguson & Slobin, 1973).

The observation that children apply past tense markers in a highly systematic manner, together with the occurrence of overgeneralizations, has led most psycholinguists to believe that the acquisition of syntax, like the acquisition of phonology, is best viewed as a process in which children actively construct rules. Experimental evidence also suggests that the acquisition of grammatical morphemes entails the use of rules. For example, Berko (1958) used an ingenious procedure to test whether children at various ages had learned the morphophonemic rules that are involved in the pluralization of nouns. She showed children pictures of a single nonsense form, and simultaneously named the form with a nonsense syllable by saying "This is a wug." Next, she showed a picture of two of the nonsense forms and asked the child to complete a sentence that required the child to pluralize the nonsense syllable. That is, she showed the picture and said "Now there is another one. There are two of them. There are two ———." The results were that the children between 4 and 5 years old correctly pluralized words like *wug* on about 75% of the trials, and children between 5½ and 7 years old responded correctly on over 95% of the trials. These results support the view that children learn linguistic rules and that older children have greater mastery of the rules than younger children.

The Development of Transformation Rules As children begin to combine words into complex sentences, they come to construct sentences that may be said to express more than one proposition. For example, they come to produce interrogative sentences such as "Why did you cut the tree?". That sentence is said to express two propositions, which may be stated as "you cut the tree" and "tell me why you did that." The production of well-formed interrogative sentences marks an important occurrence in the development of language: the development of transformation rules. As we saw in Chapter 8, transformation rules are some of the most important aspects of human language since they convert deep structures into surface structures. To examine the development of a few transformation rules, we shall consider the development of one type of interrogative sentence.

First let us examine the transformations that are involved in the linguistic derivation of adult interrogatives. One type of question we often ask is called the *yes/no question,* for it can be answered with a simple "yes" or "no." To see the transformations involved in yes/no questions, consider sentences (3) through (8).

(3) Can he cook?
(4) He can cook.
(5) Have they been sleeping?
(6) They have been sleeping.
(7) Does she see the eagle?
(8) She sees the eagle.

Sentences (3) through (8) include three interrogatives, each of which is followed by the corresponding declarative. Notice that in each of the questions, as in all yes/no questions, an auxiliary verb (for example, *can, had,* and so on) precedes the subject noun phrase. Thus, *can* precedes *he* in (3), and *Have* precedes *they* in (5). The inversion of the auxiliary verb and the subject is called the *question transformation.* In sentences that lack an auxiliary verb, for example, (8), the verb *do* is introduced into the sentence, and the *do* form is marked for number and tense (for example, *does* is present and singular, whereas *did* is past and either singular or plural). The introduction of the verb *do* occurs via the *do-insertion transformation.* Sentences such as (7) involve the do-insertion transformation, and they also involve the question transformation, which moves the auxiliary form of *do* in front of the subject.

In learning to ask yes/no questions, children pass through stages that are defined structurally in terms of the presence or absence of the transformation rules described above (Klima & Bellugi, 1966). In the first stage, children ask a small number of yes/no questions, and these questions are distinguished from declarative sentences by a rising intonation at the end of the sentence (for example, *Sit CHAIR?*). The first stage is clearly pretransformational, for there are no auxiliary verbs (and therefore no question or do-insertion transformations).

In the second stage, children's questions have become longer (*See my doggie?*), and articles and modifiers appear. However, auxiliary verbs have not yet developed, and there is no evidence for the acquisition of the question and the do-insertion transformations. Although some forms of *can* (for example, *can't*) and *do* (for example, *d'you*) occur in the second stage, these words appear in a very small number of forms and in a limited number of contexts. For example, *d'you* appeared as a single word at the beginning of questions such as *D'you want its turn?*, and forms of *do* did not occur in other contexts in which adults say it. Whereas the adult form of a *Do you want . . .* question involves the do-insertion and question transformations, the stage-two form of a *Do you want . . .* question seems to involve the operation of the following phrase-structure rules (Dale, 1976):

> Q → d'you want
> S → (Q) + NP + VP.

On a broader level, the development of transformation rules is often preceded by the development of less powerful phrase-structure rules, and this phenomenon seems to be general during the acquisition of language.

By the third stage, major changes in syntax have occurred, and the system of auxiliary verbs has developed. In yes/no questions, the subject and the auxiliary verb are correctly inverted, as in *Can I have a piece of paper?* Additionally, *do* is introduced into the sentence if it is necessary. Thus both the question and the do-insertion transformations have been acquired by the third stage. However, errors are made in adding the tense and number suffixes to the auxiliary verb, and incorrect forms such as *Does lions walk?* are produced.

At stage three, the transformations involved in the formation of adult English questions have developed, but these rules are not applied in child speech as they are in adult speech. For example, when auxiliary verbs are present in yes/no questions, they are inverted with the subject, and the children are said to have mastered the question transformation. In contrast, when auxiliary verbs are present in wh-questions (for example, *When can she come?*), they are not inverted with the subjects. Thus the question transformation is often not included in the formation of wh-questions even though that transformation has clearly been acquired by the third stage. Clearly, the domain of application of the question transformation is not the same in stage three as it is in adulthood. The important point is that it is an oversimplification to believe that once a generative rule (or an elementary operation therein: for example, addition or deletion) has been acquired, that rule can be applied in all of the required contexts. The boundaries for the application of linguistic rules, like the boundaries of nonverbal concepts, can change during development, and the boundaries that exist at a particular point in time must be determined empirically.

The Later Development of Syntax   A good bit of the acquisition of syntactic rules seems to occur between the ages of about 2 and 5 years. However, the acquisition of syntax is not complete (as was once believed) by age 5 (cf. Chomsky, C., 1969; Horgan, 1978; Palermo & Molfese, 1972). For example, children of that age have only begun to produce and understand complex sentences that contain adverbial clauses (for example, *When she was young, she lived in the jungle*), complements (for example, *Tell me what to feed the cat*), and so on. To take a different but more concrete example, most children at age 5 are unable to correctly comprehend sentences in which the subjects or objects (as indicated in the deep structure of the sentences) are not apparent in the surface structures of the sentences. For example, children under 7 years of age often fail to recognize the differences between sentences such as *The wolf is happy to bite* and *The duck is fun to bite* (Cromer, 1970). By the age of 7 almost all children correctly comprehend both types of sentence (see also Chomsky, C., 1969; Kessel, 1970).

These observations, together with many others (cf. Clark, H. H., & Clark, 1977; deVilliers & deVilliers, 1978), suggest that the ability to discern important grammatical relationships develops very slowly, and that process is by no means completed during the first few years of life. It is in many ways unsurprising that children before age 6 are unable to pick out subjects and objects in sentences such as the preceding. For one thing, in most English sentences, the subject and the object are indicated by the word order. Another consideration is that children can often rely upon nonverbal contextual factors or upon nonlinguistic knowledge to facilitate comprehension (Shatz, 1978). For example, Strohner and Nelson (1974) observed that young children understand sentences such as (9) but not (10).

(9) The baby is fed by the girl.
(10) The girl is fed by the baby.

Whereas sentence (9) corresponds to the child's apparent knowledge of who feeds whom, sentence (10) does not. The point is that children are rarely required to comprehend sentences on the basis of syntactic information alone. The importance of syntactic factors in comprehension probably increases as children are required to understand and produce sentences that describe past events, future events, hypothetical events, and so on, without the aid of contextual factors. In future studies of syntactic competence, it will be important to control carefully for the influence of nonlinguistic, contextual factors.

Semantic Development

The inadequacies of the syntactically based theories of linguistic performance (see pp. 332–339), together with the shortage of careful theory and observation in the realm of semantics, gave rise in the 1970s to a large upsurge of research into semantics and semantic development. The current literature concerning semantic development is far too voluminous to be reviewed here. For our purposes, it will be sufficient to focus upon a few aspects of semantic development that have implications for theories of the acquisition of semantics.

Semantic Components and Child Language   In the same way that some semantic theories (for example, Katz & Fodor, 1963) have represented the meanings of words as configurations of semantic features or components, theorists of semantic development (for example, Clark, E. V., 1973; Clark, H. H., & Clark, 1977) have described the development of word meanings as a process of differentiating and combining semantic components. In general, children may be said to have acquired a particular semantic component, say, *animate,* when they use words that include that component in a systematic and different way from words that do not include that component. For example, if a child can state that people, dogs, cats, birds and so on can move by themselves, but that rocks, chairs and clocks cannot, then the child shows verbal knowledge of the distinction between animate and inanimate objects and can be said to have acquired the component labelled *animate.* That knowledge is typically reflected in the production of statements such as *The girl walked home* but not *The boulder strolled away.* In short, a child can be said to have a particular semantic component when the child's verbal behavior is controlled reliably by the stimulus dimension named by the component label.

The semantic components of a language have proven to be difficult to define, for words can be broken down logically into a large number of components, but only some of these components may be "psychologically real." Some semantic components such as *male* and *female* may seem to be easily identifiable. Since these components are all that distinguish between the meanings of, say, *boy* and *girl,* they may be said to have been acquired if the child says *boy* and *girl* in the presence of the appropriate stimuli. However, upon reflection, it is apparent that a child may distinguish between boys and girls on the basis of dimensions that are odd from the viewpoint of adults (for example, the dimension of hair length), and it would then be inaccurate to say that the child has acquired the components *male* and *female.* A similar but related problem is that even if components such as *male* and *female* have been mastered by a child, they may not correspond exactly to the adult versions, and it may be a mistake to equate the components held in common by children and adults. The exact nature of the semantic components of the child are best determined by empirical means, and the methodology of studies of stimulus control (see Chapter 5) is of value in that undertaking.

Semantic Complexity and Semantic Development   Despite the preceding caveats concerning the definition of semantic components, the analysis of semantic components has contributed to the description of semantic development. For example, the order of acquisition of verbs of possession (for example, *give, take, pay, trade, buy, sell* and *spend*) is predictable on the basis of semantic complexity (Gentner, 1975), which is defined in terms of semantic components. Generally, one word may be said to be semantically more complex than another if that word includes all of the semantic components of the other, and more. Of the verbs of possession, *give* and *take* are the simplest, for they include fewer semantic components than, say, *pay* and *trade*. Whereas *give* and *take* both include a component that may be described as "transfer of an object from one person to another," *pay* and *trade* include that component and others: an obligation involving money (*pay*) or a mutual contract for exchanging goods (*trade*). Similarly, a verb such as *trade* is semantically simpler than a verb such as *sell*, for the latter includes not only the components of a transfer and a mutual contract for exchange, but also the component of an obligation involving money (cf. Bendix, 1966; Clark, H. H., & Clark, 1977). The ordering of possession verbs in terms of semantic complexity, then, is as follows:

(*give, take*) < (*pay, trade*) < (*buy, sell, spend*)

In a study of the acquisition of the verbs of possession, Gentner (1975) asked children between the ages of 3 and 9 years to give, trade or sell objects according to the instructions of the experimenter. The results were that the order of acquisition of the verbs corresponded to the ordering according to semantic complexity shown above, with the simpler verbs being acquired earlier. Specifically, *give* and *take*, which had been acquired before the experiment, were acquired before *pay* and *trade*, which were acquired before *buy, spend* and *sell*. In other studies (for example, Clark, E. V., & Garnica, 1974; Haviland & Clark, 1974), the order of acquisition of words other than possession verbs has been shown to be predictable on the basis of semantic complexity.

The exact course of later semantic development remains to be plotted. Although it is clear that children learn not only word meanings but also how to combine words in semantically appropriate ways, there is currently no precise record of the ontogeny of semantic knowledge. Despite the current limitations of our knowledge of the course of natural language development, some of the factors that may contribute to the elaboration of language have been identified, and we shall now focus upon those factors.

THE ANTECEDENTS OF LANGUAGE DEVELOPMENT BEYOND STAGE I

In keeping with our view that all behavior reflects the interplay between the biology and the experience of the organism, we shall inquire into both the phylogenetic and the ontogenetic origins of some of the more complex aspects of language. In that undertaking, we should keep in mind that as the organism develops, it becomes increasingly difficult to discern the unique contributions of phylogeny or ontogeny.

Phylogeny and the Elaboration of Language

Earlier in this chapter, we saw that extensive changes in the anatomy of peripheral structures such as the pharynx must occur before the child can produce the full range of human speech sounds. In this section, we shall see that the full development of language seems to depend upon changes in the central nervous system as well as changes in peripheral anatomy.

Cerebral specialization   In adult humans, the two cerebral hemispheres perform very different psychological functions, and the left hemisphere of most adults seems to be specialized for language. The most striking evidence that certain parts of the human brain are specialized for language comes from the study of people with "split brains" (Kinsbourne & Smith, 1974). Normally, the cerebral hemispheres are connected by a large body of fibers called the *corpus callosum*. The corpus callosum transmits information between the two hemispheres, thus permitting the hemispheres to function in a unified manner. In people with split brains, the corpus callosum has been cut (usually for the sake of controlling severe epileptic seizures), and communication between the two hemispheres is drastically reduced. Through studying the behavior of split-brain humans, one can assess separately the abilities of each half of the brain in a person whose cerebral hemispheres are connected.

Various tests of split-brain patients show that most linguistic abilities are localized in the left hemisphere. For example, in one test, the patient is instructed to stare at a dot on a screen and visual stimuli are then flashed briefly on one side of the screen. If the stimulus, for instance, a picture of a nut, is flashed on the right side of the screen, the visual information is relayed to only the left hemisphere, and the patient can report seeing a nut. In contrast, if the picture of the nut is flashed on the left side of the screen, the visual information is relayed to only the right hemisphere, but in this case the patient cannot report seeing a nut. One might think at this point that the right hemisphere is either blind or stupid. However, that is not the case, for objects shown to the right hemisphere can be retrieved by touch with the left hand, which is connected only to the right hemisphere. Furthermore, objects that are shown to the right hemisphere and then selected and held in the left hand can be neither described verbally nor selected by the right hand! Clearly, information presented to only one hemisphere is inaccessible to the other hemisphere. It is as if there were two independent persons living within the same skull.

In general, the left hemisphere is specialized for language, whereas the right hemisphere is specialized for the perception of patterns and melodies (Sperry, 1968). For example, if two different verbal stimuli are presented simultaneously to the two ears of a typical right-handed person and the person is asked to identify the stimuli that were presented, performance is better for the stimuli that were presented to the right ear. In contrast, if the stimuli were musical melodies, the person identifies the stimuli presented to the left ear better than those that had been presented to the right ear (cf. Kimura, 1964, 1973; Shankweiler & Studdert-Kennedy, 1967; Studdert-Kennedy, Shankweiler, & Pisoni, 1972). Presumably, the *right-ear advantage* with verbal stimuli results from the dominance of the connections between the right ear and the left hemisphere.

Although the left hemisphere is typically specialized for language and is dominant over the right hemisphere in performing linguistic functions, the right hemisphere does have some linguistic ability (for a review, see Nebes, 1974). For example, adults who have sustained damage to the left hemisphere can acquire the same sorts of linguistic skills as those that have been taught to chimpanzees (see Hughes, 1975; Premack & Premack, 1974); and the linguistic abilities of the right hemisphere, as measured by tests for comprehension rather than production, have turned out to be more extensive than they were formerly believed to be (Nebes, 1974).

Cerebral Specialization and Language Development   Up to the age of about 5 years, changes occur in the organization of the brain, and these changes appear to have important implications for the development of language (Krashen, S., 1975; see also Lenneberg, 1967). At birth, the part of the left hemisphere that has been shown to be involved in performing linguistic functions is larger than the corresponding part of the right hemisphere (Witelson & Pallie, 1973), but the two hemispheres are not functionally specialized as they are later (but see Molfese, Nunez, Siebert & Ramanaiah, 1976). If the left hemisphere is damaged extensively during the first few years of life, linguistic functions cease, but only temporarily. Language is then reacquired with repetition of the typical stages, and the linguistic functions are performed by the right hemisphere. However, the brain apparently loses some of its plasticity during development, and the chances of recovering from damage to the left hemisphere become progressively worse with age. The exact time at which cerebral plasticity decreases and cerebral specialization is completed is uncertain, and the estimates range from before 5 years (Witelson & Pallie, 1973) to puberty (Lenneberg, 1967). Once cerebral specialization is completed, extensive damage to the left hemisphere in most individuals produces a severe and permanent deficit in language (Penfield & Roberts, 1959). Apparently, then, part of the functioning brain must be specialized for language if language is to be acquired, and the development of language thus depends in part upon the development of cerebral specialization.[6]

The Critical Period Hypothesis   The preceding observations, together with the well-known difficulty of acquiring a second language after puberty (cf. Krashen, S., 1975), have led some (for example, Lenneberg, 1967) to postulate that the years between birth and puberty define the critical period for the development of language. However, that view, which may be called the *critical period hypothesis,* may be questioned on several grounds (Krashen, S. D., 1973). First, there is at least one well-documented case that may contradict this hypothesis (Curtiss, Fromkin, Krashen, Rigler, & Rigler, 1974; Fromkin, Krashen, Curtiss, Rigler, & Rigler, 1974). The case involved a girl named Genie who had been severely mistreated by her parents. Until the age of nearly 14 (beyond the onset of puberty), she had been isolated in a small room, deprived of all linguistic input and punished for vocalizing. In the first two years following her admission to a hospital and exposure to language, she came to speak in a manner similar to 2-year-olds, and her language development was characterized by the same stages that characterize the development of children reared in typical environments. Thus Genie clearly has at least a rudimentary capacity for language. What is unclear at present is how far her language will continue to develop. Will she master the subtleties of grammar as most children do, or is she irreparably limited linguistically? It is too soon to know, but in light of the evidence, it seems best to regard the critical period hypothesis with caution.

Another potential problem with the critical period hypothesis is that it suggests that growth processes terminate in the period during which a language may be acquired. However, it may be that the developmental gates are closed by the very development of language. For example, it is possible that cerebral specialization results from an interaction of growth processes and language development. In the case of Genie, the development of language may actually have facilitated cerebral specialization (Curtiss et al., 1974; Fromkin et al., 1974), and more research is clearly required in this area.

A third problem with the critical period hypothesis concerns some of the behavioral data upon which that hypothesis is based. Some observations have suggested that it is very difficult to learn a second language after puberty, whereas second languages are often acquired before puberty (for example, Burling, 1959; for a review, see McLaughlin, 1978) and with apparent ease. Although it is possible to account for this observation by stating that the developmental gates for the acquisition of language are closed at puberty, that account is not necessary. A variety of factors may contribute to the difficulty of learning a second language beyond puberty. Note that a situation that involves the learning of one language and then another constitutes a negative transfer paradigm (see pp. 260–261). The acquisition of one language may interfere with the development of another, and the amount of interference may increase with increases in the degree of learning of the first language (see Hakuta, 1976). Moreover, second languages are very rarely acquired under the same conditions under which the first language is typically acquired. If we were isolated from our society, placed in a novel environment with people who speak a very different language and could communicate our needs only through speech, we might rise to the task, as seemingly helpless infants do, and learn the second language readily. Finally, the results of many studies suggest that with the possible exception of phonology (Oyama, 1976), second languages are learned beyond puberty at about the same rate and in the same manner in which the first language is acquired before puberty (cf. McLaughlin, 1978). Many more controlled studies must be conducted before concluding with confidence that second language learning differs fundamentally from first language learning, particularly when the second language is learned after puberty.

Concluding comments In summary, phylogenetic factors clearly contribute to the elaboration of language, but the exact effects of these factors and their interactions with ontogenetic factors have yet to be ascertained. Until further research clarifies the locus, the range and the nature of the contribution of phylogenetic factors to the later development of language, specific hypotheses such as the critical period hypothesis are best regarded with caution.

Having considered the contribution of phylogeny to the elaboration of language, we may now examine the contribution that ontogeny makes. Specifically, we shall explore the linguistic, the cognitive and the communicative antecedents of language.

The Contribution of Linguistic Factors

Throughout this chapter, we have seen that psycholinguists have often described language acquisition as a process in which the child acts as a linguist and constructs a set of grammatical rules. More specifically, the child is believed to formulate and test hypotheses about the corpus of speech the child is exposed to.

Given the description of language development as a process of developing linguistic rules (that description is not accepted by all psychologists: cf. Skinner, 1957, 1969, 1974), several questions concerning the origins of language arise. What determines the types of rules that children formulate? What determines the orderly sequence of rule development in the acquisition of language? We shall now consider these questions further.

The Linguistic Power Hypothesis   Consider the question of what determines the types of rules that children formulate. We saw earlier that some theorists believe that part of our biological heritage for language is a predisposition to form particular types of rules. But what ontogenetic events lead the child to reject one type of rule such as phrase-structure rules in favor of other rules such as transformational rules? One suggestion is that children eventually reject phrase-structure rules in favor of transformational rules because the latter are linguistically more powerful. That suggestion may be called the *linguistic power hypothesis*. Recall that in the development of interrogation, the questions of some children (for example, those that began with *D'you want ...?*) seemed to involve a phrase structure rule. Although the rule can generate one acceptable type of adult question, that rule is not very powerful since it cannot be used to generate many different types of questions. If the child continued to formulate phrase-structure rules, many rules of limited applicability would have to be learned. On the other hand, if the child switched over to transformation rules, the child would only need to formulate three transformations that could produce the full range of questions that adults typically ask. Thus the argument is that children formulate transformation rules because these rules are more powerful than phrase-structure rules.

The trouble with this argument is that it does not explain how a child knows that transformation rules are more powerful than phrase-structure rules. Of course, one could argue that that knowledge is also part of our biological heritage. However, that argument seems too facile; it is not demanded by the available evidence (only by our lack of knowledge), and it puts the matter beyond the reach of psychological inquiry. Moreover, the argument does not address the key question of what types of linguistic input the child must be exposed to in order to formulate the appropriate transformation rules. Simple exposure to adult speech, such as person-to-person speech on television, appears to be insufficient for the development of transformation rules in children

(Sachs & Johnson, 1976). Overall, we are far from an understanding of the ontogenetic events that lead children to devise phrase-structure rules, transformation rules and so on.

The Linguistic Complexity Hypothesis   A second factor that is believed to affect the acquisition of linguistic rules is linguistic complexity. Recall that the order of acquisition of grammatical morphemes in English is predictable from both syntactic and semantic complexity. Similarly, the order of acquisition of the verbs of possession depends upon the relative semantic complexity of the verbs. The substantial correlation between linguistic complexity and the order of acquisition of the syntactic and semantic components of language has led some theorists (for example, Brown, R., 1973; Clark, H. H., & Clark, 1977) to use the complexity construct to explain the order of acquisition.

The attempt to explain the phenomena of language development on the basis of linguistic complexity encounters at least two problems. One is that linguistic complexity is often confounded with other variables. For example, the acquisition of *give* and *take* may occur before the acquisition of *buy* and *sell* because of differences in semantic complexity. However, factors other than complexity may be involved. For instance, words such as *give* and *take* may be heard by or spoken to children earlier than *buy* and *sell*. Another alternative, roughly stated, is that the child does not need to use words such as *buy* as early as words such as *take*. After all, young children do not ordinarily have to use money to obtain items. An account based upon linguistic complexity must, in order to be convincing, rule out myriad other factors (cf. Brown, R., 1973). Although that is possible in principle, it has seldom been achieved in practice.

The second problem with an account of language development in terms of linguistic complexity is that the complexity is left unexplained. Are humans structured by evolution in such a way that they will always find some linguistic stimuli more complex than others? Or does the complexity of a stimulus depend upon the types of experience the organism has had? Until answers to these questions are available, we may question the explanatory power of accounts based on linguistic complexity.

The Role of Cognition in the Elaboration of Language

The contribution of cognitive knowledge is apparent in semantic development. For example, consider how our cognitive knowledge of colors affects the meaning of color words in humans. If adults are shown an array of colors and are asked to pick out an instance of red, they pick some colors that are referred to by the word *red* more often than others. The same is true for color categories other than red (Berlin & Kay, 1969). Thus in choosing colors that are instances of particular color categories adults treat some colors as "best" instances, and these colors are called *focal colors*. Interestingly, these focal colors appear to be universal, although the color words used vary from language to language (Berlin & Kay, 1969). In studies of 3 and 4-year-olds, it has been observed that children also show a preference for the focal colors even before they can understand or produce the names of colors (also see Bornstein, 1975). Furthermore, when they begin to learn color names such as red, and are asked to pick an instance of red, they tend to pick the focal instance of red (Heider, 1971, 1972; Rosch, 1978). Thus children appear to map color names onto their knowledge of colors. Any universal aspects of the meaning of color words may result from the universality of the nonverbal knowledge children have of colors.

Just as cognitive knowledge contributes to the development of semantic knowledge, so too may it contribute to the development of syntactic knowledge. The role of cognitive knowledge in the acquisition of linguistic rules is difficult to determine through naturalistic observation, for in naturalistic settings many factors are confounded or beyond the control of the observer. It is very difficult to define either the linguistic and nonlinguistic stimuli that a person has been exposed to or the linguistic and cognitive knowledge that has arisen from experience with those stimuli. One promising strategy for dealing with the preceding problems is to study the relationship between cognitive knowledge and the acquisition of language in the controlled setting of the laboratory through the use of miniature experimental languages.

Nonlinguistic Knowledge and the Acquisition of Syntactic Rules   The contribution of cognitive knowledge to the acquisition of linguistic rules has been studied in a series of experiments by Moeser and Bregman (1972, 1973; see also Moeser & Olson, 1974; Moeser, 1975). The acquisition of various miniature languages was studied under conditions in which the words of the language either did or did not refer to figures such as colored rectangles. Figure 9.4a shows the rules, words and referents of the simplest language that was studied in the experiment. Figure 9.4b shows the phrase structure of one of the strings that is generated by the rules of that language. Some subjects were shown strings that consisted only of words, whereas other subjects were shown the same strings together with corresponding figures. Thus in one condition the strings had no referents, whereas the strings in the other had referents, as shown in Fig. 9.4c. Furthermore, the referents of the words in the latter condition were combined in ways that reflected the phrase structure of the string. For example, fet and yow are closely related in the phrase-structure of the string shown in Fig. 9.4c, and the referents of fet (green rectangle) and yow (dotted border) are also shown as closely related.

Moeser and Bregman divided their adult subjects into two groups, and they showed each subject 40 different grammatical strings either with or without the corresponding figures. Each string was presented for 5 sec on any occasion, and each string was presented a total of eight times during the first phase of the experiment. Then the subjects were given a test in which 15 pairs of strings without referents were shown and the subjects were asked to choose the grammatical string from each pair. The strings used in the test were novel combinations of the words that had been presented in the first phase. Each pair of test strings was constructed in such a way that the acquisition of each rule of the language could be assessed.

The results were that the adults who had seen the strings without the corresponding figures learned only the simplest rules of the language. On the

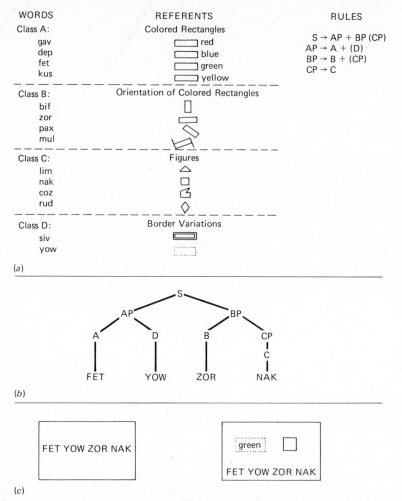

Fig. 9.4 (a) The words, referents and rules of the simplest miniature language studied by Moeser and Bregman. (b) The phrase structure of one of the strings that is generated by the rules shown in (a). (c) The same string as it was shown to the subjects in the words only and reference conditions, respectively. (From Moeser & Bregman, 1972. Copyright 1972 by Academic Press, *Journal of Verbal Learning and Verbal Behavior.*)

other hand, the subjects who had seen the same strings with the figures had learned all of the rules of the language, and fine-grained analyses of the errors revealed that they learned the rules of the language in a different way than the subjects who had seen only the strings. The subjects who had seen both figures and words first learned to emit particular words in the presence of the appropriate figures. Then they learned how the referents could be combined. Finally, they learned to use the words referring to particular aspects of the visual field in the appropriate sentence positions. In other words, those subjects first learned the appropriate word-referent relations, then they learned the relations between the referents, and then they mapped the appropriate words onto their knowledge of the reference field.

In contrast, the subjects who had seen only the linguistic strings learned according to the regularities in word order. Specifically, they learned to treat words that occurred in a given position as members of the same class, and then they learned how the classes could be combined to form sentences. Since the words from more than one class could not occur in a given sentence position, it was possible for those subjects to learn the language solely on the basis of the regularities in word order.

In further experiments, the preceding results were extended in significant ways. Experiments concerning the acquisition of more complex languages revealed that subjects who were shown only the linguistic strings learned virtually none of the rules, despite extensive practice. However, adults who saw the linguistic strings together with the figures readily learned all of the rules. Interestingly, the subjects in the reference condition who had mastered the language were able to learn how to use new words appropriately by seeing those words used in particular ways with familiar words and without reference to figures. Furthermore, Moeser and Bregman showed that the nature of the referents affected the acquisition of complex linguistic rules. Reference facilitated the learning of complex rules primarily when the relations between the figures reflected the relations between the words in the strings. Finally, Moeser and Olson (1974) showed that reference plays an important role in the acquisition of linguistic rules in 4-year-olds, just as it does in adults.

These studies suggest that reference or, more precisely, cognitive knowledge of referential relations may be critical for learning the rules of language. It appears that learning how to speak requires a good deal of learning about the events we speak of, and some linguistic rules may not be learned solely from exposure to a body of utterances (see also Macnamara, 1972). Whether the results of studies of miniature languages may be generalized fully to the conditions in which natural language acquisition occurs remains to be determined.

The preceding studies suggest that some aspects of syntactic structure may reflect relations between nonlinguistic events (see also Moeser, 1975). In a sentence such as *The green caterpillar crawled up the brown branch*, *green* and *caterpillar* are closely related. Likewise, the referents of these words are closely related. Similarly, the synonymy of sentences like *Washoe hugged the cat* and *The cat was hugged by Washoe* may result from the fact that these sentences refer to similar nonlinguistic events. It may even turn out that some universal aspects of language result in part from universal similarities in the environments that humans live in and speak of. These possibilities need to be explored further, for at least one thing is certain: If we are to understand how language is acquired, we shall have to examine carefully the relationship between the linguistic and nonlinguistic stimuli children are exposed to.

Evidence from Naturalistic Settings   The view that cognitive knowledge contributes to the elaboration of language is supported by many observations other than those concerning the acquisition of miniature language (for a review, see Bloom, L. M., & Lahey, 1978; Clark, H. H., & Clark, 1977). For example, it appears that children respond to sentences not only on the basis of the linguistic information expressed in the sentence but also on the basis of their nonlinguistic knowledge about the objects mentioned in the sentence. Whereas young children can understand sentences such as *The dog is chasing the car,* they often fail to understand sentences such as *The boot is hitting the girl* (Chapman & Miller, 1975). In general, young children may be said to follow the semantic strategy of identifying the animate entity as the subject and the inanimate entity as the object of the sentence. In turn, that semantic strategy seems to be based upon the child's knowledge of nonlinguistic events—that people can throw stones but not vice versa, that people can paint pictures but not vice versa, and so on.

Although we have only a fragmentary understanding of how syntax is acquired, it seems quite likely that knowledge of nonverbal events and relationships contributes to the learning of complex syntactic constructions. As an example, consider a sentence such as *The dog that chased the cat is panting.* If children were exposed to that type of sentence in the absence of contextual information, they would probably learn to produce and understand these sentences only with great difficulty. However, knowledge of the events described in these sentences can facilitate that learning. For example, if a child saw a dog chasing a cat and a short time later saw the dog panting, the child could use that information to interpret the sentence and specifically to determine that both *chased the cat* and *is panting* refer to *dog.* After a child has correctly understood several sentences such as this with the aid of nonverbal, contextual information, the child may be able to understand a wide variety of sentences with relative clauses without the aid of nonverbal, contextual information. The task of specifying the exact factors that lead to such positive transfer remains for future research.

Operating Principles and Language Development The intimate relationship between cognitive knowledge and language development has led developmental psycholinguists (for example, Slobin, 1973) to try to specify the operating principles or cognitive strategies that children are said to use in acquiring language. We shall consider four of these operating principles (from Slobin, 1973):

A. Look for systematic modification in the forms of words.
B. Look for grammatical markers that indicate underlying semantic distinctions clearly and make semantic sense.
C. Avoid exceptions.
D. Pay attention to the ends of words.

A variety of the phenomena of language acquisition may be said to involve these operating principles. For example, recall that in the acquisition of the past tense forms for verbs, past tense markers such as -ed are often overgeneralized to irregular verbs, thereby resulting in incorrect forms such as *comed* and *runned.* One might attempt to explain the application and the over-generalization of the -ed morpheme in terms of the operation of Principles A, B, C, and so on. However, numerous difficulties arise in that attempt. Without information about the conditions under which these principles operate, precise predictions cannot be made. Currently, only *post hoc* accounts of linguistic phenomena can be given by these principles. A related problem is that the operating principles are inferred from the linguistic phenomena they are meant to explain, and these principles are circular to that extent. Accordingly, the operating principles are best seen as descriptive rather than explanatory in nature.

A third problem is that these operating principles have sometimes been seen as describing the universal cognitive knowledge or strategies of young children. Although the principles may be inferred from the verbal behavior of children in many different cultures, they may not arise solely from phylogenetic factors. Until the antecedents of the principles have been identified, it is best not to regard them as basic structural features of young children (and see Park, 1978). Under different conditions of rearing, very different cognitive principles may emerge. Clearly, we have an immense amount to learn about the complex relationships between the environment, nonverbal behavior and verbal behavior that we speak of in terms of the relationship between cognition and language.

Communicative Antecedents of the Elaboration of Language

Whether we speak, and the manner in which we speak, are determined in large part by communicative factors. A stranger whom we might not ordinarily address asks for directions, and we respond verbally to this request. When a young child asks us why we see only black and white at night, we might give a very simple answer, whereas the same question put to us by an adult may draw a relatively sophisticated answer. As the result of our extensive histories of social and verbal interactions, our verbal behavior comes to be controlled in appropriate ways by the verbal and nonverbal stimuli provided by other members of our society. The subtleties and complexities involved in the development and maintenance of the behaviors we call communicative are attested to by the frequent failures of stimulus control ("communication breakdowns"), by the myriad levels of sophistication on which verbal interactions may proceed, and sadly by the large numbers of people whose communicative responses are consistently aberrant. Unfortunately, the subtlety and complexity of communication have made it difficult to identify and specify the effects of the discriminative, eliciting and reinforcing stimuli that are involved in communicative episodes. Accordingly, much of what we shall say in this section is speculative and suggestive rather than firmly established.

Communication and the Acquisition of Syntax   Although it is obvious that communicative factors affect what we say, when we say it, and so on, it is perhaps less obvious that these factors may contribute to the development of complex aspects of language such as syntax. Let us begin with a very simple example concerning the acquisition of function words such as the articles *a* and *the*. Adults use the definite article *the* when they speak of objects or events that are known to the listener; otherwise, they use the indefinite article *a* (Grieve, 1973). For example, if adults are asked to describe the events in a movie in which a particular object such as a box appears repeatedly, they will refer to that object as *a box* the first time they speak of it. Thereafter, the adults refer to that same object by saying *the box*. Thus adults introduce new information with the article *a*, whereas they speak of given or known objects and events with *the*.

Children begin to use both articles between the ages of 2 and 3 years. However, childrens' usage of these articles does not initially correspond to that of adults. For example, 3-year-olds who are telling a novel story to another child often (about 50% of the time) use the definite article in their first reference to an object. It is not until the age of about 9 years that they conform to the adult usage and reliably use the indefinite article in their first mention of an object (Warden, 1976). The exact factors responsible for the shift in the usage of articles have not yet been determined, but it seems likely that communicative factors are involved. For example, when *the* is used inappropriately on the first mention of a novel object such as a car, the listener may respond with a puzzled or disgruntled look and a question such as "What car?" Presumably, the first speaker will then supply the information needed to correctly interpret the reference to *the car*. After a number of similar experiences, saying *the* may come to be controlled not only by the presence of a particular object but also by (roughly speaking) the speaker's assessment of what the listener knows.

Now let us consider how communicative factors may contribute to the development of more complex aspects of syntax. Recall that during the early stages of language development, children's utterances consist of one or two words, and these utterances can often be interpreted readily with the aid of contextual information. If children can communicate effectively via two-word utterances that express only simple semantic relationships, why do they come to emit longer, syntactically complex utterances?

We believe that the answer to the preceding question is to be sought partly in the changing nature of the communicative demands that confront the child throughout development. Adults and older children modify their speech to match or stay one step above the level of linguistic development of young children (cf. Snow & Ferguson, 1977), and the attention and praise that children may receive for responding correctly to more and more complex verbal stimuli may contribute to syntactic development (but see Brown, R. & Hanlon, 1970). Similarly, as children develop, they come to talk about or request objects and events that are not immediately present, and contextual information may less often contribute to the interpretation of the child's utterances. Accordingly, the interpretation of the child's utterances must be based upon linguistic information. In a sense, the child is forced to use the appropriate syntactic devices to communicate effectively. As children develop, they talk about past events and future events, as well as present events, and they do so over the telephone and in writing, in addition to vocal, face-to-face interactions. In order to communicate effectively in that wide variety of contexts, children must use the appropriate syntactic devices such as word order, past tense markers, auxiliary verbs, and so on. In much the same way, effective communication with different people regarding a wide variety of events may depend upon the use of the appropriate sounds, words and semantic relationships and distinctions, and communicative factors may contribute substantially to semantic and phonological development.

Self-editing Responses and the Development of Grammatical Speech
What might be the specific mechanisms whereby communicative factors affect the development of complex aspects of language such as syntax? One possibility is that grammatical speech results in part from the acquisition of *self-editing responses* (see also Segal, 1975, 1977; Skinner, 1957; Winokur, 1976). We are all familiar with self-editing responses, for we often observe ourselves "thinking how to say something" or discontinuing one sentence we are speaking and producing another (see Baars, Motley, & MacKay, 1975). Self-editing responses are sometimes public, as when we proofread a paper we have written, but these responses are more often covert.

To illustrate the potential role of self-editing responses in the production of grammatical responses, consider a hypothetical episode. Two field biologists are searching for a particular type of moth in a forest. One person sees it and wishes to tell the other where to look. Even before speaking, verbal responses such as *look,* naming the moth and naming the type of tree on which it is resting might have a high probability of occurrence as the result of seeing the moth. In other words, the basic propositional content of the sentence (for example, *The moth is on the large evergreen on the right*) is determined before the sentence has actually been produced. But knowing what one wants to say is not necessarily the same as knowing how to say it effectively. Saying *Look! The moth is in the evergreen on the right* might be ineffective because of the lack of specificity, and the speaker might make that discrimination. Accordingly, the speaker might edit the covert verbal behavior in such a way as to produce the sentence *The moth is in the small hemlock tree on the right, on the third branch from the top.* Thus, although the covert editing responses of the speaker may not be directly accessible to the listener, these responses may, by modifying the verbal behavior of the speaker, indirectly affect the behavior of the listener (for further discussion see Skinner, 1957, on autoclitics and self-editing).

The editing responses that are involved when we choose which words to use, how to begin a sentence, how definite a statement to make, and so on, seem to occur quite automatically in adults. These responses and the automaticity with which they are emitted may result from an extensive set of experiences in which different responses had different communicative consequences.

Self-editing responses apparently are made by children, for they frequently emit utterances such as "She had a silly putty like me had . . . like I . . . like I did" (Slobin, 1971c). To illustrate how changes in self-editing responses could lead to syntactic development, consider the development of interrogation. Recall that the development of interrogation involves including auxiliary verbs where necessary, inverting the subject and the auxiliary verb, and so on. Self-editing responses may contribute to the development of these phenomena. For example, at an early stage in the development of interrogation, the main self-editing response that occurs in asking a question is one that modifies the pattern of intonation to produce utterances such as *Sit CHAIR?* At a later stage, other self-editing responses may lead to the production of auxiliary verbs and their inversion with subjects of the sentences, and questions such as *Does lions walk?* may then be produced. Still later, other self-editing responses may lead to agreement in the markings for singularity or plurality in nouns and verbs, thus leading to sentences such as *Do lions walk?* As a greater number of self-editing responses are acquired and emitted in the appropriate combinations and under the appropriate conditions, the child's utterances may increase in grammatical complexity. Whether the development of syntax is seen as a process of acquiring transformation rules or of acquiring self-editing responses, the critical empirical tasks remain the same: to specify the origins of verbal behavior and the conditions under which it is produced and comprehended (cf. Segal, 1977). As matters now stand, self-editing responses have a status somewhat similar to transformation rules and operating principles, for they too are unobserved and are often inferred from the behaviors that are to be explained.

Concluding Comments   We have spoken of self-editing responses as if they were private events that have the same functional status as public events. In fact, very little is now known about the antecedents of self-editing responses. Self-editing responses, like many public events and simple private events, may be governed in part by their consequences, for these responses indirectly affect the behavior of the people to whom we speak. However, there is little evidence that now supports that position. For example, it has been observed that parents verbally approve and disapprove of childrens' utterances more on the basis of the truth value of those utterances than on their grammaticality (Brown, R., Cazden, & Bellugi, 1968; see also Brown, R., & Hanlon, 1970).

These results, however, do not indicate that the consequences of verbal behavior do not contribute to syntactic development.[7] As we mentioned earlier, the study of communicative interactions has only begun. The role of communicative consequences in the development of language is best regarded as uncertain until a wide range of adult-child and child-child interactions have been studied and the discriminative and reinforcing stimuli that are involved in communicative interactions have been specified empirically. That task constitutes a major area for further research.

The Role of Imitation

The last ontogenetic factor that we shall consider is imitation. Currently, there is abundant evidence that children can be taught via conditioning procedures to imitate verbal responses (for example, Brigham & Sherman, 1968; Lovaas, 1966, 1976). Additionally, there is evidence that after several imitative responses have been established through explicit reinforcement, novel imitative responses may occur even without direct reinforcement (see pp. 268–270). The conditioning of imitative verbal responses can facilitate the linguistic development of children with various types of behavior disturbances (Garcia, Guess, & Byrnes, 1973; Guess, 1969; Schumaker & Sherman, 1970). Furthermore, verbal imitative responses are emitted frequently by many children in natural settings and without the aid of special training procedures (for example, Bloom, L. M., Hood, & Lightbrown, 1974).

Despite the preceding observations, most of the available evidence suggests that imitation does not typically contribute to syntactic development, although imitation does appear to contribute to vocabulary development. Children rarely imitate utterances that they do not produce under nonimitative conditions (Bloom, L. M., et al., 1974; Brown, R., & Bellugi, 1964; Ervin, 1964; Slobin, 1969). For example, when children who have not mastered the grammatical morphemes imitate adult utterances (such as *Fraser will be unhappy*), they typically delete those morphemes (for example, *Fraser unhappy*).

In naturalistic settings, children seem to imitate those syntactic constructions that they have recently begun to produce nonimitatively (Bloom, L. M., et al., 1974; Dale, 1976). The only reported condition under which children correctly imitate utterances that are grammatically more complex than their nonimitative utterances is one in which children imitate an adult's expansion of the child's utterance (Slobin, 1969). At present, it is not known how frequently these imitative responses occur and what their exact role in language development is.

On definitional grounds alone, it seems that imitation is not sufficient for the acquisition of complex aspects of syntax. Few if any theorists would be willing to say that a particular aspect of syntactic development such as the usage of auxiliary verbs, had occurred if the responses that had been acquired via imitation were only emitted under imitative conditions. Imitation could aid in the acquisition of auxiliary verbs, for once these verbs are produced as imitative responses they can be brought under the control of other variables. Nevertheless, the point remains that imitation alone is not sufficient for the acquisition of complex aspects of language. Furthermore, it is certain that imitation is not necessary for the development of language. Indeed, language development occurs in many individuals who seldom imitate (Bloom, L. M., et al., 1974) and full language development has been observed in individuals who cannot speak and who cannot emit imitative verbal responses (for example, Lenneberg, 1962).

In closing, it is important to recognize that many imitative responses may go unnoticed. As we saw earlier, some imitative responses may not exactly match the response of a model (for example, a child may say *dup* instead of *jump*). Moreover, complex responses such as questions are multidimensional, and an observer's imitative responses may be controlled by one dimension of a model's response but not by others (Whitehurst, 1978). For example, parents may ask questions frequently, and their children may not imitate the particular questions asked. But the children may imitate their parents by often asking questions. To specify the contribution of imitation, we need to devise more subtle measures of imitative responses than those used in the past.

SUMMARY

Most contemporary theories of language development have their roots in linguistic theories and depict language development in terms of the formation of phonological, syntactic and semantic categories (for example, phonemic categories and semantic components) and rules (for example, phonological rules and transformation rules). Thus far, case grammar shows considerable promise in the description of child language, for the deep structure categories of that theory seem to correspond to the conceptual categories of young children, whereas the deep-structural categories of transformational grammar (for example, "subject" and "object") do not. However, the problems involved in distinguishing between linguistic competence and linguistic performance make it difficult to decide which linguistic theory best applies to which aspects of child language. We may speculate that the difficulty of distinguishing between competence and performance will eventually lead to descriptive accounts of language development that, like many of the adult theories of memory and cognition that we shall next consider, do not embody that distinction.

The complexities involved in describing language development are compounded by the differences between comprehension and production during development. As in the field of memory (see especially Chapter 11), we may expect the relations between comprehension and production to figure prominently in future accounts of language development. A final problem in describing language development thoroughly is one of sampling. Very few children have been studied in the sorts of careful longitudinal studies that are needed, and those children have come from rather similar environments (white, middle-class, and so on). Since many aspects of language development result from the ontogenetic environment, a complete description of language development requires the study of many children in very different types of environment.

In exploring the antecedents of language development, theorists have often focused upon the role of explicitly linguistic factors such as syntactic and semantic complexity, linguistic power, and so forth. While the potential influence of these factors is not to be denied, they have yet to provide compelling analyses of most linguistic phenomena. To that extent, the view that the child forms and tests hypotheses on the basis of aspects of the linguistic input received should be regarded as incomplete. Of course, it should come as no surprise to find that language acquisition cannot be accounted for solely in terms of linguistic factors. As contemporary theorists have argued, language acquisition is an outcome of a vast nexus of environment-behavior interactions that are typically classified into anatomical/physiological, cognitive and communicative (as well as linguistic) categories.

The importance of phylogenetic factors is apparent in phonological de-

velopment. For example, the production of the phones belonging to the phonemes /i/, /a/ and /u/ depends upon the elongation and neuromuscular control of the supralaryngeal cavity. At a central level the development of cerebral
specialization seems to play an important role in the later development of language. However, the details of the latter process are unclear, and the question
of whether there is a critical period for the development of language remains
open. Until much more is known about the exact effects of phylogeny, it is well
to be wary of assertions about innate linguistic knowledge.

Cognitive and linguistic development occur simultaneously and interact
extensively. Before the first words occur, the child seems to be acquiring
knowledge about nonlinguistic categories such as "agent," and these categories
later appear in the child's language. Similarly, the child's early knowledge of
word meanings depends upon his or her nonlinguistic knowledge of the referents of words. Even the acquisition of complex syntactic rules seems to depend
in part upon the nonlinguistic knowledge of the objects, events and relations
that we speak of. In general, there seems to be considerable transfer of cognitive knowledge to linguistic knowledge, and language is thus said to be mapped
onto our cognitive knowledge. However, the relationship between language
and cognition is bidirectional, and just as cognitive knowledge can influence
our linguistic knowledge, so too may the opposite occur.

Although the relationships between language and cognition are diverse
and important, it is wise to remember that an aspect of language development
is not explained by showing that it is based upon a particular aspect of cognitive knowledge, for the antecedents of that cognitive knowledge must also be
ascertained. A complete account of the origins of that cognitive knowledge
must be based in part upon a thorough analysis of the environment-behavior
interactions that occur throughout life.

Broadly stated, the primary function of language is communication. In all
known human societies, people communicate via language, and considering
the importance of communication in human life it is not surprising that adults
communicate with children in the first few months of life. Atlhough the initial
communicative interchanges are typically nonverbal, these interchanges lay
the groundwork for linguistic communication. For example, the communicative functions that we call assertions and requests characterize the early nonverbal interactions of parent and child, and these functions later appear when
the child begins to speak. The development of syntax and other complex aspects of language may result in part from the increasingly subtle and complex
communicative demands that confront the child during the early years of life.

Communicative factors may help to bring about grammatical speech by
establishing a repertoire of covert self-editing responses. Although the nature
of these self-editing responses has yet to be determined, there is no question
that private events contribute importantly to the production and comprehension of grammatical speech. Since language and memory are intimately related, the analysis of private events will be of considerable importance in the
following chapters concerning memory.

NOTES

1. Imitative responses are not under discussion here, for those responses do not meet the criteria for the actual linguistic use of a word. The criteria that are used most often to define which words are used linguistically are (1) evidence of comprehension, and (2) consistent and "spontaneous" use.
2. Jakobson (1968) has proposed that phonological contrasts develop in children according to an invariant and universal sequence. However, there are too few data available to evaluate that proposal adequately, and it will not be discussed further here (for discussion see Clark, H. H., & Clark, 1977; Ferguson & Garnica, 1975; Garnica, 1973).
3. It is important to note that two-word utterances may not always express knowledge of cognitive categories such as "agent," "locative," and so on. For example, *doggie run* may occur as an imitative response. In that case, it would be inappropriate to classify this sentence as an "agent-action" construction. The general point is that categories such as "agent" are functional ones, and their membership must be defined through empirical investigation.
4. Performance in linguistic tasks is not always better in comprehension tests than in production tests (cf. deVilliers, J. G., & deVilliers, 1978).
5. For a discussion of the complications involved in making and interpreting this analysis, see Brown, R., 1973.
6. Lateralization of function may not bear any special tie to language, for central anatomical and functional asymmetries occur in species that communicate extensively but are not typically ascribed any capacity for language (for a review, see Neville, 1976). Further studies of the role of cerebral specialization in communication may help clarify the relationship between communication and language.
7. The question of the contribution of reinforcement and other conditioning processes to the development of language has generated intense controversy. For the flavor of the debate, see Chomsky (1959); MacCorquodale (1970); Richelle (1976); Salzinger (1978); Skinner (1957, 1969, 1974); Slobin (1971b).

10

Sensory and Short-Term Memory

In the preceding chapters, we have spoken of learning in considerable detail, but we have said little about memory. Our approach is consistent with history, for learning and memory have traditionally been studied as if they were different phenomena. Students of learning have typically focused on the processes involved in acquisition and extinction, and they have sought to minimize the contribution of variables that might lead to forgetting in an experiment on learning. In contrast, students of memory have concentrated their efforts on the factors that affect retention, and they have often sought to control factors that affect acquisition in their experiments concerning memory.

The distinction between learning and memory is convenient, but this distinction seems stronger in its tradition than in its substance. When we distinguish between learning and memory, we run the risk of passively adopting the view that learning and memory are completely distinct phenomena. However, even momentary reflection reveals that learning and memory are in fact different aspects of the same phenomenon. Remembering involves retaining the effects of experience over time. Similarly, learning involves retention over time, for learning is said to occur when the events that take place at one time during an organism's life influence the behavior of that organism at some later time. Thus memory is implicit in all learning (Melton, 1963; McGeoch, 1942; Postman, 1976a). To go one step further, memory is necessary for learning. There could be no learning if there were no memory, for the effects of experience could not carry over from one time to the next. Since memory is an important part of learning, we must seek to understand memory in our attempt to gain a comprehensive understanding of learning. The final two chapters of this book are therefore devoted to the analysis of memory, and specifically to the work that cognitive theorists have done concerning human memory.

In this chapter, we shall consider the basic phenomena and theories of retention over short intervals of time—for example, less than a minute. We shall begin our inquiry into memory by examining some of the historical antecedents and general characteristics of contemporary theories of memory.

AN OVERVIEW OF MEMORY

Before examining some theories of memory, let us examine the problems that confront students of memory. Consider the following hypothetical example of an everyday memory task. A stranger in a car stops and asks us for directions to city hall. In giving these directions, a complex and poorly understood sequence of events occurs. Stated in loose terms, we first comprehend the request made by the stranger. Next, we might form a visual image of the area between our present location and that of town hall. Then we use the information in that image to select a simple, direct route, and we transmit the pertinent information in verbal form to the stranger. Although the particular example we have used is fictional, the processes that are described above have been shown to be involved in remembering (cf. Baddeley, 1976; Crowder, 1976).

How did we understand the request of the stranger? How did we form the visual image, and how did we translate the visual information into a verbal form? Was forming the image a necessary part of remembering the desired information? Although we are far from having answered these questions in a satisfactory manner, several points are clear. First, even in very simple memory tasks, many of the important events that occur are private rather than public. Second, these private events are the legacy of a vast array of prior experiences, and prior experience is a factor that must be reckoned with in all studies of memory. A third point, related to the preceding ones, is that, whether by way of the legacy of phylogeny or of ontogeny, the organism plays an active role in the process of remembering. As in the analysis of learning in the experienced organism (see Chapter 7), a complete analysis of memory cannot be made solely on the basis of the contemporaneous environment. Let us consider how contemporary theorists have attempted to handle these problems.

Associationistic Theories

One contemporary type of memory theory is associationistic. This type of theory is rooted in the philosophies of Aristotle and the British associationists (for example, John Locke, David Hume, George Berkeley, and so on; cf. Rappaport, 1974) and in the pioneering experimental work of Hermann Ebbinghaus (see pp. 210–216). According to associationistic theories, memory involves the utilization or activation of existing associations, whereas forgetting occurs when a particular association is either unlearned or blocked by competing associations. For example, in attempting to recall the name of an acquaintance of long ago, we often recall one or several names other than the correct one. An associationist might attribute that forgetting to competition among associations.

The basic tenet of associationism was that complex phenomena such as images and language could be analyzed thoroughly in terms of associations that were formed through experience. Associationists sought to discover the fundamental laws of memory by studying associations under simple and well-controlled conditions in which the effects of prior experience did not intrude. Accordingly, the associationists followed the lead of Ebbinghaus and studied the acquisition and retention of nonsense syllables in seemingly simple procedures such as the paired-associate learning procedure.

Associationist theories made many valuable contributions to the study of memory, primary among which was the emphasis on rigorous experimentation and the interference theory of forgetting. Unfortunately, the associationistic theories encountered serious difficulties that eventually led to the rise of the kinds of cognitive theories that dominate the field today. On the empirical side, the effects of prior experience intruded into even the simplest and best controlled experimental arrangements devised by the associationists. For example, adults often learned pairs of nonsense syllables by forming visual images, verbal mediators, and so on (see pp. 271–273). Attempts to quantify or control for those effects of prior experience met with mixed success (for example, Horton & Kjeldergaard, 1961). On the theoretical side, Chomsky and other theorists (cf. Chomsky, N., 1957; Chomsky, N., & Miller, 1963; Miller, 1962b) persuasively challenged the assumption that associationistic theories could, at least in principle, account for the complexities of language. Chomsky's arguments were not simply negative ones, for he proposed the alternative model of transformational grammar that was believed to provide a powerful analysis of our natural language abilities. Furthermore, Chomsky argued that many facets of language could not be analyzed adequately by studying experience alone. The emphasis he put on biological factors contrasted sharply with the emphasis put by the associationists, at least implicitly, on experiential factors. It was not long before many psychologists came to believe that although the phenomena, procedures and theories of associationists are interesting and important, they cannot provide us with a complete understanding of the complex phenomena of language and memory that pervade our everyday lives.

The Impact of the Computer   Another influential consideration involved in the demise of associationistic theories concerned the development of a sophisticated computer technology in the 1950s and early 1960s. In scientific undertakings, theorists often find it conceptually advantageous to devise machine models of a particular phenomenon. For example, it has been argued that one could explain a particular psychological phenomenon such as remembering if a machine could be constructed that accurately simulates what happens when an organism remembers (Fodor, 1968; Hilgard & Bower, 1966;

Newell, 1973; but cf. Dreyfus, 1971). Consider the following statement by two eminent learning theorists:

> In designing and building a machine to simulate certain behaviors, one is in effect working out a physical embodiment of a theory about how that behavior is produced by that organism. Getting the machine to actually work and to simulate some interesting behavior is a way of demonstrating that the theory is internally consistent and that it has specified a sufficient set of mechanisms. Running a robot through one or another task is logically equivalent to deriving theorems about behavior from the theory that is modeled by the physical realization. (Hilgard & Bower, 1966, p. 382)

The computer simulation approach, like all theoretical approaches, had its own descriptive language, and that language differed considerably from that of associationism. In the language of computer theories, the computer is a system for *information processing*. Instructions, data, stimuli, and so on, are "input" or read into the computer. Then the computer, following the instructions specified by a *program,* processes or manipulates the input in particular ways. For example, if the input were a set of 10 numbers, a statistical program might have the computer add the 10 numbers and divide the sum by 10, thereby calculating the arithmetic mean of the set of numbers. Searching the information inside the machine, comparing that information to input, deciding whether the input has been encountered before, and so on, are some of the information-processing functions that are performed by computers. After the computer processes the information in the ways specified by the program, it "outputs" or reads out the end result in the form of a picture, a graph, a printout, and so on.

Theories involving computer simulation showed considerable promise for clarifying complex phenomena such as problem-solving (for example, Newell & Simon, 1962; Newell, Shaw, & Simon, 1958) and pattern recognition (for example, Selfridge & Neisser, 1960), and it was not long before theorists undertook the task of building a computer-based theory of memory that was very broad in scope (Atkinson & Shiffrin, 1968; Broadbent, 1958). The application of computer technology involved a new research strategy. This strategy was to analyze the complex phenomena on a larger, molar level rather than to break these phenomena down into constituent associations. Whereas molar analyses could have been and had been made (for example, Kohler, 1925, 1941) in earlier times, the computer provided the powerful sort of research tool needed to execute this strategy effectively. Whether the workings of complex programs can be analyzed in associationistic terms is debatable (see Suppes, 1969). What is undebatable is that most contemporary theorists of memory believe that it is not convenient or useful for research purposes to try to analyze complex phenomena solely in terms of associations (Estes, 1976). In most contemporary theories of memory, which are cognitive in nature, the processes of forming and utilizing associations are seen as important in memory, but they are not held to be the entire story (cf. Anderson & Bower, 1973). Current cognitive theorists view the organism as a processor of information who actively transforms, recombines and restructures information from the external environment. In order to introduce cognitive theories of memory and some of the related terminology, we shall consider the basic aspects of information processing.

Information Processing   In general, three *stages* of processing have been postulated. First, the input from the external environment must be translated into a usable format. The processing of information into a format that the organism or the computer can use is called *encoding* (alternatively called the process of "coding"), and the format itself is called a *memory code*. For example, when someone asks us for directions, a series of sound waves impinge upon our auditory receptors. The information from these sound waves may be translated or encoded by the memory system in various ways. The sounds that differentiate between phonemes in English may be encoded, thus forming a phonemic or phonological code. Similarly, semantic aspects of the utterance may be analyzed, and the information would then be said to have been encoded semantically.

After information has been encoded, it is then stored over time, and *storage* is the second general aspect of information processing. Stored information constitutes the knowledge of the organism that has been accumulated through experience. In giving directions to city hall, we use stored information that had been acquired from prior travels, looking at maps, and so on. Storage may be either transient or permanent, and we shall later discuss the controversy over the number and the nature of the storage processes involved in memory. The third important aspect of information processing involves the activation or utilization of stored information, and this process is called *retrieval*. For example, in forming an image of the route to city hall, we retrieved information that we had stored previously about that route. To oversimplify a bit, the retrieval process is like that of trying to find something we have filed away.

To summarize briefly, cognitive psychologists have conceived of memory as a processing system that, like a computer, actively encodes, stores and retrieves information. Having sketched the general outline of cognitive theories, we may now consider one of the major contemporary theories of memory.

A Multistore Model of Memory

In the model of human memory proposed by Atkinson and Shiffrin (1968, 1971), there are three main systems for storing information: the *sensory register,* the *short-term store* (STS) and the *long-term store* (LTS). According to the model, these three memory stores have distinct characteristics. The sensory register holds information from the environment in roughly its original or "sensory" form, but it does so only for a very brief period of time, at most a few seconds, for information in the sensory register spontaneously decays or fades away rapidly. The STS is a storage system of limited capacity that is large enough to hold, for instance, one telephone number but not three. Unlike the sensory registers, the STS holds information that has been encoded, and that information is retained over a longer period of time, for example, 15 sec. For example, a telephone number that is new to us might be encoded on the basis of how it sounds, and that phonological information would, according to the model, be stored in the STS for a short time. The LTS, unlike the sensory registers and the STS, is virtually unlimited in capacity and holds information for very long periods of time, perhaps even permanently. The LTS serves as a repository of the myriad events of the past; in general, it is the storehouse of our verbal and nonverbal knowledge. For example, information about where we live, whom we know, how to read and write, and so on, is presumably stored in the LTS. Presumably, the information in the LTS does not decay as readily as information in the STS does, but this information can be very difficult to retrieve, as anyone who has ever taken a test can readily appreciate.

According to Atkinson and Shiffrin, the sensory registers, the STS and the LTS are permanent *structural components* of the memory system. These structural components are held to be intrinsic features of the information-processing system of humans. In addition to these structural components, the memory system consists of relatively transient processes, called *control processes.* Control processes are diverse in nature, and they perform numerous functions. For example, one control process is *rehearsal,* and this control process is believed to both maintain information in the STS and transfer information to the LTS. Control processes other than rehearsal serve to organize different pieces of information or to alter the format of the information, and so on. In short, the organism acts upon information by bringing control processes to bear upon it. The control processes that the organism brings to bear upon a given set of information are determined by factors such as the nature of the task, the current stimulus conditions, and, of course, the history of the organism.

Having considered briefly both the structural features and the control processes of the memory system, we may now examine the workings of the entire information-processing system that was proposed by Atkinson and Shiffrin. This system is shown in Fig. 10.1. When an exteroceptive stimulus is presented, this stimulus is represented in a sensory register in a form best described as raw or unencoded. For example, if the printed word *wug* were presented, the letters *w, u* and *g* would be represented in one of the sensory registers in a raw visual format. Information in the sensory register is then scanned and matched with information in the LTS, as indicated by the dotted line leading from the sensory register to the LTS. If a match occurs between the information in the sensory register and the LTS, a process called *pattern recognition,* the information from the sensory register might be fed into the STS along with a verbal label from the LTS. After an item has entered the STS, it can be maintained indefinitely through the control process of rehearsal, especially if this information is encoded in terms of its phonological properties. During its stay in the STS, the information is analyzed acoustically, semantically, and so forth. When the analysis is completed, the information is stored in the LTS. Since the analyses performed in the STS require time, the probability of information being transferred to the LTS increases as a function of the duration of storage in the STS. When the information reaches the LTS, control

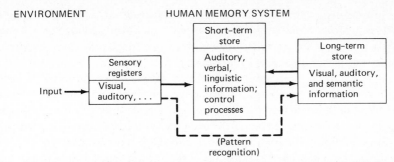

ENVIRONMENT   HUMAN MEMORY SYSTEM

Fig. 10.1   The structure of the information-processing system proposed by Atkinson & Shiffrin.   (Adapted from Atkinson & Shiffrin, 1968.)

processes determine how the information will be stored and how it will be retrieved.

According to this model, there are numerous ways in which forgetting can occur. First, information in the sensory registers *decays* or fades away very rapidly, and this information will soon be lost if it is not encoded and transferred to the STS. Similarly, the information in the STS decays and will be lost unless it is rehearsed or transferred to the LTS. Moreover, the STS has limited storage capacity, and new items that enter the STS may displace the items already in STS, thereby producing forgetting of the latter items. Finally, forgetting can occur if the information that is stored in the LTS cannot be retrieved. Difficulties in retrieving information can stem either from *interference* between similar sets of information in the LTS or from an ineffective search of the LTS. Thus forgetting can be seen as arising out of problems in encoding, storage and retrieval processes.

Problems with the Multistore Model   The multistore model reviewed above has, as we shall see, served both to organize a large body of observations and to guide and stimulate research concerning memory. However, there are a variety of problems associated with this model. Although a detailed critique of the model is premature at this point, it is worthwhile to consider here some of the general problems with this kind of model, for they are characteristic of many cognitive models of memory and have fundamental implications for how the study of memory might best proceed.

The main problem with the model described above concerns the postulation of permanent structural features of human memory. Cognitive theorists account for the complexities of the experienced organism by devising theories about the knowledge and the processing system that is inferred from overt behavior. In the case of the multistore model, the different retention functions that reliably occur under different input conditions are accounted for by postulating three memory stores that are permanent structural features of the organism. The problem is that to describe the STS and the LTS as permanent structural features of memory is to say that these stores are intrinsic properties of the human organism. But as we have seen, regularities in the behavior of humans may arise from ontogenetic as well as from phylogenetic factors. If one were to study adults with very different experiences, one might infer a very different set of structural features.

Cognitive theories in general aim to specify the capacities of the organism that determine how it can respond given exposure to a particular environment. The problem is that the adult's cognitive capacities and processes may depend upon prior experiences. Because the way in which an organism responds depends in part upon its history, there may not be a single, general answer to questions concerning how humans remember concrete words, how semantic information is organized, and so on. Accordingly, we should be very cautious in making inferences about the structural features of the memory system. Furthermore, we should continue to seek the antecedents of proposed structural features in an effort to achieve a full understanding of the memory system.

Another problem with the multistore model of memory is that it may not be necessary to postulate the existence of three memory stores. Many of the observations that have been interpreted in terms of the multistore model may also be accounted for by models that do not postulate multiple stores. As an example of the latter type of model, we shall consider the levels of processing approach proposed by Craik and Lockhart (1972; see also Craik & Tulving, 1975).

Levels of processing   Using theories of perception as a conceptual origin, Craik and Lockhart suggested that memory can be seen as a process in which incoming information is analyzed or processed on a number of different levels. For example, information is first analyzed in terms of its physical or sensory properties. When this analysis is completed, or while this analysis is going on (cf. Craik & Tulving, 1975), analysis can begin at another level, and the information might be analyzed in terms of, say, its phonological properties. The analysis can be continued through various levels or "depths" until the information has been analyzed at the deepest level, which is currently believed to be semantic in nature. According to Craik and Lockhart, the retention of information depends directly upon the depth to which that information has been processed, with deeper processing leading to longer retention.[1] Thus information that is processed at a superficial, physical level will be retained very briefly, whereas information that is processed at a semantic level may be retained for very long periods of time.

When memory is analyzed from the perspective of levels of processing, there is little need to postulate different memory stores. Numerous aspects of memory, such as the amount of time information is retained, may be seen as depending upon the level at which the information has been processed rather than on the storage of that information within a particular memory store. A more complete comparison and evaluation of the levels of processing and multistore models of memory cannot be undertaken until the next chapter. Nevertheless, the reader should keep in mind that it may be possible to analyze memory in terms of private processes without postulating multiple memory structures.

At this point, the reader might well ask what, if any, advantages follow from analyzing memory in terms of multiple levels of processing rather than multiple structures. We believe there are several advantages, the first of which concerns parsimony. Cognitive structures such as the STS and the LTS are inferred from numerous observations concerning memory, and are assumed to process information in particular ways. But if one says that a particular structure has operated only when information has been processed in just those particular ways, the cognitive structures have little explanatory value. If the only evidence for the operation of a structural component of memory is the observation that information has been processed in certain ways, the cognitive structures add little to an account based upon the processing that occurred. The postulation of a memory structure such as the STS is logically circular in the conditions described above. From the observation that information is processed in certain ways, it is inferred that a single structure underlies these sorts of processing, but the only evidence for the existence and the operation of the structure is the very occurrence of the processing. Thus if an account in terms of processes can do what an account based upon cognitive structures can do, the former account is preferred on the grounds of parsimony, for that account involves fewer assumptions.

Another advantage of analyzing memory in terms of processes lies in the avoidance of certain semantic snares. Speaking of memory in terms of structures may lead one to view memory as an entity or system of entities rather than a vast set of incredibly complex and varied processes. It is easy to lose sight of the fact that cognitive structures such as the STS and the LTS are hypothetical constructs. Indeed, after speaking of STS and LTS as storage spaces, it seems almost natural to think of these stores as actual places or anatomical loci within the organism. When cognitive structures are implicitly treated as if they correspond to anatomical structures, these cognitive structures are easily seen as permanent structural features of the organism. As we mentioned earlier, that view has not yet been substantiated empirically, and the general question of whether cognitive structures such as the STS correspond to anatomical structures must await the outcome of future research.

Furthermore, viewing memory in terms of structures can give rise to a rather static conception of memory, for structures are often spoken of as fixed entities with a given set of properties. As was emphasized by those working within the framework of Gestalt psychology (for example, Bartlett, 1932), memory is fluid, active and constructive in nature. These characteristics of memory should be reflected in a model of memory, and the levels of processing approach fares better in this regard than the multistore model does.

Concluding comments Both of the preceding information-processing models represent the attempt of cognitive psychologists to account for the complexities of the experienced organism by postulating equally complex internal processes. Although this strategy has met with considerable success and has led to the experimental analysis of many phenomena that had previously gone unstudied, we should recognize that the strategy taken by cognitive psychologists is but one way among many of attempting to deal with the intricacies of the experienced organism. At this early point, it is too soon to evaluate that strategy fully. Another strategy, which has much to recommend it, would be to analyze complex phenomena by specifying the public and private behavioral events that constitute a phenomenon such as sentence comprehension, and by making an exhaustive historical analysis of the antecedents of these events.

By and large, we shall for the sake of convenience use the terminology of information-processing models and speak of encoding, storage, retrieval, and so on. Before continuing, however, it should be noted that the terminology of processing, storage, images, and internal representations is troublesome, largely owing to its metaphorical nature. For example, to speak of visual images sometimes implies that we store static pictures inside our head. But whether images are best conceived of in terms of pictures or in terms of other processes is a matter of debate (for example, Kosslyn, 1975; Kosslyn & Pomerantz, 1977; Kosslyn, 1978; Paivio, 1971b; Pylyshyn, 1973; Skinner, 1953, 1974). Similarly, to say that information is stored suggests that this information is tucked away somewhere inside the organism. It may be that experience simply changes the organism and that the information is not literally stored away. In terms of information processing, it is possible that information storage does not involve something like a passive filing process but rather an active maintenance process whereby old information is integrated into new information systems. The general point is that much of the terminology used by contemporary cognitive theorists is metaphorical and we should carefully analyze the meaning of theoretical constructs such as "image," "storage," and so on.

Some Procedural Distinctions

For the reasons described above, we choose not to view memory in terms of structures such as the sensory register, the STS, and the LTS. However, this does not imply that we accept the levels of processing interpretation for the latter view has yet to be either formulated or tested thoroughly. The field of memory is a vast and formidable terrain that is perhaps best explored with an open attitude and an unwillingness to see through the eyes of any one theory.

In the following discussion, we will speak of memory in terms of *sensory memory, short-term memory,* and *long-term memory.* Unlike the distinction between the three memory stores, the distinctions between sensory, short-term, and long-term memories are procedural in nature. That is, these distinctions differentiate not between different memory structures but between different procedures or paradigms that have arisen in the study of memory. In sensory memory procedures, information is presented for a very brief period, typically less than one second, and the time between presentation and recall, called the retention interval, is also very brief. In contrast, long-term memory procedures often involve presenting information repeatedly and for much longer periods of time, at least on the order of seconds, and the retention interval may range anywhere from several minutes to several months. In between are short-term memory procedures, which usually involve an initial presentation for several seconds and a retention interval of up to about 30 seconds.

The procedural distinctions between sensory memory, short-term memory, and long-term memory are made primarily for reasons of convenience and say more about the behavior of experimenters than the processes involved in memory. The question of whether similar or unique processes are involved in the various memory paradigms should be settled empirically. But before questions so broad in scope can be discussed, we must first examine the basic procedures and phenomena of memory, and we shall now turn to the topic of sensory memory.

SENSORY MEMORY

The environment first makes contact with the organism at the level of the sensory receptors. Before information at the sensory level can affect the behavior of the organism, however, this information must be transmitted to the brain for further processing. For example, a visual stimulus might not exert discriminative control over behavior until the information at the level of the retina has been processed by the brain in the ways we call pattern recognition. The processing of information at the receptor level takes time, and here some potential problems arise for the organism. What if sensory information could be processed only when the physical stimulus is impinging upon the sensory receptor? In that case, the sensory information might not be processed adequately if the physical stimulus were very brief. Fortunately, we are structured in such a way that we can retain information in nearly original form long enough for recognition to occur, even when the physical stimulus is too brief to allow for recognition.

Sensory memory, the brief retention of raw, unprocessed information, is apparently a general phenomenon, at least in humans. Indeed, sensory memory has been observed in the visual (Sperling, G., 1960), auditory (Massaro, 1970) and tactile (Abramsky, Carmon, & Benton, 1971) modalities. Although it is likely that there is sensory memory for all sensory modalities, we shall restrict our discussion primarily to the visual modality, for it has been studied most thoroughly and can be used to illustrate the essential features of sensory memory.

In order to understand the process whereby sensory information is retained for further processing, we need to consider a number of questions. How much information is retained? What kinds of information are retained? How is the information forgotten? And so on. These questions are the foci of much research, and we shall consider each in examining visual sensory memory, also known as *iconic memory* (Neisser, 1967).

Visual Sensory Memory

One procedure which was first used to establish the existence of iconic memory and which is now used widely to study visual sensory memory involves exposing subjects to a visual stimulus for a very short period, say, 50 msec (one-twentieth of a sec). A tachistoscope, which is a device for controlling precisely the duration of visual stimuli, is typically used to present the stimuli. The visual stimulus might consist of a three-by-three array of letters such as the following:

M   T   F
K   Q   V
D   L   N

Following exposure to the stimulus, the subject is asked to report what was seen. Sperling (1960) used this procedure and asked adult subjects to recall as many letters as possible. The result was that the subjects could accurately report only four or five letters on the average. Does this imply that adult subjects can remember only four or five items in a sensory memory task? Did the subjects not see all of the presented letters? Or is it possible that they could only report four or five letters even though they had a brief memory of the entire display?

Interestingly, the subjects reported they could see more than they could report all at once. Thus the possibility arises that the subjects may have seen all the letters but retained them so briefly that only four or five could be reported. To test the possibility that the subjects had briefly seen and remembered more than they could report, Sperling devised an ingenious procedure called the *partial report procedure*. Whereas the previous *whole report procedure* required the subjects to report all they had seen, the partial report procedure required the subjects to report only the letters from one particular row. Immediately after the array of letters was shown, the subject heard a tone of high, medium, or low pitch, and these tones served as signals for the recall of the top, middle, or bottom rows, respectively. Thus a trial might consist of presenting the array for 50 msec followed by the presentation of a high tone. In this instance, the subject would be required to report the letters seen in the top row of the display. On other trials, the subject was required to recall letters from the other rows. Which row was to be reported varied irregularly from trial to trial, and the subjects were therefore unable to guess beforehand which row to report.

Because the subjects did not know which row to report until after the array had been presented, they had to rely on their memory of what they had seen in order to report accurately. Furthermore, if the subjects were able to report the letters of any of the three rows accurately, their memory of the items would have to include virtually all of the letters that had been presented. In other words, if the subjects had seen and briefly retained all of the items, they would be able to report the items from any particular row accurately, even though they were unable to report the letters of all rows accurately on a single trial.

The results of the experiment with the partial report procedure showed that the subjects could in fact briefly remember all they had seen, even though they could not report it all. Figure 10.2 shows the results from both the whole report and the partial report procedures for displays of various sizes. Consider

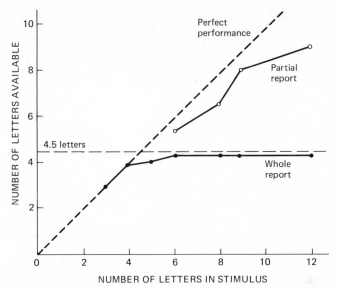

Fig. 10.2   The number of letters that can be recalled in the partial and the whole report procedures for displays of various sizes.   (After Sperling, 1960.)

the results for an array of nine letters. As Fig. 10.2 shows, the subjects in the partial report condition were able to recall almost all of the letters of any particular row. Therefore, they were able to retain all nine items when the recall signal immediately followed the stimulus display. In contrast, the subjects in the whole report condition recalled only about 50% of all presented items, despite the fact that they too must have remembered briefly (but too briefly to report) all nine items.

Why could the subjects in the whole report condition report only four or five items from an array of nine letters? This question is clarified by Fig. 10.3, which shows how the subjects performed in the partial report procedure when the delay between the stimulus array and the recall signal was increased. Figure 10.3 shows that the percentage of letters that were reported accurately decreased systematically as the recall signal was delayed longer and longer. Indeed, when the recall cue followed the stimulus array by 1.0 sec, the subjects in the partial report condition performed at the same level as the subjects in the whole report condition. These observations suggest that the subjects retained information about the entire array for a short time, but only long enough to report several letters accurately. The rapid decay of the sensory information (or the *icon* as it is sometimes called) was responsible for the poor performance in the whole report condition, for the time required to report all of the letters exceeded the storage time for the sensory information.

The observation that sensory information decays or fades rapidly has been confirmed in a variety of procedures. The exact length of retention, however, depends upon many procedural variables such as the brightness of the display, the characteristics of the visual field following exposure to the stimuli,

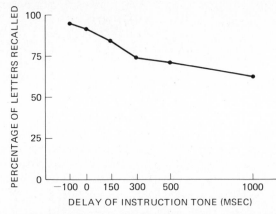

Fig. 10.3 The percentage of letters recalled in the partial report procedure as a function of the delay between the stimulus array and the recall signal. (After Sperling, 1960. Copyright 1960 by the American Psychological Association. Reprinted by permission.)

and so on (Dick, 1974; Turvey, 1978). Many estimates of the duration of iconic memory center around 250 msec (Haber & Hershenson, 1973), but additional research is required to assess the generality of this estimate.

Several important points are forthcoming from the preceding experiment. The first is that the subjects in the sensory memory task described above do briefly remember more than they can report. Although they can recall only four or five letters, they can recall *any* four or five letters from the array, thus showing that information concerning the entire array is available momentarily. The memory capacity of subjects in tasks concerning visual sensory memory appears quite large, and their capacity certainly extends beyond the four or five reported items (see Estes & Taylor, 1966, for further information concerning the capacity of iconic memory). The second point is that theories about how much subjects can remember are only as good as the methods on which they are based. The quality of an answer depends largely upon the quality of the question. In a sensory memory experiment, the whole and partial report procedures give rise to very different estimates of the capacity to remember. In our attempts to ascertain how much subjects can remember in a particular task, we should constantly remind ourselves of the possible limitations of our procedures and view our estimates of capacity as tentative and fallible.

Type of Information The information in iconic memory seems to be visual in nature. One convincing source of evidence on that point comes from studies of visual interference. For example, Averbach and Coriell (1961) presented an array of 16 letters and used either a bar or a circle to indicate which letter should be reported by the subject. Whereas the bar was presented above the letter to be reported, the circle was presented in such a way that it would have surrounded one of the letters if the array were still present. The results were that the circle actually impaired recall relative to the bar marker when it followed the array by 100 msec. Apparently, the circle acted as a masking stimulus, for the circle "erased" the letter it was intended to mark. This phenomenon, called *erasure,* may be important in eliminating relatively old visual information, thereby preventing the accumulation and confusion of old and new information (for further observations and interpretations of the erasure phenomenon see Dick, 1974; Kahneman, 1968; and Turvey, 1978). This erasure or interference effect appears to be produced only by visual stimuli, for the auditory signals used by Sperling did not produce interference. Interestingly, the interference effect has been obtained when the stimulus items were presented to one eye and the masking stimulus was presented to the other (DiLollo, Lowe, & Scott, 1973; Schiller, 1965). This observation suggests that erasure occurs to some extent at a central level rather than at the retina (but see Sakitt, 1976).

Several observations suggest that the information that is said to be in visual sensory memory is not only visual but also simple in nature and closely related to the physical characteristics of the external stimulus. In one experiment, subjects were shown an array of 12 colored letters and were asked to report only those letters of a particular color. The result was that recall was better in the partial report procedure than in a whole report procedure (Clark, S. E., 1969; von Wright, 1968, 1970; Well & Sonnenschein, 1973). Thus the subjects in an iconic memory procedure clearly retain information concerning color (Banks & Barber, 1977). Similar experiments have shown that subjects also remember information concerning the size, the shape, the brightness and the position of the presented items (Clark, S. E., 1969; Turvey & Kravetz, 1970; von Wright, 1968).

In contrast, the partial report procedure does not facilitate recall when the subjects are shown an array of letters and numbers and are asked to report only letters or only numbers (Sperling, 1960; von Wright, 1970; Well & Sonnenschein, 1973). Apparently, relatively simple sorts of information concerning color, position, size, and so on are involved in iconic memory, but the information seems not to be encoded or categorized in ways that permit the discrimination of letters from numbers. Presumably, the information in visual sensory memory must be processed to a deeper level before the discrimination between letters and numbers can be made.[2] In general, a great deal of processing must occur before the subjects can respond to the deeper aspects of information such as the semantic properties of the information.

Concluding Comments   In closing this discussion, we should note some of the problems involved in studying iconic memory, for they have implications for the study of memory in general. In many of the studies we have considered, the subjects were shown familiar stimuli and were asked to verbally report the items they had been shown (but see Eriksen & Collins, 1967). Two problems are involved in using this procedure. First, effective performance in this procedure depends not only upon iconic memory processes but also on the recoding of information into a verbal format. It is often difficult to determine whether a variable affects iconic memory processes or recoding processes, and further research is needed to define the domain of iconic memory more precisely. The second problem is that the use of highly familiar stimuli can influence the outcome of experiments on iconic memory (for example, Mewhort & Cornett, 1972).

The preceding considerations lead one to wonder how general the results of the preceding experiments are. What would happen if the subjects were shown unfamiliar stimuli and were not required to encode the information verbally? For example, the procedure might involve presenting briefly an array of unfamiliar visual stimuli and then, a short time later, presenting a single test item that may or may not have been presented in the array. The task of the subjects, called a *recognition task*, would be to press one of two buttons to indicate whether the test item was or was not from the original array. The recognition procedure might provide a more sensitive measure of how long visual information is retained in iconic memory, and might help us ascertain the generality of our current conceptions of iconic memory.

Auditory Sensory Memory

In the preceding section, we noted that much information would not affect the organism if there were no iconic memory. The temporary retention of raw, unprocessed information is important in audition, just as it is in vision. For example, time is required for the complex processing involved in the recognition of speech, and speech recognition would be very difficult at best if there were no brief retention of raw acoustic information. Fortunately, humans do seem to retain unprocessed auditory information for a brief period (Moray, Bates, & Barnett, 1965), and this type of sensory memory is sometimes called *echoic memory* (Neisser, 1967).

In order to understand echoic memory, we wish to ascertain the characteristics of echoic memory, such as the nature of the information, the duration of retention and the antecedents of forgetting. These aspects of echoic memory have been investigated recently through the following type of procedure (Massaro, 1970, 1972, 1974, 1975, 1976). First, the subjects were trained to discriminate between pure tones of 770 Hz and 870 Hz. More specifically, the subjects were exposed to a recognition procedure in which one of these two "test" tones was presented on a particular trial for 20 msec, and the subjects were to identify whether the tone they heard was the high or the low one. After the subjects had learned to identify each test tone accurately, the task was changed by presenting an intermediate tone of 820 Hz following the presentation of the test tone. The intermediate tone lasted 500 msec and acted as a "masking" tone in that it interfered with the processing of the test tones and impaired recognition.

Massaro varied the delay between the test tone and the masking tone, and he examined the effects of the masking tone upon the recognition of the test tones. The results for three individual subjects are shown in Fig. 10.4. Figure 10.4 shows that with very short delays between the test and masking tones, the recognition performance was very near the level expected on the basis of chance (50%). However, when the masking tone was delayed for 250 msec, the subjects recognized the test tones quite accurately. Clearly, the auditory infor-

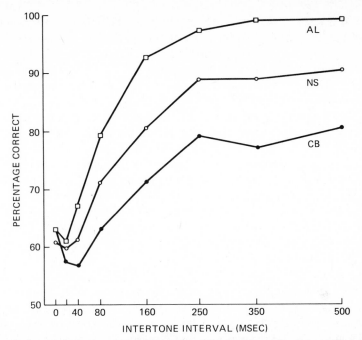

Fig. 10.4   Percentage of correct identifications of the test tones for three different subjects as a function of the delay between the test tone and the masking tone.   (From Massaro, 1972. Copyright 1972 by the American Psychological Association. Reprinted by permission.)

mation is processed *after* the presentation of the auditory stimulus, for recognition improved with the passage of time since the offset of the stimulus. Presumably, unprocessed auditory information, the *echo*, was retained and was processed during the delay between the test and masking tones. In further experiments, it was shown that the effect depicted in Fig. 10.4 depends neither on the duration of the masking tone (Massaro, 1971) nor on the similarity of the masking and test tones. Furthermore, the masking tone has similar effects to those described above even when the test tone is presented to one ear and the masking tone to the other (for a review, see Massaro, 1975).

These results help clarify several aspects of echoic memory. First, the auditory information decayed very rapidly. Recognition performance improved over intertone intervals of up to about 250 msec, but there was little improvement beyond that point. Apparently, the auditory information decayed after about 250 msec, thereby eliminating the possibility for further processing and improvements in performance. Another important point is that forgetting in echoic memory experiments results not only from decay but also from interference, for the presentation of the masking tone ended the processing of the test tone and impaired recognition. Finally, the results of the experiment showed that echoic memory, like iconic memory, involves to some extent a central process. Since the masking tone interfered with the recognition of the test tone when the tones were presented to different ears, the masking effect must have occurred at a central rather than a peripheral level.

Although the results of the preceding experiment have helped to clarify the nature of echoic memory, we are far from a deep understanding of the phenomenon. Indeed, it is difficult at this stage to decide whether or not a particular phenomenon is relevant to the study of echoic memory. The problem is the same one encountered in the study of iconic memory: Sensory memory involves the retention of raw, unprocessed or *precategorical* information, but retention cannot be measured until the information has been processed to a postcategorical level that permits the recognition or the recall of the information. Unfortunately, there is no sure assay for determining whether precategorical or postcategorical information is being studied, and one cannot be sure echoic memory is being studied. Consequently, there is controversy in the literature about the duration of echoic memory, and estimates range from under 1 sec to over 5 sec (cf. Crowder, 1976; Crowder & Morton, 1969; Neisser, 1967). Similarly, there are numerous views concerning the nature of the information involved in echoic memory (for example, Massaro, 1972; Crowder & Morton, 1969).

As we stated in our discussion of iconic memory, the procedures one uses influence the nature and the extent of processing. It is virtually certain that information at different levels of analysis is examined in the diverse procedures that have been used. Additional research is required to more specifically define and describe echoic memory and sensory memory in other modalities.

PATTERN RECOGNITION

Having discussed the retention of precategorical information, we may now consider the question of how the information in sensory memory is categorized. The process whereby unanalyzed information is identified or categorized is called *pattern recognition*. Basically, the process of pattern recognition entails comparing information retained in sensory memory to the relatively permanent information that has been acquired during the lifetime of the organism. When a match is made between the incoming sensory information and the more permanently stored information, a pattern is said to have been recognized.

Each day, we recognize with little effort innumerable visual and auditory stimuli. However, the effortlessness and the automaticity with which we recognize patterns belie the subtlety and complexity of the process. It has proven to be very difficult to devise machines that can "recognize" even a small number of words spoken by different speakers or written by different people, but not for a lack of trying. To see one of the basic problems involved, one need only to consider the diversity of the ways in which a particular word can be spoken or written. For example, consider the following variants of the letter E:

The variations of the letter E that we can recognize are virtually endless in number. If that were not so, we would experience much more difficulty in reading the handwriting of other people than we do, for the letters written by different individuals vary widely in size, shape, orientation and so on, and no two people write in exactly the same way.

The Template-Matching Hypothesis
The preceding observation bears on one theory of pattern recognition called the *template-matching hypothesis*. According to this hypothesis, the memory system stores a large number of internal representations, or templates, of objects and events that have been encountered in the past. When an external stimulus is encountered, it is compared to the stored templates, and if a match occurs, pattern recognition is said to have occurred. A simple everyday example of a template-matching system comes from the banking business, in which our checks are recognized and sorted by electronic devices. Each check has a serial number and an account number that appear in special print. The identification system involves a small number of characters (digits) that are highly distinctive and are invariant in form, orientation, and so on. Consequently, only a small number of internal templates are needed in an effective check-recognition system.

Now consider the problems encountered by the template-matching hypothesis. Recall that we are able to recognize an infinite number of different instances of a particular letter or word. The process of recognizing even the letter E could not consist of matching the stimulus letter with a miniature copy of that letter in one's memory, for the process would require that we store a template for each unique pattern we can recognize. If pattern recognition involved matching stimuli with templates, there would have to be an infinite number of templates in order for the process to be accurate. Thus the template hypothesis of pattern recognition ends up assuming what needs to be explained, for little is gained by postulating a hypothetical template for each pattern that can be recognized.

The template-matching hypothesis may be made more workable by proposing that what we store is not a template for each individual pattern but rather a small number of prototypes. Recall from our previous discussion (see pp. 284–286) that a prototype is the form that represents the central tendency of a set of stimuli. If incoming stimuli were encoded as prototypes plus permissible variations, there would be no need to postulate a large number of templates. Instead, we would be said to have a prototype for each category of stimuli we can recognize. Pattern recognition might then be seen as a process in which an incoming stimulus is compared to a small number of prototypes rather than a cumbersome number of templates (cf. Posner, 1969; Reed, 1972). As we noted previously, however, the nature of prototypes is unclear, and there is some question as to whether prototype models add anything to feature models (for example, Neuman, 1974; 1977), which we shall now consider.

Feature Detection
Currently, a good deal of evidence is converging to suggest that the phenomenon of pattern recognition comes about partly through the detection of the es-

sential features or properties of a stimulus. Each pattern that we can recognize can be seen as a configuration of elementary features, just as a phoneme can be seen as a bundle of distinctive features (see pp. 315–316; for a discussion of auditory features and speech perception, see Morse, 1974, 1978). The letters of the alphabet, for example, can be seen as configurations of about 12 features such as straight vertical lines, straight horizontal lines, closed curves, and so on.

Evidence that feature detection is involved in the recognition of patterns comes from a variety of sources. First consider the observation of what happens in a visual scanning task that requires subjects to search lists of letters as rapidly as possible to find a particular target letter that occurs in unpredictable positions in the lists. Finding the target letter clearly involves recognizing a particular pattern and rejecting others. If the recognition of the target entails the detection of elementary features, the difficulty of the scanning task should depend on the similarity of the target item to the other, nontarget items. In other words, if the subjects find the target by searching for certain features, then they should be able to find the target item faster when the nontarget items have very few features in common with the target item than when the nontarget items share many common features with target items. The greater the difference between the target and the nontarget items, the fewer the features that must be analyzed to find the target.

In fact, the time required to find a target item is influenced by the similarity of the target and the nontarget items (Neisser, 1964). For example, in searching the lists of curved letters such as *C, G* and *O*, subjects can reliably find the letter *Z* faster than they can in searching lists of straight-line letters such as *M, X* and *E*. Also, the subjects report that most of the letters in the array appear as a blur, and that is what would be expected if the subjects were analyzing selected aspects of the letters rather than the entire letters. These observations are clearly consistent with the view that the subjects recognize the target by examining various features of the letters in the search list. On the other hand, this result would not be predicted by a simple template hypothesis of pattern recognition.

In addition, an extensive amount of physiological evidence supports the view that the detection of features plays an important role in pattern recognition. For example, the visual systems of a wide variety of vertebrates contains both peripheral and central cells that respond or fire only to particular features of visual stimuli (Barlow, Narasimhan, & Rosenfeld, 1972; Hubel & Wiesel, 1962, 1968; Lettvin, Maturana, McCulloch, & Pitts, 1959). The visual cortex in cats and monkeys contains cells that respond only to vertical lines or only to horizontal lines, and so on. Interestingly, early visual experience seems to play a role in determining the tendency of some cortical cells to respond only to particular orientations (Leventhal & Hirsch, 1975; Wiesel & Hubel, 1965). Thus the presence of a particular feature detector in an adult organism does not necessarily imply that that detector is an inherent structural feature of the organism.

Of importance for this discussion is the observation that those specialized cells that respond to particular orientations of lines are relatively insensitive to the length and width of the lines. A neuron that responds to vertical lines could therefore respond to a very large number of different vertical lines. Thus insight into the question of how animals recognize an infinite number of variations of a certain pattern may come from an analysis of the characteristics of the functionally specialized neurons that act as feature detectors.

An analysis of pattern recognition in terms of feature detection has some important advantages. A feature theory of pattern recognition is very economical relative to a template hypothesis, for a small number of features can do what only a large number of templates could do. Furthermore, a feature theory can potentially account for the ability of animals to recognize patterns that are similar but not identical to those seen in the past. Finally, a feature theory can predict the complexity of certain pattern recognition tasks and can be used to predict the types of errors that are likely to occur (for example, Miller, G. A. & Nicely, 1955).

A feature theory does not, however, provide a comprehensive analysis of pattern recognition, for the context in which a particular pattern occurs is an important determinant of how a pattern is recognized.

Context and Pattern Recognition

If pattern recognition were solely a process of detecting features, the detection of particular features should invariably lead to the recognition of particular patterns. However, the detection of a set of features does not always result in the recognition of the same pattern, as Fig. 10.5a shows. Most people read the sequence of symbols in Fig. 10.5a as *THE CAT*. The middle symbol is the same in both words and thus contains exactly the same features. Nevertheless, this symbol is interpreted as *H* in the first word and as *A* in the second. Clearly, the context in which particular combinations of features occur determines how those features are responded to (cf. Norman, 1976; Palmer, 1975).

Fig. 10.5   Examples illustrating the effects of context on perception. (a) The physical stimulus of the middle "letter" is identical, yet it is perceived differently in the context of different letter arrangements. (From Neisser, 1967). (b) and (c) The fragmented physical stimulus is identical, yet it is difficult to "read" when presented alone in (b) and easy to "read" when presented in the context of (c).

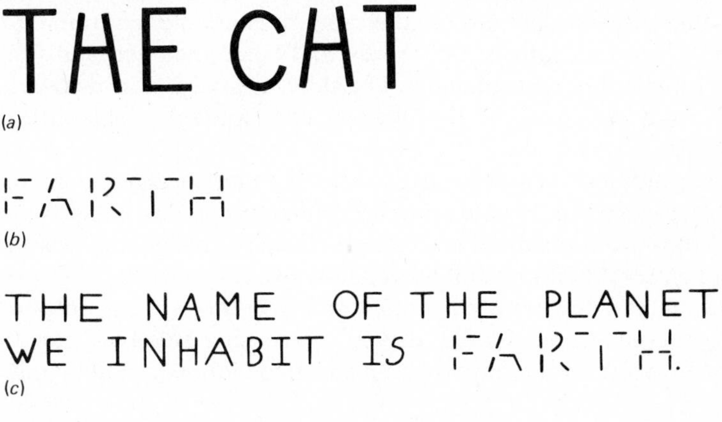

(a)

(b)

(c)

The effects of context are pervasive in the recognition of linguistic stimuli (for example, Massaro, Jones, Lipscomb, & Scholz, 1978). For example, although the same features are shown in Fig. 10.5*a* and *b,* the word *earth* is easily and reliably recognized only in the context of the sentence. The role of context in the recognition of the written word is perhaps most clearly demonstrated by an analysis of reading (Haber, 1978; Norman, 1976). Skilled readers process between 300 and 600 words per minute on the average. In order to read 600 words per minute, the reader must recognize as many as 10 words, or 50 to 70 letters each second! However, that high rate of recognition is misleading, for language is highly redundant, and from our prior experiences, we have learned well which sequences of words and letters are likely to occur in our language. Indeed, in reading, it is unnecessary to detect many features of individual words or letters since the words and letters are predictable from the context in which they occur. To appreciate the role of context in reading, try reading upside down for about 15 min. Initially, you will probably tend to read letter by letter and word by word. But as you improve, you will come to read in larger chunks such as phrases, and you tend to do so largely on the basis of the linguistic context in which the words occur.

The contribution of context to the recognition of linguistic stimuli is not restricted to the written word, for the context also plays an important role in the recognition of spoken words. For example, if meaningful words are played against a background of white noise, the words are more easily recognized when they occur as part of a meaningful sentence than when they occur alone (Miller, G. A., Heise, & Lichten, 1951).

Data-Driven and Conceptually Driven Processing Largely because of the contribution of contextual factors to pattern recognition, a distinction has been made between two types of processing: data-driven and conceptually driven. A processing system is said to be *data-driven* if the processing operations proceed from the incoming data through a series of increasingly sophisticated analyses. For example, the analysis of a written sentence would be described as data-driven if the analysis began with the stimulation of the rods and cones by the visual stimuli and then proceeded through a second stage involving the detection of features such as straight and curved lines and orientations of those lines. The process would presumably continue until combinations of features, letters and words had been analyzed and the sentence had been interpreted semantically. The flow of analysis in data-driven processing is from the data to the deeper conceptual or semantic levels of processing.

Conceptually driven processing is, as the name suggests, the opposite of data-driven processing. In conceptually driven processing, the flow of analysis proceeds from the conceptual or semantic level to the level of analysis of sensory features, combinations of features, and so on. In a sense, data-driven processing entails starting with the input and working to the deeper levels of analysis, whereas conceptually driven processing involves starting at the deeper levels of analysis and working toward shallower levels and the data.

When context affects the recognition of patterns, the knowledge that is the legacy of prior experience is utilized in the recognition process. Thus an effect of context upon pattern recognition entails conceptually driven processing.

How does conceptually driven processing occur? It is known that conceptual factors can increase both the speed of pattern recognition (for example, Meyer & Schvaneveldt, 1971; Meyer, Schvaneveldt, & Ruddy, 1974) and the accuracy of pattern recognition (Johnston & McClelland, 1973; Reicher, 1969; Wheeler, 1970). But the question remains as to how contextual factors exert the influence that they do. One possibility is that contextual factors allow for a partial and selective analysis of the features of the stimuli to be recognized (Rummelhart, 1977; Rummelhart & Siple, 1974; Smith, E. E., & Spoehr, 1974). For example, in processing the sentence *The name of the planet we inhabit is "earth,"* we can recognize the word *earth* without analyzing every feature of every letter of that word (see Fig. 10.5). The reason is that, on the basis of our knowledge derived from our previous experiences, the occurrence of *earth* is highly predictable in the context of the sentence. Presumably, when the word *earth* is expected, fewer stimulus features must be detected before the recognition of the word can occur (cf. Rummelhart & Siple, 1974).

Another possible mechanism whereby context could influence pattern recognition concerns the speed of processing. Perhaps contextual factors, rather than permitting a partial or selective analysis of features, simply speed up the detection of the relevant features and combinations of features. According to the latter view, many irrelevant features may be partially analyzed even in the presence of contextual information (cf. Shiffrin, 1976), but the relevant features may be detected more rapidly and may be subsequently analyzed further than the irrelevant features. We shall pursue the issue further in the subsequent discussion of serial and parallel processing. We mention the latter alternative here to point out that it may not be necessary to conclude that context has its effects by reducing the number of stimulus features that are analyzed.

Regardless of the processes whereby context affects pattern recognition, it is clear that both the stimuli to be recognized and the contextual stimuli that are present affect pattern recognition. In other words, both data-driven and conceptually driven processing affect the recognition of patterns. Indeed, in everyday situations, the two types of processing seem to proceed simultaneously. For example, in recognizing *earth* in *The name of the planet we inhabit is "earth,"* conceptually driven processing will very likely occur for most adult speakers of English. However, before the sentential context can affect the recognition of *earth,* we must have recognized, at least partially, the previous words of the sentence such as *the* and *name.* The recognition of the latter words is very likely to entail data-driven processing. After some data-driven processing has occurred and a meaningful, sentence-like context has been developed, conceptually driven processing can then strongly influence the recognition of the last words in the sentence.

In closing this discussion, we should note that the distinction between data-driven and conceptually driven processing is not always straightforward.

There are currently no well-established rules for distinguishing between the two types of processing. Moreover, the contribution of prior experience to pattern recognition may turn out to be too complex to be captured by the distinction between data-driven and conceptually driven processing. For example, after a particular stimulus has been processed repeatedly in a particular, conceptually driven way, the "data" may be fundamentally altered even when the stimulus is presented outside of its typical context. Since the extent to which recognition may ever be said to be truly data-driven is unclear, the distinction between data-driven and conceptually driven processing is fuzzy and remains to be clarified by further research.

Analysis-by-Synthesis   The importance of contextual factors in pattern recognition has led to the view that pattern recognition is much more than a passive process of matching inputs with either templates or features. Rather, pattern recognition appears to be an active process that is strongly influenced by one's prior experiences. Some attempts have been made to incorporate the effects of context into an active model of pattern recognition. One of these models is called the *analysis-by-synthesis* model, and it was first devised to handle the recognition of speech (Halle & Stevens, 1959; see Neisser, 1967, for a discussion of the model as it applies to both vision and audition). According to the analysis-by-synthesis model, pattern recognition is a process of construction whereby the organism synthesizes or generates internal patterns and compares them to the stimulus that is to be recognized. When a match is made, recognition is said to have occurred. The generation of internal patterns for comparison is guided by the context in which the stimulus occurs.

The details of how contextual factors actually guide the synthesis of internal patterns remains unclear, and we mention the analysis-by-synthesis model here primarily to discuss the potential benefits and limitations of computer simulation. Computer scientists have been fairly successful in combining the processes of analysis-by-synthesis and feature detection to devise a computer program that recognizes handwriting (for example, Mermelstein & Eden, 1964). The fact that a computer program based upon analysis-by-synthesis and feature detection can recognize many of the patterns that humans do is important for the following reason. If a computer program based upon a model of how humans recognize patterns could only recognize a few of the patterns humans do, the adequacy of the model would be called into question. On the other hand, if that computer program could recognize the same patterns humans do, the plausibility of the model would be increased, for the model would at least be consistent with the observations. At an early stage of research, consistency with the observations is about as much as can be required of a model. In that sense, models that integrate the processes of analysis-by-synthesis and feature detection are promising. As this type of model develops, it will be evaluated according to increasingly stringent criteria such as the ability to make precise and interesting predictions.

The preceding comments show that the computer can be more than a conceptual framework for information-processing analyses. However, a note of caution is called for at this point. The fact that a computer program can do some of the things humans do does not necessarily imply that it does those things in similar or isomorphic ways (see Fodor, 1968, for a complete discussion of the issues involved). Another problem with computer-based models is that our working models seem to forge our conceptions of memorial processes almost as much as do the observations to be explained. In principle, that may not be problematic, but in practice, our understanding of memorial processes may not progress optimally by describing what humans do only in terms of what computers do. By allowing the nature of our theories to be deeply immersed in the computer technology of the times, we may overlook the possibility that existing computers may simply lack some of the important cognitive properties that humans have. The point is not that we should distrust all computer models but that we should recognize both the potential merits and pitfalls of those models.

Selective Attention

In the preceding section, we saw that one view of the effects of contextual factors is that they may permit a partial and selective analysis of the stimuli that are to be recognized. In that view, pattern recognition involves selectively attending to some aspects of the presented stimuli but not to others. Not all theories suggest that selective attention is implicit in the process of pattern recognition, but there is little doubt that selective attention and pattern recognition are closely related. The study of pattern recognition may be advanced by an analysis of the phenomena of selective attention, and that is the purpose of this section.

Dichotic Listening   One common example of a situation in which selective attention is said to occur arises at parties and other social gatherings. Many conversations may be going on simultaneously in a crowded room, but you understand or attend to only the speech of the person with whom you are talking. Some of the complexities involved in listening to a conversation during a crowded, noisy party may be captured in the laboratory by the *dichotic-listening procedure*. In this procedure, different auditory stimuli are simultaneously presented to the two ears by means of stereophonic headphones. The listener is instructed to attend to only the information fed into one ear. As an index of compliance with the instructions, the subject is often asked to repeat each word heard or to *shadow* the message to which the subject has been instructed to attend (Broadbent, 1952).

Now consider some of the major findings that have come from this procedure. The listener is able to shadow the message in the attended ear with very few mistakes—especially if the speaking voices and the content of the two messages are different, and if the attended message is connected prose such as that found in a novel. The delivery of the shadowed message tends to be flat and unemotional and occurs after some delay with pausing between phrases, but it is essentially error-free.

What is the fate of the unshadowed message? Questioning of the subjects at the conclusion of the experiment indicated that they recalled very little, if any, of the message that they had been instructed to ignore. The content of the unshadowed message, and even the language in which it had been spoken, could not be identified. A word repeated as often as 35 times in the unshadowed message was not remembered (Moray, 1959). The subjects detected only such gross characteristics as the sex of the speaker, whether the message consisted of words or pure tones, and so on. Thus, as measured by responses to questions at the end of the session, the behavior of the subjects had been largely unaffected by the unattended message (see Cherry, 1953; Cherry & Taylor, 1954; Moray, 1959; and Treisman, 1964, for related observations).

Filter Theory From the preceding observations, it appeared that humans have a limited capacity to respond to simultaneously presented stimuli. This apparent limitation upon the organism's capacity for processing information was likened to a filter that permits only one of many incoming messages to pass at a time (Broadbent, 1957, 1958). The unattended message was "filtered out" and therefore did not affect responding.

In the early versions of filter theory, incoming messages were held to be analyzed in terms of their gross physical characteristics. As the result of filtering, only the attended message was analyzed at deeper semantic levels. But further research discredited the notion that only the physical features of the unattended message were analyzed. For example, if the word *good* occurs in the unshadowed message and is differentially paired with one conceptual class of shadowed words (for example, the class of human nouns), words in that class are produced more frequently in a test conducted at the end of the session (Konecni & Slamecka, 1972). That effect could not occur if the subject were responsive only to the gross physical aspects of the unshadowed message. Similar results were obtained in studies in which shadowed words were preceded by unshadowed words that were related in meaning. Specifically, there was a small (80 msec) but reliable decrease in the speed with which the shadowed word was spoken (Lewis, J., 1970).

In a similar vein, it was observed that if the listener's name was spoken in the unshadowed message, it was often recognized (Moray, 1959). Even more striking was the result obtained with phrases such as the following.

Shadowed message: . . . crept out of . . . flowers . . .
Unshadowed message: . . . brightly colored . . . the swamp . . .

The listener would be apt to say "crept out of the swamp" even though the last part of the statement had been presented to only the unattended ear (Triesman, 1960; cf. MacKay, 1973). Thus the experience of the subject with the grammatical and semantic aspects of language overrode the instructions to attend to only one ear. Finally, if the listener were unexpectedly stopped in the middle of the shadowing task, the last few words of the unshadowed message could be recalled if questioning occurred within 30 sec of the interruption (Norman, 1969). All of these findings indicate that the meaning of the unshadowed message can affect performance, although the effect is not detectable when measured by recall at the end of the experiment.

Although various efforts have been made to accommodate these unruly findings through more complex conceptions of how a filter might operate (cf. Deutsch, J.A. & Deutsch, 1963; Moray, 1970; Triesman, 1969), many investigators (for example, Hirst, Neisser, & Spelke, 1978; Norman & Bobrow, 1975; Neisser, 1976) have questioned whether a filter theory can in principle account for the complexities of selective attention. Filter theories are based upon the assumption that humans have a limited capacity for processing simultaneously present stimuli. However, with extended experience the apparent capacity of the organism may change. For example, novices to the dichotic listening task detect numbers in the unshadowed message only 4% of the time. But a well-practiced subject may detect the numbers 83% of the time (Underwood, G., 1974). The complex relationships between capacity and experience have posed serious problems for filter theories, and some contemporary theories of attention have diverged sharply from filter theories. We shall examine one of those theories in our discussion of the relationship between pattern recognition and attention, but first let us consider more thoroughly the relationships between capacity and experience.

Capacity and Experience   Many everyday examples of the changing ability to respond to multiple inputs are available. If you remember the concentration required when you were first learning to drive a car and how you now sometimes drive from one place to another with nary a thought for the specific movements required in driving, then you can appreciate the change that experience can produce. Experience produces what has been called *automaticity,* the capability to engage in an interaction with the environment in the relative absence of awareness (Norman, 1976). As automaticity develops through repeated experience, attentional effects also change, as the following experiment illustrates.

Subjects were told to attend to one of two messages being given simultaneously over both earphones. Note that this is not a dichotic listening procedure since both messages were presented to each ear. It is a more difficult task to follow a message under the circumstances just described. In addition to attending to one of the messages, a light in front of the subject would intermittently increase in intensity. When the light intensity increased, the subjects were instructed to press a button as rapidly as possible. The time required to press the button, the reaction time, was recorded (Johnston & Heinz, 1974, cited in Norman, 1976).

The purpose of the experiment was to determine how the reaction time to detect the light change varied with the familiarity of the message being attended to. Speaking loosely, increases in reaction time were interpreted to mean that following the message required some attention; hence, there was less attention available for detection of the light. As might be anticipated, when the message was made familiar by presenting it to the subject many times before the experiment, the reaction time was short. When the message was unfamiliar, the reaction time to the light was increased. Thus, whatever limitations in processing capacity exist, they are altered by experience.

Through the use of techniques such as the monitoring of multiple aspects of performance, including responses at the physiological level, progress is being made in the experimental analysis of processes underlying attentional effects (Posner, 1974, 1978). Through such work, the possibility, the extent and the nature of capacity limitations in the genesis of attentional effects may be explored.

Pattern Recognition and Attention

In this section, we shall examine the evidence for and against attentional involvement in pattern recognition, and we shall see that the role of attention in pattern recognition may depend upon the conditions under which pattern recognition occurs. Recall that pattern recognition involves the detection of features from the information in sensory memory. One way to pose the question of attentional involvement is to ask whether the feature detection process is serial in nature. Do adults extract features from the information in sensory memory one after another, or can many features be detected simultaneously? If features are analyzed one at a time, then *serial scanning* is said to have occurred. If many features are extracted or detected simultaneously, then *parallel scanning* is said to have occurred. Since serial scanning by definition entails a selective, one-at-a-time analysis of features, selective attention (but not necessarily conscious attention) is implicit in serial scanning. To the extent that selective attention is implicit in the process of pattern recognition, we may expect to find evidence of serial scanning. But to the extent that attention does not enter into the process of pattern recognition, we may expect to find evidence of parallel scanning.

Serial and Parallel Scanning One strategy that has often been utilized in determining whether information is scanned in a serial or a parallel manner is to assess the effects of display size upon the detection of target items (Estes & Taylor, 1966; Sternberg, 1975). For example, Estes and Taylor (1966) used a tachistoscope to expose subjects to arrays of 8, 12, or 16 letters for 50 msec. The task of the subjects was to search for the letters B and F, and to indicate which letter they detected by pressing one of two keys. The results of the experiment were that as the display size increased from 8 to 16 letters, the proportion of correct detections decreased. This observation is consistent with the view that the information in visual sensory memory is scanned serially. Recall that the latter information decays rapidly. If serial scanning were occurring, more time would be required to find the target letter in a large display than in a smaller display, for more items would have to be scanned in the former case. As the display size increases, it becomes more likely that the sensory information will decay before the target letter is reached in a serial scan. Thus, if the sensory information were scanned serially, detection should become less accurate as the display size is increased, and that is exactly what was observed. (For additional evidence for serial scanning see Bryden, 1960, 1966; Estes & Wessel, 1966; Mewhort & Cornett, 1972.)

The preceding observations should not lead to the view that serial scanning inevitably occurs in the types of letter detection procedures described above. Under some conditions, variations in display size do not affect performance. For example, if the target and the nontarget items are physically dissimilar (for example, T as opposed to O and G), variations in display size have no effect upon detection performance (Gardner, G. T., 1973; Estes, 1972; Shiffrin & Gardner, 1972). In general, when the target and nontarget items are similar, serial scanning seems to occur, but when the target and nontarget items are dissimilar, parallel scanning seems to occur. (For additional evidence of parallel scanning see Shiffrin, 1976; Shiffrin & Schneider, 1977; Wolford, Wessel, & Estes 1968.)

Parallel Processing and the Focus of Attention   At this point, a dilemma has arisen. On one hand, some evidence supports the view that attention is involved in pattern recognition and that the scanning occurs serially, presumably because of a limited processing capacity at the perceptual level. On the other hand, some evidence supports the view that scanning occurs in parallel and without attentional limitations. In an attempt to resolve this dilemma, theorists have formulated numerous interpretations of the data. One interpretation entails the postulation of distinct stages of processing that are characterized by different processing capacities (for example, Gardner, G. T., 1973; Shiffrin, 1976). According to this account, the information from sensory memory is extracted in a parallel manner and without any limitations upon processing capacity at that stage. In that view, the processing that occurs following pattern recognition is subject to the limitations of processing capacity. More specifically, it has been argued that after information has been recognized, it is processed in short-term memory, which has a limited processing capacity. Presumably, the limited processing capacity of short-term memory necessitates serial processing. According to this view, then, the occurrence of serial scanning and the phenomena of selective attention result from the limited capacity of short-term memory.

To clarify the preceding approach, consider how the model applies to the observation that the speed of performance in a letter-detection task decreases as the display size is increased, but only when the nontarget items are similar to the target item. By assuming that pattern recognition involves parallel scanning and no limitations of processing capacity, one accounts for the finding that increasing the display size does not affect reaction time when the target and nontarget items are dissimilar. The effects of increasing the display size when the target and nontarget items are similar can be accounted for by assuming that after the letters in the display have been scanned in parallel and recognized, decisions must be made in short-term memory as to whether the target letter occurred. When these items are confusable, the decisions are made difficult and, because of the limited processing capacity of short-term memory, the decisions are presumably made in a serial manner.

The preceding account is consistent with many observations (see Shiffrin, 1976). However, that account is difficult to test, for there is no established way of determining empirically whether a variable such as similarity of target and nontarget items affects processes at the level of pattern recognition or at the level of short-term memory. Consequently, the account can currently be made only in a *post hoc* manner and involves assuming that the occurrence of serial processing reflects the limited capacity of short-term memory. Furthermore, the account rests on the assumption that the capacity of short-term memory is inherently limited. As we saw earlier, the postulation of inherent capacity limitations carries many dangers and often fails to capture the complex relations between processing capacity and experience. Finally, the account seems to be unparsimonious since the data can be accounted for without postulating two different processing mechanisms with different capacities. We shall now consider an alternative account that is based upon a distinction between data-limited and resource-limited processes.

Data-Limited and Resource-Limited Processes   Norman and Bobrow (1975) have defined *resource-limited* tasks as those in which performance can be improved by devoting additional processing resources to the task. Playing chess is a resource-limited task since the harder one tries, at least up to some level, the better one performs. Understanding a lecture is also a resource-limited task in that one's understanding often improves the more cognitive resources one devotes to the task. In contrast to resource-limited tasks, *data-limited* tasks are those in which performance is independent of processing resources. On a data-limited task, performance will not improve no matter how much harder one tries or how much more one practices. Examples of data-limited tasks would include the detection of suprathreshold sounds in a quiet room or the application of one's automobile brakes upon seeing a red light ahead under conditions of high visibility and light traffic.

It is important to notice that each particular task may be both resource-limited and data-limited. In loose terms, the task of applying one's brakes in the presence of a red light is resource-limited in that performance may be improved up to a point by devoting more attention to the task. However, a point will eventually be reached beyond which no improvements in performance will occur no matter how much more attention and effort are devoted to the task. At the latter point, the task is said to have become data-limited and can no longer be said to be resource-limited. Another important consideration is that tasks may differ widely in the points at which they become data-limited. For example, both playing chess and detecting the occurrence of tones may initially be resource-limited tasks. But the detection task may become data-limited much sooner than the chess-playing task, for the detection task would require the allocation of fewer resources to become data-limited than the chess-playing task would.

In order to extend the distinction between resource-limited and data-limited tasks to the observations concerning pattern recognition and the role of attention, two assumptions have been made, both of which are common to a wide variety of models. The first assumption is that the total amount of processing resources is finite. In other words, there is a limited central processing capacity. The second assumption is that subjects are flexible in how they allocate their processing resources. A very complicated task will demand more resources than a very simple task. The distinction between data-limited and resource-limited processes, together with the preceding assumptions, shall hereafter be called the *resource allocation model.*

Figure 10.6 shows how the model may be applied to the observations concerning serial and parallel scanning described above. Function A shows performance on a task (Task A) that is data-limited over most of the range of resources that may be devoted to it. Although this function is hypothetical, it might correspond to performance in a relatively simple task such as detecting a particular target letter from an array of unconfusable letters. Performance on this task at point (1) is said to be data-limited, since performance does not improve when additional resources are allocated to the task, as at point (2). If performance on the task were measured at points (1) and (2), the speed and accuracy of detection might be very high. Under these conditions, one might be led to postulate that the processing that occurs during the performance of Task A is automatic and free from all limitations upon processing capacity. But note that such a conclusion would not be justified, for performance before point (1) was resource-limited and would not have appeared to be free of capacity limitations. The main point is that capacity limitations will not be apparent to an experimenter who measures performance in the range at which performance is data-limited. To ascertain the presence or absence of capacity limitations, one must measure performance throughout the entire range of resource allocation. That is clearly hard to do, but the point remains that capacity limitations may go unnoticed when performance is measured only in the region in which it has become data-limited.

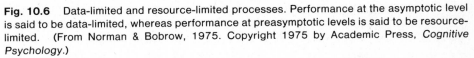

Fig. 10.6   Data-limited and resource-limited processes. Performance at the asymptotic level is said to be data-limited, whereas performance at preasymptotic levels is said to be resource-limited.   (From Norman & Bobrow, 1975. Copyright 1975 by Academic Press, *Cognitive Psychology.*)

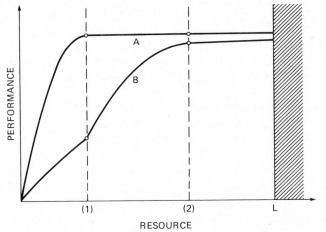

Now consider performance on a more difficult task, such as one that involves the detection of a particular target letter in an array of highly confusable letters, Task B. As shown in Function B of Fig. 10.6, at point (1) performance is considerably poorer than performance on the easier task shown by Function A. Specifically, the speed and accuracy of detection at point (1) might be quite low. Under these conditions, detection would occur slowly and inaccurately, and one might conclude that the processing that occurs in Task B is necessarily subject to severe limitations of capacity and that the processing occurs in a serial rather than a parallel manner. However, this conclusion would be erroneous, for the allocation of additional resources to the performance of the task could significantly improve performance, as shown in Function B at point (2). If performance on Tasks A and B were measured at point (2), there would appear to be no differences either in processing capacity or in the mode of processing (that is, serial or parallel). Indeed, Neisser (1974) has shown that, given sufficient practice and presumably the allocation of sufficient resources, adults can search for 10 letters in a large array of similar letters as rapidly as they can search for one letter. The main point is that performance may at a particular point in time appear to suffer from intrinsic limitations of processing capacity, but in fact the imperfect performance may result simply from the failure to allocate sufficient resources to the task.

On a broader level, one must be very cautious and do extensive experimental work before accounting for phenomena in terms of the presence or absence of intrinsic limitations of processing capacity. Those intrinsic limitations may exist, but they may often be inferred erroneously from performance that is resource-limited. Conversely, the absence of capacity limitations may often be erroneously inferred from performance that is data-limited. In a sense, then, the entire question of capacity limitations and attentional involvement in pattern recognition must be left open until performance has been investigated over a broad range of resource allocation. One prominent theorist (Kintsch, 1977) in the field of memory has summarized matters succinctly:

> There is no need for a model with two separate processing units, one for perceptual analysis without capacity limitations and one with capacity limitations for the "higher" mental operations. One central processor, with strictly limited resources, is all that is required to explain the experimental observations, if one keeps in mind that different processes become data limited at different resource levels. (Kintsch, 1977, p. 139)

Merits of the Resource Allocation Model   One advantage of the model is its relative parsimony. For example, in the preceding discussion we saw that the model could be used to interpret the data concerning pattern recognition without postulating two separate processing units with different capacities. Furthermore, the model recognizes the difficulties involved in attributing behavioral phenomena to intrinsic limitations of processing capacity. The model leads one to investigate the effects of a wide variety of experiences and training conditions before drawing conclusions regarding the intrinsic capacities and limitations of the organism. In a similar vein, the model makes it clear that theoretical constructs such as the short-term store or the stages of information processing are postulated primarily for the sake of convenience. The information-processing system is described as a set of possible resources that can be utilized in different behavioral tasks. Processing may be seen as a continuous stream, and terms such as "sensory memory," "short-term memory," and "shallow level of processing" are labels that identify the apparently important products of the continuous stream of processing (for further discussion of this view see Kintsch, 1977; Norman & Bobrow, 1975; Norman, 1976).

Applications to Attention Another benefit conferred by the resource allocation model is that it may help to interpret some of the complexities of attention. Recall that under some conditions, adults can simultaneously perform two tasks such as reading a familiar passage and detecting the presence of a light. This observation poses problems for attentional models that involve strictly serial processing and strict limitations upon processing capacity. In contrast, the ability to perform two tasks simultaneously is accommodated nicely by the resource allocation model. According to this model, doing two things simultaneously is possible as long as neither task requires a very high percentage of the available processing resources. If this restriction is met, the available cognitive resources may be allocated to the two tasks in such a way that both may be performed efficiently at the same time. Within this framework, then, it is not surprising that adults can read a familiar passage and simultaneously perform well on a light-detection task. But when the passage is difficult and a high percentage of the processing resources are devoted to reading, there are insufficient resources available for effective performance on the light-detection task.

The resource allocation model provides an interpretation of some of the complex relationships between apparent capacity and experience. For example, at a particular point in time an organism may be unable to simultaneously read a prose passage and detect the occurrence of a light, and one might say that the person lacks the capacity to do both concurrently. But the inability to do both may not result from inherent limitations on processing capacity, and the situation may change radically with additional experience. Through experience, the organism may come to allocate the cognitive resources in a more effective manner and may learn to perform both tasks simultaneously. Thus many changes in apparent capacity may in fact result from changes in the allocation of processing resources.

Much remains to be learned about how organisms come to allocate their cognitive resources in the ways that they do. In the study of resource allocation, the phenomenon of automaticity may figure prominently. When a task becomes well learned, performance may require fewer resources than it once did and may become "automatic." Although the nature and antecedents of automaticity are presently unclear, the analysis of that phenomenon may help us to understand the complex relationships between resource allocation and performance.

Problems with the Resource Allocation Model Of course, the resource allocation model is not completely meritorious. The central problem is that it is difficult to determine empirically when performance is data-limited and when it is resource-limited. When performance on a task has reached asymptote and no change in performance results from many attempts to allocate more resources to the task, one might conclude that performance is data-limited. But how does one know for sure that performance will be unaffected by the allocation of further resources? A related problem is that data limitations and resource limitations are inferred directly from the performances they are intended to explain. Thus the distinction is circular to some extent, and if the appropriate caution is not exercised, the distinction may be used to account for many phenomena in solely a *post hoc* manner.

A fundamental question that the model raises is whether it is advisable given our present state of knowledge to formulate accounts in terms of resource limitations. The processing resources that an organism has may depend upon its prior experiences. Particular resource limitations may not be intrinsic properties of organisms and may partially result from prior experience. The crucial point is that we do not yet know very much about the contribution of experience to the phenomena observed in studies of letter detection (pattern recognition) and dichotic listening (attention). By interpreting behavioral phenomena in terms of the presence or absence of resource limitations, we may mistakenly accept the common properties of organisms that arise from the complex effects of prior experience as intrinsic structural properties of the organisms.

The resolution of the preceding problems must come from further theoretical and empirical research. For the present, we may view the distinction between data-limited and resource-limited processes as a useful heuristic for interpreting the phenomena of pattern recognition and attention. As we proceed to the topic of short-term memory, we should also keep in mind the limitations of any framework that includes assumptions about intrinsic limitations (or lack thereof) of processing capacity.

SHORT-TERM MEMORY

Up to this point, we have seen that the organism and the environment first make contact when the organism takes in raw, sensory information. Whereas much of that information is lost through rapid decay or through interference, some information is categorized or recognized. We may now ask what happens to the categorized information. Clearly not all categorized information is retained. Almost everyone has had the experience of looking up a phone number and then forgetting it before dialing it. What are the factors that facilitate or impair the retention of categorized information that has just been acquired? This question is the central focus of research concerning short-term memory. Even to begin to answer the question, we need to ask several related questions. How is categorized information that is retained for brief periods of time represented or encoded? How much of that information can be retained over the short run? How is it retrieved? And so on. An understanding of short-term memory must come from the consideration of each of these questions and it is to that task that we now turn.

Encoding and Short-Term Memory

To ask how information is encoded is to ask how it is represented inside the memory system. A stimulus such as a printed word may be encoded in numerous ways. For example, the word *bat* may be encoded on the basis of its visual features, on the basis of how it sounds, on the basis of its various meanings, and so on. The question of how a particular stimulus is encoded must be decided empirically, for there is often a discrepancy between the way the experimenter encodes the stimulus and the way in which the subject encodes the stimulus.

To determine how a stimulus has been encoded, experimenters have used procedures that are very similar to those used to identify which properties of a stimulus control the responding of nonhumans. Experimenters have often adopted the strategy of analyzing errors to determine how a stimulus has been encoded. For example, if a subject recalled *dog* instead of *collie,* that error would indicate that, to some extent, *collie* had been encoded semantically. A variation upon this strategy is to vary the stimulus along particular dimensions and then observe how many errors are made. For example, to test whether a subject was encoding letters such as *F* on the basis of their acoustic properties, one could test whether more errors occurred when letters similar in sound (for example, *V*) or similar in appearance (for example, *E*) were presented simultaneously. With these procedures in mind, let us now examine the different types of encoding that can occur in short-term memory tasks.

Phonological Encoding   Quite often information is encoded in a verbal form. Since it is unclear whether the verbal code is acoustic (Conrad, R., 1964) or articulatory (Hintzman, 1967; for a discussion of this issue see Crowder, 1976), we shall use the more general phrase "phonological encoding." Evidence for phonological encoding has come primarily from an analysis of the types of errors that the subjects make in short-term memory experiments. For instance, if adult humans are briefly shown a series of six letters and asked to write them down immediately after presentation, certain sorts of errors occur more frequently than others. Specifically, the errors consisted mainly of recalling letters that sounded like the presented letters (Conrad, R., 1964). Thus, when the correct letter was *V,* the subjects were more likely to err by recalling *B* or *C* than by recalling *X* or *M.* Although the subjects were likely to confuse letters that sounded alike, they seldom confused letters that looked alike, for letters such as *E* and *F* were seldom confused with each other. Furthermore, if the subjects were asked to recall a string of letters that were phonologically similar, they correctly recalled fewer letters than when the presented letters were phonologically dissimilar (Conrad, R. & Hull, 1964). These data show clearly that phonological encoding occurs even when the items to be recalled are presented visually.

Why might visually presented information come to be encoded phonologically? One possibilty is that short-term retention necessarily involves phonological encoding. Indeed, this view at one time had considerable support (for example, Waugh & Norman, 1965; Baddeley & Dale, 1966; Baddeley, 1972). However, a more likely possibility is that information is often encoded phonologically and whether it is or not depends upon the prior experiences of the subjects. For example, 10-year-olds often label verbally and rehearse the visual stimuli they are asked to remember, whereas children at the ages of five or six years tend not to (for a review, see Hagen & Stanovich, 1977). Adults and older children typically have had extensive experience with reading, and this experience may lead them to encode visual stimuli in a phonological form. One observation that supports this notion comes from the study of memory in children. Three- to 5-year-olds can remember short lists of phonologically similar words about as well as lists of phonologically dissimilar words. However, at the age of 6 years, the age at which many children learn to read, children remember phonologically different words better than phonologically similar words, and that difference increases with age (Conrad, R., 1972).

Further support for the view that the occurrence of phonological encoding has antecedents in the experiences of the individual comes from investigations of how deaf individuals encode strings of visually presented letters. An analysis of the errors made by deaf persons shows that they encode on the basis of neither the phonological nor the visual properties of the letters (Conrad, R. & Rush, 1965). Although the exact nature of the encoding for deaf subjects is unknown, some sort of finger-spelling code does seem to be involved in the retention of letters (Locke & Locke, 1971). Similarly, the errors that deaf people make in recalling words are related to the gestures that are used to produce the corresponding Ameslan signs (Bellugi, Klima, & Siple, 1975). Interestingly, deaf children who had learned to speak intelligibly confused phonologically similar letters more often than did deaf children whose speech was unintelligible.

Another determinant of the occurrence of phonological encoding is the nature of the procedure that is used to examine short-term memory (Estes, 1973; Tell, 1972). For example, phonological encoding does not occur when adults are required to say *the* repeatedly as they view a series of letters that they have been instructed to remember (Murray, 1967). The level of recall in this situation is quite high even though the requirements of the procedure prevented phonological encoding. These results show that the information involved in studies of short-term memory can be encoded in a variety of ways, and the past experiences of the subjects and the nature of the current task jointly determine how information will be encoded. We will now consider the types of encoding other than the phonological.

Visual Encoding The occurrence of visual encoding has been observed in numerous experiments concerning short-term memory (for example, Bartram, 1978; den Heyer & Barrett, 1971; Posner, 1969; Posner, Boies, Eichelman, & Taylor, 1969; Proctor, 1978; for a review, see Kroll, 1975). One of the most interesting demonstrations of visual encoding has come from studies of "mental"

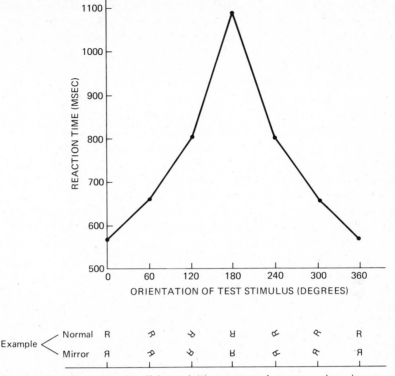

Fig. 10.7 Reaction times for classifying a letter as normal or as a mirror image.   (After Cooper & Shepard, 1973.)

rotation (Shepard & Metzler, 1971; Cooper & Shepard, 1973). To avoid some of the semantic problems inherent in the use of the word "mental," we shall speak of covert rather than mental rotation.

In one study of covert rotation (Cooper & Shepard, 1973), subjects were shown an alphabetic letter that was often not in the normal upright position. The letter, such as R, was rotated various degrees from the upright position and was sometimes presented as a mirror image, say, Я. On each of a series of trials, a letter was presented in various orientations and the task of the subject was to press one button as fast as possible if the letter was normal and to press another button if the letter was a mirror image.

The results of the experiment, shown in Fig. 10.7, were that the reaction times increased as a function of the difference in orientation between the presented letter and that letter in the normal upright position. The greater the angular departure of the test letter from the normal upright position, the longer the reaction times were. These data, together with the verbal behavior of the subjects, suggested that the subjects formed an image of the test stimulus, rotated that image to the typical upright orientation, and then decided whether the imagined letter was normal. That interpretation has been supported in numerous subsequent experiments (cf. Cooper, 1975).

For our purposes, the important point is that performance in the preceding task seemed to require a short-term visual code. After a visual image of the stimulus had been formed, that image was apparently rotated on a covert level. When and how often visual encoding occurs is presently unknown, but it seems clear that the visual encoding and transformation of stimuli can occur in short-term memory procedures.

Semantic Encoding   We have seen that the nature of the errors made by subjects in studies of short-term memory help to clarify the way information is encoded. If the errors in a short-term memory task were shown to depend upon the meaning of the remembered items, that would indicate that semantic encoding is involved in short-term memory. Whereas earlier evidence suggested that semantic encoding is not involved in short-term memory (for example, Baddeley & Dale, 1966), more recent evidence suggests the opposite (Shulman, 1970, 1971, 1972; Wetherick, 1975; Wickens, 1972).

One observation of semantic encoding comes from an experiment (Shulman, 1972) in which adult subjects were exposed to 10 spoken words at the rate of two words per sec on each of a number of trials. Immediately following the 10th word on each trial, the subject saw either *I* or *M* followed in turn by a probe word. When the probe word was preceded by the *I*, the subject was to indicate whether the probe word was identical to one of the 10 words that had been heard on that trial. When the probe word was preceded by *M*, the subject was to indicate whether the probe word had the same meaning as one of the 10 words. Thus a particular trial might proceed as follows. First, the subject hears 10 words such as *big, dull, sacred, pile, . . . shy.* Then the letter *M* might be presented visually followed by the probe word *holy.* Since the *M* indicates that the task is to determine whether one of the 10 words is a synonym of the probe word *holy,* and since *holy* and *sacred* are synonymous, the correct response on that trial would be "yes."

The results of main interest were that the subjects performed above the chance level in indicating whether the probe word was the same or meant the same as one of the 10 words presented on a trial. Additionally, judgments of identity and synonymity occurred rapidly and usually within one sec of the presentation of the probe word. Just as importantly, many errors made by the subjects were predictable on the basis of the meaning or semantic aspects of the probe word. For example, on trials in which the probe word was a synonym of one of the words in the list and the subject was supposed to indicate whether that probe word had actually occurred in the list, the subjects often erred by saying "yes." Presumably, the semantic similarity of the probe word and the synonym in the list led the subjects to confuse the semantically related words as identical. The occurrence of semantically based errors, together with the ability of the subjects to rapidly discriminate the synonymity of the probe words and list words, shows that the words in the experiment were encoded semantically to some extent (but see Baddeley, 1972, for an alternative viewpoint).

Concluding Comments   The question of how information is encoded is similar to questions concerning the nature of the stimulus that controls responding (pp. 196–199). Just as it is a mistake to contend that behavior is controlled only by the absolute values of stimuli or only by the relations between stimuli, so too is it a mistake to contend that the information involved in short-term memory is encoded only in a phonological format or only in a visual format. The information involved in short-term memory can be encoded in a phonological, visual or semantic format. Other evidence suggests that short-term memory can also involve encoding in olfactory (Engen, Kuisma, & Eimas, 1973), motor (Adams & Dijkstra, 1966) and spatial (Healy, 1974) formats. Rather than search for the one nature of encoding, we should seek the antecedents of encoding and ask how information will be encoded under various contemporary conditions and following various types of past experience.

Unfortunately, the antecedents of encoding are currently unknown, and we can offer only a few speculative remarks concerning the phylogeny and ontogeny of encoding. The contribution of phylogenetic factors to encoding are perhaps most apparent in the occurrence of phonological encoding, for the occurrence of phonological encoding is attributable in part to the biological factors that underlie language in humans (see pp. 362–363). However, the exact ways in which biological factors contribute to the different encoding processes are unclear.

Many unresolved questions concerning the ontogenetic antecedents of encoding also remain. Why might a particular set of visual stimuli come to be encoded, say, phonologically rather than visually, or vice versa? That question is especially enigmatic since encoding processes are private and are inaccessible to those with whom we interact. One possibility is that the occurrence of a particular type of encoding is governed by its indirect consequences. For example, attempts to remember complex visual stimuli often fail when those stimuli are encoded in a verbal rather than a visual form. Many a novice at art has had the experience of being unable to recognize a particular painting that originally had been seen and encoded by means of brief verbal description. Perhaps a series of similar experiences would lead to a decreased probability that a complex visual stimulus would be encoded solely on a verbal level.

Conversely, it may be that the probability of encoding stimuli in a particular way will increase if encoding in that way somehow increases the probability of remembering the relevant information. For example, encoding a phone number phonologically permits one to covertly rehearse the number, which increases the probability of recalling the number. In general, training individuals to rehearse often improves recall (Hagen & Stanovich, 1977). The reinforcement received for dialing the number or telling it to someone else may strengthen not only the overt behavior but also the private events such as the phonological encoding and rehearsal that preceded it.

More generally, then, the way information is encoded may depend upon the effects of the encoding. If encoding in a particular manner facilitates the emission of an overt response that is reinforced, the probability of encoding similar information in that way will subsequently be increased. However, the preceding comments should be viewed as suggestive rather than compelling, for a great deal of further research is needed to clarify this topic.

Organization and Short-Term Memory

Despite the problems involved in making and testing assumptions about limitations in processing capacity, considerable evidence suggests that we have a limited capacity to remember over the short run. As an example, read the following string of letters at a rate of about one letter per second and then try to recall them.

o i r o l d a o v i f n r e o t n m a

If you are like most adults, you had trouble remembering all of the letters. Most adults can remember correctly a string of about seven random letters or digits, but beyond that point errors begin to occur. Our ability to remember information over short time intervals is clearly limited, and our span or capacity of short-term memory is said to be about seven plus or minus two items (Miller, G. A., 1956).

Chunking Although the span of short-term memory is about seven items, we can nevertheless remember many more than seven digits or letters over the short run. Through an organizational process called chunking, a whole series of items such as letters can be recoded or grouped into a single, higher-order item called a *chunk* (for a discussion of the problem of defining chunks see Simon, 1974). For example, the string of 19 individual letters listed above can be reorganized into two higher-order chunks: *information overload*. These words are clearly remembered more easily than the random collection of the individual letters they are composed of.

To illustrate the contribution of chunking to short-term memory, consider an experiment by Miller (1956). When adults were asked to remember strings of briefly presented binary digits (for example, 1010001101110101001), they were unable to recall more than about seven digits. Then the adults were instructed to break a string of binary digits up into groups of three digits and to then name each group in the following way:

000 = 0	100 = 4
001 = 1	101 = 5
010 = 2	110 = 6
011 = 3	111 = 7

By using this scheme, which entails converting binary numbers to octal numbers, the subjects could recode a long string of binary digits into a shorter string or chunk of octal digits. For example, a string of binary digits such as 011010011100101001111 could be broken up into the groups 011, 010, 011, 100, 101, 001 and 111. In turn, these groups could be recoded into the sequence 3234517. The results were that adults who used this recoding strategy remembered many more binary digits than those who did not use this strategy. Some adults who used the recoding strategy successfully recalled strings of up to forty binary digits. The use of such recoding schemes is hardly an esoteric phenomenon, for we often use our knowledge of language to group series of letters into informationally rich units such as words.

Recoding can facilitate the retention of relatively large amounts of information, but recoding in a sense does not increase the span of short-term memory. Adult humans can remember only about seven new items whether those items are single digits, letters, or chunks of digits or letters. For example, we can remember about seven short words as well as seven single, randomly ordered letters even though the list of seven words contains many more letters than the list of letters does (with the help of a friend, you can confirm this for yourself). Although recoding does not change our ability to remember about seven items, recoding into informationally rich items does permit the retention of more information (for a discussion of information theory see Shannon & Weaver, 1949). Thus recoding partially alleviates the problem of our limited capacity to remember over the short run.

Properties of Chunks   Having seen that the formation of informationally rich chunks makes a significant contribution to short-term memory, we may inquire further into the nature of these chunks. The first important point is that a chunk is a functional unit of memory. To say that a set of items, such as a string of three digits, acts as a functional unit of memory means that these items tend to be recalled together and are affected in similar ways by particular factors. Thus when one of the digits is recalled there is a high probability of recalling the other digits belonging to that unit. For example, if a string of 12 digits such as 83 592 61 748 31 is presented, the digits within each group of two or three digits form a functional unit. The digits 5, 9 and 2 are said to belong to a functional unit since the probability of recalling the 9 was higher when the 5 had been recalled than when the 5 had not been recalled. Similarly, the 2 is more likely to be recalled if the 9 has been recalled, and so on (Bower, 1972). Moreover, the items within a group tend to be recalled at the same time (Bower & Winzenz, 1969) and with very short pauses between the recall of successive items (Chase, W. G., & Simon, 1973; for further discussion of functional units of memory, see Shimp, 1976).

Another noteworthy aspect of chunks is that they can be based on numerous types of information. For example, one who is competent in a particular language can chunk sequences of letters or even sequences of words on the basis of knowledge of the rules of syntax (for example, Johnson, N. F., 1968; see pp. 332–335). As another example, the skill of the master chess player rests in part with the ability to form large chunks of visual information, such as frequently occurring attack formations, on the basis of knowledge of chess (Chase & Simon, 1973; Simon & Gilmartin, 1973). Similarly, the retention of lists of words over short intervals of time is often improved by forming a visual image of the referent of those words (Paivio & Begg, 1971; Paivio & Smythe, 1971; cf. Paivio, 1975a, for a review of the role of imagery in short-term memory). In general, chunks can consist of many different types of information such as linguistic, visual, motoric and so on. Furthermore, chunks can be based upon factors as diverse as rhythm and syntax that serve to structure or organize information.

In most instances, chunks are based upon information that is retained over long periods of time and is therefore said to be involved in long-term memory. Thus the process of chunking is one in which knowledge of relatively distant events is brought to bear upon the information involved in short-term memory. The fact that chunking reflects the contribution of information retained over long intervals has important implications for the study of memory. First, memory is an active process that entails much more than a passive absorption of new information by the organism. Rather, the organism makes a substantial contribution to short-term memory by organizing and recoding information and by generally bringing knowledge of past events to bear upon the retention of that information. Second, the study of short-term memory must to some extent include an analysis of the contribution of information retained over the long run. In other words, we need to understand the relationship between short-term and long-term memory before we can fully understand what are now seen as aspects of short-term memory.

Concluding Comments   We have seen that chunking facilitates short-term memory in that it allows more information to be retained. We have also seen that chunking involves the use of information that has been stored over relatively long intervals of time. The fundamental question that now arises is this: What are the antecedents of chunking? The problem of how different items come to belong to the same functional unit of memory resembles the problem of how different responses come to function as members of the same operant. In both instances, the problem may be seen as that of how different behaviors come to belong to a single behavioral unit. And in both instances, two general types of antecedents may be sought: phylogenetic and ontogenetic. However, the antecedents of chunking and other organizational phenomena have not yet been identified, and therein lies an important area for future research.

FORGETTING AND SHORT-TERM MEMORY

As we can all readily appreciate, one of the most ubiquitous characteristics of short-term memory is lack of permanence. Indeed, we forget recently learned names, phone numbers and shopping items so frequently that forgetting seems to be inevitable. But is forgetting really inevitable? Is there a set time limit on the duration of short-term memory? Why does forgetting occur at all? These questions have recently been the focus of a great deal of research.

Most of the studies of forgetting in short-term memory involve the following kind of procedure, which was first devised by Brown (1958) and by Peterson and Peterson (1959). On each of a series of trials, a sequence of three consonants such as M V K is presented briefly to the subject. Immediately following the presentation of the consonants, the subject hears a three-digit number such as 491. The task of the subject is to count backward by threes from that number until a recall cue is presented, whereupon the subject tries to re-call the three consonants. The time between the presentation of the conso-nants and the cue to recall the consonants is called the retention interval; this interval is usually varied systematically over trials for each subject. The task of counting backwards by threes is called a *distractor task* since it helps to pre-vent the subject from attending to and rehearsing the consonants during the retention interval. If rehearsal were allowed to occur, there would be no for-getting (Brown, J. A., 1958), for a verbal stimulus can be retained indefinitely through covert rehearsal. Moreover, information that is rehearsed repeatedly may be retained or forgotten in fundamentally different ways from informa-tion that is not rehearsed repeatedly, and only the latter type of information lies within the domain of short-term memory. Therefore, studies of forgetting in short-term memory have come to include a distractor task that is designed to prevent rehearsal during the retention interval.

The results of one of the first studies of forgetting in short-term memory (Peterson & Peterson, 1959) are shown in Fig. 10.8. With a short retention inter-val of 3 sec, a high percentage of the verbal information was recalled accu-rately. However, a substantial amount of forgetting occurred as the duration of the retention intervals increased. Indeed, when the retention interval lasted 18 sec, almost all of the verbal information was forgotten.

Why were the consonants forgotten over the span of 18 sec? One possi-bility is that the verbal information spontaneously decayed with the passage of time (Peterson & Peterson, 1959); this account is called the *decay theory* of for-getting. According to the decay theory, forgetting is a passive process that inev-itably occurs when rehearsal is prevented. Since the decay theory attributes forgetting to the gradual fading of stored information over time, decay theory accounts for forgetting in terms of storage processes rather than encoding or

Fig. 10.8 The percentage of items recalled correctly as a function of the retention interval duration. (From Peterson & Peterson, 1959. Copyright 1959 by the American Psychological Association. Reprinted by permission.)

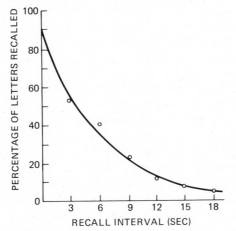

retrieval processes. Basically, the decay theory asserts that it is the nature of the adult organism to lose verbal information spontaneously over time. Thus this theory holds that the duration of short-term memory is relatively constant in the absence of rehearsal. Specifically, the duration of short-term memory is held to be about 15 sec.

One problem with decay theory is that it is extremely difficult to test. The reason is that the events that occur in the retention interval may produce forgetting. Thus if forgetting occurred during an 18-sec retention interval, the forgetting could have resulted from either the passage of time or from the events that occurred during the retention interval. The problem is compounded by the fact that the distractor task, which must be included to prevent rehearsal, may also produce forgetting. Although no completely acceptable resolution to the problem has been achieved, the best controlled studies to date (Reitman, 1974; Shiffrin, 1973; Shiffrin & Cook, 1978; Wingfield & Byrnes, 1972) suggest that decay does to some extent produce forgetting in short-term memory experiments. Decay theory does not, however, provide a complete account of forgetting. Much forgetting results from the events that occur as time passes, and the effects of decay may interact with the effects of the intervening events (Shiffrin & Cook, 1978). We shall now pursue further the effects of intervening events upon retention.

Interference Theory

In general, the view that forgetting results from the events that occur as time passes is called the *interference theory* of forgetting (McGeough, 1942), and the events that occur as time passes are said to interfere with the retention of the learned items. According to interference theory, forgetting can result from events that either precede or follow the presentation of the items that are to be remembered by the subject. When the recall of learned information is impaired by the events that preceded the learning of that information, *proactive interference* or *proactive inhibition* is said to have occurred. On the other hand, when the recall of learned information is hindered by the events that followed the learning of that information, *retroactive interference* or *retroactive inhibition* is said to have occurred.

Proactive Interference   First consider the role of proactive interference. In the preceding experiment concerning short-term memory, there were two potential sources of proactive interference. One source consisted of the events that occurred before the experiment began. Adults have had extensive experiences outside of the laboratory, and those experiences could possibly produce proactive interference. Thus, just as the results of all learning experiments may be affected by the prior experiences of the subjects, so too might the results of all memory experiments be affected by the prior experiences of the subjects. Another potential source of proactive interference consists of the events that occur within the experimental procedure. The retention of the stimuli presented on a particular trial may be influenced not only by events occurring within that trial but also by the events that occurred on the preceding trials of the experiment. If proactive interference were produced by the events within the experiment, then retention on the first few trials might differ considerably from retention on the later trials, for the later trials were preceded by a greater number of potentially interfering events.

In fact, later experiments have shown that proactive interference from events within the experiment is a fundamental antecedent of the forgetting observed in experiments concerning short-term memory (Loess, 1964; Loess & Waugh, 1967; Keppel & Underwood, 1962). Keppel and Underwood (1962) noted that in the original study by Peterson and Peterson (1959), there were two practice trials executed before the experiment began. Thus the possibility existed that the forgetting observed in the trials of the experiment resulted from proactive interference from the events that occurred in the practice trials. This possibility was consistent with the results of other experiments that had shown that a substantial amount of proactive interference could be produced by a small number of events. Therefore, Keppel and Underwood repeated the experiment of Peterson and Peterson, but they omitted the practice trials and took a closer look at retention over the first few trials. The experiment was designed so that each of the first three trials was equally likely to involve a retention interval of either 3, 9 or 18 sec.

If proactive interference from events within the experiment were responsible for forgetting, little forgetting should occur on the first trial, for there were no experimental events preceding that trial that could produce interference. The results of the experiment were that no forgetting occurred on the first trial even at the 18-sec retention interval. In contrast, a considerable amount of forgetting occurred on the second and third trials of the experiment. Clearly, the amount of forgetting depended not only upon the duration of the retention interval but also upon the events that preceded a particular trial.

These results show that proactive interference is a major determinant of forgetting in short-term memory tasks and that the account in terms of decay theory is at best incomplete. Furthermore, these results show the problems that arise in postulating that the duration of short-term memory is set at a value such as 15 sec. How long information is retained depends upon how much proactive interference has occurred, and thus upon the experience of the organism rather than upon how much time has elapsed. Indeed, the time between trials seems to be as important as the duration of the retention interval, for little forgetting occurs with a retention interval of 15 sec when there are several minutes between trials (Loess & Waugh, 1967).

Although the amount of forgetting on a trial in a short-term memory task clearly depends upon the number of preceding trials, the amount of forgetting also depends on the similarity of the events that occur over trials. For example, Wickens, Born, and Allen (1963) performed an experiment which, like the preceding study, consisted of only a few trials. On each of four consecutive trials, the control group was given different sets of three consonants to remember. In contrast, the first three trials for the experimental group involved different sets of three digits, whereas the fourth trial involved three consonants. Thus the fourth trial was the same for both groups. But for the control group, the events on the fourth trial were very similar to those of the preceding trials since similar stimuli were used. For the experimental group, the events on the fourth trial were very different from those of the first three trials since different stimuli were presented.

The results of the experiment, shown in Fig. 10.9, were that the probability of recalling the consonants on the fourth trial was very high for the experimental group but not for the control group. Indeed, the probability of recall for the control group decreased on the fourth trial just as on the second and third trials. In other words, the amount of proactive interference increased over the four trials for the control group. On the other hand, proactive interference increased over trials for the experimental group, but only for the first three trials. When a different type of material was introduced on the fourth trial, the probability of recall was as high as for the first trial when there was no proactive interference produced by events within the experiment. This observation has been called *release from proactive inhibition* (see Wickens, 1972, for a review), and it clearly shows that the amount of proactive interference depends upon the similarity of the events that occurred over trials.

Forgetting was characterized as a problem of storage by decay theory, but the forgetting that results from proactive interference seems to involve difficulties in retrieval rather than storage. For example, recent evidence indicates that the phenomenon of release from proactive interference reflects events that occur at the time of retrieval. In one experiment (Gardiner, Craik, & Birtwistle, 1972), the subjects were exposed to four successive trials that involved items from the same general class. Specifically, the items from the first three trials were names of garden flowers such as *pansy* and *tulip*, whereas the items for the fourth trial were names of wild flowers such as *daisy* and *dandelion*. The

Fig. 10.9 The probability of recall over the four trials. The filled circles and the solid line show the performance of the control group on each trial. The open circle shows the performance of the experimental group on the fourth trial. Release from proactive interference is shown by the difference in the performance of the two groups on the fourth trial.   (From Wickens, Born, & Allen, 1963. Copyright 1963 by Academic Press, *Journal of Verbal Learning and Verbal Behavior*.)

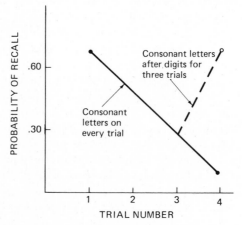

subjects were divided into three groups. The control group was exposed to the four trials without special instructions. However, the two experimental groups received instructions that the items on the fourth trial differed from those of preceding trials. One of the latter groups received the instructions before the fourth trial began, whereas the other group received the instructions at the time during the fourth trial when the items were to be recalled.

The results of the experiment were that the level of recall on the fourth trial was high and about equal for the experimental groups, but not for the control group that had been given no special instructions. In fact, the level of recall for the control group was lower on the fourth trial than it had been on the first three trials. Thus proactive interference increased over trials for the control group. In contrast, the level of recall decreased over the first three trials for the experimental groups but increased on the fourth trial. In other words, the phenomenon of release from proactive interference occurred on the fourth trial for both experimental groups. Presumably, the lack of release from proactive interference for the control group resulted from the high degree of similarity between the items from the different trials. The release from proactive interference for the experimental groups occurred only because they were told about the differences between the items on the various trials. The important point is that since the release from proactive interference occurred when the instructions were given at the time of recall, this release must have occurred at the time of retrieval for that group. Although there is some controversy over the exact mechanisms involved in proactive interference (cf. Dillon & Thomas, 1975), the results of numerous studies (for example, Bennett, 1975; Loftus & Patterson, 1975) support the view that proactive interference involves retrieval processes.

Retroactive Interference   Having examined the contribution of proactive interference to forgetting in experiments concerning short-term memory, we can now consider the contribution of retroactive interference. That retroactive interference contributes to forgetting is shown clearly in an experiment by Wickelgren (1965; see also Deutsch, D., 1970; Waugh & Norman, 1965). On each trial of this experiment, four letters were presented at a rate of two per second; these letters were to be recalled at the end of a retention interval of 4 sec. During the retention interval, eight letters were presented, again at a rate of two per second, and the subjects wrote down these letters as they were presented. The phonological similarity of the letters presented in the retention interval was varied in such a way that either 0, 2, or 4 of the letters in the retention interval shared a phonological feature with the letters that the subjects were instructed to remember. The results were that the level of retention decreased as a function of how many phonologically similar letters occurred in the retention interval. With 0, 2, and 4 similar letters in the retention interval, the percentage of letters correctly recalled was 68.4, 60.5 and 49.8, respectively. Thus the events that intervene between the time of presentation and the time of recall can clearly produce forgetting. Furthermore, as was the case for proactive interference, the amount of forgetting that occurred depended on the similarity of the information in the retention interval to that which was to be remembered.

How similar the information in the retention interval is to the information that is to be remembered depends upon how the latter information is encoded. For example, if the subjects in the experiment above had encoded the letters visually rather than phonologically, the amount of forgetting probably would not have depended upon the phonological features of the letters that were presented in the retention interval. Instead, the visual features of the letters presented in the retention interval could have produced retroactive interference. In general, then, the source of interference depends upon how the subject encodes the information the subject is trying to remember. A complete analysis of forgetting must recognize the importance of encoding as well as the experiences that occur between the presentation and the recall of the stimuli.

The amount of retroactive interference depends not only upon the similarity of the information presented in the retention interval but also upon the complexity of the information processing task that fills the retention interval (Dillon & Reid, 1969; Posner & Rossman, 1965; Watkins, Watkins, Craik, & Muzuryk, 1973). For example, Crowder (1967) presented five words followed by a distractor task that involved rapidly pressing keys that corresponded to flashing lights. In the control condition, there was a simple relationship between the lights and the keys in that the first light signalled the subject to press the first key, the second light signalled the subject to push the second key, and so on. For the experimental group, the distractor task was more difficult. For that group, the order of the lights differed from that of the keys so that the first light signalled the subject to press, for instance, the seventh key, and so on. The result of primary interest was that significantly more forgetting occurred in the experimental condition that involved the more difficult distractor task. These results show that the events occurring in the retention interval can produce forgetting even when they bear little similarity to the items the subject is instructed to remember. Why the difficulty of the distractor task affects recall is unknown, but one possibility is that difficult tasks are more effective in preventing rehearsal than are simpler tasks.

To the extent that forgetting results from factors such as the difficulty of the processing that occurs between presentation and recall, forgetting may be viewed as the result of limited processing capacity. Accordingly, the analysis of forgetting may be advanced through the application of models of processing capacity such as the resource allocation model (see pp. 438–442). Additionally, the analysis of forgetting may benefit from the study of retrieval, and we shall now focus upon that topic.

RETRIEVAL AND SHORT-TERM MEMORY

Much of the information concerning retrieval in short-term memory procedures has come from the following kind of task, which was devised by Sternberg (1966, 1967, 1969, 1975). First, a series of, for example, four digits was presented visually for 1 or 2 sec. This series of digits may be called the memory set. Then, after 2 sec, a test digit was presented. On some trials, the test digit was a member of the memory set, whereas on other trials the test digit was not a member of the memory set. The task of the subject was to indicate by pressing one of two buttons as rapidly as possible whether or not the test stimulus belonged to the memory set for that trial. For example, if the memory set were the series 5 3 9 2 and the test digit were 9, the correct response would be a press of the "yes" button. In this type of task, the subjects typically make very few errors since the number of items in the memory set does not exceed the memory span, and the retention interval is very brief and is free of interfering events. The dependent variable of primary interest is the reaction time, which is defined as the amount of time between the presentation of the test digit and the response of the subject.

Before we discuss the results of the foregoing procedure, we need to consider the various stages of processing that might be involved in this task. In general terms, three stages seem to be involved in determining whether the test digit belonged to the memory set. First, the test digit must be encoded. Then, the information concerning the test digit must be compared with the information about the digits in the memory set. On the basis of the results of the comparison process, a response must be made. Of these three stages, the comparison stage is most pertinent to the topic of retrieval, and we will therefore focus on that stage.

In order to study the comparison process that is involved in retrieval, it is necessary to vary the task in such a way that the comparison process will be affected while the processes involved in encoding and responding will be held constant. One way to achieve that end is to vary the number of digits in the memory set. As the size of the memory set increases, the subject has more items which must be compared with the test digit, and so the comparison process might be affected as the size of the memory set changes. Just as importantly, changes in the size of the memory set should not affect the processes involved in encoding the information and making an overt response.

The Serial-Exhaustive Model

Now consider what happens when the size of the memory set is varied. Figure 10.10 shows that the reaction time increases as a linear function of the size of the memory set. According to Sternberg (1966), this observation shows that the comparisons of the test digit with the digits in the memory set are performed in a serial rather than a parallel manner. If numerous comparisons could be carried out simultaneously, five comparisons should presumably require no more time than one comparison, and the reaction times would therefore remain constant as the size of the memory set increased. If, on the other hand, the comparisons were performed serially and each comparison required about the same amount of time, the reaction time should increase as the size of the memory set increases, for more comparisons must be made and each additional comparison adds to the reaction time. The slope of the best-fitting line for the data shown in Fig. 10.10 indicates that each comparison required about 38

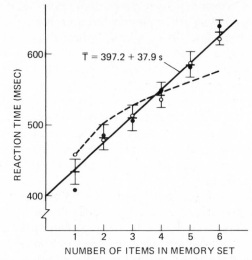

Fig. 10.10 The mean reaction time for positive responses (filled circles) and negative responses (open circles) for memory sets of various sizes. (After Sternberg, 1966. Copyright 1966 by the American Association for the Advancement of Science.)

msec. On the basis of these observations, Sternberg concluded that the comparison aspect of retrieval in this recognition task is a serial process that occurs at a very high speed of about 26 items per second.

Besides wanting to know whether the comparison process is serial or parallel in nature, experimenters have sought to know whether the probe item is compared with all or only some items in the memory set. If the test digit is compared to every item in the memory set, the comparison process is said to be *exhaustive*. An exhaustive search would be expected on trials with negative outcomes since the only way the subject could determine that the test digit did not belong to the memory set would be to compare the test digit to every item in the memory set. However, an exhaustive search might not be required when the test digit matched an item in the memory set (that is, on positive trials). Since on the average the test digit matches an item in the middle of the memory set (the position of a matching item in the memory set is typically varied systematically), it would seem that only half as many comparisons must be made on positive than on negative trials. Once a match has been made on a positive trial, no more comparisons need to be made and the search could be terminated before the entire memory set is searched. If the search ends when a match is made, the search is said to be *self-terminating* rather than exhaustive. Since on positive trials fewer items would be scanned in a self-terminating search than in an exhaustive search, the reaction times would be lower in the self-terminating search. More specifically, if the search were self-terminating, the slope of the reaction time function would be half of what it would be if the search were exhaustive.

Since an exhaustive search would be expected on negative trials, one could compare the slopes for positive and negative trials to determine whether the search on positive trials were self-terminating or exhaustive. If the slopes for positive and negative trials were equal, the search on positive trials would presumably be exhaustive, like the search on negative trials. If, on the other hand, the slope for positive trials was half the slope for the negative trials, the search would appear to be self-terminating. As Fig. 10.10 shows, the slopes for positive and negative trials were about equal, and Sternberg concluded that the comparison process was not only serial but also exhaustive.

The conclusion that the search was exhaustive seems counterintuitive. Why should all of the items be scanned on a positive trial even when a match has been made? Although there is no satisfactory answer to this question, one possibility is that the comparison process we have been discussing actually consists of two components: comparison and decision. If the subjects could compare items at a very rapid rate but could decide upon the outcome of those comparisons only at a slow rate, the occurrence of exhaustive scanning might help to reduce the reaction time. In a self-terminating search, each item would be compared with the probe, and a decision would be made for each item. In an exhaustive search, however, all of the comparisons could be made, and then one decision could be made. Thus fewer of the slow decisions would have to be made in an exhaustive search, and the response could perhaps be made faster by first executing all of the comparisons and then making a decision and responding. However, this line of reasoning is best viewed as suggestive until there is independent evidence that shows that the time required to make comparisons is indeed less than the time required to make decisions.

Problems with the Serial-Exhaustive Model   The conclusion that the comparison process is both serial and exhaustive is consistent with the data shown in Fig. 10.10, but this conclusion is not the only plausible account of those data. For example, the observation that the reaction time increases as a linear function of the size of the memory set is consistent not only with models of serial processing but also with certain models of parallel processing (Corcoran, 1971; Townsend, 1971). Assume that the subject has a limited capacity for processing information and that all items in the memory set receive equal amounts of that capacity at the same time. When few items are in the memory set, a relatively large amount of the processing capacity is devoted to each item and the items can be processed rapidly. However, when more items are in the memory set, a relatively small amount of the processing capacity is devoted to each item, and the items are therefore processed more slowly. Although the items are processed in parallel in both instances, the reaction time should increase with the size of the memory set. Thus the data shown in Fig. 10.10 are consistent with certain models of both serial and parallel processing.

Furthermore, the conclusion that the comparison process is serial and exhaustive is inconsistent with certain observations (see Sternberg, 1975, for a discussion of how to deal with the contradictory evidence). For example, reaction time depends not only upon the size of the memory set but also upon the location of a matching item within the memory set (Burrows & Okada, 1971; Clifton & Birenbaum, 1970; Cocoran, 1971; Raeburn, 1974). When the probe item matches, for example, the last item in the memory set, the reaction time is much lower than it is when the probe matches an item in the middle of the set. In other words, serial position effects occur in the standard procedure used to study scanning. On the surface, the occurrence of serial-position effects conflicts with the view that scanning is exhaustive (for an alternative model that is consistent with this observation, see Atkinson & Juola, 1974). However, it should be recalled that performance on the recognition task involves both encoding and retrieval processes. One could argue that the serial-position effects involve not retrieval processes but encoding processes. Perhaps when the probe item matches the last item in the memory set, the probe item is encoded more rapidly than when the probe item matches an item from the middle of the memory set. The plausibility of that alternative illustrates an important point: In a particular memory experiment, the inferred stages of processing such as encoding and retrieval are confounded. In general, it is very difficult to empirically distinguish between the stages of information-processing (cf. Postman, 1976a).

Returning to the issue of the locus of serial position effects, we shall consider whether those effects result from encoding processes. If they do, then they do not contradict the serial-exhaustive model, for the latter is a model of how retrieval occurs. In the absence of a way to distinguish directly between encoding and retrieval phenomena, we shall have to evaluate the issue partly on the basis of the internal consistency of the serial-exhaustive model.

The serial-exhaustive model accounts for the functions shown in Fig. 10.10 by postulating a serial and exhaustive scanning process. But what if those linear and parallel functions were obtained from the same experiment in which serial-position effects occurred? In that case, the serial-exhaustive model cannot be applied consistently, for the model accounts for the linear and parallel functions in terms of retrieval and assumes that encoding processes are constant. If the model did not assume that encoding processes were constant, regardless of the serial position of the matching items, the model could not account for the linear and parallel reaction time functions that it was intended to account for. In fact, both the linear and parallel functions and the serial position effects have been reported in the same experiment (see Sternberg, 1975, for a review). We may conclude that at least in some experiments, serial position effects have occurred and cannot be explained by the serial-exhaustive model.

The last problem with the serial-exhaustive model that we shall consider is that the model does not apply to all procedures that require scanning (Shiffrin, 1976; Sternberg, 1975). For example, as subjects become well-practiced, the function relating reaction time to set size changes from linearity to curvilinearity (Simpson, 1972). Moreover, Neisser & Lazar (1964; see also Sperling, Budiansky, Spivak, & Johnson, 1971) observed that, given extensive practice, subjects could search for 10 items as fast as they could for only one item.

It seems unwise at this point to try to depict retrieval as involving only one particular process such as serial and exhaustive scanning. The human organism is too flexible as a processor of information to be characterized as a

serial-exhaustive or a parallel and self-terminating scanner. Much of the flexibility of the organism seems to arise from the varied experiences that organisms can have. To capture the flexibility of the organism, models of retrieval,
like models of other cognitive processes, should be designed to account for the
diverse effects of experience.

SUMMARY

We began this chapter by examining some of the historical roots of contemporary theories of memory. The early experimental analyses of memory were
guided by associationistic theories that analyzed memory in terms of the formation and utilization of associations. The experimental strategy followed by
associationists was to study relatively simple memory phenomena before
studying relatively complex phenomena. To implement that strategy within
the context of their theoretical approach, the associationists sought to eliminate or control the effects of prior experience. They often studied memory for
nonsense materials and rarely confronted directly complex memory phenomena such as constructing and using images, sentences, stories, and so on.

The domination of the field of memory by associationistic theories ended
in the early 1960s because of conflicting evidence, effective criticism from
theorists such as Chomsky, the formulation of promising theories that directly
confronted the complexities of language and memory, the development of the
computer technology, and so on. The contemporary theories of memory are
information-processing theories that differ radically from their associationistic
predecessors in their emphasis upon the active role played by the organism.

Contemporary memory theorists have in general adopted the strategy of
studying complex phenomena directly rather than studying first the simple
and then the complex. Information-processing theories, like their associationistic predecessors, have not always dealt adequately with the complex effects
of prior experience. Questions have often been posed in forms such as "what is
the nature of encoding in short-term memory?", "what is the nature of retrieval from short-term memory?", and so on. Questions such as the preceding
seem to cast the organism into a mold it does not really fit. Both encoding and
retrieval processes are affected by the prior experiences of the organism, and
the answers to questions such as "what is the nature of encoding" must be as
rich and diverse as the effects of experience seem to be.

The field of memory has been divided for the purposes of experimental
analysis into the subareas of sensory memory, short-term memory and long-
term memory, and three stages of information-processing—encoding, storage
and retrieval—have been postulated. Although the preceding distinctions are
often drawn, they are far from clear, and this problem will loom large in our
discussion of long-term memory. For now, let us grant these distinctions tentatively and turn to some of the substantive comments concerning sensory and
short-term memory.

Sensory memory involves the retention of relatively large amounts of information that is precategorical in form and specific to a particular modality.
Much of the information involved in sensory memory is forgotten as the result

of either rapid decay or interference. Some of the information is retained through a rapid scanning process whereby pattern recognition occurs. In the recognition or categorization of the information from sensory memory, both feature detection and the analysis of context appear to be fundamental. The process of pattern recognition does not necessarily involve selective attention, but the issue is complicated by the complex relationship between processing capacity and experience. In both pattern recognition and attention, information may or may not be processed in a selective manner. Selective processing is best understood not in terms of the filtering of information but rather in terms of the failure or the inability to devote sufficient processing resources to two tasks simultaneously.

The categorized information that is involved in short-term memory may be encoded phonologically, visually, semantically, and so on. The nature of encoding in short-term memory, like many other phenomena discussed earlier in this text, seems to depend upon both phylogenetic and ontogenetic factors such as the nature of the task and the prior experiences of the organism. The capacity of short-term memory appears limited, but through organizational processes such as chunking and imagery, large amounts of information can be remembered over the short run. Forgetting in short-term memory may result in part from decay, but seems to stem primarily from experiential factors such as proactive and retroactive interference. Much of what appears to be forgetting may actually involve difficulty in retrieving information. Retrieval has been described as a serial, self-terminating process. However, parallel processing does appear to occur under conditions of extended practice, and we conclude that the diverse effects of experience must be incorporated more fully into models of retrieval.

NOTES

1. In more recent formulations (for example, Craik & Tulving, 1975), "deeper processing" has to some extent come to mean "more elaborate processing." The latter phrase implies that processing need not progress through a sequence of stages in a serial manner. Rather, processing can occur at a variety of levels simultaneously, and there can be differences in how elaborate the processing on the different levels is.
2. This is not to say that the categorical information is not included in iconic memory. Although that is perhaps the most straightforward interpretation of the data, there is a possibility that categorical information is retained but decays during the encoding of the cue to recall either letters or numbers.

11
Long-Term Memory

INTRODUCTION

The ability to remember over long periods of time is central to most aspects of human life. Without long-term memory, the events and objects in our world would appear far less stable and familiar than they now do. In a sense, we would be creatures without a past, trapped within the boundaries of the moment, confronted with unending change and uncertainty. There would be neither language nor culture, and learning would play a far less significant role in our lives.

What is the nature of this ability that is so central in our lives yet so pervasive as simply to be taken for granted? To answer this question, we need to consider how the information in long-term memory is represented, how it is forgotten, how it is retrieved, and so on. Each of these topics shall be taken up in this chapter, and we shall begin with an analysis of encoding.

ENCODING AND LONG-TERM MEMORY

As we mentioned in the preceding chapter, encoding is the process whereby information is categorized and represented within the organism. The analysis of encoding is fundamental for an understanding of long-term memory, for the way information is encoded determines how that information is retrieved, how it is forgotten, and so on.

In this section, we first consider the types of information involved in long-term memory; we shall find that the memory codes involved in long-term memory are both diverse and flexible. Then we examine the implications of encoding for retention. This topic will lead us into a discussion of the role of organizational factors in long-term memory. We shall see that information can be encoded and organized through a variety of processes such as repetition, imagery, linguistic mediation and abstract semantic coding. Our discussion of encoding concludes with an examination of those encoding processes.

The Dimensions of Encoding

A large amount of experimental work has shown that many different types of information can be remembered over the long run (cf. Bower, 1967; Underwood, 1969; Wickens, 1970). For example, adults can remember how often a word has occurred, where and when it occurred, the modality in which it occurred, its meaning, and so forth. In other words, there are a multiplicity of encoding dimensions involved in long-term memory, and those dimensions include the temporal, the spatial, the frequency, the modality and the semantic dimensions.

Although it is possible to remember many different types of information concerning a stimulus such as a word, that stimulus may not always be encoded along all possible dimensions (cf. Underwood, 1969). Under some conditions, a word may be encoded along only the dimension of meaning, whereas under other conditions the same word may be encoded along numerous dimensions. For an adult, a word is not a unitary event since a particular word such as *rejuvenate* may be encoded visually on one occasion and semantically on a different occasion. Accordingly, the way in which a stimulus is encoded is best determined by empirical observation rather than by intuition.

A discussion of all the different types of information that can be involved in long-term memory is beyond the scope of this chapter (for full discussions see Kintsch, 1977; Tulving & Bower, 1974; Underwood, 1969; Wickens, 1972). However, in order to analyze theoretical issues such as the nature of visual imagery and the relationship between short-term and long-term memory, we need to consider the experimental evidence concerning the involvement of visual, phonological and semantic information in long-term memory.

Visual Information   One source of evidence that shows that visual information is involved in long-term memory has come from studies of the ability of adults to recognize pictures. For example, Shepard (1967) gave adults an inspection series of 612 colored pictures of various objects. The subjects inspected the pictures for as long as they wished, but the average time that the subjects actually spent looking at a picture was 5.9 sec. After the subjects had looked at all of the pictures, they were given two recognition tests. One test was given immediately after the subjects finished inspecting the pictures, and the second test was given following a delay of either two hours, three days, one week or four months. In each of the recognition tests, 68 pairs of pictures were presented. The two pictures in each test pair were shown simultaneously, and the task of the subjects was to indicate which one had been presented before as part of the inspection series. Different sets of 68 pictures were used in the two recognition tests.

The results of the experiment were that the pictures were recognized with a high degree of accuracy when the delay between the inspection series and the recognition test was short; the level of accuracy decreased over long delays. Nevertheless, the subjects correctly recognized about 58% of the pictures even when the retention interval was 120 days long. These results are consistent with the results of several other studies (for example, Nickerson, 1968; Paivio & Csapo, 1973; Standing, Conezio, & Haber, 1970) in showing that adults can remember large numbers of pictures over relatively long periods of time. In one study (Standing, 1973), retention for pictures was very good even for a set of thousands of pictures! There is probably no determinable limit to the number of pictures we can remember, particularly if the pictures are seen more than once.

The observation that adults have a highly developed ability to remember pictures suggests that long-term memory can involve visual information. (For further evidence on this issue see Baddeley, 1976; Crowder, 1976.) However, the possibility exists that adults remember pictures by describing those pictures verbally on a covert level and then remembering the verbal descriptions. If that were the case, the ability to remember large numbers of pictures could not be interpreted as showing that visual information is involved in long-term memory. For several reasons, however, it seems unlikely that the retention of many pictures can be accounted for solely in terms of verbal recoding. For example, the ability of adults to remember pictures exceeds their ability to remember the names of the objects that are shown in the pictures (Paivio & Csapo, 1973). Furthermore, adults are very adept at recognizing pictures when the pictures, for instance, pictures of snowflakes, are very similar and are given very similar verbal descriptions by the subjects who view them (Goldstein & Chance, 1970). Although the retention of verbal descriptions may contribute to our ability to remember pictures (Carmichael, Hogan, & Walter, 1932), we apparently can remember pictures in the absence of distinctive verbal descriptions.

Phonological Information   As we noted earlier, experiments have shown that short-term memory can involve semantic as well as phonological types of information. Similarly, recent experiments have demonstrated that phonological information is involved in long-term memory.

Nelson and Rothbart (1972) used a transfer task to test for the long-term retention of phonological information. In the first phase of the experiment, the subjects were exposed to a paired-associate task. The items used in that task were 24 pairs of numbers and words such as 27–tacks and 13–pray. The pairs were presented repeatedly until there had been one trial in which the subject correctly spelled each of the words that went with each of the numbers. At the end of that learning phase, the subjects left the laboratory without knowing they would later be asked to return for a test of retention.

Four weeks later, the subjects returned to participate in the second phase of the experiment. They were given a relearning task that consisted of a single trial in which the stimuli were the same numbers that had been used in the first task. The response items used in the relearning task were either identical to the old response items (for example, tacks and pray), or they were homophones of the old response items (for example tax and prey), or they were unrelated to the old response items (for example, *jury*). Thus some of the pairs in the relearning task were identical to those of the original learning task. Other pairs in the relearning task included identical stimuli and responses that sounded similar to those from the first task (for example, 27–*tacks* and 27–*tax*). Finally, some pairs in the relearning task consisted of the same stimuli from the original task and responses that were unrelated to those used in the first task (for example 27–*jury*). If the subjects remembered none of the phonological information concerning the original words, the phonologically similar responses should be as difficult to learn as the unrelated responses.

The results were that performance on the relearning trial was clearly best for those pairs that were identical to those of the first task. Moreover, the least amount of relearning occurred for the pairs that included responses that were unrelated to the old responses. Of central importance for our purposes, the subjects learned more pairs of numbers and homophones than of numbers and unrelated words. Thus the subjects must have remembered some of the phonological properties of the original words over the interval of four weeks.

It now seems that phonological information is involved in long-term memory, and this conclusion fits with our earlier observations concerning the tip-of-the-tongue phenomenon (see pp. 341–342; for further evidence see Bruce & Crowley, 1970; Dallett, 1966). Indeed, this information must underlie our ability to produce and understand language, to recognize accents, and so on. These observations conflict with the view that there are separate short-term and long-term stores that differ with respect to the type of encoding that occurs.

Semantic Information   Many types of evidence have shown that semantic information is involved in long-term memory. One source of evidence on this point has been studies of free recall. In the *free recall* procedure, the subjects are typically exposed to a series of words and then, following a retention interval, are asked to recall the words in any order. In an experiment by Bousfield (1953), adults were exposed to a list of 60 words that belonged to one of four categories: animals, names, professions, and vegetables. There were 15 words from each category, and the words were presented in a random order, thereby preventing all of the words from one category from occurring in a block. Thus part of the list might have been *lettuce, beet, John, cat, doctor, robin, Mike, radish*.

Interestingly, when the subjects recalled the words, they tended to recall words from the same category together, even though those words had not been presented together by the experimenter. This tendency to recall the words from a category together is called *categorical clustering* (Bousfield, 1953). Since the categories were defined on the basis of meaning, the occurrence of categorical clustering indicates that the subjects remembered semantic information.[1]

Another type of evidence that shows that semantic information is involved in long-term memory comes from the study of word recognition. If adults are shown a series of words and are then given a series of test words and are asked to indicate which words had been presented earlier, they often make errors in recognition. Just as "slips of the tongue" are revealing, so too are recognition errors. Subjects most often err by incorrectly recognizing test words that are semantically related to the originally presented words (Anisfeld & Knapp, 1968; Grossman & Eagle, 1970). Thus those errors indicate that it is the meaning of the words that is remembered by the subjects.

Concluding Comments   In concluding our discussion of the types of information that are involved in long-term memory, it is important to note that adults are very flexible in the ways they encode information. It is an oversimplification to contend that humans can encode only or even primarily one type of information for long-term memory. Whereas in some situations information concerning the visual characteristics or the time of occurrence may be encoded, in other situations semantic information may be encoded. For example, when sentences are presented in the context of a meaningful paragraph, subjects most often remember the meaning rather than the form of the sentence (Sachs, 1967). However, when a series of unrelated sentences are presented, subjects do remember something about the form of the sentences such as whether they were of the active or passive voice (Anderson, 1974; see also Bates, Masling, & Kintsch, 1978; Begg & Paivio, 1969; Keenan, MacWhinney, & Mahew, 1977).

Another important point is that encoding involves responding to the stimuli presented by the experimenter, and adult subjects may remember not only what stimuli were presented but also how they responded to them. In other words, adults seem to remember the encoding operations that were performed on the information presented by the experimenter. For example, in one study (Kolers & Ostry, 1974) adults were shown sentences in normal type, upside down, backwards, and so on. After a retention interval of over one month, the subjects were able to recognize whether a particular sentence had originally been presented upside down, in normal typography, and so on. The extent to which memory for encoding operations facilitates retention of the encoded information is uncertain, but this issue should be clarified as research intensifies on our next topic of discussion, the effects of encoding upon retention.

The Nature of Encoding as an Antecedent of Retention

The dimensions along which information is encoded determine what is remembered. A particular word such as *baboon* may be encoded along visual, phonological or semantic dimensions (or combinations thereof), thereby making it possible to remember either visual, phonological or semantic information concerning that word.

Just as the nature of encoding determines what is remembered, so too may the nature of encoding help to determine the level of retention. However, this view is easier to state than to test, for an obvious but stubborn problem is encountered in testing how the nature of encoding affects retention. Specifically, if the subjects are given a list of items to remember, the experimenter may have little control over how the items are encoded (cf. Postman, 1976a). Even if the subjects are instructed to encode in a particular way, they may disobey the instructions and engage in additional processing if they know they will later be asked to recall the items. More generally, the problem is that adults actively try to figure out what the purpose of the experiment is, and they often try to behave in ways that they think will be consistent with the desires of the experimenter (Rosenthal, 1966). Thus it is unwise for the experimenter to believe that the subjects are doing only what they have been instructed to do.

One commonly used strategy for handling the foregoing problem is to use *incidental learning* paradigms to study memory (cf. Hyde & Jenkins, 1973; Till & Jenkins, 1973). Basically, incidental learning paradigms entail deceiving subjects into believing that the goal of the experiment is to study how they perform some cover task, when in fact the purpose is to study memory. By varying the nature of the cover task, one can gain some degree of control over how the subjects process the information. And by deceiving the subjects about the purpose of the experiment, one can help to prevent the subjects from encoding information in ways other than those desired by the experimenter, for the subjects may have little reason to believe that the experimenter will test for retention.

Craik and Tulving (1975) have used an incidental learning paradigm to test whether the nature of encoding determines the level of retention. In that study, the subjects were told that the experiment concerned perception and the speed of reaction. The experiment included 60 trials, each of which began with the presentation of a question about the word that immediately followed. The words used were common nouns and each was presented visually for 200 msec. The task of the subjects was to answer the question about the word as rapidly as possible by immediately pressing either a "yes" button or a "no" button.

The purpose of the questions was to induce the subjects to encode the words in particular ways. On different trials, one of three types of question was asked. To induce the subjects to encode the physical characteristics of the word, for instance, *table,* the experimenters asked a question such as "Is the word in capital letters?" To bring about the phonological encoding of a word such as *crate,* the experimenters asked a question such as "Does the word rhyme with WEIGHT?" Similarly, to induce semantic encoding, the subjects were given a question such as "Would the word fit the sentence: 'They met a _____ in the street'?" Following the series of 60 trials with questions and answers, the subjects were unexpectedly given a recognition test for the words. The recognition test consisted of 180 words, including the 60 original words and 120 distractor items. In that test, the task of the subjects was to indicate which words had been presented originally.

The results of the experiment, shown in Fig. 11.1, were that the level of retention varied systematically as a function of the level of encoding. Retention was poorest for the words that had been encoded on a physical level. Retention was greatest for the words that had been encoded on a semantic level. Finally, retention was intermediate for the words that had been encoded pho-

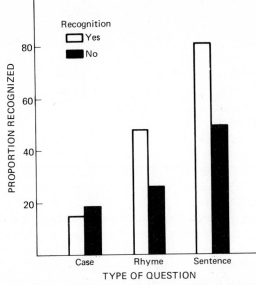

Fig. 11.1   The proportion of words correctly recognized as a function of the type of question.   (From Craik & Tulving, 1975. Copyright 1975 by the American Psychological Association. Reprinted by permission.)

nologically. Clearly, the level of retention depends upon the manner in which the information is processed, regardless of whether the subjects intentionally try to remember the information. If the information is processed on a superficially, nonsemantic level, retention is generally poor, but if the information is processed on a deeper semantic level, retention is generally good (cf. Hyde & Jenkins, 1973; Lockhart, Craik, & Jacoby, 1976; Walsh & Jenkins, 1973).

Recently, Craik and Tulving (1975; see also Lockhart, et al., 1976) have suggested that the analysis of memory in terms of levels of processing should be modified to include the elaborateness as well as the level of encoding. Specifically, they suggested that stimuli are processed through a series of levels, but that at any particular level the stimulus may be processed fully or only partially. Thus a stimulus might not be analyzed fully in terms of its physical features before it is analyzed in terms of its semantic features. Furthermore, words that are processed on the same level, such as the semantic level, may be processed in different degrees of elaborateness. For example, less elaborate semantic processing may be required to determine whether a word fits into a simple sentence such as *The _____ is torn* than into a more complex sentence such as *The small lady angrily picked up the red _____* . Research conducted to date indicates that more elaborately processed items are remembered better than those that are less elaborately processed.

Some Unresolved Problems   Although many observations are consistent with the view that retention is a function of the depth and elaborateness of encoding, this view does have some problematic features. One of the main problems is that there is no clear way of defining the level or elaborateness of encoding that is engendered by a particular task (Baddeley, 1978; Nelson, T. O., 1977; Postman, 1976a). For example, what level of encoding is occasioned by a task that requires the subjects to estimate the frequency with which particular words are used in the English language? There is no clear answer to this question, and it is perhaps tempting to use the level of retention for the rated words as a gauge of the level at which they were processed. However, it is circular to assert that the level of processing determines retention and to then infer the level of processing from the results of retention tests.

What is needed is a way of determining the level of encoding independently of tests for retention. This need is partially satisfied by the use of the incidental learning procedure, for this procedure does yield some control over how the subjects act upon information. Nevertheless, the incidental learning procedure does not really provide an independent definition of the level of encoding (Postman, 1976a). First, the subjects in an incidental learning procedure may process information in ways other than those that are requested by the experimenter. Adults are seldom so obliging as to do only what they have been asked to, and in an experimental task that requires only phonological processing, they may engage in some semantic processing. Second, in an incidental learning paradigm, the definition of the level of encoding rests with the intuition of the experimenter. Needless to say, intuition is too fallible a guide in situations that involve tasks such as estimating how often a particular word is used. In the future, it may be wise to try to define the level of encoding in an independent and empirical manner (Seamon & Virostek, 1978). One might ascertain whether information had been encoded, say, phonologically or semantically by examining the types of events that could produce retroactive interference.

The second major problem is that in much of the current research on encoding and retention, several variables may be confounded (Baddeley, 1978; Nelson, T. O., 1977; Nelson, T. O., & Vining, 1978; Postman, 1976a). For example, the superiority of semantic encoding over phonological encoding depends to some extent on the nature of the retention test (Morris, Bransford, & Franks, 1977; see also Stein, 1978). In one experiment (Morris et al., 1977), subjects performed tasks that required either semantic or phonological processing of words. Then the subjects were given two types of retention test. In the semantic test, the task was to identify words that were semantically equivalent to the words that had been presented earlier. In the phonological test, the task was to identify words that rhymed with the previously presented words. The results were that the words that had been processed semantically were remembered well on the semantic retention test but not on the phonological retention test. Conversely, the words that had been processed phonologically were remembered well on the phonological test but not on the semantic test. Thus the effects of the level of encoding depend upon how retention is tested. The poor retention for phonologically encoded information that has been observed in many studies may be due to the type of retention test given rather than any intrinsic inferiority of phonological processing. These observations remind us that a retention test is not a neutral measuring device, and the observed level of retention reflects as much about our ingenuity in testing as it does about the effects of encoding. In any memory experiment, encoding, storage and retrieval are potentially confounded, and a factor that appears to affect encoding processes may affect retrieval processes, or both.

A third problem with the view that retention is a function of the level and elaborateness of processing is that it remains unclear as to *why* different levels of processing give rise to different degrees of retention. Is information that is processed on a semantic level better organized than information that is processed on a nonsemantic level? Is semantic information more accessible than nonsemantic information (cf. Lockhart et al., 1976)? The fact that semantic information is remembered better than nonsemantic information is not explained in a deep way by referring to levels of processing, for the effects of the different levels still need to be explained.

These comments are not meant to imply that the analysis of memory in terms of levels of encoding is fruitless. Indeed, this analysis contains an important germ of truth: Memory depends upon the nature of the private events the subject brings to bear upon the information that is to be remembered. Moreover, the analysis in terms of levels of processing is consistent with the flexible and diverse nature of encoding in humans. Nevertheless, the levels-of-processing analysis is best seen not as a refined and powerful theory but as a working hypothesis that can help to guide research and to make some rough, qualitative predictions about memory. One topic that will be of central importance in future attempts to clarify the effects of encoding is organization; this topic will now be considered.

Encoding and Organization

In the preceding chapter, we saw that organization is important in short-term memory in that organizing or chunking information permits one to overcome the problem of our limited capacity to remember over the short run. In this chapter, we have seen that long-term retention is facilitated by encoding information elaborately. To say that information is encoded elaborately is to some extent to say that the information is somehow organized or related to previously acquired information, and students of memory have sought to analyze the nature and the effects of organization (Bower, 1972; Cofer, 1965; Tulving & Donaldson, 1972).

It has proved to be difficult to study organization, for the nature of the experimental procedure often interferes with the observations that bear most directly on the topic of organization. For example, the paired-associate learning procedure requires the subject to recall a particular item in the presence of particular stimulus item that is presented by the experimenter. In the paired-associate procedure, the experimenter has imposed many constraints upon what the subject can do. The subject is required to relate only pairs of items and is not free to recall the learned items in any order. Thus the experimenter has no way of knowing whether the subject has somehow grouped together the words from different pairs. Thus the paired-associate procedure does not permit one to see the organization that might be present.

In order to study organization, it is clearly important for the experimenter to use a procedure that imposes few constraints upon the behavior of the subjects. One such procedure that has been utilized extensively in recent years is the free recall procedure (cf. Tulving, 1968). This procedure usually involves presenting a list of items for a short time and, following a retention interval, asking the subjects to recall the items in any order.

Subjective Organization The occurrence of categorical clustering that was examined previously shows that subjects actively organize information when they learn a list of words. Given that organization occurs, two important questions arise. First, is the organization of information a general phenomenon, or is it restricted to situations that involve items that fall into several classes? Second, is organization a necessary condition for the long-term retention of information?

To pursue these questions, consider an experiment by Tulving (1962). In an effort to determine whether organization is a general phenomenon, Tulving studied the free recall of a list of 16 unrelated words. The experiment consisted of 16 trials, and on each trial a list of 16 two-syllable nouns was presented at a rate of one word per sec. Following the presentation of each list, there was a brief recall period in which the subjects were to recall as many words as possible and in any order they wished. The order in which the words were presented varied from trial to trial. Since the words in the list were not related in any obvious way, the organization of the words at recall could not be assessed by looking at the extent to which the subjects recalled together the words of common categories that were defined by the experimenter. Rather, the organization of words at recall was assessed by measuring the extent to which the subjects recalled pairs of items together on different trials. If two words such as *lagoon* and *cent* followed each other in recall on trial n and again on trial n + 1 for a particular subject, those words were said to have formed a subjectively organized unit for trial n + 1. Tulving developed a quantitative index of the amount of subjective organization, and this index was based upon the tendency to recall certain pairs of items in succession over different trials.

The results of the experiment are shown in Fig. 11.2, in which the mean number of words recalled over trials is plotted together with the amount of subjective organization that occurred over trials. As Fig. 11.2 shows, the number of words recalled increased over trials. As the number of words recalled increased, so did the amount of subjective organization. Indeed, for individual subjects there were relatively high correlations between the amount of subjective organization and the amount recalled. (For an analysis of organization in individual subjects see Buschke, 1976.) These results suggest that organization is a general phenomenon that occurs even for lists of unrelated words.

The preceding observation and conclusion have significant methodological and theoretical implications. The main methodological implication is that just as it is an error to believe that nonsense syllables are meaningless (see pp. 214–216), so too is it an error to contend that the words in a list are ever really unrelated. Because of the diversity of the prior experiences adults have had, organization may be idiosyncratic and imposed upon materials that appear to be unrelated, and it seems wise in experimental work to avoid assum-

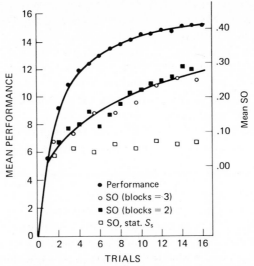

Fig. 11.2   The mean number of words recalled and the amount of subjective organization (SO) over trials in a free recall task.   (From Tulving, 1962. Copyright 1962 by the American Psychological Association. Reprinted by permission.)

ing that the words of any list are unrelated. In short, the presence or absence of relationships between items must be determined not by assumption but by observation.

The principal theoretical implication of the preceding observations is that organization may be central to learning and remembering. Indeed, it has been suggested (for example, Mandler, G., 1967; Mandler, G., 1970) that organization is necessary for learning.[2] According to this view, we have an intrinsically limited capacity for memory, and we can come to remember large amounts of information only by organizing information into larger and larger units. This position is supported by some evidence (Mandler, G., 1967; Mandler, G., & Pearlstone, 1966), particularly by the high correlation between measures of organization and recall. Needless to say, however, the high correlation need not imply causation. Additionally, there have been reports of instances in which the level of recall was high while the level of organization was low (for example, Puff, 1970; Shapiro & Bell, 1970). Before the issue may be settled, better measures of organization need to be devised, and many different types of tasks must be studied in greater detail.

Organization as a Sufficient Condition   At present, the most that may be said confidently is that organization is sufficient to facilitate retention. Consider the following noncorrelational study of the relation between organization and retention (Bower, Clark, Lesgold, & Winzenz, 1969). The subjects in the experiment were divided into an experimental and a control group. Both groups were required to learn a list of 112 words. These words belonged to one of four conceptual hierarchies; one of those hierarchies is shown in Fig. 11.3. The subjects in the experimental group were shown on each of four trials a series of four cards. Each card showed one conceptual hierarchy and included 28 words. The subjects in the control group were also shown four cards on four successive trials. The cards shown to the control group also contained 28 of the 112 words, but those words were selected on a random basis. Thus the words shown to the control group were not grouped according to their conceptual relatedness. The results of the experiment were that at the end of four trials, the subjects in the experimental group recalled almost all 120 words correctly. In contrast, the subjects in the control group recalled only half as many words correctly. Organization clearly may facilitate retention. Conversely, disrupting the organization of items may impair retention (Allen, 1968; Bower, Lesgold, & Tieman, 1969).

Concluding Comments   Several important questions concerning organization remain unanswered, and those questions merit careful analysis in the future. For example, what are the antecedents of organization? To some extent, the facilitation of retention by organization is a transfer phenomenon,[3] but the exact ontogenetic antecedents of organizational effects have yet to be identified. Moreover, the phylogenetic antecedents of organization are unknown, and we can only speculate about how the structure of the environments of our predecessors have contributed to our current tendencies and abilities to organize information. (For further discussion see Bower, 1972.) Another important question is this: Why does organization affect retention? It does not help to try to explain the effects of organization in terms of the elaborateness of processing, for the effects of the elaborateness of processing are themselves unexplained. No answer to this question is yet available. However, it seems likely that an adequate answer will require an understanding of the various mechanisms whereby information is encoded and organized, and we shall now consider those mechanisms.

Mechanisms of Encoding

In our discussion of memory, we have seen repeatedly that encoding is both active and flexible in nature. Humans can encode information in a variety of

Fig. 11.3   The conceptual hierarchy for "minerals."   (From Bower, Clark, Lesgold, & Winzenz, 1969. Copyright 1969 by Academic Press, *Journal of Verbal Learning and Verbal Behavior*.)

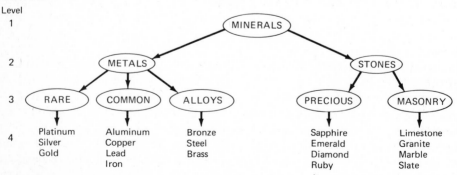

ways, including rote repetition, the formation of visual images, the use of a linguistic mediator such as a story and so on. In other words, the complex effects of past experience always intrude into any contemporary memory task, and we say that the subject uses a variety of strategies or mechanisms for encoding information.

Rehearsal   One of the simplest but least exciting ways of encoding information for long-term retention is to keep rehearsing or repeating information again and again. A variety of studies have provided support for the view that rehearsal facilitates long-term retention (for example, Hebb, 1961; Hellyer, 1962; Hintzman, 1976; Murdock & Metcalfe, 1978). Of course, it is not easy to determine the relation between rehearsal and long-term retention, for rehearsal is often covert. One strategy that has proven to be useful in the study of rehearsal is to require that the subject rehearse overtly rather than covertly. This strategy has helped to clarify the role of rehearsal in one of the oldest and most puzzling of all memory phenomena: the serial position effect.

First consider a study by Rundus and Atkinson (1970). In that experiment, each subject was shown a series of 11 lists of 20 unrelated nouns. Each item in a particular list was presented for 5 sec, and the subjects were instructed to learn the words in the list by rehearsing aloud the word that was being shown and any of the other words they wished to rehearse. Following the presentation of a list, there was a retention test in which the subjects were asked to write down in any order as many words from that list as possible.

The results of the experiment are shown in Fig. 11.4. The probability of recalling an item varied as a function of the position in which that item had been presented. The observation that the probability of recall depends upon the position in which an item was presented is called the *serial position effect.* Some reliable and salient features of the serial position effect are that the items at the beginning and the end of the list are remembered better than items from the middle of the list. The high level of retention for the items at the beginning of the list is called the *primacy effect,* and the high level of retention for the items at the end of the list is called the *recency effect.* As Fig. 11.4 shows, there is a close correspondence between the amount of rehearsal and the level of retention for all but the last items in the lists. In other words, the primacy effect seems to depend upon the amount of rehearsal, whereas the recency effect does not. Presumably, the recency effect results from the tendency of the subjects to begin the retention test by recalling the last items that had been presented, and those last items lie within the span of short-term memory (Glanzer & Cunitz, 1966). It is as if the subjects first "unload" the final, poorly rehearsed items and then go back to recall the better rehearsed items from the beginning of the list.

To test more precisely the relationship between the amount of rehearsal and the degree of long-term retention, subsequent experiments of a similar nature have investigated retention over intervals of up to three weeks (Rundus, Loftus, & Atkinson, 1970; see also Dark & Loftus, 1976). Just as in the preceding experiment, the probability of remembering an item depended upon how many

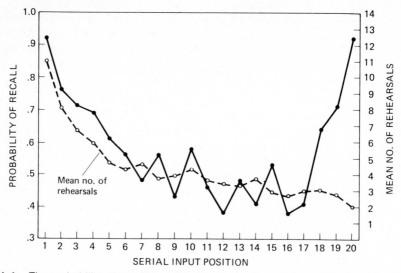

Fig. 11.4 The probability of recalling an item as a function of the position in which the item was presented and the mean number of rehearsals for that item. (From Rundus & Atkinson, 1970. Copyright 1970 by Academic Press, *Journal of Verbal Learning and Verbal Behavior.*)

times that item had been rehearsed. Furthermore, whereas the last items in the presented list are recalled well at short retention intervals (the recency effect), those same items are recalled worse than any other items at long retention intervals (Craik, 1970). In other words, when the recall test was delayed, there was a *negative recency effect*. At long retention intervals, then, the shape of the serial position function is accounted for nicely by the amount of rehearsal devoted to items at the various positions in a list.

As we mentioned above, delaying the retention test eliminates the recency effect, and instead produces a negative recency effect while leaving the primacy effect unchanged. The lack of rehearsal may account for the negative recency effect, but it does not account for the recency effect. Why is it that at short retention intervals, the probability of recalling the last items in a list is high despite the small amount of rehearsal devoted to them? According to the multistore model of memory, the last items are retained in the short-term store and can be remembered without rehearsal for brief periods of time. At long retention intervals, the information has been lost from the short-term store and was not transferred via rehearsal to the long-term store. Accordingly, retention of the last items is poor.

Despite the plausibility of the preceding analysis, the primacy and recency effects may be accounted for without postulating different memory stores (cf. Bernbach, 1975; Bjork & Whitten, 1974). For example, it is possible that the different effects of the retention interval upon the first and last items result from differences in the amount of interference that those items are exposed to. Since many items follow the first few, the initial items are (at least potentially) subjected to a good deal of retroactive interference even when the retention test is immediate. In contrast, the last few items are subjected to retroactive interference only during the delayed retention interval that involves some distracting activity. Thus the last few items could be affected more than the first items by the events in the retention interval (cf. Grunenberg, 1970; Wickelgren, 1973). The important point is that a phenomenon that can be accounted for in terms of storage in different memory stores may also be accounted for in terms of retrieval processes such as those involved in interference (see Bjork & Whitten, 1974). And in general, many of the phenomena that are accounted for by the multistore model may be explained in other ways without suggesting different memorial stores or processes (cf. Wickelgren, 1973).

At one time, multistore theorists hoped for a relatively simple relationship between repetition and memory. However, the relationship between repetition and memory has proven to be surprisingly intricate. For example, the effects of repetition upon retention depend upon the amount of time that passes between the repetitions of a particular item (cf. Hintzman, 1974; Melton, 1967, 1970). If the repetitions of an item follow each other closely in time, the increase in the probability of recalling the item is less than would have occurred if the repetitions of an item were further separated in time. This phenomenon is called the *lag effect*.

Different Types of Rehearsal   To further complicate the view that repetition facilitates retention, there are conditions under which rehearsal does not facilitate long-term retention (Jacoby & Bartz, 1972; Jacoby, 1973; Modigliani & Seamon, 1974; Rundus, 1977; Woodward, Bjork, & Jongeward, 1973).[4] For example, Craik and Watkins (1973) presented subjects with a series of lists and told them that they would be asked to recall the last four words in each list. The subjects were also told that if they needed to rehearse the last four words, they were to do so aloud. After some lists, a test of free recall was given immediately, whereas after other lists, there was a 15-sec delay between the end of the list and the free recall test. Following the presentation and recall of all of the lists, an unannounced, final test of retention for all of the words was given. The results were that the probability of recalling an item in the final test of retention did not depend upon how much that item had been rehearsed. Indeed, there was more rehearsal of the items in the lists for which there had been a delayed recall test, but the final level of retention for those items was poor, just as it was for the items that had been rehearsed less.

These results have led to the view that there are two types of rehearsal: *maintenance rehearsal* and *elaborative rehearsal* (Craik & Lockhart, 1972; Craik & Watkins, 1973). Both types of rehearsal involve the repetition of an item over and over, either overtly or covertly. Maintenance rehearsal involves processing information at a particular level, and it does not facilitate long-term recall (although some evidence suggests that maintenance rehearsal does facilitate recognition; cf. Nelson, T. O., 1977; Woodward, Bjork, & Jongeward, 1973).

In contrast, elaborative rehearsal involves organizing the repeated information and fitting it in with information from past experiences, and elaborative rehearsal improves long-term retention.

The distinction between maintenance and elaborative rehearsal corresponds roughly to the distinction between elaborative and nonelaborative processing. The observation that only elaborative rehearsal improves long-term retention is consistent with the view that long-term retention comes about as the result of deep, elaborative processing. However, as we saw earlier, there is no clear definition of what constitutes "elaborative" processing and it is circular to observe that rehearsal facilitated retention and then to infer that retention was improved by the occurrence of elaborative rehearsal. This problem complicates attempts to test the claim that maintenance rehearsal does not facilitate long-term retention. For instance, in some studies (for example, Glenberg, Smith, & Green, 1977; Nelson, T. O., 1977; Woodward, Bjork, & Jongeward, 1973), it has been shown that the repetition of items at a phonological level of processing does enhance retention, and this observation has been interpreted as conflicting with the view that maintenance rehearsal does not affect long-term retention (cf. Nelson, T. O., 1977). But since there is no way to be certain that the subjects actually engaged in maintenance rather than elaborative rehearsal, the proper interpretation of this observation is unclear. It is simply too soon to say for sure whether long-term retention is facilitated only by elaborative rehearsal. Although we can conclude that rehearsal can facilitate retention, we must also conclude that more research is needed to determine the conditions under which rehearsal does enhance long-term memory. That research will have important implications for the levels-of-processing analysis of memory.

Natural Language Mediation Another mechanism for encoding stimuli for long-term retention reflects the contribution of past experience with natural languages. The process of encoding through natural language mediation involves transforming or incorporating stimuli into words or sentences that are part of our language and are already well learned (see pp. 271–272). For example, in trying to remember the nonsense syllable *wod*, one might transform *wod* into the word *wood,* and we would then say that natural language mediation had occurred. As another example of natural language mediation, if subjects were to learn pairs of words such as *truth* and *fallible,* they might construct a sentential mediator such as *The truths of science are fallible.*

The question that now arises is whether natural language mediation enhances long-term retention, and a study of Montague, Adams and Kiess (1966) bears on that issue. In this experiment, a list of 96 pairs of nonsense syllables was presented, and each pair was presented for either 15 or 30 sec. Some of the pairs were high in rated meaningfulness (as defined by Noble, 1961), whereas other pairs were low in rated meaningfulness. The subjects were told that they would later be asked to recall the pairs. The subjects were also instructed to write down any natural language mediator that occurred to them for a particular pair while that pair was shown. Following a retention interval of 24 hr, a test of retention was given. In that test, the stimulus item from each of the pairs was presented, and the task of the subject was to recall the other term of the pair and the mediator that had been constructed for that pair.

The main results of the study were twofold. First, the probability of forming a mediator increased as the amount of study time and the association value of the syllables in the pairs increased. Apparently, it takes time to devise a mediator, and the ease of devising a mediator depends upon the meaningfulness of the items. The second important result was that the level of retention depended upon whether a mediator had been formed for a pair and whether the mediator was recalled at the time of the retention test. In analyzing the results of the test, the pairs were divided into three classes: pairs for which no mediator had been given originally; pairs for which a mediator had been given and later forgotten; and pairs for which a mediator had been given originally and remembered at the time of the test. As Fig. 11.5 shows, the level of retention was high for the pairs for which a natural language mediator had been devised and remembered. In contrast, retention was poor when the mediator was not recalled. Similarly, retention was poor for those pairs for which no mediator had been given. This observation is consistent with the finding that instructions to use mediators in a paired-associate task give rise to better retention than do instructions to learn pairs through rote repetition (Paivio, 1971b).

It is possible that the differences in retention for the different classes of word pairs described above are actually not differences in retention but rather differences in the original degree of learning. However, this interpretation is made less plausible by the observation that whereas nonsense syllables learned either by rote or by mediation are remembered very well in an immediate retention test, the syllables learned by mediation are better remembered after a retention interval of 30 sec (Kiess, 1968).

The preceding observations show that just as mediation can facilitate

Fig. 11.5   The mean percentage of items that were correctly recalled as a function of the association value of the mediator and whether the mediator was recalled.   (After Montague, Adams, & Kiess, 1966.)

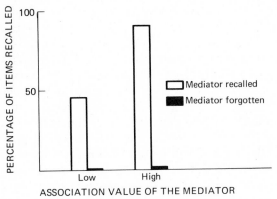

learning, so too can it facilitate retention. However, mediation enhances retention only if the mediator is remembered, and only if the original item can be reconstructed from the mediator. Thus, it becomes important to ascertain what determines whether one remembers a mediator and its relation to the original stimulus. Although this topic is largely unexplored, one important variable is the complexity and the number of transformations that are made to form natural language mediators (Prytulak, 1971). If the transformation is very simple and direct (for example, *lov* to *love*), the level of retention is high, but retention is worse when the transformations are more numerous and complex.

An important task of future research in this area is to determine the antecedents of the formation and use of natural language mediators, and historical analyses will undoubtedly be beneficial. Another important aim is to specify the inner processes that underlie the formation and use of linguistic mediators. The search for those processes will assume significant proportions as we next examine encoding via imagery.

Imagery   Imagery has long been believed to be an important determinant of long-term retention. For example, in ancient Greek times, mnemonic systems based upon visual imagery were used widely by orators. Indeed, these mnemonic systems were often taught by the teachers of rhetoric, for at that time writing was expensive and uncommon, and speeches had to be memorized.

One mnemonic system that was used by the Greek orators was called the *method of loci* (cf. Yates, 1966); this system is best illustrated by an example. Suppose you have a list of 20 items to remember, and two of those items are *wood* and *television.* Now imagine in vivid detail the rooms of a house in which you have lived for a long time. Next, form an image of each of the items to be remembered, and picture each item in a distinct location in your house. For the words *wood* and *television,* one might form an image of one's family watching a favorite show with a warm, glowing fire in the fireplace. In trying to recall the 20 items, you should take an imaginary walk through the house and recall the items in each of the imagined locations.

Although the method of loci may seem an unnecessarily complicated one, this system seems to work well after it has been practiced (Groninger, 1971) and has been used by many professional mnemonists (Baddeley, 1976). This method and other mnemonic systems are important on an applied level in that they may facilitate the learning and retention of, for example, the vocabulary of a foreign language (Atkinson, 1975). At present, we have only begun to explore the educational uses of mnemonic systems and of theories of memory.

Imagery and Long-Term Retention   Although considerable evidence shows that imagery contributes to the acquisition of information (Paivio, 1971b), the role of imagery in retention is difficult to assess, as the following experiment shows. Begg and Robertson (1973) had subjects learn two lists of 25 words. One list contained concrete nouns such as *elephant, clock,* and *board,* whereas the other list contained abstract nouns such as *fact, competence,* and *banality;* the concrete and abstract nouns were about equal in their frequency of occurrence. The concrete nouns evoke covert images more easily and quickly than do the abstract nouns (cf. Paivio, Yuille, & Madigan, 1968). The concrete nouns are said to be high in imagery value, whereas the abstract nouns are said to be low in imagery value. Each list was presented in the following way. On the first trial, one word was presented and the subjects were then asked to recall that word. On the second trial, the word from the first trial was presented with another word in a random order, and the subjects were asked to recall both words. On the third trial, the words from the first two trials were presented along with a third word, and so on. This procedure continued until all 25 words had been presented and the subjects had attempted to recall those words. Tests of retention for both the concrete and the abstract nouns were given either 48 or 72 hr following the completion of the learning procedure.

The results of the experiment are shown in Fig. 11.6. For both the 48-hr and the 72-hr retention intervals, the proportion of concrete words that were correctly recalled exceeded the proportion of abstract words that were correctly recalled. Furthermore, the level of subjective organization was much higher among the concrete words recalled than among the abstract words recalled. These results were interpreted as showing that covert imagery, as measured by the scales provided by Paivio, Yuille, and Madigan (1968), facilitates both the long-term retention and the organization of verbal information. (For a review of the effects of imagery on retention see Paivio, 1975a).

Although the preceding experiment may seem to show that imagery influences long-term retention, the interpretation of the experiment is complicated by methodological problems (Postman, 1976a). In studies of retention, the level of retention is often confounded with the level of acquisition (cf. Underwood, 1954, 1964, for discussions of the problem and how to deal with it). If in the study by Begg and Robertson there had been differences in the degree of

Fig. 11.6   Retention of concrete and abstract words 48 and 72 hr after learning.   (From Begg & Robertson. 1973. Copyright 1973 by Academic Press, *Journal of Verbal Learning and Verbal Behavior.*)

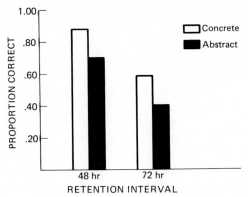

learning for the abstract and concrete words, what appeared to be a difference in long-term retention for those words might have in fact reflected differences in the degree of original learning. Begg and Robertson attempted to equate the degree of learning for the concrete and the abstract words by using the special learning procedure described above. In their procedure, a single word was first presented, followed by that word and a second one, and so on through the lists. This minimized the occurrence of errors, and over all 25 trials, the proportion of correct responses was .95 for concrete words and .94 for abstract words. However, the occurrence of a small and approximately equal number of errors in both conditions may not indicate equivalent degrees of learning in the two conditions. For example, assume that items that have been learned and can be accurately recalled in the learning task can differ somewhat in "strength" or level of acquisition. This assumption is not unreasonable, for even in everyday tasks such as learning the names of 10 people, we may be more certain of some of our correct responses than of others, and these responses may differ with respect to the level of acquisition. When the preceding assumption is made, one becomes uncertain as to whether the level of acquisition actually was equivalent for the abstract and concrete words. Thus the most appropriate conclusion that may be drawn at this time is that imagery may facilitate long-term retention, but that further research is needed to separate the effects upon acquisition and retention (cf. Postman & Burns, 1973).

On a different level, one may argue that the effects of imagery upon memory are implicit in the effects of imagery upon acquisition. To the extent that memory is implicit within learning (see pp. 409–410), the effects of imagery upon acquisition also constitute effects upon memory. Contemporary studies have identified imagery as one of the chief determinants of acquisition in adult humans, and adults often report spontaneously that they use imagery to remember concrete nouns (Paivio, 1969). Because of the strong and pervasive effects of imagery, it is important to control for the effects of imagery in investigating the effects of verbal factors such as the level of meaningfulness, the degree of conceptual relatedness among words, and so on (Paivio, 1971a, 1971b).

Theoretical Analyses of Imagery Having seen that imagery facilitates long-term memory, we may ask how the effects of imagery may be explained (see Kieras, 1978, and Paivio, 1975a, for a full discussion of this issue). One explanation of imagery is based upon the concept of organization. For example, Begg and Robertson (1973; see also Begg, 1972, 1973) have argued that imagery enhances retention by integrating discrete verbal items into a single functional unit of memory. The notion that imagery facilitates retention as the result of its organizational function is supported by the results of experiments by Bower (1972). In these experiments, the effects of interactive and noninteractive imagery were compared. An interactive image for the words *girl* and *bicycle* might involve imagining a girl riding a bicycle. In contrast, a noninteractive image for these words might involve imagining a room in which there was a girl on one side and a bicycle on the other. The results were that interactive imagery facilitated learning and retention much more than noninteractive imagery did. Although it seems clear that organization does contribute to the effects of imagery, the effects of organization upon memory are to a large extent in need of explanation. Furthermore, it is unclear whether interactive images always benefit retention more than noninteractive images, or whether interactive images facilitate retention mainly when the objects that are imagined as interacting have previously been seen interacting frequently. It is too early to accept the view that the effects of imagery can be accounted for in terms of organization, and further research on this topic is clearly needed.

Another explanation of the effects of imagery, proposed by Paivio (1969, 1971a, 1971b, 1975a, 1975b; see also Paivio & Csapo, 1973), is called the *dual-coding theory*. According to the dual-coding theory, humans have two independent systems for processing information: the imaginal system and the verbal system. The imaginal system is specialized for the encoding, storage and retrieval of nonverbal information that is sensory or spatial (in the case of vision) in nature. On the other hand, the verbal system is specialized for the processing of information that is linguistic and nonspatial in nature.[5] Presumably, different cerebral hemispheres are involved in imaginal and verbal processing. Just as the left hemisphere in most adults is specialized for the processing of linguistic information (recall the split-brain studies (see pp. 392–393), so the right hemisphere is specialized for processing nonverbal, imaginal information (cf. Kimura, 1973; Milner, 1968; Ornstein, 1978).

According to Paivio (1971b), the imaginal and verbal systems are richly interconnected even though they are independent. If the two systems were unconnected (as in the split-brain preparation), we would be unable to describe our images, to form an image of something named by a word, and so on. Because the two systems are connected, adults can process a word such as *bicycle* both verbally and imaginally. Thus concrete words can be encoded in two different ways and in two different systems. In contrast, abstract words do not readily give rise to images, and they are encoded only (or primarily) in the verbal system. Presumably, then, words that are high in imagery value are better remembered than words that are low in imagery value because the former words are represented in two independent codes that add together to improve retention.

Evidence in support of the dual-coding theory comes from a variety of sources (Kosslyn, 1978; Nelson, D. L., & Brooks, 1973; Paivio & Csapo, 1973; Rowe, 1973). For example, it has been observed that performance of tasks that are thought to involve visual imagery is impaired more by the simultaneous performance of a visual distracting task than by the performance of a verbal distracting task (Brooks, 1967, 1968; see also Allen, Marcell, & Anderson, 1978). Presumably, activity in the imaginal processing system is interfered with by simultaneous visual processing, but verbal processing is less disruptive since it occurs in the other (verbal) processing system.

The dual-coding theory is also consistent with evidence that imaginal processing is functionally similar to the processing that occurs in the perception of visual scenes (for example, Podgorny & Shepard, 1978). For example, it takes time to scan across large distances while viewing a scene. Similarly, it takes time to scan across imagined scenes (for a review, see Kosslyn, 1978). In one experiment (Kosslyn, Ball, & Reiser, 1978), people were shown and asked to imagine three letters of the alphabet lying at different points along a line. Two of the letters were of one case (upper or lower), and the third was of the opposite case. The line was removed after it had been studied, and the subject was asked to form an image of one end of the line. Then one letter was named, and the subject was to scan the imagined line for that letter and push one of two buttons indicating the case of the letter. The result of main interest was that reaction times increased in proportion to the distance that was scanned. Apparently, people scan visual images as they do actual scenes, and this suggests that the information processed imaginally is visual or spatial in nature.

The dual-coding theory is generally in keeping with the physiological evidence concerning the specialization of the cerebral hemispheres. The theory also accommodates the observation that we can easily recognize pictures and other visual stimuli even when they are difficult to name distinctively. Nevertheless, it is not altogether clear why a single imaginal system should be postulated, for imagery may be auditory or tactile as well as visual. There may turn out to be different imaginal processing systems. The occurrence of imagery in nonvisual modalities may account for the observation that people who have been blind throughout life learn and remember concrete words better than abstract words (Coltheart & Glick, 1974).

On the other hand, the dual-coding theory is not supported by all of the available evidence. For example, the learning and retention of words is facilitated equally well by making up an image or a sentence that connects a pair of words (Bobrow & Bower, 1969). Moreover, subjects who learn some word pairs through imagery and other pairs through the generation of sentences have difficulty remembering which encoding strategy they used (Bower, Munoz & Arnold, 1972; cited in Anderson & Bower, 1973). Another problem is that the effect of imagery variables may be confounded with the effects of other variables that have not yet been defined precisely (Galbraith & Underwood, 1973; Schnorr & Atkinson, 1970).

On a deeper level, it may not be possible to evaluate the dual-coding theory solely on empirical grounds. Some theorists (for example, Kieras, 1978; Pylyshyn, 1973) have argued that the dual-coding theory does not provide a satisfactory explanation of the effects of imagery variables. The argument turns on the observation that images are constructed or generated from underlying information (Pylyshyn, 1973). To see this for yourself, form a visual image of a child effortlessly riding up a very steep mountain on a bicycle, towing along a two-ton truck behind. The image you formed was surely constructed since you have most likely never witnessed such an episode. Forming that image is not like looking up a picture stored in memory. Rather, it seems to entail using your knowledge of children, trucks, and so on to actively generate an image.

Now consider the implications for the dual-coding theory. Since images are often constructed, it seems that the effects of imagery variables upon memory are better explained in terms of the processes that lead to the production of images rather than in terms of the images themselves (Anderson, 1978; Kieras, 1978; Pylyshyn, 1973). An important implication of this view is that conscious phenomena such as images may be products of underlying processes of which we are not and cannot be conscious. At any rate, the dual-coding theory does not specify what these underlying processes are and is therefore held by some (Kieras, 1978; Pylyshyn, 1973) to provide an inadequate explanation of performance in memorial tasks. At present, most theories that do specify the underlying processes do not entail the assumption of two independent memory codes (Kieras, 1978), and we shall now consider these theories briefly.

Imagery and the Representation of Knowledge   In Chapter 8, we saw that knowledge may be represented in a propositional format. Recall that a proposition consists of two concepts and a term that specifies the relationship between them. We shall not explore propositional knowledge in detail here. For our purposes, it is sufficient to note that many theorists who are attempting to build computer models that simulate human cognitive processes believe that all knowledge, whether perceptual or abstract, can be represented in terms of propositions (Anderson, 1978; Anderson & Bower, 1973; Kieras, 1978; Pylyshyn, 1973; Simon, 1972). In other words, it seems possible to represent all knowledge in a propositional format. This theory, which is called the *propositional-coding theory,* asserts that it is unnecessary to postulate two independent memory codes as the dual-coding theory does.

It is important to recognize that the propositional coding theory does not hold that verbal and imaginal information are represented in identical ways. For example, semantic (verbal) and perceptual (imaginal) representations may differ in the number of connections between concepts in the representation (Kieras, 1978). In terms of the levels-of-processing analysis, perceptual-imaginal representations may constitute more elaborate encodings that include more interconnections between concepts. Furthermore, the propositions that represent perceptual and semantic knowledge may contain different concepts and relations. For example, the relations that describe a visual scene may have no direct semantic counterparts. In summary, the propositional-coding theory asserts that perceptual-imaginal and semantic-verbal knowledge is unitary and propositional in nature, but the theory allows for differences in the types of relations expressed and in the number of connections between concepts.

The propositional-coding theory is believed by many theorists to have advantages over a dual-coding theory. One advantage is parsimony. If the propositional-coding theory can do all that the dual-coding theory can, it is preferred on grounds of simplicity since it assumes one memory code rather than two. Another possible advantage of the propositional-coding theory is that it readily accommodates the observation that sentences and images may be based upon common conceptual information. For example, in forming a visual image of a girl riding a bicycle up a steep hill, we might use our knowledge of the positions in which humans can ride bikes, the relationship between pedalling and moving, and so on. This same general conceptual information might also be used to construct the sentence *The girl rode the bicycle up the steep hill.*

The most significant advantage of the propositional-coding theory is that it can in principle provide the basis for successful computer simulations of forming images, comprehending sentences, and so on (Anderson, 1978; Anderson & Bower, 1973; Kintsch & van Dijk, 1978; Pylyshyn, 1973). Thus, the propositional-coding theory is capable of specifying the mechanisms that underlie visual and verbal retention. In principle, then, the propositional-coding theory may provide a stronger explanation of the effects of imagery than the dual-coding theory can (Kieras, 1978).

The problem with the preceding argument is that the assumption of two independent codes may yet provide the basis for models of memory that do specify the mechanisms involved in processing images and sentences (Anderson, 1978; Kosslyn, 1978). At this point, there is no fully adequate model of verbal and imaginal phenomena, and it would be premature to reject the dual-coding theory. Interestingly, propositional-coding and dual-coding models may eventually prove to be equivalent in their power and consistency with experimental observations (Anderson, 1978). The resolution of this dilemma, however, must await the outcome of additional research. In our subsequent discussion of semantic memory, we shall pursue further the question of how information is represented in the memory system.

Abstract Semantic Coding The sentences that we utter and comprehend, much like the images we form, may be based upon abstract conceptual and semantic information (see pp. 343–346). Some evidence consistent with this position comes from studies of memory for sentences and for connected discourse such as paragraphs, stories, and so on (for example, Bartlett, 1932; Kintsch & van Dijk, 1978; Sachs, 1967).

Bransford and Franks (1971) presented subjects with a list of sentences that together made up four different stories. Each story consisted of what may be loosely called four elementary ideas. For example, the story told by sentence (1) consists of the elementary ideas expressed in sentences (2) through (5).

(1) The ants in the kitchen ate the sweet jelly which was on the table.
(2) The ants were in the kitchen.
(3) The jelly was on the table.
(4) The jelly was sweet.
(5) The ants ate the jelly.

The subjects were not exposed to sentences such as sentence (1) above, but were exposed to sentences that included either one, two or three of the elementary ideas. An example of a sentence that includes three elementary ideas is *The ants in the kitchen ate the jelly.* The specific procedure used in the experiment by Bransford and Franks was as follows. The experimenter read aloud a list of 24 sentences, six from each of the four stories. The sentences from the four stories were presented in a random order, so that the sentences relevant to a particular story did not follow each other. Following each sentence, the subjects were given a simple question to answer about the sentence. For example, if the sentence were *The rock rolled down the mountain,* it would be followed by the question *Did what?* The subjects were not instructed to remember the sentences, but they were nevertheless given a recognition test 5 min later. The recognition test consisted of 28 sentences, some of which were new and some of which had been presented earlier. Some of the test sentences included ideas from the stories, whereas other test sentences differed in meaning from the original sentences. The test sentences contained either one, two, three or four elementary ideas. The task of the subjects was to indicate whether each test sentence was new or old and to indicate on a five-point scale how confident they were of their answer.

The results of the study were that many of the novel test sentences were incorrectly recognized. Indeed, most of the subjects said they had previously seen the sentences that included all four elementary ideas, even though those sentences had never been presented in the original phase of the experiment. Furthermore, the subjects were most confident that they had previously heard the sentences that contained all four elementary ideas. Finally, the subjects rarely erred by recognizing a test sentence that differed in meaning from the original sentence.

Several important conclusions can be drawn from the foregoing observations. First, the subjects clearly retained information concerning the meaning of the sentences, but they remembered little concerning the exact form of the sentences. Second, the semantic information from the different sentences that together composed a story was integrated into an abstract format over time, for the subjects were (mistakenly) very confident they had previously seen the sentences that contained all four elementary ideas (for an alternative interpretation, see Flagg, 1976). In a sense the subjects remembered more than they had heard. In remembering the meaning of sentences, stories and so on, the experienced human responds in a manner that is best described as active and constructive. As we have emphasized previously, this manner of responding reflects the contribution of prior experience to the behavior of the adult organism.

Studies such as that of Bransford and Franks are also important in that they may provide insights into the memorial processes involved in situations often encountered outside of the laboratory. Humans may bring different processes to bear upon the task of remembering a list of words as opposed to a spoken story or a passage from a book. Thus studies of long-term memory for sentences and connected discourse are needed to ascertain the generality of the principles of memory that have come from studies of memory for lists of words. Moreover, these studies are needed to clarify how we remember the connected discourse that is ubiquitous in our lives (see Kintch, 1977, for a discussion of memory for connected discourse).

Concluding Comments   We have now considered in some depth various mechanisms or strategies of encoding, but we have said little about what determines the use of these strategies. Although a great deal remains to be learned about the ontogenetic antecedents of encoding, it is well established that certain features of the contemporaneous environment influence how information is encoded. For example, the nature of the retention test that is given affects how information is encoded. Specifically, recognition occurs more rapidly and more accurately when the subjects are led through instruction or repeated testing to expect a recognition test rather than a free recall test (Carey & Lockhart, 1973; Tversky, 1973; see Lockhart, Craik, & Jacoby, 1976, for further discussion). Apparently, the ways in which subjects retrieve information affect how they subsequently encode information. If phonological encoding is very effective in a particular experimental procedure, phonological encoding may tend to occur thereafter rather than another level of encoding that is less effective (for example, Jacoby & Bartz, 1972; Mazuryk & Lockhart, 1974). Thus the type of encoding that occurs may depend upon the consequences of that encoding that are implicit in all retention tests. An important goal for future research is to specify the historical and contemporaneous consequences that affect encoding.

STRUCTURAL MODELS OF LONG-TERM MEMORY

In the preceding section, we noted that words, sentences, and images are generated from underlying information and that a full understanding of the effects of imaginal and verbal mediation must come from the study of that information. The information that underlies words and images has come to be called *semantic memory* (Tulving, 1972). The study of semantic memory is concerned with our long-term conceptual and linguistic knowledge of the world. For example, answering questions such as *Can pigeons fly?* or *Do fish breathe?* requires the use of our conceptual knowledge about pigeons and fish, the meanings of the words *fish, breathe,* and so on. The study of semantic memory does not concern *episodic* information, which is temporal or spatial in nature. Our memory of what we had for dinner last Wednesday or where we last saw a particular friend is based upon episodic information in that it concerns events that occurred at a particular time and place. Of course, our semantic and conceptual knowledge of birds is based partly upon episodic information from personal experience. Episodic and semantic information are best seen not as strictly dichotomous but as points on a continuum that differ in the importance of temporal and spatial information in distinguishing and/or retrieving stored information. A great number and variety of models of semantic memory have been proposed (for a review see Smith, E. E., 1978). A full discussion of the various models of semantic memory is beyond the scope of this text. For our purposes it will be sufficient to examine one seminal network model of semantic memory.

A Hierarchical Network Model of Semantic Memory

Collins and Quillian (1969; 1972; see also Collins & Loftus, 1975) have proposed a model of semantic memory that is concerned with our memory for words and their meanings. According to this model, the information involved in semantic memory is organized hierarchically, as shown in Fig. 11.7. Semantic memory is depicted as a network of concepts that are connected with other words by pointers. Each word or concept is represented by a particular node in the network. The meaning of a particular word is given by the configuration of pointers that connect that word with other words. Some pointers indicate the properties of a word. For example, the properties of *canary* are *can sing* and *is yellow*. Other pointers indicate the category name or the superset of *canary*: *bird*. As Fig. 11.7 shows, the properties *has wings, can fly* and *has feathers* are stored with the word *bird*, for these properties are general characteristics of birds. Thus properties such as *has wings* and *has feathers* need not be stored for each kind of bird. It is much more economical to store with each type of bird the unique properties of that bird, and to store the general properties of birds at the level of the word *bird*. By organizing information in a hierarchy in which there is little redundancy, a relatively large amount of information can be stored in a relatively small amount of space.

It should be noted that the pointers in the model of Collins and Quillian correspond roughly to associations, and many network theories of semantic memory have an associationistic flavor (cf. Anderson & Bower, 1973). However, the associations in these theories are complex in that they can specify numerous types of relationships between words such as *is a property of* and *is a superset of*. Thus the associationism that is inherent in some contemporary models of semantic memory is very different from the more traditional associationistic models.

In addition to specifying some of the structure of the information involved in semantic memory, the model of Collins and Quillian makes predictions about how people go about comprehending and verifying simple sentences. For example, if one were asked whether the statement *A canary can sing* is true, one would only need to find the word *canary* and retrieve the properties stored with that word. In contrast, to verify a statement such as *A ca-*

Fig. 11.7   A portion of the semantic memory network for a three-level hierarchy.   (From Collins & Quillian, 1969. Copyright 1969 by Academic Press, *Journal of Verbal Learning and Verbal Behavior*.)

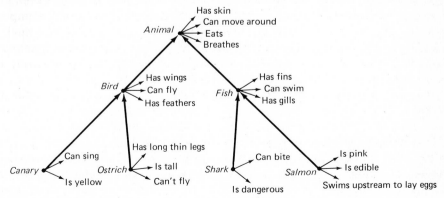

nary can fly, one would have to first find the word *canary* and then move up one level to the word *bird* before retrieving the property *can fly.* Assuming that it takes time to move from one level to another, it should take longer to verify that *A canary can fly* than to verify that *A canary can sing.* Similarly, it should take longer to verify that *A canary has skin* than to verify that *A canary can fly.*

To test these predictions, Collins and Quillian presented a series of propositions such as *A canary can fly, A pine is barley,* and *Tennis is a game.* The task of the subjects was to indicate by pushing one of two buttons as rapidly as possible whether a particular statement was true or false. The main result of their experiment was that the time to decide that a statement is true increased as a function of the number of levels the subject had to go through to verify that statement. Thus more time was required to verify *A canary is an animal* than *A canary is a bird.* Similarly, it took longer to verify *A canary can fly* than *A canary is a bird,* presumably because both statements involve information stored at the level of *bird,* and additional time is required to retrieve *can fly* from that level.

A Critique of the Hierarchical Network Model   The model proposed by Collins and Quillian is important in that it provides an account of how we verify simple sentences and attempts to specify the structure of our semantic and conceptual knowledge.

However, the model is problematic in several regards. First, there are alternative accounts of the observations it is intended to explain (Conrad, C., 1972; Freedman & Loftus, 1971; Wilkins, 1971). For example, Landauer and Meyer (1972) have argued that it takes longer to verify *A canary is an animal* than *A canary is a bird* because there are more animals than birds. It may take longer to retrieve information from large categories such as *animal* than from small categories such as *bird.* Thus, the observations made by Collins and Quillian could be accounted for in terms of the relationship between category size and reaction time.

Another problem is that some observations are not readily accounted for by the hierarchical network model. Consider the typicality effects that we discussed in Chapter 7. Recall that some members of a category are judged to be more typical than other members. For example, *robin* and *chicken* both belong to the category *bird,* but *robin* is judged to be a more typical bird than a *chicken.* In determining whether instances belong to a category, subjects respond faster to typical instances than to atypical ones. Thus subjects verify *A robin is a bird* faster than *A chicken is a bird* (Smith, E. E., 1967; Wilkins, 1971). That should not happen according to the hierarchical model, for the same distance in the hierarchy presumably has to be traversed in both instances (but see Collins, A. C., & Loftus, 1975). Furthermore, subjects take longer to verify *A bear is a mammal* than *A bear is an animal* (Rips, Shoben, & Smith, 1973; Smith, E. E., Shoben, & Rips, 1974). This result is the opposite of what the hierarchical network model predicts, for *animal* is more levels above *bear* than is *mammal.*

A third problem confronting the hierarchical network model concerns the assumption of a hierarchical memory structure. Why assume that properties such as *has wings* are stored at the general level (at the *bird* node) rather than with numerous instances of birds? Although the hierarchical memory structure is economical, it may be arranged in a more logical manner than is the human memory system. Semantic information may be stored in a highly redundant manner for some individuals but not for others. Additionally, there may be large individual differences in the structure of knowledge, for knowledge of the relationships between the concepts *animal, mammal, primate,* and so on, may vary according to one's experiences.

A Revised Network Model   The preceding problems have led to the revision of the model described above. In the revised model (Collins, A. C., & Loftus, 1975), the semantic memory network is no longer structured hierarchically. Rather, the memory system is depicted as a network that contains interconnected concepts and clusters of concepts, as shown in Fig. 11.8. The more closely related two concepts are, the more links there are between them. The path between two concepts is short if they are closely related with regard to a particular property; the less closely related two concepts are, the longer the path between them.

Now consider the main processing assumptions of the model. The first is that the links differ in accessibility or strength, and it takes less time to traverse

Fig. 11.8   A portion of a semantic memory network in which shorter lines indicate greater semantic relatedness.   (After Collins & Loftus, 1975.)

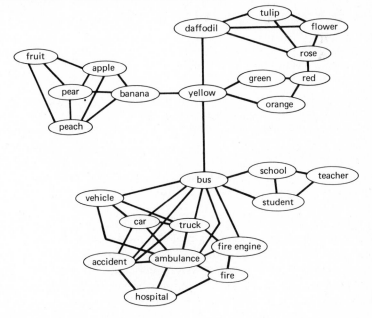

a strong path than a weak one. Presumably, the accessibility or strength of a link depends upon how often that link is used. The second assumption is that when a concept is processed, activation spreads out from that concept in proportion to the strength of activation and the strength of the paths emanating from the concept. Because of the latter assumption, this model may be referred to as the *spreading-activation model*. The final assumption relevant here is that a particular amount of activation is required for making a decision, and the threshold level of activation at a point can be reached through the summation of activation spreading from related points.

The functioning of the model may be illustrated by considering how it accounts for typicality effects. As ratings of typicality show, *robin* is more typical of the category *bird* than *chicken* is. Presumably, the path from *robin* to *bird* is more accessible than the path between *chicken* and *bird*. Consequently, activation will spread faster between *robin* and *bird*, and *A robin is a bird* will be verified faster than *A chicken is a bird* (for further discussion, see Collins, A. C. & Loftus, 1975).

As another example, consider how the model applies to *semantic priming effects* (Meyer & Schvaneveldt, 1971; Meyer, Schvaneveldt & Ruddy, 1974; Rosch, 1978). If adults are asked to classify letter strings as either words or nonwords, they do so faster if they have just seen a semantically similar word. For example, adults classify *butter* as a word faster if they have just classified *bread* than if they have just classified *nurse*. In deciding whether *bread* is a word, the *bread* concept was activated, and the activation presumably spread from that concept to related concepts, one of which is *butter*. Thus the concept *butter* is already activated at the time the word *butter* is presented. Consequently, the threshold level of activation required for a decision on that word is reached faster. In contrast, *nurse* and *butter* are unrelated; no activation spreads between those concepts, and the reaction time to *butter* is not facilitated by the prior presentation of *nurse*.

The spreading-activation model has not been evaluated fully, yet it does have substantial advantages over the hierarchical network model. For one thing, the structure of the memorial network is not defined by logical, hierarchical relationships. Rather, the relationships between concepts depend upon the experiences of the individual and the structure of the environment to which one is exposed. The varying degrees of relatedness between concepts is embodied in the model by the number and length of the interconnecting pathways. Moreover, the model can account for typicality and priming effects in the manner described above. Finally, the model has considerable generality (for comparisons to other models see Collins, A.C.,& Loftus, 1975; Smith, E. E., 1978).

On the other hand, numerous difficulties confront the spreading-activation model. The principal problem is that the model provides no independent determination of either the relatedness of concepts or the accessibility of pathways between them. If the relatedness of concepts and the accessibility of pathways must be inferrred from the observations to be explained, the model is circular and lacks predictive power. Fortunately, this problem may be alleviated partly by using independent judgments such as typicality ratings to empirically define conceptual relatedness and accessibility (see Caramazza, Hersh, & Torgerson, 1976; Deese, 1962; Rips et al., 1973; Smith, E. E., et al., 1974; Smith, E. E., 1978). However, it should be remembered that observed relationships between typicality and the time required to verify sentences is correlational in nature, and it is premature at this point to assume the relationship is causal.

Concluding Comments   We have only begun to explore the intricacies of the structure and processing of semantic and conceptual information. Although the models we have discussed are helping to organize observations and guide research, they should address several issues further. In Chapter 7, we pointed out the problem of contextual variation: A concept or the meaning of a word may change with the context in which it occurs. In the same way, it is possible that the relationships we see between concepts are context-dependent. For example, in the context of making decisions about weight, a small car may appear distantly related to a large bus. But in the context of deciding how to travel to work, those two concepts may be closely related. Future models of semantic memory might represent conceptual networks as multidimensional in nature. The relatedness and accessibility of concepts might differ across dimensions, and contextual factors might determine the dimensions in which activation occurs.

Another issue for future research concerns the dynamic nature of our knowledge. Our conceptual and semantic knowledge often changes, and models of semantic memory should eventually be able to predict these changes (Hopf-Weichel, 1977). Furthermore, future research should evaluate whether experience leads to the formation of fundamentally different conceptual structures.[6] These investigations should enhance our understanding of the effects of experience upon retention and of the relationships between structure and function in memory.

FORGETTING AND LONG-TERM MEMORY

As the reader is well aware, theories in psychology are often highly specific to a particular experimental paradigm. Fortunately, theories of forgetting provide an exception to this schizoid rule, for the same theories that have been applied to forgetting in short-term memory procedures have also been applied to forgetting in long-term memory procedures. Indeed, both the decay and the interference theories of forgetting originated in the study of long-term memory. Recall that the decay theory of forgetting, like the saying "Time heals a broken heart," attributes forgetting to the passage of time. In contrast, the interference theory identifies the events that occur during time as the antecedents of forgetting. Finally, there is another theory (Tulving, 1974), called the *theory of cue-dependent forgetting*, that attributes forgetting to the inability to retrieve information that is involved in long-term memory.

In this discussion, we shall primarily be concerned with the interference theory and the theory of cue-dependent forgetting. This is not to deny that decay contributes to forgetting, but as we saw previously the decay theory is very difficult to test. Consider an early experiment on forgetting (Jenkins, J. G., & Dallenbach, 1924). Adults learned several lists of 10 nonsense syllables, and then there was a retention interval of 1, 2, 4, or 8 hrs. During the retention intervals, the subjects either slept or engaged in their usual waking activities. At the end of each retention interval, the subjects were given a free recall test.

The results were that retention declined as the retention interval increased, and more forgetting occurred in the waking condition than in the sleeping condition. Some forgetting occurred in the sleep condition, and this result might be attributed to decay. On the other hand, however, the forgetting that occurred in the sleep condition could have resulted from interference produced by dreams or from the stimulation that can occur during periods of light sleep. Indeed, most of the forgetting that occurs during sleep occurs during the stage of sleep that is highly correlated with rapid eye movements and dreaming (Yaroush, Sullivan, & Ekstrand, 1971).

To establish that decay contributes to forgetting, it is necessary to eliminate all sources of interference from the retention interval. This in turn requires a full understanding of the conditions under which interference occurs; this understanding has not yet been achieved. Moreover, testing the decay theory requires that one distinguish empirically between storage and retrieval processes. In fact, there is currently no sure way of distinguishing between storage and retrieval processes (Postman, 1976a). Consequently, the decay theory cannot yet be tested adequately, and there is little convincing evidence that decay actually does produce forgetting.

The Interference Theory of Forgetting

A great deal of evidence supports the view that interference is a major antecedent of forgetting in experiments concerning long-term memory (for reviews of the massive literature concerning interference, see Crowder, 1976; McGeoch, 1942; Postman, 1971, 1976b; Postman & Underwood, 1973). The contribution of retroactive interference to forgetting was shown in an early experiment by Müller and Pilzecker (1900; cited in Woodworth, 1938). This study illustrates the typical procedure that is used to study retroactive interference in long-term memory. The subjects were divided into experimental and control groups, and each group learned the same original list of verbal items. The experimental group then learned a second list of items while the control group rested. Finally, both groups were asked to recall the items from the original list. The result was that the control group recalled more of the words than did the experimental group; this effect defines the phenomenon of retroactive interference. Apparently, the items from the second list interfered with the retention of items from the first list. Later research (for example, Bugelski & Cadwallader, 1956; Dallet, 1962) has shown that the occurrence and the magnitude of retroactive interference depend upon the similarity of the items in the first and second lists. In general, the same conditions that lead to negative transfer (see pp. 263–268) also lead to retroactive interference.

The contribution of proactive interference to forgetting is best illustrated by an insightful paper by Underwood (1957). Underwood noted that a large amount of forgetting (up to 75% of what had been learned) was often observed following the learning of a single list of nonsense syllables and a retention interval of 24 hr. It seemed unlikely that the mere 25% level of retention could be attributed to retroactive interference from the events that occurred outside of the laboratory. Accordingly, Underwood focused on the events that occur within the laboratory, and he made a fascinating discovery. In previous research, it had been standard practice for each subject to serve in various conditions of the experiment for the purpose of counterbalancing. However, this guaranteed that the subjects learned numerous lists before the one for which retention was measured after 24 hr. Thus there was a possibility that the large amount of forgetting after 24 hr resulted from interference from previously learned information rather than from the events that occurred in the retention interval. To assess this possibility, Underwood examined the procedures and results of numerous published experiments to see if the amount of forgetting was related to the number of previously learned lists.

The results of the analysis, shown in Fig. 11.9, were that retention decreased sharply as a function of the number of lists that had been learned previously. Interestingly, very little forgetting occurred when no lists preceded that for which retention was tested.[7] Clearly, long-term memory for a list of items depends upon the events that precede the learning of the list. This conclusion was also supported by the results of experiments designed to directly determine the role of previous learning upon the retention of items that were learned at a later time (cf. Underwood, 1957). In addition to showing the impor-

Fig. 11.9   The percentage of items correctly recalled as a function of the number of lists that were previously learned. The data points shown came from different published reports by different experimenters.   (From Underwood, 1957. Copyright 1957 by the American Psychological Association. Reprinted by permission.)

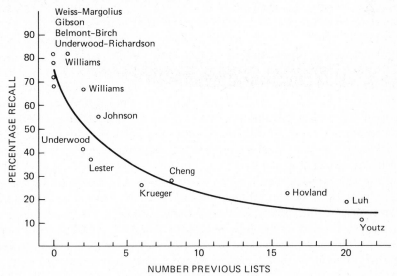

tance of proactive interference, these results show that significant discoveries and theories can come from looking at old observations in a new way, as well as from making new observations. Furthermore, these results support the view that seemingly unimportant procedural details can determine the outcome of one's experimental inquiries.

A Componential Analysis of Interference Effects   When the interference theory of forgetting was first formulated, the effects of interference were attributed to response competition at the time of recall (McGeoch, 1942). How response competition can lead to interference can be seen by examining what might happen in a paired-associate procedure, such as the A-D, A-B paradigm that produces large amounts of retroactive interference. In this procedure, subjects learn first an A-D list, then an A-B list, and finally they are asked to recall the items for the A-D list. Suppose one of the A-D items was *KOJ-14* and the corresponding A-B item was *KOJ-26*. In the retention test for the A-D list, the subject would be shown items such as *KOJ*, but might tend to recall the response item *26* from the most recently learned list rather than recall the correct reponse, *14*. In this case, one could say that the recall of *26* blocked or competed with the recall of *14*, and the incorrect recall of *26* would be called an interlist intrusion. The idea that interference results from competition between responses is consistent with some of our everyday experiences. For example, most of us have had the experience of trying to recall the name of a person or the title of a book only to find the correct response blocked by other names or titles.

The view that interference effects result from response competition was tested in a classic study by Melton and Irwin (1940). The original learning task consisted of five trials of the method of serial anticipation in which there were 18 nonsense syllables to be learned. The interpolated or second learning task consisted of either 5, 10, 20, or 40 trials with a different list of nonsense syllables. Finally, the subjects relearned the original list. The amount of retroactive interference was defined as the difference in recall between one of the groups that had been exposed to both learning tasks and the control group that had been exposed only to the original learning task.

The main results of the experiment, shown in Fig. 11.10, were twofold. First, the amount of retroactive interference clearly depended upon the number of trials on the interpolated learning task. As the number of trials on the interpolated list increased, the amount of retroactive interference at first increased and then leveled off or even decreased. In order to determine whether the observed retroactive interference was attributable to response competition, the number of interlist intrusions was plotted as a function of the number of trials on the interpolated list. As Fig. 11.10 shows, the number of interlist intrusions at first increased and then decreased to a low level. The important observation was that the amount of retroactive interference remained high even when very few interlist intrusions occurred. Thus, the amount of retroactive interference did not depend solely upon response competition, at least as measured by interlist intrusions. Despite the relatively infrequent occurrence of overt interlist intrusions, one could contend that much of the observed forget-

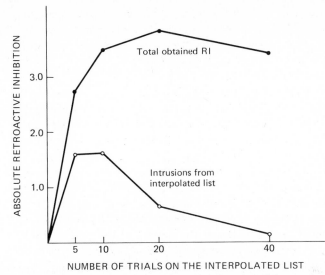

Fig. 11.10   The amount of retroactive interference as a function of the number of trials on the interpolated list. The absolute amount of retroactive interference is defined as the difference in recall for the experimental group and a control group that learned only one list. Also shown are the interlist intrusions that occurred.   (After Melton & Irwin, 1940.)

ting resulted from competition from covert interlist intrusions. However, in the absence of some measure of the hypothesized covert intrusions, this argument would clearly be *post hoc* and devoid of explanatory value. By inducing subjects to talk aloud rather than to themselves (as in the studies of rehearsal discussed previously), it might be possible to attain a more accurate measure of interlist intrusions.

On the basis of these observations, Melton and Irwin concluded that response competition contributes to the phenomenon of retroactive interference, but that some other factor must also be involved. This other factor was tentatively identified as *unlearning* of the items of the original list. Thus response competition and unlearning were the postulated components of retroactive interference. The unlearning of the items from the original list was believed to occur as follows. During the learning of the interpolated list, the items from the first list were incorrectly recalled either overtly or covertly. Since these incorrect responses were not reinforced, they underwent extinction and are said to be "unlearned."

The analogy between unlearning and extinction was a distant one at best. Nevertheless, it had important implications. For example, if the responses from the first list undergo extinction during the learning of the second list, spontaneous recovery should occur for those responses following the passage of time. If spontaneous recovery occurred, there should be an increase in the retention of items from the first list with increases in the duration of the interval between the interpolated task and the test of retention. In fact, this prediction has been confirmed (Underwood, 1948; Briggs, 1954).

In an effort to test directly whether the first-list responses are unlearned in a retroactive interference procedure, Barnes and Underwood (1959) sought to separate the effects of unlearning and response competition. Accordingly, they devised a modification of the standard A-D, A-B procedure for studying retroactive interference. Specifically, following the presentations of the second (A-B) list, the subjects were given the "A" terms from the lists and were given 2 min to recall both the response items from both lists. Since there was an opportunity for both the "D" and "B" responses to occur, competition between the "D" and "B" items should have been minimal. With response competition minimized, any inability to recall the "D" items would presumably result from the unlearning of those items.

The results of the experiment were that as the number of trials on the second list increased, the number of responses that could be recalled from the first list decreased. This observation is consistent with the view that the responses from the first list were unlearned during the acquisition of the second list. Clearly, these results support the view that both unlearning and response competition contribute to retroactive interference.

The component processes of response competition and unlearning originally appeared to provide a comprehensive account of both the proactive and the retroactive interference effects (cf. Postman, 1961), and we will briefly summarize how these effects were accounted for. The procedures used to study retroactive and proactive interference and the sources of interference in these procedures are outlined in Fig. 11.11.[8] In the retroactive interference procedure, the "D" responses in the experimental condition presumably undergo extinction or unlearning during the learning of the A-B list. In the recall test, retention for the A-D items is poor relative to the control condition for two reasons. First, the D-list responses were unlearned to some extent, and sec-

Fig. 11.11 The retroactive (a) and proactive (b) interference designs together with the postulated basis for interference in each case.

RI	PROCEDURE				SOURCE OF INTERFERENCE FOR EXP. GROUP
Exp.	Learn A–D	Learn A–B	Ret. In.	Recall A–D	1. Unlearning of A–D during learning of A–B list
Control	Learn A–D	(Rest)	Ret. In.	Recall A–D	2. Competition between B and D list responses

Time⟶

(a)

PI	PROCEDURE				SOURCE OF INTERFERENCE FOR EXP. GROUP
Exp.	Learn A–D	Learn A–B	Ret. In.	Recall A–B	1. Competition between B list responses and D list responses that spontaneously recover
Control	(Rest)	Learn A–B	Ret. In.	Recall A–B	

Time⟶

(b)

ondly, the recently learned "B" responses intrude and compete with the recall of the "D" responses.

Proactive interference was believed to result from only competition, and in the following way. The "D" responses were presumably unlearned in the proactive interference procedure during the learning of the A-B list. In the recall test, retention for the A-B items is poor relative to the control condition. The reason is that the unlearned "D" responses spontaneously recover as time passes, and those "D" responses block or compete with the recall of the "B" responses. It should be noted that the response competition that occurs in the proactive interference procedure stems from the unlearning and the eventual recovery of the originally learned "D" responses.

Problems with the Unlearning-Competition Analysis   Although the analysis of retroactive and proactive interference in terms of unlearning and competition originally appeared promising, this analysis later encountered numerous difficulties (cf. Postman & Underwood, 1973; Postman, 1976b). For example, the spontaneous recovery of the "D" responses predicted by the unlearning hypothesis has not been observed in all experiments. Koppenaal (1963) exposed subjects to an A-D, A-B procedure and tested for the retention of the A-D list following retention intervals of various lengths. During the recall test, the "A" items were provided, and the subjects were asked to recall both the "D" and the "B" responses. Spontaneous recovery was defined as an increase over time in the level of retention for the "D" responses either absolutely or relative to a control group that learned only A-D. However, there was no evidence for spontaneous recovery, and the absence of spontaneous recovery has been documented in other experiments (for example, Ceraso & Henderson, 1965; Houston, 1966). In other experiments (for example, Forrester, 1970; Postman, Stark, & Fraser, 1968; Shulman & Martin, 1970; see Brown, A. S., 1976, for a review), spontaneous recovery has been observed for very short retention intervals of about 30 min. Overall, spontaneous recovery has not been established experimentally as the general phenomenon it needs to be if it is to be used to account for proactive interference. (Recall that the spontaneous recovery of "D" responses is the source of competition in the PI procedure.) Furthermore, the phenomenon of spontaneous recovery can in principle provide only a weak account of proactive interference, for spontaneous recovery itself needs to be explained (see pp. 205–206).

A major problem with the analysis of interference effects in terms of unlearning and competition concerns the concept of unlearning. In the standard procedure for studying retroactive interference, for instance, the subjects are asked to recall the "D" responses in the presence of the "A" items. Postman and Stark (1969) modified this procedure by making the test for the retention of the "D" items a recognition test rather than a recall test. Specifically, an "A" item was shown with a set of "D" items, as in a multiple-choice test, and the subject had to pick the correct "D" item. The results of this procedure contrasted sharply with the results of the standard recall procedure: There was no retroactive interference in the A-D, A-B paradigm! Clearly, the "D" responses had not been unlearned. Rather, the "D" items seemed to have been unavailable at the time of recall. In more recent experiments (for example, Petrich, 1974; Sanders, Whitaker, & Cofer, 1974), retroactive interference has been observed in recognition tests, but the magnitude of the effects has consistently been small. Apparently, retroactive interference occurs not because the subject unlearns which "B" item goes with which "A" item, but because the "D" terms were unavailable. This observation, together with the observations concerning spontaneous recovery, weaken the analogy between unlearning and extinction. Furthermore, the observation that the "D" responses were not unlearned significantly undermined the attempt to account for interference, particularly proactive interference, in terms of competition and unlearning.

Response-Set Interference When the experimental data showed that the "D" responses had not been unlearned or extinguished, there was a large conceptual gap in the interference theory of forgetting. It was not long before there were fresh attempts to account for the phenomena that had initially been attributed to the factor of unlearning. The main alternative to the hypothesis of unlearning is called the hypothesis of response-set interference (Postman et al., 1968). The unlearning hypothesis attributed interference in the A-D, A-B procedure to the extinction of the "D" responses that had been controlled by the "A" stimuli. In contrast, the hypothesis of response-set interference attributed interference to the suppression or unavailability of the entire set of "D" responses.

To illustrate how interference could result from the suppression of an entire set of responses, consider what might happen in the A-D, A-B procedure. The A-D list is first learned, and the "D" responses come to be activated by a "selector mechanism" (Underwood & Schulz, 1960). This selector mechanism that makes the "D" responses available switches over to activate only the "B" responses during the learning of the A-B list, and the "D" responses are then suppressed. It is as if the subject were blocking out the entire set of "D" responses. The selector mechanism was assumed to have some inertia in that it required time to switch from one set of responses to another.

The hypothesis of response-set interference is consistent with numerous observations. For example, this view is consistent with the observations concerning retroactive interference. Presumably, retroactive interference results from the inertia of the selector mechanism. Soon after the learning of the A-B list, the selector is still activating the "B" responses, thereby interfering with the recall of the entire set of "D" responses. Following a long retention interval, the inertia of the selector mechanism would supposedly have decreased, thus leading to a decreased amount of retroactive interference. Furthermore, the hypothesis of response-set interference can account for the lack of retroactive interference in the recognition tests used by Postman and Stark (1969). Specifically, when the "D" responses are made available as in a recognition test, the selector mechanism will be bypassed and the correct responses can be made.

However, the hypothesis of response-set interference does not (and was not intended to) account for all interference effects. Just as interference can result from the suppression of whole sets of responses, so too can it result from competition between specific responses that are controlled by the same "A" stimulus. For example, retroactive interference occurs in the A-Br, A-B procedure (Postman & Stark, 1969), in which the same responses occur in both lists, but are paired with different stimuli. Since the set of first-list responses are not suppressed during the learning of the second list, the retroactive interference that occurs cannot be attributed to response-set interference. (For other results in a similar vein, see Delprato, 1971; Wichowut & Martin, 1971). The occurrence of retroactive interference in the A-Br, A-B procedure could be accounted for either in terms of unlearning or in terms of competition between responses. At any rate, the general message is that retroactive interference may arise from factors that affect entire sets of responses, and factors that affect specific pairs of items.

The Problem of Proactive Interferences   As we saw earlier, the original component analysis of interference in terms of unlearning and response competition applied to both proactive and retroactive interference (see Fig. 11.11). However, when the concept of unlearning was brought into question, the original component analysis could no longer account for proactive interference. The reason was that proactive interference had been seen as arising from the competition of the "D" responses with the "B" responses at the time of recall. This competition in turn supposedly resulted from the unlearning and the eventual recovery of the "D" responses. Thus the weakening of the unlearning hypothesis made it difficult to explain why response competition occurred at the time of recall in the proactive interference procedure. To the extent that unlearning occurs, competition between responses could also occur. However, the magnitude of pair-specific unlearning effects is typically too small to account for the very large effects of proactive interference.

The later concept of response-set interference helped to account for retroactive interference, but this hypothesis does not seem to apply to proactive interference. Indeed, the suppression of the "D" responses in the A-D, A-B procedure should lead to the *absence* of proactive interference, for the inertia of the selector mechanism should improve the retention of the "B" responses. Thus the possibility arises that proactive and retroactive interference are very different and must be accounted for in different ways. This possibility is consistent with the observation that whereas very little retroactive interference occurs in multiple-choice tests of recognition, substantial proactive interference occurs when recognition tests are used to measure retention (Postman, Stark, & Burns, 1974).

One plausible account for the occurrence of proactive interference is the hypothesis of *list differentiation* (list differentiation may also be relevant to retroactive interference; cf. Briggs, 1957). According to this hypothesis, proactive interference results from the inability of the subject to discriminate between the responses of the most recently learned list and the items from previously learned lists. Presumably, the "D" responses in the A-D, A-B procedure compete with the recall of the "B" responses due to the failure to distinguish the list membership of the "D" and "B" responses. Support for this view comes from studies (Underwood & Ekstrand, 1966, 1967; Underwood & Freund, 1968; Warren, 1974; see also Winograd, 1968), in which the factors that lead to a loss of differentiation also lead to an increase in the amount of proactive interference. For example, Underwood and Freund (1968) observed that in the A-D, A-B procedure, more proactive interference occurred when there was a short amount of time between the two learning tasks than when there was a long time separating those tasks. Presumably, a long delay between the two tasks facilitates a temporal discrimination between the two lists, thereby reducing the amount of proactive interference. The fact that a temporal differentiation between lists reduces proactive interference makes sense when one considers that the time of presentation is one of the only differences between lists in an A-D, A-B paradigm. Indeed, the A-D, A-B procedure can be seen as a conditional discrimination task, for in the presence of one set of temporal and contextual stimuli the "D" responses are "correct," in another set of temporal stimuli the "B" responses are "correct," and the "A" stimuli remain constant.

A Critique of Interference Theory We may now examine some of the problems that are encountered by the theory. The first problem is that the theory sometimes assumes what needs to be explained. For example, retroactive interference has sometimes been attributed to the actions of an internal selector mechanism that activates and suppresses sets of responses. However, the properties of that mechanism, such as its presumed inertia, are only assumed. The only evidence that the mechanism has those properties is that soon after learning an A-B list the response items from a previously learned A-D list are difficult to recall. This, however, is the very phenomenon that needs to be explained, and therefore the account in terms of the selector mechanism is circular.

Recently, the conceptual tools of interference theory have come to include such diverse terms as list differentiation, response-set interference, response competition, and unlearning. However, it is unclear how these different factors operate in different situations, and two problems follow from this consideration. One is that precise predictions cannot be generated easily, whereas *post hoc* accounts of data can. Another problem is that the theory may be inconsistent in certain instances. For example, in the A-D, A-B procedure, the mechanism of response selection is held to bring about a suppression of "D" responses during the learning of the A-B list. The suppression of "D" responses would lead to the occurrence of a large amount of retroactive interference and to no proactive interference. How, then, does proactive interference occur? One could argue that a loss of list differentiation leads to proactive interference. If a loss of list differentiation occurs in the A-D, A-B procedure used to study proactive interference, however, it must also occur in the A-D, A-B procedure used to study retroactive interference, and here a problem arises. If there were a loss of list differentiation in the procedure used to study retroactive interference, how could the mechanism of response selection operate? Logically, it seems that some degree of list differentiation is required for the selection of either "D" or "B" responses. Thus it is difficult to see how the factors of list differentiation and response-set interference can be invoked in a consistent manner to account for proactive and retroactive interference.

Finally, there is some question as to how general an account of forgetting can be provided by interference theory. Can a theory that was formulated to account for forgetting in laboratory procedures such as the paired-associate procedure account for how we forget the forms of sentences we have heard, the thesis of a book we have read, and so on? Although effects such as retroactive interference have been observed in tasks that involve prose learning (for example, Crouse, 1971), it is too early to tell whether these effects and others (cf. Shiffrin, 1970) can be adequately explained in terms of competition, response-set interference, and so forth.

The foregoing criticisms of interference theory do not imply that the theory is in principle incapable of accounting for the forgetting that occurs over the long run. As Postman and Underwood (1973) have noted, however, it remains to be seen whether interference effects will be best accounted for in terms of concepts such as response-set interference or in terms of radically different concepts (for example, Greeno, James, & DaPolito, 1971; Martin, 1971).

The Theory of Cue-Dependent Forgetting

Throughout our discussion of forgetting, we have seen repeatedly that forgetting often stems from an inability to retrieve information that has been learned, rather than from the failure of storage processes such as decay. Indeed, the forgetting that results from factors such as response competition and response-set interference reflects a failure to retrieve information. Since forgetting often seems to involve problems in retrieving information, the possibility arises that the origins of forgetting could be elucidated considerably by the study of retrieval.

From the view that forgetting reflects a failure of retrieval, it follows that phenomena such as retroactive interference should not occur if effective retrieval cues are provided. Evidence concerning this prediction comes from a study by Tulving and Psotka (1971). In the pertinent condition of their experiment, the subjects learned a series of six lists of words. Each list included 24 words which belonged to obvious categories. In each list, there were six different categories, and the words in each category were grouped together to make the categories apparent. An example of part of one of the lists would be as follows: *zinc, copper, aluminum, bronze, orange, apple, pear, melon, hut, cottage, tent, hotel.* . . . Each list was presented three times in succession, and a test of free recall was then given for that list. After each list had been presented and retention had been tested, two tests of overall retention were given. In one type of overall test, the subjects were asked to recall all of the words from all of the lists that had been presented. In the other type of overall test, called a "cued-recall" test, the subjects were again asked to recall all the words they had seen, but they were given the names of all the categories (for example, *metals, fruits, buildings,* and so on) that had been used.

The results of the experiment were that in the overall retention test for which no retrieval cues were presented (that is, noncued recall), the level of retention was much lower than it had been in the original test of free recall. Additionally, the level of retention in the noncued overall recall test decreased as a function of the number of lists that intervened between the presentation of a list and the noncued, overall test of recall. In other words, the learning of the later lists retroactively interfered with the retention of the earlier lists. However, this retroactive interference effect was virtually eliminated when the retrieval cues were presented, for the level of retention in the cued-recall test was very similar to that in the original test of free recall.

According to Tulving (1974), whether or not forgetting occurs depends largely upon the presence or absence of effective retrieval cues. In other words, much of forgetting is said to be cue-dependent, and the account of forgetting in terms of retrieval cues is therefore called the theory of cue-dependent forgetting. The theory of cue-dependent forgetting could help to account for the beneficial effects upon memory of encoding strategies such as imagery. Specifically, the facilitation of memory by imagery, organization and so on may result from the generation and use of effective retrieval cues.

Furthermore, this theory could help to account for phenomena such as the retroactive interference that occurs in an A-D, A-B procedure. As we noted earlier, the discrimination as to whether a response item belongs to the "D" or the "B" list must be made on the basis of temporal and contextual or "background" stimuli present during the presentation of the lists. Thus the possibility arises that there would be less retroactive interference in this procedure if the appropriate temporal and contextual cues were presented at the time of retrieval. Indeed, some evidence is consistent with this view (Abernathy, 1940; Bilodeau & Scholsberg, 1951; Greenspoon & Ranyard, 1957).

The theory of cue-dependent forgetting by itself has little predictive or explanatory power, for the conditions under which stimuli facilitate retrieval are not specified. It thus should come as no surprise that the theory of cue-dependent forgetting is part of a broader theory of retrieval called the theory of encoding specificity (Thomson & Tulving, 1970; Tulving & Thomson, 1973), which shall be examined in the following section.

RETRIEVAL AND LONG-TERM MEMORY

From the preceding discussion, it seems clear that a deep understanding of remembering and forgetting depends in part upon an analysis of retrieval. In this section, we shall first consider the relationship between encoding and retrieval, and then will examine the component processes that are involved in retrieval.

The Relation Between Encoding and Retrieval

In our previous discussions, we have for the sake of convenience spoken of encoding and retrieval as if they were independent. However, the independence of encoding and retrieval resides primarily in the procedures that are used to study memory. We say that a variable affects encoding if that variable exerts its effect during the presentation of the stimuli that are to be remembered. Similarly, we say that a variable affects retrieval if that variable has an effect at the time of a retention test. Although encoding and retrieval may be independent on a procedural level, they are, as we shall see, independent for the experimenter but not for the organism under study.

Encoding Specificity   The view that encoding and retrieval are closely related is perhaps best captured in what may be called the *theory of encoding specificity*. This theory was originally formulated to provide a broad account of the effects of retrieval cues upon retention. It asserts that there is a close relationship between encoding and retrieval, and it makes predictions about the conditions under which stimuli will facilitate retrieval. The central thesis of the theory of encoding specificity is perhaps best stated by Tulving and Thomson (1973):

> What is stored is determined by what is perceived and how it is encoded, and what is stored determines what retrieval cues are effective in providing access to what is stored. (p. 353)

Thus this theory asserts that successful retrieval depends upon the presence of stimuli that provide information that was present at the time of encoding. For example, suppose subjects were shown a long list of words to remember, part of which is as follows:

fruit–apple

pear

banana

weapon–knife

gun

spear

The theory of encoding specificity would predict that words such as *fruit* and *weapon* would be very effective retrieval cues since those words had been present at the time of encoding. Indeed, words such as *fruit* and *weapon* facilitate retrieval even if, as in the experiment by Tulving and Psotka (1971), they had not been explicitly presented at the time of encoding. According to the theory of encoding specificity, the names of the categories or the information that underlies those names must have been present *implicitly* at the time of encoding. This account becomes plausible when one recalls that the members of a category were presented together to make the category obvious. However, this account is clearly *post hoc,* and does not provide direct support for the theory of encoding specificity.

In an effort to directly test the theory of encoding specificity, Thomson and Tulving (1970) sought to control the potential retrieval cues that were present at the time of encoding. To prevent the subjects from generating implicit retrieval cues, they presented at the time of encoding a potential retrieval cue along with each word that was to be remembered. The potential retrieval cues were either weak or strong associates (as measured by norms of free-association) of the words that were to be remembered. The subjects were given three different lists of words, each of which contained 24 pairs of cue words and "target" words (that is, words that were to be remembered). In each pair, the cue word was uncapitalized whereas the target word was capitalized. An example of part of one of the lists is as follows:

(1) ground–COLD
(2) want–NEED
(3) sky–BLUE
(4) swift–GO

The cue words *ground* and *swift* are weak associates of their respective target words, whereas *want* and *sky* are strong associates of their target words. The subjects were told to remember the target words, and they were also told that attending to the cue words might help them in their task.

Following the presentation of a list of words, the subjects were given a cued-recall test of retention. In that test, the cue words were presented and the task of the subject was to recall the target words. This procedure for presenting and testing words was followed for the first two lists that were presented. However, for the third list a different recall procedure was used. Specifically, some of the cues that were presented at the time of recall differed from the originally presented cues. Of the items that had been paired with weak cues (for example, *ground–COLD*), recall was sometimes tested with the same weak cues but at other times was tested with "strong" cues (for example, *hot*, which is a strong cue for *cold*) that had not been presented before. Similarly, recall for the items that had been presented with strong cues (for example, *sky–BLUE*) was sometimes tested with the same strong cue and sometimes with a weak, novel cue (for example, *pretty*, which is a weak cue for *blue*). According to the theory of encoding specificity, the only effective retrieval cues should be those that were present both at the time of encoding and at the time of recall.

The results for the third list of the experiment are shown in Table 11.1. The level of recall was high when the cues that were presented at the time of retrieval had also been present at the time of encoding. When both cues were

TABLE 11.1 Probability of Recall

Input Cue	Output cue	
	Strong	Weak
Strong	.833	.035
Weak	.326	.729

Note: The probability of recall as a function of the type of cue (weak or strong associates of the items to be recalled) that was present at the time of encoding (input) or at the time of retrieval (output).
Source: After Thomson & Tulving, 1970.

strong associates of the target words, the proportion of target words that were recalled was .84, and when both cues were weak associates of the target words, the proportion of target words recalled was .73. In contrast, the level of recall was low when the retrieval cues had not been presented at the time of encoding. In fact, the level of recall in the latter condition did not differ significantly from the level of recall in conditions for which no retrieval cues had been presented (Thomson & Tulving, 1970). These results support the theory of encoding specificity since they show that regardless of the relationship between a cue and a target word, the effectiveness of a retrieval cue depends primarily (but not exclusively; note that of the novel cues that were presented at the time of retrieval, the strong cues were more effective than the weak cues) upon whether that cue had been presented (and encoded) at the time when the target words were encoded.

Now consider the implications of this theory for the theory of cue-dependent forgetting that we examined in the preceding section. The theory of encoding specificity can predict some of the conditions under which retrieval cues will facilitate retrieval, and to that extent the theory adds predictive power to the theory of cue-dependent forgetting. However, some questions remain about the validity and the generality of the theory of encoding specificity (cf. Postman, 1976a; Santa & Lamwers, 1974; but see also Tulving & Wiseman, 1975; Watkins & Tulving, 1975). Until these questions are resolved, it will not be possible to evaluate adequately the theory of cue-dependent forgetting.

Some Common Ground for the Fields of Learning and Memory   Regardless of the outcome of the controversy concerning the theory of encoding specificity, the observations described above show that encoding and retrieval are importantly related. At this point, it is instructive to try to relate the phenomenon of memory to one of the fundamental phenomena of learning: the phenomenon of stimulus control. Saying that the probability of a response is affected by the presence of a controlling stimulus is similar to saying that the probability of recall is affected by the presence of a stimulus that has been encoded along with the "target" stimuli. In both instances, the basic observations are very similar. First, a response is brought under stimulus control at a particular time, and it can then be said that the stimulus has been encoded. Second, at some later time, the probability that the response will recur depends upon the presence or absence of the original encoded or controlling stimuli. In other words, the probability of recall depends on the reinstatement of some of the originally encoded information. Clearly, some of the observations and distinctions that have been made by students of learning and memory bear some measure of similarity. An important task for the future is to combine some of the theories of learning and memory so that they can contribute to each other and enhance our understanding of both public and private events.

Recognition and Recall

In the preceding discussions of memory, recall and recognition procedures have been used as tools for measuring retention. In this section, recall and recognition shall become the substance rather than the tools of our inquiry, for questions concerning the relationship between recognition and recall are directly related to questions concerning the nature of retrieval.

Let us first consider the question of whether recall and recognition involve similar processes. To the extent that recognition and recall involve similar processes, they should be affected in the same way by numerous variables. Indeed, there are many variables that have similar effects upon both recall and recognition. For example, retroactive interference impairs retention in both recognition and recall procedures, and repeated presentations of items can facilitate both the recognition and the recall of those items (see Kintsch, 1970, for a review). Moreover, the context in which items are presented influences both the recognition and recall of those items. For example, the word *jam* is poorly recognized if it is first presented in the pair *strawberry–JAM* and later in a recognition test in the pair *traffic–JAM* (Light, L. L. & Carter-Sobell, 1970). The effects of context upon recall are illustrated by the evidence discussed earlier that supports the encoding specificity theory. Specifically, the level of recall for words is higher when those words are encoded and recalled in the context of associates that function as retrieval cues.

Although some variables have similar effects upon recognition and recall, there are variables that affect recognition and recall differently. One such variable is the frequency of occurrence of words in books, magazines, and so on. Whereas words that occur infrequently in everyday discourse are recognized better than words that occur frequently, the opposite is true for recall (Hall, 1954; Kinsbourne & George, 1974; McCormack & Swenson, 1972). Another variable that affects recognition and recall differently is organization. For example, subjects who are exposed to lists of highly organized words (as determined by category norms) recall many more words than subjects who are exposed to lists of words that are not highly organized. On the other hand, there is typically no difference in the recognition performance of subjects who have been exposed to lists that are high or low in organization (Kintsch, 1968, 1970). While some studies have reported effects of organization upon recognition (Mandler, 1972; Mandler & Boeck, 1974), the important point for our present purpose is that it is well documented that organization affects recognition and recall differently in particular procedures.

The Generation-Recognition Model   The observation that some variables affect recall and recognition differently has led some theorists (for example, Anderson & Bower, 1972, 1974; Kintsch, 1970) to postulate that recall and recognition involve some similar and some different processes. The models proposed by the latter theorists vary with respect to details and the terms used to describe the hypothesized processes, but since these models are similar, they will be collectively referred to here for the sake of convenience as the generation-recognition model. According to the model, recall involves two processes, whereas recognition involves only one. Specifically, recall involves both a *generation* and a *recognition* process, whereas recognition involves only a decision process. Generation is described as a search process that involves traversing the hypothetical pathways between items stored in memory and generating possible candidates for recall. The recognition process involves deciding whether the item is part of the list or episode that one is attempting to recall. Thus recall is seen as consisting of two stages or processes: First, items are generated, and then a decision is made about which items should be produced overtly in the retention test. On the other hand, recognition is seen as involving no generation or search process, but only the decision process, for the item is presented to the subject who has simply to decide whether or not the item belonged to the list or episode the subject is trying to remember. A considerable amount of research (for example, Atkinson & Juola, 1973; Underwood, 1972; for reviews, see Crowder, 1976; Kintsch, 1977) indicates that the decisions involved in recognition are based upon information concerning the frequency or familiarity of the items that have been presented.

Having described the generation-recognition model, we may now examine how this model accounts for the observations that some variables have similar effects upon recall and recognition, whereas other variables do not. The finding that variables such as word frequency have opposite effects on recall and recognition is accounted for in the following manner. A variable such as word frequency may affect both the hypothesized generation and decision processes, but in opposite ways. For example, low word frequency may facilitate the decision process, but may also impede the generation process. Since low word frequency facilitates the decision process, the level of recognition for infrequent words should be very high, for recognition involves only the decision process. In contrast, recall is held to entail both generation and decision processes, and the beneficial effects of low word frequency upon the decision process may be offset by the negative effects of low word frequency upon the generation process. Consequently, the level of recall for infrequent words may be quite low relative to the level of recognition.

Of course, some variables may have similar rather than opposite effects upon the generation and decision processes, or they may have substantial effects on the decision process but not on the generation process. In these instances, the variables that are manipulated would have similar effects upon recognition and recall. In summary, the generation-recognition model is consistent with the observation that some variables have similar effects upon recall and recognition, whereas other variables have different effects upon recall and recognition.

Problems with the Generation-Recognition Model   Although the generation-recognition model is consistent with the observations described above, the model currently confronts theoretical and empirical problems. The theoretical difficulty is that there exists no widely agreed upon way of experimentally separating the proposed generation and recognition processes (but see Anderson & Bower, 1972; see also Tulving, 1976). How does one know whether a variable affects only the recognition process or only the generation process?

And if a variable affects both processes, how does one determine the magnitude and the direction of those effects? In the absence of precise measures of the two processes, it is difficult to predict the exact effects of a variable upon recall and recognition. As a result, the model is difficult to test, and it lacks predictive power.

Another problem is that the model is contradicted by some observations. If recall has generation and decision components and recognition has only the decision component, it follows that recognition should, if anything, be easier than recall. The level of recall should never exceed the level of recognition since whatever items one decides to produce in the recall test, one should also decide to mark in the recognition test. To test whether the level of recall can exceed the level of recognition, Tulving and Thomson (1973) performed the following experiment. The subjects first learned a list of 24 target words, each of which was paired with a cue word that was a weak associate. Some examples of those pairs are as follows:

beat–PAIN
lady–QUEEN
plant–BUG

After learning the list, the subjects were given 24 words that were strong associates of the target words (for example, *ache, king* and *plant* are said to be strong associates of *PAIN, QUEEN* and *BUG,* respectively). As in a free-association test, the subjects were asked to write down several words that were suggested by the strong associates. Thus the subject might have responded to the strong associates in the following way:

(1) *ache*–back, strain, pain, aspirin
(2) *king*–queen, castle, knight, servant
(3) *plant*–garden, tomato, squash, corn

Notice that the words *ache* and *king* occasioned the target words from the list that had been learned. When the subjects had responded to the strong associates, they were asked to recognize any words that were members of the originally learned list. Following this recognition test, the subjects were given a cued-recall test in which the cue words from the learning task (for example, *beat, lady, plant*) were presented and the subjects were to recall the appropriate target words.

The main results of the experiment were that many of the target words that were generated on the free-association test were not recognized by the subjects. Moreover, many of the words that had not been recognized were recalled later in the cued-recall test. Thus the subjects recalled many of the target words that they had been unable to recognize. For the reasons mentioned earlier, this observation conflicts with the view that recall consists of generation and decision components, whereas recognition includes only the decision component (see also Flexser & Tulving, 1978; Tulving, 1976; Watkins & Tulving, 1975).[9] This observation necessitated a revision of the generation-recognition model, and we shall next consider this revision.

Encoding and the Generation-Recognition Model   The proposed modification of the generation-recognition model of retrieval involves bringing together what is known about the nature of encoding and the relationship between encoding and retrieval (Anderson & Bower, 1974; Kintsch, 1978; Martin, 1975; Pellegrino & Salzberg, 1975). Specifically, words are held to be encoded not as words per se but rather as collections of semantic, acoustic, visual and other features. When a word occurs in one context, a particular configuration of features may be encoded, whereas when that same word occurs in a different context, a very different configuration of features may be encoded. Now, as the theory of encoding specificity suggests, there is a close relation between encoding and retrieval. The fact that a word is presented in a recognition test does not guarantee access to the configuration of features that was encoded. Whether a word is recognized will depend on whether the same features that were encoded are activated in the recognition test.

What, the perceptive reader may ask, determines whether the same features that were encoded are activated in a recognition test? The best answer that is currently available is this: context (cf. Light, L. L., Kimble, & Pellegrino, 1975, for a review). As we stated previously, contextual factors strongly affect both recognition and recall. The contexts of the recognition and the recall tests used by Tulving and Thomson were quite different, and that difference could have produced better recall than recognition. Only the recall test provided the contextual stimuli (the "cue" words) that had been present at the time of encoding. If those same contextual stimuli are present in the recognition test, the level of recognition equals the level of recall, in keeping with the generation-recognition model of retrieval (Wallace, 1978).

Concluding Comments   It is too early to attempt a complete evaluation of the generation-recognition model. At this point, the model is best regarded as a useful working hypothesis rather than a powerful and well-articulated model.

Any complete theory of retrieval shall have to address several unresolved issues. Among those issues is whether it is fruitful to place recognition and recall into different conceptual or procedural classes. Several lines of evidence (Mandler, 1972; Mandler & Boeck, 1974) suggest that within a particular recognition test, the subjects process different items in different ways. Indeed, when the subjects are uncertain about a particular item, they try to recall the item just as they would on a recall test, and variables such as organization facilitate the recognition of exactly those items. In the future, it may be unwise to assume that all recognition tasks engender one particular process or that all recall tasks are fundamentally similar. A comprehensive analysis of retrieval must incorporate the diversity of the strategies for encoding and retrieval that adults may engage in.

SUMMARY

The phenomena of long-term memory, like the phenomena of short-term memory, have in recent times been analyzed within the framework of the information-processing model. Experimentation within the information-processing framework has shown that humans can encode many different types of information (for example, visual, phonological and semantic) for long-term retention, and that specific events or episodes may be encoded along one or numerous dimensions. Generally, information that is encoded elaboratively on a semantic level is remembered better than information that is encoded on a less elaborate and shallow level. However, the analysis of the contribution of encoding processes to retention is currently hindered by the lack of procedures for determining how information has been encoded and for separating the effects of encoding and retrieval processes.

Information that is encoded elaboratively is, in ways that are not yet clear, organized with the information from one's prior experiences. Although we know that information can be organized by forming interactive images, natural language mediators, and so on, we know little about the information and the processing that underlies those images and mediators. Furthermore, not much is known about the antecedents of the various mechanisms for encoding information. Although the nature of the information and the type of retention test in part determine how information is encoded, it seems likely that a complete understanding of encoding must include an analysis of the history of the organism. When the study of memory comes to include an historical analysis of the organism under investigation, the fields of learning and memory may be integrated, thereby leading to a broad experimental analysis of public and private events.

The field of memory is characterized by a variety of structural models. Some general models divide the memory system into separate long-term and short-term stores. Other more specific models are designed to characterize the nature and the structure of the information that constitutes our knowledge of the world. We have seen that there are two general problems with those models. First, the structures that are postulated are sometimes based solely on the observations they are intended to explain. Second, the structural models are sometimes nonhistorical in that they do not provide for the possibility that different experiences could give rise to different structures. In the study of both learning and memory, it will be important to determine how behavior is structured and how behavior comes to be structured in this way.

We have seen that although it is difficult to separate experimentally encoding, storage and retrieval processes, many observations suggest that forgetting involves failures of retrieval. According to the interference theory of forgetting, some of the problems in retrieval arise from response competition, response-set interference, and a failure to discriminate between events that occur at different times. Although these processes have been shown to contribute to forgetting, the interference theory of forgetting is troublesome in a variety of ways, and new theories of forgetting are emerging. One of those theories is the theory of cue-dependent forgetting, which attributes forgetting to the absence of information that was present at the time of encoding. Although this theory has yet to be adequately evaluated, it does embody the fact that there is an important relation between encoding and retrieval, and this relationship is now recognized by models of retrieval such as the generation-recognition model. In the future, we may hope to see models of retrieval that will help to explain forgetting and help to specify various retrieval strategies, their relationship to encoding strategies, and so on. As comprehensive theories of retrieval are approximated, we may expect to see increased concern over the historical antecedents of retrieval strategies. This concern should serve not only to further unite theories of encoding and retrieval, but also to synthesize theories of learning with theories of memory.

NOTES

1. Another plausible interpretation is that the words from a category were recalled together because they were verbal associates of each other, not because they were related semantically in a deeper sense. However, categorical clustering has been observed for lists of words that are not associated but have categorical relationships (Bousfield & Puff, 1964; Cofer, 1965).
2. Another possibility is that organization is a correlate of a high level of retention but that the organization is not an antecedent of retention. In other words, a factor that facilitates retention may also facilitate organization. In that case, organization and retention would appear related when in fact the organization is a correlate rather than a cause of retention. The merits of this view remain to be determined.
3. For some evidence that suggests that organization can, depending upon the subject's prior experience and the nature of the task, produce negative as well as positive transfer, see Tulving (1966, 1968; Tulving & Osler, 1968). But see Baddeley (1976) and Wood (1972) for discussions of the problems involved in interpreting this evidence.
4. The evidence presented by Rundus and his colleagues is correlational in nature, and there is the possibility that it is not rehearsal that facilitates retention. Rather, some other factor may lead to a high level of both repetition and retention. However, this interpretation is made less plausible by the noncorrelational evidence that shows a direct relation between repetition and long-term retention (for example, Hebb, 1961).
5. For a discussion of the two processing systems and their relationship during development, see Bruner, Olver, and Greenfield (1966).
6. Although the models proposed by Anderson and Bower (1973) and by Rummelhart, Lindsay, and Norman (1972) can acquire a new information, these models do not provide for the possibility of developing fundamentally different structures.
7. The forgetting that did occur was attributed to interference from extraexperimental situations. However, there is little experimental support for that view (cf. Underwood & Postman, 1960).
8. Note that if one desired to compare the magnitude of the effects of retroactive and proactive interference, the PI procedure would be reversed so that the experimental group would learn the A-B list first. Then both groups would learn the second list and, after a retention interval, recall the A-D list. In the latter procedure, the experimental groups in both the PI and RI paradigms would receive retention tests on the same list (that is, the A-D list).
9. Although that observation does seem to depend upon the type of stimuli that are used (cf. Reder, Anderson, & Bjork, 1974), it has been shown not to depend upon the particular procedure that was used by Tulving and Thomson (cf. Watkins & Tulving, 1975; Wiseman & Tulving, 1975).

References and Author Index

Page numbers for the author index appear in boldface following each reference.

Aaronson, D., and Scarborough, H. S. 1976. Performance theories for sentence coding: Some quantitative evidence. *Journal of Experimental Psychology: Human Perception and Performance, 2*:56–70. **(334)**

Abernathy, E. M. 1940. The effect of changed environmental conditions upon the results of college examinations. *Journal of Psychology, 10*:293–301. **(504)**

Abramsky, O.; Carmon, A.; and Benton, A. L. 1971. Masking of and by tactile pressure stimuli. *Perception and Psychophysics, 10*:353–355. **(419)**

Adams, J. A. 1961. The second facet of forgetting: A review of warm-up decrement. *Psychological Bulletin, 58*:257–273. **(206)**

Adams, J. A. 1971. A closed-loop theory of motor learning. *Journal of Motor Behavior, 3*:111–149. **(154)**

Adams, J. A., and Dijkstra, S. 1966. Short-term memory for motor responses. *Journal of Experimental Psychology, 71*:314–318. **(447)**

Akmajian, A., and Heny, F. 1975. *An introduction to the principles of transformational syntax.* Cambridge, Mass.: M.I.T. Press. **(330)**

Alberts, E., and Ehrenfreund, D. 1951. Transposition in children as a function of age. *Journal of Experimental Psychology, 41*:30–38. **(198)**

Alcock, J. 1975. *Animal behavior: An evolutionary approach.* Sunderland, Mass.: Sinauer Associates. **(17, 18)**

Allen, M. 1968. Rehearsal strategies and response cueing as determinants of organization in free recall. *Journal of Verbal Learning and Verbal Behavior, 7*:58–63. **(474)**

Allen, T. W.; Marcell, M. M.; and Anderson, P. 1978. Modality-specific interference with verbal and nonverbal stimulus information. *Memory and Cognition, 6*:184–188. **(483)**

Allison, J. 1976. Contrast, induction, facilitation, suppression, and conservation. *Journal of the Experimental Analysis of Behavior, 25*:185–198. **(225)**

Allyon, T.; Haughton, E.; and Hughes, H. B. 1965. Interpretation of symptoms: Fact or fiction. *Behavior Research and Therapy, 3*:1–7. **(223)**

Amsel, A. 1958. The role of frustrative nonreward in noncontinuous reward situations. *Psychological Bulletin, 55*:102–119. **(241, 249, 250)**

Amsel, A. 1967. Partial reinforcement effects on vigor and persistence. In K. W. Spence and J. T. Spence (Eds.), *The psychology of learning and motivation,* Vol. I. New York: Academic Press. **(249, 254)**

Amsel, A. 1972. Behavioral habituation, counter-conditioning, and a general theory of persistence. In A. H. Black and W. F. Prokasy (Eds.), *Classical conditioning. II: Current research and theory.* Englewood Cliffs, N.J.: Prentice-Hall. **(249)**

Amsel, A., and Roussel, J. 1952. Motivational properties of frustration: I. Effect on running response of the addition of frustration to the motivational complex. *Journal of Experimental Psychology, 43*:363–368. **(250, 251)**

Anderson, J. R. 1974. Verbatim and propositional representation of sentences in immediate and long-term memory. *Journal of Verbal Learning and Verbal Behavior, 13*:149–162. **(467)**

Anderson, J. R. 1978. Arguments concerning representations for mental imagery. *Psychological Review, 85*:249–277. **(485, 486)**

Anderson, J. R., and Bower, G. H. 1972. Recognition and retrieval processes in free recall. *Psychological Review, 79*:97–123. **(508, 509)**

Anderson, J. R., and Bower, G. H. 1973. *Human associative memory*. New York: Holt, Rinehart and Winston. **(412, 485, 489)**

Anderson, J. R., and Bower, G. H. 1974. A propositional theory of recognition memory. *Memory and Cognition, 2*:406–412. **(486, 508, 511, 513)**

Anger, D. 1956. The dependence of interresponse times upon the relative reinforcement of different interresponse times. *Journal of Experimental Psychology, 52*:145–161. **(184)**

Anger, D. 1963. The role of temporal discriminations in the reinforcement of Sidman avoidance behavior. *Journal of the Experimental Analysis of Behavior, 6*:477–506. **(207)**

Anglin, J. M. 1977. *Word, object and conceptual development*. New York: Norton. **(281, 284, 287)**

Anisfeld, M., and Knapp, M. 1968. Association, synonymity, and directionality in false recognition. *Journal of Experimental Psychology, 77*:171–179. **(467)**

Annau, Z., and Kamin, L. J. 1961. The conditioned emotional response as a function of the intensity of the US. *Journal of Comparative and Physiological Psychology, 54*:428–432. **(110)**

Antelman, S. M., and Caggiula, A. R. 1977. Norepinephrine-dopamine interactions and behavior. *Science, 195*:646–653. **(224, 231)**

Archer, E. J. 1962. Concept identification as a function of obviousness of relevant and irrelevant information. *Journal of Experimental Psychology, 63*:616–520. **(295)**

Atkinson, R. C. 1975. Mnemotechnics in second-language learning. *American Psychologist, 30*:821–828. **(480)**

Atkinson, R. C., and Estes, W. K. 1963. Stimulus sampling theory. In R. D. Luce, R. R. Bush, and E. Galanter (Eds.), *Handbook of mathematical psychology*, Vol. 2. New York: Wiley. Pp. 121–268. **(187)**

Atkinson, R. C., and Juola, J. F. 1973. Factors influencing speed and accuracy of word recognition. In S. Kornblum (Ed.), *Attention and performance IV*. New York: Academic Press. **(509)**

Atkinson, R. C., and Juola, J. F. 1974. Search and decision processes in recognition memory. In D. H. Krantz, R. C. Atkinson, R. D. Luce, and P. Suppes (Eds.), *Contemporary developments in mathematical psychology*, Vol. 1. San Francisco: Freeman. Pp. 242–293. **(460)**

Atkinson, R. C., and Shiffrin, R. M. 1968. Human memory: A proposed system and its control processes. In K. W. Spence and J. T. Spence (Eds.), *The psychology of learning and motivation*. Vol. 2. New York: Academic Press. Pp. 89–195. **(412, 413, 415)**

Atkinson, R. C., and Shiffrin, R. M. 1971. The control of short-term memory. *Scientific American, 225*:82–90. **(413)**

Atkinson, R. C.; Bower, G. H.; and Crothers, E. J. 1965. *An Introduction to mathematical learning theory*. New York: Wiley. **(157)**

Atkinson, R. C., and Wilson, H. A. (Eds.) 1969. *Computer-assisted instruction: A book of readings*. New York: Academic Press. **(152)**

Attneave, F. 1957. Transfer of experience with a class-schema to identification learning of patterns and shapes. *Journal of Experimental Psychology, 54*:81–88. **(286)**

Autor, S. M. 1969. The strength of conditioned reinforcers as a function of frequency and probability of reinforcement. In D. P. Hendry (Ed.), *Conditioned reinforcement*. Homewood, Ill.: Dorsey Press. Pp. 127–162. **(172)**

Averbach, E., and Coriell, A. S. 1961. Short-term memory in vision. *Bell System Technical Journal, 40*:309–328. **(422)**

Ayllon, T., and Azrin, N. 1968. *The token economy: A motivational system for therapy and rehabilitation.* Englewood Cliffs, N.J.: Prentice-Hall. **(176)**

Ayllon, T., and Haughton, E. 1962. Control of the behavior of schizophrenic patients by food. *Journal of the Experimental Analysis of Behavior, 5:343–349.* **(175)**

Ayres, J. J. B.; Benedict, J. O.; and Witcher, E. S. 1975. Systematic manipulation of individual events in a truly random control in rats. *Journal of Comparative and Physiological Psychology, 88:97–103.* **(116)**

Azrin, N. H. 1956. Some effects of two intermittent schedules of immediate and nonimmediate punishment. *Journal of Psychology, 42:3–21.* **(132)**

Azrin, N. H. 1970. Punishment of elicited aggression. *Journal of the Experimental Analysis of Behavior, 14:7–10.* **(162)**

Azrin, N. H., and Holz, W. C. 1966. Punishment. In W. K. Honig (Ed.), *Operant behavior: Areas of research and application.* Englewood Cliffs, N.J.: Prentice-Hall. Pp. 380–447. **(135, 229)**

Azrin, N. H.; Hutchinson, R. R.; and Hake, D. F. 1966. Extinction-induced aggression. *Journal of the Experimental Analysis of Behavior, 9:191–204.* **(261)**

Azrin, N. H.; Hutchinson, R. R.; and Hake, D. F. 1967. Attack, avoidance, and escape reactions to aversive shock. *Journal of the Experimental Analysis of Behavior, 10:131–148.* **(229, 244)**

Azrin, N. H.; Hutchinson, R. P.; and McLaughlin, R. 1965. The opportunity for aggression as an operant reinforcer during aversive stimulation. *Journal of the Experimental Analysis of Behavior, 8:171–180.* **(229)**

Baars, B. J.; Motley, M. T.; and MacKay, D. G. 1975. Output editing for lexical status in artificially elicited slips of the tongue. *Journal of Verbal Learning and Verbal Behavior, 14:382–391.* **(403)**

Babkin, B. P. 1949. *Pavlov.* Chicago: University of Chicago Press. **(88)**

Bachrach, A. J.; Erwin, W. J.; and Mohr, J. P. 1965. The control of eating behavior in an anorexic by operant conditioning techniques. In L. P. Ullmann and L. Krasner (Eds.), *Case Studies in Behavior Modification.* New York: Holt, Rinehart and Winston. **(28)**

Baddeley, A. D. 1972. Retrieval rules and semantic coding in short-term memory. *Psychological Bulletin, 78:379–385.* **(444, 446)**

Baddeley, A. D. 1976. *The psychology of memory.* New York: Basic Books. **(409, 465, 480, 513)**

Baddeley, A. D. 1978. The trouble with levels: A reexamination of Craik and Lockhart's framework for memory research. *Psychological Review, 85:139–152.* **(470)**

Baddeley, A. D., and Dale, H. C. A. 1966. The effect of semantic similarity on retroactive interference in long- and short-term memory. *Journal of Verbal Learning and Verbal Behavior, 5:417–420.* **(444, 446)**

Baer, D. M.; Peterson, R. F.; and Sherman, J. A. 1967. Development of imitation by reinforcing behavioral similarity to a model. *Journal of the Experimental Analysis of Behavior, 10:405–416.* **(268)**

Bandura, A. 1969. *Principles of behavior modification.* New York: Holt, Rinehart and Winston. **(247)**

Bandura, A. 1971a. Vicarious and self-reinforcement processes. In K. Glaser (Ed.), *The nature of reinforcement.* Columbus, Ohio: Merrill. **(270)**

Bandura, A. 1971b. Analysis of modeling processes. In A. Bandura (Ed.), *Psychological modeling.* New York: Lieber-Atherton. Pp. 1–62. **(270)**

Bandura, A. 1976. Self-reinforcement: Theoretical and methodological considerations. *Behaviorism, 4:135–156.* **(270)**

Bandura, A., and Walters, R. H. 1963. *Social learning and personality development.* New York: Holt, Rinehart and Winston. **(247)**

Banks, W. P., and Barber, G. 1977. Color information in iconic memory. *Psychological Review, 84:536–546.* **(423)**

Barclay, J. R. 1972. Non-categorical perception of a voiced stop: A replication. *Perception and Psychophysics, 11:269–273.* **(321)**

Barlow, H. B.; Narasimhan, R.; and Rosenfeld, A. 1972. Visual pattern analysis in machines and animals. *Science, 177*:567–575. **(428)**

Barnes, J. M., and Underwood, B. J. 1959. "Fate" of first-list associations in transfer theory. *Journal of Experimental Psychology, 58*:97–105. **(272, 498)**

Bartlett, F. C. 1932. *Remembering: A study in experimental and social psychology.* Cambridge, England: Cambridge University Press. **(417, 486)**

Bartram, D. J. 1978. Post-iconic storage: Chunking in the reproduction of briefly displayed visual patterns. *Cognitive Psychology, 10*:324–355. **(444)**

Bass, M. J., and Hull, C. L. 1934. The irradiation of a tactile conditioned reflex in man. *Journal of Comparative Psychology, 55*:473–481. **(182)**

Bates, E. 1976. *Language and context: The acquisition of pragmatics.* New York: Academic Press. **(360)**

Bates, E.; Masling, M.; and Kintsch, W. 1978. Reconition memory for aspects of dialogue. *Journal of Experimental Psychology: Human Learning and Memory,* 4:187–197. **(467)**

Bates, M., and Humphrey, P. S. (Eds.) 1956. *The Darwin reader.* New York: Scribner. **(38)**

Bateson, P. P. G. 1971. Imprinting. In H. Moltz (Ed.), *The ontogeny of vertebrate behavior.* New York: Academic Press. **(67)**

Battig, W. F. 1968. Paired-associate learning. In T. R. Dixon and D. L. Horton (Eds.), *Verbal behavior and general behavior theory.* Englewood Cliffs, N.J.: Prentice-Hall. **(271)**

Bauer, J., and Held, R. 1975. Comparison of visually guided reaching in normal and deprived infant monkeys. *Journal of Experimental Psychology: Animal Behavior Processes,* 1:298–308. **(155)**

Baum, W. M. 1974. Chained concurrent schedules: Reinforcement as situation transition. *Journal of the Experimental Analysis of Behavior, 22*:91–101. **(172)**

Beach, F. A. 1947. A review of physiological and psychological studies of sexual behavior in mammals. *Physiological Review, 27*:240–307. **(68)**

Beach, F. A. 1967. Cerebral and hormonal control of reflexive mechanisms involved in copulatory behavior. *Physiological Review, 47*:289–316. **(69)**

Beach, F. A., and Jordan, L. 1956. Sexual exhaustion and recovery in the male rat. *Quarterly Journal of Experimental Psychology, 8*:121–133. **(69)**

Beagley, W. K., and Holley, T. L. 1977. Hypothalamic stimulation facilitates contralateral visual control of a learned response. *Science, 196*:321–322. **(231)**

Beck, E. C., and Doty, R. W. 1957. Conditioned flexion reflexes acquired during combined catelepsy and de-afferentation. *Journal of Comparative and Physiological Psychology, 50*:211–216. **(114)**

Begg, I. 1972. Recall of meaningful phrases. *Journal of Verbal Learning and Verbal Behavior, 11*:431–439. **(482)**

Begg, I. 1973. Imagery and integration in the recall of words. *Canadian Journal of Psychology, 27*:159–167. **(482)**

Begg, I., and Paivio, A. 1969. Imagery and sentence meaning. *Journal of Verbal Learning and Verbal Behavior, 8*:821–827. **(467)**

Begg, I., and Robertson, R. 1973. Imagery and long term retention. *Journal of Verbal Learning and Verbal Behavior, 12*:689–700. **(480, 481, 482)**

Bellugi, U., and Fischer, S. A. 1972. A comparison of sign language and spoken language. *Cognition, 1*:173–200. **(348, 353, 373)**

Bellugi, U., and Klima, E. S. 1972. The roots of language in the sign talk of the deaf. *Psychology Today, 6*:61–76. **(373)**

Bellugi, U., and Klima, E. 1975. Aspects of sign language and its structure. In J. F. Kavanagh and J. E. Cutting (Eds.), *The role of speech in language.* Cambridge, Mass.: M.I.T. Press. Pp. 171–203. **(348, 353, 373)**

Bellugi, U.; Klima, E. S.; and Siple, P. 1975. Remembering in signs. *Cognition: International Journal of Cognitive Psychology, 3*:93–125. **(444)**

Bendix, E. H. 1966. *Componential analysis of general vocabulary: The semantic structure of a set of verbs in English, Hindi and Japanese.* The Hague: Mouton. **(391)**

Benedict, J. O. 1975. Response-shock delay as a reinforcer in avoidance behavior. *Journal of the Experimental Analysis of Behavior, 24*:323–332. **(208)**

Benedict, J. O., and Ayres, J. J. B. 1972. Factors affecting conditioning in the truly random control procedure in the rat. *Journal of Comparative and Physiological Psychology,* 78:323–330. **(116)**

Beninger, R. J.; Bellisle, F.; and Milner, P. M. 1977. Schedule control of behavior reinforced by electrical stimulation of the brain. *Science, 196:*547–549. **(230)**

Beninger, R. J., and Milner, P. M. 1977. Effects of signalled and unsignalled brain stimulation, water, and sucrose reinforcement on running behavior in rats. *Journal of Comparative and Physiological Psychology,* 91:1272–1283. **(231)**

Bennett, R. W. 1975. Proactive interference in short-term memory: Fundamental forgetting processes. *Journal of Verbal Learning and Verbal Behavior,* 14:123–144. **(455)**

Berko, J. 1958. The child's learning of English morphology. *Word, 14:*150–177. **(386)**

Berlin, B., and Kay, P. 1969. *Basic color terms: Their universality and evolution.* Berkeley and Los Angeles: University of California Press. **(396)**

Bermant, G., and Westbrook, W. H. 1966. Peripheral factors in the regulation of sexual contact by females. *Journal of Comparative and Physiological Psychology,* 61:244–250. **(81)**

Bernbach, H. A. 1975. Rate of presentation in free recall: A problem for two-stage memory theories. *Journal of Experimental Psychology: Human Learning and Memory,* 1:18–22. **(476)**

Bersch, P. J. 1951. The influence of two variables upon the establishment of a secondary reinforcer for operant responses. *Journal of Experimental Psychology,* 41:62–73. **(172)**

Bertrand, M. 1969. The behavioural repertoire of the stumptail macaque. *Bibliography of Primatology,* 11:1–273. **(69)**

Bessemer, D. W., and Stollnitz, F. 1971. Retention of discriminations and an analysis of learning set. In A. M. Schrier and F. Stollnitz (eds.), *Behavior of nonhuman primates,* Vol. 4. New York: Academic Press. Pp. 1–58. **(302)**

Best, M. R. 1975. Conditioned and latent inhibition in taste-aversion learning: Classifying the role of learned safety. *Journal of Experimental Psychology—Animal Behavior Processes,* 104:97–113. **(113)**

Best, P. J.; Best, M. R.; and Mickley, G. A. 1973. Conditioned aversion to distinct environmental stimuli resulting from gastrointestinal distress. *Journal of Comparative and Physiological Psychology,* 85:250–257. **(113)**

Bever, T. G. 1970. The cognitive basis for linguistic structures. In J. R. Hayes (Ed.), *Cognition and the development of language.* New York: Wiley. Pp. 279–352. **(344)**

Bilodeau, I. M. 1966. *Acquisition of skill.* New York: Academic Press. **(154)**

Bilodeau, I., and Schlosberg, H. 1951. Similarity in stimulating conditions as a variable in retroactive inhibition. *Journal of Experimental Psychology,* 41:199–204. **(504)**

Birch, H. 1945. The relation of previous experience to insightful problem-solving. *Journal of Comparative and Physiological Psychology,* 38:367–383. **(303)**

Bitterman, M. E. 1965. Phyletic differences in learning. *American Psychologist,* 20:396–410. **(304)**

Bitterman, M. E. 1975. The comparative analysis of learning. *Science, 188:*699–709. **(113)**

Bjork, K. A., and Whitten, W. B. 1974. Recency-sensitive retrieval processes in long-term free recall. *Cognitive Psychology,* 6:173–189. **(476, 477)**

Black, A. H., and de Toledo, L. 1972. The relationship among classically conditioned responses: Heart rate and skeletal behavior. In A. H. Black and W. F. Prokosy (Eds.), *Classical conditioning II: Current research and theory.* Englewood Cliffs, N.J.: Prentice-Hall. Pp. 290–311. **(110)**

Bloom, J. M., and Capaldi, E. J. 1961. The behavior of rats in relation to complex patterns of partial reinforcement. *Journal of Comparative and Physiological Psychology,* 54:261–265. **(252)**

Bloom, K. 1977. Patterning of infant vocal behavior. *Journal of Experimental Child Psychology,* 23:367–377. **(364)**

Bloom, L. M. 1970. *Language development: Form and function in emerging grammars.* Cambridge, Mass.: M.I.T. Press. **(374, 376)**

Bloom, L. M. 1973. *One word at a time: The use of single word utterances before syntax.* The Hague: Mouton. **(353, 369)**

Bloom, L. M.; Hood, L.; and Lightbown, P. 1974. Imitation in language development: If, when and why. *Cognitive Psychology*, 6:380–420. **(405)**

Bloom, L., and Lahey, M. 1978. *Language development and language disorders*. New York: Wiley. **(368, 371, 379, 400)**

Bloomberg, R., and Webb, W. B. 1949. Various degrees within a single drive as cues for spatial response learning in the white rat. *Journal of Experimental Psychology*, 39:628–636. **(228)**

Bloomfield, T. M. 1969. Behavioral contrast and the peak shift. In R. M. Gilbert and N. S. Sutherland (Eds.), *Animal discrimination learning*. New York: Academic Press. Pp. 215–241. **(193)**

Blough, D. S. 1963. Interresponse time as a function of continuous variable: A new method and some data. *Journal of the Experimental Analysis of Behavior*, 6:237–246. **(186)**

Blough, D. S. 1975. Steady state data and a quantitative model of operant generalization and discrimination. *Journal of Experimental Psychology: Animal Behavior Processes*, 104:3–21. **(200, 201)**

Blumenthal, A. L. 1967. Prompted recall of sentences. *Journal of Verbal Learning and Verbal Behavior*, 6:203–206. **(335)**

Blumenthal, A. L., and Boakes, R. 1967. Prompted recall of sentences: A further study. *Journal of Verbal Learning and Verbal Behavior*, 6:674–676. **(335)**

Bobrow, S. A., and Bower, G. H. 1969. Comprehension and recall of sentences. *Journal of Experimental Psychology*, 80:455–461. **(484)**

Boe, E. E., and Church, R. M. 1967. Permanent effects of punishment during extinction. *Journal of Comparative and Physiological Psychology*, 63:486–492. **(135)**

Bolinger, D. L. 1965. The atomization of meaning. *Language*, 41:555–573. **(340)**

Bolles, R. C. 1962. A psychophysical study of hunger in the rat. *Journal of Experimental Psychology*, 63:387–390. **(228)**

Bolles, R. C. 1967. *Theory of motivation*. 1st ed. New York: Harper & Row. **(172, 221)**

Bolles, R. C. 1970. Species-specific defense reactions and avoidance learning. *Psychological Review*, 77:32–48. **(43, 126, 161, 162, 210)**

Bolles, R. C. 1972. The avoidance learning problem. In G. H. Bower (Ed.), *The psychology of learning and motivation*, Vol. 6. New York: Academic Press. **(210)**

Bolles, R. C. 1975. *Theory of motivation*. 2nd ed. New York: Harper & Row. **(173, 208, 217)**

Bolles, R. C., and Popp, R. J., Jr. 1964. Parameters affecting the acquisition of Sidman avoidance. *Journal of the Experimental Analysis of Behavior*, 7:315–321. **(208)**

Bolles, R. C., and Riley, A. L. 1973. Freezing as an avoidance response. *Learning and Motivation*, 4:268–275. **(209)**

Boneau, C. A. 1958. The interstimulus interval and the latency of the conditioned eyelid response. *Journal of Experimental Psychology*, 56:464–472. **(111)**

Borgealt, A. J.; Donahoe, J. W.; and Weinstein, A. 1972. Effects of delayed and trace components of a compound CS on conditioned suppression and heart rate. *Psychonomic Science*, 26:13–15. **(110)**

Boring, E. G. 1950. *A history of experimental psychology*. Englewood Cliffs, N.J.: Prentice-Hall. **(211, 218)**

Bornstein, M. H. 1975. Qualities of color vision in infancy. *Journal of Experimental Child Psychology*, 19:401–419. **(397)**

Bourne, L. E., Jr. 1966. *Human conceptual behavior*. Boston: Allyn and Bacon. **(282, 298)**

Bourne, L. E., Jr. 1967. Learning and utilization of conceptual rules. In B. Kleinmuntz (Ed.), *Concepts and the structure of memory*. New York: Wiley. Pp. 1–32. **(289, 291)**

Bourne, L. E., Jr., and Guy, D. E. 1968. Learning conceptual rules: I. Some inter-rule transfer effects. *Journal of Experimental Psychology*, 76:423–429. **(290)**

Bourne, L. E., Jr.; Ekstrand, B. R.; and Dominowski, R. L. 1971. *The psychology of thinking*. Englewood Cliffs, N.J.: Prentice-Hall. **(288, 290, 298, 307)**

Bousfield, W. A. 1953. The occurrence of clustering in the recall of randomly arranged associates. *Journal of General Psychology*, 49:229–240. **(466)**

Bousfield, W. A., and Puff, C. R. 1964. Clustering as a function of response dominance. *Journal of Experimental Psychology*, 67:76–79. **(513)**

Bower, G. H. 1967. A multicomponent theory of the memory trace. In K. W. Spence and

J. T. Spence (eds.), *The psychology of learning and motivation: Advances in research and theory*, Vol. 1. New York: Academic Press. Pp. 299–325. **(464)**

Bower, G. H. 1972. Mental imagery and associative learning. In L. W. Gregg (Ed.), *Cognition in learning and memory*. New York: Wiley. Pp. 51–88. **(449, 471, 474, 482)**

Bower, G. H., and Grusec, T. 1964. Effect of prior Pavlovian discrimination training upon learning an operant discrimination. *Journal of the Experimental Analysis of Behavior*, 7:401–404. **(155, 266)**

Bower, G. H., and Trabasso, T. R. 1964. Concept identification. In R. C. Atkinson (Ed.), *Studies in mathematical psychology*. Stanford: Stanford University Press. Pp. 32–94. **(307)**

Bower, G. H., and Winzenz, D. 1969. Group structure, coding, and memory for digit series. *Journal of Experimental Psychology Monograph*, 80:1–17. **(449)**

Bower, G. H.; Clark, M. C.; Lesgold, A. M.; and Winzenz, D. 1969. Hierarchical retrieval schemes in recall of categorized word lists. *Journal of Verbal Learning and Verbal Behavior*, 8:323–343. **(473)**

Bower, G. H.; Lesgold, A. M.; and Tieman, D. 1969. Grouping operations in free recall. *Journal of Verbal Learning and Verbal Behavior*, 8:481–493. **(474)**

Bower, G. H.; Munoz, R.; and Arnold, P. G. 1972. On distinguishing semantic and imaginal mnemonics. Unpublished study, cited in J. R. Anderson and G. H. Bower, *Human associative memory*. New York: Holt, Rinehart and Winston, 1973. **(484)**

Bowerman, M. 1973. *Early syntactic development: A cross-linguistic study with special reference to Finnish*. Cambridge: Cambridge University Press. **(372)**

Bowerman, M. 1976. Semantic factors in the acquisition of rules for word use and sentence construction. In D. M. Morehead and A. E. Morehead (Eds.), *Normal and deficient child language*. Baltimore: University Park Press. Pp. 99–179. **(369, 373)**

Bowlby, J. 1969. *Attachment and loss*. Vol. 1. *Attachment*. New York: Basic Books. **(66)**

Bracewell, R. J., and Black, A. H. 1974. The effects of restraint and noncontingent preshock on subsequent escape learning in the rat. *Learning and Motivation*, 5:53–69. **(245)**

Braine, M. D. S. 1963. The ontogeny of English phrase structure: The first phase. *Language*, 39:1–13. **(350, 354)**

Braine, M. D. S. 1971. The acquisition of language in infant and child. In C. Reed (Ed.), *The learning of language*. Englewood Cliffs, N.J.: Prentice-Hall. Pp. 7–95. **(353)**

Braine, M. D. S. 1974. Length constraints, reduction rules, and holophrastic processes in children's word combinations. *Journal of Verbal Learning and Verbal Behavior*, 13:448–456. **(375)**

Braine, M. D. S. 1976. Children's first word combinations. *Monographs of the Society for Research in Child Development*, 41: Serial No. 164. **(372, 373, 375)**

Braine, M. D. S., and Wells, R. S. 1978. Case-like categories in children: The actor and some related categories. *Cognitive Psychology*, 10:100–122. **(367, 373, 377)**

Bransford, J. D., and Franks, J. J. 1971. The abstraction of linguistic ideas. *Cognitive Psychology*, 12:331–350. **(486)**

Breland, K., and Breland, M. 1961. The misbehavior of organisms. *American Psychologist*, 16:661–664. **(161)**

Breland, K., and Breland, M. 1966. *Animal behavior*. New York: Macmillan. **(162)**

Brewer, W. F. 1974. There is no convincing evidence for operant or classical conditioning in adult humans. In W. B. Weimer and D. S. Palermo (Eds.), *Cognition and the symbolic process*. Hillsdale, N.J.: Erlbaum. Pp. 1–42. **(272, 274)**

Briggs, G. E. 1954. Acquisition, extinction, and recovery functions in retroactive inhibition. *Journal of Experimental Psychology*, 47:285–293. **(497)**

Briggs, G. E. 1957. Retroactive inhibition as a function of the degree of original and interpolated learning. *Journal of Experimental Psychology*. 53:60–67. **(501)**

Brigham, T. A., and Sherman, J. A. 1968. An experimental analysis of verbal imitation in preschool children. *Journal of Applied Behavior Analysis*, 1:151–158. **(268, 404)**

Brindley, C.; Clarke, P.; Hutt, C.; Robinson, I.; and Wethei, E. 1973. Sex differences in the activities and social interactions of nursery school children. In R. P. Michael and J. H. Crook (Eds.), *Comparative ecology and behavior of primates*. New York: Academic Press. **(69)**

Broadbent, D. E. 1952. Speaking and listening simultaneously. *Journal of Experimental Psychology*, 43:267–273. **(433)**

Broadbent, D. E. 1957. A mechanical model for human attention and immediate memory. *Psychological Review*, 64:204–215. **(434)**

Broadbent, D. E. 1958. *Perception and communication.* London: Pergamon Press. **(412, 434)**

Brogden, W. J. 1939. Sensory preconditioning. *Journal of Experimental Psychology*, 25:323–332. **(110)**

Brogden, W. J.; Lipman, E. A.; and Culler, E. 1938. The role of incentive in conditioning and extinction. *American Journal of Psychology*, 51:109–117. **(111)**

Brooks, L. 1967. The suppression of visualization by reading. *Quarterly Journal of Experimental Psychology*, 19:280–299. **(483)**

Brooks, L. R. 1968. Spatial and verbal components in the act of recall. *Canadian Journal of Psychology*, 22:349–368. **(483)**

Brooks, L. 1978. Nonanalytic concept formation and memory for instances. In Eleanor Rosch and Barbara B. Lloyd (Eds.), *Cognition and Categorization.* Hillsdale, N.J.: Lawrence Erlbaum Associates. Pp. 169–211. **(297, 298, 300, 301)**

Brown, A. S. 1974. Examination of hypothesis sampling theory. *Psychological Bulletin*, 81:773–790. **(304, 307)**

Brown, A. S. 1976. Spontaneous recovery in human learning. *Psychological Bulletin*, 83:321–338. **(499)**

Brown, F. G., and Archer, E. J. 1956. Concept identification as a function of task complexity and distribution of practice. *Journal of Experimental Psychology*, 52:316–327. **(295)**

Brown, J. A. 1958. Some tests of the decay theory of immediate memory. *Quarterly Journal of Experimental Psychology*, 10:12–21. **(450, 451)**

Brown, J. S. 1965. Generalization and discrimination. In D. I. Mostofsky (Ed.), *Stimulus generalization.* Stanford, Calif.: Stanford University Press. Pp. 7–23. **(170)**

Brown, J. S. 1969. Factors affecting self-punitive locomotor behavior. In B. A. Campbell and R. M. Church (Eds.), *Punishment and aversive behavior.* Englewood Cliffs, N.J.: Prentice-Hall. Pp. 167–514. **(246)**

Brown, P. L., and Jenkins, H. M. 1968. Autoshaping of the pigeon's key-peck. *Journal of the Experimental Analysis of Behavior*, 11:1–8. **(160)**

Brown, R. 1968. The development of *Wh* questions in child speech. *Journal of Verbal Learning and Verbal Behavior*, 7:277–290. **(352)**

Brown, R. 1970. The first sentences of child and chimpanzee. In R. Brown (Ed.), *Psycholinguistics.* New York: Free Press. Pp. 208–231. **(351, 352, 353, 354, 372)**

Brown, R. 1973. *A first language: The early stages.* Cambridge, Mass.: Harvard University Press. **(351, 352, 353, 354, 355, 369, 372, 373, 374, 375, 382, 385, 386, 396, 408)**

Brown, R., and Bellugi, U. 1964. Three processes in the child's acquisition of syntax. *Harvard Educational Review*, 34:133–151. **(405)**

Brown, R., and Hanlon, C. 1970. Derivational complexity and order of acquisition in child speech. In J. R. Hayes (Ed.), *Cognition and the development of language.* New York: Wiley. Pp. 11–53. **(402, 404)**

Brown, R., and Herrnstein, R. J. 1975. *Psychology.* Boston: Little, Brown. **(355)**

Brown, R., and McNeill, D. 1966. The "tip of the tongue" phenomenon. *Journal of Verbal Learning and Verbal Behavior*, 5:325–337. **(341)**

Brown, R.; Cazden, C. B.; and Bellugi, U. 1969. The child's grammar from I to III. In J. P. Hill (Ed.), *Minnesota symposium on child psychology*, Vol. 2. Minneapolis: University of Minnesota Press. Pp. 28–73. **(404)**

Brown, R. T., and Logan, F. A. 1965. Generalized partial reinforcement effect. *Journal of Comparative and Physiological Psychology*, 60:64–69. **(254)**

Bruce, D., and Crowley, J. J. 1970. Acoustic similarity effects on retrieval from secondary memory. *Quarterly Journal of Experimental Psychology*, 9:190–196. **(466)**

Bruner, A. 1965. UCS properties in classical conditioning of the albino rabbit's nictitative membrane response. *Journal of Experimental Psychology*, 69:186–192. **(114)**

Bruner, A. 1969. Reinforcement strength in classical conditioning of leg flexion, freezing, and heart rate in cats. *Conditional Reflex*, 4:24–31. **(111)**

Bruner, J. S. 1974/5. From communication to language—A psychological perspective. *Cognition, 3*:225–287. **(364)**

Bruner, J. S. 1975. The ontogenesis of speech acts. *Journal of Child Language,* 2:1–19. **(360, 361, 366)**

Bruner, J. S.; Goodnow, J. J.; and Austin, G. A. 1956. *A study of thinking.* New York: Wiley. **(287, 289, 298)**

Bruner, J. S.; Olver, R. R.; and Greenfield, P. M. 1966. *Studies in cognitive growth.* New York: Wiley. **(513)**

Brunswick, E. 1939. Probability as a determiner of rat behavior. *Journal of Experimental Psychology, 25*:175–197. **(248)**

Bryden, M. P. 1960. Tachistoscopic recognition of non-alphabetical material. *Canadian Journal of Psychology, 14*:78–86. **(437)**

Bryden, M. P. 1966. Accuracy and order of report in tachistoscopic recognition. *Canadian Journal of Psychology, 20*:262–272. **(437)**

Buchwald, A. M. 1969. Effects of "right" and "wrong" on subsequent behavior. *Psychological Review, 76*:132–143. **(38)**

Bugelski, B. R., and Cadwallader, T. C. 1956. A reappraisal of the transfer and retroaction surface. *Journal of Experimental Psychology, 52*:360–365. **(494)**

Bugelski, B. R., and Scharlock, D. P. 1952. An experimental demonstration of unconscious mediated association. *Journal of Experimental Psychology, 44*:334–338. **(271)**

Burling, R. 1959. Language development of a Garo- and English-speaking child. *Word,* 15:45–68. **(394)**

Burrows, D., and Okada, R. 1971. Serial position effects in high-speed memory search. *Perception and Psychophysics, 10*:305–308. **(459)**

Burstein, K. R., and Moeser, S. 1971. The informational value of a distinctive stimulus associated with the initiation of acquisition trials. *Learning and Motivation,* 2:228–234. **(206)**

Buschke, H. 1976. Learning is organized by chunking. *Journal of Verbal Learning and Verbal Behavior, 15*:313–324. **(472)**

Bush, R. R., and Mosteller, F. 1951. A mathematical model for simple learning. *Psychological Review, 58*:313, 323. **(187)**

Bush, R. R., and Mosteller, F. 1955. *Stochastic models for learning.* New York: Wiley. **(156)**

Bushnell, M. C., and Weiss, S. J. 1978. Microanalysis of variable-interval performance during stimulus compounding. *Animal Learning and Behavior, 6*:66–71. **(196)**

Butler, R. A. 1954. Incentive conditions which influence visual exploration. *Journal of Experimental Psychology, 48*:19–23. **(82)**

Butter, C. M. 1963. Stimulus generalization along one and two dimensions in pigeons. *Journal of Experimental Psychology, 65*:339–346. **(189)**

Butter, C. M., and Thomas, D. R. 1958. Secondary reinforcement as a function of the amount of primary reinforcement. *Journal of Comparative and Physiological Psychology, 51*:346–348. **(172)**

Butterfield, E. C., and Cairns, G. F. 1974. Discussion summary: infant reception research. In R. L. Schiefelbusch and L. L. Lloyd (Eds.), *Language perspectives: acquisition, retardation and intervention.* Baltimore: University Park Press. **(362)**

Bykov, K. M., and Gantt, W. H. (Eds.) 1957. *The cerebral cortex and the internal organs.* New York: Chemical Publishing Company. **(90)**

Cahoon, D. D. 1968. Symptom substitution and the behavior therapies. *Psychological Bulletin, 69*:149–156. **(39)**

Cairns, H. S., and Cairns, C. E. 1976. *Psycholinguistics.* New York: Holt, Rinehart and Winston. **(329, 344)**

Camp, D. S.; Raymond, G. A.; and Church, R. M. 1967. Temporal relationship between response and punishment. *Journal of Experimental Psychology, 74*:114–123. **(132)**

Campbell, B. A., and Sheffield, F. D. 1953. Relation of random activity to food deprivation. *Journal of Comparative and Physiological Psychology, 46*:320–322. **(225)**

Campbell, P. E.; Crumbaugh, C. M.; Rhodus, D. M.; and Knouse, S. B. 1971. Magnitude of partial reward and amount of training in the rat: An hypothesis of sequential effects. *Journal of Comparative and Physiological Psychology, 75*:120–128. **(252)**

Cantor, M. B. 1971. Signaled reinforcing brain stimulation facilitates operant behavior under schedules of intermittent reinforcement. *Science, 174*:610–613. **(115)**

Capaldi, E. J. 1966. Partial reinforcement: A hypothesis of sequential effects. *Psychological Review, 73*:459–477. **(249, 252)**

Capaldi, E. J. 1967. A sequential hypothesis of instrumental learning. In K. W. Spence and J. T. Spence (Eds.), *The psychology of learning and motivation*, Vol. 1. New York: Academic Press. Pp. 67–156. **(249, 252)**

Capaldi, E. J. 1971. Memory and learning: A sequential viewpoint. In W. K. Honig and P. H. R. James (Eds.), *Animal memory*. New York: Academic Press. Pp. 111–154. **(249, 253, 254)**

Capaldi, E. J., and Stanley, L. R. 1963. Temporal properties of reinforcement after-effects. *Journal of Experimental Psychology, 65*:169–175. **(252)**

Capaldi, E. J., and Waters, R. W. 1970. Conditioning and nonconditioning interpretations of small-trial phenomena. *Journal of Experimental Psychology, 84*:518–522. **(252)**

Capaldi, E. J.; Hart, D.; and Stanley, L. R. 1963. Effect of intertrial reinforcement on the aftereffect of nonreinforcement and resistance to extinction. *Journal of Experimental Psychology, 65*:70–74. **(253)**

Caramazza, A.; Hersh, H.; and Torgerson, W. S. 1976. Subjective structures and operations in semantic memory. *Journal of Verbal Learning and Verbal Behavior, 15*:103–118. **(493)**

Carew, T. J., and Kupferman, I. 1974. The influence of different natural environments on habituation in *Aplysia californica. Behavioral Biology, 12*:339–345. **(54)**

Carey, S. T., and Lockhart, R. S. 1973. Encoding differences in recognition and recall. *Memory and Cognition* 1:297–300. **(488)**

Carmichael, L. C.; Hogan, H. P.; and Walter, A. A. 1932. An experimental study of language on the reproduction of visually perceived form. *Journal of Experimental Psychology* 15:73–86. **(465)**

Carr, A., and Coleman, P. J. 1974. Sea floor spreading and the odyssey of the green turtle. *Nature, 249*:128–130. **(42)**

Carter, A. L. 1975. Development of the presyntactic communication system: A case study. *Journal of Child Language, 2*:233–250. **(360)**

Catania, A. C. 1971a. Elicitation, reinforcement, and stimulus control. In R. Glaser (Ed.), *The nature of reinforcement*. New York: Academic Press. Pp. 196–220. **(35, 154, 221)**

Catania, A. C. 1971b. Reinforcement schedules: The role of responses preceding the one that produces the reinforcer. *Journal of the Experimental Analysis of Behavior* 15:271–287. **(130)**

Catania, A. C. 1972. Chomsky's formal analysis of natural languages: A behavioral translation. *Behaviorism,* 1:1–15. **(311)**

Catania, A. C. 1973a. The nature of learning. In J. A. Nevin and G. S. Reynolds (Eds.), *The study of behavior*. Glenview, Ill.: Scott, Foresman. Pp. 31–68. **(154)**

Catania, A. C. 1973b. The psychologies of structure, function and development. *American Psychologist, 28*, 434–443. **(154, 311, 359)**

Catania, A. C. 1975. The myth of self-reinforcement. *Behaviorism, 3*, 192–199. **(270)**

Catania, A. C. 1976. Self-reinforcement revisited. *Behaviorism,* 4:157–162. **(270)**

Catania, A. C., and Cutts, D. 1963. Experimental control of superstitious responding in humans. *Journal of the Experimental Analysis of Behavior, 6*:203–208. **(29)**

Cautela, J. R. 1965. The problem of backward conditioning. *Journal of Psychology, 60*:135–144. **(97)**

Cegarvske, C. F.; Thompson, R. F.; Patterson, M. M.; and Gormezano, I. 1976. Mechanisms of efferent neuronal control of the reflex nictitating membrane response in the rabbit. *Journal of Comparative and Physiological Psychology, 90*:411–423. **(113)**

Ceraso, J., and Henderson, A. 1965. Unavailability and associative loss in RI and PI. *Journal of Experimental Psychology, 70*:300–303. **(499)**

Chamove, A.; Harlow, H. F.; and Mitchell, G. D. 1967. Sex differences in the infant-directed behavior of preadolescent rhesus monkeys. *Child Development, 38*:329–335. **(69)**

Chapman, R. S., and Miller, J. F. 1975. Word order in early two and three word utterances. Does production precede comprehension? *Journal of Speech and Hearing Research,* 18:355–371. **(400)**

Chase, S. 1968. Selectivity in multidimensional stimulus control. *Journal of Comparative and Physiological Psychology,* 66:787–792. **(138, 202)**

Chase, W. G., and Simon, H. A. 1973. Perception in chess. *Cognitive Psychology,* 4:55–81. **(449)**

Chatterjee, B. B., and Eriksen, C. W. 1960. Conditioning and generalization of GSR as a function of awareness. *Journal of Abnormal and Social Psychology,* 60:349–403. **(277)**

Cherek, D. R., and Pickens, R. 1970. Schedule-induced aggression as a function of fixed-ratio value. *Journal of the Experimental Analysis of Behavior,* 14:309–311. **(243)**

Cherek, D. R.; Thompson, T.; and Heistad, G. T. 1973. Responding maintained by the opportunity to attack during an interval food reinforcement schedule. *Journal of the Experimental Analysis of Behavior,* 19:113–124. **(243, 244)**

Cherry, E. C. 1953. Some experiments on the recognition of speech, with one and with two ears. *Journal of the Acoustical Society of America,* 25:975–979. **(434)**

Cherry, E. C., and Taylor, W. K. 1954. Some further experiments on the recognition of speech with one and two ears. *Journal of the Acoustical Society of America,* 26:554–559. **(434)**

Chomsky, C. 1969. *The acquisition of syntax in children from 5 to 10.* Cambridge, Mass.: M.I.T. Press. **(389)**

Chomsky, N. 1957. *Syntactic structures.* The Hague: Mouton. **(312, 324, 325, 327, 328, 330, 336, 338, 359, 411)**

Chomsky, N. 1959. A review of B. F. Skinner's *Verbal behavior. Language,* 35:26–58. **(408)**

Chomsky, N. 1965. *Aspects of the theory of syntax.* Cambridge, Mass.: M.I.T. Press. **(312, 324, 328, 329, 330, 331, 332, 338, 359, 379)**

Chomsky, N. 1971. Deep structure, surface structure and semantic interpretation. In D. D. Steinberg and L. A. Jokobovits (Eds.), *Semantics: An interdisciplinary reader in philosophy, linguistics and psychology.* London: Cambridge University Press. Pp. 183–216. **(332, 338)**

Chomsky, N. 1972. *Language and mind.* New York: Harcourt Brace Jovanovich. **(310, 311, 378, 379)**

Chomsky, N. 1975. *Reflections on language.* New York: Pantheon Books. **(312, 332, 359)**

Chomsky, N. 1976. On the biological basis of language capacities. In R. W. Rieber (Ed.), *The neuropsychology of language.* New York: Plenum Press. **(359)**

Chomsky, N., and Halle, M. 1968. *The sound pattern of English.* New York: Harper & Row. **(315, 316)**

Chomsky, N., and Miller, G. A. 1963. Introduction to the formal analysis of natural languages. In R. D. Luce, R. R. Bush, and E. Galanter (Eds.), *Handbook of mathematical psychology,* Vol. II. New York: Wiley. **(411)**

Chumbley, J. 1969. Hypothesis memory in concept learning. *Journal of Mathematical Psychology,* 6:528–540. **(307)**

Chung, S., and Herrnstein, R. J. 1967. Choice and delay of reinforcement. *Journal of the Experimental Analysis of Behavior,* 10:67–74. **(147)**

Church, R. M. 1964. Systematic effect of random error in the yoked control design. *Psychological Bulletin,* 62:122–131. **(127)**

Church, R. M. 1969. Response suppression. In B. A. Campbell and R. M. Church (Eds.), *Punishment and aversive behavior.* Englewood Cliffs, N.J.: Prentice-Hall. Pp. 111–156. **(132)**

Clark, E. V. 1973. What's in a word? On the child's acquisition of semantics in his first language. In T. E. Moore (Ed.), *Cognitive development and the acquisition of language.* New York: Academic Press. Pp. 65–110. **(360, 390)**

Clark, E. V. 1975. Knowledge, context, and strategy in the acquisition of meaning. In D. P. Dato (Ed.), *Georgetown University round table on languages and linguisitics 1975.* Washington, D.C.: Georgetown University Press. Pp. 77–98. **(369)**

Clark, E. V., and Garnica, O. K. 1974. Is he coming or going? On the acquisition of deictic verbs. *Journal of Verbal Learning and Verbal Behavior, 13*:559–572. **(391)**

Clark, F. C. 1958. The effect of deprivation and frequency of reinforcement on variable-interval responding. *Journal of the Experimental Analysis of Behavior, 1*:221–227. **(133, 226, 227)**

Clark, F. C. 1972. Some procedural effects in operant discrimination reversal. *Psychological Record, 22*:83–101. **(304)**

Clark, H. H., and Clark, E. V. 1977. *Psychology and language.* New York: Harcourt Brace Jovanovich. **(311, 334, 338, 342, 344, 360, 365, 368, 369, 370, 373, 379, 381, 382, 383, 384, 389, 390, 391, 396, 400, 408)**

Clark, S. E. 1969. Retrieval of color information from preperceptual memory. *Journal of Experimental Psychology 82*:263–266. **(423)**

Clifton, C., Jr., and Birenbaum, S. 1970. Effects of serial position and delay of probe in a memory scan task. *Journal of Experimental Psychology, 86*:69–76. **(459)**

Cofer, C. N. 1965. On some factors in the organizational characteristics of free recall. *American Psychologist, 20*:261–272. **(471, 513)**

Cohen, P. S. 1968. Punishment: The interactive effects of delay and intensity of shock. *Journal of the Experimental Analysis of Behavior, 11*:789–799. **(131)**

Colavita, F. B. 1965. Dual function of the US in classical salivary conditioning. *Journal of Comparative and Physiological Psychology, 60*:218–222. **(114)**

Cole, R. A., and Scott, B. 1972. Distinctive feature control of decision time: Same-different judgments of simultaneously heard phonemes. *Perception and Psychophysics, 12*:91–94. **(322)**

Coleman, S. R., and Gormezano, I. 1971. Classical conditioning of the rabbit's (*Oryctolagus cuniculus*) nictitating membrane response under symmetrical CS-US interval shifts. *Journal of Comparative and Physiological Psychology, 77*:447–455. **(111)**

Collier, G.; Hirsch, E.; and Kanarek, R. 1977. The operant revisited. In W. K. Honig and J. E. R. Staddon (Eds.), *Handbook of operant behavior.* Englewood Cliffs, N.J.: Prentice-Hall. Pp. 28–52. **(224)**

Collins, A. M., and Loftus, E. R. 1975. A spreading-activation theory of semantic processing. *Psychological Review, 82*:407–428. **(488, 490, 491, 492)**

Collins, A. M., and Quillian, M. R. 1969. Retrieval time from semantic memory. *Journal of Verbal Learning and Verbal Behavior, 8*:240–247. **(488, 489)**

Collins, A. M., and Quillian, M. R. 1972. How to make a language user. In E. Tulving and W. Donaldson (Eds.), *Organization of memory.* New York: Academic Press. **(488)**

Collins, J. P. 1974. Generalization and decision theory. Unpublished doctoral dissertation, University of Massachusetts. **(186, 194, 195)**

Coltheart, M., and Glick, M. J. 1974. Visual imagery: A case study. *Quarterly Journal of Experimental Psychology, 26*:438–453. **(484)**

Conrad, C. 1972. Cognitive economy in semantic memory. *Journal of Experimental Psychology, 92*:149–154. **(490)**

Conrad, R. 1964. Acoustic confusions in immediate memory. *British Journal of Psychology, 55*:75–84. **(443)**

Conrad, R. 1972. Short-term memory in the deaf: A test for speech coding. *British Journal of Psychology, 63*:173–180. **(444)**

Conrad, R., and Hull, A. S. 1964. Information, acoustic confusion and memory span. *British Journal of Psychology, 55*:429–432. **(443)**

Conrad, R., and Rush, M. L. 1965. On the nature of short-term memory encoding by the deaf. *Journal of Speech and Hearing Disorders, 30*:336–343. **(444)**

Cooper, L. A. 1975. Mental rotation of random two-dimensional shapes. *Cognitive Psychology, 7*:20–43. **(445)**

Cooper, L. A., and Shepard, R. N. 1973. Chronometric studies of the rotation of mental images. In W. G. Chase (Ed.), *Visual information processing.* New York: Academic Press. Pp. 75–176. **(445)**

Corcoran, D. W. J. 1971. *Pattern recognition.* Baltimore: Penguin Books. **(459)**

Corey, J. R., and Shamow, J. 1972. The effects of fading on the acquisition and retention of oral reading. *Journal of Applied Behavior Analysis, 5*:311–315. **(194)**

Corrigan, R. 1978. Language development as related to stage 6 object permanence development. *Journal of Child Language,* 5:173–189. **(367)**

Cotton, J. W. 1953. Running time as a function of amount of food deprivation. *Journal of Experimental Psychology,* 46:188–198. **(133, 226)**

Cousins, L. S.; Zamble, E. D.; Tait, R. W.; and Suboski, M.D. 1971. Sensory preconditioning in curarized rats. *Journal of Comparative and Physiological Psychology,* 77:152–154. **(110)**

Cowles, J. T. 1937. Food tokens as incentives for learning by chimpanzees. *Comparative Psychology Monographs,* 14(5, No. 71). **(175)**

Craik, F. I. M. 1970. The fate of primary items in free recall. *Journal of Verbal Learning and Verbal Behavior,* 9:143–148. **(476)**

Craik, F. I. M., and Lockhart, R. S. 1972. Levels of processing: A framework for memory research. *Journal of Verbal Learning and Verbal Behavior,* 11:671–684. **(416, 477)**

Craik, F. I. M., and Tulving, E. 1975. Depth of processing and the retention of words in episodic memory. *Journal of Experimental Psychology: General,* 104:268–294. **(416, 462, 468, 469)**

Craik, F. I. M., and Watkins, M. J. 1973. The role of rehearsal in short-term memory. *Journal of Verbal Learning and Verbal Behavior,* 12:599–607. **(477)**

Creelman, M. B. 1966. *The experimental investigation of meaning: A review of the literature.* New York: Springer-Verlag. **(277)**

Crites, R. J.; Harris, R. T.; Rosenquist, H.; and Thomas, D. R. 1967. Response patterning during stimulus generalization in the rat. *Journal of the Experimental Analysis of Behavior,* 10:165–168. **(186)**

Cromer, R. F. 1970. Children are nice to understand: Surface structure clues for the recovery of a deep structure. *British Journal of Psychology,* 61:397–408. **(389)**

Crouse, J. H. 1971. Retroactive interference in reading prose materials. *Journal of Educational Psychology,* 62:39–44. **(503)**

Crowder, R. G. 1967. Short-term memory for words with a perceptual-motor interpolated activity. *Journal of Verbal Learning and Verbal Behavior,* 6:753–761. **(456)**

Crowder, R. G. 1976. *Principles of learning and memory.* Hillsdale, N.J.: Lawrence Erlbaum Associates. **(409, 426, 465, 494, 509)**

Crowder, R. G., and Morton, J. 1969. Precategorical acoustic storage (PAS). *Perception and Psychophysics,* 5:365–373. **(426)**

Crowley, M. A. 1979. The allocation of time to temporally defined behaviors: Responding during stimulus generalization. *Journal of the Experimental Analysis of Behavior,* in press. **(186, 196)**

Cullen, E. 1957. Adaptations in the kittiwake to cliff nesting. *Ibis,* 99:275–302. **(17)**

Cumming, W. W., and Eckerman, D. A. 1965. Stimulus control of a differentiated operant. *Psychonomic Science,* 3:313–314. **(186, 196)**

Curtiss, S.; Fromkin, V.; Krashen, S.; Rigler, D.; and Rigler, M. 1974. The linguistic development of Genie. *Language,* 50:528–554. **(393, 394)**

Dale, P. S. 1976. *Language development.* New York: Holt, Rinehart and Winston. **(365, 374, 388, 405)**

Dallet, K. M. 1962. The transfer surface re-examined. *Journal of Verbal Learning and Verbal Behavior,* 1:91–94. **(264, 494)**

Dallet, K. M. 1966. Effects of within-list and between list acoustic similarity in the learning and retention of paired associates. *Journal of Experimental Psychology,* 72:667–677. **(466)**

D'Amato, M. R. 1955. Secondary reinforcement and magnitude of primary reinforcement. *Journal of Comparative and Physiological Psychology,* 48:378–380. **(172)**

D'Amato, M. R.; Fazzaro, J.; and Etkin, M. 1968. Discriminated barpress avoidance, maintenance and extinction in rats as a function of shock intensity. *Journal of Comparative and Physiological Psychology,* 63:351–354. **(209)**

Darby, C. C., and Riopelle, A. J. 1959. Observation learning in the rhesus monkey. *Journal of Comparative and Physiological Psychology,* 52:94–98. **(302)**

Dark, V. J., and Loftus, G. R. 1976. The role of rehearsal in long-term memory performance. *Journal of Verbal Learning and Verbal Behavior,* 15:479–490. **(475)**

Davenport, J. W. 1956. Choice behavior as a function of drive strength and rate of learning. Unpublished doctoral dissertation, State University of Iowa. **(226, 227)**

Davis, M. 1970a. Interstimulus interval and startle response habituation with a "control" for total time during training. *Psychonomic Science,* 20:39–41. **(57)**

Davis, M. 1970b. Effects of interstimulus interval length and variability on startle-response habituation in the rat. *Journal of Comparative and Physiological Psychology,* 72:177–192. **(51, 55)**

Davis, M., and Sollberger, A. 1971. Twenty-four hour periodicity of the startle response in rats. *Psychonomic Science,* 25:37–39. **(49)**

Davis, M., and Wagner, A. R. 1969. Habituation of startle response under incremental sequence of stimulus intensities. *Journal of Comparative and Physiological Psychology,* 67:486–492. **(49, 50)**

Dawkins, R. 1976. *The selfish gene.* New York: Oxford University Press. **(17)**

Dawson, M. E. 1970. Cognition and conditioning: Effects of masking the CS-UCS contingency on human GSR classical conditioning. *Journal of Experimental Psychology,* 85:389–396. **(274)**

Dawson, M. E., and Biferno, N. A. 1973. Concurrent measurement of awareness and electrodermal classical conditioning. *Journal of Experimental Psychology,* 101:55–62. **(274)**

Dawson, M. E., and Grings, W. W. 1968. Comparison of classical conditioning and relational learning. *Journal of Experimental Psychology,* 76:227–231. **(274)**

Dawson, M. E., and Reardon, P. 1969. Effects of facilitory and inhibitory sets on GSR conditioning and extinction. *Journal of Experimental Psychology,* 82:462–466. **(273)**

Dawson, M. E., and Reardon, P. 1973. Construct validity of recall and recognition postconditioning measures of awareness. *Journal of Experimental Psychology,* 98:308–315. **(277)**

Deese, J. 1962. On the structure of associative meaning. *Psychological Review,* 69:161–175. **(493)**

De Laguna, G. 1927. *Speech: Its function and development.* New Haven: Yale University Press. **(368)**

Delprato, D. J. 1971. Specific-pair interference on recall and associative-matching retention tests. *American Journal of Psychology,* 84:185–193. **(501)**

den Heyer, K., and Barrett, B. 1971. Selective loss of visual and verbal information in STM by means of visual and verbal interpolated tasks. *Psychonomic Science,* 25:100–102. **(444)**

DeNike, L. D. 1964. The temporal relationship between awareness and performance in verbal conditioning. *Journal of Experimental Psychology,* 68:521–529. **(274)**

DeNike, L. D., and Spielberger, C. D. 1963. Induced mediating states in verbal conditioning. *Journal of Verbal Learning and Verbal Behavior,* 1:339–345. **(274)**

Denny, M. R. 1946. The role of secondary reinforcement in a partial reinforcement learning situation. *Journal of Experimental Psychology,* 36:373–389. **(249)**

Denny, M. R. 1967. A learning model. In W. C. Corning and S. C. Ratner (Eds.), *Chemistry of learning.* New York: Plenum. **(172)**

Detier, V. G. 1976. *To know a fly.* Cambridge, Mass.: Harvard University Press. **(224)**

Deutsch, D. 1970. Tones and numbers: Specificity of interference in immediate memory. *Science,* 168:1604–1604. **(455)**

Deutsch, J. A., and DiCara, L. 1967. Hunger and extinction in intracranial self-stimulation. *Journal of Comparative and Physiological Psychology,* 63:344–347. **(230)**

Deutsch, J. A., and Deutsch, D. 1963. Attention: Some theoretical considerations. *Psychological Review,* 70:80–90. **(435)**

Deutsch, W., and Pechman, T. 1978. Ihr, dir or mir? On the acquisition of pronouns in German children. *Cognition,* 6:155–168. **(385)**

DeValois, R. L., and Jacobs, G. H. 1968. Primate color vision. *Science,* 162:533–540. **(304)**

de Villiers, J. G., and de Villiers, P. A. 1978. *Language acquisition.* Cambridge, Mass.: Harvard University Press. **(351, 368, 369, 371, 380, 381, 382, 383, 385, 389, 408)**

de Villiers, P. A. 1974. The law of effect and avoidance: A quantitative relationship between response rate and shock-frequency reduction. *Journal of the Experimental Analysis of Behavior, 21*:223–235. **(146, 147)**

de Villiers, P. A. 1977. Choice in concurrent schedules and a quantitative formulation of the law of effect. In W. K. Honig and J. E. R. Staddon (Eds.), *Handbook of operant behavior*. Englewood Cliffs, N.J.: Prentice-Hall. **(147)**

Devine, J. V. 1970. Stimulus attributes and training procedures in learning-set formation of rhesus and cebus monkeys. *Journal of Comparative and Physiological Psychology, 73*:62–67. **(304)**

Dews, P. B. 1962. The effect of multiple S^Δ periods on responding on a fixed interval schedule. *Journal of the Experimental Analysis of Behavior, 5*:369–374. **(238, 239)**

Dews, P. B. 1970. The theory of fixed-interval responding. In W. N. Schoenfeld (Ed.), *The theory of reinforcement schedules*. Englewood Cliffs, N.J.: Prentice-Hall. Pp. 43–61. **(239)**

Dewsbury, D. A. 1975. Diversity and adaptation in rodent copulatory behavior. *Science, 190*:947–954. **(69)**

Dick, A. O. 1974. Iconic memory and its relation to perceptual processing and other memory mechanisms. *Perception and Psychophysics, 16*:575–596. **(422, 423)**

Dillon, R. F., and Reid, L. S. 1969. Short-term memory as a function of information processing during the retention interval. *Journal of Experimental Psychology, 81*:261–269. **(456)**

Dillon, R. F., and Thomas, H. 1975. The role of response confusion in proactive interference. *Journal of Verbal Learning and Verbal Behavior, 14*:603–615. **(455)**

DiLollo, V.; Lowe, D. G.; and Scott, J. P., Jr. 1974. Backward masking and interference with the processing of brief visual displays. *Journal of Experimental Psychology, 103*:934–940. **(423)**

Dinsmoor, J. A. 1950. A quantitative comparison of the discriminative and reinforcing functions of a stimulus. *Journal of Experimental Psychology, 40*:458–472. **(172)**

Dixon, P. W., and Oakes, W. F. 1965. Effects of intertrial activity in the relationship between awareness and verbal operant conditioning. *Journal of Experimental Psychology, 69*:152–157. **(274)**

Dodd, B. 1975. Children's understanding of their own phonological forms. *Quarterly Journal of Experimental Psychology, 27*:165–172. **(383, 384)**

Dodd, D. H.; Kinsman, R. A.; Klipp, R. D.; and Bourne, L. E., Jr. 1971. Effect of logic pretraining on conceptual rule learning. *Journal of Experimental Psychology, 88*:119–122. **(290)**

Donahoe, J. W. 1970. Stimulus control within response sequences. In J. H. Reynierse (Ed.), *Current issues in animal learning*. Lincoln: University of Nebraska Press. Pp. 233–293. **(125, 236, 238)**

Donahoe, J. W. 1977. Some implications of a relational principle of reinforcement. *Journal of the Experimental Analysis of Behavior, 27*:341–350. **(141, 144, 147)**

Donahoe, J. W., and Miller, L. R. 1975. A finite-state analysis of stimulus control. Paper presented at the meetings of the Psychonomic Society, November, 1975, at Denver, Colorado. **(196)**

Donahoe, J. W.; Schulte, V. G.; and Moulton, A. E. 1968. Stimulus control of approach behavior. *Journal of Experimental Psychology, 78*:21–30. **(236)**

Dore, J. 1975. Holophrases, speech acts and language universals. *Journal of Child Language, 2*:21–40. **(364)**

Dore, J.; Franklin, M.; Miller, R.; and Ramer, A. 1976. Transitional phenomena in early language acquisition. *Journal of Child Language, 3*:13–28. **(364)**

Dreyfus, H. L. 1971. *What computers can't do: A critique of artificial reason*. New York: Harper & Row. **(412)**

Dunham, P. J. 1971. Punishment: Method and theory. *Psychological Review, 78*: 58–70. **(146, 209)**

Dunham, P. J. 1972. Some effects of punishment upon unpunished responding. *Journal of the Experimental Analysis of Behavior, 17*:443–450. **(209)**

Dunham, P. J. 1977. The nature of reinforcing stimuli. In W. K. Honig and J. E. R. Staddon (Eds.), *Handbook of operant behavior*. Englewood Cliffs, N.J.: Prentice-Hall. **(144, 225)**

Dunham, P. J. 1978. Changes in unpunished responding during response-contingent punishment. *Animal Learning and Behavior,* 6:174–180. **(146)**

Dunn, R. F. 1968. Anxiety and verbal concept learning. *Journal of Experimental Psychology,* 76:286–290. **(298)**

Dyer, J. C., and Meyer, P. A. 1976. Facilitation of simple concept identification through mnemonic instruction. *Journal of Experimental Psychology: Human Learning and Memory,* 2:767–773. **(300)**

Dykman, R. A. 1976. Conditioning as sensitization. *The Pavlovian Journal of Biological Science,* 11:24–36. **(93)**

Ebbinghaus, H. 1885. *Memory: A contribution to experimental psychology.* Translated by H. A. Ruger and C. E. Bussenius. New York: Dover, 1964. **(211, 213, 214)**

Edwards, D. 1973. Sensory-motor intelligence and semantic relations in early child grammar. *Cognition,* 2:395–434. **(368)**

Ehrenfreund, D. 1952. A study of the transposition gradient. *Journal of Experimental Psychology,* 43:81–87. **(198)**

Eibl-Eibesfeldt, I. 1975. *Ethology: The biology of behavior.* New York: Holt, Rinehart, and Winston. **(65, 74)**

Eimas, P. D. 1975a. Auditory and phonetic coding of the cues for speech: Discrimination of the [r-l] distinction by young infants. *Perception and Psychophysics,* 18:341–347. **(361)**

Eimas, P. D. 1975b. Speech perception in early infancy. In L. B. Cohen & P. Salapatek (Eds.), *Infant perception: From sensation to cognition,* Vol. 2. New York: Academic Press. Pp. 193–231. **(361)**

Eimas, P.; Siqueland, E. R.; Jusczyk, K. P.; and Vigorito, J. 1971. Speech perception in infants. *Science,* 171:303–306. **(361)**

Eiseley, L. 1958. *Darwin's century.* Garden City, N.Y.: Doubleday. **(38)**

Ellison, G. D. and Konorski, J. 1964. Separation of the salivary and motor responses in instrumental conditioning. *Science,* 146:1071–1072. **(172)**

Engberg, L. A.; Hansen, G. A.; Welker, R. L.; and Thomas, D. R. 1972. Acquisition of keypecking via autoshaping as a function of prior experience. *Science,* 178:1002–1004. **(245)**

Engen, T.; Kuisma, J. E.; and Eimas, P. D. 1973. Short-term memory of odors. *Journal of Experimental Psychology,* 99:222–225. **(447)**

Entwisle, D. R., and Frasure, N. E. 1974. A contradiction resolved: Children's processing of syntactic cues. *Developmental Psychology,* 10:852–857. **(342)**

Erickson, J. R., and Zajkowski, M. M. 1967. Learning several concept-identification problems concurrently: A test of the sampling-with-replacement assumption. *Journal of Experimental Psychology,* 74:212–218. **(307)**

Eriksen, C. W. 1958. Unconscious processes. In M. R. Jones (Ed.), *Nebraska symposium on motivation.* Lincoln: University of Nebraska Press. Pp. 169–227. **(277)**

Eriksen, C. W., and Collins, J. F. 1967. Sensory traces versus the psychological moment in the temporal organization of form. *Journal of Experimental Psychology,* 77:376–382. **(423)**

Ervin, S. M. 1964. Imitation and structural change in children's language. In E. H. Lenneberg (Ed.), *New directions in the study of language.* Cambridge, Mass.: M.I.T. Press. **(386, 405)**

Ervin-Tripp, S. 1970. Discourse agreement: How children answer questions. In J. R. Hayes (Ed.), *Cognition and the development of language.* New York: Wiley. Pp. 79–107. **(352)**

Escalona, S. K. 1973. Basic modes of social interaction: Their emergence and patterning during the first two years of life. *Merrill-Palmer Quarterly,* 19:204–232. **(360)**

Estes, W. K. 1949. Generalization of secondary reinforcement from the primary drive. *Journal of Comparative and Physiological Psychology,* 42:286–295. **(174)**

Estes, W. K. 1950. Toward a statistical theory of learning. *Psychological Review,* 57:94–107. **(156)**

Estes, W. K. 1955. Statistical theory of spontaneous recovery and regression. *Psychological Review,* 62:145–154. **(206)**

Estes, W. K. 1956. The problem of inference from curves based on group data. *Psychological Bulletin*, 53:134–140. **(74)**

Estes, W. K. 1958. Stimulus-response theory of drive. In M. R. Jones (Ed.), *Nebraska symposium on motivation*. Lincoln: University of Nebraska Press. **(228)**

Estes, W. K. 1959. Component and pattern models with Markovian interpretations. In R. R. Bush and W. K. Estes (Eds.), *Studies in mathematical learning theory*. Stanford, Calif.: Stanford University Press. **(150)**

Estes, W. K. 1960. Learning theory and the new "mental chemistry." *Psychological Review*, 67:207–233. **(156)**

Estes, W. K. 1972. Interactions of signal and background variables in visual processing. *Perception and Psychophysics*, 12:278–286. **(437)**

Estes, W. K. 1973. Phonetic coding and rehearsal in short-term memory for letter strings. *Journal of Verbal Learning and Verbal Behavior*, 12:360–372. **(444)**

Estes, W. K. 1976. Introduction to Volume 4. In W. K. Estes (Ed.), *Handbook of learning and cognitive processes. Vol. 4. Attention and memory*. Hillsdale, N.J.: Lawrence Erlbaum Associates. Pp. 1–16. **(412)**

Estes, W. K., and Skinner, B. F. 1941. Some quantitative properties of anxiety. *Journal of Experimental Psychology*, 29:390–400. **(107)**

Estes, W. K., and Taylor, H. A. 1966. Visual detection in relation to display size and redundancy of critical elements. *Perception and Psychophysics*, 1:9–16. **(422, 436)**

Estes, W. K., and Wessel, D. L. 1966. Reaction time in relation to display size and correctness of response in forced-choice visual signal detection. *Perception and Psychophysics*, 1:369–373. **(437)**

Eysenck, M. W. 1976. Arousal, learning, and memory. *Psychological Bulletin*, 83:389–404. **(229)**

Falk, J. L. 1961. Production of polydipsia in normal rats by an intermittent food schedule. *Science*, 133:195–196. **(231)**

Falk, J. L. 1966. Schedule-induced polydipsia as a function of fixed interval length. *Journal of the Experimental Analysis of Behavior*, 9:37–39. **(232)**

Falk, J. L. 1967. Control of schedule-induced polydipsia: Type, size, and spacing of meals. *Journal of the Experimental Analysis of Behavior*, 10:199–206. **(232)**

Falk, J. L. 1969. Conditions producing psychogenic polydipsia in animals. *Annals of the New York Academy of Sciences*, 157:569–593. **(232)**

Falk, J. L. 1971. The nature and determinants of adjunctive behavior. *Physiology and Behavior*, 6:577–588. **(126, 232)**

Falk, J. L. 1972. The nature and determinants of adjunctive behavior. In R. M. Gilbert and J. D. Keehn (Eds.), *Schedule effects: Drugs, drinking, and aggression*. Toronto: University of Toronto Press. Pp. 148–173. **(232)**

Falk, J. L. 1977. The origin and functions of adjunctive behavior. *Animal Learning and Behavior*, 5:325–335. **(232, 233)**

Fantino, E. 1973. Aversive control. In J. A. Nevin and G. S. Reynolds (Eds.), *The study of behavior*. Glenview, Ill.: Scott, Foresman. Pp. 239–275. **(132)**

Fantino, E. J.; Sharp, D.; and Cole, M. 1966. Factors facilitating level press avoidance. *Journal of Comparative and Physiological Psychology*, 62:214–217. **(210)**

Farris, H. E. 1967. Classical conditioning of courting behavior in the Japanese quail, *Coturnix coturnix japonica*. *Journal of the Experimental Analysis of Behavior*, 10:213–217. **(81)**

Ferguson, C. A., and Farwell, C. B. 1975. Words and sounds in early language acquisition. *Language*, 51:419–439. **(384)**

Ferguson, C. A., and Garnica, O. K. 1975. Theories of phonological development. In E. H. Lenneberg and E. Lenneberg (Eds.), *Foundations of language development: A multidisciplinary approach*, Vol. I. New York: Academic Press. Pp. 153–180. **(408)**

Ferguson, C. A., and Slobin, D. I. (Eds.) 1973. *Studies of child language development*. New York: Holt, Rinehart and Winston. **(386)**

Ferster, C. B., and DeMyer, M. K. 1962. A method for the experimental analysis of the behavior of autistic children. *American Journal of Orthopsychiatry*, 32:89–98. **(170)**

Ferster, C. B., and Skinner, B. F. 1957. *Schedules of reinforcement.* Englewood Cliffs, N.J.: Prentice-Hall. **(126, 147, 233, 234, 235, 237, 244, 248)**

Fillmore, C. J. 1968. The case for case. In E. Bach and R. T. Harms (Eds.), *Universals of linguistic theory.* New York: Holt, Rinehart and Winston. Pp. 1–90. **(341, 375)**

Fillmore, C. J. 1971. Verbs of judging: An exercise in semantic description. In C. J. Fillmore and D. T. Langendoen (Eds.), *Studies in linguistic semantics.* New York: Holt, Rinehart, and Winston. Pp. 273–296. **(375)**

Flagg, P. W. 1976. Semantic integration in sentence memory. *Journal of Verbal Learning and Verbal Behavior,* 15:491–504. **(487)**

Flavell, J. H. 1977. *Cognitive development.* Englewood Cliffs, N.J.: Prentice-Hall. **(287, 298, 380)**

Fleshler, M., and Hoffman, H. S. 1962. A progression for generating variable-interval schedules. *Journal of the Experimental Analysis of Behavior,* 5:529–531. **(147)**

Flexser, A. J., and Tulving, E. 1978. Retrieval independence in recognition and recall. *Psychological Review,* 85:153–171. **(510)**

Flory, R. 1969. Attack behavior as a function of minimum inter-food interval. *Journal of the Experimental Analysis of Behavior,* 12:825–828. **(232, 233, 243)**

Flynn, J. P. 1967. The neural basis of aggression in cats. In D. C. Glass (Ed.), *Neurophysiology and emotion.* New York: Rockefeller University Press. Pp. 40–60. **(229)**

Flynn, J. P. 1976. Neural basis of threat and attack. In R. G. Grenell and S. Gabay (Eds.), *Biological foundations of Psychiatry,* vol. 1. New York: Raven Press. Pp. 273–295. **(229)**

Flynn, J. P.; Vanegas, H.; Foote, W.; and Edwards, S. 1970. Neural mechanisms involved in a cat's attack on a rat. In R. E. Whalen, R. F. Thompson, M. Verzeano, and N. M. Weinberger (Eds.), *The neural control of behavior.* New York: Academic Press. Pp. 135–173. **(229, 231)**

Fodor, J. A. 1968. *Psychological explanation: An introduction to the philosophy of psychology.* New York: Random House. **(411, 433)**

Fodor, J. A. 1975. *The language of thought.* New York: Crowell. **(281)**

Fodor, J. A., and Garrett, M. 1966. Some reflections on competence and performance. In J. Lyons and R. J. Wales (Eds.), *Psycholinguistics papers.* Edinburgh: University of Edinburgh Press. **(336, 344)**

Foree, D. D., and LoLordo, V. M. 1973. Attention in the pigeon: The differential effects of food-getting vs. shock-avoidance procedures. *Journal of Comparative and Physiological Psychology,* 85:551–558. **(162)**

Foree, D. D., and LoLordo, V. M. 1975. Stimulus-reinforcer interactions in the pigeon: The role of electric shock and the avoidance contingency. *Journal of Experimental Psychology: Animal Behavior Processes,* 104:39–46. **(162)**

Forrester, W. E. 1970. Retroactive inhibition and spontaneous recovery in the A-B, D-C paradigm. *Journal of Verbal Learning and Verbal Behavior,* 9:525–528. **(499)**

Fourcin, A. J. 1975. Language development in the absence of expressive speech. In E. H. Lenneberg and E. Lenneberg (Eds.), *Foundations of language development,* Vol. 2. New York: Academic Press. Pp. 263–268. **(365)**

Fouts, R. S. 1972. The use of guidance in teaching sign language to a chimpanzee. *Journal of Comparative and Physiological Psychology,* 80:515–522. **(348)**

Fouts, R. S. 1974. Language: Origins, definitions and chimpanzees. *Journal of Human Evolution,* 3:475–482. **(355)**

Fouts, R. S., and Couch, J. B. 1976. Cultural evolution of learned language in chimpanzees. In Martin E. Hahn and Edward C. Simmel (Eds.), *Communicative Behavior and Evolution.* New York: Academic Press. Pp. 141–161. **(353)**

Fowler, H., and Miller, N. E. 1963. Facilitation and inhibition of runway performance by hind- and forepaw shock of various intensities. *Journal of Comparative and Physiological Psychology,* 56:801–805. **(161)**

Fowler, H., and Trapold, M. A. 1962. Escape performance as a function of delay of reinforcement. *Journal of Experimental Psychology,* 63:464–467. **(146)**

Francis, W. Nelson. 1958. *The Structure of American English.* New York: Ronald Press. **(363)**

Franks, J. J., and Bransford, J. D. 1971. Abstraction of visual patterns. *Journal of Experimental Psychology*, 90:65–74. **(286)**

Freed, E. X., and Hymovitz, N. 1969. A fortuitous observation regarding "psychogenic" polydipsia. *Psychological Reports*, 24:224–226. **(233)**

Freedman, J. L., and Loftus, E. F. 1971. Retrieval of words from long-term memory. *Journal of Verbal Learning and Verbal Behavior*, 10:107–115. **(490)**

Freibergs, V., and Tulving, E. 1961. The effect of practice on utilization of information from positive and negative instances in concept identification. *Canadian Journal of Psychology*, 15:101–106. **(294)**

Frey, P. W.; Maisiak, R.; and Dague, G. 1976. Unconditioned stimulus characteristics in rabbit eyelid conditioning. *Journal of Experimental Psychology: Animal Behavior Processes*, 2:175–190. **(114)**

Friedman, M. I., and Striker, E. M. 1976. The physiological psychology of hunger: A physiological perspective. *Psychological Review*, 83:409–431. **(224)**

Friedman, R., and Iwai, J. 1976. Genetic predisposition and stress-induced hypertension. *Science*, 193:161–162. **(33)**

Frieman, J. P. 1965. The use of pups as positive reinforcement in mice. *Proceedings of the 73rd Annual Convention of the American Psychological Association.* Pp. 131–132. **(82)**

Frieman, J., and Goyette, C. H. 1973. Transfer of training across stimulus modality and response class. *Journal of Experimental Psychology*, 97:235–241. **(155, 203)**

Fromkin, V. (Ed.) 1973. *Speech errors as linguistic evidence*. The Hague: Mouton. **(321)**

Fromkin, V.; Krashen, S.; Curtiss, S.; Rigler, D.; and Rigler, M. 1974. The development of language in Genie: A case of language acquisition beyond the "critical period." *Brain and Language*, 1:81–107. **(393, 394)**

Fuhrer, M. J., and Baer, P. E. 1965. Differential classical conditioning: Verbalization of stimulus contingencies. *Science*, 150:1479–1481. **(274)**

Galbraith, R. C., and Underwood, B. J. 1973. Perceived frequency of concrete and abstract words. *Memory and Cognition*, 1:56–60. **(484)**

Gallup, G. 1970. Chimpanzees: Self-recognition. *Science*, 167:86–87. **(276)**

Gallup, G. G., Jr. 1977. Self-recognition in primates. A comparative approach to the bidirectional properties of consciousness. *American Psychologist*, 32:329–338. **(276)**

Gamzu, E., and Schwartz, B. 1973. The maintenance of keypecking by stimulus-contingent and response-independent food presentations. *Journal of the Experimental Analysis of Behavior*, 19:65–72. **(193)**

Garcia, E.; Baer, D. M.; and Firestone, I. 1971. The development of generalized imitation within experimentally determined boundaries. *Journal of Applied Behavioral Analysis*, 4:101–112. **(270)**

Garcia, E.; Guess, D.; and Byrnes, J. 1973. Development of syntax in a retarded girl using procedures of imitation, reinforcement, and modelling. *Journal of Applied Behavior Analysis*, 6:299–310. **(405)**

Garcia, J., and Koelling, R. A. 1966. Relation of cue to consequence in avoidance learning. *Psychonomic Science*, 4:123–124. **(113)**

Gardiner, J. H.; Craik, F. I. M.; and Birtwistle, J. 1972. Retrieval cues and release from proactive inhibition. *Journal of Verbal Learning and Verbal Behavior*, 11:778–783. **(454)**

Gardner, B. T., and Gardner, R. A. 1971. Two-way communication with an infant chimpanzee. In A. M. Schrier and F. Stollnitz (Eds.), *Behavior of nonhuman primates*, Vol. 4. New York: Academic Press. Pp. 117–184. **(347, 351, 352, 353)**

Gardner, B. T., and Gardner, A. 1974. Comparing the early utterances of child and chimpanzee. In A. D. Pick (Ed.), *Minnesota symposia on child psychology*, Vol. 8. Minneapolis: The University of Minnesota Press. **(347, 350, 351, 352)**

Gardner, B. T., and Gardner, R. A. 1975. Evidence for sentence constituents in the early utterances of child and chimpanzee. *Journal of Experimental Psychology: General*, 104:244–267. **(347, 352, 354)**

Gardner, E. T., and Lewis, P. 1976. Negative reinforcement with shock-frequency increase. *Journal of the Experimental Analysis of Behavior*, 25:3–14. **(208)**

Gardner, G. T. 1973. Evidence for independent parallel channels in tachistoscopic perception. *Cognitive Psychology*, 4:130–155. **(437)**

Garner, W. R. 1962. *Uncertainty and structure as psychological concepts*. New York: Wiley. **(292)**

Garnica, O. K. 1973. The development of phonemic speech perception. In T. E. Moore (Ed.), *Cognitive development and the acquisition of language*. New York: Academic Press. Pp. 215–222. **(408)**

Garrett, M., and Fodor, J. 1968. Psychological theories and linguistic constructs. In T. R. Dixon and D. L. Horton (Eds.), *Verbal behavior and general behavior theory*. Engle-wood Cliffs, N.J.: Prentice-Hall. **(336)**

Garvey, C. 1975. Requests and responses in children's speech. *Journal of Child Language*, 2:41–63. **(366)**

Gavalas, R. J. 1967. Operant reinforcement of an autonomic response: Two studies. *Journal of the Experimental Analysis of Behavior*, 10:119–130. **(274)**

Gentner, D. 1975. Evidence for the psychological reality of semantic components: The verbs of possession. In D. A. Norman, D. E. Rumelhart, and the LNR Research Group. *Explorations in cognition*. San Francisco: Freeman. Pp. 211–246. **(390, 391)**

Gentry, W. D. 1968. Fixed-ratio schedule-induced aggression. *Journal of the Experimental Analysis of Behavior*, 11:813–817. **(243)**

Gerall, A. A., and Obrist, P. A. 1962. Classical conditioning of the pupillary dilation response of normal and curarized cats. *Journal of Comparative and Physiological Psychology*, 55:486–491. **(114)**

German, D. C., and Bowden, D. M. 1974. Catecholamine systems as the neural substrate for intracranial self-stimulation: A hypothesis. *Brain Research*, 73:381–319. **(224)**

Gewirtz, J. L. 1961. A learning analysis of the effects of normal stimulation, privation and deprivation on the acquisition of social motivation and attachment. In B. M. Foss (Ed.), *Determinants of infant behavior*, Vol. 1. London: Methuen. **(70)**

Gewirtz, J. L. 1971a. The roles of overt responding and extrinsic reinforcement in "self-" and "vicarious-reinforcement" phenomena and in "observational learning" and imitation. In R. Glaser (Ed.), *The nature of reinforcement*. New York: Academic Press. Pp. 279–309. **(270)**

Gewirtz, J. L. 1971b. Conditional responding as a paradigm for observational, imitative learning and vicarious-reinforcement. In H. W. Reese (Ed.), *Advances in child development and behavior*, Vol. 6. New York: Academic Press. Pp. 273–304. **(270)**

Gewirtz, J. L. 1978. Social learning in early human development. In A. Charles Catania and Thomas A. Brigham (Eds.), *Handbook of Applied Behavior Analysis*. New York: Irvington. Pp. 105–141. **(270, 360)**

Gibbs, C. M.; Latham, S. B.; and Gormezano, I. 1978. Classical conditioning of the rabbit nictitating membrane response: Effects of reinforcement schedule on response maintenance and resistance to extinction. *Animal Learning and Behavior*, 6:209–215. **(248, 249)**

Gibson, E. J. 1940. A systematic application of the concepts of generalization and differentiation to verbal learning. *Psychological Review*, 47:196–229. **(264)**

Gill, T. V., and Rumbaugh, D. M. 1974. Mastery of naming skills by a chimpanzee. *Journal of Human Evolution*, 3:483–492. **(349)**

Gillan, D. J., and Domjan, M. 1977. Taste-aversion conditioning with expected versus unexpected drug treatment. *Journal of Experimental Psychology: Animal Behavior Processes*, 3:297–309. **(163)**

Glanzer, M., and Cunitz, A. R. 1966. Two storage mechanisms in free recall. *Journal of Verbal Learning and Verbal Behavior*, 5:351–360. **(475)**

Glazer, H. I., and Weiss, J. M. 1976a. Long-term and transitory interference effects. *Journal of Experimental Psychology: Animal Behavior Processes*, 2:191–201. **(245)**

Glazer, H. I., and Weiss, J. M. 1976b. Long-term interference effect: An alternative to "learned helplessness." *Journal of Experimental Psychology: Animal Behavior Processes*, 2:202–213. **(245)**

Glenberg, A.; Smith, S.; and Green, C. 1977. Type I rehearsal: Maintenance and more. *Journal of Verbal Learning and Verbal Behavior*, 16:339–352. **(478)**

Glickman, S. E., and Schiff, B. B. 1967. A biological theory of reinforcement. *Psychological Review,* 74:81–109. **(28)**

Glucksberg, S., and Danks, J. H. 1975. *Experimental psycholinguistics.* New York: Wiley. **(336)**

Gogan, P. 1970. The startle and orienting reactions in man. A study of their characteristics and habituation. *Brain Research,* 18:117–135. **(50)**

Goggin, J., and Martin, E. 1970. Forced stimulus encoding and retroactive interference. *Journal of Experimental Psychology,* 84:131–136. **(266)**

Gold, R. M. 1973. Hypothalamic obesity: The myth of the ventromedial nucleus. *Science,* 182:448–450. **(224)**

Goldstein, A. G., and Chance, J. E. 1970. Visual recognition memory for complex configurations. *Perception and Psychophysics,* 9:237–241. **(465)**

Gollub, L. R. 1958. The chaining of fixed-interval schedules. Unpublished doctoral dissertation, Harvard University. **(173)**

Gollub, L. R. 1977. Conditioned reinforcement: Schedule effects. In W. K. Honig and J. E. R. Staddon (Eds.), *Handbook of operant behavior.* Englewood Cliffs, N.J.: Prentice-Hall. Pp. 288–312. **(176)**

Goodman, N. 1972. On likeness of meaning. In N. Goodman (Ed.), *Problems and projects.* New York: Bobbs-Merrill. **(281)**

Gormezano, I. 1966. Classical conditioning. In J. B. Sidowski (Ed.), *Experimental methods and instrumentation in psychology.* New York: McGraw-Hill. Pp. 385–420. **(89, 92, 95)**

Gormezano, I. 1972. Investigations of defense and reward conditioning in the rabbit. In A. H. Black and W. F. Prokasy (Eds.), *Classical conditioning II: Current research and theory.* Englewood Cliffs, N.J.: Prentice-Hall. Pp. 151–181. **(95, 100)**

Gormezano, I., and Coleman, S. R. 1973. The law of effect and CR contingent modification of the UCS. *Conditional Reflex,* 8:41–56. **(111)**

Gormezano, I., and Kehoe, E. J. 1975. Classical conditioning: Some methodological and conceptual issues. In W. K. Estes (Ed.), *Handbook of learning and cognitive processes,* Vol. 2. Hillsdale, N.J.: Lawrence Erlbaum Associates. Pp. 143–179. **(90)**

Gormezano, I., and Moore, J. W. 1969. Classical conditioning. In M. H. Marx (Ed.), *Learning: Processes.* New York: Macmillan. **(89, 97, 100, 114)**

Gormezano, I.; Schneiderman, N.; Deaux, E. B.; and Fuentes, I. 1962. Nictitating membrane: Classical conditioning and extinction in the albino rabbit. *Science,* 138:33–34. **(95)**

Gottlieb, G. 1971. *Development of species identification.* Chicago: University of Chicago Press. **(67)**

Gottlieb, G. 1975. Development of species identification in ducklings: I. Nature of perceptual deficit caused by embryonic auditory deprivation. *Journal of Comparative and Physiological Psychology,* 89:387–399. **(67)**

Goudie, A. J.; Thornton, E. W.; and Wheeler, T. J. 1976. Drug pretreatment effects in drug induced taste aversions. *Psychopharmacology, Biochemistry, & Behavior,* 4:629–633. **(114)**

Gough, P. B. 1965. Grammatical transformation and speed of understanding. *Journal of Verbal Learning and Verbal Behavior,* 4:107–111. **(336)**

Graham, F. K. 1973. Habituation and dishabituation of responses innervated by the autonomic nervous system. In H. V. S. Peeke and M. J. Herz (Eds.), *Habituation,* Vol. I. New York: Academic Press. Pp. 163–218. **(58, 63)**

Grant, D. A. 1943. The pseudo-conditioned eyelid response. *Journal of Experimental Psychology,* 32:139–149. **(93)**

Grant, D. A. 1964. Classical and instrumental conditioning. In A. W. Melton (Ed.), *Categories of human learning.* New York: Academic Press. Pp. 1–31. **(89, 92)**

Grant, D. A. 1972. A preliminary model for processing information conveyed by verbal conditioned stimuli in classical conditioning. In A. H. Black and W. F. Prokasy (Eds.), *Classical conditioning II. Current research and theory.* Englewood Cliffs, N.J.: Prentice-Hall. **(90, 94)**

Grant, D. A., and Adams, J. K. 1944. "Alpha" conditioning in the eyelid. *Journal of Experimental Psychology,* 34:136–142. **(93)**

Grant, D. A., and Norris, E. B. 1947. Eyelid conditioning as influenced by the presence of sensitized Beta-responses. *Journal of Experimental Psychology, 37*:423–433. **(92)**

Gray, V. A. 1976. Stimulus control of differential-reinforcement-of-low-rate responding. *Journal of the Experimental Analysis of Behavior, 25*:199–207. **(183, 184)**

Green, D. M., and Swets, J. A. 1966. *Signal detection theory and psychophysics.* New York: Wiley. **(287)**

Greenberg, J. H., and Jenkins, J. J. 1964. Studies in the psychological correlates of the sound system of American English. *Word, 20*:157–177. **(321)**

Greene, J. 1972. *Psycholinguistics.* Baltimore: Penguin Books. **(335, 336)**

Greenfield, P. M., and Smith, J. H. 1976. *The structure of communication in early language development.* New York: Academic Press. **(365, 366)**

Greeno, J. G.; James, C. T.; and DaPolito, F. J. 1971. A cognitive interpretation of negative transfer and forgetting of paired associates. *Journal of Verbal Learning and Verbal Behavior, 10*:331–345. **(503)**

Greenspoon, J., and Ranyard, R. 1957. Stimulus conditions and retroactive inhibition. *Journal of Experimental Psychology, 53*:55–59. **(504)**

Grice, G. R. 1948. The relation of secondary reinforcement to delayed reward in visual discrimination learning. *Journal of Experimental Psychology, 38*:1–16. **(131)**

Grice, G. R., and Hunter, J. J. 1964. Stimulus intensity effects depend upon the type of experimental design. *Psychological Review, 71*:247–256. **(100)**

Grieve, R. 1973. Definiteness in discourse. *Language and Speech, 16*:365–372. **(402)**

Grings, W. W., and Lockhart, R. A. 1963. Effects of "anxiety-lessening" instructions and differential set development on the extinction of GSR. *Journal of Experimental Psychology, 66*:292–299. **(273)**

Groninger, L. D. 1971. Mnemonic imagery and forgetting. *Psychonomic Science, 23*:161–163. **(480)**

Grossman, L., and Eagle, M. 1970. Synonymity, antonymity, and association in false recognition responses. *Journal of Experimental Psychology, 83*:244–248. **(467)**

Grover, D. E.; Horton, D. L.; and Cunningham, M., Jr. 1967. Mediated facilitation and interference in a four-stage paradigm. *Journal of Verbal Learning and Verbal Behavior, 6*:42–46. **(271)**

Groves, P. M., and Thompson, R. F. 1970. Habituation: A dual-process theory. *Psychological Review, 77*:419–450. **(51, 58, 60, 64)**

Groves, P. M., and Thompson, R. F. 1973. A dual-process theory of habituation: Neural mechanisms. In H. V. S. Peeke and M. J. Herz (Eds.), *Habituation,* Vol. II. New York: Academic Press. Pp. 175–206. **(64)**

Grunenberg, M. M. 1970. A dichotomous theory of memory—Unproved and unprovable? *Acta Psychologica, 34*:489–496. **(477)**

Guess, D. A. 1969. A functional analysis of receptive language and productive speech. *Journal of Applied Behavior Analysis, 2*:55–64. **(405)**

Guthrie, E. R. 1935. *The psychology of learning.* New York: Harper & Row. **(120, 187, 206, 228)**

Guttman, N., and Kalish, H. I. 1956. Discriminability and stimulus generalization. *Journal of Experimental Psychology, 51*:79–88. **(177, 178)**

Gynther, M. D. 1957. Differential eyelid conditioning as a function of stimulus similarity and strength of response to the CS. *Journal of Experimental Psychology, 53*:408–416. **(191)**

Haber, R. N. 1978. Visual perception. In Mark R. Rosenweig and Lyman W. Porter (Eds.), *Annual Review of Psychology, 29*:31–59. **(430)**

Haber, R. N., and Hershenson, M. 1973. *The psychology of visual perception.* New York: Holt, Rinehart and Winston. **(422)**

Hagen, J. W., and Stanovich, K. G. 1977. Memory: Strategies of acquisition. In Robert V. Kail, Jr. and John W. Hagen (Eds.), *Perspectives on the development of memory and cognition.* Hillsdale, N.J.: Lawrence Erlbaum. Pp. 89–112. **(444, 447)**

Hakuta, K. 1976. A case study of a Japanese child learning English. *Language Learning, 26*:321–351. **(394)**

Hall, J. F. 1951. Studies in secondary reinforcement: I. Secondary reinforcement as a function of the frequency of primary reinforcement. *Journal of Comparative and Physiological Psychology*, 44:246–251. **(172)**

Hall, J. F. 1954. Learning as a function of word frequency. *American Journal of Psychology*, 67:138–140. **(508)**

Hall, J. F. 1971. *Verbal learning and retention*. Philadelphia: Lippincott. **(214)**

Hall, J. F. 1976. *Classical conditioning and instrumental learning: A contemporary approach*. Philadelphia: Lippincott. **(133)**

Halle, M., and Stevens, K. N. 1959. Analysis by synthesis. In W. Wathen-Dunn and L. E. Wood (Eds.), *Proceedings of the Seminar on Speech Comprehension and Processing*. Bedford, Mass.: Air Force Cambridge Research Laboratories. **(432)**

Halliday, M. A. K. 1975. *Learning how to mean: Explorations in the development of language*. London: Edward Arnold. **(364)**

Halmi, K. A.; Powers, P.; and Cunningham, S. 1975. Treatment of anorexia nervosa with behavior modification. *Archives of General Psychiatry*, 32:93–96. **(39)**

Halpern, J., and Poon, L. 1970. Human partial reinforcement extinction effects: An information-processing development from Capaldi's sequential theory. *Journal of Experimental Psychology Monograph*, 89:201–227. **(254)**

Hamilton, C. E. 1950. The relationship between length of interval separating two learning tasks and performance on the second task. *Journal of Experimental Psychology*, 40:423–438. **(252)**

Hamilton, R. J. 1943. Retroactive facilitation as a function of degree of generalization between tasks. *Journal of Experimental Psychology*, 32:353–376. **(264)**

Hamilton, W. 1964. The genetical theory of social behavior, I, II. *Journal of Theoretical Biology*, 7:1–52. **(38)**

Hamilton, W. D. 1971. Selection of selfish and altruistic behavior in some extreme models. In J. F. Eisenberg and W. S. Dillon (Eds.), *Man and beast: Comparative social behavior*. Washington, D.C.: Smithsonian Institution Press. Pp. 57–91. **(65)**

Hanby, J. P. 1972. The sociosexual nature of mounting and related behaviors in a confined troop of Japanese macaques (*Macaca fuscata*). Ph.D. thesis, University of Chicago. **(68)**

Hanson, E. W. 1966. The development of maternal and infant behavior in the rhesus monkey. *Behaviour*, 27:109–149. **(70)**

Hanson, H. M. 1959. Effects of discrimination training on stimulus generalization. *Journal of Experimental Psychology*, 58:321–334. **(192)**

Harlow, H. F. 1949. The formation of learning sets. *Psychological Review*, 56:51–65. **(301)**

Harlow, H. F. 1950. Analysis of discrimination learning by monkeys. *Journal of Experimental Psychology*, 40:26–39. **(301, 302)**

Harlow, H. F. 1959. Learning set and error factor theory. In S. Koch (Ed.), *Psychology: A study of a science*. New York: McGraw-Hill. **(302, 303)**

Harlow, H. F. 1962. The heterosexual affectional system in monkeys. *American Psychologist*, 17:1–9. **(67, 68, 70)**

Harlow, H. F., and Harlow, M. K. 1965. The affectional systems. In A. M. Schrier, H. F. Harlow, and F. Stollnitz (Eds.), *Behavior of nonhuman primates*, Vol. 2. New York: Academic Press. **(70)**

Harlow, H. F., and Harlow, M. K. 1969. Effects of various mother-infant relationships on rhesus monkey behaviors. In B. M. Foss (Eds.), *Determinants of infant behavior*, Vol. 4. London: Methuen. **(68)**

Harlow, H. F., and Suomi, S. J. 1971a. From thought to therapy: Lessons from a primate laboratory. *American Scientist*, 59:538–549. **(68)**

Harlow, H. F., and Suomi, S. J. 1971b. Social recovery by isolation-reared monkeys. *Proceedings of the National Academy of Sciences*, 68:1534–1538. **(68)**

Harris, J. D. 1943. Habituatory response decrement in the intact organism. *Psychological Bulletin*, 40:385–422. **(49, 50)**

Harter, S. 1965. Discrimination learning set in children as a function of IQ and MA. *Journal of Experimental Child Psychology*, 2:31–43. **(298)**

Harvey, C. B., and Wickens, D. D. 1971. Effect of instructions on responsiveness to the CS and to the UCS in GSR conditioning. *Journal of Experimental Psychology*, 87:137–140. **(273)**

Harvey, C. B., and Wickens, D. D. 1973. Effects of cognitive control processes on the classically conditioned galvanic skin response. *Journal of Experimental Psychology,* 101:278–282. **(273)**

Hatton, H. M.; Berg, W. K.; and Graham, F. K. 1970. Effects of acoustic rise time on heart rate response. *Psychonomic Science,* 19:101–103. **(46)**

Haviland, S. E., and Clark, H. H. 1974. What's new? Acquiring new information as a process in comprehension. *Journal of Verbal Learning and Verbal Behavior,* 13:512–521. **(391)**

Hawkes, L., and Shimp, C. P. 1975. Reinforcement of behavioral patterns: Shaping a scallop. *Journal of the Experimental Analysis of Behavior,* 23:3–16. **(240)**

Hayes, C. 1951. *The ape in our house.* New York: Harper & Row. **(347)**

Healy, A. F. 1974. Separating item from order information in short-term memory. *Journal of Verbal Learning and Verbal Behavior,* 13:644–655. **(447)**

Healy, A. F., and Cutting, J. E. 1976. Units of speech perception: Phoneme and syllable. *Journal of Verbal Learning and Verbal Behavior,* 15:73–84. **(324)**

Hearst, E. 1969. Excitation, inhibition, and discrimination learning. In N. J. Mackintosh and W. K. Honig (Eds.), *Fundamental issues in associative learning.* Halifax: Dalhousie University Press. Pp. 1–41. **(198)**

Hearst, E. 1975a. Pavlovian conditioning and directed movements. In G. Bower (Ed.), *The psychology of learning and motivation,* Vol. 9. New York: Academic Press. Pp. 215–262. **(162)**

Hearst, E. 1975b. The classical-instrumental distinction: Reflexes, voluntary behavior, and categories of associative learning. In W. K. Estes (Ed.), *Handbook of learning and cognitive processes,* Vol. 2. Hillsdale, N.J.: Lawrence Erlbaum Associates. Pp. 181–223. **(162)**

Hearst, E., and Jenkins, H. M. 1974. *Sign-tracking: The stimulus-reinforcer relation and directed action.* Austin, Texas: The Psychonomic Society. **(162, 193)**

Hearst, E.; Besley, S.; and Farthing, G. W. 1970. Inhibition and stimulus control of operant behavior. *Journal of the Experimental Analysis of Behavior* 14:373–409. **(177)**

Heath, R. G., and Mickle, W. A. 1960. Evaluation of seven years' experience with depth electrode studies in human subjects. In E. R. Ramey and D. S. O'Doherty (Eds.), *Electrical studies on the unanesthetized brain.* New York: Harper & Row. **(230)**

Hebb, D. O. 1961. Distinctive features of learning in the higher animal. In J. F. Delafresnaye (Ed.), *Brain mechanisms and learning.* London: Oxford University Press. **(475, 513)**

Hefferline, R. F., and Bruno, L. J. J. 1971. The psychophysiology of private events. In A. Jacobs and L. B. Sachs (Eds.), *The psychology of private events.* New York: Academic Press. Pp. 163–192. **(275)**

Hefferline, R. F.; Bruno, L. J.; and Davidowitz, J. 1971. Feedback control of covert behavior. In K. J. Connolly (Ed.), *Mechanisms of motor skill development.* New York: Academic Press. **(275, 276)**

Hefferline, R. F.; Kennan, B.; and Harford, R. A. 1959. Escape and avoidance conditioning in human subjects with and without their observation of the response. *Science,* 130:1338–1339. **(275)**

Heidbreder, E. 1946. The attainment of concepts: I. Terminology and methodology. *Journal of General Psychology,* 35:173–189. **(282, 298)**

Heider, E. R. 1971. "Focal" color areas and the development of color names. *Developmental Psychology,* 4:447–455. **(397)**

Heider, E. R. 1972. Universals in color naming and memory. *Journal of Experimental Psychology,* 93:10–20. **(397)**

Hein, A., and Diamond, R. M. 1972. Locomotor space as a prerequisite for acquiring visually guided reaching in kitten. *Journal of Comparative and Physiological Psychology,* 81:394–398. **(155)**

Heinemann, E. G., and Rudolph, R. L. 1963. The effect of discrimination training on the gradient of stimulus generalization. *American Journal of Psychology,* 76:653–658. **(180)**

Hellyer, S. 1962. Supplementary report: Frequency of stimulus presentation and short-term decrement in recall. *Journal of Experimental Psychology,* 64:650. **(475)**

Hemmes, N. 1973. Behavioral contrast in pigeons depends upon the operant. *Journal of Comparative and Physiological Psychology, 85*:171–178. **(193)**

Hendry, D. P. (Ed.) 1969. *Conditioned reinforcement.* Homewood, Ill.: Dorsey Press. **(83, 176)**

Herbert, J. A., and Krantz, D. L. 1965. Transposition: A re-evaluation. *Psychological Bulletin, 63*:244–257. **(218)**

Herman, L., and Arbeit, W. R. 1973. Stimulus control and auditory discrimination learning sets in the bottlenose dolphin. *Journal of the Experimental Analysis of Behavior, 19*:379–394. **(303)**

Herriot, P. 1969. The comprehension of active and passive sentences as a function of pragmatic expectations. *Journal of Verbal Learning and Verbal Behavior, 8*:166–169. **(337)**

Herrnstein, R. J. 1961. Relative and absolute strength of response as a function of frequency of reinforcement. *Journal of the Experimental Analysis of Behavior, 4*:267–272. **(148)**

Herrnstein, R. J. 1966. Superstition: A corollary of the principles of operant conditioning. In W. K. Honig (Ed.), *Operant behavior: Areas of research and application.* Englewood Cliffs, N.J.: Prentice-Hall. Pp. 33–51. **(166)**

Herrnstein, R. J. 1969. Method and theory in the study of avoidance. *Psychological Review, 76*:49–69. **(208)**

Herrnstein, R. J. 1970. On the law of effect. *Journal of the Experimental Analysis of Behavior, 13*:243–266. **(146, 147)**

Herrnstein, R. J., and Hineline, P. N. 1966. Negative reinforcement as shock-frequency reduction. *Journal of the Experimental Analysis of Behavior, 9*:421–430. **(207)**

Herrnstein, R. J., and Loveland, D. H. 1964. Complex visual concept in the pigeon. *Science, 146*:549–551. **(282)**

Herrnstein, R. J.; Loveland, D. H.; and Cable, C. 1976. Natural concepts in pigeons. *Journal of Experimental Psychology: Animal Behavior Processes, 2*:285–302. **(282)**

Hess, E. H. 1956. Natural preferences of chicks and ducks for objects of different colors. *Psychological Reports, 2*:477–483. **(178)**

Hess, W. R. 1956. *Hypothalmus and thalamus documentary pictures.* Stuttgart: Thienne. **(230)**

Hewes, G. W. 1977. Language origin theories. In D. Rumbaugh (Ed.), *Language learning by a chimpanzee. The Lana Project.* New York: Academic Press. Pp. 3–54. **(310, 356)**

Hickis, C. F.; Robles, L.; and Thomas, D. R. 1977. Contextual stimuli and memory retrieval in pigeons. *Animal Learning and Behavior, 5*:161–168. **(204)**

Hilgard, E. R., and Bower, G. H. 1966. *Theories of Learning.* 3rd ed. Englewood Cliffs, N.J.: Prentice-Hall. **(38, 411, 412)**

Hilgard, E. R., and Bower, G. H. 1975. *Theories of learning,* 4th ed. Englewood Cliffs, N.J.: Prentice-Hall. **(38)**

Hill, F. A. 1967. Effects of instructions and subject's need for approval on the conditioned galvanic skin response. *Journal of Experimental Psychology, 73*:461–467. **(273)**

Hinde, R. A. 1959. Behaviour and speciation in birds and lower vertebrates. *Biological Review, 34*:85–128. **(71)**

Hinde, R. A. 1966. *Animal behavior: A synthesis of ethology and comparative psychology.* New York: McGraw-Hill. **(49)**

Hinde, R. A. 1970. Behavioural habituation. In G. Horn and R. A. Hinde. *Short-term changes in neural activity and behaviour.* New York: Cambridge University Press. **(54, 58)**

Hinde, R. A. 1974. *Biological basis of human social behaviour.* New York: McGraw-Hill. **(65, 70, 72, 229)**

Hinde, R. A., and Stevenson-Hinde, J. (Eds.) 1973. *Constraints on learning: Limitations and predispositions.* New York: Academic Press. **(43, 162)**

Hinde, R. A., and White, L. E. 1974. Dynamics of a relationship: Rhesus mother-infant ventro-ventral contact. *Journal of Comparative and Physiological Psychology, 86*:8–23. **(70)**

Hinde, R. A.; Rowell, T. E.; and Spencer-Booth, Y. 1964. Behaviour of socially living rhesus monkeys in their first six months. *Proceedings of the Zoological Society of London, 143*:609-649. **(69)**

Hineline, P. N. 1970. Negative reinforcement without shock reduction. *Journal of the Experimental Analysis of Behavior. 14*:259-268. **(208)**

Hintzman, D. L. 1967. Articulatory coding in short-term memory. *Journal of Verbal Learning and Verbal Behavior, 6*:312-316. **(443)**

Hintzman, D. L. 1974. Theoretical implications of the spacing effect. In R. L. Solso (Ed.), *Theories in cognitive psychology: The Loyola Symposium.* Potomac, Md.; Earlbaum. **(477)**

Hintzman, D. L. 1976. Repetition and memory. In G. H. Bower (Ed.), *The psychology of learning and motivation,* Vol. 10. New York: Academic Press. Pp. 47-93. **(475)**

Hirst, W.; Neisser, U.; and Spelke, E. 1978. Divided attention. *Human Nature, 1*:54-61. **(435)**

Hockett, C. F. 1958. *A course in modern linguistics.* New York: Macmillan. **(316)**

Hodos, W., and Campbell, C. B. 1969. Scala naturae: Why there is no theory in comparative psychology. *Psychological Review, 76*:337-350. **(17, 303)**

Hoebel, B. G. 1968. Inhibition and disinhibition of self-stimulation and feeding: Hypothalamic control and post-ingestional factors. *Journal of Comparative and Psychological Psychology, 66*:89-100. **(230)**

Hoffman, H. S., and Ratner, A. M. 1973. A reinforcement model of imprinting: Implications for socialization in monkeys and men. *Psychological Review, 80*:527-544. **(66)**

Hoffman, H. S., and Searle, J. L. 1968. Acoustic and temporal factors in the evocation of startle. *Journal of the Acoustical Society of America, 43*:269-282. **(49)**

Hoffman, H. S., and Solomon, R. L. 1974. An opponent process theory of motivation: III. Some affective dynamics in imprinting. *Learning and Motivation, 5*:149-164. **(224)**

Hoffman, H. S.; Barrett, J.; Ratner, A. M.; and Singer, P. 1972. Conditioned suppression of distress calls in imprinted ducklings. *Journal of Comparative and Physiological Psychology, 80*:357-364. **(81)**

Hoffman, H. S.; Searle, J. L.; Toffey, S.; and Kozma, F., Jr. 1966. Behavioral control by an imprinted stimulus. *Journal of the Experimental Analysis of Behavior, 9*:177-189. **(81)**

Hogan, J. A. 1967. Fighting and reinforcement in the Siamese fighting fish. (*Betta splendous*). *Journal of Comparative and Physiological Psychology, 64*:356-359. **(81)**

Holland, P. C. 1977. Conditioned stimulus as a determinant of the form of the Pavolvian conditioned response. *Journal of Experimental Psychology: Animal Behavior Processes, 3*:77-104. **(112)**

Hollard, V., and Davison, M. C. 1971. Preference for qualitatively different reinforcers. *Journal of the Experimental Analysis of Behavior, 16*:375-380. **(230)**

Holstein, S. B., and Hundt, A. G. 1965. Reinforcement of intracranial self-stimulation by licking. *Psychonomic Science, 3*:17-18. **(230)**

Holz, W. C., and Azrin, N. H. 1961. Discriminative properties of punishment. *Journal of the Experimental Analysis of Behavior, 4*:225-232. **(169)**

Homa, D. 1978. Abstraction of ill-defined form. *Journal of Experimental Psychology: Human Learning and Memory, 4*:407-416. **(296)**

Homa, D., and Vosburgh, R. 1976. Category breadth and the abstraction of prototypical information. *Journal of Experimental Psychology: Human Learning and Memory, 2*:322-330. **(296)**

Homme, L. E.; DeBaca, P. C.; Devine, J. V.; Steinhorst, R.; and Rickert, E. J. 1963. Use of the Premack principle in controlling the behavior of nursery school children. *Journal of the Experimental Analysis of Behavior, 6*:544. **(144)**

Honig, W. K. 1962. Prediction of preference, transposition, and transposition-reversal from the generalization gradient. *Journal of Experimental Psychology, 64*:239-248. **(196, 198)**

Honig, W. K. 1965. Discrimination, generalization, and transfer on the basis of stimulus differences. In D. I. Mostofsky (Ed.), *Stimulus generalization.* Stanford, Calif.: Stanford University Press. **(199)**

Honig, W. K. 1969. Attentional factors governing stimulus control. In R. Gilbert and N. S.

Sutherland (Eds.), *Discrimination learning*. New York: Academic Press. Pp. 35–62. **(203)**

Honig, W. K. 1970. Attention and the modulation of stimulus control. In D. I. Mostofsky (Ed.), *Attention: Contemporary theory and analysis*. Englewood Cliffs, N.J.: Prentice-Hall. Pp. 193–238. **(190)**

Honig, W. K.; Boneau, C. A.; Burstein, K. R.; and Pennypacker, H. C. 1963. Positive and negative generalization gradients obtained after equivalent training conditions. *Journal of Comparative and Physiological Psychology*, 56:111–116. **(182, 183)**

Hoogland, R.; Morris, D.; and Tinbergen, N. 1957. The spines of sticklebacks (*Gasterosteus* and *Pygosteus*) as means of defense against predators (*Perca* and *Esox*). *Behaviour*, 10:205–236. **(71, 72)**

Hopf-Weichel, R. 1977. Reorganization in semantic memory: An interpretation of the facilitation effect. *Journal of Verbal Learning and Verbal Behavior*, 16:261–275. **(493)**

Horgan, D. 1978. The development of the full passive. *Journal of Child Language*, 5:65–80. **(389)**

Horlington, M. 1968. A method for measuring acoustic startle response latency and magnitude in rats: Detection of a single stimulus effect using latency measurements. *Physiology and Behavior*, 3:839–944. **(46, 47, 55)**

Horn, G. 1967. Neuronal mechanisms of habituation. *Nature*, 215:707–711. **(74)**

Horton, D. L., and Kjeldergaard, P. M. 1961. An experimental analysis of associative factors in mediated generalization. *Psychological Monographs*, 75:11 (No. 515). **(271, 411)**

Houston, J. P. 1964. S-R stimulus selection and strength of R-S association. *Journal of Experimental Psychology*, 68:563–566. **(264)**

Houston, J. P. 1966. Verbal transfer as a function of $S_T R_2$ and S_2-R_1 interlist similarity. *Journal of Experimental Psychology*, 71:222–235. **(264, 499)**

Hovland, C. I. 1952. A "communication analysis" of concept learning. *Psychological Review*, 59:461–472. **(293)**

Hovland, C. I., and Weiss, W. 1953. Transmission of information concerning concepts through positive and negative instances. *Journal of Experimental Psychology*, 45:165–182. **(294)**

Hubel, D. H., and Wiesel, T. N. 1962. Receptive fields, binocular interaction, and functional architecture in the cat's visual cortex. *Journal of Physiology*, 160:106–154. **(428)**

Hubel, D. H., and Wiesel, T. N. 1968. Receptive fields and functional architecture of monkey striate cortex. *Journal of Physiology*, 195:215–243. **(428)**

Hughes, J. 1975. Acquisition of a nonvocal "language" by aphasic children. *Cognition*, 3:41–55. **(393)**

Hull, C. L. 1920. Quantitative aspects of the evolution of concepts: An experimental study. *Psychological Monographs*, 28:1 (No. 123). **(192, 295)**

Hull, C. L. 1933. Differential habituation to internal stimuli in the albino rat. *Journal of Comparative Psychology*, 16:255–273. **(228)**

Hull, C. L. 1934. The concept of the habit-family hierarchy and maze learning. *Psychological Review*, 41:33–54. **(164)**

Hull, C. L. 1943. *Principles of behavior*. Englewood Cliffs, N.J.: Prentice-Hall. **(60, 84, 104, 120, 138, 156, 172, 177, 206, 255)**

Hull, C. L. 1952. *A behavior system*. New Haven: Yale University Press. **(302)**

Humphreys, L. G. 1939. The effect of random alternation of reinforcement on the acquisition and exinction of conditioned eyelid reactions. *Journal of Experimental Psychology*, 25:141–158. **(248, 249)**

Hunt, E. B. 1962. *Concept learning: An information processing problem*. New York: Wiley. **(292)**

Hunt, H. F., and Brady, J. V. 1955. Some effects of punishment and intercurrent "anxiety" on a simple operant. *Journal of Comparative and Physiological Psychology*, 48:305–310. **(108)**

Hunter, M. W., III, and Kamil, A. C. 1971. Object discrimination learning set and hypothesis behavior in the northern bluejay (*Cyanocitta cristata*). *Psychonomic Science*, 22:271–273. **(303)**

Hurlock, E. B. 1950. *Child development*. New York: McGraw-Hill. **(134)**

Hutchinson, R. R., and Emley, G. S. 1977. Electric shock produced drinking in the squirrel monkey. *Journal of the Experimental Analysis of Behavior, 28*:1–12. **(232)**

Hutchinson, R. R.; Renfrew, J. W.; and Young, G. A. 1971. Effects of long-term shock and associated stimuli on aggressive and manual response. *Journal of the Experimental Analysis of Behavior, 15*:141–166. **(250)**

Hutt, P. J. 1954. Rate of bar pressing as a function of quality and quantity of food reward. *Journal of Comparative and Physiological Psychology, 47*:235–239. **(133)**

Hyde, T. S., and Jenkins, J. J. 1973. Recall of words as a function of semantic, graphic, and syntactic orienting tasks. *Journal of Verbal Learning and Verbal Behavior, 12*:471–480. **(468, 469)**

Immelman, K. 1972. Sexual and other long-term aspects of imprinting in birds and other species. In D. S. Lehrman, R. A. Hinde, and E. Shaw (Eds.), *Advances in the study of behavior*, Vol. 4. New York: Academic Press. **(67)**

Ingram, D. 1971. Transitivity in child language. *Language, 47*:888–910. **(360)**

Ison, J. R., and Hammond, G. R. 1971. Modification of the startle reflex in the rat. *Journal of Comparative and Physiological Psychology, 75*:435–452. **(93)**

Ison, J. R., and Leonard, D. W. 1971. Effects of auditory stimuli on the nictitating membrane reflex of the rabbit (*Oryctolagus cuniculus*). *Journal of Comparative and Physiological Psychology, 75*:157–164. **(93)**

Ivanov-Smolensky, A. G. 1933. *Methods of investigation of conditioned reflexes in man*. (In Russian.) Moscow: Medqiz (Medical State Press). **(90)**

Jacoby, L. L. 1973. Test appropriate strategies in retention of categorized lists. *Journal of Verbal Learning and Verbal Behavior, 12*:675–687. **(477)**

Jacoby, L. L., and Bartz, W. H. 1972. Encoding processes and the negative recency effect. *Journal of Verbal Learning and Verbal Behavior, 11*:561–565. **(477, 488)**

Jakobson, R. 1968. *Child language, aphasia and phonological universals*. The Hague: Mouton Publishers. **(365, 408)**

Jakobson, R.; Fant, C.; and Halle, M. 1963. *Preliminaries to speech analysis: The distinctive features and their correlates*. Cambridge, Mass.: M.I.T. Press. **(315, 316)**

James, W. 1890. *The principles of psychology*. New York: Holt, Rinehart and Winston. **(80, 147, 202)**

James, W. 1902. *Varieties of religious experience*. New York: Macmillan. **(221)**

Jenkins, H. M. 1962. Resistance to extinction when partial reinforcement is followed by regular reinforcement. *Journal of Experimental Psychology, 64*:441–450. **(254)**

Jenkins, H. M. 1970. Sequential organization in schedules of reinforcement. In W. N. Schoenfeld (Ed.), *Theories of reinforcement schedules*. Englewood Cliffs, N.J.: Prentice-Hall. Pp. 63–109. **(240)**

Jenkins, H. M. 1977. Sensitivity of different response systems to stimulus-reinforcer and response-reinforcer relations. In H. Davis and H. M. B. Hurwitz (Eds.), *Operant Pavlovian interactions*. New York: Lawrence Ehrlbaum Association. Pp. 47–62. **(127, 162)**

Jenkins, H. M., and Harrison, R. H. 1960. Effect of discrimination training on auditory generalization. *Journal of Experimental Psychology, 59*:246–253. **(179, 180)**

Jenkins, H. M., and Harrison, R. H. 1962. Generalization gradients of inhibition following auditory discrimination learning. *Journal of the Experimental Analysis of Behavior, 5*:434–441. **(182)**

Jenkins, H. M., and Moore, B. R. 1973. The form of the auto-shaped response with food or water reinforcers. *Journal of the Experimental Analysis of Behavior. 20*:163–181. **(160)**

Jenkins, H. M., and Sainesbury, R. S. 1969. The development of stimulus control through differential reinforcement. In N. J. Mackintosh and W. K. Honig (Eds.), *Fundamental issues in associative learning*. Halifax, Nova Scotia: Dalhousie University Press. Pp. 123–161. **(189)**

Jenkins, J. G., and Dallenbach, K. H. 1924. Oblivescence during sleep and waking. *American Journal of Psychology, 35*:605–612. **(494)**

Jenkins, J. J. 1963. Mediated associations: Paradigms and situations. In C. N. Cofer and B. S. Musgrave (Eds.), *Verbal behavior and learning: Problems and processes.* New York: McGraw-Hill. **(271)**

Jenkins, W. O. 1950. A temporal gradient of derived reinforcement. *American Journal of Psychology,* 63:237–243. **(172)**

Jenkins, W. O., and Stanley, J. C., Jr. 1950. Partial reinforcement: A review and critique. *Psychological Bulletin,* 47:193–204. **(249)**

John, E. R. 1967. *Mechanisms of memory.* New York: Academic Press. **(28, 187)**

Johnson, D. F. 1970. Determiners of selective attention in the pigeon. *Journal of Comparative and Physiological Psychology,* 70:298–307. **(138, 202)**

Johnson, E. S. 1978. Validation of concept-learning strategies. *Journal of Experimental Psychology: General,* 107:237–265. **(299, 301)**

Johnson, H. J., and Schwartz, G. E. 1967. Suppression of GSR activity through operant reinforcement. *Journal of Experimental Psychology,* 75:307–312. **(274)**

Johnson, N. F. 1965a. Linguistic models and functional units of language behavior. In L. Rosenberg (Ed.), *Directions in psycholinguistics.* New York: Macmillan. **(333)**

Johnson, N. F. 1965b. The psychological reality of phrase structure rules. *Journal of Verbal Learning and Verbal Behavior.* 4:469–475. **(333)**

Johnson, N. F. 1968. Sequential verbal behavior. In T. R. Dixon and D. L. Horton (Eds.), *Verbal behavior and general behavior theory.* Englewood Cliffs, N.J.: Prentice-Hall. Pp. 421–450. **(334, 449)**

Johnston, J. C., and McClelland, J. L. 1973. Visual factors in word perception. *Perception and Psychophysics,* 14:365–370. **(431)**

Jonçich, G. 1968. *The sane positivists: A biography of Edward L. Thorndike.* Middletown, Conn.: Wesleyan University Press. **(38)**

Jung, J. 1963. Effects of response meaningfulness (m) on transfer of training under two different paradigms. *Journal of Experimental Psychology,* 65:377–384. **(264)**

Jusczyk, K. P.; Rosner, B.; Cutting, J.; Foard, C.; and Smith, L. 1977. Categorical perception of nonspeech sounds by two-month-old infants. *Perception and Psychophysics,* 21:50–54. **(321)**

Kachanoff, R.; Leveille, R.; McLelland, J. P.; and Wayner, M. J. 1973. Schedule induced behavior in humans. *Physiology and Behavior,* 11:395–398. **(232)**

Kahneman, D. 1968. Method, findings and theory in studies of visual masking. *Psychological Bulletin,* 70:404–425. **(423)**

Kalish, H. I. 1969. Stimulus generalization. In M. H. Marx (Ed.), *Learning: Processes.* Toronto, Ontario: Macmillan. Pp. 207–297. **(218)**

Kalish, H. I., and Haber, A. 1965. Prediction of discrimination from generalization following variations in deprivation level. *Journal of Comparative and Physiological Psychology,* 60:125–128. **(228)**

Kamin, L. J. 1956. The effects of termination of the CS and avoidance of the US on avoidance learning. *Journal of Comparative and Physiological Psychology,* 49:420–424. **(207)**

Kamin, L. J. 1957. The effects of termination of the CS and avoidance of the US on avoidance learning: An extention. *Canadian Journal of Psychology,* 11:48–56. **(207)**

Kamin, L. J. 1968. Attention-like processes in classical conditioning. In M. R. Jones (Ed.), *Miami symposium on the prediction of behavior: Aversive stimulation.* Miami: University of Miami Press. **(101, 103, 107)**

Kamin, L. J. 1969. Predictability, surprise, attention and conditioning. In B. A. Campbell and R. M. Church (Eds.), *Punishment and aversive behavior.* New York: Appleton-Century-Crofts. Pp 279–296. **(101, 103)**

Kamin, L. J., and Gaoini, S. J. 1974. Compound conditioned emotional response conditioning with differentially salient elements in rats. *Journal of Comparative and Physiological Psychology,* 87:591–597. **(202)**

Kamin, L. J.; Brimer, C. J.; and Black, A. N. 1963. Conditioned suppression as a monitor of fear of the CS in the course of avoidance training. *Journal of Comparative and Physiological Psychology,* 56:497–501. **(207)**

Kandel, E. R., and Spencer, W. A. 1968. Cellular neurophysiological approaches in the study of learning. *Physiological Reviews, 48*:65–134. **(62)**

Karen, R. L. 1974. *An introduction to behavior theory and its applications.* New York: Harper & Row. **(153)**

Katz, J. J., and Fodor, J. A. 1963. The structure of a semantic theory. *Language, 39*:170–210. **(339, 390)**

Kausler, D. H. 1974. *Psychology of verbal learning and memory.* New York: Academic Press. **(271)**

Kausler, D. H., and Kanoti, G. A. 1963. R-S learning and negative transfer effects with a mixed list. *Journal of Experimental Psychology, 65*:201–205. **(264)**

Kazdin, A. E. 1975. *Behavior modification in applied settings.* Homewood, Ill.: Dorsey Press. **(176)**

Kear, J. 1962. Food selection in finches with special reference to interspecific differences. *Proceedings of Zoological Society of London, 138*:163–204. **(71)**

Keehn, J. D. 1969. Consciousness, discrimination and the stimulus control of behavior. In R. M. Gilbert and N. S. Sutherland (Eds.), *Animal discrimination learning.* New York: Academic Press. Pp. 273–298. **(274)**

Keenan, J. M.; MacWhinney, B.; and Mayhew, D. 1977. Pragmatics in memory: A study of natural conversation. *Journal of Verbal Learning and Verbal Behavior, 16*:549–560. **(467)**

Kelleher, R. T. 1958. Fixed-ratio schedules of conditioned reinforcement with chimpanzees. *Journal of the Experimental Analysis of Behavior, 1*:87–102. **(175)**

Kelleher, R. T. 1966. Conditioned reinforcement in second-order schedules. *Journal of the Experimental Analysis of Behavior, 9*:475–485. **(173)**

Kelleher, R. T., and Gollub, L. R. 1962. A review of positive conditioned reinforcement. *Journal of the Experimental Analysis of Behavior,* Supplement 5:543–597. **(83, 147, 172, 176, 217)**

Kelleher, R. T., and Morse, W. H. 1968. Schedules using noxious stimuli: III. Responding maintained with response-produced electric shock. *Journal of the Experimental Analysis of Behavior, 11*:819–838. **(245)**

Keller, F. S., and Schoenfeld, W. N. 1950. *Principles of psychology.* Englewood Cliffs, N.J.: Prentice-Hall. **(172, 236, 279)**

Keller, J. V., and Gollub, L. R. 1977. Duration and rate of reinforcement as determinants of concurrent responding. *Journal of the Experimental Analysis of Behavior, 28*:145–153. **(147)**

Keller, R. J.; Ayres, J. J. B.; and Mahoney, W. J. 1977. Brief versus extended exposure to truly random control procedures. *Journal of Experimental Psychology: Animal Behavior Processes, 3*:53–65. **(166)**

Kellogg, R. T.; Robbins, D. W.; and Bourne, L. E., Jr. 1978. Memory for intratrial events in feature identification. *Journal of Experimental Psychology: Human Learning and Memory, 4*:256–265. **(307)**

Kellogg, W. N. 1968. Communication and language in the home-raised chimpanzee. *Science, 162*:423–427. **(347)**

Kendler, H. H. and Kendler, T. S. 1975. From discrimination learning to cognitive development: A neobehavioristic odyssey. In W. K. Estes (Ed.), *Handbook of learning and cognitive processes. Vol. I.* Hillsdale, N.J.: Lawrence Erlbaum Associates. Pp. 191–247. **(296)**

Kennedy, T. D. 1970. Verbal conditioning without awareness: The use of programmed reinforcement and recurring assessment of awareness. *Journal of Experimental Psychology, 84*:487–494. **(274)**

Kennedy, T. D. 1971. Reinforcement frequency, task characteristics, and interval of awareness assessment as factors in verbal conditioning without awareness. *Journal of Experimental Psychology, 88*:103–112. **(274)**

Keppel, G., and Underwood, B. J. 1962. Proactive inhibition in short-term retention of single items. *Journal of Verbal Learning and Verbal Behavior, 1*:153–161. **(453)**

Kessel, F. S. 1970. The role of syntax in children's comprehension from ages six to ten. *Monographs of the Society for Research in Child Development, 35*:No. 6(Serial No. 139). **(389)**

Kettlewell, N. M., and Papsdorf, J. D. 1971. A role for cutaneous afferents in classical conditioning in rabbits. *Journal of Comparative and Physiological Psychology*, 75:239–247. **(114)**

Kieras, D. 1978. Beyond pictures and words: Alternative information-processing models for imagery effects in verbal memory. *Psychological Bulletin*, 85:532–554. **(482, 484, 485, 486)**

Kiess, H. O. 1968. Effects of natural language mediators on short-term memory. *Journal of Experimental Psychology*, 77:7–13. **(479)**

Killeen, P. 1972. The matching law. *Journal of the Experimental Analysis of Behavior*, 17:489–495. **(144)**

Killeen, P. 1975. On the temporal control of behavior. *Psychological Review*, 82:89–115. **(39, 232)**

Killeen, P. R.; Hanson, S. J.; and Osborne, S. R. 1978. Arousal: its genesis and manifestation as response rate. *Psychological Review*, 85:571–581. **(233)**

Kimble, G. A. 1961. *Hilgard and Marquis' conditioning and learning*. Englewood Cliffs, N.J.: Prentice-Hall. **(89, 92, 97, 100)**

Kimmel, H. D., and Burns, R. A. 1975. Adaptational aspects of conditioning. In W. K. Estes (Ed.), *Handbook of learning and cognitive processes*, vol. 2. Hillsdale, N.J.: Ehrlenbaum. Pp. 99–142. **(164)**

Kimura, D. 1964. Left-right differences in the perception of melody. *Quarterly Journal of Experimental Psychology*, 14:355–358. **(392)**

Kimura, D. 1973. The asymmetry of the human brain. *Scientific American*, 228:70–78. **(392, 483)**

King, G. D. 1974. Wheel running in the rat induced by a fixed-time presentation of water. *Animal Learning and Behavior*, 2:325–328. **(232)**

Kinsbourne, M., and George, J. 1974. The mechanism of the word-frequency effect on recognition memory. *Journal of Verbal Learning and Verbal Behavior*, 13:63–69. **(508)**

Kinsbourne, M., and Smith, W. L. (Eds.). 1974. *Hemispheric disconnection and cerebral function*. Springfield, Ill.: Thomas. **(392)**

Kintsch, W. 1968. Recognition and free recall of organized lists. *Journal of Experimental Psychology*, 78:481–487. **(508)**

Kintsch, W. 1970. *Learning, memory and conceptual processes*. New York: Wiley. **(508)**

Kintsch, W. 1977. *Memory and cognition*. New York: Wiley. **(298, 440, 441, 464, 487, 509)**

Kintsch, W. 1978. More on recognition failure of recallable words: Implications for generation-recognition models. *Psychological Review*, 85:470–473. **(511)**

Kintsch, W., and van Dijk, T. A. 1978. Toward a model of text comprehension and production. *Psychological Review*, 85:363–394. **(343, 486)**

Klein, M., and Rilling, M. 1972. Effects of response-shock interval and shock intensity on free-operant avoidance responding in the pigeon. *Journal of the Experimental Analysis of Behavior*, 18:293–304. **(210)**

Klein, M., and Rilling, M. 1974. Generalization of free-operant avoidance behavior in pigeons. *Journal of the Experimental Analysis of Behavior*, 21:75–88. **(209)**

Klein, R. M. 1959. Intermittent primary reinforcement as a parameter of secondary reinforcement. *Journal of Experimental Psychology*, 58:423–427. **(174)**

Klima, E. S., and Bellugi, U. 1966. Syntactic regularities in the speech of children. In J. Lyons and R. J. Wales (Eds.), *Psycholinguistics papers*. Edinburgh: Edinburgh University Press. Pp. 183–208. **(388)**

Kohler, W. 1918. Nachweis einfacher Struktur funktionen beim Schimpansen und beim Haushuhn. *Abb. d. konigl Preuss. Ak. d. Wissen*, 2:1–101. Translated and condensed in W. D. Ellis (Ed.), *A source book of Gestalt psychology*. New York: Harcourt Brace Jovanovich, 1938. Pp. 217–227. **(196)**

Kohler, W. 1925. *The mentality of apes*. London: Routledge & Kegan. **(412)**

Kohler, W. 1941. On the nature of associations. *Proceedings of the American Philosophical Society*, 84:489–502. **(412)**

Kohn, M. 1951. Satiation of hunger from food injected directly into the stomach versus food ingested by mouth. *Journal of Comparative and Physiological Psychology*, 44:412–422. **(140)**

Kolers, P. A., and Ostry, D. J. 1974. Time course of loss of information regarding pattern analyzing operations. *Journal of Verbal Learning and Verbal Behavior,* 13:599–612. **(467)**

Konecni, V. J., and Slamecka, N. J. 1972. Awareness in verbal nonoperant conditioning: An approach through dichotic listening. *Journal of Experimental Psychology,* 94:248–254. **(434)**

Konorski, J. 1967. *Integrative activity of the brain.* Chicago: University of Chicago Press. **(90, 111, 114)**

Konorski, J., and Miller, S. 1937. On two types of conditioned reflex. *Journal of General Psychology,* 16:264–272. **(78, 120, 164, 166)**

Kopp, J., and Lane, H. L. 1968. Hue discrimination related to linguistic habits. *Psychonomic Science,* 11:61–62. **(321)**

Koppenaal, R. J. 1963. Time change in the strength of A-B, A-C lists; spontaneous recovery? *Journal of Verbal Learning and Verbal Behavior,* 2:310–319. **(499)**

Kosslyn, S. M. 1975. Information representation in visual images. *Cognitive Psychology,* 7:341–370. **(418)**

Kosslyn, S. M. 1978. Imagery and internal representation. In Eleanor Rosch and Barbara B. Lloyd (Eds.), *Cognition and Categorization.* Hillsdale, N.J.: Lawrence Erlbaum Associates. Pp. 217–257. **(418, 483, 484, 485)**

Kosslyn, S. M.; Ball, T. M.; and Reiser, B. J. 1978. Visual images preserve metric spatial information: Evidence from studies of image scanning. *Journal of Experimental Psychology: Human Perception and Performance,* 4:47–60. **(484)**

Kosslyn, S. M., and Pomerantz, J. R. 1977. Imagery, propositions, and the form of internal representations. *Cognitive Psychology,* 8:52–76. **(418)**

Kraeling, D. 1961. Analysis of amount of reward as a variable in learning. *Journal of Comparative and Physiological Psychology,* 54:560–565. **(133, 134, 150)**

Krashen, S. 1973. Lateralization, language learning and the critical period: Some new evidence. *Language Learning,* 23:63–74. **(393)**

Krashen, S. 1975. The critical period for language acquisition and its possible bases. *Developmental Psycholinguistics and Communication Disorders,* 263:1–287. **(393)**

Krasner, L., and Ullman, L. P. (Eds.) 1965. *Research in behavior modification.* New York: Holt, Rinehart, and Winston. **(247)**

Krechevsky, I. 1932. "Hypotheses" in rats. *Psychological Review,* 38:516–532. **(189)**

Krechevsky, I. 1933. Hereditary nature of "hypotheses." *Journal of Comparative Psychology,* 16:99–116. **(22)**

Kremer, E. F. 1978. The Rescorla-Wagner model: Losses in associative strength in compound conditioned stimuli. *Journal of Experimental Psychology: Animal Behavior Processes,* 4:22–36. **(202)**

Kroll, N. E. 1975. Visual short-term memory. In D. Deutsch and J. A. Deutsch (Eds.), *Short-term memory.* New York: Academic Press. **(444)**

Kuenne, M. R. 1946. Experimental investigation of the relation of language to transposition behavior in young children. *Journal of Experimental Psychology,* 36:471–490. **(198)**

Kuhl, P. K., and Miller, J. D. 1975. Speech perception by the chinchilla: Voiced-voiceless distinction in alveolar plosive consonants. *Science,* 190:69–72. **(321, 361)**

Kuo, Z. Y. 1967. *The dynamics of behavior development.* New York: Random House. **(43)**

Kupferman, I. 1975. Neurophysiology of learning. *Annual Review of Psychology,* 26:367–391. **(28)**

Lakoff, A. 1971. On generative semantics. In D. Steinberg and L. Jakobovits (Eds.), *Semantics.* London: Cambridge University Press. **(341)**

Landauer, T. K., and Meyer, D. E. 1972. Category size and semantic memory retrieval. *Journal of Verbal Learning and Verbal Behavior,* 11:539–549. **(490)**

Landis, C., and Hunt, W. A. 1939. *The startle pattern.* New York: Farrar, Straus & Giroux. New York: Johnson Reprint Corp., 1968, reprint ed. **(46, 50)**

Lashley, K. S., and Wade, M. 1946. The Pavlovian theory of generalization. *Psychological Review,* 53:72–87. **(177, 189)**

Lasky, R. E., and Kallio, K. D. 1978. Transformation rules in concept learning. *Memory and Cognition,* 6:491–495. **(285, 286)**

Laties, V. G.; Weiss, B.; and Weiss, A. B. 1969. Further observations on overt "mediating" behavior and the discrimination of time. *Journal of the Experimental Analysis of Behavior,* 12:43–57. **(146)**

Lawick-Goodall, J. van. 1968. The behavior of free-living chimpanzees in the Gombe Stream Reserve. *Animal Behavior Monographs,* 1:161–233. **(347)**

Lawrence, D. H. 1950. Acquired distinctiveness of cues: II. Selective association in a constant stimulus situation. *Journal of Experimental Psychology,* 40:175–188. **(155, 189, 203)**

Lawrence, D. H., and DeRivera, J. 1954. Evidence for relational transposition. *Journal of Comparative and Physiological Psychology,* 47:465–471. **(199)**

Lawry, J. A.; Lupo, V.; Overmeier, J. J.; Kochevar, J.; Hollis, K. L.; and Anderson, D. C. 1978. Interference with avoidance behavior as a function of qualitative properties of inescapable shock. *Animal Learning and Behavior,* 6:147–154. **(245)**

Leeper, R. 1935. The role of motivation in learning: A study of the phenomenon of differential motivational control of the utilization of habits. *Journal of Genetic Psychology,* 46:3–40. **(228)**

Lehner, G. F. J. 1941. A study of the extinction of unconditioned reflexes. *Journal of Experimental Psychology,* 29:435–456. **(55)**

Lehrman, D. S. 1970. Semantic and conceptual issues in the nature-nurture problem. In L. R. Aronson, E. Tobach, D. S. Lehrman, and J. S. Rosenblatt (Eds.), *Development and evolution in behavior.* San Francisco: Freeman. **(43)**

Lenneberg, E. H. 1962. Understanding language without ability to speak: A case report. *Journal of Abnormal and Social Psychology* 65:419–425. **(365, 405)**

Lenneberg, E. H. 1967. *Biological foundations of language.* New York: Wiley. **(310, 358, 359, 362, 363, 378, 379, 393)**

Lettvin, J. Y.; Maturana, H. R.; McCulloch, W. S.; and Pitts, W. H. 1959. What the frog's eye tells the frog's brain. *Proceedings of the Institute of Radio Engineers* 47:1940–1951. **(428)**

Levelt, W. J. M. 1970. Hierarchical clustering algorithm in the psychology of grammar. In G. B. Flores and W. J. M. Levelt (Eds.), *Advances in Psycholinguistcs.* Amsterdam: North Holland Publishing, 1970. Pp. 101–140. **(324)**

Leventhal, A. G., and Hirsch, H. V. 1975. Cortical effect of selective exposure to diagonal lines. *Science,* 190:902–904. **(428)**

Levine, M. 1959. A model of hypothesis behavior in discrimination learning set. *Psychological Review,* 66:353–366. **(303)**

Levine, M. 1965. Hypothesis behavior. In A. M. Schrier, H. F. Harlow, and F. Stollnitz (Eds.), *Behavior of nonhuman primates,* Vol. 1. New York: Academic Press. Pp. 97–127. **(303)**

Levine, M. 1966. Hypothesis behavior by humans during discrimination learning. *Journal of Experimental Psychology,* 71:331–338. **(289, 304, 305, 306, 307)**

Levine, M. 1969. Neo-noncontinuity theory. In G. H. Bower and J. T. Spence (Eds.), *The psychology of learning and motivation,* Vol. 3. New York: Academic Press. Pp. 101–134. **(304, 306)**

Levison, P. K., and Flynn, J. P. 1965. The objects attacked by cats during stimulation of the hypothalamus. *Animal Behaviour,* 13:217–220. **(230)**

Lewis, D. J. 1960. Partial reinforcement: A selective review of the literature since 1950. *Psychological Bulletin,* 57:1–28. **(249)**

Lewis, J. 1970. Semantic processing of unattended messages using dichotic listening. *Journal of Experimental Psychology,* 35:225–228. **(434)**

Lewis, Michael, and Rosenblum, Leonard A. (Eds.) 1977. *Interaction, conversation and the development of language.* New York: Wiley. **(380, 381)**

Liberman, A. M. 1970. The grammars of speech and language. *Cognitive Psychology,* 1:301–323. **(322)**

Liberman, A. M.; Cooper, F.; Shankweiler, D.; and Studdert-Kennedy, M. 1967. Perception of the speech code. *Psychological Review,* 74:431–459. **(321, 322, 323)**

Liberman, A. M.; Harris, K. S.; Hoffman, H. S.; and Griffith, B. C. 1957. The discrimination of speech sounds within and across phoneme boundaries. *Journal of Experimental Psychology,* 54:358–368. **(318, 319)**

Liberman, A. M.; Mattingly, I. G.; and Turvey, M. T. 1972. Language codes and memory codes. In A. W. Melton and E. Martin (Eds.), *Coding processes in human memory*. New York: Holt, Rinehart and Winston. Pp. 307–334. **(317, 322)**

Liddell, H. S.; James, W. T.; and Anderson, O. D. 1935. The comparative physiology of the conditioned motor reflex. *Comparative Psychology Monographs*, 11:1, Serial No. 51. **(112)**

Lieberman, P. 1973. On the evolution of language: A unified view. *Cognition*, 2:59–94. **(362)**

Lieberman, P. 1975. *On the origins of language: An introduction to the evolution of human speech*. New York: Macmillan. **(362)**

Light, L. L., and Carter-Sobell, L. 1970. Effects of changed semantic context on recognition memory. *Journal of Verbal Learning and Verbal Behavior*, 9:1–11. **(508)**

Light, L. L.; Kimble, G. A.; and Pellegrino, J. W. 1975. Comments on "Episodic memory: When recognition fails" by Watkins and Tulving. *Journal of Experimental Psychology: General*, 104(1):30–36. **(511)**

Limber, J. 1976. Unravelling competence, performance and pragmatics in the speech of young children. *Journal of Child Language*, 3:309–318. **(369)**

Linden, E. 1975. *Apes, men and language*. New York: Dutton. **(349, 350, 353, 354)**

Lisker, L., and Abramson, A. 1964. A cross-language study of voicing in initial stops: Acoustical measurements. *Word*, 20:384–422. **(356)**

Littman, R. A. 1958. Motives, history, and causes. In M. R. Jones (Eds.), *Nebraska symposium on motivation*. Lincoln, Neb.: University of Nebraska Press. Pp. 114–167. **(222)**

Lockard, J. S. 1963. Choice of a warning signal or no warning signal in an unavoidable shock situation. *Journal of Comparative and Physiological Psychology*, 56:526–530. **(115)**

Locke, J. L., and Locke, V. L. 1971. Deaf children's phonetic, visual, and dactylic coding in a grapheme recall task. *Journal of Experimental Psychology*, 89:142–146. **(444)**

Lockhart, R. S.; Craik, F. I. M.; and Jacoby, L. 1976. Depth of processing, recognition and recall. In J. Brown (Ed.), *Recognition and recall*. New York: Wiley. Pp. 75–102. **(469, 471, 488)**

Loess, H. 1964. Proactive inhibition in short-term memory. *Journal of Verbal Learning and Verbal Behavior*, 3:362–368. **(453)**

Loess, H., and Waugh, N. C. 1967. Short-term memory and intertrial interval. *Journal of Verbal Learning and Verbal Behavior*, 6:455–460. **(453)**

Loftus, G. R., and Patterson, K. K. 1975. Components of short-term proactive interference. *Journal of Verbal Learning and Verbal Behavior*, 14:105–121. **(455)**

Logan, F. A. 1956. A micromolar approach to behavior theory. *Psychological Review*, 63:63–73. **(154)**

Logan, F. A. 1960. *Incentive*. New Haven: Yale University Press. **(128, 129)**

Logan, F. A. 1965. Decision making by rats: Delay versus amount of reward. *Journal of Comparative and Physiological Psychology*, 59:1–12. **(149)**

Logan, F. A. 1966. Transfer of discrimination. *Journal of Experimental Psychology*, 71:616–618. **(254, 266)**

LoLordo, V. M. 1969. Positive conditioned reinforcement from aversive situations. *Psychological Bulletin*, 72:193–203. **(173)**

LoLordo, V. M., and Furrow, D. R. 1976. Control by the auditory or visual element of a compound discriminative stimulus: effects of feedback. *Journal of the Experimental Analysis of Behavior*, 25:251–256. **(162)**

Long, J. B.; McNamara, H. J.; and Gardner, J. O. 1965. Resistance to extinction after variable training as a function of multiple associations. *Journal of Comparative and Physiological Psychology*, 60:252–255. **(174)**

Lorenz, K. 1935. Der Kumpan in der Umwelt des Vogels. *Journal of Ornithology*, 83:137–413. **(66)**

Loucks, R. B. 1933. An appraisal of Pavlov's systematization of behavior from the experimental viewpoint. *Journal of Comparative Psychology*, 15:1–47. **(177)**

Lovaas, O. I. 1966. A program for the establishment of speech in psychotic children. In J. K. Wing (Ed.), *Childhood autism*. New York: Macmillan. **(404)**

Lovaas, O. I. 1976. *Language acquisition programs for nonlinguistic children.* New York: Irvington. **(268, 404)**

Lovaas, O. I.; Berberich, J. P.; Perloff, B. F.; and Schaeffer, B. 1966. Acquisition of imitative speech by schizophrenic children. *Science, 151:*705–707. **(268)**

Lowe, C. F., and Harzem, P. 1977. Species differences in temporal control of behavior. *Journal of the Experimental Analysis of Behavior, 28:*189–201. **(163)**

Lubow, R. E., and Moore, A. V. 1959. Latent inhibition: The effect of nonreinforced preexposure to the conditioned stimulus. *Journal of Comparative and Physiological Psychology, 52:*415–419. **(92)**

Lyons, J. 1968. *Introduction to theoretical linguistics.* Cambridge: Cambridge University Press. **(316)**

MacCorquodale, K. 1970. On Chomsky's review of Skinner's "Verbal Behavior." *Journal of the Experimental Analysis of Behavior, 13:*83–99. **(408)**

MacDonnell, M. F., and Flynn, J. P. 1966. Control of sensory fields by stimulation of hypothalamus. *Science, 152:*1406–1408. **(230)**

MacFarlane, D. A. 1930. The role of kinesthesis in maze learning. *University of California Publications in Psychology, 4:*277–305. **(155)**

MacKay, D. G. 1970. Spoonerisms: The structure of errors in the serial order of speech. *Neuropsychologia, 8:*323–350. **(321)**

MacKay, D. G. 1973. Aspects of the theory of comprehension, memory and attention. *Quarterly Journal of Experimental Psychology, 25:*22–40. **(434)**

Mackintosh, N. J. 1974. *The psychology of animal learning.* New York: Academic Press. **(83, 127, 132, 172, 209, 217, 218, 240, 248, 302)**

Mackintosh, N. J. 1975. A theory of attention: Variations in the associability of stimuli with reinforcement. *Psychological Review, 82:*276–298. **(189, 203)**

Mackintosh, N. J. 1977. Stimulus control: Attentional factors. In W. K. Honig and J. E. R. Staddon (Eds.), *Handbook of operant behavior.* Englewood Cliffs, N.J.: Prentice-Hall. Pp. 481–513. **(204)**

Mackintosh, N. J., and Honig, W. K. 1970. Blocking and enhancement of stimulus control in pigeons. *Journal of Comparative and Physiological Psychology, 73:*78–83. **(138)**

Mackintosh, N. J., and Little, L. 1970. An analysis of transfer along a continuum. *Canadian Journal of Psychology, 24:*362–369. **(266)**

Macnamara, J. 1972. Cognitive basis of language learning in infants. *Psychological Review, 79:*1–13. **(368, 399)**

Mahoney, K.; Van Wagenen, R. K.; and Meyerson, L. 1971. Toilet training of normal and retarded children. *Journal of Applied Behavior Analysis, 4:*173–181. **(266)**

Mahoney, W. J., and Ayres, J. J. B. 1976. One-trial simultaneous and backward fear conditioning as reflected in conditioned suppression of licking in rats. *Animal Learning and Behavior, 4:*357–362. **(97)**

Maier, S. F., and Seligman, M. E. P. 1976. Learned helplessness: Theory and evidence. *Journal of Experimental Psychology: General, 105:*3–46. **(245)**

Mandler, G. 1967. Organization and memory. In K. W. Spence and J. T. Spence (Eds.), *The psychology of learning and motivation,* Vol. 1. New York: Academic Press. **(473)**

Mandler, G. 1970. Words, lists and categories: An experimental view of organized memory. In J. L. Cowan (Ed.), *Studies in thought and language.* Tucson, Ariz.: University of Arizona Press. **(473)**

Mandler, G. 1972. Organization and recognition. In E. Tulving and W. Donaldson (Eds.), *Organization of memory.* New York: Academic Press. **(508, 511)**

Mandler, G., and Boeck, W. J. 1974. Retrieval processes in recognition. *Memory and Cognition, 2:*613–615. **(508, 511)**

Mandler, G., and Heinemann, S. H. 1956. Effect of over-learning of a verbal response on transfer of training. *Journal of Experimental Psychology, 51:*39–46. **(266)**

Mandler, G., and Pearlstone, Z. 1966. Free and constrained concept learning and subsequent recall. *Journal of Verbal Learning and Verbal Behavior, 5:*126–131. **(473)**

Marchant, H. G., III, and Moore, J. W. 1973. Blocking of the rabbit's conditioned nictitating membrane response in Kamin two-stage paradigm. *Journal of Experimental Psychology, 101:*155–158. **(102)**

Marcucella, H., and MacDonall, J. S. 1977. A molecular analysis of multiple schedule interactions: negative contrast. *Journal of the Experimental Analysis of Behavior,* 28:71–82. **(193)**

Marler, P. 1970a. Birdsong and speech development: Could there be parallels? *American Scientist,* 58:669–673. **(356)**

Marler, P. 1970b. A comparative approach to vocal development: Song learning in the white-crowned sparrow. *Journal of Comparative and Physiological Psychology,* 71:1–25. **(270)**

Marler, P. 1975. On the origin of speech from animal sounds. In J. F. Kavanagh and J. E. Cutting (Eds.), *The role of speech in language.* Cambridge, Mass.: M.I.T. Press. Pp. 11–37. **(356)**

Marler, P. 1976. On animal aggression. *American Psychologist,* 106:239–246. **(229)**

Marler, P. 1977. Sensory templates, vocal perception, and development. In Michael Lewis and Leonard A. Rosenblum (Eds.), *Interaction, Conversation, and the Development of Language.* New York: Wiley. Pp. 95–114. **(310)**

Marsh, G. 1969. An evaluation of three explanations for the transfer of discrimination effect. *Journal of Comparative and Physiological Psychology,* 68:268–275. **(266)**

Marsh, G. 1972. Prediction of peak shift in pigeons from gradients of excitation and inhibition. *Journal of Comparative and Physiological Psychology,* 81:262–266. **(198)**

Marsh, R.; Hoffman, H. S.; and Stitt, C. L. 1973. Temporal integration in the acoustic startle reflex of the rat. *Journal of Comparative and Physiological Psychology,* 82:507–511. **(47, 48)**

Marsh, R. R.; Hoffman, H. S.; and Stitt, C. L. 1976. Eyeblink inhibition by monaural and binaural stimulation: One ear is better than two. *Science,* 192:390–391. **(93)**

Martin, E. 1967. Relation between stimulus recognition and paired-associate learning. *Journal of Experimental Psychology,* 74:500–505. **(265)**

Martin, E. 1968. Stimulus meaningfulness and paired-associate transfer: An encoding variability hypothesis. *Psychological Review,* 75:421–441. **(266)**

Martin, E. 1971. Verbal learning theory and independent retrieval phenomena. *Psychological Review,* 78:314–332. **(503)**

Martin, E. 1972. Stimulus encoding in learning and transfer. In A. W. Melton and E. Martin (Eds.), *Coding processes in human memory.* New York: Holt, Rinehart and Winston. **(266)**

Martin, E. 1975. Generation-recognition theory and the encoding specificity principle. *Psychological Review,* 82:150–153. **(511)**

Martin, E., and Noreen, D. P. 1974. Serial learning: Identification of subjective subsequences. *Cognitive Psychology,* 6:421–435. **(216)**

Massaro, D. W. 1970. Preperceptual auditory images. *Journal of Experimental Psychology,* 85:411–417. **(419, 424)**

Massaro, D. W. 1971. Effect of masking tone duration on preperceptual auditory images. *Journal of Experimental Psychology,* 87:146–148. **(425)**

Massaro, D. W. 1972. Preperceptual images, processing time, and perceptual units in auditory perception. *Psychological Review,* 72:124–145. **(424, 425, 426)**

Massaro, D. W. 1974. Perceptual units in speech recognition. *Journal of Experimental Psychology,* 102:199–208. **(424)**

Massaro, D. W. 1975. Acoustic features in speech perception. In D. W. Massaro (Ed.), *Understanding language.* New York: Academic Press. Pp. 129–150. **(319, 323, 424, 425)**

Massaro, D. W. 1976. Auditory information processing. In W. K. Estes (Ed.), *Handbook of learning and cognitive processes.* Vol. 4. *Attention and memory.* Hillsdale, N.J.: Lawrence Erlbaum Associates. Pp. 275–320. **(323, 357, 424)**

Massaro, D. W.; Jones, R. D.; Lipscomb, C.; and Scholz, R. 1978. Role of prior knowledge on naming and lexical decisions with good and poor stimulus information. *Journal of Experimental Psychology: Human Learning and Memory,* 4:498–512. **(430)**

Matthews, W. A. 1968. Transformational complexity and short-term recall. *Language and Speech,* 11:120–128. **(336)**

Mattson, M., and Moore, J. W. 1964. Intertrial responding and CS intensity in classical eyelid conditioning. *Journal of Experimental Psychology,* 68:396–401. **(100)**

Mazuryk, G. F., and Lockhart, R. S. 1974. Negative recency and levels of processing in free recall. *Canadian Journal of Psychology, 28*:114–123. **(488)**

McCawley, J. 1968. The role of semantics in grammar. In E. Bach and R. Harms (Eds.), *Universals in linguistic theory*. New York: Holt, Rinehart and Winston. **(341, 376)**

McClearn, G. E. 1963. The inheritance of behavior. In L. J. Postman (Ed.), *Psychology in the making*. New York: Knopf. Pp. 144–252. **(20, 21, 22)**

McClearn, G. E., and DeFries, J. C. 1973. *Introduction to behavioral genetics*. San Francisco: Freeman. **(21)**

McClelland, D. C. 1961. *The achieving society*. Princeton: Van Nostrand. **(247)**

McClelland, D. C.; Atkinson, J. W.; Clark, R. A.; and Lowell, E. L. 1953. *The achievement motive*. Englewood Cliffs, N.J.: Prentice-Hall. **(247)**

McClelland, D. C., and McGowan, D. R. 1953. The effect of variable food reinforcement on the strength of a secondary reward. *Journal of Comparative and Physiological Psychology, 46*:80–86. **(174)**

McCloskey, M., and Glucksberg, S. 1978. Natural categories: Well-defined or fuzzy sets? *Memory and Cognition, 6*:462–472. **(283)**

McCormack, P. D., and Swenson, A. L. 1972. Recognition memory for common and rare words. *Journal of Experimental Psychology, 95*:72–77. **(508)**

McGeoch, J. A. 1942. *The psychology of human learning*. New York: McKay. **(409, 452, 494, 496)**

McGeoch, J. A., and Irion, A. L. 1952. *The psychology of human learning*, 2nd ed. New York: McKay. **(214)**

McKearney, J. W. 1969. Fixed-interval schedules of electric shock presentation: Extinction and recovery of performance under different shock intensities and fixed-interval durations. *Journal of the Experimental Analysis of Behavior, 12*:301–314. **(245)**

McLaughlin, B. 1978. *Second-language acquisition in childhood*. Hillsdale, N.J.: Lawrence Erlbaum Associates. **(394)**

McNamara, H. J., and Wike, E. L. 1958. The effects of irregular learning conditions upon the rate and permanence of learning. *Journal of Comparative and Physiological Psychology, 51*:363–366. **(174)**

McNeill, D. 1970. *The acquisition of language: The study of developmental psycholinguistics*. New York: Harper & Row. **(310, 378)**

McSweeney, F. K. 1978. Negative behavioral contrast on multiple treadle-press schedules. *Journal of the Experimental Analysis of Behavior, 29*:463–474. **(193)**

Medin, D. L., and Schaffer, M. M. 1978. Context theory of classification learning. *Psychological Review, 85*:207–238. **(298)**

Mednick, J. A., and Halpern, S. 1962. Ease of concept attainment as a function of associative rank. *Journal of Experimental Psychology, 64*:628–630. **(296)**

Mehler, J. 1963. Some effects of grammatical transformations on the recall of English sentences. *Journal of Verbal Learning and Verbal Behavior, 2*:250–262. **(336)**

Mellgren, R. L., and Ost, J. W. P. 1969. Transfer of Pavlovian differential conditioning to an operant discrimination. *Journal of Comparative and Physiological Psychology, 67*:390–394. **(266)**

Melton, A. W. 1963. Implications of short-term memory for a general theory of memory. *Journal of Verbal Learning and Verbal Behavior, 2*:1–21. **(409)**

Melton, A. W. 1967. Repetition and retrieval from memory. *Science, 158*:532. **(477)**

Melton, A. W. 1970. The situation with respect to the spacing of repetitions in memory. *Journal of Verbal Learning and Verbal Behavior, 9*:546–606. **(477)**

Melton, A. W., and Irwin, J. M. 1940. The influence of degree of interpolated learning on retroactive inhibition and the overt transfer of specific responses. *American Journal of Psychology, 53*:173–203. **(496, 497)**

Melvin, K. B., and Martin, R. C. 1966. Facilitative effects of two modes of punishment on resistance to extinction. *Journal of Comparative and Physiological Psychology, 62*:491–494. **(246)**

Mendelson, J., and Chorover, S. L. 1965. Lateral hypothalamic stimulation in satiated rats: T-maze learning for food. *Science, 149*:559–561. **(231)**

Merikle, P. M. 1968. Paired-associate transfer as a function of stimulus and response meaningfulness. *Psychological Reports, 22*:131–138. **(266)**

Mermelstein, P., and Eden, M. 1964. Experiments on computer recognition of connected handwritten words. *Information and Control, 7*:250–270. **(432)**

Mewhort, D. J., and Cornett, S. 1972. Scanning and the familiarity effect in tachistoscopic recognition. *Canadian Journal of Psychology, 26*:181–189. **(424, 437)**

Meyer, D. E., and Schvaneveldt, R. W. 1971. Facilitation in recognizing pairs of words: Evidence of a dependence between retrieval operations. *Journal of Experimental Psychology, 90*:227–234. **(431, 492)**

Meyer, D. E.; Schvaneveldt, R. W.; and Ruddy, M. G. 1974. Functions of phonemic and graphic codes in visual word recognition. *Memory and Cognition, 2*:309–321. **(431, 492)**

Michael, J. 1975. Positive and negative reinforcement, a distinction that is no longer necessary; or a better way to talk about bad things. *Behaviorism, 3*:33–44. **(164)**

Migler, B. 1964. Effects of averaging data during stimulus generalization. *Journal of the Experimental Analysis of Behavior, 7*:303–307. **(186, 187)**

Miles, C. G. 1970. Blocking the acquisition of control by an auditory stimulus with pretraining on brightness. *Psychonomic Science, 19*:133–134. **(138)**

Miles, R. C. 1956. The relative effectiveness of secondary reinforcers throughout deprivation and habit-strength parameters. *Journal of Comparative and Physiological Psychology, 49*:126–130. **(172, 174)**

Miller, G.; Galanter, E.; and Pribram, K. 1960. *Plans and the structure of behavior.* New York: Holt, Rinehart and Winston. **(357)**

Miller, G. A. 1956. The magical number seven plus or minus two: Some limits on our capacity for processing information. *Psychological Review, 63*:81–97. **(448)**

Miller, G. A. 1962a. *Psychology: The science of mental life.* New York: Harper & Row. **(88)**

Miller, G. A. 1962b. Some psychological studies of grammar. *American Psychologist, 17*:748–862. **(336, 411)**

Miller, G. A., and Johnson-Laird, P. N. 1976. *Language and perception.* Cambridge, Mass.: Harvard University Press. **(281)**

Miller, G. A., and McKean, K. O. 1964. A chronometric study of some relations between sentences. *Quarterly Journal of Experimental Psychology, 16*:297–308. **(336)**

Miller, G. A., and Nicely, P. 1955. An analysis of perceptual confusions among some English consonants. *Journal of the Acoustical Society of America, 27*:338–352. **(322, 429)**

Miller, G. A.; Heise, G. A.; and Lichten, W. 1951. The intelligibility of speech as a function of the context of the test materials. *Journal of Experimental Psychology, 41*:329–335. **(430)**

Miller, J. S., and Gollub, L. R. 1974. Adjunctive and operant bolt pecking in the pigeon. *Psychological Record, 24*:203–208. **(232)**

Miller, N. E. 1948. Studies of fear as an acquirable drive. *Journal of Experimental Psychology, 38*:89–101. **(207)**

Miller, N. E. 1963. Some reflections on the law of effect produce a new alternative to drive reduction. In M. R. Jones (Ed.), *Nebraska symposium on motivation.* Lincoln, Neb.: University of Nebraska Press. **(139, 140)**

Miller, N. E. 1969. Learning of visceral and glandular responses. *Science, 163*:434–443. **(164)**

Miller, N. E. 1978. Biofeedback and visceral learning. *Annual Review of Psychology, 29*:373–404. **(164)**

Miller, N. E., and Carmona, A. 1967. Modification of a visceral response, salivation in thirsty dogs, by instrumental conditioning with water reward. *Journal of Comparative and Physiological Psychology, 63*:1–6. **(161)**

Miller, N. E., and DiCara, L. 1967. Instrumental learning of heart-rate changes in curarized rats: Shaping and specificity to discriminative stimulus. *Journal of Comparative and Psychological Psychology, 63*:12–19. **(164)**

Miller, N. E., and Dollard, J. C. 1941. *Special learning and imitation.* New Haven: Yale University Press. **(139, 247)**

Miller, N. E., and Dworkin, B. R. 1974. Visceral learning: Recent difficulties with curarized rats and significant problems for human research. In P. A. Obrist, A. H. Black,

J. Brener, and L. V. DiCara (Eds.), *Cardiovascular psychophysiology: Current issues in response mechanisms, biofeedback, and methodology*. Chicago: Aldine. **(164)**

Miller, N. E., and Kessen, M. L. 1952. Reward effects of food by stomach fistula compared with those of food via mouth. *Journal of Comparative and Physiological Psychology, 45*:555–564. **(140)**

Milner, B. 1968. Disorders of memory after brain lesions in man. *Neuropsychologia, 6*:175–179. **(483)**

Missakian, E. A. 1969. Reproductive behavior of socially deprived rhesus monkeys. *Journal of Comparative and Physiological Psychology, 69*:403–407. **(67)**

Mitchell, D.; Kirschbaum, E. H.; and Perry, R. L. 1975. Effects of neophobia and habituation on the poison-induced avoidance of exteroceptive stimuli in the rat. *Journal of Experimental Psychology: Animal Behavior Processes, 104*:47–55. **(113)**

Modigliani, V., and Seamon, J. G. 1974. Transfer of information from short-term to long-term memory. *Journal of Experimental Psychology, 102*:768–772. **(477)**

Moeser, S. D. 1975. Iconic factors and language word order. *Journal of Verbal Learning and Verbal Behavior, 14*:43–55. **(397, 399)**

Moeser, S. D., and Bregman, A. S. 1972. The role of reference in the acquisition of a minature artificial language. *Journal of Verbal Learning and Verbal Behavior, 11*:759–769. **(397, 398)**

Moeser, S. D., and Bregman, A. S. 1973. Imagery and language acquisition. *Journal of Verbal Learning and Verbal Behavior, 12*:91–98. **(397)**

Moeser, S. D., and Olson, J. 1974. The role of reference in children's acquisition of a miniature artificial language. *Journal of Experimental Child Psychology, 17*:204–218. **(397, 399)**

Molfese, D. L.; Nunez, V.; Seibert, S. M.; and Ramanaiah, N. V. 1976. Cerebral asymmetry: Changes in factors affecting its development. *Annals of the New York Academy of Science, 280*:821–833. **(393)**

Moltz, H. 1963. Imprinting: An epigenetic approach. *Psychological Review, 70*:123–138. **(66)**

Montague, W. E. 1972. Elaborative strategies in verbal learning and memory. In G. A. Bower (Ed.), *The psychology of learning and motivation*, Vol. 6. New York: Academic Press. Pp. 225–302. **(271)**

Montague, W. E.; Adams, J. A.; and Kiess, H. O. 1966. Forgetting and natural language mediation. *Journal of Experimental Psychology, 72*:829–833. **(478, 479)**

Moore, B. R. 1973. The role of directed Pavlovian reactions in simple instrumental learning in the pigeon. In R. A. Hinde and J. Stevenson-Hinde (Eds.), *Constraints on learning*. New York: Academic Press. Pp. 159–186. **(160)**

Moore, J. W. 1972. Stimulus control: Studies of auditory generalization in rabbits. In A. H. Black and W. F. Prokasy (Eds.), *Classical conditioning II: Current research and theory*. Englewood Cliffs, N.J.: Prentice-Hall. Pp. 206–230. **(190, 191)**

Moore, J. W. 1978. Brain processes and conditioning. In A. Dickinson and R. A. Boakes (Eds.), *Associative mechanisms in conditioning: A memorial volume for Jerzy Konorski*. Hillsdale, N.J.: Lawrence Erlbaum Associates. **(104)**

Moore, J. W., and Gormezano, I. 1961. Yoked comparisons of instrumental and classical eyelid conditioning. *Journal of Experimental Psychology, 62*:552–559. **(126)**

Moore, T. E. (Ed.) 1973. *Cognitive development and the acquisition of language*. New York: Academic Press. **(366)**

Moorehead, A. 1969. *Darwin and the Beagle*. London: Hamish Hamilton Ltd. **(38)**

Moray, N. 1959. Attention in dichotic listening: Affective cues and the influence of instructions. *Quarterly Journal of Experimental Psychology, 11*:56–60. **(434)**

Moray, N. 1970. *Attention: Selective processes in vision and hearing*. New York: Academic Press. **(189, 435)**

Moray, N.; Bates, A.; and Barnett, T. 1965. Experiments on the four-eared man. *Journal of the Acoustical Society of America, 38*:196–201 **(424)**

Morris, C. C.; Bransford, J. D.; and Franks, J. J. 1977. Levels of processing versus transfer appropriate processing. *Journal of Verbal Learning and Verbal Behavior, 16*:519–533. **(470)**

Morse, P. A. 1974. Infant speech perception: A preliminary model and review of the literature. In R. L. Schiefelbusch and L. L. Lloyd (Eds.), *Language perspectives: acquisition, retardation, and intervention*. Baltimore: University Park Press. **(361, 428)**

Morse, P. A. 1978. Infant speech perception: origins, processes and *Alpha Centauri*. In F. Minifie and L. Lloyd (Eds.), *Communicative and cognitive abilities: early behavioral assessment*. Baltimore: University Park Press. **(361, 428)**

Morse, W. H. 1966. Intermittent reinforcement. In W. K. Honig (Ed.), *Operant behavior: Areas of research and application*. Englewood Cliffs, N.J.: Prentice-Hall. Pp. 52–108. **(185, 237, 240)**

Morse, W. H., and Kelleher, R. T. 1977. Determinants of reinforcement and punishment. In W. K. Honig and J. E. R. Staddon (Eds.), *Handbook of operant behavior*. Englewood Cliffs, N.J.: Prentice-Hall. Pp. 174–200. **(245, 246)**

Morse, W. H., and Skinner, B. F. 1957. A second type of superstition in the pigeon. *American Journal of Psychology*, 70:308–311. **(167)**

Morse, W. H., and Skinner, B. F. 1958. Some factors involved in the stimulus control of operant behavior. *Journal of the Experimental Analysis of Behavior*, 1:103–107. **(125)**

Mowrer, O. H. 1947. On the dual nature of learning—A reinterpretation of "conditioning" and "problem-solving." *Harvard Educational Review*, 17:102–148. **(164, 207)**

Mowrer, O. H. 1950. *Learning theory and personality dynamics*. New York: Ronald Press. **(247)**

Mowrer, O. H. 1960. *Learning theory and behavior*. New York: Wiley. **(173)**

Mowrer, O. H., and Aiken, E. G. 1954. Contiguity vs. drive reduction in conditioned fear: Temporal variations in conditioned and unconditioned stimulus. *American Journal of Psychology*, 67:26–28. **(172)**

Mowrer, O. H., and Jones, H. M. 1945. Habit strength as a function of the pattern of reinforcement. *Journal of Experimental Psychology*, 35:293–311. **(249)**

Müller, G. E., and Pilzeker, A. 1900. Experimentelle Beiträge zur Lehre vom Gedachtnis. *Zeitschrift fur Psychologie*. Supplement No. 1. **(494)**

Murdock, B., and Metcalfe, J. 1978. Controlled rehearsal in single-trial free recall. *Journal of Verbal Learning and Verbal Behavior*, 17:309–324. **(475)**

Murray, D. J. 1967. The role of speech responses in short-term memory. *Canadian Journal of Psychology*, 21:263–276. **(444)**

Nahinsky, I. D., and Oeschger, D. E. 1975. The influence of specific stimulus information on the concept learning process. *Journal of Experimental Psychology: Human Learning and Memory*, 1:660–670. **(298)**

Nebes, R. D. 1974. Hemispheric specialization in commisurotimized man. *Psychological Bulletin*, 81:1–14. **(373)**

Neisser, U. 1964. Visual search. *Scientific American*, 210:94–102. **(424)**

Neisser, U. 1967. *Cognitive psychology*. Englewood Cliffs, N.J.: Prentice-Hall. **(419, 424, 426, 429, 432)**

Neisser, U. 1974. Practiced card sorting for multiple targets. *Memory and Cognition*, 2:781–785. **(440)**

Neisser, U. 1976. *Cognition and Reality*. San Francisco: W. H. Freeman. **(435)**

Neisser, U., and Lazar, R. 1964. Searching for novel targets. *Perceptual and Motor Skills*, 19:427–432. **(460)**

Neisser, U., and Weene, P. 1962. Hierarchies in concept attainment. *Journal of Experimental Psychology*, 64:644–645. **(289)**

Nelson, D. L., and Brooks, D. H. 1973. Functional independence of pictures and their verbal memory codes. *Journal of Experimental Psychology*, 98:44–48. **(483)**

Nelson, K. 1973. Structure and strategy in learning to talk. *Monographs of the Society for Research in Child Development*, 38:(Serial No. 149). **(365)**

Nelson, K. 1974. Concept, word, and sentence: Interrelations in acquisition and development. *Psychological Review*, 81:267–285. **(369)**

Nelson, T. O. 1977. Repetition and depth of processing. *Journal of Verbal Learning and Verbal Behavior*, 16:151–171. **(470, 477, 478)**

Nelson, T. O., and Rothbart, R. 1972. Acoustic savings for items forgotten from long-term memory. *Journal of Experimental Psychology*, 93:357–360. **(465)**

Nelson, T. O., and Vining, S. K. 1978. Effect of semantic versus structural processing on long-term retention. *Journal of Experimental Psychology: Human Learning and Memory,* 4:198–209. **(470)**

Neumann, P. G. 1974. An attribute frequency model for the abstraction of prototypes. *Memory and Cognition,* 2:241–248. **(286, 292, 427)**

Neumann, P. G. 1977. Visual prototype formation with discontinuous representation of dimensions of variability. *Memory and Cognition,* 5:187–197. **(286, 292, 308, 427)**

Neville, H. J. 1976. The functional significance of cerebral specialization. In R. W. Rieber (Ed.), *The Neuropsychology of Language.* New York: Plenum Press. Pp. 193–227. **(408)**

Nevin, J. A. 1973. Conditioned reinforcement. In J. A. Nevin and G. S. Reynolds (Eds.), *The study of behavior.* Glenview, Ill.: Scott, Foresman. Pp. 154–198. **(172, 173, 176)**

Newell, A. 1973. Artificial intelligence and the concept of mind. In R. C. Schank and K. M. Colby (Eds.), *Computer models of thought and language.* San Francisco: Freeman. Pp. 1–60. **(412)**

Newell, A., and Simon, H. A. 1962. Computer simulation of human thinking. *Science,* 134:2011–2017. **(412)**

Newell, A.; Shaw, J. C.; and Simon, H. A. 1958. Elements of a theory of human problem solving. *Psychological Review,* 65:151–166. **(412)**

Newman, J. R., and Grice, G. R. 1965. Stimulus generalization as a function of drive level, and the relation between two measures of response strength. *Journal of Experimental Psychology,* 69:357–362. **(226)**

Nickerson, R. S. 1968. A note on long-term recognition memory for picture material. *Psychonomic Science,* 11:58. **(465)**

Ninio, A., and Bruner, J. 1978. The achievement and antecedents of labelling. *Journal of Child Language,* 5:1–15. **(366)**

Noble, C. E. 1952. An analysis of meaning. *Psychological Review,* 59:421–430. **(215)**

Norman, D. A. 1969. Memory while shadowing. *Quarterly Journal of Experimental Psychology,* 21:85–93. **(434)**

Norman, D. A. 1976. *Memory and attention.* 2nd ed. New York: Wiley. **(429, 430, 435, 441)**

Norman, D. A., and Bobrow, D. G. 1975. On data limited and resources limited processes. *Cognitive Psychology,* 7:44–64. **(435, 438, 439, 441)**

Oakes, W. F. 1967. Verbal operant conditioning, intertrial activity, awareness, and the extended interview. *Journal of Personality and Social Psychology,* 6:198–202. **(274)**

Oden, G. C. 1977. Fuzziness in semantic memory: Choosing exemplars of subjective categories. *Memory and Cognition,* 5:198–204. **(283)**

Ohman, A.; Fredrikson, M.; Hugdahl, K.; and Rimmo, P. A. 1976. The premise of equipotentiality in human classical conditioning: Conditioned electrodermal responses to potentially phobic stimuli. *Journal of Experimental Psychology: General Psychology,* 105:313–337. **(113)**

Olds, J. 1958. Satiation effects in self-stimulation of the brain. *Journal of Comparative and Physiological Psychology,* 51:321–324. **(230)**

Olds, J., and Milner, P. 1954. Positive reinforcement produced by electrical stimulation of septal area and other regions of rat brain. *Journal of Comparative and Physiological Psychology,* 47:419–427. **(140, 230)**

Olds, J.; Allan, W. S.; and Briese, E. 1971. Differentiation of hypothalamic drive and reward centers. *American Journal of Physiology,* 221:368–375. **(230)**

Oller, D. K.; Wieman, L. A.; Doyle, W. J.; and Ross, C. 1976. Infant babbling and speech. *Journal of Child Language,* 3:1–11. **(365)**

Olney, R. L., and Scholnick, E. K. 1978. An experimental investigation of adult perception of one-word utterances. *Journal of Child Language,* 5:131–142. **(369)**

Olson, G. M. 1973. Developmental changes in memory and the acquisition of language. In T. E. Moore (Ed.), *Cognitive development and the acquisition of language.* New York: Academic Press. Pp. 145–157. **(369)**

Oppenheim, R. W. 1968. Color preferences in the pecking response of newly hatched ducks (*Anas platyrynchos*). *Journal of Comparative and Physiological Psychology Monograph Supplement,* 66:No. 3, 1–17. **(178)**

Orne, M. J. 1962. On the social psychology of the psychological experiment: With particular reference to demand characteristics and their implications. *American Psychologist*, 17:776–783. **(277)**

Ornstein, R. 1978. The split and whole brain. *Human Nature*, 1:76–83. **(483)**

Osgood, C. E. 1946. Stimulus similarity and interference in learning. *Journal of Experimental Psychology*, 36:277–301. **(264)**

Osgood, C. E. 1949. The similarity paradox in human learning: A resolution. *Psychological Review*, 56:132–143. **(264)**

Osgood, C. E. 1953. *Method and theory in experimental psychology*. New York: Oxford University Press. **(55, 261)**

Overmeier, J. B. and Seligman, M. E. P. 1967. Effects of inescapable shock upon subsequent escape and avoidance responding. *Journal of Comparative and Physiological Psychology*, 63:28–33. **(245)**

Oyama, S. 1976. A sensitive period for the acquisition of a nonnative phonological system. *Journal of Psycholinguistic Research*, 5:261–284. **(394)**

Paivio, A. 1969. Mental imagery in associative learning and memory. *Psychological Review*, 76:241–263. **(271, 482, 483)**

Paivio, A. 1971a. Imagery and language. In S. J. Segal (Ed.), *Imagery: Current cognitive approaches*. New York: Academic Press. Pp. 7–32. **(482, 483)**

Paivio, A. 1971b. *Imagery and verbal processes*. New York: Holt, Rinehart and Winston. **(271, 418, 480, 482, 483)**

Paivio, A. 1975a. Imagery and long-term memory. In A. Kennedy and A. Wilkes (Eds.), *Studies in long-term memory*. New York: Wiley. Pp. 57–88. **(449, 481, 482, 483)**

Paivio, A. 1975b. Coding distinctions and repetition effects in memory. In G. H. Bower (Ed.), *The psychology of learning and motivation*, Vol. 4. New York: Academic Press. Pp. 179–214. **(483)**

Paivio, A., and Begg, I. 1971. Imagery and associative overlap in short-term memory. *Journal of Experimental Psychology*, 89:40–45. **(449)**

Paivio, A., and Csapo, K. 1973. Picture superiority in free recall: Imagery or dual coding? *Cognitive Psychology*, 5:176–206. **(465, 483)**

Paivio, A., and Smythe, P. C. 1971. Word imagery, frequency and meaningfulness in short-term memory. *Psychonomic Science*, 22:333–235. **(449)**

Paivio, A.; Yuille, J. C.; and Madigan, S. A. 1968. Concreteness, imagery and meaningfulness values for 925 nouns. *Journal of Experimental Psychology Monograph Supplement*, 76:No. 1, Part 2. **(481)**

Palermo, D. S., and Molfese, D. L. 1972. Language acquisition from age five onward. *Psychological Bulletin*, 78:409–428. **(389)**

Palmer, S. E. 1975. Visual perception and world knowledge. In D. A. Norman, D. E. Rummelhart, and the LNR Research Group (Eds.) *Explorations in cognition*. San Francisco: Freeman. **(429)**

Palmer, S. E. 1978. Fundamental aspects of cognitive representation. In Eleanor Rosch and Barbara B. Lloyd (Eds.), *Cognition and Categorization*. Hillsdale, N.J.: Lawrence Erlbaum Associates. Pp. 259–303. **(286, 308)**

Park, T. 1978. Plurals in child speech. *Journal of Child Language*, 5:237–250. **(401)**

Patterson, F. G. 1978. The gestures of a gorilla: Language acquisition in another Pongid. *Brain and Language*, 5:72–97. **(349, 353)**

Patterson, I. J. 1965. Timing and spacing of broods in the black-headed gull *Larus ridibundus*, *Ibis*, 107:433–457. **(17)**

Patterson, M. M. 1970. Classical conditioning of the rabbit's (*Oryctolagus cuniculus*) nictitating membrane response with fluctuating ISI and intracranial CS. *Journal of Comparative and Physiological Psychology*, 72:193–202. **(112)**

Patterson, M. M.; Olah, J.; and Clement, J. 1977. Classical nictitating membrane conditioning in the awake, normal, restrained cat. *Science*, 196:1124–1126. **(95)**

Pavlov, I. P. 1906. The scientific investigation of the psychical facilities or processes in the higher animals. *Science*, 24:613–619. **(87)**

Pavlov, I. P. 1927. *Conditioned reflexes*. New York: Oxford University Press. Reprint. New York: Dover, 1960. **(45, 77, 83, 87, 111, 133, 166, 182, 193, 206, 241, 255, 266)**

Pavlov, I. P. 1928. *Lectures on conditioned reflexes*. Vol. I. New York: International Publishers. **(86, 87, 88)**

Pavlov, I. P. 1941. *Conditioned reflexes and psychiatry*. New York: International Publishers. **(86)**

Pearce, J. M., and Dickinson, A. 1975. Pavlovian counterconditioning: Changing the suppressive properties of shock by association with food. *Journal of Experimental Psychology: Animal Behavior Processes*, 104:170–177. **(86)**

Peeke, H. V. S., and Peeke, S. C. 1973. Habituation in fish with special reference to intraspecific aggressive behavior. In H. V. S. Peeke and M. J. Herz (Eds.), *Habituation*, Vol. I. New York: Academic Press. Pp. 59–83. **(54)**

Peeke, H. V. S., and Veno, G. 1973. Stimulus specificity of habituated aggression in three-spine sticklebacks (*Gasterosteus aculeatus*). *Behavioral Biology*, 8:427–432. **(58)**

Pellegrino, J. W., and Salzberg, P. M. 1975. Encoding specificity in cued recall and context recognition. *Journal of Experimental Psychology: Human Learning and Memory*, 104:261–270. **(511)**

Penfield, W., and Roberts, L. 1959. *Speech and brain mechanisms*. Princeton: Princeton University Press. **(393)**

Perfetti, C. A. 1973. Retrieval of sentence relations: Semantic vs. syntactic deep structure. *Cognition*, 2:95–106. **(355)**

Peterson, L. R., and Peterson, M. J. 1959. Short-term retention of individual verbal items. *Journal of Experimental Psychology*, 58:193–198. **(450, 451, 453)**

Peterson, N. 1960. Control of behavior by presentation of an imprinted stimulus. *Science*, 132:1395–1396. **(81)**

Peterson, R. F. 1968. Some experiments on the organization of a class of imitative behaviors. *Journal of Applied Behavior Analysis*, 1:225–235. **(270)**

Peterson, R. F., and Whitehurst, G. J. 1971. A variable influencing the performance of nonreinforced imitative behaviors. *Journal of Applied Behavior Analysis*, 4:1–9. **(270)**

Petrich, J. A. 1974. Retroactive inhibition under a multiple-choice procedure. *American Journal of Psychology*, 87:335–349. **(500)**

Petrinovich, L. 1973. A species-meaningful analysis of habituation. In H. V. S. Peeke and M. J. Herz (Eds.), *Habituation*, Vol. I. New York: Academic Press. Pp. 141–161. **(54)**

Phares, E. J. 1976. *Locus of control in personality*. Morristown, N.J.: General Learning Press. **(247)**

Phillips, J. R. 1973. Syntax and vocabulary of mothers' speech to young children: Age and sex comparisons. *Child Development*, 44:182–185. **(381)**

Piaget, J. 1951. *Play, dreams, and imitations in childhood* (Translation of *La formation du symbole chez l'enfant*). New York: Norton. **(366)**

Piaget, J. 1953. *The origins of intelligence in the child*. London: Routledge & Kegan Paul. **(287, 366)**

Piaget, J. 1955a. *The child's construction of reality*. London: Routledge & Kegan Paul. **(366)**

Piaget, J. 1955b. *The language and thought of the child*. Translated by M. Gabain. New York: New American Library (Meridian Books). **(368)**

Pierrel, R., and Sherman, J. G. 1963. Barnabus, the rat with college training. *Brown Alumni Monthly*, February 1963, pp. 8–12. Providence, R.I.: Brown University. **(153)**

Pisoni, D. B. 1973. Auditory and phonetic memory codes in the discrimination of consonants and vowels. *Perception and Psychophysics*, 13:253–260. **(321)**

Pisoni, D. B. 1977. Identification and discrimination of the relative onset time of two-component tones: Implications for voicing perception in stops. *Journal of the Acoustical Society of America*, 61:1352–1361. **(321)**

Pisoni, D. B., and Lazarus, J. H. 1974. Categorical and non-categorical modes of speech perception along the voicing continuum. *Journal of the Acoustical Society of America*, 55. **(321)**

Pisoni, D. B., and Tash, J. 1974. Reaction times to comparisons within and across phonetic categories. *Perception and Psychophysics* 15:285–290. **(321)**

Platt, J. R. 1964. Strong inference. *Science*, 146:347–353. **(38)**

Platt, J. R. Interresponse-time shaping by variable-interval interresponse-time reinforcement contingencies. *Journal of the Experimental Analysis of Behavior, 31*:3–14. **(238)**

Pliskoff, S. S., and Hawkins, T. D. 1967. A method for increasing the reinforcement magnitude of intracranial stimulation. *Journal of the Experimental Analysis of Behavior, 10*:281–289. **(230)**

Podgorny, P., and Shepard, R. N. 1978. Functional representations common to visual perception and imagination. *Journal of Experimental Psychology: Human Perception and Performance, 4*:21–35. **(483)**

Polanyi, M. 1966. *The tacit dimension.* Garden City, N.Y.: Doubleday. **(298)**

Posner, M. I. 1969. Abstraction and the process of recognition. In J. T. Spence and G. H. Bower (Eds.), *Advances in learning and motivation,* Vol. 3. New York: Academic Press. **(285, 287, 296, 427, 444)**

Posner, M. I. 1970. Retention of abstract ideas. *Journal of Experimental Psychology, 83*:304–308. **(285)**

Posner, M. I. 1973. *Cognition: An introduction.* Glenview, Illinois: Scott, Foresman, 1973. **(285)**

Posner, M. I. 1974. Psychobiology of attention. In C. Blakemore and M. S. Gazzaniga (Eds.), *The handbook of psychobiology.* New York: Academic Press. **(189, 202, 436)**

Posner, M. L. 1978. *Chronometric explorations of mind.* Hillsdale, N.J.: Lawrence Erlbaum Associates. **(436)**

Posner, M. I., and Keele, S. W. 1968. On the genesis of abstract ideas. *Journal of Experimental Psychology, 77*:353–363. **(285, 295)**

Posner, M. I., and Rossman, E. 1965. Effect of size and location of information transforms upon short-term retention. *Journal of Experimental Psychology, 70*:496–505. **(456)**

Posner, M. I.; Boies, L. J.; Eichelman, W. H.; and Taylor, R. L. 1969. Retention of visual and name codes of single letters. *Journal of Experimental Psychology Monograph, 79*:1, Part 2. **(444)**

Postman, L. 1961. The present status of interference theory. In C. N. Cofer (Ed.), *Verbal learning and verbal behavior.* New York: McGraw-Hill. Pp. 152–178. **(498)**

Postman, L. 1962. Transfer of training as a function of experimental paradigm and degree of first-list learning. *Journal of Verbal Learning and Verbal Behavior, 1*:109–118. **(264)**

Postman, L. 1969. Experimental analysis of learning to learn. In G. H. Bower and J. T. Spence (Eds.), *The psychology of learning and motivation,* Vol. 3. New York: Academic Press. **(261, 262, 263, 302)**

Postman, L. 1971. Transfer, interference and forgetting. In J. W. Kling and L. A. Riggs (Eds.), *Woodworth and Schlosberg's experimental psychology,* 3rd ed. New York: Holt, Rinehart and Winston. Pp. 1019–1132. **(261, 263, 264, 266, 267, 271, 494)**

Postman, L. 1976a. Methodology of human learning. In W. K. Estes (Ed.), *Handbook of learning and cognitive processes.* Vol. 3. *Approaches to human learning and memory.* Hillsdale, N.J.: Lawrence Erlbaum Associates. Pp. 11–70. **(409, 460, 468, 470, 481, 494, 507)**

Postman, L. 1976b. Interference theory revisited. In J. Brown (Ed.), *Recall and recognition.* New York: Wiley. Pp. 157–182. **(494, 499)**

Postman, L., and Burns, S. 1973. Experimental analysis of coding processes. *Memory and Cognition, 1*:503–507. **(482)**

Postman, L., and Schwartz, M. 1964. Studies of learning to learn: 1. Transfer as a function of method of practice and class of verbal materials. *Journal of Verbal Learning and Verbal Behavior, 3*:37–49. **(302)**

Postman, L., and Stark, K. 1969. The role of response availability in transfer and interference. *Journal of Experimental Psychology, 79*:168–177. **(499, 500, 501)**

Postman, L., and Underwood, B. J. 1973. Critical issues in interference theory. *Memory and Cognition, 1*:19–40. **(266, 494, 499, 503)**

Postman, L.; Stark, K.; and Burns, S. 1974. Sources of proactive inhibition on unpaced tests of retention. *American Journal of Psychology, 87*:33–56. **(501)**

Postman, L.; Stark, K.; and Fraser, J. 1968. Temporal changes in interference. *Journal of Verbal Learning and Verbal Behavior, 7*:672–694. **(499, 500)**

Potts, G. M. 1977. Integrating new and old information. *Journal of Verbal Learning and Verbal Behavior*, 16:365–370. **(271)**

Premack, D. 1959. Toward empirical behavioral laws: I. Positive reinforcement. *Psychological Review*, 66:219–233. **(141, 142)**

Premack, D. 1963. Prediction of the comparative reinforcement values of running and drinking. *Science*, 139:1062–1063. **(143)**

Premack, D. 1965. Reinforcement theory. In D. Levine (Ed.), *Nebraska symposium on motivation*. Lincoln University of Nebraska Press. **(133, 140, 141, 144, 225)**

Premack, D. 1969. On some boundary conditions of contrast. In J. Tapp (Ed.), *Reinforcement and behavior*. New York: Academic Press. Pp. 120–195. **(193)**

Premack, D. 1970. A functional analysis of language. *Journal of the Experimental Analysis of Behavior*, 14:107–125. **(354)**

Premack, D. 1971a. Catching up with common sense or two sides of a generalization: Reinforcement and punishment. In R. Glaser (Ed.), *The nature of reinforcement*. New York: Academic Press. **(132, 140, 141, 143, 144)**

Premack, D. 1971b. Language in chimpanzee? *Science*, 172:808–822. **(354)**

Premack, D. 1971c. On the assessment of language competence in the chimpanzee. In A. M. Schrier and F. Stollnitz (Eds.), *Behavior of nonhuman primates*. New York: Academic Press. **(354)**

Premack, D. 1973. Cognitive principles? In F. J. McGuigan and D. B. Lumsden (Eds.), *Contemporary approaches to conditioning and learning*. New York: Wiley. Pp. 287–310. **(354)**

Premack, D. 1976. *Intelligence in ape and man*. Hillsdale, N.J.: Lawrence Erlbaum Associates. **(354, 355, 356, 368)**

Premack, D., and Premack, A. J. 1974. Teaching visual language to apes and language deficient persons. In R. L. Schiefelbusch and L. L. Lloyd (Eds.), *Language perspectives*. Baltimore: University Park Press. **(393)**

Premack, D.; Schaeffer, R. W.; and Hundt, A. 1964. Reinforcement of drinking by running: Effect of fixed ratio and reinforcement time. *Journal of the Experimental Analysis of Behavior*, 7:91–96. **(143)**

Premack, D.; Woodruff, G.; and Kennel, K. 1978. Paper-marking test for chimpanzee: Simple control for social cues. *Science*, 202:903–905. **(354)**

Pribram, K. H., and Broadbent, D. E. (Eds.) 1970. *Biology of memory*. New York: Academic Press. **(28)**

Proctor, R. W. 1978. Attention and modality-specific interference in visual short-term memory. *Journal of Experimental Psychology: Human Learning and Memory*, 4:239–245. **(444)**

Prokasy, W. F.; Ebel, H. C.; and Thompson, D. D. 1963. Response shaping at long interstimulus intervals in classical eyelid conditioning. *Journal of Experimental Psychology*, 66:138–142. **(111)**

Prokasy, W. F., and Harsany, M. A. 1968. Two-phase model for human classical conditioning. *Journal of Experimental Psychology*, 78:359–368. **(100)**

Prytulak, L. S. 1971. Natural language mediation. *Cognitive Psychology*, 2:1–56. **(480)**

Pubols, B. H., Jr. 1960. Incentive magnitude, learning, and performance in animals. *Psychological Bulletin*, 57:89–115. **(133)**

Puff, C. R. 1970. Role of clustering in free recall. *Journal of Experimental Psychology*, 86:384–386. **(473)**

Pylyshyn, Z. W. 1973. What the mind's eye tells the mind's brain: A critique of mental imagery. *Psychological Bulletin*, 80:1–24. **(271, 367, 418, 484, 485, 486)**

Quinsey, V. L. 1971. Conditioned suppression with no CS-US contingency in the rat. *Canadian Journal of Psychology*, 25:69–82. **(116)**

Rachlin, H. 1973. Contrast and matching. *Psychological Review*, 80:217–234. **(193)**

Rachlin, H., and Herrnstein, R. J. 1969. Hedonism revisited: On the negative law of effect. In B. A. Campbell and R. M. Church (Eds.), *Punishment and aversive behavior*. Englewood Cliffs, N.J.: Prentice-Hall. Pp. 83–109. **(132)**

Raeburn, V. P. 1974. Priorities in item recognition. *Memory and Cognition,* 2:663–669. **(459)**

Ramos, A.; Schwartz, E. L.; and John, E. R. 1976. Stable and plastic unit discharge patterns during behavioral generalization. *Science, 192*:393–396. **(187)**

Rappaport, D. 1974. *The history of the concept of association of ideas.* New York: International Universities Press. **(410)**

Ratner, S. C. 1970. Habituation: Research and theory. In J. Reynierse (Ed.), *Current issues in animal learning.* Lincoln: University of Nebraska Press. **(74)**

Razran, G. 1939. A quantitative study of meaning by a conditioned salivary technique (semantic conditioning). *Science, 90*:89–91. **(90)**

Razran, G. 1949. Stimulus generalization of conditioned responses. *Psychological Bulletin,* 46:337–365. **(177)**

Razran, G. 1961. The observable unconscious and the inferable conscious in current Soviet psychophysiology: Interoceptive conditioning, semantic conditioning, and the orienting reflex. *Psychological Review, 68*:81–147. **(90)**

Reder, L. M.; Anderson, J. R.; and Bjork, R. A. 1974. A semantic interpretation of encoding specificity. *Journal of Experimental Psychology, 102*:648–656. **(513)**

Reed, S. K. 1972. Pattern recognition and categorization. *Cognitive Psychology,* 3:382–467. **(286, 307, 427)**

Reese, E. 1971. Born to succeed: *Behavioral procedures for education.* Part 1: Concept of number; Part 2: Arithmetic. Box 625, Northampton, Mass.: Hanover Communications. **(34)**

Reese, E. P. 1977. *Human behavior: Analysis and application.* Dubuque, Iowa: Brown. **(128, 194)**

Reicher, G. M. 1969. Perceptual recognition as a function of meaningfulness of stimulus material. *Journal of Experimental Psychology, 81*:275–280. **(431)**

Reinhold, D. B., and Perkins, C. C., Jr. 1955. Stimulus generalization following different methods of training. *Journal of Experimental Psychology, 49*:423–427. **(203)**

Reitman, J. S. 1974. Without surreptitious rehearsal information in short-term memory decays. *Journal of Verbal Learning and Verbal Behavior, 13*:365–377. **(452)**

Rescorla, R. A. 1967. Pavlovian conditioning and its proper control procedures. *Psychological Review, 74*:71–80. **(116)**

Rescorla, R. A. 1971. Variation in the effectiveness of reinforcement and nonreinforcement following prior inhibitory conditioning. *Learning and Motivation,* 2:113–123. **(202)**

Rescorla, R. A. 1972. Informational variables in Pavlovian conditioning. In G. H. Bower (Ed.), *The psychology of learning and motivation,* Vol. 6. New York: Academic Press. **(102, 203)**

Rescorla, R. A. 1973. Effect of UCS habituation following conditioning. *Journal of Comparative and Physiological Psychology, 82*:137–143. **(217)**

Rescorla, R. A. 1977. Pavlovian second-order conditioning: Some implications for instrumental behavior. In H. Davis and H. M. B. Hurwitz (Eds.), *Operant-Pavlovian interactions.* Hillsdale, N.J.: Lawrence Erlbaum Associates. Pp. 133–164. **(83, 217)**

Rescorla, R. A. 1979. Aspects of the reinforcer learned in second-order Pavlovian conditioning. *Journal of Experimental Psychology: Animal Behavior Processes,* 5:79–95. **(217)**

Rescorla, R. A., and Solomon, R. L. 1967. Two-process learning theory: Relationship between Pavlovian conditioning and instrumental learning. *Psychological Review,* 74:151–182. **(207)**

Rescorla, R. A., and Wagner, A. R. 1972. A theory of Pavlovian conditioning: Variations in the effectiveness of reinforcement and nonreinforcement. In A. H. Black and W. F. Prokasy (Eds.), *Classical conditioning II: Current research and theory.* Englewood Cliffs, N.J.: Prentice-Hall. Pp. 64–99. **(102, 104, 113, 116, 181)**

Restle, F. 1958. Toward a quantitative description of learning set data. *Psychological Review, 65*:77–91. **(302)**

Restle, F. 1962. The selection of strategies in cue learning. *Psychological Review,* 69:329–343. **(307)**

Restle, F., and Greeno, J. G. 1970. *Introduction to mathematical psychology.* Reading, Mass.: Addison-Wesley. **(156, 157)**

Revusky, S. 1971. The role of interference in association over a delay. In W. Honig and H. James (Eds.), *Animal memory.* New York: Academic Press. **(113, 163)**

Revusky, S., and Garcia, J. 1970. Learned associations over long delays. In G. H. Bower (Ed.), *The psychology of learning and motivation,* Vol. 4. New York: Academic Press. Pp. 1–84. **(113, 136)**

Reynierse, J. H.; Scavio, M. J., Jr.; and Ulness, J. D. 1970. An ethological analysis of classically conditioned fear. In J. H. Reynierse (Ed.), *Current issues in animal learning.* Lincoln: University of Nebraska Press. Pp. 33–54. **(110)**

Reynolds, G. S. 1961a. Attention in the pigeon. *Journal of the Experimental Analysis of Behavior,* 4:203–208. **(189)**

Reynolds, G. S. 1961b. Behavioral contrast. *Journal of the Experimental Analysis of Behavior,* 4:57–71. **(193)**

Reynolds, G. S., and MacLeod, A. 1970. On the theory of interresponse-time reinforcement. In G. H. Bower (Ed.), *The psychology of learning and motivation,* Vol. 4. New York: Academic Press. Pp. 85–107. **(238)**

Richardson, J., and Brown, B. L. 1966. Mediated transfer in paired-associate learning as a function of presentation rate and stimulus meaningfulness. *Journal of Experimental Psychology,* 72:820–828. **(264, 265)**

Richardson, W. K. 1973. A test of the effectiveness of the differential-reinforcement-of-low-rate schedule. *Journal of the Experimental Analysis of Behavior,* 20:385–392. **(238)**

Richelle, M. 1976. Formal and functional analysis of verbal behavior: Notes on the debate between Chomsky and Skinner. *Behaviorism,* 4:209–221. **(408)**

Ricks, D. M. 1975. Vocal communication in preverbal normal and autistic children. In N. O'Connor (Ed.), *Language cognitive deficits and retardation.* London: Butterworth. Pp. 75–80. **(360)**

Riley, D. A. 1958. The nature of the effective stimulus in animal discrimination learning: transposition reconsidered, *Psychological Review,* 65:1–7. **(199)**

Riley, D. A. 1968. *Discrimination learning.* Boston: Allyn & Bacon. **(218)**

Rilling, M. 1967. Number of responses as a stimulus in fixed-interval and fixed-ratio schedules. *Journal of Comparative and Physiological Psychology,* 63:60–65. **(238)**

Rilling, M. E. 1977. Stimulus control and inhibitory processes. In W. K. Honig and J. E. R. Staddon (Eds.), *A Handbook of operant conditioning.* Englewood Cliffs, N.J.: Prentice-Hall. **(218, 255)**

Rilling, M.; Askew, H. R.; Ahlskog, J. E.; and Kramer, T. J. 1969. Aversive properties of the negative stimulus in a successive discrimination. *Journal of the Experimental Analysis of Behavior,* 12:917–932. **(244)**

Rilling, M., and McDiarmid, C. 1965. Signal detection in fixed-ratio schedules. *Science,* 148:526–527. **(238)**

Rips, L. J.; Shoben, E. J.; and Smith, E. E. 1973. Semantic distance and the verification of semantic relations. *Journal of Verbal Learning and Verbal Behavior,* 12:1–20. **(283, 490, 493)**

Rizley, R. C., and Rescorla, R. A. 1972. Associations in second-order conditioning and sensory preconditioning. *Journal of Comparative and Physiological Psychology,* 81:1–11. **(217)**

Robbins, D. 1971. Partial reinforcement: A selective review of the alleyway literature since 1960. *Psychological Bulletin,* 76:415–431. **(249)**

Robbins, D.; Barresi, J.; Compton, P.; Russo, M.; and Smith, M. A. 1978. The genesis and use of exemplar vs. prototype knowledge in abstract category learning. *Memory and Cognition,* 6:473–480. **(298)**

Roberts, W. W. 1970. Hypothalamic mechanisms for motivational and species-typical behavior. In R. E. Whalen, R. F. Thompson, M. Verzeano, and N. M. Weinberger (Eds.), *The neural control of behavior.* New York: Academic Press. Pp. 175–206. **(299)**

Roberts, W. W., and Bergquist, E. H. 1968. Attack elicited by hypothalamic stimulation in cats raised in social isolation. *Journal of Comparative and Physiological Psychology,* 66:590–595. **(230)**

Rosch, E. 1974. Linguistic relativity. In A. Silverstein (Ed.), *Human communication: Theoretical perspectives.* New York: Halsted Press. Pp. 95–121. **(283)**

Rosch, E. 1975. Cognitive representations of semantic categories. *Journal of Experimental Psychology: General,* 104:192–253. **(283)**

Rosch. E. 1978. Principles of categorization. In Eleanor Rosch and Barbara B. Lloyd (Eds.), *Cognition and Categorization.* Hillsdale, N.J.: Lawrence Erlbaum Associates. Pp. 27–48. **(282, 283, 286, 291, 293, 308, 397, 492)**

Rosch, E., and Mervis, C. B. 1975. Family resemblances: Studies in the internal structure of categories. *Cognitive Psychology,* 7:573–605. **(282, 283, 286, 292)**

Rosch, E.; Simpson, C.; and Miller, R. S. 1976a. Structural bases of typicality effects. *Journal of Experimental Psychology: Human Perception and Performance,* 2:491–502. **(283, 287, 291, 292)**

Rosch, E.; Mervis, C. B.; Gray, W.; Johnson, D.; and Boyes-Braem, P. 1976b. Basic objects in natural categories. *Cognitive Psychology,* 8:382–439. **(284, 292, 293)**

Rosellini, R. A., and Seligman, M. E. P. 1978. Role of shock intensity in the learned helplessness paradigm. *Animal Learning and Behavior,* 6:143–146. **(245)**

Rosenblum, L. A. 1971. The ontogeny of mother-infant relations in macaques. In H. Moltz (Ed.), *The ontogeny of vertebrate behavior.* New York: Academic Press. **(70)**

Rosenfeld, H. M., and Baer, D. M. 1969. Unnoticed verbal conditioning of an aware experimenter by a more aware subject. The double-agent effect. *Psychological Review,* 76:425–432. **(274)**

Rosenfeld, H. M., and Baer, D. M. 1970. Unbiased and unnoticed verbal conditioning: The double-agent robot procedure. *Journal of the Experimental Analysis of Behavior,* 14:99–107. **(275)**

Rosenthal, R. 1966. *Experimenter effects in behavioral research.* Englewood Cliffs, N.J.: Prentice-Hall. **(277, 468)**

Ross, L. E., and Ross, S. M. 1972. Conditional stimulus parameters and the interstimulus interval: The processing of CS information in differential conditioning. In A. H. Black and W. F. Prokasy (Eds.), *Classical conditioning II: Current research and theory.* Englewood Cliffs, N.J.: Prentice-Hall. Pp. 182–205. **(191)**

Rotter, J. B. 1966. Generalized expectancies for internal versus external control of reinforcement. *Psychological Monographs,* 80:Whole No. 609. **(246)**

Routh, D. 1969. Conditioning of vocal response differentiation in infants. *Developmental Psychology,* 1:219–225. **(364)**

Rowe, E. J. 1973. Verbalization effects in discrimination learning of pictures and words. *Canadian Journal of Psychology,* 27:184–190. **(483)**

Rowland, N. E., and Antelman, S. M. 1976. Stress induced hyperphagia and obesity in rats: A possible model for understanding human obesity. *Science,* 191:310–312. **(231)**

Rozin, P., and Kalat, J. W. 1971. Specific hungers and poison avoidance as adaptive specializations of learning. *Psychological Review,* 78:459–486. **(113, 139)**

Rubel, E. W., and Rosenthal, M. H. 1975. The ontogeny of auditory frequency generalization in the chicken. *Journal of Experimental Psychology: Animal Behavior Processes,* 1:28–297. **(58, 59)**

Rudolph, R. L., and Van Houten, R. 1977. Auditory stimulus control in pigeons: Jenkins and Harrison (1960) revisited. *Journal of the Experimental Analysis of Behavior,* 27:327–330. **(217)**

Rudy, J. W. 1974. Stimulus selection in animal conditioning and paired-associate learning: Variations in the associative process. *Journal of Verbal Learning and Verbal Behavior,* 13:282–296. **(204)**

Rumbaugh, D. M. (Ed.) 1977. *Language learning by a chimpanzee. The Lana project.* New York: Academic Press. **(354, 431)**

Rummelhart, D. 1977. Introduction to human information processing. New York: Wiley. **(431)**

Rummelhart, D. E., and Siple, P. 1974. Process of recognizing tachistoscopically presented words. *Psychological Review,* 81:99–118. **(431)**

Rummelhart, D. E.; Lindsay, P. H.; and Norman, D. A. 1972. A process model for long-term memory. In E. Tulving and W. Donaldson (Eds.), *Organization of memory.* New York: Academic Press. Pp. 197–246. **(343, 344, 513)**

Rundus, D. 1977. Maintenance rehearsal and single-level processing. *Journal of Verbal Learning and Verbal Behavior,* 16:665–682. **(477)**

Rundus, D., and Atkinson, R. C. 1970. Rehearsal processes in free recall: A procedure for direct observation. *Journal of Verbal Learning and Verbal Behavior,* 9:99–105. **(475, 476)**

Rundus, D.; Loftus, G.; and Atkinson, R. C. 1970. Immediate free recall and three-week delayed recognition. *Journal of Verbal Learning and Verbal Behavior,* 9:684–688. **(475)**

Russek, M. 1971. Hepatic receptors and the neurophysiological mechanisms controlling feeding behavior. In S. Ehrenpreis and O. C. Solnitzky (Eds.), *Neurosciences research,* Vol. 4. New York: Academic Press. **(224)**

Russell, W. A., and Storms, L. H. 1955. Implicit verbal chaining in paired-associate learning. *Journal of Experimental Psychology,* 49:287–293. **(272)**

Sachs, J. S. 1967. Recognition memory for syntactic and semantic aspects of connected discourse. *Perception and Psychophysics,* 2:437–442. **(467, 486)**

Sachs, J. S., and Johnson, M. 1976. Language development in a hearing child of deaf parents. In W. von Raffler Engel and Y. LeBrun (Eds.), *Baby talk and infant speech (Neurolinguistics 5).* Amsterdam: Swets & Zeitlinger. Pp. 246–252. **(382, 396)**

Sachs, J. S.; Brown, R.; and Salerno, R. A. 1976. Adults' speech to children. In W. van Raffler Engel and Y. LeBrun (Eds.), *Baby talk and infant speech (Neurolinguistics 5).* Amsterdam: Swets & Zeitlinger. Pp. 240–245. **(381)**

Sachs, J., and Truswell, L. 1978. Comprehension of two-word instructions by children in the one-word stage. *Journal of Child Language,* 5:17–24. **(368)**

Sakitt, B. 1976. Iconic memory. *Psychological Review,* 83:257–276. **(423)**

Saltzman, I. J. 1949. Maze learning in the absence of primary reinforcement. *Journal of Comparative and Physiological Psychology,* 42:161–173. **(173)**

Salzinger, K. 1978. Language behavior. In A. Charles Catania and Thomas A. Brigham (Eds.), *Handbook of Applied Behavior Analysis.* New York: Irvington. Pp. 275–321. **(313, 359, 408)**

Sanders, A. F.; Whitaker, L.; and Cofer, C. N. 1974. Evidence for retroactive interference in recognition from reaction time. *Journal of Experimental Psychology,* 102:1126. **(500)**

Santa, J. L., and Lamwers, L. L. 1974. Encoding specificity: Fact or artifact. *Journal of Verbal Learning and Verbal Behavior,* 13:412–423. **(507)**

Sargent, J. D.; Green, E. E.; and Walters, E. D. 1973. Preliminary report on the use of autogenic feedback training in the treatment of migraine and tension headaches. *Psychosomatic Medicine,* 35:129–135. **(276)**

Savin, H. B., and Perchonock, E. 1965. Grammatical structure and the immediate recall of English sentences. *Journal of Verbal Learning and Verbal Behavior,* 4:348–353. **(336)**

Schiller, P. H. 1952. Innate constituents of complex responses in primates. *Psychological Review,* 59:177–191. **(303)**

Schiller, P. H. 1965. Monoptic and dichoptic visual masking by patterns and flashes. *Journal of Experimental Psychology,* 69:193–199. **(423)**

Schlesinger, H. S., and Meadow, M. P. 1972. *Sound and sign.* Berkeley: University of California Press. **(348)**

Schlesinger, I. M. 1974. Relational concepts underlying language. In R. L. Schiefelbusch and L. L. Lloyd (Eds.), *Language perspectives—Acquisition, retardation and intervention.* Baltimore: University Park Press. pp. 129–151. **(373)**

Schlesinger, I. M. 1977. The role of cognitive development and linguistic input in language acquisition. *Journal of Child Language,* 4:153–169. **(379)**

Schneiderman, N. 1966. Interstimulus interval function of the nictitating membrane response of the rabbit under delay vs. trace conditioning. *Journal of Comparative and Physiological Psychology,* 62:397–402. **(99, 111)**

Schneiderman, N. 1972. Response system divergencies in aversive classical conditioning.

In A. H. Black and W. F. Prokasy (Eds.), *Classical conditioning II*. Englewood Cliffs, N.J.: Prentice-Hall. **(93, 99)**

Schneiderman, N.; Fuentes, I.; and Gormezano, I. 1962. Acquisition and extinction of the classically conditioned eyelid response in the albino rabbit. *Science, 136*:650–652. **(95)**

Schneirla, T. C. 1949. Levels in the psychological capacities of animals. In R. W. Sellars, V. J. Sellars, and M. Farber (Eds.), *Philosophy of the future*. New York: Macmillan. **(43, 72)**

Schneirla, T. C. 1956. Interrelationships of the "innate" and the "acquired" in instinctive behavior. In *L'instinct dans le comportement des animaux et de l'homme*. Paris: Masson & Cie, Pp. 387–452. Reprinted in P. H. Klopfer and J. P. Hailman (Eds.), *Function and evolution of behavior*. Reading, Mass.: Addison-Wesley, 1972. **(72)**

Schnorr, J. A., and Atkinson, R. C. 1970. Study position and item differences in the short- and long-run retention of paired associates learned by imagery. *Journal of Verbal Learning and Verbal Behavior, 9*:614–622. **(484)**

Schoenfeld, W. N. 1950. An experimental approach to anxiety, escape, and avoidance behavior. In P. H. Hock and J. Zubin (Eds.), *Anxiety*. New York: Grune & Stratton. Pp. 70–99. **(207)**

Schoenfeld, W. N. 1969. "Avoidance" in behavior theory. *Journal of the Experimental Analysis of Behavior, 12*:897–904. **(146)**

Schoenfeld, W. N.; Cole, B. K.; Blaustein, J.; Lachter, G. D.; Martin, J. M.; and Vickery, C. 1972. *Stimulus schedules: The t-r systems*. New York: Harper & Row. **(240)**

Schoenfeld, W. N., and Farmer, J. 1970. Reinforcement schedules and the "behavior stream." In W. N. Schoenfeld (Ed.), *The theory of reinforcement schedules*. Englewood Cliffs, N.J.: Prentice-Hall. Pp. 215–245. **(80)**

Schroeder, S. R., and Holland, J. G. 1969. Reinforcement of eye movements with concurrent schedules. *Journal of the Experimental Analysis of Behavior, 12*:897–904. **(146)**

Schumaker, J., and Sherman, J. A. 1970. Training generative verb usage by imitation and reinforcement procedures. *Journal of Applied Behavior Analysis, 3*:273–287. **(405)**

Schuster, C. R., and Woods, J. H. 1966. Schedule-induced polydipsia in the rhesus monkey. *Psychological Reports, 19*:823–828. **(232)**

Schusterman, R. J. 1962. Transfer effects of successive discrimination reversal training in chimpanzees. *Science, 137*:422–423. **(302, 303)**

Schusterman, R. J. 1964. Successive discrimination-reversal training and multiple discrimination training in one-trial learning by chimpanzees. *Journal of Comparative and Physiological Psychology, 58*:153–156. **(302)**

Schwartz, B., and Gamzu, E. 1977. Pavlovian control of operant behavior: an analysis of autoshaping and its implications for operant conditioning. in W. K. Honing and J. E. R. Staddon (Eds.), *Handbook of operant conditioning*. New York: Prentice-Hall. Pp. 53–97. **(193)**

Schwenn, E., and Postman, L. 1967. Studies of learning to learn: V. Gains in performance as a function of warm-up and associative practice. *Journal of Verbal Learning and Verbal Behavior, 6*:565–573. **(262, 263)**

Seamon, J. G., and Virostek, S. 1978. Memory performance and subject-defined depth of processing. *Memory and Cognition, 6*:283–287. **(470)**

Searles, L. V. 1949. The organization of hereditary maze brightness and maze dullness. *Genetic Psychology Monographs, 39*:279–375. **(22)**

Sechenov, I. M. 1863. *Reflexes of the brain*. Reprint. Cambridge, Mass.: M.I.T. Press, 1965. **(60, 86)**

Segal, E. 1977. Toward a coherent psychology of language. In W. K. Honig and J. E. R. Staddon (Eds.), *Handbook of operant behavior*. Englewood Cliffs, N.J.: Prentice-Hall. Pp. 628–654. **(311, 359, 403, 404)**

Segal, E. F. 1975. Psycholinguistics discover the operant: A review of Roger Brown's *A First Language: The Early Stages*. *Journal of the Experimental Analysis of Behavior, 23*:149–158. **(359, 403)**

Selfridge, O. G., and Neisser, U. 1960. Pattern recognition by machine. *Scientific American, 203*:60–68. **(412)**

Seligman, M. E. P. 1966. CS redundancy and secondary punishment. *Journal of Experimental Psychology,* 72:546–550. **(173)**

Seligman, M. E. P. 1970. On the generality of the laws of learning. *Psychological Review,* 77:406–418. **(113, 162)**

Seligman, M. E. P. 1975. *Helplessness.* San Francisco: Freeman. **(246)**

Seligman, M. E. P., and Hager, J. L. (Eds.). 1972. *Biological boundaries of learning.* Englewood Cliffs, N.J.: Prentice-Hall. **(43, 113, 162)**

Seligman, M. E. P.; Maier, S. F.; and Solomon, R. L. 1971. Unpredictable and uncontrollable aversive events. In F. R. Brush (Ed.), *Aversive conditioning and learning.* New York: Academic Press. Pp. 347–400. **(245)**

Senkowski, P. C., and Denny, M. R. 1977. Frustration-mediated learning of a bar-press response. *Animal Learning and Behavior,* 5:373–376. **(250)**

Sewall, W. R., and Kendall, S. B. 1965. A note on interresponse time distributions during generalization testing. *Psychonomic Science,* 3:95–96. **(185, 186)**

Seward, J. P., and Levy, N. 1953. Choice-point behavior as a function of secondary reinforcement with relevant drive satiated. *Journal of Comparative and Physiological Psychology,* 46:334–338. **(174)**

Shakow, D. 1930. Hermann Ebbinghaus. *American Journal of Psychology,* 42:505–518. **(218)**

Shanab, M. E., and Peterson, J. L. 1969. Polydipsia in the pigeon. *Psychonomic Science,* 15:51–52. **(233)**

Shankweiler, D., and Studdert-Kennedy, M. 1967. Identification of consonants and vowels presented to left and right ears. *Quarterly Journal of Experimental Psychology,* 19:59–63. **(392)**

Shannon, C. E., and Weaver, W. 1949. *The mathematical theory of communication.* Urbana: University of Illinois Press. **(449)**

Shapiro, D., and Crider, A. 1967. Operant electrodermal conditioning under multiple schedules of reinforcement. *Psychophysiology,* 4:168–175. **(274)**

Shapiro, M. M. 1960. Respondent salivary conditioning during operant lever pressing in dogs. *Science,* 132:619–620. **(160)**

Shapiro, M. M. 1962. Temporal relationship between salivation and lever pressing with differential reinforcement of low rates. *Journal of Comparative and Physiological Psychology,* 55:456–571. **(160)**

Shapiro, M. M., and Herendeen, D. L. 1975. Food-reinforced inhibition of conditioned salivation in dogs. *Journal of Comparative and Physiological Psychology,* 88:628–632. **(162)**

Shaprio, S. I., and Bell, J. A. 1970. Subjective organization and free-recall: Performance of high, moderate and low organizers. *Psychonomic Science,* 21:71–72. **(473)**

Shatz, M. 1978. Children's comprehension of their mother's question-directives. *Journal of Child Language,* 5:39–46. **(389)**

Sheafor, P. J. 1975. "Pseudoconditioned" jaw movements of the rabbit reflect associations conditioned to contextual background cues. *Journal of Experimental Psychology: Animal Behavior Processes,* 104:245–260. **(93)**

Sheffield, F. D. 1965. Relation between classical conditioning and instrumental conditioning. In W. F. Prokasy (Ed.), *Classical conditioning: A symposium.* Englewood Cliffs, N.J.: Prentice-Hall. **(127, 145, 162)**

Sheffield, F. D., and Campbell, B. A. 1954. The role of experience in the "spontaneous" activity of hungry rats. *Journal of Comparative and Physiological Psychology,* 47:97–100. **(225)**

Sheffield, F. D., and Roby, T. B. 1950. Reward value of a non-nutritive sweet taste. *Journal of Comparative and Physiological Psychology,* 43:471–481. **(139)**

Sheffield, F. D.; Roby, T. B.; and Campbell, B. A. 1954. Drive reduction vs. consummatory behavior as determinants of reinforcement. *Journal of Comparative and Physiological Psychology,* 47:349–354. **(139)**

Sheffield, F. D.; Wulff, J. J.; and Backer, R. 1951. Reward value of copulation without sex drive reduction. *Journal of Comparative and Physiological Psychology,* 44:3–8. **(81, 139)**

Sheffield, V. F. 1949. Extinction as a function of partial reinforcement and distribution of practice. *Journal of Experimental Psychology, 39:*511–526. **(249)**

Shepard, R. N. 1967. Recognition memory for words, sentences, and pictures. *Journal of Verbal Learning and Verbal Behavior, 6:*156–163. **(464)**

Shepard, R. N., and Metzler, J. 1971. Mental rotation of three-dimensional objects. *Science, 171:*701–703. **(445)**

Sherrington, C. 1947. *The integrative action of the nervous system.* 2nd ed. New Haven: Yale University Press. **(44, 60)**

Shettleworth, S. J. 1972. Constraints on learning. In D. S. Lehrman, R. A. Hinde, and E. Shaw (Eds.), *Advances in the study of behavior.* New York: Academic Press. Pp. 175–198. **(43, 113, 162)**

Shettleworth, S. J. 1975. Reinforcement and the organization of behavior in golden hamsters: Hunger, environment, and food reinforcement. *Journal of Experimental Psychology: Animal Behavior Processes, 104:*56–87. **(161)**

Shick, K. 1971. Operants. *Journal of the Experimental Analysis of Behavior, 15:*413–423. **(155, 164)**

Shiffrin, R. M. 1970. Memory search. In D. A. Norman (Ed.), *Models of human memory.* New York: Academic Press. **(503)**

Shiffrin, R. M. 1973. Information persistence in short-term memory. *Journal of Experimental Psychology, 100:*39–49. **(452)**

Shiffrin, R. M. 1976. Capacity limitations in information processing, attention, and memory. In W. K. Estes (Ed.), *Handbook of learning and cognitive processes. Volume 4. Attention and memory.* Hillsdale, N.J.: Lawrence Erlbaum Associates. Pp. 177–236. **(431, 437, 438, 460)**

Shiffrin, R. M., and Cook, J. R. 1978. Short-term forgetting of item and order information. *Journal of Verbal Learning and Verbal Behavior, 17:*189–218. **(452)**

Shiffrin, R. M., and Gardner, G. T. 1972. Visual processing capacity and attentional controls. *Journal of Experimental Psychology, 93:*72–82. **(437)**

Shiffrin, R. M., and Schneider, W. 1977. Controlled and automatic human information processing: II. Perceptual learning, automatic attending and a general theory. *Psychological Review, 84:*127–190. **(437)**

Shimp, C. P. 1975. Perspectives on the behavioral unit: Choice behavior in animals. In W. K. Estes (Ed.), *Handbook of learning and cognitive processes,* Vol. 2. Hillsdale, N.J.: Lawrence Erlbaum Associates. Pp. 225–268. **(241)**

Shimp, C. P. 1976. Organization in memory and behavior. *Journal of the Experimental Analysis of Behavior, 26:*113–130. **(241, 449)**

Shulman, H. G. 1970. Encoding and retention of semantic and phonemic information in short-term memory. *Journal of Verbal Learning and Verbal Behavior, 9:*499–508. **(446)**

Shulman, H. G. 1971. Similarity effects in short-term memory. *Psychological Bulletin, 75:*399–415. **(446)**

Shulman, H. G. 1972. Semantic confusion errors in short-term memory. *Journal of Verbal Learning and Verbal Behavior, 11:*221–227. **(446)**

Shulman, H. G., and Martin, E. 1970. Effects of response-set similarity on unlearning and spontaneous recovery. *Journal of Experimental Psychology, 86:*230–235. **(499)**

Sidman, M. 1953. Two temporal parameters of the maintenance of avoidance behavior by the white rat. *Journal of Comparative and Physiological Psychology, 46:*253–261. **(207)**

Sidman, M. 1960. *Tactics of scientific research: Evaluating experimental data in psychology.* New York: Basic Books. **(74)**

Sidman, M. 1962. Reduction of shock frequency as reinforcement for avoidance behavior. *Journal of the Experimental Analysis of Behavior, 5:*247–257. **(207)**

Siegel, S. 1975. Evidence from rats that morphine tolerance is a learned response. *Journal of Comparative and Physiological Psychology, 89:*498–506. **(188)**

Siegel, S. 1977. Morphine tolerance acquisition as an associative process. *Journal of Experimental Psychology: Animal Behavior Processes, 3:*1–13. **(188)**

Siegel, S. In press. Learning and psychopharmacology. In M. E. Jarvik (Ed.), *Psychopharmacology in the practice of medicine.* Englewood Cliffs, N.J.: Prentice-Hall. **(188)**

Siegal, S., and Domjam, M. 1971. Backward conditioning as an inhibitory procedure. *Learning and Motivation,* 2:1–11. **(103)**

Silberberg, A., and Adler, N. 1974. Modulation of the copulatory sequence of the male rat by a schedule of reinforcement. *Science, 185:*374–376. **(69)**

Silver, D. S.; Saltz, E.; and Modigliani, V. 1970. Awareness and hypothesis testing in concept and operant learning. *Journal of Experimental Psychology, 84:*198–203. **(274)**

Simon, H. A. 1972. What is visual imagery? An information processing interpretation. In L. W. Gregg (Ed.), *Cognition in learning and memory.* New York: Wiley. Pp. 183–204. **(485)**

Simon, H. A. 1974. How big is a chunk? *Science, 183:*482–488. **(448)**

Simon, H. A., and Gilmartin, K. A. 1973. A simulation of memory for chess positions. *Cognitive Psychology, 5:*29–46. **(449)**

Simons, R. C.; Bobbit, R. A.; and Jensen, G. D. 1967. An experimental study of mother m. nemestrina's responses to infant vocalizations. *American Zoologist, 7:*112. **(69)**

Simpson, P. J. 1972. High-speed memory scanning: Stability and generality. *Journal of Experimental Psychology, 96:*239–246. **(460)**

Sinclair-de Zwart, H. 1973. Language acquisition and cognitive development. In T. E. Moore (Ed.), *Cognitive development and the acquisition of language.* New York: Academic Press. Pp. 9–25. **(366)**

Skinner, B. F. 1933. The abolishment of a discrimination. *Proceedings of the National Academy of Science, 8:*114–129. **(234)**

Skinner, B. F. 1937. Two types of conditioned reflex: A reply to Konorski and Miller. *Journal of General Psychology, 16:*272–279. **(164)**

Skinner, B. F. 1938. *The behavior of organisms.* Englewood Cliffs, N.J.: Prentice-Hall. **(83, 120, 154, 164, 172, 193, 243, 248, 250, 255)**

Skinner, B. F. 1945. The operational analysis of psychological terms. *Psychological Review, 52:*270–277. **(276)**

Skinner, B. F. 1948. Superstition in the pigeon. *Journal of Experimental Psychology, 38:*168–172. **(29, 30)**

Skinner, B. F. 1950. Are theories of learning necessary? *Psychological Review, 57:*193–216. **(206)**

Skinner, B. F. 1953. *Science and human behavior.* New York: Macmillan. **(156, 164, 174, 214, 270, 276, 359, 418)**

Skinner, B. F. 1954. The science of learning and the art of teaching. *Harvard Educational Review, 24:*86–97. **(152)**

Skinner, B. F. 1957. *Verbal behavior.* Englewood Cliffs, N.J.: Prentice-Hall. **(270, 276, 359, 365, 367, 395, 403, 408)**

Skinner, B. F. 1959. A case history of scientific method. In S. Koch (Ed.), *Psychology: A study of a science,* Vol. II. New York: McGraw-Hill. **(87, 234)**

Skinner, B. F. 1964. Behaviorism at fifty. In T. W. Wann (Ed.), *Behaviorism and phenomenology.* Chicago: University of Chicago Press. Pp. 79–96. **(214, 367)**

Skinner, B. F. 1966. The ontogeny and phylogeny of behavior. *Science, 153:*1203–1213. **(43, 164)**

Skinner, B. F. 1968. *The technology of teaching.* Englewood Cliffs, N.J.: Prentice-Hall. **(266, 270)**

Skinner, B. F. 1969. *Contingencies of reinforcement.* Englewood Cliffs, N.J.: Prentice-Hall. **(164, 395, 408)**

Skinner, B. F. 1971. *Beyond freedom and dignity.* New York: Knopf. **(30, 31)**

Skinner, B. F. 1974. *About behaviorism.* New York: Knopf. **(214, 271, 276, 313, 359, 367, 395, 408, 418)**

Skinner, B. F. 1975. The shaping of phylogenetic behavior. *Journal of the Experimental Analysis of Behavior, 24:*117–120. **(42)**

Slobin, D. I. 1966. Grammatical transformations and sentence comprehension in childhood and adulthood. *Journal of Verbal Learning and Verbal Behavior, 5:*219–227. **(337)**

Slobin, D. I. 1969. Imitation and grammatical development in children. In N. S. Endler, L. R. Boulten, and H. Osser (Eds.), *Contemporary issues in developmental psychology.* New York: Holt, Rinehart and Winston. **(405)**

Slobin, D. I. 1971a. Developmental psycholinguistics. In W. O. Dingwall (Ed.), *A survey of linguistic science*. College Park: University of Maryland Press. Pp. 298–410. **(332)**

Slobin, D. I. (Ed.) 1971b. *The ontogenesis of grammar*. New York: Academic Press. **(408)**

Slobin, D. I. 1971c. *Psycholinguistics*. Glenview, Ill.: Scott, Foresman. **(403)**

Slobin, D. I. 1973. Cognitive pre-requisites for the acquisition of grammar. In C. A. Ferguson and D. I. Slobin (Eds.), *Studies of child language development*. New York: Holt, Rinehart and Winston. Pp. 175–208. **(353, 366, 373, 379, 400)**

Sluckin, W. 1965. *Imprinting and early learning*. Chicago: Aldine. **(81)**

Smith, E. E. 1967. Effects of familiarity on stimulus recognition and categorization. *Journal of Experimental Psychology, 74*:324–332. **(490)**

Smith, E. E. 1978. Theories of semantic memory. In W. K. Estes (Ed.), *Handbook of learning and cognitive processes*, Vol. 6. Hillsdale, N.J.: Lawrence Erlbaum Associates. **(488, 492, 493)**

Smith, E. E., and Spoehr, K. T. 1974. The perception of printed English: A theoretical perspective. In B. H. Kantowitz (Ed.), *Human information processing: Tutorials in performance and cognition*. Hillsdale, N.J.: Lawrence Erlbaum Associates. **(431)**

Smith, E. E.; Shoben, E. J.; and Rips, L. J. 1974. Structure and process in semantic memory: A feature model for semantic decisions. *Psychological Review, 81*:214–241. **(283, 490, 493)**

Smith, J. B., and Clark, F. C. 1974. Intercurrent and reinforced behavior under multiple spaced-responding schedules. *Journal of the Experimental Analysis of Behavior, 21*:445–454. **(232)**

Smith, J. C., and Roll, D. L. 1967. Trace conditioning with X-rays as the aversive stimulus. *Psychonomic Science, 9*:11–12. **(113)**

Smith, M. C. 1968. CS-US interval and US intensity in classical conditioning of the rabbit's nictitating membrane response. *Journal of Comparative and Physiological Psychology, 66*:679–687. **(96, 97, 98, 100, 111)**

Smith, M. C.; Coleman, S. P.; and Gormezano, I. 1969. Classical conditioning of the rabbit's nictitating membrane response at backward, simultaneous, and forward CS-US intervals. *Journal of Comparative and Physiological Psychology, 69*:226–231. **(96, 97)**

Smith, N. V. 1973. *The acquisition of phonology: A case study*. Cambridge: Cambridge University Press. **(383, 384)**

Smith, N. V. 1975. Universal tendencies in the child's acquisition of phonology. In N. O'Connor (Ed.), *Language, cognitive deficits, and retardation*. London: Butterworth. Pp. 47–65. **(384)**

Smoke, K. L. 1933. Negative instances in concept learning. *Journal of Experimental Psychology, 16*:583–588. **(293)**

Snow, C. E. 1977. The development of conversation between mothers and babies. *Journal of Child Language, 4*:1–22. **(368, 380)**

Snow, C. E., and Ferguson, C. A. (Eds.) 1977. *Talking to children: Language input and acquisition*. Cambridge: Cambridge University Press. **(381, 402)**

Sokolov, E. N. 1963. *Perception and the conditioned reflex*. New York: Pergamon Press. **(45, 58, 74)**

Solomon, R. L., and Corbit, J. D. 1974. An opponent-process theory of motivation: I. Temporal dynamics of affect. *Psychological Bulletin, 81*:119–145. **(224)**

Solomon, R. L., and Turner, L. H. 1962. Discriminative classical conditioning in dogs paralyzed by curare can later control discriminative avoidance responses in the normal state. *Psychological Review, 69*:202–219. **(114)**

Spear, N. E.; Hill, W. F.; and O'Sullivan, D. J. 1965. Acquisition and extinction after initial trials without reward. *Journal of Experimental Psychology, 69*:25–29. **(252)**

Spence, K. W. 1937. The differential response in animals to stimuli within a single dimension. *Psychological Review, 44*:430–444. **(60, 189, 197, 198, 250)**

Spence, K. W. 1956. *Behavior theory and conditioning*. New Haven: Yale University Press. **(91, 92, 129, 130)**

Spence, K. W. 1960. *Behavior theory and learning*. Englewood Cliffs, N.J.: Prentice-Hall. **(243)**

Spence, K. W. 1966. Cognitive and drive factors in the extinction of the conditioned eye blink in human subjects. *Psychological Review,* 73:445–458. **(273)**

Spence, K. W., and Platt, J. R. 1967. Effects of partial reinforcement on acquisition and extinction of the conditioned eyeblink in a masking situation. *Journal of Experimental Psychology,* 74:259–263. **(94)**

Spence, K. W.; Haggard, D. F.; and Ross, L. E. 1958. UCS intensity and the associative (habit) strength of the eyelid CR. *Journal of Experimental Psychology,* 55:404–411. **(100, 150)**

Spencer-Booth, Y. 1968. The behavior of group companions toward rhesus monkey infants. *Animal Behaviour,* 16:541–557. **(69)**

Sperling, G. 1960. The information available in brief visual presentations. *Psychological Monographs,* 74:No. 498. **(419, 420, 421, 422, 423)**

Sperling, G.; Budiansky, J.; Spivak, J. G.; and Johnson, M. C. 1971. Extremely rapid visual search: The maximum rate of scanning letters for the presence of a numeral. *Science,* 174:307–311. **(460)**

Sperry, R. W. 1968. Hemisphere deconnection and unity in conscious awareness. *American Psychologist,* 23:723–733. **(392)**

Spielberger, C. D., and De Nike, L. D. 1966. Descriptive behaviorism versus cognitive theory in verbal operant conditioning. *Psychological Review,* 73:306–326. **(274)**

Spivey, J. E. 1967. Resistance to extinction as a function of number of N-R transitions and percentage of reinforcement. *Journal of Experimental Psychology,* 75:43–48. **(253)**

Spivey, J. E., and Hess, D. T. 1968. Effect of partial reinforcement trial sequences on extinction performance. *Psychonomic Science,* 10:375–376. **(253)**

Staats, A.; Finley, J.; Minke, K. A.; Wolf, M.; and Brooks, C. 1964. A reinforcer system and experimental procedure for the laboratory study of reading acquisition. *Child Development,* 35:209–231. **(170)**

Staddon, J. E. R. 1970. Temporal effects of reinforcement: A negative "frustration" effect. *Learning and Motivation,* 1:227–247. **(239, 249)**

Staddon, J. E. R. 1974. Temporal control, attention, and memory. *Psychological Review,* 81:375–391. **(239)**

Staddon, J. E. R. 1976. Schedule-induced behavior. In W. K. Honig and J. E. R. Staddon (Eds.), *Handbook of operant behavior.* Englewood Cliffs, N.J.: Prentice-Hall. Pp. 125–152. **(232)**

Staddon, J. E. R., and Innis, N. K. 1969. Reinforcement omission on fixed-interval schedules. *Journal of the Experimental Analysis of Behavior,* 12:689–700. **(239, 249)**

Staddon, J. E. R., and Simmelhag, V. L. 1971. The "superstition" experiment: A reexamination of its implications for the principles of adaptive behavior. *Psychological Review,* 78:3–43. **(39, 126, 232)**

Standing, L. 1973. Learning 10,000 pictures. *Quarterly Journal of Experimental Psychology,* 25:207–222. **(465)**

Standing, L.; Conezio, J.; and Haber, R. N. 1970. Perception and memory for pictures: Single-trial learning of 2560 visual stimuli. *Psychonomic Science,* 19:73–74. **(465)**

Stark, R. E.; Rose, S. N.; and McLagen, M. 1975. Features of infant sounds: The first eight weeks of life. *Journal of Child Language,* 2:205–222. **(360)**

Stein, B. S. 1978. Depth of processing reexamined: the effects of the precision of encoding and test appropriateness. *Journal of Verbal Learning and Verbal Behavior,* 17:165–174. **(470)**

Steinberg, D. D., and Jakobovits, L. A. (Eds.) 1971. *Semantics: An interdisciplinary reader in philosophy, linguistics, and psychology.* London: Cambridge University Press. **(341)**

Steinman, W. M. 1970a. The social control of generalized imitation. *Journal of Applied Behavior Analysis,* 3:159–167. **(270)**

Steinman, W. M. 1970b. Generalized imitation and the discrimination hypothesis. *Journal of Experimental Child Psychology,* 10:79–99. **(270)**

Sterman, M. B. 1973. Neurophysiologic and clinical studies of sensorimotor EEG biofeedback training: Some effects on epilepsy. *Seminars in Psychiatry,* 5:507–525. **(276)**

Stern, R. M., and Lewis, N. L. 1968. Ability of actors to control their GSRs and express emotions. *Psychophysiology,* 4:294–299. **(273)**

Sternberg, S. 1966. High-speed scanning in human memory. *Science, 153*:652–654. **(456, 457, 458)**

Sternberg, S. 1967. Two operations in character recognition: Some evidence from reaction-time measurements. *Perception and Psychophysics, 2*:45–53. **(456)**

Sternberg, S. 1969. The discovery of processing stages: Extensions of Donder's method. *Acta Psychologica, 30*:276–315. **(456)**

Sternberg, S. 1975. Memory scanning: New findings and current controversies. *Quarterly Journal of Experimental Psychology, 27*:1–32. **(436, 456, 459, 460)**

Stevens, K. N., and House, A. S. 1972. Speech perception. In J. V. Tobias (Ed.), *Foundations of modern auditory theory*, Vol. 2. New York: Academic Press. Pp. 3–62. **(316)**

Stitt, C. L.; Hoffman, H. S.; and Marsh, R. 1973. Modification of the rat's startle reaction by termination of antecedent acoustic signals. *Journal of Comparative and Physiological Psychology, 84*:207–215. **(51)**

Streeter, L. A., and Landauer, T. K. 1975. Effects of learning English as a second language on the acquisition of a new phonemic contrast. Paper presented at the 89th Meeting of the Acoustical Society of America at Austin, Texas, 1975. **(321)**

Strohner, H., and Nelson, K. E. 1974. The young child's development of sentence comprehension: Influence of event probability, nonverbal context, syntactic form, and strategies. *Child Development, 45*:567–576. **(389)**

Strong, P. N., Jr. 1966. Comparative studies in simple oddity learning: II. Children, adults and seniles. *Psychonomic Science, 6*:459–460. **(298)**

Stubbs, A. 1969. Contiguity of briefly presented stimuli with food reinforcement. *Journal of the Experimental Analysis of Behavior, 12*:271–278. **(172)**

Stubbs, D. A. 1971. Second-order schedules and the problem of conditioned reinforcement. *Journal of the Experimental Analysis of Behavior, 16*:289–313. **(173)**

Studdert-Kennedy, M. 1974. The perception of speech. In T. A. Sebeok (Ed.), *Current trends in linguistics, Vol. 12: Linguistics and adjacent arts and sciences*. The Hague: Mouton. Pp. 2349–2385. **(322)**

Studdert-Kennedy, M. and Shankweiler, D. 1970. Hemispheric specialization for speech perception. *Journal of the Acoustical Society of America, 48*:597–594. **(322)**

Studdert-Kennedy, M.; Shankweiler, D.; and Pisoni, D. 1972. Auditory and phonetic processes in speech perception: Evidence from a dichotic study. *Cognitive Psychology, 3*:455–466. **(392)**

Sulzer, B., and Mayer, G. R. 1977. *Behavioral procedures with children and youth*. New York: Holt, Rinehart and Winston. **(128, 194)**

Suppes, P. 1969. Stimulus-response theory of finite automata. *Journal of Mathematical Psychology, 6*:327–355. **(412)**

Suppes, P., and Ginsberg, R. 1963. A fundamental property of all-or-none models. *Psychological Review, 70*:139–161. **(157)**

Teghtsoonian, R., and Campbell, B. A. 1960. Random activity of the rat during food deprivation as a function of environment. *Journal of Comparative and Physiological Psychology, 53*:242–244. **(225)**

Teitelbaum, P., and Epstein, A. N. 1962. The lateral hypothalamic syndrome. *Psychological Review, 69*:74–90. **(224)**

Teleki, G. 1973. *The predatory behavior of wild chimpanzees*. Lewisburg, Pa.: Bucknell University Press. **(347)**

Tell, P. M. 1972. The role of certain acoustic and semantic factors at short and long retention intervals. *Journal of Verbal Learning and Verbal Behavior, 11*:455–464. **(444)**

Terhune, J. G. 1978. The relationship between momentary response probabilities and momentary reinforcement effects. *Animal Learning and Behavior, 6*:187–192. **(225)**

Terhune, J. G., and Premack, D. 1975. Comparison of reinforcement and punishment functions produced by the same contingent event in the same subjects. *Learning and Motivation, 5*:221–230. **(143)**

Terrace, H. S. 1963a. Discrimination learning with and without "errors." *Journal of the Experimental Analysis of Behavior, 6*:1–27. **(193, 255)**

Terrace, H. S. 1963b. Errorless transfer of a discrimination across two continua. *Journal of the Experimental Analysis of Behavior, 6*:223–232. **(193)**

Terrace, H. S. 1966. Stimulus control. In W. K. Honig (Ed.), *Operant behavior: Areas of research and application.* Englewood Cliffs, N.J.: Prentice-Hall. Pp. 271–344. **(218, 255)**

Terrace, H. S. 1968. Discrimination learning, the peak shift and behavioral contrast. *Journal of the Experimental Analysis of Behavior, 11:727–741.* **(193)**

Terrace, H. S. 1975. Evidence for the innate basis of the hue dimension in the duckling. *Journal of the Experimental Analysis of Behavior, 24:79–87.* **(178)**

Terrace, H. S. 1979. Is problem-solving language? *Journal of the Experimental Analysis of Behavior, 31:161–175.* **(355)**

Teyler, T. J.; Baum, W. M.; and Patterson, M. M. 1975. Behavioral and biological issues in the learning paradigm. *Physiological Psychology, 3:65–72.* **(93)**

Theois, J. 1962. The partial reinforcement effect sustained through blocks of continuous reinforcement. *Journal of Experimental Psychology, 64:1–6.* **(254)**

Theios, J., and Brelsford, J. W., Jr. 1966. A Markov model for classical conditioning: Application to eyeblink conditioning in rabbits. *Psychological Review, 73:393–408.* **(157)**

Thiessen, D. D. 1972. *Gene organization and behavior.* New York: Random House. **(34)**

Thiessen, D. D. 1976. *The evolution and chemistry of aggression.* Springfield, Ill.: Thomas. **(229)**

Thomas, D. R. 1962. The effects of drive and discrimination training on stimulus generalization. *Journal of Experimental Psychology, 64:24–28.* **(261)**

Thomas, D. R. 1970. Stimulus selection, attention, and related matters. In J. H. Reynierse (Ed.), *Current issues in animal learning,* Lincoln: University of Nebraska Press. Pp. 311–356. **(203)**

Thomas, D. R., and Caronite, S. C. 1964. Stimulus generalization of a positive conditioned reinforcer: II. Effects of discrimination training. *Journal of Experimental Psychology, 68:402–406.* **(171)**

Thomas, D. R., and DeCapito, A. 1966. Role of stimulus labeling in stimulus generalization. *Journal of Experimental Psychology, 71:913–915.* **(198)**

Thomas, D. R.; Freeman, F.; Svinicki, J. G.; Burr, D. E. S.; and Lyons, J. 1970. Effects of extradimensional training on stimulus generalization. *Journal of Experimental Psychology Monographs, 83:1,* Part 2. **(189, 203)**

Thompson, R. F. 1965. The neural basis of stimulus generalization. In D. I. Mostofsky (Ed.), *Stimulus generalization.* Stanford, Calif.: Stanford University Press. Pp. 154–178. **(187)**

Thompson, R. F. 1976. The search for the engram. *American Psychologist, 31:209–227.* **(28, 104, 106)**

Thompson, R. F., and Spencer, W. A. 1966. Habituation: A model phenomenon for the study of neuronal substrates of behavior. *Psychological Review, 73:16–43.* **(55, 60)**

Thompson, R. F.; Groves, P. M.; Teyler, T. J.; and Roemer, R. A. 1973. A dual-process theory of habituation. In H. V. S. Peeke and M. J. Herz (Eds.), *Habituation,* Vol. I. New York: Academic Press. Pp. 239–272. **(54, 58, 60, 61, 62)**

Thompson, T., and Sturm, T. 1965. Classical conditioning of aggressive display in Siamese fighting fish. *Journal of the Experimental Analysis of Behavior, 8:397–403.* **(81)**

Thomson, D. M., and Tulving, E. 1970. Associative encoding and retrieval: Weak and strong cues. *Journal of Experimental Psychology, 86:255–262.* **(504, 505, 506, 507)**

Thorndike, E. L. 1898. Animal intelligence: An experimental study of the associative processes in animals. *The Psychological Review Monograph Supplements 2, 4:* No. 8. Pp. 1–74. **(24, 43)**

Thorndike, E. L. 1903. *Educational psychology.* New York: Lemcke & Buechner. **(187)**

Thorndike, E. L. 1911 *Animal intelligence.* New York: Macmillan. **(38)**

Thorndike, E. L. 1931. *Human learning.* Englewood Cliffs, N.J.: Prentice-Hall. **(38)**

Thorpe, W. H. 1963. *Learning and instinct in animals.* Cambridge, Mass.: Harvard University Press. **(49)**

Thune, L. E. 1950. The effect of different types of preliminary activities on subsequent learning of paired-associate material. *Journal of Experimental Psychology, 40:423–438.* **(262)**

Thurstone, L. L. 1930. The learning function. *Journal of Genetic Psychology, 3:469–493.* **(156)**

Till, R. E., and Jenkins, J. J. 1973. The effects of cued orienting tasks on the free recall of words. *Journal of Verbal Learning and Verbal Behavior*, 12:489–498. **(468)**

Timberlake, W., and Allison, J. 1974. Response deprivation: An empirical approach to instrumental performance. *Psychological Review*, 81:146–164. **(133, 144, 225)**

Timberlake, W., and Grant, D. L. 1975. Autoshaping in rats to the presentation of another rat predicting food. *Science*, 190:690–692. **(111)**

Tinbergen, N. 1952. "Derived" activities; their causation, biological significance, origin, and emancipation during evolution. *Quarterly Review of Biology*, 27:1–32. **(232)**

Tinbergen, N. 1964. The evolution of signalling devices. In W. Etkin (Ed.), *Social behavior and evolution among vertebrates*. Chicago: University of Chicago Press. Pp. 206–230. **(232)**

Tinbergen, N.; Broekhuysen, G. J.; Feekes, F.; Houghton, J. C. W.; Kruuk, H.; and Szulc, E. 1962. Egg shell removal by the black-headed gull, *Larus ridibundus* L.: A behaviour component of camouflage. *Behavior*, 19:74–118. **(17, 19)**

Tolman, E. C. 1932. *Purposive behavior in animals and men*. Englewood Cliffs, N.J.: Prentice-Hall. **(104, 120, 156)**

Tolman, E. C. 1938. The determiners of behavior at a choice point. *Psychological Review*, 45:1–41. **(147)**

Tolman, E. C., and Brunswik, E. 1935. The organism and the causal texture of the environment. *Psychological Review*, 42:43–77. **(234)**

Tomie, A. 1976. Interference with autoshaping by prior context conditioning. *Journal of Experimental Psychology: Animal Behavior Processes*, 2:323–334. **(204)**

Townsend, J. T. 1971. A note on the identifiability of parallel and serial processes. *Perception and Psychophysics*, 10:161–163. **(459)**

Trabasso, T. R., and Bower, G. H. 1964. Memory in concept identification. *Psychonomic Science*, 1:133–134. **(307)**

Trabasso, I, and Bower, G. H. 1968. *Attention in learning: Theory and research*. New York: Wiley. **(189)**

Tracy, W. K. 1970. Wavelength generalization and preference in monochromatically reared ducklings. *Journal of the Experimental Analysis of Behavior*, 13:153–178. **(178)**

Trapold, M. A., and Overmier, J. B. 1972. The second learning process in instrumental learning. In A. H. Black and W. F. Prokasy (Eds.), *Classical conditioning II: Current research and theory*. Englewood Cliffs, N.J.: Prentice-Hall. **(155, 266)**

Treisman, A. M. 1960. Contextual cues in selective listening. *Quarterly Journal of Experimental Psychology*, 12:242–248. **(434)**

Treisman, A. M. 1964. Selective attention in man. *British Medical Bulletin*, 20:12–16. **(434)**

Treisman, A. M. 1969. Strategies and models of selective attention. *Psychological Review*, 76:282–299. **(435)**

Trivers, R. 1971. The evolution of reciprocal altruism. *Quarterly Review of Biology*, 46:35–57. **(38)**

Trivers, R. L., and Hare, H. 1976. Haplodiploidy and the evolution of the social insects. *Science*, 191:249–263. **(38)**

Trowill, J. A.; Panksepp, J.; and Gandleman, R. 1969. An incentive model of rewarding brain stimulation. *Psychological Review*, 76:264–281. **(230)**

Tulving, E. 1962. Subjective organization in free recall of unrelated words. *Psychological Review*, 69:344–354. **(472, 473)**

Tulving, E. 1966. Subjective organization and the effects of repetition in multitrial free recall verbal learning. *Journal of Verbal Learning and Verbal Behavior*, 5:193–197. **(513)**

Tulving, E. 1968. Theoretical issues in free recall. In T. R. Dixon and D. L. Horton (Eds.), *Verbal behavior and general behavior theory*. Englewood Cliffs, N.J.: Prentice-Hall, Pp. 2–36. **(472, 513)**

Tulving, E. 1972. Episodic and semantic memory. In E. Tulving and W. Donaldson (Eds.), *Organization of memory*. New York: Academic Press. Pp. 381–403. **(488)**

Tulving, E. 1974. Cue-dependent forgetting. *American Scientist*, 62:74–82. **(493, 504)**

Tulving, E. 1976. Ecphoric processes in recall and recognition. In J. Brown (Ed.), *Recall and recognition*. New York: Wiley. Pp. 37–74. **(509, 510)**

Tulving, E., and Bower, G. H. 1974. The logic of memory representations. In G. H. Bower (Ed.), *The psychology of learning and motivation: Advances in research and theory*, Vol. 8. New York: Academic Press. **(464)**

Tulving, E., and Donaldson, W. (Eds.), 1972. *Organization of memory*. New York: Academic Press. **(471)**

Tulving, E., and Osler, S. 1968. Effectiveness of retrieval cues in memory for words. *Journal of Experimental Psychology*, 77:593–601. **(513)**

Tulving, E., and Psotka, J. 1971. Retroactive inhibition in free recall: Inaccessibility of information available in the memory store. *Journal of Experimental Psychology*, 87:1–8. **(503, 505)**

Tulving, E., and Thomson, D. M. 1973. Encoding specificity and retrieval processes in episodic memory. *Psychological Review*, 80:352–373. **(254, 504, 505, 510)**

Tulving, E., and Wiseman, S. 1975. Relation between recognition and recognition failure of recallable words. *Bulletin of the Psychonomic Society*, 6:78–82. **(507)**

Turvey, M. T. 1978. Visual processing and short-term memory. In W. K. Estes (Ed.), *Handbook of learning and cognitive processes*. Hillsdale, N.J.: Lawrence Erlbaum Associates. Pp. 91–142. **(422, 423)**

Turvey, M. T., and Kravetz, S. 1970. Retrieval from iconic memory with shape as the selection criterion. *Perception and Psychophysics*, 80:171–172. **(423)**

Tversky, B. 1973. Encoding processes in recognition and recall. *Cognitive Psychology*, 5:275–287. **(488)**

Uhl, C. N. 1973. Eliminating behavior with omission and extinction after varying amounts of training. *Animal Learning and Behavior*, 1:237–240. **(145)**

Underwood, B. J. 1948. Retroactive and proactive inhibition after five and forty eight hours. *Journal of Experimental Psychology*, 38:29–38. **(497)**

Underwood, B. J. 1954. Speed of learning and amount retained: A consideration of methodology. *Psychological Bulletin*, 51:276–282. **(481)**

Underwood, B. J. 1957. Interference and forgetting. *Psychological Review*, 64:48–60. **(495)**

Underwood, B. J. 1964. Degree of learning and the measurement of forgetting. *Journal of Verbal Learning and Verbal Behavior*, 3:112–129. **(481)**

Underwood, B. J. 1966. *Experimental psychology*. Englewood Cliffs, N.J.: Prentice-Hall. **(261)**

Underwood, B. J. 1969. Attributes of memory. *Psychological Review*, 76:559–573. **(464)**

Underwood, B. J. 1972. Word recognition memory and frequency information. *Journal of Experimental Psychology*, 94:276–283. **(509)**

Underwood, B. J., and Ekstrand, B. R. 1966. An analysis of some shortcomings in the interference theory of forgetting. *Psychological Review*, 73:540–549. **(502)**

Underwood, B. J. and Ekstrand, B. R. 1967. Studies of distributed practice: xxix. Differentiation and proactive inhibition. *Journal of Experimental Psychology*, 74:574–580. **(502)**

Underwood, B. J., and Freund, J. S. 1968. Effect of temporal separation of two-tasks on proactive inhibition. *Journal of Experimental Psychology*, 78:50–54. **(502)**

Underwood, B. J., and Postman, L. 1960. Extra-experimental sources of interference in forgetting. *Psychological Review*, 67:73–95. **(513)**

Underwood, B. J., and Richardson, J. 1956a. Verbal concept learning as a function of instructions and dominance level. *Journal of Experimental Psychology*, 51:229–239. **(296)**

Underwood, B. J., and Richardson, J. 1956b. The influence of meaningfulness, intralist similarity, and serial position on retention. *Journal of Experimental Psychology*, 52:119–126. **(215)**

Underwood, B. J., and Schulz, R. W. 1960. *Meaningfulness and verbal learning*. Philadelphia: Lippincott. **(500)**

Underwood, G. 1974. Moray vs. the rest: The effects of extended shadowing practice. *Quarterly Journal of Experimental Psychology*, 26:368–372. **(435)**

Valenstein, E. S.; Cox, V. C.; and Kakolewski, J. W. 1968. Modification of motivated behavior elicited by electrical stimulation of the hypothalamus. *Science, 157*:552–554. **(230, 231)**

Valenstein, E. S.; Cox, V. C.; and Kakolewski, J. W. 1969. The hypothalamus and motivated behavior. In J. T. Tapp (Ed.), *Reinforcement and behavior.* New York: Academic Press. Pp. 242–285. **(230)**

Valenstein, E. S.; Cox, V. C.; and Kakolewski, J. W. 1970. Re-examination of the role of the hypothalamus in motivation. *Psychological Review, 77*:16–31. **(230)**

VanDercar, D. H., and Schneiderman, N. 1967. Interstimulus interval functions in different response systems during classical discrimination conditioning of rabbits. *Psychonomic Science, 9*:9–10. **(97)**

vom Saal, W., and Jenkins, H. M. 1970. Blocking the development of stimulus control. *Learning and Motivation, 1*:52–64. **(137)**

von Holst, E., and von Saint-Paul, U. 1963. On the functional organization of drives. *Animal Behavior, 11*:1–20. **(230)**

von Wright, J. 1968. Selection in visual immediate memory. *Quarterly Journal of Experimental Psychology, 20*:62–68. **(423)**

von Wright, J. M. 1970. On selection in visual immediate memory. *Acta Psychologica, 33*:280–292. **(423)**

Voronin, L. G.; Leontiev, A. N.; Luria, A. R.; Sokolov, E. N.; and Vinogradova, O. S. 1965. *Orienting reflex and exploratory behavior.* Washington, D.C.: American Institute of Biological Sciences. **(45)**

Wade, G. N. 1972. Gonadal hormones and behavioral regulation of body weight. *Physiology and Behavior, 8*:523–534. **(224)**

Wagner, A. R. 1959. The role of reinforcement and nonreinforcement in an "apparent frustration effect." *Journal of Experimental Psychology, 57*:130–136. **(250)**

Wagner, A. R. 1969. Stimulus selection and a "modified continuity theory." In G. H. Bower and J. T. Spence (Eds.), *The psychology of learning and motivation,* Vol. 3. New York: Academic Press. **(102)**

Wagner, A. R. 1975. Priming in STM: An information processing mechanism for self-generated or retrieval-generated depression in performance. In T. J. Tighe and R. N. Leaton (Eds.), *Habituation: Perspectives from child development, animal behavior, and neurophysiology.* Hillsdale, N.J.: Lawrence Erlbaum Associates. **(74)**

Wagner, A. R.; Logan, F. A.; Haberlandt, K.; and Price, T. 1968. Stimulus selection in animal discrimination learning. *Journal of Experimental Psychology, 76*:171–180. **(203)**

Wagner, A. R., and Rescorla, R. A. 1972. Inhibition in Pavlovian conditioning. In R. A. Boakes and M. S. Halliday (Eds.), *Inhibition and learning.* New York: Academic Press. **(102, 181)**

Wahlsten, D. L., and Cole, M. 1972. Classical and avoidance training of leg flexion in the dog. In A. H. Black and W. H. Prokasy (Eds.), *Classical conditioning II: Research and theory.* Englewood Cliffs, N.J.: Prentice-Hall. Pp. 379–408. **(111)**

Walker, E. L. 1958. Action decrement and its relation to learning. *Psychological Review, 65*:129–142. **(229)**

Walker, E. L. 1967. Arousal and the memory trace. In D. P. Kimble (Ed.), *The organization of recall.* New York: Academy of Sciences. **(229)**

Wallace, M., and Singer, G. 1976. Adjunctive behavior and smoking induced by a maze solving schedule in humans. *Physiology and Behavior, 17*:849–852. **(232)**

Wallace, W. P. 1978. Recognition failure of recallable words and recognizable words. *Journal of Experimental Psychology: Human Learning and Memory, 4*:441–452. **(511)**

Walsh, D. A., and Jenkins, J. J. 1973. Effects of orienting tasks on free recall in incidental learning: "Difficulty," "effort," and "process" explanations. *Journal of Verbal Learning and Verbal Behavior, 12*:481–488. **(469)**

Ward, L. B. 1937. Reminiscence and rote learning. *Psychological Monographs, 49*:No. 220. **(302)**

Warden, D. A. 1976. The influence of context on children's use of identifying expressions and references. *British Journal of Psychology, 67*:101–102. **(402)**

Warren, J. M. 1965. Primate learning in comparative perspective. In A. M. Schrier, H. F. Harlow, and F. Stollnitz (Eds.), *Behavior of nonhuman primates*, Vol. 1. New York: Academic Press. Pp. 249–281. **(303)**

Warren, L. C. 1974. An analysis of proactive inhibition in a cued recall task. *Journal of Experimental Psychology*, 103:131–138. **(502)**

Waters, R. S., and Wilson, W. A., Jr. 1976. Speech perception by rhesus monkeys: The voicing distinction in synthesized labial and velar stop consonants. *Perception and Psychophysics*, 19:285–289. **(361)**

Watkins, M. J., and Tulving, E. 1975. Episodic memory: When recognition fails. *Journal of Experimental Psychology: General*, 104:5–20. **(510, 513)**

Watkins, M. J.; Watkins, O. C.; Craik, L. I. M.; and Mazuryk, G. 1973. Effect of verbal distraction on short-term storage. *Journal of Experimental Psychology*, 101:296–300. **(456)**

Watson, J. B. 1913. Psychology as the behaviorist views it. *Psychological Review*, 20:158–177. **(87, 214)**

Watson, J. B. 1914. *Behavior: An introduction to comparative psychology*. New York: Holt, Rinehart and Winston. **(87)**

Watson, J. B. 1924. *Behaviorism*. New York: Norton. **(43)**

Watson, R. I. 1971. *The great psychologists*. Philadelphia: Lippincott. **(212, 218)**

Waugh, N. C., and Norman, D. A. 1965. Primary memory. *Psychological Review*, 72:89–104. **(444, 455)**

Waxler, C. Z., and Yarrow, M. R. 1970. Factors influencing imitative learning in preschool children. *Journal of Experimental Child Psychology*, 9:115–130. **(270)**

Wayner, M. J.; Singer, G.; Cimino, K.; Stein, J.; and Dworkin, L. 1975. Adjunctive behavior induced by different conditions of wheel running. *Physiology and Behavior*, 14:507–510. **(232)**

Wegener, A. 1966. *The origin of continents and oceans*. New York: Dover. **(42)**

Weimer, W. B. 1973. Psycholinguistics and Plato's paradoxes of the Meno. *American Psychologist*, 28:15–33. **(91)**

Weinstock, S. 1954. Resistance to extinction of a running response following partial reinforcement under widely spaced trials. *Journal of Comparative and Physiological Psychology*, 47:318–322. **(254)**

Weisman, R. G., and Davis, E. R. 1976. Interresponse time analysis of behavioral interaction. *Bulletin of the Psychonomic Society*, 8:27–29. **(195)**

Weisman, R. G., and Litner, J. S. 1969. Positive conditioned reinforcement of Sidman avoidance in rats. *Journal of Comparative and Physiological Psychology*, 68:597–603. **(209)**

Weiss, B. 1970. The fine structure of operant behavior during transition states. In W. N. Schoenfeld (Ed.), *The theory of reinforcement schedules*. Englewood Cliffs, N.J.: Prentice-Hall. Pp. 277–311. **(158, 244)**

Weiss, K. M. 1978. A comparison of forward and backward procedures for the acquisition of response chains in humans. *Journal of the Experimental Analysis of Behavior*, 29:255–259. **(153)**

Weiss, S. J. 1976. Multiple schedule control of free-operant avoidance: The contribution of response rate and incentive relations between schedule components. *Learning and Motivation*, 7:477–516. **(196)**

Weiss, S. J. 1977. The isolation of stimulus-reinforcer associations established with multiple schedules. *Animal Learning and Behavior*, 5:421–429. **(196)**

Weiss, S. J. 1978. Discriminated response and incentive processes in operant conditioning: A two-factor model of stimulus control. *Journal of the Experimental Analysis of Behavior*, 30:361–381. **(196)**

Welker, R. L., and McAuley, K. 1978. Reductions in resistance to extinction and spontaneous recovery as a function of changes in transportational and contextual stimuli. *Animal Learning and Behavior*, in press. **(205, 206)**

Well, A. D., and Sonnenschein, B. 1973. Effects of irrelevant stimulus dimensions on selection in immediate memory. *Journal of Experimental Psychology*, 99:283–285. **(423)**

Wells, H. 1963. Effects of transfer and problem structure in disjunctive concept formation. *Journal of Experimental Psychology,* 65:63–69. **(289)**

Wessells, M. G. 1973. Errorless discrimination, autoshaping, and conditioned inhibition, *Science,* 182:941–943. **(255)**

Wessells, M. G. 1974. The effects of reinforcement upon the prepecking behaviors of pigeons in the autoshaping experiment. *Journal of the Experimental Analysis of Behavior,* 21:125–144. **(162)**

Wetherick, N. E. 1975. The role of semantic information in short-term memory. *Journal of Verbal Learning and Verbal Behavior,* 14:471–480. **(446)**

Whalen, R. E. 1971. The ontogeny of sexuality. In H. Moltz (Ed.), *The ontogeny of vertebrate behavior.* New York: Academic Press. **(68)**

Wheeler, D. D. 1970. Processes in word recognition. *Cognitive Psychology,* 1:59–85. **(431)**

Whitehurst, G. J. 1972. Production of novel and grammatical utterances by young children. *Journal of Experimental Child Psychology,* 13:502–515. **(380)**

Whitehurst, G. J. 1978. Observational learning. In A. Charles Catania and Thomas A. Brigham (Eds.), *Handbook of applied behavior analysis.* New York: Irvington. Pp. 142–178. **(384, 405)**

Whitlow, T. W. 1975. Short-term memory in habituation and dishabituation. *Journal of Experimental Psychology: Animal Behavior Processes,* 104:189–206. **(74)**

Whorf, B. L. 1956. *Language, thought, and reality.* Cambridge, Mass.: M.I.T. Press. **(371)**

Wichawut, C., and Martin E. 1971. Independence of A-B and A-C associations in retroaction. *Journal of Verbal Learning and Verbal Behavior,* 10:316–321. **(501)**

Wickelgren, W. A. 1965. Acoustic similarity and retroactive interference in short-term memory. *Journal of Verbal Learning and Verbal Behavior,* 4:53–61. **(455)**

Wickelgren, W. A. 1973. The long and short of memory. *Psychological Bulletin,* 80:425–438. **(477)**

Wickens, D. D. 1970. Encoding categories of words: An empirical approach to meaning. *Psychological Review,* 77:1–15. **(464)**

Wickens, D. D. 1972. Characteristics of word encoding. In A. Melton and E. Martin (Eds.), *Coding processes in human memory.* New York: Holt, Rinehart and Winston. **(446, 454, 464)**

Wickens, D. D., and Cross, H. A. 1963. Resistance to extinction as a function of temporal relations during sensory preconditioning. *Journal of Experimental Psychology,* 65:206–211. **(110)**

Wickens, D. D.; Born, D. G.; and Allen, C. K. 1963. Proactive inhibition and item similarity in short-term memory. *Journal of Verbal Learning and Verbal Behavior,* 2:440–445. **(453, 454)**

Wieman, L. A. 1976. Stress patterns of early child language. *Journal of Child Language,* 3:283–286. **(373)**

Wiesel, T. N. and Hubel, D. H. 1965. Comparison of the effects of unilateral and bilateral eye closure on cortical unit responses in kittens. *Journal of Neurophysiology,* 28:1029–1040. **(428)**

Wike, E. L. 1966. *Secondary reinforcement.* New York: Harper & Row. **(176)**

Wilder, L. 1975. Articulatory and acoustic characteristics of speech sounds. In D. W. Massaro (Ed.), *Understanding language.* New York: Academic Press. Pp. 31–76. **(318)**

Wilkins, A. 1971. Conjoint frequency, category size, and categorization time. *Journal of Verbal Learning and Verbal Behavior,* 10:382–385. **(490)**

Williams, D. R., and Williams, H. 1969. Auto-maintenance in the pigeon: Sustained pecking despite contingent nonreinforcement. *Journal of the Experimental Analysis of Behavior,* 12:511–520. **(127, 161)**

Willner, J. A. 1978. Blocking of a taste aversion by prior pairings of exteroceptive stimuli with illness. *Learning and Motivation,* 9:125–140. **(113)**

Wilson, C. J., and Groves, D. M. 1973. Refractory period and habituation of acoustic startle response in rats. *Journal of Comparative and Physiological Psychology,* 83:492–498. **(51)**

Wilson, D. S. 1975. A theory of group selection. *Proceedings of the National Academy of Sciences,* 72:143–146. **(38)**

Wilson, E. O. 1975. *Sociobiology*. Cambridge, Mass.: Harvard University Press. **(38, 65, 71, 72)**

Wingfield, A., and Byrnes, D. L. 1972. Decay of information in short-term memory. *Science, 176*:490–492. **(452)**

Winograd, E. 1968. List differentiation, recall, and category similarity. *Journal of Experimental Psychology, 78*:510–515. **(502)**

Winokur, S. 1976. *A primer of verbal behavior: An operant view*. Englewood Cliffs, N.J.: Prentice-Hall. **(366, 403)**

Wise, K. L.; Wise, L. A.; and Zimmerman, R. R. 1974. Piagetian object permanence in the infant rhesus monkey. *Developmental Psychology, 10*:429–437. **(367)**

Wiseman, S., and Tulving, E. 1975. A test of confusion theory of encoding specificity. *Journal of Verbal Learning and Verbal Behavior, 14*:370–381. **(507, 513)**

Witelson, S., and Pallie, W. 1973. Left hemisphere specialization for language in the newborn. *Brain, 96*:641–646. **(393)**

Wittgenstein, L. 1953. *Philosophical investigations*. New York: Macmillan. **(282)**

Wolfe, J. B. 1936. Effectiveness of token rewards for chimpanzees. *Comparative Psychology Monographs, 12*:5, No. 60. **(175)**

Wolff, P. H. 1966. The natural history of crying and other vocalization in early infancy. In B. M. Foss (Ed.), *Determinants of infant behavior*, Vol. 4. London: Methuen. Pp. 81–109. **(360)**

Wolford, G. L.; Wessel, D. L.; and Estes, W. K. 1968. Further evidence concerning scanning and sampling assumptions of visual detection models. *Perception and Psychophysics, 3*:439–444. **(437)**

Wolpe, J. 1958. Psychotherapy by reciprocal inhibition. Stanford, Calif.: Stanford University Press. **(85, 247)**

Wolpe, J. 1973. *The practice of behavior therapy*. New York: Pergamon. **(247)**

Wood, G. 1972. Organizational processes and free recall. In E. Tulving and W. Donaldson (Eds.), *Organization of memory*. New York: Academic Press. Pp. 49–91. **(513)**

Woodward, A. E.; Bjork, R. A.; and Jongeward, R. H. 1973. Recall and recognition as a function of primary rehearsal. *Journal of Verbal Learning and Verbal Behavior, 12*:608–614. **(477, 478)**

Woodworth, R. S. 1909. Hermann Ebbinghaus. *The Journal of Philosophy, 6*:253–256. **(211, 218)**

Woodworth, R. S. 1938. *Experimental psychology*. New York: Holt, Rinehart and Winston. **(494)**

Wyckoff, L. B. 1959. Toward a quantitative theory of secondary reinforcement. *Psychological Review, 66*:68–78. **(172)**

Yamaguchi, H. G. 1952. Gradients of drive stimulus (S_D) intensity generalization. *Journal of Experimental Psychology, 43*:298–304. **(228)**

Yaroush, R.; Sullivan, M. J.; and Ekstrand, B. R. 1971. The effect of sleep on memory. II: Differential effect of the first and second half of the night. *Journal of Experimental Psychology, 88*:361–366. **(494)**

Yates, F. A. 1966. *The Greek art of memory*. Chicago: University of Chicago Press. **(480)**

Yerkes, R. M., and Morgulis, S. 1909. The method of Pavlovian animal psychology. *Psychological Bulletin, 6*:257–273. **(87)**

Young, P. T. 1959. The role of the affective processes in learning and motivation. *Psychological Review, 66*:104–125. **(139)**

Young, R-A.; Cegavske, C. F.; and Thompson, R. F. 1976. Tone-induced changes in excitability of abducens motoneurons and of the reflex path of nictitating membrane response in rabbit (*Oryctalagus cuniculus*). *Journal of Comparative and Physiological Psychology, 90*:424–434. **(93)**

Young, R. K. 1968. Serial learning. In T. R. Dixon and D. L. Horton (Eds.), *Verbal behavior and general behavior theory*. Englewood Cliffs, N.J.: Prentice-Hall. Pp. 122–148. **(215)**

Zeigler, H. P., and Karten, H. J. 1974. Central trigeminal structures and the lateral hypothalamic syndrome in the rat. *Science, 186*:636–637. **(224)**

Zeiler, M. D. 1971. Eliminating behavior with reinforcement. *Journal of the Experimental Analysis of Behavior, 16*:401–405. **(127, 145)**

Zeiler, M. D. 1976. Positive reinforcement and the elimination of reinforced responses. *Journal of the Experimental Analysis of Behavior, 26*:37–44. **(145)**

Zeiler, M. D. 1977. Schedules of reinforcement: The controlling variables. In W. K. Honig and J. E. R. Staddon (Eds.), *Handbook of operant behavior*. Englewood Cliffs, N.J.: Prentice-Hall. Pp. 201–232. **(237)**

Zimmerman, D. W. 1959. Sustained performance in rats based on secondary reinforcement. *Journal of Comparative and Physiological Psychology, 52*:353–358. **(174)**

Subject Index

Cerebral specialization. *See also* Right-ear advantage; Split-brain research
  and dual-coding theory of imagery, 483
  and language development, 392–394
Chaining, 152–154
Choice procedure, 218
  theoretical analysis of, 146–149
Chunking. *See* Organization
Classical procedure
  acquisition, 158
  basic findings, 94–100
  complexities, 106–115
  control procedures, 92–94
  defining contingency, 76
  limitations of, 117
  model preparation, 95
  paradigms, 91–92
  physiological mechanisms of, 106
  relation to instrumental conditioning, 78–80
  terminology, 88–89
  theoretical analysis of, 101–106
  uncontrolled factors, 121
Cognition
  definition of cognitive psychology, 344–346
  and development of syntax, 397–400
  early stages of cognitive development, 366–368
  and early word combinations, 379–380
  and the competence-performance distinction, 344–346
  interaction with communicative and semantic factors in language development, 370–371
  and semantic universals, 396
Communication
  babbling and, 364–365
  between chimpanzees and humans, 346–355
  crying and, 360
  and origins of assertions and requests, 360–361, 366–367
  communication pressure and language development, 366, 380–382, 401–404
  and language, 351, 359
Competence. *See* Linguistic competence
Compound conditioning, 90
Comprehension. *See also* Recognition
  gap between comprehension and production, 361, 383–384
  processing strategies and, 334–335
  semantic factors and, 337
  syntactic factors and, 336
Computer. *See also* Information processing
  program, 412
  simulation and theorizing, 411–412, 432–433, 486
Computer-assisted instruction, 152
Concept formation. *See also* Attribute-rule hypothesis; Concepts; Hypothesis-testing; Prototype-transformation hypothesis; Strategies
  environmental structure, information and, 292–294
  methods of reception and selection, 288–289
  object permanence, 367
  procedural determinants of, 296–298
  role of errors in, 302, 306
  stimulus variables and, 295–296
  typicality and, 291–294
Concepts. *See also* Attribute-rule hypothesis; Concept formation; Prototype-transformation hypothesis
  conceptual behavior, 278
  contextual-variation in, 287–288
  family resemblance in, 282–283
  fuzzy boundaries of, 283

internal structure of, 283–284
  and propositions, 343
Conceptually-driven processing, 430–432
Conditioned reinforcement
  basic experiment, 83–84
  in delay of reinforcement, 130–131
  generalized, 174
  and human behavior, 173
  relation to elicitation, 171–172
  and schedules of reinforcement, 173–174
  token reinforcers, 175–176
  variables affecting, 172–173
Conditioned response (CR), 111–112
Conditioned stimulus (CS), 100
Conditioned suppression, 107–111, 132
Consummatory response, 139
Context. *See also* Background stimuli; Recall; Recognition
  contextual variation in concepts, 287–288
  context-conditioned variation and language, 322–323
  contextual variation and semantic memory, 493
  interpreting children's utterances, 370, 372–373
  nonlinguistic context and the development of syntax, 397–400
  pattern recognition and, 429–432
Contiguity
  in classical conditioning, 101
  in instrumental conditioning, 136–137
Continental drift, 42
Contingency
  definition of, 68
  of reinforcement, 31
  of survival, 31
  three-term, 166
Contrast, 217
  behavioral contrast, 193
Control processes. *See* Multistore model of memory
Control variable, 5
Correlational view of conditioning, 116
Counterconditioning, 85–86
Critical (sensitive) period, 66
Cross-fostering experiment, 66
CS-UCS interval, 96–99
Cue-dependent forgetting. *See also* Encoding specificity
  retrieval cues and forgetting, 503–504
  retroactive interference and, 504
  theory of, 503–507
Cumulative records, 109–110

Darwin, Charles, 23, 28, 162
  biography, 13–15, 38
  and mechanism of heredity, 28
  and Pavlov, 86
Darwin's finches, 14, 71
Data-driven processing, 430–432
Data-limited processes. *See* Resource allocation model
Decay theory of forgetting
  long-term memory and, 493–494
  problems in testing, 452, 495
  sensory memory and, 415, 421–422
  short-term memory and, 451–452
Decibel (db), 46
Delay of punishment, 131–132
Delay of reinforcement, 121–122, 128–129
  theoretical analysis of, 129–131
Delayed conditioning, 91, 99
Depression, 246

80 81 82 9 8 7 6 5 4 3 2